WITHDRAWN FROM
TSC LIBRARY

W9-DEJ-621

DATE DUE

HIGHSMITH #45115

OXFORD HISTORY OF MODERN EUROPE

OXFORD HISTORY OF MODERN EUROPE

The Struggle for Mastery in Europe 1848–1918
Available in paperback
A. J. P. Taylor

The Russian Empire 1801–1917
Available in paperback
Hugh Seton-Watson

A History of French Passions
Available in paperback in two volumes
Ambition, Love, and Politics
Intellect, Taste, and Anxiety
Theodore Zeldin

Germany 1866–1945
Available in paperback
Gordon A. Craig

The Low Countries 1780–1940
E. H. Kossman

Spain 1808–1975
Available in paperback
Raymond Carr

German History 1770–1866
Available in paperback
James J. Sheehan

A People Apart: A Political History of the Jews in Europe 1789–1939
Available in paperback
David Vital

The Transformation of European Politics 1763–1848
Available in paperback
Paul W. Schroeder

**The Lights that Failed
European International History
1919–1933**
Forthcoming in paperback
Zara Steiner

Bulgaria

R. J. CRAMPTON

OXFORD
UNIVERSITY PRESS

OXFORD

UNIVERSITY PRESS

Great Clarendon Street, Oxford OX2 6DP

Oxford University Press is a department of the University of Oxford.
It furthers the University's objective of excellence in research, scholarship,
and education by publishing worldwide in

Oxford New York

Auckland Cape Town Dar es Salaam Hong Kong Karachi
Kuala Lumpur Madrid Melbourne Mexico City Nairobi
New Delhi Shanghai Taipei Toronto

With offices in

Argentina Austria Brazil Chile Czech Republic France Greece
Guatemala Hungary Italy Japan Poland Portugal Singapore
South Korea Switzerland Thailand Turkey Ukraine Vietnam

Oxford is a registered trade mark of Oxford University Press
in the UK and in certain other countries

Published in the United States
by Oxford University Press Inc., New York

© R. J. Crampton 2007

The moral rights of the author have been asserted
Database right Oxford University Press (maker)

First published 2007

All rights reserved. No part of this publication may be reproduced,
stored in a retrieval system, or transmitted, in any form or by any means,
without the prior permission in writing of Oxford University Press,
or as expressly permitted by law, or under terms agreed with the appropriate
reprographics rights organization. Enquiries concerning reproduction
outside the scope of the above should be sent to the Rights Department,
Oxford University Press, at the address above

You must not circulate this book in any other binding or cover
and you must impose the same condition on any acquirer

British Library Cataloguing in Publication Data
Data available

Library of Congress Cataloging in Publication Data
Data available

Typeset by Newgen Imaging Systems (P) Ltd., Chennai, India
Printed in Great Britain
on acid-free paper by
Biddles Ltd., King's Lynn, Norfolk

ISBN 978–0–19–820514–2

1 3 5 7 9 10 8 6 4 2

To
Alf and Margaret Smyth
For friendship and laughter in the past and, I hope,
the future

Preface

If the writer of the Oxford History of Modern Europe volume on Bulgaria is required to define his terms he is in difficulties. History as a discipline has evolved rapidly over the last three decades; many of those trained in earlier years at times find themselves on unfamiliar and sometimes baffling territory when reading the works of the younger generation. 'Modern' used to be a straightforward concept meaning the most up-to-date, so that a Victorian engineer and a 1950s car worker could both consider themselves living in the modern age. Now modern has come to mean a chronologically defined era and we live in the 'post-modernist age'; more unfamiliarity and bafflement ensue. It might be thought that 'Oxford' at least was immune from change, but can we be so sure of that given the malevolent, misguided intentions towards the University of mendacious and frequently ignorant politicians?

And that leaves 'Bulgaria'. As the following pages I hope will show 'Bulgaria' and 'Bulgarian' have been fluid concepts. In its long history the state has ranged territorially far and wide across the Balkans, and even in the shorter time frame of its modern existence the question of where its borders should be drawn has seldom been absent from the minds of many Bulgarians. And who are the 'Bulgarians'? What makes a 'Bulgarian'? At times the answer would have depended primarily on which church he or she attended, though now language would be a more likely indicator. But that is not as simple as might at first be thought. The Slav languages of south-eastern Europe frequently merge imperceptibly from one to another. Croats and Bosnians now insist on the distinction between their speech and that of the Serbs, a distinction rarely emphasized or largely muted before the 1990s. There is a linguistic transition belt between Bulgarian and Macedonian which is only one of the indications of the great problem of Bulgaria's relationship vis-à-vis the Macedonians. Whether Macedonia is or is not part of Bulgaria has for long been debated, and no doubt the debate will continue, between historians if not on a wider plane. It is impossible to be objective on this question. To me it seems that in some historic epochs Macedonia has been part of Bulgaria and in others, as at present, it is not. I do not intend this as a value judge-ment. As I wrote in an earlier work, 'as an Englishman, educated for some time in Ireland, and married to a southern Irish Protestant of moderate nationalist views, I know better than to attempt to champion any one side in the multi-faceted Macedonian problem.'[1] What I have tried to do is to treat as 'Bulgarians' those who at the time considered themselves to be 'Bulgarians' and to deal too with events and issues which affected Bulgaria and the Bulgarians. The text says little about Bulgarian culture except where that has a direct bearing on political history. Bulgarian art, literature, film, and music are subjects which deserve their own separate treatments by experts in those fields; for a non-expert to write upon them would be to demean the subjects themselves as well as to short-change the reader.

To write about a foreign nation requires a great deal of presumption. The outsider can never see events and evolutions with the same eyes as the insider, but an outside view can add to the total understanding of those phenomena.

This book concentrates on the period since the 1820s when the emergence of the modern Bulgarian nation, by my definition or lack of it, began to emerge. But the genesis of the modern nation cannot be described without some reference to previous eras of Bulgarian history and thus a brief introduction to those earlier eras has been provided. It was decided to conclude the story with the final decision on Bulgaria's entry into the European Union. This, as the Epilogue suggests, is a major event in that it seems to anchor Bulgaria more firmly than it has ever been in Europe.

The use of dates in Bulgarian history is a source of difficulty. The Orthodox, or Julian, calendar was twelve days behind the western or Gregorian system in the nineteenth century and thirteen days in arrears in the twentieth. The Bulgarian state used the Julian calendar until April 1916 and in the following text all dates before the change of calendar are given in the Julian form.

Transliteration too poses problems. This book is intended primarily for those who have an interest in the history of south-eastern Europe but do not know all or any of the local languages. In questions such as

[1] Richard J. Crampton, *Bulgaria 1878–1918. A History*, (Boulder, Colo.: East European Monographs no. 138, distributed by Columbia University Press, 1983), 81 n.

transliteration, abbreviations, and toponyms therefore simplicity and clarity have been given a higher priority than strict accuracy; those who will wish or need to refer to the Slavonic original will be able to recognize and rectify my inconsistencies or inaccuracies. I have used the system set out on page xxii, which varies somewhat from the Library of Congress method widely used by other scholars and publishers. Similarly, when using abbreviations I have used the English-language initials in almost all cases, hence BANU rather than BZNS; but there are a handful of initials which have become common usage even amongst non-Bulgarian speakers, BAN and NDK being among them. Most Balkan topographic names have many variants, each local language frequently having its own word for a river, mountain range, town, or even village. By and large, the Bulgarian name has been used with its most frequently used other version being given when the name is first cited. This does not, however, apply to major European cities such as Paris, Vienna, and Moscow. For the largest cities there has also been an attempt to avoid anachronisms which are too glaring; thus, before 1922 Constantinople has been preferred to Istanbul and Smyrna to Izmir.

Acknowledgements

All academics depend on libraries and their staffs. My work would have been impossible without them, and my thanks go to them all and above all to those in the Bodleian Library in Oxford.

Some academics might think or say that they are burdened by teaching and students. I do not. I have been privileged in Oxford to deal mainly with graduate students and their work has hugely expanded my knowledge, whilst their enthusiasm and commitment have been both a reward and an encouragement. I would therefore like to thank those of them who have worked or are working on Bulgarian themes. They are Patricia Curtis, Kyril Drezov, Tressa Gipe, Daniela Kalkandjieva, Ivan Krŭstev, Yavor Siderov, and Matthew Tejada. Examining theses for other universities has brought me into contact with young scholars whose work has made and is making great contributions to scholarship. My own work would have been impoverished without their help and I wish to thank the following, even though our first encounter in the doctoral viva might have been intimidating for them: Svetla Baloutzova, Vesselin Dimitrov, Rositsa Guentcheva, Milena Mahon, Spyridion Ploumidis, Bernd Rechel, and Marieta Stankova; mention must be made too of the work of Teodora Parveva from the Central European University in Budapest, and of Dimitŭr Bechev of Oxford. I would also like to thank Irina Dimitrova Gigova of the University of Illinois at Urbana-Champaign for allowing me to read her wonderful doctoral thesis.

My academic colleagues too must be thanked for their comradeship. Over the years I have derived enormous pleasure and benefit from the companionship and conversation of colleagues, including, among many others, Archie Brown, Richard Caplan, Richard Clogg, Anne Deighton, John Dunbabin, Robert Evans, Timothy Garton Ash, Michael Hurst, Alex Pravda, Adam Roberts, and Robert Service. Outside the UK equal benefit has derived from the friendship of John Lampe, Gale Stokes, and Sam Williamson. Amongst the many Bulgarian colleagues who have helped me with their scholarship and/or friendship are Rumen Daskalov, Rumen Genov, Zina Markova, Andreĭ Pantev, Tsvetana Todorova, and Aleksandŭr Velichkov. The hospitality and friendship of Sasho and

Daniela Shŭrbanov and Aglika Markova have meant more to me than I can express in words. Successive British ambassadors have also provided encouragement and/or hospitality and jovial company over the years and I would like to thank in particular Richard Thomas, Richard Stagg, Jeremy Hill, and the late Roger Short. The good will, bonhomie, and help provided many years ago in Sofia by Edward Clay have not been forgotten.

Dr Vesselin Dimitrov of the London School of Economics provided expert and invaluable advice on a number of occasions during the preparation of this work, and for this I am deeply grateful.

I owe a particular debt to Professor Martin Mintchev of the University of Calgary who read this manuscript and made hugely useful and important comments on it. I wish I knew as much about engineering as he does about Bulgarian history.

Over the many years in which this book has been in the making Oxford University Press has provided a number of advisers and editors, all of whom have shown exemplary expertise, consideration, and patience; the last, but by no means least of this honourable line being Samantha Skyrme and Rupert Cousens. The proofs have been read by Kate Williams and my good friend and fellow villager, Robin Burleigh. I owe them an enormous debt. They have eliminated many errors and infelicities. For those that remain I alone am responsible.

The support, patience, and forbearance of my wife of forty-odd years remains the greatest of all the favours I have enjoyed, and is followed by the fun and stimulus provided by the company of our two sons, Will and Ben.

Contents

Preface   vii
Acknowledgements   x
List of Maps   xviii
List of Tables   xix
Abbreviations   xx
Transliteration scheme   xxii

Prologue   1

1. Origins   6
   1. Bulgaria and the Bulgarians   6
   2. Bulgaria before the Ottoman conquest   11
   3. The Bulgarians under Ottoman Rule   18

2. The Bulgarian National Renaissance, I. Introduction   23
   1. The pre-renaissance   25
   2. The *kŭrdjaliĭstvo*   32
   3. Population movements   35

3. The Bulgarian National Renaissance, II. The Cultural
   Revival and the Creation of the Modern Bulgarian State   41
   1. The Tanzimat and the modernization of the
      Ottoman system   41
   2. The education movement   49
   3. Language and the press   55
   4. The campaign for a Bulgarian Church   63
   5. The revolutionary and political movements   81

4. The Tŭrnovo Constitution and the Reign of
   Prince Alexander, 1878–1886   96
   1. The Tŭrnovo constitution and political instability,
      1879–1881   96
   2. Prince Alexander's attempted authoritarian rule,
      1881–1883   107

3. The restoration of the Tŭrnovo constitution and
   the rule of the liberals, 1883–1885   113
4. The national question, and the unification of
   Bulgaria and Eastern Rumelia, 1878–1885   116
5. War with Serbia and the deposition of
   Prince Alexander, 1885–1886   123
6. The election of Prince Ferdinand   128

5. **Stefan Stambolov, Prince Ferdinand, and the Quest for
   Recognition, 1887–1896**   133

   1. Stambolov ascendant, 1887–1890   134
   2. The decline and fall of Stambolov, 1890–1894   138
   3. The recognition of Prince Ferdinand,
      1894–1896   143
   4. Parties, *partizanstvo,* and the political system   146

6. **Prince Ferdinand's Personal Rule, 1896–1912**   150

   1. The Macedonian question, 1894–1898   150
   2. The ORC fiasco, 1894–1899   153
   3. The agrarian crisis and the birth of BANU,
      1899–1901   157
   4. Money and Macedonia, 1900–1903   162
   5. The Ilinden rising and the second stambolovist
      government, 1903–1908   166
   6. The government of Malinov and the declaration of
      independence, 1907–1911   174
   7. The growth of political radicalism   179

7. **Bulgaria at War, 1912–1918**   190

   1. Constitutional change and the formation of the
      Balkan league   190
   2. The first Balkan war   196
   3. The second Balkan war: the first 'national catastrophe'   198
   4. From Balkan to European war   204
   5. Bulgaria and the first world war: the commitment to
      the central powers   206
   6. Bulgaria in the first world war: the second
      'national catastrophe'   210

8. **Between Two Wars, 1919–1941**   220
   1. The treaty of Neuilly-sur-Seine   221
   2. The agrarians versus the communists, 1919–1920   222
   3. BANU in power, 1920–1923   224
   4. The tsankovist terror, 1923–1926   236
   5. The government of the Democratic Alliance,
     1926–1931   239
   6. The People's Bloc and the great depression,
     1931–1934   240
   7. The zvenari government, 19 May 1934–January 1935   245
   8. The personal regime of King Boris, 1935–1941   248

9. **Bulgaria and the Second World War, 1941–1944**   258
   1. The occupied territories   258
   2. Domestic politics during the war   262
   3. Bulgaria's military participation in the war   267
   4. The regency and the end of the 'symbolic' war   270
   5. Internal opposition: the Fatherland Front, and the
     partisan movement   274
   6. Bulgaria's exit from the war   277

10. **Social and Economic Factors, 1878–1944**   282
   1. Demography   282
   2. Stability and change   284
   3. The persistence and dominance of the
     small peasant proprietor   287
   4. Standards of living in rural areas   289
   5. Agricultural backwardness   291
   6. Urban growth   295
   7. Industrial development   298
   8. The state and industry   301
   9. Public health   305
   10. The position of women in Bulgarian society   305

11. **The Communist Acquisition of Power, 1944–1948**   308
   1. The first purges, September 1944–May 1945   308
   2. The communists versus the agrarians,
     May–November 1945   312

3. The communist offensive, December
   1945–October 1946   314
4. The communists embattled, October
   1946–February 1947   316
5. The peace treaty and the elimination of Petkov,
   February–September 1947   321
6. The communists assume total control,
   September–December 1947   323

12. **The Communists in Power, I. The Rule of Terror,
   the Reign of Vŭlko Chervenkov, and the Rise of Todor
   Zhivkov, 1948–1965**   327
   1. The transformation of the social and economic order   327
   2. The terror and the stalinist purges   333
   3. Vŭlko Chervenkov and the sovietization of Bulgaria,
      1949–1953   340
   4. The 'new course' in Bulgaria, 1953–1956   343
   5. The April plenum 1956   345
   6. Zhivkov versus Yugov, 1956–1962   347
13. **The Communists in Power, II. The Rule of Todor Zhivkov,
   1965–1989**   352
   1. Todor Zhivkov   352
   2. Building socialism   354
   3. 'Mature' or 'real existing socialism' in Bulgaria   356
   4. Zhivkov ascendant, 1965–1975   358
   5. Zhivkov's external policies   363
   6. The amazing career of Lyudmila Zhivkova   367
   7. The decline of communist power; the collapse of
      the economic strategy   370
   8. The decline of communist power: the
      'regenerative process'   375
   9. The decline of party authority, 1975–1985   379
   10. The collapse of the Zhivkov regime, 1985–1989   381

14. **Post-Communist Bulgaria, 1989–2005**   389
   1. Devising a new constitution, December
      1989–July 1991   389
   2. Treading water, October 1991–January 1995   395

3. The BSP government, January 1995–April 1997   400
4. The Kostov government and movement towards
   the EU and NATO, April 1997–June 2001   407
5. Government by 'the king' and entry into NATO
   and the EU, June 2001–June 2005   415
6. Postscript: the elections of 2005   420

15. **The Minority and Demographic Questions**   422

1. The Muslims: Turks and Pomaks, 1878–1989   426
2. The other minorities, 1878–1944   433
3. The minorities under communist rule,
   1944–1989   436
4. The minorities since 1989   438
5. Recent demographic decline   443

Epilogue: Bulgaria between East and West   445

Appendix. Bulgarian Political Parties, 1878–1934   449

Bibliographical Notes   456

  General histories   456
  The Bulgarian national revival   459
  From the liberation to the end of the first world war   463
  From the end of the first to the end of the second
  world war   469
  Social and economic development from
  1878 to 1944   473
  The years of communist domination, 1944–1989   474
  Bulgaria since 1989   479
  Minorities and ethnic questions   479

Index   483

List of Maps

1. The Balkans   5
2. The Bulgarian renaissance   22
3. Bulgaria: main towns and railway lines   40
4. Bulgaria's frontiers, 1878–1919   189
5. Bulgaria in the second world war   257

List of Tables

10.1	Total population	283
10.2	Rural and urban populations	283
10.3	Distribution of landholdings by size, percentage of total	287
13.1	Percentage average annual growth rate of Net Material Product, 1950–1970	354
13.2	Average annual growth in Net Material Product in percentages, 1950–1989	372
15.1	The population of Bulgaria by ethnic identity, 1880/4–2001	424
15.2	Total population, 1880/4–2004	443

Abbreviations

ACC	Allied Control Commission
AIC	Agro-Industrial Complex
ANS	Alliance for National Salvation
BAN	Bulgarian Academy of Sciences
BANU	Bulgarian Agrarian National Union
BANU-NP	Bulgarian Agrarian National Union—Nikola Petkov
BCP	Bulgarian Communist Party
BDZh	Bulgarian State Railways
BNB	Bulgarian National Bank
BRCC	Bulgarian Revolutionary Central Committee
BRSDP	Bulgarian Workers' Social Democratic Party
BSP	Bulgarian Socialist Party
BTK	Bulgarian Telecommunications Company
BWP	Bulgarian Workers' Party
CC	Central Committee
CITUB	Confederation of Independent Trade Unions in Bulgaria
CLS	compulsory labour service
CPSU	Communist Party of the Soviet Union
CSCE	Commission on Security and Cooperation in Europe
DP	Democratic Party
DS	*Dŭrzhavna Sigurnost* ('State Security', i.e. the secret police)
EEC	European Economic Community
EU	European Union
FF	Fatherland Front
fyp	five-year plan
GNA	grand national assembly
IMF	International Monetary Fund
IMRO	Internal Macedonian-Adrianople Revolutionary Organization

MRF	Movement for Rights and Freedoms
MTS	motor tractor station
NDK	National Palace of Culture, Sofia
NEM	New Economic Mechanism
NLP	National Liberal Party
NMP	net material product
NMSS	National Movement Simeon II
NSM	National Social Movement
ORC	Oriental Railway Company
PR	proportional representation
PRM	People's Republic of Macedonia
RDP	Radical Democratic Party
SCBC	Secret Central Bulgarian Committee
SDP	Social Democratic Party
SOE	Special Operations Executive
TKZS	collective farm (Also used in the text for state farm)
UDF	Union of Democratic Forces
UtDF	United Democratic Forces
VMORO	See IMRO
VMRO	See IMRO

Transliteration scheme

А	a
Б	b
В	v
Г	g
Д	d
Е	e
ж	zh, but Дж as 'dj'
з	z
и	i
й	ĭ
к	k
л	l
м	m
н	n
о	o
п	p
р	r
с	s
т	t
у	u
ф	f
х	h, but 'kh' in Russian and Ukrainian words
ц	ts
ч	ch
ш	sh
щ	sht, but 'shch' in Russian and Ukrainian words
ъ	ŭ
ь	not transliterated at the end of words, but 'y' when used in conjunction with 'o'
ю	yu
я	ya

The Russian letter, 'ы' is transliterated as 'y'.

Prologue

In Great Britain during the second half of the twentieth century Bulgaria was probably the least known of all the East European states. Even Albania, under the egregious leadership of Enver Hoxha, seemed to receive more media coverage. Only with the occasional scandal, such as the murder of Georgi Markov, was this apparent indifference abandoned and this ignorance dented.

This was not a recent phenomenon. Such a statement would not have been contested in his time by Constantin Jireček, a Czech Slavicist who served for a while as minister of education in the newly created Bulgarian principality, and who wrote in the early 1890s, 'Despite its position between Constantinople and central Europe's greatest waterways research into Bulgaria is only just beginning.'[1] According to Jireček Bulgaria was little known even in Russia. Despite the fact that Turgenev had based Insarov in *On the Eve* on the Bulgarian nationalist activist Nikolai Kitanov, and notwithstanding a Pan Slav crusade on behalf of the Bulgarians, Jireček, in the foreword to the Russian edition of his *Istoriya na bŭlgarite* (History of the Bulgarians), written in the climacteric year of 1878, described the Bulgarian nation as one 'sadly so little known to the Russian public'.[2]

Ignorance in the English-speaking world was even greater. A few Bulgarian merchants established links with Britain, the Geshov family, for example, traded with and visited Manchester, but the Bulgarian mercantile presence was never strong or influential. Bulgaria flashed vividly across the political stage in 1876 when, following the April uprising of that year, Gladstone produced his famous pamphlet on *The Bulgarian Horrors and the Question of the East*. There was practical aid as

[1] Dr Constantin Jireček, *Das Fürstenthum Bulgarien: Seine Bodengestaltung, Natur, Bevölkerung, wirtschafliche Zustände, geistige Cultur, Staatsverfassung, Staatsverwaltung und neueste Geschichte* (Vienna: F. Tempsky, 1891), iii.

[2] Cited from the Bulgarian edition of his *Istoriya na bŭlgarite*, (Sofia: Nauka i izkustvo, 1978), 31.

well as political sympathy for the Bulgarians. A number of British volunteers, including Lady Strangford, worked with and for the National Aid Society in hospitals in Karlovo, Rusé and elsewhere in the Balkans.[3] Other welfare action followed subsequent upheavals. An uprising in Macedonia in 1903 produced a great work of scholarship from H. N. Brailsford[4] but it also prompted further aid work by Britons in Bulgaria, including, for example, that of the little-known Miriam King Lewis who distributed relief to refugees in Burgas.[5] After the first world war Lord Atholl built a village in Bulgaria for refugees from Macedonia, the village, Atolovo, being named after him.[6] Another virtually unknown British helper of Bulgarians in distress was an Englishwoman who looked after the families of Georgi Dimitrov and Vasil Tanev during the Leipzig trial following the burning of the Reichstag in 1933. She brought newspapers, including some Russian and Bulgarian ones, which enabled the detained to learn how much of a stir the case was causing in the world; she also informed the British Anti-Fascist Committee of their fate after the trial.[7]

Charity, be it by individuals or by institutions, could not overcome political realities. And in the twentieth century these drove Bulgaria and the Anglo-Saxon world apart. At the international level Bulgaria's significance was never contested. 'It is clear', wrote the British foreign secretary Sir Edward Grey in April 1915, 'that the key to the situation in the Balkans lies in Sofia',[8] and during the next great European conflict a former British minister to Bulgaria expressed a similar opinion, noting that 'to approach any Balkan problem without taking Bulgaria into account is merely to deal with the periphery and to ignore what has so

---

[3] Details can be found in Dorothy Anderson, *The Balkan Volunteers* (London: Hutchinson, 1968).

[4] The work is H. N. Brailsford, *Macedonia, its Races and their Future* (London: Methuen, 1906); for Brailsford's work in Macedonia, see F. M. Leventhal, *The Last Dissenter; H. N. Brailsford and His World* (Oxford: Clarendon Press, 1985), 46–59.

[5] Dimitŭr Popnikolov, *Preobrazhenskoto vŭstanie: lichni spomeni i po spomeni na voĭvodata Yani Popov*, second, enlarged edition (Sofia: Otechestven Front, 1982), 117.

[6] Dinyu Sharlanov and Polya Meshkova (eds.), *Sŭvetnitsite na Tsar Boris III Naroden sŭd; Doznaniya* (Sofia: Riana Press, 1993), 238.

[7] Blagoi Popov, *Ot Protsesa v Laiptsig do lagerite v Sibir* (Sofia: Hristo Botev, 1991), 94–5. Popov was also convicted at Leipzig and went with Dimitrov and Tanev to the Soviet Union. He was later interned in the Gulag.

[8] Ivan Ilchev (ed.), *D-r Vasil Radoslavov: Dnevni Belezhki, 1914–1916* (Sofia: Kliment Ohridski, 1993), 129.

often proved in the past to be the central core'.[9] Bulgaria's calculation in both world wars had been that the Germans could offer more than the other side, and thus Bulgaria lost the sympathy of Germany's adversaries; the United States ambassador to Greece during the second world war dismissed Bulgaria as 'the most consistently double-dealing of all the Balkan states';[10] Sir Winston Churchill described the Bulgarians as 'a peccant people'[11] and told Stalin that he ' "could not give a damn about Bulgaria." '[12]

Underlying and complicating the lack of political rapport between Bulgaria and Britain was the absence of cultural contact. Bulgaria did not have a vociferous and powerful diaspora in the west, such as that enjoyed, and utilized, by the Greeks. A few Bulgarians did, however, make an impact on the west, and one of them sagely isolated another reason why there was so little awareness in the west of Bulgaria and the Bulgarians. Again with Bulgaria's southern neighbour in mind, he wrote, 'Greek public relations have always been good from Homer down through Byron, while we had no poets to sing our exploits.'[13] The lack of cultural links was, and to a considerable extent still is, most notable in the world of the creative arts. The *Oxford Companion to English Literature in Translation*, mentions only three major works of Bulgarian literature published in English translation in Britain between the 1860s and the outbreak of the first world war.[14] Although George Bernard Shaw gave

[9] Sir George Rendel to Anthony Eden, 19 December 1942. Quoted in Graham Ross (ed.), *The Foreign Office and the Kremlin: British Documents on Anglo-Soviet Relations 1941–1945* (Cambridge: Cambridge University Press, 1984), 117.

[10] John O. Iatrides (ed.) *Ambassador MacVeagh Reports: Greece 1933–1947* (Princeton: Princeton University Press, 1980), 600.

[11] National Archives, Kew, London. PREM 3 79/1, 125. Extract from Chiefs of Staff meeting, 19 October 1943.

[12] Vladimir Volkov, 'The Soviet Leadership and Southeastern Europe', in Norman Naimark and Leonid Gibianskii (eds.), *The Establishment of Communist Regimes in Eastern Europe, 1944–1949* (Boulder, Colo.: Westview Press, 1997), 55–72, 61. Volkov quotes from a Soviet archival source. The remark was made during Churchill's meeting with Stalin in Moscow in October 1944.

[13] Ivan D. Stancioff, *Diplomat and Gardener. Memoirs* (Sofia: Petrikov Publishers, 1998), 22.

[14] This was stated by Professor Michael Holman in a message posted on the Bulgarian Studies Group website on 4 January 2006. The message was part of a discussion centred on the paucity of English translations of Bulgarian works of literature. For details of the Bulgarian Studies Group, see Bulgarian_Studies@yahoogroups.com.

Bulgaria fleeting fame by setting *Arms and the Man* in the Serbo-Bulgarian war of 1885 other references to the country in British literature are few and usually disparaging. Swinburne used the word 'Bulgarian' as a code for 'homosexual',[15] whilst Evelyn Waugh lampooned a Bulgarian priest in *Put Out More Flags*.[16] If there was relatively little interest from the western side, the Bulgarian intelligentsia did not cultivate British links as assiduously as it did those with other European cultures. As a great historian of the Bulgarian national revival has observed, in the nineteenth and early twentieth century 'the Anglo-Saxon university was unknown to Bulgarian youth. Thus yet again Bulgarian culture was deprived of the intellectual attainments of the great Anglo-Saxon school, of contact with the spirit of the Victorian era.'[17] Shortly after the first world war a major Bulgarian critic and scholar regretted that of all the foreign influences on Bulgarian culture, 'the English has been the weakest. One day we shall understand how much we have lost because of the distance, not merely geographically, between us and England.'[18]

That distance is still too great, even though Bulgaria is now on the threshold of membership of the European Union (EU). It is hoped that the following pages might do something to lessen this regrettable divide.

[15] Roger Hudson (ed.), *The Lyttelton Hart-Davis Letters. A Selection. Correspondence between George Lyttelton and Rupert Hart-Davis, 1955–1962*, ed. Rupert Hart-Davis (London: John Murray, 2001), 324.

[16] 'I am the Archimandrite Antonius . . . I have been telling your office clergymen about my expulsing. The Bulgar peoples say it was for fornications, but it was for politics. They are not expulsing from Sofia for fornications unless there is politics too.' Evelyn Waugh, *Put out More Flags*, (London: Penguin, 1942), 67.

[17] Nikolai Genchev, *Ochertsi: Sotsialno-psihologicheski tipove vǔv bǔlgarskata istoriya*, (Sofia: Septemvri, 1987), 153.

[18] Boyan Penev, 'Nashata inteligentisya. Fragmenti', *Zlatorog*, 5/1 (1924), in Ivan Elenkov and Rumen Daskalov (compilers), *Zashto sme takiva? V tǔrsene na bǔlgarskata kulturna identichnost*, (Sofia: Prosveta, 1994), 131–43, 142.

Map 1. The Balkans

1

Origins

1. BULGARIA AND THE BULGARIANS

When President Zhelyu Zhelev of Bulgaria visited President Askar Akaev of Kirghizia in July 1993 he was told:

Honoured Bulgarian friends, many centuries—perhaps millennia—before you became Christians and we Muslims, we both knelt before the same god, Tangra. And even now, were you to go out into the steppe and ask an ordinary Kazakh shepherd whose is that mountain over there whose peak is always covered in snow and shrouded in mists, he will answer: that is the Bulgarians' mountain, that's where their god lives.[1]

This is only one illustration of the fact that, as is the case with most other nations of modern Europe, the geographic spread of the Bulgarian state and nation have varied considerably with time. Again in conformity with other European models, the confines of the Bulgarian nation and state have rarely been coterminous. The Bulgarian state seldom, if ever, contained only Bulgarians and, conversely, it equally infrequently encompassed all Bulgarians; even at the opening of the twenty-first century there were Bulgarian communities in Serbia, Romania, Albania, Russia, Ukraine, Moldova, and Turkey, with émigré groups scattered throughout the world.

As President Akaev's remarks indicate the geographic origin of the Bulgarians is believed to be in the fastness of central Asia, and not till the seventh century AD did the so-called Proto-Bulgars cross the Danube and enter the area which now bears their name. Ethnically they were an amalgam of various elements—the word *bulgar* is derived from a Turkic

[1] Zhelyu Zhelev, *V Golyamata Politika* (Sofia: Trud Press, 1998), 239.

verb meaning 'to mix'—and the process of mixing was to continue in the coming centuries, albeit slowly, as the Proto-Bulgars mingled with the resident Slavs who had begun settling south of the Danube in the fifth century. The Proto-Bulgars' ability to mix meant that little survived of their language beyond a score or so words. Some of their customs, however, were more long-lasting, and in the nineteenth and early twentieth centuries some villages in Bulgaria still followed the Proto-Bulgarian custom of erecting large stones, or 'babi', on which, as in Proto-Bulgarian days, candles were lit.[2]

When the Proto-Bulgars arrived in the Balkans the area was already far from ethnically homogeneous. To the south of the Balkan mountains the Thracians mixed with Roman settlers whilst there were Greek settlements throughout the region, but particularly on the coast where they remained until the twentieth century. Cultural mixing continued in succeeding centuries as a result of incursions by a series of tribes, including Avars, Huns, Tatars, Pechenegs, and Magyars; in the Serbo-Bulgarian war of 1885 troops from southern Bulgaria were colloquially known as 'Pechenegs'[3] whilst the Magyar legacy lingered in a number of topographic names, a gazetteer published in 1987 listing seven settlements in Bulgaria whose name began with 'Madj' and a further seven which had names beginning with 'Mag'.[4]

A major redrawing of the ethnic contours followed the invasion of the Ottomans in the second half of the fourteenth century. By the end of that century all present-day Bulgaria had fallen under Ottoman domination and the conquest was followed by widespread colonization by Turks and other Muslims, including Tatars. Large proportions of present-day Bulgaria soon had sizeable Turkish minorities. Though assimilation was not common a cultural *modus vivendi* was achieved and even as late as 1878 it was a general rule of thumb that east of the river Yantra the Christians spoke Turkish whilst west of it the Turks spoke Bulgarian.[5]

---

[2] Popnikolov, *Preobrazhenskoto vŭstanie*, 14–15.

[3] Elena Statelova and Radoslav Popov (eds.), *Spomeni za Sŭedinenieto ot 1885g* (Sofia: Otechestven Front, 1980), 239. One Bulgarian memoir writer speaks of the great courage shown in the 1885 war by 'the Pechenegs of the Harmanli company'. Nikola Genadiev, *Memoari*, vol.i, with an introduction by Stoĭcho Grŭncharov (Sofia: Otechestven Front, 1985), first published in 1923, 131.

[4] *Gazetteer of Bulgaria* (Washington, DC: Defense Mapping Agency, 1987), 311–12.

[5] Konstantin Irichek, *Pŭtuvane po Bŭlgariya* (Sofia: Nauka i izkustvo, 1974), 86.

The cultural *modus vivendi* was based on the principle of ultimate Muslim superiority over but tolerance of other religions, though some Bulgarians did accept the new and dominant creed without losing their Bulgarian language, these Pomaks, as they were named, becoming a distinct community. There were also communities of Turkish speaking Christians, or Gagauze.

There were many other ethnic elements in the multicultural construct that was the Ottoman empire in Europe. Nomadic shepherds moved across the peninsula and transhumance brought groups such as the Vlachs and the Karakachans into the Bulgarian lands where some of them settled; even in the 1970s there were Vlachs in the Vidin area who did not speak Bulgarian. Jewish communities were established, the largest being in Rusé. Gypsies entered the Bulgarian lands shortly after the Ottoman conquest.

This racial and religious complexity was made possible in part by the Pax Ottomanica but some later additions to the cultural mix were made possible or necessary by disorder and war. After the Crimean war the Ottoman government decided to strengthen the Muslim element on its northern European border by settling communities of Circassians whose former homes had been in tsarist Russia; their presence was short-lived, most of them leaving Bulgaria after the Russo-Turkish war of 1877–8. Many Armenians fled persecution in the late nineteenth and early twentieth centuries, and after the civil war in Russia 30,000 White Russians made their home in Bulgaria, as had a number of sailors from the battleship *Potemkin* in 1905. There were also more exotic incomers such as the Russian Old Believers who arrived in the 1830s and whose descendants still made up the entire population of two villages in 1961.[6] In the early twentieth century a number of German settlers arrived from southern Russia, Volhynia, and Transylvania to settle near Tsaribrod; they were of such mixed origins that in one village the church services combined Roman Catholic and Lutheran practices.[7] In the final stages of communist rule in Bulgaria the growing shortage of labour was made good by immigration from other socialist countries. In the census of 1985

[6] Stefan Troebst, 'Nationale Minderheiten', in Klaus-Detlev Grothusen (ed.), *Bulgarien*, Südosteuropa-Handbuch, no. 6 (Göttingen: Vandenhoeck & Ruprecht, 1990), 474–89, 483.

[7] Joachim Gerstenberg, *Bulgarien Бългaрия: Ein Reisebuch* (Hamburg: Broschek & Co., 1940), 33–4.

'Cuban' and 'Vietnamese' were amongst the twelve categories which respondents could choose for their 'nationality'; virtually all the Vietnamese left after 1989.[8]

The Bulgarian communities outside the confines of what is now the Republic of Bulgaria contributed hugely to the evolution of the nation and the foundation of the state. Nor did their contribution end with the liberation from Ottoman rule. Discounting two Russians who were invited by the prince in the early 1880s to become minister president, of the forty-five Bulgarians who fulfilled that office between 1878 and 2005 seven were born outside the territory of the present (2006) republic; two were from Bessarabia, and one each from what is now Romania, Russia, Ukraine, the (Former Yugoslav) Republic of Macedonia, and Greece.

The existence of Bulgarian communities outside what was to become the Bulgarian state was frequently the consequence of political upheaval. Thousands of Bulgarians took part in the Hungarian resistance to the Ottoman advance into central Europe, as they did in the defence of Moldavia and Wallachia. In the latter there were large Bulgarian settlements which were constantly refreshed by further waves of immigration.[9] These usually followed rebellions against Ottoman rule in the Bulgarian lands when whole communities fled the retribution which followed the suppression of the rising. The most notable example was that of the inhabitants of Chiprovets. This mining area in the north-west of present-day Bulgaria had seen an influx of Saxons who had become absorbed linguistically into the indigenous Bulgarian communities but had retained their Catholicism; after a failed uprising in 1688 many left for the Banat of Temesvar where their descendants are still to be found in the twenty-first century. The wars of the eighteenth and early nineteenth century between Russia and the Ottoman empire saw large scale, though not always permanent emigration of Bulgarians to southern Russia, Bessarabia, and Ukraine; in the 1920s in Ukraine, the 'Dimitŭr Blagoev' kolkhoz, named after the founder of the Bulgarian socialist movement, consisted entirely of ethnic Bulgarians.[10] And in the late nineteenth and early twentieth centuries thousands of Bulgarians, particularly those left

[8] For census categories, see Dimitŭr Arkadiev, 'Izuchavane na etnicheskiya sŭstav pri prebroyavaneto na naselenieto v Bŭlgariya', *Naselenie*, 6 (1992), 47–57.

[9] Plamen Pavlov and Ivan Tyutyundjiev, *Bŭlgarite i osmanskoto zavoevanie; (krayat na xiii-sredata na xv v)* (Veliko Tŭrnovo: Slovo, 1995), 126.

[10] Blagoĭ Popov, *Ot Protsesa*, 241.

under Ottoman rule after the treaty of Berlin in 1878, sought a new life in north America, whilst after 1945 smaller emigrations took place to western Europe and north and south America.

Not all Bulgarians who left the Bulgarian lands did so because of upheaval and war. Bulgarian merchants ranged widely into central Europe, though the fact that many of them wrote and frequently spoke Greek for professional reasons has meant that their numbers cannot be accurately estimated. More easily identifiable were those Bulgarians who went abroad 'on *pechalba*' (profit) to work, either seasonally or permanently, their main destinations being Romania, Austria-Hungary, Russia, Serbia, and Asiatic Turkey. They worked mainly as gardeners and harvesters; in 1880 there were an estimated 12,000 Bulgarians working seasonally outside Bulgaria, and at the end of the nineteenth century around 10,000 seasonal workers were reported to pass each year between Bulgaria and Macedonia.[11] Some workers established colonies abroad. The Bulgarians of Budapest, most of whom were or had been migrant horticultural labourers, formed their own society in 1914 to care for the Bulgarian church and schools in the city; the society was still flourishing after the war and in 1922 opened the new Ivan Vazov school for Bulgarian-speaking children.[12] In 1944 an entire quarter of Sarajevo was said to be inhabited by Bulgarians.[13] In the 1960s many Bulgarians left their native land to work in the Soviet Union, particularly in the timber industry in the Komi region, and in 1973 a separate communist party committee was created in Moscow for Bulgarians resident in the Soviet Union.

In historic terms the most important of the Bulgarian communities outside the Bulgarian lands were those of Bucharest, Braila, and, above all, Constantinople. These communities were to play a vital role in the promotion of the idea of Bulgarian nationality, but that idea, not least because of the proximity and influence of the imperial Ottoman capital, did not develop strongly until the 1840s. Petŭr Beron who produced the first Bulgarian textbook in the 1820s, called himself a Thracian not a Bulgarian,[14] and even in the second half of the nineteenth century many

---

[11] Georgi Georgiev, *Osvobozhdenieto i etnokulturnoto razvitie na bŭlgarskiya narod 1877–1900* (Sofia: BAN, 1979), 26.

[12] Konstantin Gŭrdev, *Bŭlgariya i Ungariya, 1923–1941* (Sofia: Nauka i izkustvo, 1988), 19–20.

[13] Stoyan Iliev, *Iz spomenite mi* (Sofia: Georgi Pobedonosets, 1993), 246.

[14] Ivan Duĭchev, *Pŭteki ot utroto: Ochertsi za srednovekovnata bŭlgarska kultura* (Sofia: Otechestvo, 1985), 222.

Bulgarians living in the Balkan mountains called the Thracian planes 'Romanjá' and those who lived there 'Romanéc' and 'Romanká', names used originally for the Byzantine empire and its inhabitants.[15]

Nor had national identity solidified entirely by the mid-twentieth century. In Macedonia and the borderlands between Bulgaria and Serbia the languages and the cultures merged gradually and distinction between them was frequently difficult if not impossible. Language was seldom a useful guide and local inhabitants would often grow up speaking four or even five native languages: Bulgarian, Serbian, Macedonian, Turkish, Greek, Albanian, and Ladino were the most common. A Bulgarian officer billeted on a family in occupied Serbia during the second world war asked the small daughter of the household if she was Bulgarian or Serbian; she told him she was Serbian, 'but my mother and father told me that if you were to ask me what I was, I was to say that I was Bulgarian. With you I am Bulgarian, at home I am Serbian.'[16]

2. BULGARIA BEFORE THE OTTOMAN CONQUEST

Byzantium and its proximity conditioned Bulgaria's development for almost a millennium. In the first century of its existence the Proto-Bulgarian empire, founded in 681 and based first in Pliska to the north of the Balkan mountains, expanded its territories to the south-west and even more so to the north-west, reaching its greatest extent under Khan Omurtag, who ruled from 814 to 831.

The most important developments in the first empire, however, were cultural rather than military. In 864 Khan Boris made the momentous decision to impose Christianity upon his subjects. Bulgaria was by this time almost isolated in Europe in clinging to paganism and acceptance of the dominant faith would make easier the diplomatic and commercial exchanges the empire needed, not least with Byzantium. A more important consideration was the effect conversion would have within Bulgaria itself. The Slavs whom the Proto-Bulgars had conquered were Christian; the Proto-Bulgar nobility who ruled over them were pagan, but as territorial expansion brought more Christians into the state the

---

[15] Jireček, *Fürstenthum*, 8.   [16] Iliev, *Spomenite*, 190.

Proto-Bulgars became an ever smaller minority in their own land. Conversion would please the large number of Christians and if the Byzantine pattern were followed the Church would reinforce the power of the Khan and the central state apparatus against the nobility. To impose a common faith should also help fuse Proto-Bulgar and Slav into a single cultural unit. This proved to be a protracted process with Proto-Bulgar and Slav continuing to live in separate communities for decades, but in the long run a new and more homogeneous system did emerge. The Slavs were now more prepared to accept the state because it was Christian, whilst the Proto-Bulgars had less to fear from Christianity because it was no longer divorced from the state. No single act did more, in the long run, to weld Christian Slav and Proto-Bulgar into a Bulgarian people than the conversion of 864.

The conversion did pose one dilemma which was to be felt more than once in subsequent Bulgarian history: should Bulgaria face east or west? To the east the Byzantine model posed the threat that the Bulgarian Church and Bulgarian culture might be overwhelmed and suffocated by their huge neighbour, and that the Church would become an arm of the Byzantine state and would be used to subvert Bulgaria from within. This fear was reinforced after 864 when the Byzantine Church, to which the Bulgarian had been affiliated, refused Bulgaria the right to have its own patriarch as head of the Church or even to nominate its own bishops. In disappointment Boris turned to the west and dispatched delegates to Rome to find out what terms were on offer from the Pope. The delegates were also to ask for clarification of certain points of doctrine and Christian practice, but when Rome proved as adamant as Byzantium in its opposition to a Bulgarian patriarch Boris concluded that Bulgaria would be more threatened by an alienated Byzantium than an offended Rome, and therefore decided that Bulgaria should become part of the eastern half of Christianity. In 869–70 a council in the imperial capital drew up the regulations for the organization of the Bulgarian Church which was to be headed by an archbishop appointed by the Patriarch in Constantinople (Byzantium).

If the amalgamation of Christian Slav and pagan Proto-Bulgar was a slow process another consequence of conversion was much more immediate. In 862 the ruler of Moravia had asked that an alphabet be devised for use amongst his own Slavic people so that the cultural influence of the Franks and Germans could be contained. The challenge was taken up by the monks Cyril and Methodius whose Cyrillic alphabet was drawn up in the second half of the ninth century. If it helped stem Frankish and German influence in Moravia, its function in Bulgaria was to contain Greek cultural pressures. The newly converted country had few priests of its own and many were imported from Greek-speaking Byzantium. Not for the last time in the history of Bulgaria this import-ation of foreign advisers and assistants caused tensions and the availability of a Slavonic alphabet made the training of slavophone priests easier. An assembly of Bulgarian notables decreed in 893 that Bulgarian be the liturgical language of the Church in Bulgaria.

The introduction of the Cyrillic alphabet also facilitated the appearance of a Bulgarian literature, lay as well as secular. By the end of the ninth century Bulgarian had mostly replaced Greek as the written language[17] and a large and flourishing school of learning in Bulgarian had been established by St Kliment of Ohrid, after whom Sofia University was to be named a thousand years later.

The first Bulgarian empire reached its apogee, if not its greatest territorial extent, at the turn of the ninth and tenth centuries under Simeon the Great (893–927). Brought up in Constantinople he was familiar with contemporary and ancient literature and was originally destined for a clerical career, his father intending him to be the head of the Bulgarian Church.[18] This aim was frustrated by a palace coup which put Simeon on the temporal rather than the spiritual throne. He spent much of the early and late years of his reign fighting the empire in which he had been nurtured and twice he led armies to the walls of Constantinople itself. Also, in 918 he proclaimed an independent Bulgarian Patriarchate. This the Byzantine emperor accepted in a treaty of 927,[19] an agreement which also recognized Simeon as *basileus*, or emperor, and obliged the Byzantines to accord greater deference to Bulgarian than to any other foreign representatives.[20]

Within Bulgaria itself Simeon's reign saw a flowering of culture with such figures as the monk Hrabŭr, Ivan (John) the Exarch, and Konstantin

[17] David Marshall Lang, *The Bulgarians: From Pagan Times to the Ottoman Conquest* (London: Thames & Hudson, 1976), 61; Robert Browning, *Byzantium and Bulgaria: A Comparative Study across the Early Medieval Frontier* (London: Temple Smith, 1975), 61–75.

[18] Petŭr Mutafchiev, *Kniga za bŭlgarite* (Sofia: BAN, 1987), 181.

[19] Duĭchev, *Pŭteki*, 55.

[20] Petŭr Angelov, *Bŭlgarskata srednovekovna diplomatsiya* (Sofia: Nauka i izkustvo, 1988), 175–6.

of Preslav adding lustre to the court which was moved to Preslav, a city which, Simeon calculated, would be more free of semi-pagan, noble, and Proto-Bulgar influence than Pliska.[21]

Despite Simeon's attainments Bulgaria suffered from a number of systemic weaknesses. Perhaps the most serious was its lack of any naval power, or of any realization amongst its ruling elite of how command of the sea might act as a guarantor of state power.[22] The Proto-Bulgars never escaped the land-locked mentality which they brought with them from the central Asian steppes and this left the Black Sea under Byzantine domination, and the problem was compounded by the fact that Bulgaria then, as now, did not control the mouth of any of the major rivers which ran through it. Even had the Proto-Bulgars or any of the rulers after Boris I wished to establish a maritime presence, commercial or military, it is doubtful whether they could have done so, because another debilitating weakness of the Bulgarian khanate was its low technological base. Relatively few industries developed between the seventh and the eleventh centuries and the Bulgarian empire did not even produce its own currency, relying instead on that of Byzantium.

A further underlying weakness was the tendency towards rejectionism. Before the conversion to Christianity the Slavs had not felt at one with the state, and many Proto-Bulgar nobles had a similar feeling after 864. In the days immediately after the conversion some Christian Slavs also felt ill-at-ease because their new priests were Greek rather than Bulgarian. The tendency towards rejection of, or at least indifference to the state and temporal affairs was strengthened by two religious movements which gained particular strength in Bulgaria. The first was hermitism. Imported from Armenia and Syria this became widespread in Bulgaria and a hermit, Ivan Rilski, who lived from the late 880s until 947, became, and remains, the national saint. An even more widespread phenomenon was bogomilism. To the bogomils the temporal world was the creation of Satan whilst the spiritual was made by God, who had sent his Son, Jesus Christ, to show the world humility and the way to salvation. In times of social hardship it was a popular creed for peasants who were disillusioned with self-enriching and haughty clerics. But if bogomilism met spiritual and social needs it posed political difficulties. In preaching that all

[21] Vassil Gyuzelev, 'The Bulgarian Medieval State: Seventh to Fourteenth Centuries', *Southeastern Europe*, 8/1–2 (1981), 19–39, 21.   [22] Genchev, *Ochertsi*, 28.

institutions were evil it inculcated a contempt for the state and the Church and fostered a form of indifference which made it difficult to mobilize the population in defence of the state.

By the middle of the tenth century Bulgaria was in decline. Renewed wars in the north and yet again with Byzantium weakened it and in 971 the Byzantines took Preslav. The Bulgarian capital moved to the west but never settled for long in any centre and despite a military resurgence and further territorial expansion under Tsar Samuil (997–1014) the Bulgarian state was doomed. In 1014 its armies were defeated in battle on the slope of Mount Belasitsa in present-day Macedonia. Legend has it that the victorious Byzantine emperor earned himself the sobriquet of 'Basil the Bulgar-Slayer' by blinding ninety-nine in every hundred Bulgarian captives and leaving the hundredth with one eye to guide his comrades home.

The legend was probably created in order to intimidate would-be invaders from the north and to increase the prestige of later emperors in Constantinople, and it was much exploited in the early twentieth century when Greek and Bulgarian aspirations again clashed in Macedonia.[23] The Bulgarian state lasted for four years after Belasitsa after which it was gradually incorporated into the Byzantine empire. There it remained until the late twelfth century when social tensions occasioned by the increased taxation made necessary by the empire's wars, precipitated protest and eventual revolt. In 1187 the second Bulgarian empire was established with its capital in Tŭrnovo. A separate Bulgarian church was also established in 1235.

The second empire, like the first, could not escape wars either to defend itself against invaders such as the Magyars or to expand its territories. At its greatest extent, after the victory of Tsar Ivan Asen II (1218–41) at the battle of Klokotnitsa in 1230, it stretched from the Black Sea to the Aegean and the Adriatic. However, external threats soon reappeared. In 1261 the Magyars took Vidin for a short period. In the fourteenth century Bulgaria was threatened from the west by the Serbs and then by the Ottomans who had entered the Balkans in the 1340s and who in 1389 smashed the most powerful Christian army, that of the Serbs, in the battle of Kosovo Polje. In July 1393 Tŭrnovo fell after

[23] See Paul Stephenson, *The Legend of Basil the Bulgarslayer* (Cambridge: Cambridge University Press), 2003.

a three-month siege and with it the Bulgarian empire collapsed, though it
lingered for three more years in Vidin, and some form of Bulgarian state
probably continued to exist in the Dobrudja until 1399.[24]

The second Bulgarian empire, again like the first, had to decide
whether it should align with the west or the east in religious affairs. The
diverging practices of the eastern and western churches had led to their
formal separation in the great schism of 1054. Hostility towards and
suspicion of the west was greatly increased in 1204 when the Crusaders
had taken and sacked Constantinople. It was largely to fend off this
menace that the Bulgarian Tsar Kaloyan (1197–1207) concluded an
agreement with the Pope under which the Bulgarians acknowledged the
Roman pontiff's supreme authority in matters religious, whilst the latter
agreed that there would be little if any interference in internal Bulgarian
affairs. After his victory at Klokotnitsa Ivan Asen II concluded a treaty
with Byzantium which allowed the Greeks to take the lion's share of
and conquests which a joint war against the Crusaders might bring;
the condition was that the Greeks recognize the independence of the
Bulgarian Church and its Patriarch. Having secured this concession Ivan
Asen negotiated successfully with the papacy for a similar recognition by
the western Church. From 1235 Bulgaria had its own Patriarch who was
head of a fully independent Church. One of its first preoccupations
was to stress that it was a Bulgarian as opposed to a Greek or Roman
institution. This, together with the fact that there was no sizeable lay
intelligentsia, made the Church the main exponent and defender of a
separate, Bulgarian culture.

The Bulgarian Orthodox Church under the second empire produced
two masterpieces of medieval art, the frescoes at Boyana near Sofia, begun
in 1259 and now a protected UNESCO site, and the Ivan Alexander
Gospels, an illustrated manuscript now on display in the British Museum.

If it produced major works of art the second empire also reproduced
many of the faults of the first. Once again there was no attempt to
establish any authority over the sea; even today most Bulgarian words for
winds and almost all those to do with seafaring are of foreign, mainly
Italian origin.[25] The development of a navy brought technological
expertise and advance to other states but not to the second Bulgarian

---

[24] Pavlov and Tyutyundjiev, *Bŭlgarite*, 101–13.
[25] Duĭchev, *Pŭteki*, 139.

empire where manufacturing was so little advanced that the empire did not produce its own coinage until the reign of Ivan Asen II, preferring to rely until then, as the first empire had done, on that of its largest neighbour. Economic and social development was also held back by the relative lack of urbanization; there was no great city with even the capital, Tŭrnovo, never having more than 12,000 inhabitants. And despite the glories of the small church at Boyana, the second Bulgarian empire produced no great non-military official building, lay or secular.[26]

In the second empire, as in the first, bogomilism was a divisive factor. It was condemned by a council in Tŭrnovo in 1211. In later years hesychism appeared, a movement which also called upon its followers to abjure the world and to seek a life devoted to silent contemplation. Like bogomilism, hesychism lessened the commitment of the individual to society and the state thus fostering a form of individual withdrawal or inward migration. Such a mentality did not encourage commitment to the defence of the realm or of the Church. More importantly, perhaps, those who withdrew from a fallen world had no desire to change it. For that reason, the debates on the nature of spiritual and temporal authority, which did so much to stimulate the Reformation in the west, did not take place in Bulgaria, though whether it would have done so had the Ottoman conquest not severed Bulgaria's links with the rest of Europe is open to debate.

In its political organization the second empire was, like the Byzantine state upon which it modelled itself, highly centralized. Power was deemed to stem directly from God and was invested in the crown. The crown controlled ecclesiastical appointments and there were few if any 'troublesome priests' to worry a Bulgarian monarch. Nor were the nobility a threat to his authority. Land in itself did not bestow power. It was in plentiful supply and landed property was not the origin but the consequence of local power. That power was bestowed by the crown, and therefore a noble's priority was not to expand his landed possessions but to keep on the right side of the monarch. This did not make for the rebellious nobility of the west but created a subservient, administrative caste.

The nobility's chance to augment its power came with the recurrent wars of the fourteenth century. So preoccupied with battle were the rulers

[26] Genchev, *Ochertsi*, 34–6.

of this century that they could not prevent the nobility flexing their local, political muscle. Furthermore, the cost of the wars forced the government to increase taxation whilst the growing freedom of the nobility allowed them too to extract levies from the peasantry. The result was growing social discontent just at the moment when grave external dangers called for the maximum degree of internal cohesion and commitment to the defence of the empire.

An empire weakened by internal migration, by the growing power of the nobility, and by the enfeeblement of an overtaxed peasantry could not withstand the impact of Ottoman armies already dizzy with success and driven by a religious fervour which encouraged commitment rather than withdrawal.

3. THE BULGARIANS UNDER OTTOMAN RULE

The collapse of the second Bulgarian empire in the 1390s ushered in almost half a millennium of foreign domination. It has been argued that for three centuries at least Ottoman rule offered security, toleration, and relatively moderate taxation, and was therefore for many a welcome change from the plundering exactions and the increasing political instability of the last decades of the second empire. If that were the case, there was, in historic terms, a high price to pay.

In the first place the Ottoman conquest separated Bulgaria together with the rest of the Balkans from their previous and natural associations with the Slav and Orthodox world, and from their connections with a central and western Europe which was just beginning the Renaissance; for centuries the Balkans were kept away from the path of European progress. In the second place, cultural unity was fractured. There was a considerable degree of colonization. The Bulgarian lands were rich and near the imperial capital, Constantinople. This proved an attraction not only to Turks but also to Greeks, Jews, and to a lesser degree Armenians, all of whom came to play a large part in the commerce of the Bulgarian lands. The Ottomans did not insist that the conquered convert to Islam except on rare occasions, usually after outbreaks of unrest and disobedience amongst the Christian population. Other forced conversions occurred in the latter half of the seventeenth century when the empire's campaigns in central Europe made it dangerous to leave Christian villagers in control of all the strategically vital passes through the Balkan mountains. There were also instances of individuals or communities converting voluntarily, sometimes to preserve property ownership or to extend their possessions at the expense of non-converted Christian villages, or even to receive pensions or benefit payments from the state. When communities accepted Islam they seldom abandoned their Bulgarian language and thus the Bulgarian-speaking Muslims, or Pomaks, appeared.

The conquest meant the immediate destruction of the Bulgarian state, monarchy, Church, and nobility. The Tŭrnovo Patriarchate was dissolved and although that of Ohrid was allowed to continue as technically a Bulgarian institution it was almost totally under the domination of the Greek Patriarchate in Constantinople. The dissolution of the Church meant the loss of links with the past, of the historic memory contained in buildings, icons, books, etc. Immediately after the conquest these survived only in remote monasteries. The nobility also disappeared. Some were killed, some fled, and others accepted Islam in order to remain on their lands and were rapidly absorbed into the Ottoman social and political system. A number of the lesser nobility retained some of their former powers, operating under the new rulers but retaining for a while the Bulgarian title of *kmet* (mayor) or *knyaz* (prince).

The Church also suffered after the conquest because the Bulgarian element in the towns decreased. At first the Bulgarians fled from or were chased out of their urban centres, taking refuge in the hills and more remote regions of the countryside. When more stable times returned Turkish, Greek, and other colonization of the towns meant that there were few economic niches which the Bulgarians could fill. In consequence, the churches were for the most part deprived of the sources of revenue available in the towns.

A further blow to Bulgarian cultural identity came in the mid-fifteenth century. In 1454, the year after the fall of Constantinople, the Ottoman authorities introduced a new administrative system under which the empire was divided into a number of religious communities or 'millets'. Within each millet the respective religious community enjoyed considerable powers of self-regulation in questions such as education, family law, and, of course, religious affairs. The head of each religious community, the *milletbashi*, was directly responsible to the Ottoman authorities who required him to ensure the good behaviour of his flock. The system had distinct advantages. It granted freedom of worship and it enabled a multi-faith system to operate reasonably smoothly. For the sultan and the Sublime Porte, the Ottoman administrative centre, it had the advantage of devolving contentious issues concerning religious observance to the faith communities themselves. The blow to the Bulgarians, however, came from the fact that they were included in the Orthodox millet whose *milletbashi* was the Patriarch in Constantinople, who was invariably a Greek.

The millet system did much to prevent religious intolerance and the forms of persecution rampant in central and western Europe, but it did not propagate equality. The Muslim millet was always to enjoy superiority, which resulted in a series of restrictions on Christians. Many of these were minor and insignificant, for example that which prevented Christians becoming tanners because that had been Mohammed's profession, but it was a real disadvantage in any legal confrontation with a Muslim because in such cases *sheriya* law was always to take precedence. Taxation was also a greater burden for non-Muslims than for Muslims, and European Christians were subjected to the *devshirme*. This was levied at intervals and took Christian boys aged between 7 and 14 who were then converted to Islam and trained to serve in the Janissary corps which provided the sultan's civilian and military elite.

In social structure the Ottoman system inherited much from the Byzantine. Land was still owned by the head of state, now the sultan. Some estates, *hass* land, remained in his direct possession. Other estates, the *timars*, were rented out to *spahis* who were required to provide troops in proportion to the amount of land held. *Spahis* in one area were put under the command of a *beglerbeg* who also served as the civil governor of that area. The land was worked by the peasants, or *raya*, a word which originally applied to all peasants but which later came to mean non-Muslim tenants. The centralization of power was even greater under the Ottoman than under the Byzantine or Bulgarian empires. This was in no small measure the result of the fact that the sultan was also Caliph-ul-Islam, or the spiritual leader of Islam.

Under this system Bulgarian identity was maintained primarily in the small and more remote villages and monasteries. Whereas in the towns Turkish, Greek, Armenian, and other languages tended to dominate commercial exchanges, in the villages Bulgarian survived, as did Bulgarian names and the observance of Bulgarian customs and religious holidays. It was the women in particular who preserved the language, passing it and the Bulgarian folk memory on to their offspring in the cradle and the nursery. The preservation of Bulgarian culture was also helped by the fact that the more remote communities saw little of the Ottoman administrators or tax collectors. In the monasteries, particularly those far from the cities and the main lines of communication, Bulgarian books and manuscripts were preserved as were traditional crafts such as religious painting and bookbinding. Education too was maintained in the monastery cell schools which prepared priests for service in the villages.

Another important preserver of Bulgarian identity was the specialist village. The Ottoman authorities charged some villages with specific functions. Some were made responsible for ensuring that vital mountain passes were safe for the movement of troops and merchants, but other tasks were more exotic with a number being responsible for supplying birds to the sultan's falconries and one, Dedovo, being required to deliver two barrels of water per day to nearby Plovdiv. Turks were not allowed to settle in specialized villages which, because they were not taxed, were relatively wealthy; they were also allowed to regulate the fulfilment of their obligations on their own without any interference from the governmental authorities. These essentially autonomous villages therefore remained Bulgarian in nature and at the same time acquired an expertise in self-management.

Neither the preservation of a sense of cultural identity nor the acquisition of the habit of self-management, however, could produce anything which might be regarded as a national revival in the modern sense.

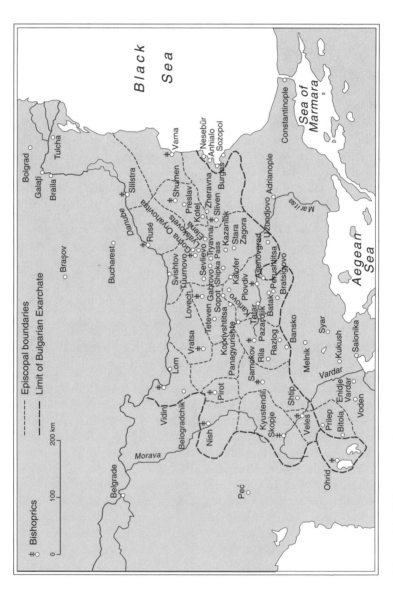

Map 2. The Bulgarian renaissance

2

The Bulgarian National Renaissance,
I. Introduction

The Bulgarian national revival, or 'vŭzrazhdane' in Bulgarian, exhibits many of the features of other nationalist reawakenings: a cultural quickening, the 'apostles' and 'awakeners', the emergence of an 'imagined community', the need for a committed social group with sufficient material wealth to further the cause, the importance of external as well as internal factors, and the equal or probably greater importance of 'the defining other'. But despite the intriguing work of the political scientists Bulgarian nationalism, like all other nationalisms, is *sui generis*. As with all other nationalisms, it was conditioned by historical, social, cultural, political, and international factors whose relative strengths and juxtapositions were unique; in few other nationalist movements, for example, did ecclesiastical affairs play so determining a role, and, conversely, in very few others did social grievances and inequalities play so minor a part. Furthermore, although the Bulgarian national state was a successor state of the Ottoman empire, the national revival which made that state possible, was, ironically, less the result of the empire's decline than of its regeneration.

The factors which were involved in the vŭzrazhdane were: economic and, to a lesser degree, social changes which provided the material base on which a national cultural edifice could be constructed; the increasing desire for education in Bulgarian which initially meant education in Bulgarian as well as Greek but which later became a demand for education in Bulgarian rather than Greek; the spread of literacy and the appearance of a Bulgarian periodical and newspaper press; the appearance of a distinct, modern literature; the growth in the authority of local communal organizations; and the eventual insistence that the Bulgarians must have a separate Bulgarian Church. The demand for political independence and the creation of a Bulgarian nation state appeared relatively late in the process.

The evolution of the vŭzrazhdane was conditioned by political and economic developments outside as well as within the Ottoman empire. The Bulgarian communities established beyond the Bulgarian lands played a hugely important role in the vŭzrazhdane; the actions and achievements of other ethnic and religious groups within all parts of the empire, Asian as well as European, had an effect on the Bulgarians; and because the Ottoman empire was so much the focus of diplomatic and strategic thinking amongst the great powers, when Bulgarian affairs became critical they were inevitably hugely influenced by developments on the international level.

The periodization of the vŭzrazhdane poses problems. The eighteenth century witnessed the first stirrings of a cultural revival but it hardly had a sufficient economic and social basis on which to construct the apparatus of a modern nation, and, furthermore, much of the economic advance and social change seen in the Bulgarian lands in that century were nullified by the *kŭrdjaliĭstvo*, or the political disorders which destabilized European Turkey at the end of the century. In this period the cultural advance of the Bulgarians was cauterized by the decline of Ottoman power. It is therefore appropriate to talk of a pre-renaissance in the eighteenth century which was cut short by the disorders which lasted, with differing degrees of intensity and with significant geographic variations, from the mid-1770s to the early-1820s.

With the restructuring of the Ottoman empire from the mid-1820s there re-emerged, but in much more developed form than in the previous century, the nascent Bulgarian wealthy elements which could provide the funds for cultural regeneration. That regeneration asserted itself primarily in the field of education and then in the campaign for a separate, Bulgarian Church. Frequently, in both campaigns, the Bulgarians found themselves pitted against not Ottoman state power but Greek cultural predominance exercised mainly through the Oecumenical Patriarchate in Constantinople.

The national revival and the confrontation with the Greek cultural world began during the 1830s and intensified markedly in the 1840s as the Bulgarian press became established and as Bulgarian communal authorities assumed greater responsibilities; these decades saw within the Bulgarian communities both an intensification of the process of modernization and a greater concentration on and consciousness of Bulgarian as opposed to Greek or Ottoman institutions and practices. The declaration of ecclesiastical independence by the Bulgarians on Easter Day 1860 brought a further intensification of the Bulgarian-Greek dispute and for another dozen years the two sides sought, unsuccessfully, for a solution to the church problem. The failure to secure satisfactory recognition of their ecclesiastical independence forced Bulgarians to ask whether they had to rely on external support, and if so from where, a question complicated by Russia's weakness after the Crimean war. And it was partly the frustrations of the protracted struggle to secure recognition of ecclesiastical independence which turned a number of powerful and influential Bulgarians in the direction of a political struggle aimed at the creation of an independent nation state.

1. THE PRE-RENAISSANCE

The first stirrings of a renewed Bulgarian national consciousness in the eighteenth century were made possible first by the military decline of the Ottoman empire. This allowed European Christian empires to expand into former Ottoman territory, whilst the cost of the wars involved precipitated structural changes in the Ottoman system. The advance of the Christian empires extended European influence, economic, cultural, and political, into European Turkey. For most of the eighteenth century these influences had little impact on the Bulgarians, though other social and economic changes were making their communities stronger and more self-confident. Cultural self-awareness was also increasing. This was registered first in the emergence of a literary form which attempted to break away from the Old Church Slavonic in which liturgical texts and most previous Bulgarian material had been written. Subsequently, there emerged figures with a sense of history who rediscovered the past glories of the first and second Bulgarian empires. The direct influence of these first apostles was small because literacy was little developed, because there were no facilities for printing their writings, and, most importantly, because their emergence was almost coincidental with the *kŭrdjaliĭstvo* which did so much to disrupt Bulgarian economic and cultural development.

Structural changes within the Ottoman empire

The Ottoman failure to take Vienna in 1683 marked the end of the empire's territorial expansion. In the succeeding decades, though frontiers fluctuated, the Habsburgs repossessed Hungary and Transylvania and in 1774 were awarded part of the Bukovina; for a while they were also in occupation of Wallachia and of Belgrade. Towards the end of the century the treaty of Kutchuk Kainardji, which ended the Russo-Ottoman war of 1769–74, initiated important long-term changes in that the Straits were opened to Russian merchant vessels and, more importantly, Russia was given the right to intervene diplomatically in Constantinople to safeguard the well-being of the Ottoman empire's Orthodox Christians. During the Russo-Ottoman war of 1787 to 1792 the tsar's forces took control of Moldavia and Wallachia, whilst those of his Habsburg ally occupied Bosnia. During the French revolutionary wars Dalmatia was incorporated into the Habsburg domains, whilst the Ionian islands were administered by the French and the Russians before becoming a British responsibility after the wars. Modern ideas reached the Balkans through these areas, but the most lasting impact on the Bulgarian lands was to be made by the Russo-Turkish war of 1806 to 1812.

The demands of war brought about important changes in the Ottoman empire. The *spahis* had originally held land in order to wage war and this most of them had been prepared to do because war brought conquest and plunder. When war became unprofitable the *spahi* tended more and more to regard his land not as a means to raise troops for war but as a source of wealth and profit in its own right. As the *spahi* became less central to the raising of the Ottoman armies the Janissaries became more so. Once a highly disciplined, dependable, elite force forbidden to marry, and recruited through the *devshirme*, by the mid-eighteenth century the Janissaries had for long been in decline. Since before the end of the seventeenth century they been allowed to marry and were becoming a self-perpetuating professional caste replenished from within rather than refreshed from without by the introduction of the talented young; the last *devshirme* was levied in the Bulgarian lands in 1685.[1] By the late eighteenth century many of them had come to defy the central

---

[1] Dennis P. Hupchick, *The Bulgarians in the Seventeenth Century: Slavic Orthodox Society and Culture under Ottoman Rule* (Jefferson, NC: McFarland, 1993), 34.

government and establish their own satrapies. And they had sufficient political muscle in Constantinople to block most reforms which might encroach upon their privileges.

A critical problem for the empire in the seventeenth and eighteenth centuries was how to raise the money to wage its wars. By the late seventeenth century the need for extra revenue and the declining functionality of the *spahi* had led to the replacement of the *beglerbeg* with a new official, the *vali* whose area of jurisdiction was the newly created unit of government, the 'vilayet'. The main function of the *vali* was to raise revenue for the central government and as the financial situation of the empire deteriorated the exactions of the *vali* inevitably increased. The financial burden fell mainly on the peasant and the townsman. Matters were made worse by the fact that many official responsibilities, including tax collection, were being put out to tender. The selling of office provided a useful source of supplementary revenue for the sultan and his government but the tax farmer used his position for self-enrichment and so increased the total tax burden on the peasant; tax farming also tended to increase the brutality of the tax collecting process.

High-ranking state offices were frequently bought by wealthy and influential Greeks, many of whom lived in the Phanar district of Constantinople. The holders of the highest positions recouped the costs involved in purchasing their office by selling the subordinate posts within their own jurisdiction. These officials of the second rank did likewise so the sale of office percolated down through the administrative system to the lowest level where, of course, there were no subordinate posts to sell and the purchasers of these basic offices therefore exacted the costs of their positions from the taxpayers. The phanariot Greeks bought high office in the Orthodox Church as well as in the Ottoman state apparatus.

This had two important consequences. The first was the spread into the ecclesiastical domain of the venality inherent in the selling of office. The second was that it increased yet further Greek influence within the Oecumenical Patriarchate and when Greek nationalism began to stir in the second half of the eighteenth century this could produce attempts to hellenize non-Greek communities. In the 1750s the Patriarch Samuel strove to entrench Greek influence by, for example, ordering the burning of books and manuscripts in Slavonic. The nominally independent Serbian Patriarchate in Peć was incorporated into the Oecumenical Patriarchate in Constantinople in 1766 and in 1767 the Bulgarian

Patriarchate at Ohrid suffered a similar fate. In the late eighteenth and early nineteenth centuries the Bulgarians' defining other was frequently a Greek cleric rather than an Ottoman political official.

The Bulgarians in the eighteenth century

Christian victories over the Ottoman armies brought about a considerable expansion of trade between south-eastern Europe and the remainder of the continent. In this the Bulgarian lands took a major share; by the end of the eighteenth century they accounted for approximately a fifth of the empire's trade although covering only an eighth of its total area. Cotton from Macedonia was sold widely in Saxony in the first half of the century, and large quantities of wool from the same area were on sale in the Leipzig fair of 1729. Other export items included wool, *abas* (a coarse-grained cloth) honey, and wax. The growth of trade, however, had little impact on the methods of production. Even in one of the most profitable sectors of agriculture, stock raising, there was little in the way of capitalization. Flocks were mostly reared by traditional methods, frequently being driven considerable distances between summer and winter pastures, and then to the markets in Adrianople (Edirne) and Constantinople. As both these centres had large Muslim populations sheep were the main animals produced and a number of Bulgarian communities made sizeable profits from *djelepchiĭstvo*, or sheep trading.

The sheep rearers were usually organized into guilds, or *esnafs*, and these institutions also dominated manufacturing. They were to become a vitally important factor in the *vŭzrazhdane*. The guilds had a long history as well as an important future. The Turkish traveller Evliya Chelebi recorded that there were 880 workshop stalls in Plovdiv market at the end the seventeenth century and most of these would have been associated with a guild.[2] The oldest of the guilds, as well as the most important, was that of the *aba* makers in Plovdiv. Its records, kept in Greek until the 1850s, are extant from 1685 but it existed, as did others, long before that. It declined somewhat in the 1760s and 1770s but flourished again from the mid-1800s and in 1817 witnessed its largest ever assembly when over a thousand members took part. Little is known about the ethnic composition of the guilds, though there was a tendency towards ethnic specialization.

[2] Genchev, *Ochertsi*, 91–2.

In the gold-mining guilds around Tŭrnovo, for example, Bulgarians predominated from as early as the seventeenth century, and in 1739 an Ottoman document referred to the competition a new Bulgarian shoemakers' guild presented to Sofia's Turkish shoemakers.

Examples such as these indicate that in the eighteenth century the Bulgarian element in the towns was increasing. This was in part the result of demographic factors. There seems to have been a decline in both Muslim birth-rates and Christian death-rates. The reasons for this are obscure and explanations have ranged from the varying ethnic susceptibilities to plague to the widespread Muslim practice of abortion. That migration took place from surrounding villages into towns is proved not only by the competition suffered by the Turkish shoemakers of Sofia but also by local court registers in that and other towns, for example Rusé and Vidin, all of which contain details of sales of land by Muslim townsmen to Christian incomers, whilst the surviving guild records show an increase in the number of members with obviously Bulgarian names. In some towns the local Bulgarians, usually operating through their guilds, erected distinctive new buildings such as covered markets, workshops, or even urban towers; the latter appeared in Shumen in 1741, Sevlievo in 1777, Elena in 1812, and Tryavna in 1813.

The erection of urban towers was significant in the Ottoman context because Christians were not allowed to have buildings which were as high as the local mosque, and therefore the towers could be taken as an assertion of greater cultural self-awareness and self-confidence on the part of the Christians. There were other similar signs.

The first cultural stirrings

The beginnings of European expansion into the Balkans had triggered a quickening of cultural activities amongst Bulgarian Catholics in centres such as Vienna, Zagreb, and Novi Sad. At the same time within the Bulgarian lands the first very tentative steps were being taken towards greater interchange of information and opinion within those lands. In the late seventeenth and early eighteenth century a new form of literature appeared with the *damaskini*, or homilies. These were addressed to the laity as well as to the clergy and the deity, and they were written in what philologists have come to call 'new Bulgarian' which incorporated some demotic elements into the staid, medieval Bulgarian still used in clerical writings; a number of compilers of the *damaskini* emphasized the usefulness of literacy and called for the translation of texts in Old Church Slavonic and Greek into everyday Bulgarian.[3] Some new Bulgarian writing was to be found in copies of ancient hagiographies which were still being produced and some of which contained information on Bulgarian saints and rulers of the erstwhile Bulgarian kingdoms.

The hagiographies were produced by monks in monastic scriptoria, but the monasteries were far from being closed, introspective institutions. They owned properties scattered throughout the Bulgarian lands and the *taxidioti*, or monks who travelled to collect revenues from monastic properties, brought to the villages news of happenings in the wider world, and took back to the monasteries the feelings and views of the villagers. Some monks also served as itinerant teachers.

Others travelled for scholastic purposes. A number of Bulgarian monks found their way to the great Orthodox centre at Sremski Karlovtsi in present-day Serbia where they exchanged information with monks and clerics from other parts of the Orthodox world. Here worked Hristofor Zhefarovich and Parteniĭ Pavlovich. The latter was a native of Silistra but had travelled widely in order, as he explained in his autobiography, to escape the slavery of his homeland; he was also one of a number of contemporaries to express faith in the liberating mission of Russia. It was one of the first indications of the belief that linguistic affinities and above all a common faith made Russia the natural patron of the Bulgarians.

The early 'apostles'

In addition to the *damaskini* the monasteries also produced histories. One, *A Short History of the Bulgarian Slavic People*, was written by Spiridon of Gabrovo and another emerged from the monastery at Zograf on Mount Athos founded in the fifteenth century by refugees from Tŭrnovo. The latter was used by the most important of all eighteenth century Bulgarian writers, Paisiĭ Hilendarski.

Paisiĭ was born in 1722 in Bansko and in his early twenties went to Mount Athos, where he became a monk in the monastery of Hilendar, hence his name. He became a *taxidiot*, his experiences in the Bulgarian

---

[3] See Donka Petkanova-Toteva, *Damaskinite v bŭlgarskata literatura* (Sofia: BAN, 1965).

villages making him more and more concerned at the low cultural standing of the Bulgarians compared to the Greeks. Paisiĭ read and travelled widely. He is known to have consulted Russian manuscripts in Sremski Karlovtsi in 1761 but his passions were most inflamed by the ancient Bulgarian texts he studied in Hilendar and in the nearby monastery of Zograf. Paisiĭ poured his knowledge and his passions into *A Slavonic-Bulgarian History of the Peoples, Tsars, Saints, and of all their Deeds and of the Bulgarian Way of Life*, a work which, though steeped in nostalgia for past institutions, had some prescriptions for the future. Paisiĭ insisted that he had written his text 'for the ordinary Bulgarian' and for 'the benefit of the whole Bulgarian nation', and thus some contemporary idioms were to be found in his writing, a feature which helped to make his the most important of the works produced by Bulgarian writers in the eighteenth century.

The manuscript had two main purposes. The first was to recall and relate the greatness of the past Bulgarian empires: the Bulgarians, he said, were the first Slavs to have kings, the first to have a patriarch, and the first to adopt Christianity; and their empire was the largest of the medieval Slav empires. Paisiĭ's second purpose was to issue a plea for greater self-confidence and self-assertion on the part of the Bulgarians, whom he first castigated for their cultural submissiveness and their apparent inferiority complex vis-à-vis the Greeks, after which he urged the Bulgarians to cherish their own culture. Rather than learning Greek the Bulgarian should, he wrote, 'know your own nation and language and study in your own tongue' and should 'keep close to your heart your race and your Bulgarian homeland'.

After completing his manuscript Paisiĭ again travelled throughout the Balkans, this time with the express intent of proselytizing. On Mount Athos in 1765 he met his most influential disciple: Stoĭko Vladislavov, usually known by his clerical name of Sofroniĭ Vrachanski (of Vratsa). Born in Kotel in 1739 of a family of wealthy cattle drovers he had been sent, at the insistence of local leaders, to be educated in Athos. Greatly inspired by Paisiĭ he subsequently had a copy of the latter's great work placed in his own church in Vratsa where Sofroniĭ had been made bishop. Sofroniĭ acted upon Paisiĭ's injunctions and in Vratsa delighted his congregation by preaching in Bulgarian rather than Greek. He was later to press the need for more writing in 'ordinary Bulgarian'.

There can be little doubt that Paisiĭ inspired other Bulgarians besides Sofroniĭ. The writer Petko Slaveĭkov wrote that Paisiĭ had made him 'set myself a new task: to save my nation, to instil patriotism. Reading and copying this book set my aspirations and my activities on a new course.'[4] Sixty copies of his manuscript survive, which would suggest that more were made, the extant examples being found in Bulgarian communities from Macedonia to Bessarabia. Paisiĭ's influence was far from immediate. His book was not printed until an edition appeared in Budapest in 1844 and the work was anonymous, the true author not being established until 1871 through the work of the Bulgarian historian, Marin Drinov.

Paisiĭ's was not the only work to be copied. On average once every two years between 1810 and 1844 a copy was made of *Aleksandriyata*. This large work was a romanticized version of the life of Alexander the Great but adapted to contemporary conditions and in some copies the eponymous hero was presented as a Christian Slav fighting against the Turks. The Bulgarian 'imagined community' was beginning to take shape.

One of the reasons why the works of Paisiĭ and others were relatively neglected was the disruption brought to the Bulgarian lands by the *kŭrdjaliĭstvo*.

2. THE *KŬRDJALIĬSTVO*

The disorders which affected the Balkans in the last quarter of the eighteenth century had two main characteristics: illegal land acquisition and a collapse of central government authority.

In the second half of the century there was an acceleration of the process by which individuals established control over landed property and over those who lived upon it. At times this land might be acquired because plague had removed the existing tenants, and if land were left untilled for a certain period it could then be sold and its new owners would often impose new conditions on the tenants. Other new landlords assumed control over the land of their debtors, a practice which the sultan attempted to forbid in 1795. Other properties were taken by *ayani*, or power-brokers, who already controlled the local civil and financial administrations, this combination of fiscal and landed power being particularly potent; peasants on the newly acquired land were then subjected to ruinous taxation forcing many of them to relinquish their

---

[4] Quoted in Krasimira Daskalova, *Bŭlgarskiyat uchitel prez vŭzrazhdaneto* (Sofia: Kliment Ohridski, 1997), 197.

existing rights and subordinate themselves entirely to the new landlord. The latter often recruited armed irregulars, or *kŭrdjalĭ*. Their task was to reinforce the landlords' authority or, in many cases, to force reluctant villagers to surrender their title deeds so that a landlord's property acquired piecemeal in dispersed pockets could be joined into a compact holding.

Much of the process of land acquisition by the *ayani* and others had contravened the Ottoman legal code but by the third quarter of the eighteenth century the government was hardly in a position to resist the rise of the local warlords. Wars were frequently lost, which meant a decrease in the prestige and authority of the government; and even if a war were not lost, it created financial demands which were just as debilitating. To make matters worse, the end of a war usually produced large numbers of ill-disciplined and unemployed troops wandering around the Balkans and living off the land. Many of these were recruited by the warlords.

The disorders were worst near centres of wealth. These included the largest cities, the *kŭrdjalĭstvo* affecting the area around Adrianople and even those nearer the imperial capital itself. Major roads, too, were a source of potential wealth, villages and towns near to them being vulnerable to attack or incorporation into the fief of a warlord, as were many coastal areas. The plains, because of their wealth and their accessibility, were more at risk than mountainous areas, the term *kŭrdjalĭ* being derived from a Turkish word meaning plains. The rich lands of southern Bulgaria, the Vardar valley, the Aegean coast, and the Thracian plain were all seriously affected.

At times the *kŭrdjalĭstvo* brought great destruction and deprivation at the hands both of the warlords and of the troops sent to oppose them. An ill-disciplined force of some 100,000 Ottoman soldiers sent in a vain attempt to bring the local warlord, Osman Pazvantoglu, to heel wreaked such havoc in the Vidin district that so many people died or fled that the despairing bishop found that there were not enough people left to raise taxes sufficient for his upkeep. In Sofia in 1800 so many had fled from the local disorders that the poll tax, one of the most important items of government revenue, could not be levied. In 1801 Grozyu, the priest of All Saints' Church Teteven, recorded laconically that soldiers had burnt the church and killed 'half the village', men, women, and children alike.[5]

---

[5] Bistra A. Tsvetkova, 'Turskiyat felodalizŭm i polozhenieto na bŭlgarskiya narod do nachaloto na xix v', *Istoricheski Pregled*, 11/1 (1955), 59–86, 85.

Efforts were made to contain the disorders. Sultan Selim III attempted to reimpose central authority in 1791 but had little success. Equally ineffective was legislation to ban the foundation of new private estates and to insist that land worked by peasants could not be sold without the permission of the Porte. At times force was used to try to bring the warlords to heel, but the effort required was huge and enormously costly; in 1801 the sultan had to deploy between 6,000 and 7,000 troops and two cannon to deal with the *kŭrdjalii* near Karlovo, which was not a badly affected area. Shortly after this, the outbreak of the first Serbian revolt in 1804, itself primarily the result of the exactions of local *ayani*, imposed further strains upon the central government and diverted troops which might otherwise have been employed in containing the disorders.

The Russo-Turkish war of 1806 to 1812 had a similar effect in diverting the state's resources. The *kŭrdjaliĭstvo* was still in full spate in Thrace in the 1800s; from 1810 to 1812 the Plovdiv district was held by Kara Mustafa and as late as 1816 the Adrianople *sanjak* was in the same position, as was Stara Zagora, whilst a band of 300 was active in the Burgas area.

Peace with Russia in 1812 and an accommodation with the Serbs in 1814 meant that at last order began to be restored. In 1813 Vidin was brought back under government control and by the 1820s not even the outbreak of the Greek war of independence could halt the gradual reimposition of central authority. In 1826 the sultan's sudden and extremely violent dissolution of those arch opponents of central government power, the Janissaries, laid to rest any doubt that the era of disorders was over.

The *kŭrdjaliĭstvo* truncated many of the developments which had fostered the growing cultural awareness of the Bulgarians. Trade, particularly with Europe, was disrupted, the accumulation of wealth in many centres ceased, and the peaceful transmission of the ideas of Paisiĭ and his followers was made much more difficult. On the other hand, ironically, the *kŭrdjaliĭstvo* initiated or accelerated other processes which were to benefit the Bulgarian *vŭzrazhdane*.

During the *kŭrdjaliĭstvo* many communities organized a messenger service to warn other villages of the approach of a marauding band; most villages of southern Bulgaria and Thrace had done this by the end of the century. Government officials seldom had the time or inclination to take part themselves in preparing the defences of individual settlements and therefore the considerable work and organization involved was left to the villagers themselves. Few seem to have concluded at this juncture that the *kŭrdjaliĭstvo* showed the fragility and ultimate vulnerability of the Ottoman system, but the habits and experience gained in organizing their defence persisted in many communities after the end of the disorders. Vratsa, for example, which was to be the first community to refuse to pay taxes to its bishop, had organized itself against the ravages of Pazvantoglu.

In some cases villagers did not have the time or resources to organize their defence and simply fled from the marauders. A Russian diplomatic report of 1802 speaks of a mass exodus of peasants from the plains of Thrace to the Black Sea coast. Other victims of the *kŭrdjaliĭstvo* took refuge in nearby towns, not least in the imperial capital and in so doing increased the Bulgarian elements in those towns. Many others, reversing a population drift under way in the eighteenth century, took refuge in the villages and small towns of the mountainous areas which were generally less susceptible to attack. These towns were also less ethnically diverse than those in the plains and some, such as Koprivshtitsa, Elena, and Panagyurishte, were almost entirely Bulgarian. In many the disorders were distant enough for some manufacturing and commerce to survive and even expand, and these settlements, particularly those such as Karlovo, Kazanlŭk, Kalofer, and Koprivshtitsa in the foothills of the Balkan mountains, were to play a major role in the vŭzrazhdane in the following century.

3. POPULATION MOVEMENTS

The *kŭrdjaliĭstvo* had strengthened not only the Bulgarian element in the small mountain towns but also another element which was to play a vital role in the vŭzrazhdane, the Bulgarian communities in exile. During the disorders, and especially at the conclusion of the Russo-Turkish war of 1806 to 1812, up to a 100,000 Bulgarians fled north of the Danube to Wallachia, Moldavia, and Bessarabia, and there were 80,000 Bulgarians in southern Russia in 1818. Some who had moved to Wallachia had been attracted by exemption from various taxes, such as those on sheep and long-horned cattle, a concession introduced by the Russian administrator in the province in 1809.

This was not a new phenomenon for previous periods of disorder had caused emigration, particularly when the local population had shown signs of disaffection with or hostility to the Ottoman authorities. As early as the fifteenth century records speak of up to 70 per cent of village lands in the Bulgarian areas being vacant because so many villagers had fled. Wars and local uprisings, the latter often occurring during the former and being prompted by the hope that invading armies might dislodge the Ottoman regime, were often the cause of major population movement. The Bulgarian community in Braila, which was to play a vital part in the later stages of the national revival, had its origins in the emigration which followed an abortive rising around Tŭrnovo in 1598, whilst, as has been noted, the Bulgarians in the Banat of Temesvar were descendants of émigrés who had fled their homes after the rising around Chiprovets in 1688. After the wars of the late 1730s some 20,000 Bulgarians moved into Wallachia, and after the Russo-Turkish war of 1768 to 1774 there were an estimated 160,000 Bulgarians in the province. In 1811 the leaders of those who fled during the Russo-Turkish war then being fought addressed a petition to Tsar Alexander I asking for Russian protection for the émigré Bulgarians. The petition also asked for the rights to trade freely, and to have religious services and schools in their own language.[6]

In times of prolonged disorder the Bulgarian lands were not harmed by mass emigration, and in the long term this process greatly assisted the national revival. A number of émigré communities gradually grew in wealth and, having retained a consciousness of their original culture and region, became significant benefactors to the national revival. Of the ninety Bulgarian newspapers and periodicals published between 1844 and 1878 a third were published outside the Ottoman empire,[7] and it was in the Bulgarian community in Braila, for example, that the organization which eventually became the Bulgarian Academy of Sciences (BAN) was established; it was also in Romania that the Georgiev brothers made the money which was to fund the institution which became the University of Sofia. The Bulgarian communities in Bucharest and Odessa were also influential in the vŭzrazhdane but none played a greater role than that in Constantinople, which in the nineteenth century held the greatest

[6] For the 1811 petition see Stefan Doĭnov, *Bŭlgarskoto natsionalno-osvoboditelno dvizhenie 1800–1812* (Sofia: BAN, 1979), 181–3.

[7] Steven Ashley, 'Bulgarian Nationalism (1830–1876): The Ideals and Careers of Ivan Bogorov, Georgi Rakovski, and Pencho Slaveĭkov', D.Phil. thesis (Oxford, 1984), 182.

concentration of urban Bulgarians anywhere. When Catherine the Great compiled her encyclopaedia of world languages Bulgarian was not amongst the 279 listed,[8] nor were the Bulgarians mentioned in the treaty of Bucharest which regulated the Balkans after the Russo-Turkish war of 1806–12; fifty years later the increasingly wealthy and vocal émigré Bulgarian communities would have ensured that their voice was heard.

Emigration was not always entirely beneficial. The largest exodus of Bulgarians took place immediately after the Russo-Turkish war of 1828 to 1829 when as many as a quarter of a million Bulgarians were said to have moved north of the Danube. Even some Macedonians joined the exodus although their region was hardly affected by the upheavals of the war. The emigration of 1829 was a highly organized affair. When the Russian armies withdrew from south of the Balkans in that year Romanian landowners, or boyars, sent agents into the Bulgarian lands to recruit peasants to serve on their estates, whilst some Bulgarian communities sent representatives to look for places where they and their fellow citizens might settle and work. The Russian governor of Wallachia and Moldavia from 1828 to 1834, Count Pavel Kiselev, helped the emigrants by establishing three regular crossing points, each equipped with quarantine facilities, and by organizing welfare services, tax exemptions, and grain distribution for those moving northward. Some of the migrants soon returned. They were induced to do so by concessions offered by the Ottoman regime which agreed to pay those returning compensation for their lost harvests; they were also motivated by discontent because they found they were required to pay labour dues to the boyar and tax to the Wallachian authorities.

Despite the return of some of the migrants the exodus had harmful effects. Large areas of the eastern Bulgarian lands, especially south of the Balkan mountains, were depopulated and many of those who had left had come from economically relatively advanced areas and communities whose economic progress was slowed by this loss of labour and markets. These effects of the emigration were still clearly visible a decade later. In 1841 Blanqui noted that when travelling between Vidin and Belogradchik he did not meet a living soul, reflecting that 'en cas de malheur la Valachie n'est pas loin';[9] even the western lands had suffered,

[8] Dennis P. Hupchick, *The Pen and the Sword; Studies in Bulgarian History by James F. Clarke* (Boulder, Colo.: East European Monographs no. 252, distributed by Columbia University Press, 1988), 190.

[9] J. A. Blanqui, *Voyage en Bulgarie pendant l'anné 1841* (Paris, 1843), 149.

he continued, noting that in the Sofia plain 'quelques rares champs de blé et de mais attestent seuls la présence de l'homme'.[10]

The exodus of 1829–30, though the largest in Bulgarian history, was not the last. In 1841 peasants in the north-west of Bulgaria revolted against increasing taxes, and both during the rising and its suppression many of them left. The government, concerned at the depopulation of an area which was now near the periphery of the empire, then sought to woo the departed back with schemes to help them resettle and recover their possessions. There were renewed fears of depopulation after a further rising in the Nish vilayet in 1850.

Other population movements also affected the progress of the Bulgarian national revival. After the Crimean war the Ottoman government, anxious to strengthen its northern border, planted communities of Circassians in the Danubian plain. They, with the Tatars who had been settled in previous decades, diluted the Bulgarian population in the area; according to Pencho Slaveĭkov they perpetrated horrors equivalent to those of the Vikings in western Europe.[11] A number of Christians left when Circassians were settled in or near their villages, claiming that it was no longer safe to send their children out to tend the animals; the rich sheep and goat rearers near Vratsa were said to have been ruined by the Circassians. Some of the displaced Christians moved to the Crimea whence some of the new settlers had come. The move was not always successful and a German who travelled in the area in the 1860s and 1870s found near Lovech a number of Bulgarian families who had moved to the Crimea in 1861 but had then returned only to find their original properties had been taken by Tatars; the returnees had been forced to live as troglodytes.[12]

Mass emigration was no doubt made more acceptable to Bulgarians because there was already by the end of the eighteenth century a considerable fluidity in the labour force. The seasonal movement of labour had increased considerably during the second half of the eighteenth century and there was a particular drift of market gardeners to Constantinople. By the second quarter of the nineteenth century workers were moving from

---

[10] J. A. Blanqui, *Voyage en Bulgarie pendant l'anné 1841*, 184.

[11] Pencho Slaveĭkov, 'Bŭlgarskata narodna pesen', in Elenkov and Daskalov, *Zashto sme takiva?*, 49–72, 63.

[12] F. Kanitz, *Donau-Bulgarien und der Balkan: Historisch-geographisch-ethnographische Reisestudien aus den Jahren 1860–1879*, enlarged edition, 3 vols. (Leipzig: H. Fries, 1882), ii. 25.

areas of relatively high population to those where labour was scarce, often because of emigration; thousands of labourers from Tŭrnovo, Gorna Oryahovitsa, and Lyaskovets travelled each harvest season to the Dobrudja, southern Bulgaria, and Thrace. The Ottoman authorities even issued orders for the movement of labour; Tŭrnovo, for instance, was required to supply 3,000 harvesters for work in the Dobrudja. After the war of 1828 to 1829 shepherds from the Kotel area began taking their flocks to the Dobrudja where they rented pastures from Turkish townsmen; the flocks were huge, some of them of up to 30,000 animals, and by the liberation of 1878 there were 450,000 sheep from the Kotel area in the Dobrudja. As in the eighteenth century, many of the sheep were still driven hundreds of miles to the south for sale in the markets of Adrianople and Constantinople. Other patterns of seasonal movement were from the Stara Planina to the Danubian plain and the Dobrudja, and from western Bulgaria and the Sredna Gora to the Maritsa valley, the Sea of Marmara, and even to the Aegean, whilst from western and northern Macedonia workers moved to the towns of Salonika, Bitola (Monastir), and Prilep, to southern and northern Bulgaria, or even as far afield as Wallachia. The migratory workers were usually organized into gangs run for profit by gang leaders and the numbers involved were large; in 1854 from the Elena area alone 3,230 harvesters went to work in the imperial and other estates of southern Thrace. Nor was the movement confined to the Bulgarian lands and the Ottoman empire in Europe. Bulgarians went to work in Romania, Russia, the Habsburg empire, and other states; over 40,000 foreign labourers, many of them Bulgarian, went to work in Serbia in the early 1870s. By far the majority of these seasonal labourers worked in the agrarian sector; in a number of European cities they were nicknamed 'gardeners' because so many worked on smallholdings in or near the towns.

Population fluidity had both positive and negative impacts on the vŭzrazhdane. The people who moved, particularly if they went outside the empire or to cosmopolitan centres within it, came into contact with ideas from a wider, more modern world; if they became wealthy they could use their money to further those ideas, and they could also bring Bulgarian issues to the notice of foreign nations. For those anxious to press for political independence, however, population fluidity helped to weaken the identification of ethnicity with territory, and the modern form of European, political nationalism can scarcely exist without claim to complete and unchallenged national sovereignty in a defined geographic area.

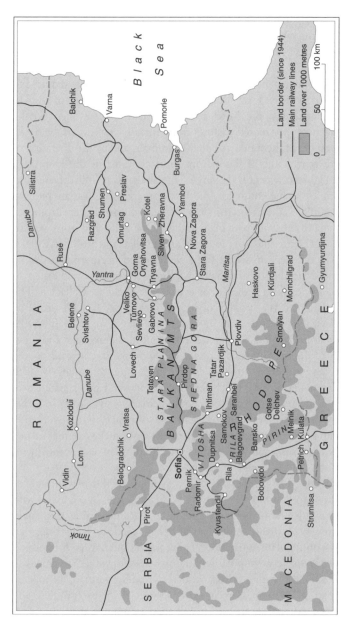

Map 3. Bulgaria: main towns and railway lines

3

The Bulgarian National Renaissance, II.
The Cultural Revival and the Creation
of the Modern Bulgarian State

The factors which made possible the emergence of Bulgarian national feeling, and its organization into an effective force in Ottoman affairs, were stability within the empire itself and the modernization of its political structure, and the generation amongst the Bulgarians themselves of a sense of national identity. For the latter what was needed, said the pioneer nationalist of the 1860s, Georgi Rakovski, was 'a national church, schools, and a press'.[1]

1. THE TANZIMAT AND THE MODERNIZATION OF THE OTTOMAN SYSTEM

The Bulgarian vŭzrazhdane would have been much more difficult, if not impossible, without the Tanzimat, the major restructuring of the Ottoman empire which began in the mid-1820s with the suppression of the Janissaries. Reform was delayed by the Greek war of independence and more so by the Russo-Turkish war of 1828–9, but by the mid-1830s it had picked up momentum. The Bulgarians were particularly affected by two aspects of Ottoman reconstruction: the expansion of trade with Europe and the creation of a professional Ottoman army. These two factors combined to increase the wealth of the Bulgarian lands and to

[1] Mari A. Firkatian, *The Forest Traveler: Georgi Stoikov Rakovski and Bulgarian Nationalism*, Balkan Studies no. 5, general editor Eran Fraenkel (New York: Peter Lang, 1996), 104. Firkatian is quoting an archival source.

stimulate gradual social change, and thus to provide the economic basis for cultural regeneration.

Under the old regime Ottoman trade had been hampered both by a government monopoly on grain which the authorities bought at low prices, and by the practice of granting export licences only when home demand had been satisfied. In 1815, however, the Porte concluded a trade treaty with the Habsburg monarchy which removed existing restrictions on Austrian vessels using the Danube. Deregulation had begun and the regulations governing the grain trade eased. In 1830 a further agreement between Constantinople and Vienna gave Austrian vessels the sole right to trade on the river; the Danube Shipping Company, founded in Vienna in 1834, made full use of this privilege. A trade treaty with Britain in 1838 increased the demand for Ottoman grains, as did similar treaties with France, the USA, and other states. Svishtov, which had suffered massive depopulation in the *kŭrdjaliĭstvo* and during the 1828–9 war, recovered to become a major exchange point for trade along the Danube and by the 1870s was so well connected with the European commercial market that it was severely affected by the European financial crisis of 1873.

The second major influence on the Bulgarian lands produced by the Ottoman reforms came as a result of the creation of a regular, standing army. It had a twofold impact. The first was to bring about a restructuring of the landholding system which produced unrest in isolated areas of the Bulgarian lands; the second was to trigger an economic boom which benefited most Bulgarian manufacturing communities.

The introduction of a standing army meant the end of the ancient, and long-decayed *timar* system with the *spahi* as the provider of soldiers. With the hatt-i-sherif, or 'charter of liberties', of 1839 the government began to codify the changes this implied. A major function of this enactment was to transfer the rights and responsibilities of landholding from the *spahi* to the state. Furthermore, most taxes, and in particular the tithe, were no longer to be collected by the landlord; each village was now to draw up a precise and clear inventory of individual holdings and on the basis of this the state tax collector would assess how much the village should pay. At the same time, in an effort to contain previous evils, private tax collection, or tax farming, was outlawed.

Some private estates did appear as a result of the 1839 reform because some *spahis*, with the connivance of local officials, managed to make themselves owners of the land they had previously held from the sultan.

This process was prevalent in the north-west around Nish and Vidin and in the south-west near Kyustendil, where the new landlords imposed various forms of exploitative tenure. However, the new owners seldom transformed their holdings into 'chifliks', or commercialized estates, where production, which was aimed at the market, was determined by the owner rather than the peasants who worked the land. In fact, even taking into account developments in the north- and south-west the ending of the *spahi's* rights meant in effect that the vast majority of Bulgarians became small freeholders who had the right to grow what they wished, how they wished. Even an assiduous and distinguished marxist scholar noted that 'the mass of the rural population of the pre-liberation Bulgarian lands consisted of small commodity producers who owned their own land...'[2]

The reforms did, however, increase the total amount of tax paid and in some areas the new tax collectors conspired with the former *spahis* and private tax collectors to increase the levies; there were even instances of the new tax being levied in addition to rather than instead of the old, and, once again, this was a problem most prevalent in the Nish, Vidin, and Kyustendil areas. These irregularities were an example of the Ottoman empire's perennial problem of the lack of central government control over its local representatives and the consequent gap between the content of legislation and the reality of its enforcement. It was a problem which did not entirely disappear with the creation of the new Bulgarian state in 1878.

The increased burden of taxation and the exploitative tenures were the main causes of the outbursts of unrest in Vidin in 1841 and Nish in 1850. But these were isolated outbursts and the Bulgarian revolutionaries of the nineteenth century paid little attention to social issues and, unlike their Bosnian counterparts, had no cause to demand the dissolution of large estates. The creation of the small, self-sufficient peasant produced, outside the Nish and Vidin areas, a social stability which enabled the Bulgarian cultural renaissance to assume a predominantly cultural form.

The contented peasantry was the base on which the *vŭzrazhdane* was built. The superstructure was the work of the Bulgarian intelligentsia and the latter could not have become the force it was without the economic

---

[2] Nikolaĭ Todorov, 'Po nyakoĭ vŭprosi za ikonomichskoto razvitie i za zarazhdaneto na kapitalizma v bŭlgarskite zemi pod tursko vladichestvo', *Istoricheski Pregled*, 17/6 (1961), 87–105, 98.

boom enjoyed in the Bulgarian communities in the second and third quarters of the nineteenth century.

The economic boom was triggered by the introduction of a standing army because it was primarily to the Bulgarian manufacturing communities that the Ottoman authorities turned to provide the cloth necessary for the army's uniforms. This created demand for *aba*, from which the uniforms were made, and for *gaitan*, the braid which decorated them. Both were produced mainly in the Bulgarian lands. In 1828 an Ottoman government official concluded an agreement with the tailors of Sliven for the supply of 10,000 uniforms. The development of textile manufacturing in Sliven stimulated the production of *aba* in other towns. In Zheravna in the Kotel area the once huge flocks of sheep began to decline as the inhabitants concentrated more and more on the production of *aba*; by the 1840s their guild masters were known in Constantinople and Smyrna (Izmir) and a third of the population of Zheravna was engaged in the manufacturing of clothes and shoes. Plovdiv fared even better. A large number of successful *aba* producing houses were to be found in the city and many of them prospered far and wide; the house of Koyumdjioglu, whose Plovdiv branch is now the town's ethnographic museum, had its headquarters in Vienna whilst the concern founded by Konstantin Mandradzhioglu exported *aba* to India and was still operating in Calcutta in the 1920s. Another famous Plovdiv figure was Atanas Gyumyushgerdan who was well established as a merchant and moneylender by 1820 and was to become hugely rich through the sale of cloth to the Ottoman army.

The expansion of trade in cloth prompted the first, faltering moves towards mechanized production in Bulgaria. In 1836, with government financial help, a Sliven cloth maker, Zhelyazkov, set up a water-powered mill and in 1847 Gyumyushgerdan built a steam-driven factory in the foothills of the Rhodope mountains. The economic boom of the 1830s and 1840s encouraged some localities to specialize. Plovdiv concentrated on *aba* whilst metalworking was strong in Gabrovo and Samokov. Sliven, in addition to the manufacture of cloth, was also renowned for its metalworking, particularly in the production of weapons.

Specialization and the mechanization of production, however, did not spread widely and the latter was unpopular. The failings of the Zhelyazkov plant in Sliven were ascribed to the curses put on it by the petty producers it had harmed, whilst in 1851 a workshop in Samokov which had installed automatic carding machines was attacked by local weavers and spinners; the women could be pacified only after the local *zaptiehs*, or gendarmes, had promised that the offending machines would be removed. So little advanced was economic activity in many of the Bulgarian lands that even in the 1870s Macedonian merchants arrived in Vienna bringing their wares on the backs of 400 camels.

If it did not precipitate widespread changes in the methods of production the economic revival of the 1830s and thereafter acted as a massive stimulus to the traditional workshops, and their expansion brought about a noticeable increase in the Bulgarian element in between fifty and sixty of the larger urban settlements in the Balkans. By the middle of the nineteenth century there were between ninety and a hundred different varieties of workshop production, many of which were now reliant on demand from the Ottoman army and the new and rapidly expanding central state apparatus. Panagyurishte in the 1850s, for example, had 569 workshops; the largest number, 120, were involved in processing the goats' hair from which *gaitan* was made; 69 made *aba*.[3]

A distinguishing feature of the Bulgarian economic revival was that wealth flowed into the coffers of the guilds as much as into the pockets of individuals. The government officials who went to Sliven in 1828 negotiated not with individual concerns but with the local guild masters. The authorities had for decades been using the guilds as the means to implement central government policies. By the early nineteenth century the Porte had allowed the guild organizations of the sheep rearers to collect the sheep tax whilst the collection of taxes from the workshops in Sofia in the early nineteenth century was entrusted to the town's guilds. Almost all who were active in the workshops belonged to the appropriate guild and the guilds were rigidly organized with the traditional hierarchy of master, journeyman, and apprentice, with only the high master having the power to use the guild's funds. If in the early nineteenth century the guilds sometimes took account of ethnic differences they performed important social welfare functions for all guild members and their families, women in this respect enjoying equal rights with men. And no one, not even the central government, dared interfere in the internal affairs of the guilds. With their immunity from outside interference and

---

[3] Nikolaĭ Genchev, *Bŭlgarsko vŭzrazhdane*, 3rd, rev. edn. (Sofia: Otechestven Front, 1988), 131.

their accumulating experience in local administration, the guilds were ideally placed, once national consciousness had developed, to become vehicles for the articulation and assertion of national demands.

The Tanzimat and the creation of the new army not only brought greater prosperity to the Bulgarian lands, they also created the peace and stability which allowed the new wealth to be used. In the second quarter of the nineteenth century a number of affluent merchants built more and larger houses, but more conspicuous were the new public buildings such as clock towers, schools, elaborate fountains, covered markets, and houses for schoolteachers, most of which were financed by the guilds. So too was the building or rebuilding of churches. In the second quarter of the nineteenth century a number of villages rebuilt their old single-aisled churches, the new ones being larger, three-aisled, and much more richly decorated; in the 1840s the church in Tatar Pazardjik, built entirely of brick, was said to be the only one in the Ottoman empire allowed to have a bell and to be higher than 5 metres. The monasteries also benefited from the guilds' largesse, none more so than the great establishment at Rila, which had to be entirely rebuilt after a disastrous fire in 1833. Guilds, towns, and villages from throughout the Bulgarian lands contributed to the reconstruction; the coordination of this effort did much to promote a sense of national community. In the long run, the monasteries returned to the nation as much as they received from it: 'Our monasteries, great and small', wrote a distinguished Bulgarian historian, 'are more than just museums and repositories of manuscripts, books, and works of art. They are national sanctuaries which for centuries on end, in the most difficult and fateful times for our people, preserved our spiritual culture and were centres of the national spirit and consciousness.'[4]

Like the guilds, local communal institutions also benefited from the Tanzimat, once again with important long-term consequences for the vŭzrazhdane. During the eighteenth century, and especially during the *kŭrdjaliĭstvo*, customary law and the communal family, or 'zadruga', declined and local communal bodies took over their administrative functions, whilst at the same time often assuming responsibility for the community's defence. A weakened central government also frequently entrusted to local communes tasks such as the collection of taxes. During the war of 1828–9 such practices still existed; a British soldier who was in

---

[4] Duĭchev, *Pŭteki*, 183.

Bulgaria when the Russian army entered the area recorded that, 'The affairs of the Bulgarians are referred, in each village, to a junta of old men, who may be considered, in the absence of the Turkish authorities, as a sort of provisional government...'[5]

The communal councils evolved in haphazard fashion and were therefore varied in nature, but they were nearly all closely connected to and dominated by the local church. Legislation in 1839 produced greater cohesion. It gave the town populations the right to have a representative with the local authorities, a development which entrenched the communities in the local administration system. The reform also began to distance the communal council from the church. In the first place, the fact that the councils were now to be elected diminished clerical influence to some degree. Secondly, the reform extended the purview of the local councils. They were now to be responsible not only for the upkeep of churches but also for the care of public buildings, as well as for education, some judicial functions, and, in a number of cases, for the collection of taxes from the Bulgarian population. By the 1860s communal authorities in the towns were lending money, employing teachers, sending gifted students to study abroad, owning and renting shops, and running local cultural institutions. Often, in an uncoordinated fashion, these functions spread out to nearby Bulgarian village communities and so the councils evolved into a form of intermediary between the Bulgarian population and the Turkish civil and Greek ecclesiastical authorities; thus, 'Communal self-government became the cradle of democracy for the Bulgarians.'[6]

Communal self-government was an important factor in the growth of Bulgarian national consciousness. By the 1850s tensions between Bulgarian and Greek had increased appreciably, as is indicated by the fact that in 1856 the large *aba* makers' guild in Plovdiv split on ethnic lines, the Greeks and Bulgarians henceforth having separate organizations. In these circumstances control of the local council was a powerful weapon. The early Bulgarian nationalist Dobri Chintulov had been educated in a Greek school in Sliven in the 1830s and by the time of the Crimean war was teaching, in Bulgarian, in the town; after the war, however, the town council once more passed into Greek control and he

---

[5] Major George Keppel, *Narrative of a Journey across the Balcan* (London: Henry Colburn and Richard Bentley, 1831), i. 307.   [6] Genchev, *Vŭzrazhdane*, 141.

was forced to leave his job. He returned in 1862 when a Bulgarian majority was once more established.[7]

Within the Bulgarian elements in the councils an important social development was seen. In general the guild organizations remained the most powerful element of a local council but to an increasing degree the older establishment within the Bulgarian communities, the *chorbadjiǔ*, was challenged by the younger new, wealthy elements of merchant, manufacturer, and, later, the educated.

The *chorbadjiǔ* were later demonized by nationalist and marxist historians alike. The original *chorbadjiya* was the commander of a basic military unit within the Janissary Corps, the unit in which the whole professional and social life of the member of the corps was lived, this giving the *chorbadjiya* almost absolute power over the ordinary member. In the late eighteenth century when the large sheep rearing groups appeared there was a similar relationship between the small shepherd and the owner of a large herd. This social connotation of the word was used by the Bulgarians when searching for a term which would most exactly describe the position of the herd owners in relation to those directly subordinated to them. The use of the word spread to other occupations and organizations which had similar clearly defined power differentials; the records of the Sofia commune show that although it was first used only in 1816 it had by 1821 become standard terminology. This was true elsewhere; the word 'rapidly drove out those other terms which Bulgarians in the eighteenth century had used to describe those who exercised economic power and social influence'.[8] The *chorbadjiya* was often entrusted with tax collection and made responsible for keeping order by the Ottoman authorities, thus making him an authoritarian figure as well as a representative of the authorities; Christians working on the *chorbadjiya*'s land would often consider him, though a Christian, a worse oppressor than the Turkish landowner, and there are a number of records of *chorbadjiǔ* being murdered. The *chorbadjiǔ* of Elena were particularly reviled by later historians, though some of them took part in widespread protests against Ottoman power in 1835.

---

[7] Nikola Tabakov (ed.), *Dobri Chintulov: Stani, Stani, yunak balkanski; stihotvoreniya, rechi, pisma; Spomeni na Dobri Chintulov* (Sofia: Bŭlgarski Pisatel, 1973), 100.

[8] Tsvetana Georgieva, 'Za genezisa na burzhoaznite elementi v sotsialnata struktura na Bŭlgarite', *Istoricheski Pregled*, 33/2 (1977), 87–90, 90.

The tension between the *chorbadjii* and the newer elements within the communal councils was one of a number of clashes between what in Bulgaria became known as the 'old' and the 'young', terms which are convenient if not entirely accurate.

2. THE EDUCATION MOVEMENT

Both the communal councils and the guilds played a major role in one of the vŭzrazhdane's most important processes, the creation of a Bulgarian educational system.

In the first three centuries of Ottoman rule there was little education in Bulgarian apart from that provided in cell schools located within monasteries. From the end of the seventeenth century a small number of cell schools began to appear in the larger towns either in outposts of the larger monasteries or attached to the local church. At the end of the eighteenth century the first lay cell schools had appeared with some of them beginning to edge away from a curriculum based on the needs of the church to give lessons in arithmetic, history, geography, elementary natural science, and, in some cases, 'good manners'.[9]

Paisii had enjoined his countrymen to 'know your own language and study in your own tongue' and Sofronii urged his flock not to give money to churches and monasteries but to use it to establish schools, including lay schools. But there was a long way to go before the Bulgarians had anything approximating to a modern, secular system of education, and well into the nineteenth century 'The adjective "Greek" was thought of by many as equivalent to "educated" '.[10] In Sofronii's day education was predominantly religious, and it was virtually all in Greek. Three essential stages were therefore necessary to create a modern, nationally based system: to move away from cell to mutual schools; to concentrate on education in Bulgarian; and finally to establish class schools.

The first step was slowly taken. The number of cell schools actually increased from 142 in 1762 to 235 in 1835 but there was not as yet enough local, Bulgarian wealth for this trend to develop on a widespread

---

[9] Krasimira Daskalova, *Gramotnost, knizhnina, chitateli, chetene v Bŭlgariya na prehoda kŭm modernoto vreme* (Sofia: LIK, 1999), 46.
[10] Charles Moser, *A History of Bulgarian Literature, 865–1944* (The Hague: Mouton, 1972), 37.

scale. Furthermore, schools teaching in Greek were still more numerous, better funded, and more advanced in their teaching, with the result that many Bulgarians who could afford to educate their children sent them to schools teaching in Greek. It was in fact the Greeks who fostered the move away from cell schools, and it was Greek schools which provided the training ground for most of the prominent figures of the vŭzrazhdane, including Sofroniĭ Vrachanski, Georgi Rakovski, Petŭr Beron, Neofit Rilski, Stoyan Chomakov, Neofit Bozveli, Ilarion Makariopolski, Ivan Seliminski, Hristaki Pavlovich, Raĭno Popovich, Konstantin Fotinov, Vasil Aprilov, Ivan Dobrovski, and many others.

The second stage of educational evolution, the move towards education in Bulgarian, began as a reaction against excessive Greek influence in the schools. The first step was to establish Greek-Bulgarian lay schools, the first of which was set up in Svishtov in 1815. Initially most of the teaching was in Greek but by the 1830s it had been pushed back to second place, thanks in large measure to Neofit Bozveli, a monk and former pupil of Sofroniĭ who went to teach in the school in 1824; he never returned to his monastery but spent the remainder of his life furthering the cultural reawakening of the Bulgarians. The second Greek-Bulgarian school was opened in Kotel in 1819 by Raĭno Popovich who in 1826 moved to Karlovo to set up one of the most famous of all the Hellenic-Bulgarian schools, its alumni including Rakovski, Evlogi Georgiev, Gavril Krŭstevich, and Botyo Petkov. There was even a Hellenic-Bulgarian school in the French quarter of Smyrna where there was a small Bulgarian mercantile community. It was opened in 1828 by Konstantin Fotinov.

Despite the advance of teaching in Bulgarian there were Bulgarians who believed that Greek should remain the major vehicle of education; for Popovich Greek was, as English was for Daniel O'Connell, more widespread and more suitable for use in commerce and public affairs. When Popovich established his school in Karlovo in 1826 teaching was entirely in Greek, and Greek flourished until the late 1840s and early 1850s, particularly in larger towns such as Plovdiv, Melnik, Tŭrnovo, Adrianople, Bitola, and Prilep. By the mid-1850s, however, the majority of Bulgarian communities provided education in Bulgarian for their children.

The move towards education in Bulgarian was also prompted by external influences. After their basic schooling a number of the early apostles had studied abroad: Petŭr Beron in Heidelberg and Munich; Ivan

Seliminski, Stoyan Chomakov, and Nikola Pikolo in Italy; and Aleksandŭr Eksarh and Gavril Krŭstevich in Paris. From these came modern ideas of education, even if the transmitter remained abroad as did Beron, Pikolo, and, for many years, Eksarh. The Russian government also became anxious to help, though here the secular element was less prevalent. In 1816 it decided to help the children of the Serbian leaders to study in Russia, and this privilege was later extended to Bulgarians.

The largest incentive to education in Bulgarian, however, came unintentionally from the Greeks who, particularly in and after the Greek war of independence, had become pan-Hellenes and proselytizers for hellenism. By the 1830s the first cohort of the modern Bulgarian intelligentsia had emerged, most of them having been educated in Greek schools. Although, or perhaps because it was largely educated in Greek schools, the emerging Bulgarian intelligentsia was not prepared to accept hellenization and the unthinking assumptions of cultural superiority which went with it; Stoyan Chomakov, born in Koprivshtitsa in 1819 of a wealthy family of cattle drovers and tax collectors, was educated in his home town but had been gravely offended by textbooks which referred to Bulgarians as a barbaric tribe which once lived in the area.[11]

The response of Chomakov, and the many like him who reacted against Greek cultural hegemonialism, was to encourage lay schools which taught in demotic Bulgarian as well as, or in place of Greek. The first opened in Gabrovo in 1835. The school was typical of the vŭzrazhdane in that it was the product of external as well as internal influences, the idea for the school having come originally from Bulgarians in Odessa who were helped by Bulgarian merchants in Bucharest; but the project would have been impossible had the citizens of Gabrovo itself not contributed generously. The first teacher was Neofit Rilski, who until 1833 was teaching in a Greek school in Bucharest. He compiled a special Bulgarian grammar which was printed in Serbia with the cooperation of Miloš Obrenović whilst books, exercise books, and slates were sent from Russia by Nikolaĭ Palauzov and Vasil Aprilov, originally a graecophone who had made a fortune as a vodka merchant in Odessa. Given the lack of qualified teachers instruction was by the mutual method. The school proved hugely popular and attracted pupils from all over the Bulgarian

---

[11] Toncho Zhechev, *Bŭlgarskiyat Velikden ili strastite bŭlgarski*, 6th celebratory edn. (Sofia: Marin Drinov, 1995), 242–5.

lands. Within a decade fifty-three similar, mutual schools had been set up in places such as Svishtov, Koprivshtitsa, Plovdiv, Veles, Kazanlŭk, Karlovo, Sopot, Kalofer, Panagyurishte, Sofia, Tŭrnovo, Tryavna, Kotel, Rusé, and Skopje. The mutual schools were not evenly spread but tended to concentrate in the economically most advanced regions of northern Bulgaria, the Danubian plain, and on both sides of the Balkan range; there were only three in Macedonia.

Secular education in Bulgarian was not confined to boys. In some of the early schools girls studied with boys but in 1841 in Sliven the first school opened for girls only. Others followed soon in Vratsa, Lovech, Sofia, Svishtov, Kotel, Elena, Shumen, and Tŭrnovo; by 1853 there were thirty-five and by 1878 ninety similar mutual schools for girls. By the latter date there were also nineteen all-girl class schools. Many schools benefited from the generosity of the educational pioneer Petŭr Beron who every year from 1840 to 1855 sent money and equipment to help girls' education. Other benefactions, particularly scholarships for gifted girls, came from the forty or so women's societies founded in Bulgaria between 1856 and 1878. Female literacy was well enough established in Constantinople by 1871 to persuade Petko Slaveĭkov to edit *Ruzhitsa ili red knizhki za zhenite* (Peony, or a series of booklets for ladies), the first journal in Bulgarian specially designed for women. It was not a commercial success and folded within the year.[12] The first woman to have received higher education is said to be Atanasya Golovina (1850–1933), who was born in Kishinev in Moldavia and studied medicine in Zürich and Paris before working as a doctor specializing in psychiatry in Sofia, Varna, Plovdiv, and Lovech. She was also to publish a number of learned articles.[13]

The move from mutual to class schools was the final stage of the educational revolution amongst the Bulgarians. In 1840 the Gabrovo school was restructured on a class rather than mutual basis and the first school to be founded specifically on this system was set up by Naĭden Gerov in Koprivshtitsa in 1846. Others soon followed, the most important being that in Plovdiv, established by wealthy merchants in the

---

[12] For the emergence of education for females, see Zdravka Konstantinova, *Dŭrzhavnost predi dŭrzhava: svrŭhfunktsii na bŭlgarskata vŭzrozhdenska zhurnalistika* (Sofia: Kliment Ohridski, 2000), 126, 140 ff..

[13] Nadezhda Bŭrzakova, 'Pisma na prof. Ivan Shishmanov do prof. d-r Parashkev Stoyanov', *Izvestiya na Dŭrzhavnite Arhivi*, 16 (1968), 173–223, 221 n. 108.

city in 1850. It was to have a powerful, modernizing influence in the Bulgarian communities in Macedonia and Thrace. As with the founding of the mutual schools, external factors were important.

The need for class schools was preached initially by the increasing number of Bulgarians educated abroad. By the liberation some 700 Bulgarians had received higher education in Russia, and about a third of all educated Bulgarians went to Russian universities or theological colleges. From the end of the 1830s Russian interest in the Balkans increased with Bulgaria as its focal point, the Bulgarian community in Odessa being active in promoting the Bulgarian cause, especially in education. The seminary in Odessa, along with that in Kiev and the University in Moscow, were the main centres of attraction for Bulgarian students. It was not only higher education that was available in Russia. In 1847 there were eighty-eight boys' and one girls' school together with agrarian institutions in southern Russia and Bessarabia. Russian money also provided a huge number of textbooks and financed many teaching posts in Bulgaria as well as scholarships for Bulgarian students to study in Russia.

The majority of those with secondary and higher education, however, obtained it elsewhere than in Russia. Figures produced in Odessa showed that 233 men and 24 women received higher degrees in Russia before 1878; far more graduated from institutions in Constantinople and western Europe. French influence grew appreciably in the 1840s when scholarships to study in France were first offered to Bulgarian students; in 1848 a Papal Encyclical stressing the unity of Christianity under Rome encouraged French Catholic activity, as, in the 1850s, did Louis Napoleon's desire to strengthen French influence abroad. The main institutions promoting French education were to be found in Constantinople; by the liberation of 1878 the Lycée in Galata Sarai and the Catholic College in Bebek had trained over 200 Bulgarians. An approximately equal number of Bulgarians, some of whom were to play a major role in the vŭzrazhdane and the post-liberation Bulgarian state, had passed through the classrooms of Robert College, an American Protestant foundation, teaching in English, which opened in Constantinople in 1863. A number of Catholic and Protestant schools were established throughout the Bulgarian lands between the end of the Crimean war and the liberation of 1878; the Catholic were more numerous but in general the Protestant were better equipped and were regarded by the Bulgarians as superior. It also has to be noted that not all those who went abroad returned to Bulgaria. A study in 1995 calculated that of the 370 individuals who studied abroad whose subsequent careers were known 123 returned to Bulgaria after finishing their education, 180 remained abroad, and 62 worked abroad more than they did in Bulgaria.[14]

Within the Bulgarian communities, in Constantinople and elsewhere, the guilds and the local councils were an essential factor in educational advance. They were invariably involved in the schools' foundation and subsequently financed the employment of teachers and the construction and maintenance of school buildings. They also provided scholarships for the needy. Moma Vasilyov, later a prominent civil servant in Bulgaria, recorded in his memoirs that he could continue his education in the Plovdiv gymnasium after the death of his father, a priest, in 1873 only because the cobblers' guild in his home town of Teteven sent him the necessary funds.[15] The council in Shumen was paying for the education of 375 poor children in 1877, and a decade earlier the guilds and council of Plovdiv were financing five students in Paris, four in Vienna, seven in Russia, two in Britain, and forty in Constantinople. In Tulcha in the Dobrudja the council implemented a suggestion of Todor Ikonomov's that the villages of the diocese be allowed to have only one pub each, the revenues from the renting of which would be used to help finance local schools.[16]

Between the end of the Napoleonic and the Crimean wars Bulgarian schools had undergone a transformation from the medieval cell to the modern secular school in which teaching in contemporary Bulgarian predominated. The statistics are impressive. From the 1830s to the liberation some 2,000 schools were established in the Bulgarian lands of which over a hundred were for girls. In the 1870s there were around 1,500 elementary schools, fifty co-educational mutual schools, and three gymnasia, in Bolgrad, Plovdiv, and Gabrovo; and there were 1,379 teachers in the small Bulgarian principality in 1879. There were some specialized schools, including a commercial school in Svishtov, teacher-training institutes in Shtip and Prilep, and theological schools in

---

[14] Rumen Daskalov, *Mezhdu iztoka i zapada; bŭlgarski kulturni dilemi* (Sofia: LIK, 1998), 233 n. 15.

[15] Toma Vasilyov, *Zhivot i Spomeni* (Sofia: Pridvorna, 1938), 13.

[16] Zina Markova, *Bŭlgarskata Ekzarhiya, 1870–1879* (Sofia: BAN, 1989), 184.

Samokov and at the Petropavlovsk monastery near Lyaskovets. Most towns by the 1870s had more than one school. In 1874 Svishtov's boys' and girls' schools educated 411 and 186 pupils respectively, its high school employed thirteen male and seven female teachers who offered classes to ninety male and forty-six female pupils in history, general and Bulgarian, in grammar, physics, botany, algebra, geometry, Turkish, French, religious studies, and philosophy. In 1871 Gabrovo had six boys' and two girls' schools with between them over 1,500 pupils, many of whom came from other parts of Bulgaria.

The teaching provided in these schools may not always have been of the highest quality; in the cell schools a good voice was at least as important as an aptitude for teaching, and even by 1905 only 27.91 per cent of the adult population could read and write, but despite this the achievements of the Bulgarian educational revival were remarkable. And they were all the more remarkable when measured against the obstacles educational development faced. One, clearly, was the established power of Greek culture in both the Church and the existing schools. But there were also structural problems within the Bulgarian world which were much more difficult to overcome. Immediately after the Napoleonic wars there were no textbooks, nor was there either an agreed form of the literary language in which they could be written, or the printing presses on which they might be printed. The first textbook in Bulgarian was produced by Petŭr Beron and appeared in 1824; the *Riben Bukvar* or 'Fish ABC', so called because of the motif on its back cover, contained information on a host of subjects from ancient philosophy to natural history. Other textbooks followed, very often financed by Bulgarians abroad, and used literary forms closer to the spoken language, but the lack of an agreed form of Bulgarian was a severe hindrance.

3. LANGUAGE AND THE PRESS

The need for a standard literary form of Bulgarian was generally accepted by the 1820s but the debate on what it should be was long and often bitter. It was complicated by the fact that until the 1820s most written Bulgarian was in archaic form, with writers such as Paisiĭ not even maintaining an internal consistency of usage; in addition to this, the linguistic variants in émigré communities evolved different forms, whilst in the Bulgarian lands themselves there was a wide variation in dialect. Some early educational apostles argued that Bulgarian should retain the case endings which were becoming obsolete in the spoken language, whilst others, most notably Yuri Venelin, urged that the post-substantive definite article should be jettisoned to make Bulgarian more akin to other Slav languages, especially Russian. Until Drinov established the identity of Paisiĭ, Venelin was amongst the most prominent of the early Bulgarian enlighteners who did much to bring the existence of the Bulgarian language to the notice of other scholars, but his proposals for the literary language would have made it almost a dialect of Russian and for that reason they found few adherents. Others, including Neofit Rilski, favoured making Old Church Slavonic the basis of the written language, and there was another school, which included Raĭno Popovich and Konstantin Fotinov, which argued that the basis should be Greek so that Bulgarians would have contact with the glories of ancient civilization. In later years the determination to resist archaic forms and foreign usages increased.

By the 1840s no one seriously advocated either Old Church Slavonic or Greek, and younger activists such as Ivan Bogorov were especially vigilant against Russian influences. Bogorov himself wrote the first Bulgarian grammar in contemporary, spoken Bulgarian, *Pŭrvichka bŭlgarska gramatika* (An Elementary Bulgarian Grammar) published in Bucharest in 1844. The case for the contemporary language was strengthened first by Naĭden Gerov who in 1846 began work on what was to be his six-volume *Rechnik na bŭlgarski ezik* (Dictionary of the Bulgarian Language) which included both written and spoken versions of the language, and then in 1852 by the 22-year-old Dragan Tsankov who, together with his brother Anton, published a grammar in German; it was the first grammar of Bulgarian in a Latin script or in a foreign language. But it was not till the 1870s that a decision was finally taken to base the written language on the Gabrovo dialect. A literary language in Bulgaria's case was therefore as much if not more the consequence than the cause of the expansion of education and the creation of that standard literary form was one of the greatest benefits the educational movement brought to Bulgaria.

Together with the development of education came the foundation of other cultural institutions and activities. The *chitalishte*, an institution first seen in Serbia, was one of the most important of them. The word means 'reading area' and the founding document of the first Bulgarian *chitalishte*, set up in Svishtov in 1856, stated that part of its function was 'to provide a municipal library which would hold books, newspapers and periodicals in Bulgarian, Russian, French, German, Romanian, Serbian, and Greek.'[17] The *chitalishta* provided much more than a place to read. Many offered classes to teach adult illiterates to read and write; the *chitalishta* also became places where village or district meetings could be held, sometimes even being chosen as the venue for secret, conspiratorial gatherings; and during the vŭzrazhdane over eighty of them staged theatrical presentations and two of them, those in Svishtov and Silistra, had their own amateur dramatic groups. They were to be found not only in the Bulgarian lands themselves but also in the émigré communities, that in Bucharest having been set up at the instigation of the later revolutionary leader, Georgi Rakovski. Most *chitalishta* were founded with money provided by rich émigré merchants and by Russian cultural or welfare societies. In addition to *chitalishta* many towns, including Koprivshtitsa, Kazanlŭk, Svishtov, Tryavna, Gabrovo, Elena, Sopot, Panagyurishte, Tŭrnovo, Karlovo, Kotel, Sofia, Pazardjik, Plovdiv, Lom, Lovech, and Bolgrad also opened small libraries.

One impulse towards the foundation of the *chitalishta* and libraries was the increase in the publication of material in Bulgarian in the 1850s. This was a late feature of the vŭzrazhdane. In the second half of the sixteenth century a Bulgarian printer, Yakov Kraĭkov, had been active in Venice and over twenty books in a form of Bulgarian had been produced in Braşov. In 1651 Filip Stanislavov's *Abagar* was published in Rome but it was representative of 'new' rather than contemporary Bulgarian. The first book published in the latter was Sofroniĭ Vrachanski's *Nedelnik* (from the word for Sunday), a collection of ninety-six sermons, which appeared in Bucharest in 1806. Partly because of the *kŭrdjaliĭstvo*, and also because the Ottoman authorities banned the printing of books in the Bulgarian lands, Sofroniĭ's work had few imitators and the publication of books remained a rarity, only nine being issued between 1821 and 1830 and forty-two between 1831 and 1840. That reading was rare even as late as the 1830s can be seen in the introduction to a book by Konstantin Fotinov who addressed himself to his 'dear listeners' rather than his readers; it is to be presumed that his work was read aloud in groups. Greater economic prosperity and, even more so, the growth of education

---

[17] Konstantinova, *Dŭrzhavnost*, 181.

increased demand, particularly for school textbooks, and between 1841
and 1850 143 Bulgarian books appeared. In the 1850s the number was
291 and in the 1860s 709. Many of these books, even in the later decades,
were published outside the Bulgarian lands. By the mid-nineteenth
century bookshops had begun to appear and by the liberation they were
established in twenty Bulgarian towns, the most famous store being that
of Hristo Gandev in Plovdiv. Some books were also distributed by mail
order, though the waiting times for delivery were long, a matter of
months for books in Bulgarian and sometimes years for those in foreign
languages. For many Bulgarians reading was difficult not only because
books were hard to come by, but also because their homes had poor
lighting and could offer nowhere to read in peace, an additional reason for
valuing the *chitalishta*.

Another factor delaying the development of Bulgarian book production
was the lack of printing presses. The first Bulgarian printing press was not
established until 1840 and its origins once again point to the importance
of external factors in the *vŭzrazhdane*. It was established not in the
Bulgarian lands but in Smyrna and was owned by a Greek who had
imported Slav type from the United States at the request of the British
and Foreign Bible Society. The same year also saw the setting up of the
first Bulgarian press in European Turkey. Established in Salonika it
produced mainly religious items, and especially bibles in vernacular
Bulgarian, the first time these had been mass produced. Religious works,
this time prayer books, were also the main item printed on the first
Bulgarian press established in Constantinople in 1848. In 1861 in
Bolgrad the head of the local gymnasium, Dimitŭr Mutev, set up a press
with Latin and Cyrillic type which proved one of the most productive of
all printing presses until the area fell under Russian administration after
the treaty of Berlin. So important did Dragan Tsankov consider presses
that he became a printer himself to learn the trade before buying a press
of his own, his intention being to produce in Svishtov a paper to rival the
dominant *Tsarigradski Vestnik* (Constantinople Herald), which he
considered too moderate.[18]

The press in Bolgrad like those in Smyrna, Salonika, and Constantinople,
concentrated on religious material but all four also produced secular

---

[18] Margarita Kovacheva, *Dragan Tsankov. Obshtestvenik, Politik, Diplomat do 1878*
(Sofia: Nauka i izkustvo, 1982), 33, 66 ff..

works, including periodicals. The first attempt to publish a Bulgarian periodical was made in Constantinople in 1837 but came to nothing, not least because at that time there were no Bulgarian printing facilities in the city. When the first Bulgarian periodical, *Lyuboslovie* (Love of Words), appeared it was printed on the Smyrna press and edited by Konstantin Fotinov. Like many periodicals it did not enjoy a long life, in this case not least because it was written in an archaic form of Bulgarian. *Tsarigradski Vestnik*, printed on the presses established by the Bulgarian commune in the city in 1848 and edited by Ivan Bogorov, was much more successful and, running from 1848 to 1862, was the longest lived of all the vŭzrazhdane journals.

Unlike *Tsarigradski Vestnik* the majority of the vŭzrazhdane periodicals were short-lived. Of the fifty newspapers and forty periodicals which began publication before the liberation, only five lasted more than five years; twenty of the newspapers and eleven of the periodicals were published outside the Ottoman empire. Yet, despite their ephemeral nature, they were of huge importance. By the late 1840s the various factions and trends which were emerging in the Bulgarian communities had recognized the need to have their own publications. In 1849 the board of trustees managing the newly founded Bulgarian church in Constantinople began publishing their own paper, *Sŭvetnik* (Adviser), to counteract the views both of Aleksandŭr Eksarh, the leader of the 'young', pro-Russian radicals as expressed in his *Tsarigradski Vestnik*, and of the increasingly pro-French and pro-Catholic *Bŭlgariya* (Bulgaria) edited by Dragan Tsankov.

The newspapers and journals were intended not only to plead political causes. Their more profound purpose was to educate the Bulgarians and, even more importantly, to propagate amongst them a sense of civic commitment and national consciousness. The intention of *Lyuboslovie* was to turn a cultural into a civil movement and Bogorov, the editor of *Bŭlgarski Orel* (Bulgarian Eagle), published in Leipzig in 1846 and 1847, said his paper's function was 'to inform our people, like our neighbours the Romanians, Serbs and Greeks, of civil organization'. Bogorov was guided by the maxim he cited at the beginning of his autobiography, 'First we have to make Bulgarians, then Bulgaria'.[19] Petko Slaveĭkov believed that the two foundations of a nation are its schools and its newspapers,

---

[19] Konstantinova, *Dŭrzhavnost*, 22–6, 26.

whilst Georgi Rakovski, who was to begin the insurrectionary movement in the 1860s, stated in his autobiography, 'My first and last resolution was to stage an open struggle against the Turkish government through the press and with the sword.'[20]

The development of national consciousness was also promoted by the almanacs and calendars which were a prominent feature of Bulgarian publication throughout the nineteenth century. This was particularly the case for Bulgarians living outside the Bulgarian lands; all émigré communities of any size, be they in Romania, Russia, or the United States, published their own almanacs or calendars.

National consciousness during the vŭzrazhdane was represented not merely in education and publication. Various forms of Bulgarian art also appeared. The 1840s saw changes in the style of painting in churches with the old, lifeless formalism beginning to give way to portraits of real human beings rather than stylized stereotypes; in some paintings there were even secular figures to the side of the main subject with these figures at times being portrayed not only as Bulgarians but as Bulgarians who were suffering under 'the yoke'.[21] The first school of Bulgarian church painting appeared in Tryavna and was followed by one in the Bansko-Razlog area, though the most famous was that established in Svishtov by the greatest of Bulgarian church artists, Zahari Zograf (1810–53).

Architecture, ecclesiastical and lay, also developed national styles. The rebuilding of Rila monastery and the creation of new foundations such as that at Rozhen near Gorna Djumaya exhibited this trend. In the 1830s both the growing wealth of the Bulgarian communities and the relaxation of previous restrictions on non-Muslim buildings encouraged the construction of churches with a distinct Bulgarian style. They were large with big, light spaces, highly decorated altars and the new, fresh style of painting. Examples of this development were to be seen in the church in the Preobrazhenski monastery (1835), in St Nikola's, Tŭrnovo (1836), in The Holy Virgin, Tatar Pazardjik (1837), and most notably in the church in Rila, begun after the great fire of 1833 and completed in 1837. Leading artists and craftsmen from throughout the Bulgarian lands

---

[20] Konstantinova, *Dŭrzhavnost*, 59.

[21] 'The Yoke', or *igoto*, was the standard term used by the Bulgarian nationalists, including those of the communist era, to describe the experience of Ottoman rule. After 1989 some historians attempted to change the terminology but without conspicuous success.

contributed to this work which therefore encapsulated all the important aspects of early renaissance art.

A distinct Bulgarian style also appeared in secular architecture. Schools provided an ideal outlet for the expression of this style, an excellent example of which was to be seen in Plovdiv's St Cyril and Methodius School completed in the 1850s. Domestic architecture also underwent a transformation as wealthy manufacturers or merchants built new houses. These ceased to be single-storeyed, with small windows facing inwards, and became two- or three-storeyed with larger windows facing outwards and with decorated façades; the ground floor, rather than providing winter quarters for animals, was more frequently a workshop or shop. Many are still to be seen in towns such as Koprivshtitsa.

Although there is little evidence that Herder was widely read in Bulgaria a number of Bulgarians began to take an interest in their folklore. The Serbian scholar Vuk Karadjić had published some Bulgarian folk songs in 1822, as did Venelin in 1849, but the most important early compilation was that of Ivan Bogorov, whose *Bŭlgarski pesni i poslovitsi* (Bulgarian Songs and Sayings) was published in Pest in 1842; it was translated into English and published by Elias Riggs as 'Popular Bulgarian Songs and Proverbs', in the *American Presbyterian Review* in 1863. The Miladinov brothers from Macedonia published a large collection of folk songs in Zagreb in 1861 and in the same year one edited by Lyuben Karavelov appeared in Moscow.

The development of Bulgarian cultural and artistic awareness during the vŭzrazhdane was greatly aided by learned societies. The first such organization, the Philological Society, had been founded in Braşov by Vasil Nenovich in 1823 to promote the use of Bulgarian as a literary medium and to stimulate the publication of books in Bulgarian. Given the lack of an educated Bulgarian public and of publishing facilities, this had little effect and it was, like the ninety cultural societies established between the 1820s and 1878, as short-lived as most newspapers. Yet some societies had considerable influence. In Constantinople in 1856 Dragan Tsankov established the Society for Bulgarian Literature, the first society for Bulgarian scholars, writers, and men of letters. Between 1857 and 1862 it published the bi-weekly *Bŭlgarski Knizhitsi* (Bulgarian Papers), which at the height of its popularity had as many as 600 subscribers. The learned societies were particularly important in providing links between the various figures and institutions of the emerging Bulgarian intelligentsia.

After the liberation a number of societies moved into the new principality, the most important of these being the Bulgarian Literary Society founded in Braila in 1869 from which was to emerge the Bulgarian Academy of Sciences. The learned and literary societies were frequently supported by the many other associations formed before the liberation. The most numerous of these were those set up by school pupils; that in Gabrovo held forty public readings in four months.[22]

The cultural societies were a manifestation of a growing new, Bulgarian intelligentsia. This intelligentsia had its highest representatives in the writers who created modern Bulgarian literature in the period of the vŭzrazhdane, even if not all of them were advocates of action on the political front.

Bulgarian literature appeared first in verse form in the mid-1840s, particularly with the work of Naĭden Gerov, whose 'Stoyan i Rada' (Stoyan and Rada) was published in Odessa in 1845. There was greater nationalist content in the work of Dobri Chintulov, a native of Sliven, whose 'Stani, stani, yunak balkanski' (Arise, arise, Balkan hero), awoke nationalist feelings in many young Bulgarians. After the Crimean war Chintulov's nationalist hopes declined, the major work of his later period, 'Patriot', recounting the story of a revolutionary who had devoted his life to a cause he now saw as lost. The other major poet of the pre-liberation period, Petko Slaveĭkov, was devoted to Bulgarian folklore and traditions but his work had little of the nationalist, political passions which inspired Chintulov and in 1875 he wrote a deeply pessimistic piece, 'Ne Sme Narod' (We are not a People), which stated that the Bulgarians would never be able to form a modern nation. Much in contrast to this was the exuberant nationalism of Georgi Rakovski's poetry; his 'Gorski Pŭtnik' (Forest Traveller), published in 1868, though dated 1867, called upon Bulgarians to take to the hills and fight the Turks as did the haiduts of old;[23] at the same time the poem painted lurid pictures of oppression by the Turks. On the very eve of the liberation Bulgarian nationalist poetry reached its apogee with the work of the nationalist, socialist, and eventual martyr, Hristo Botev. He had no equal as a poet and few works could have had greater impact than his 'Obesvaneto na Vasil Levski' (The Hanging

---

[22] Raina Gavrilova, *Bulgarian Urban Culture in the Eighteenth and Nineteenth Centuries*, (Cranbury, NJ: Susquehanna University Press, 1999), 195–6.

[23] For the haiduts, see below, p. 83.

of Vasil Levski); a collection of Botev's poems and other works, *Pesni i Stihotvoreniya* (Songs and Verse) appeared in 1875, a time of intense nationalist passion.

Bulgarian prose writing did not establish itself firmly until the 1860s, its major practitioner being Vasil Drumev, later Metropolitan Kliment of Tŭrnovo. His most important works were his early adventure novel, *Neshtastna Familya* (Unhappy Family), which appeared in 1860, and his autobiographical *Uchenik i Blagodateli* (Pupil and Benefactors) of 1865. He also wrote a number of plays, the most important being *Ivanko ubietsŭt na Asenya I* (Ivanko the murderer of Asen I), which described how Petŭr returned reluctantly to Bulgaria to remove Ivanko whose authoritarian policies were driving his country towards civil war. Drumev was a nationalist activist as well as a writer. He was a co-founder of the Bulgarian Literary Society in Braila and was a member of the first Bulgarian Legion established in Belgrade in the early 1860s.

4. THE CAMPAIGN FOR A BULGARIAN CHURCH

Bulgarian efforts to secure their own national church organization ran parallel with the strivings for education in their own language. There were a number of similarities between the educational and the church campaigns: the major confrontation was with Greek cultural influences; the Bulgarian communities outside the Ottoman empire contributed greatly to the eventual success of the campaign; and there was a sharpening of the confrontation in the 1840s. Until the 1840s the demands of the Bulgarians had been prompted by anger at clerical taxation and corruption, but after 1840 the demand for services in Bulgarian was made with ever increasing intensity. The church struggle achieved a notable success in 1849 with the establishment of a separate Bulgarian church in Constantinople and with what amounted to a unilateral declaration of independence by that church on behalf of all Bulgarians in 1860. After 1860 the chief objective was to secure recognition by the Porte and the Patriarchate of the separate Bulgarian Church as a discrete institution. This struggle was only partially successful because whilst the Porte stated in 1870 that a separate Bulgarian Exarchate should be created the Patriarchate refused to recognize it and in 1872 denounced the Exarchate as schismatic. The strivings to achieve a national Church both influenced and were influenced by the emerging sense of Bulgarian national consciousness. The Church needed the nation to free it from Greek domination; the nation needed the Church because with no secular aristocracy and with a commercial bourgeoisie that was still highly hellenized it had no other cultural leaders. So central to the national movement did the Bulgarian Church become that even in the 1930s the Catholics of Plovdiv, who were descendents of the bogomils, did not refer to themselves as 'Bulgarians'; only the Orthodox were 'Bulgarian'.[24]

Three European Churches outside Constantinople had previously claimed autocephalous and subsequently patriarchal status: the Bulgarian Church at Tŭrnovo during the second empire; the Serbian Church at Peć; and the Bulgarian Church at Ohrid after the Ottoman conquest of Bulgaria. This separate status was less de jure than de facto, the Churches' distance from Constantinople rather than any striving for national independence being a major reason why they remained distinct. Peć lost its separate status in 1463, regained it in 1557, and lost it a second time in 1766. Ohrid was incorporated into the Oecumenical Patriarchate in Constantinople in 1767.

The incorporation of the two independent patriarchates was intended to rationalize and make more efficient the administration of the Orthodox Church and had little to do with any sense of Greek nationalism. There is scant evidence that the Christians affected by the measure felt any immediate need for complaint. Feelings hardened in the late eighteenth century when, prompted by ideas imported from western and central Europe, Greek nationalism began to stir and more and more Greek bishops and priests were appointed to Slav dioceses and parishes; sometimes even confession had to be heard through an interpreter, and in 1784 a Serb, Gerasim Zelić, demanded that Slav rather than Greek priests be nominated for Slav-speaking parishes. But after that the disorders of the *kŭrdjaliĭstvo* meant that the few protests which were voiced were not heard. It was not until the 1820s that serious agitation took place.

When the agitation began it was more a social or economic than an ethnic protest, the main complaint being not the race but the venality of the clerics. By the third decade of the nineteenth century the taxes many Bulgarian villages paid to the Church were twice as high as those exacted

---

[24] Naĭden Sheĭtanov, 'Duhŭt na otritsanie u bŭlgarina', in Elenkov and Daskalov, *Zashto sme takiva?*, 270–9, 276.

by the state, frequently because of the greed of the local bishop. In 1825 the inhabitants of Skopje complained about the rapacity of their (Greek) bishop, and there were much more substantial protests in Vratsa in the same year. Here the citizens refused to pay their church taxes because of the seemingly limitless greed and corruption of their bishop, Metodi, a Greek. Their demands were not conceded and in the increasingly bitter struggle the leader of the Bulgarians, Dimitraki Hadjitoshev, was executed in Vidin in 1827 and some of his supporters exiled.

The Vratsa protest was primarily the work of Hadjitoshev and had little effect outside the diocese because the conflict between Bulgarian and Greek interests had not yet become an ethnic one. Bulgarians and Greeks in Plovdiv gratefully accepted the offer of their bishop to mediate between them, and Greek bishops sometimes allowed services in Bulgarian. Even in the school question Greek and Bulgarian could cooperate, and the foundation stone for the school in Gabrovo was laid by the Greek metropolitan of Tŭrnovo, Ilarion Kritski.[25] Nor, in the early years of the revival, did support for education in Bulgarian mean hostility to the Church; Aprilov, the founder of the school in Gabrovo and Neofit Rilski, its first teacher, were to remain committed to the Patriarchate.

Despite Aprilov's and Rilski's continuing attachment to the Patriarchate the gap between Bulgarian and Greek in ecclesiastical affairs began to widen. One cause of this was the fact that in 1831 Russian diplomatic pressure in Constantinople persuaded the Patriarchate to recognize the autonomy of the Serbian Church and two years later the Orthodox Church in the Kingdom of Greece secured autocephalous status. The Ottoman system had classified its subjects by religion, each recognized faith being granted its own millet. The decisions of 1831 and 1833 implied that the Orthodox community consisted of different, separable ethnic groups and if the Greeks themselves could be seen as one such group why, asked some Bulgarians, should not the Bulgarians?

This question was increasingly posed in the 1840s. During that decade not only did tensions between Bulgarian and Greek in the ecclesiastical sector rise rapidly, but the advances in the church campaign brought, for the first time, virtual recognition of the existence of a modern Bulgarian nation and the first institutions representing that nation. The Patriarchate,

[25] Petko Totev (ed.), *Sŭchineniya* (Sofia: Bŭlgarski Pisatel, 1968); this is a Bulgarian version, entitled *Dennitsa na novobŭlgarskoto obrazovanie, V. E. Aprilov*, of the Russian original published in Odessa in 1841.

sensing the tide rising against it, became more assertive. In Plovdiv Bishop Nikifor, who had hitherto favoured teaching in Bulgarian, ordered the destruction of all gospels in Bulgarian, whilst the Patriarchate banned any further translations of the New Testament into Bulgarian. In a number of churches and monasteries, including some on Athos, ancient as well as recent religious works in Bulgarian were destroyed.

One reason for the rising tension between Bulgarian and Greek was that an ever larger number of Bulgarian priests were being trained in the Slav-dominated seminaries of Russia rather than in the hellenized ones in the Balkans; at the same time a number of Bulgarian communities outside the empire began to take up the call for the appointment of Bulgarian clergy in Bulgarian parishes and dioceses. Responding to a petition in 1838 the tsar agreed to admit three Bulgarian monks to the seminary at Kishinev, one of them being the former bishop of Ohrid, Natanail. In 1840 the first permanent Russian bursaries were founded, two for the seminary in Kherson and two for that in Odessa. Twenty more were set up in 1846 for Moscow, St Petersburg, and Kiev. In the church question, as in education, the Bulgarians of Odessa were particularly active. In 1843 a 'general assembly' of over forty young Bulgarians decided to do all in their power to ensure Bulgarians had their own bishop and the Bulgarian community in the city arranged for four scholarships for Bulgarians to train in Odessa's seminary. The Odessa Bulgarians also gave the tsar's advisers a list of thirty-three Bulgarians whom they considered fit to be made bishops.

In the Bulgarian lands the growing antagonism between Bulgarian flock and Greek cleric was seen in the outburst of social unrest in Vidin in 1840 when the protesters included amongst their demands one that they should have 'bishops who at least understand our language'. But the tension was most clearly seen in the archdiocese of Tŭrnovo, the largest in Bulgaria. Ilarion Kritski had died in 1838 and the Patriarchate appointed as his successor Panaret, an ill-educated hellenist. Sixteen parishes protested and in 1840 sent a delegation to Constantinople with the request that Panaret be replaced by Neofit Bozveli. The Porte agreed and persuaded the Patriarch to remove Panaret who, however, was replaced by another Greek, Neofit Vizantios, with Bozveli as his second in command, though the latter was immediately banished to a monastery from which he did not return until 1844. The machinations in Constantinople sparked off demonstrations in Tŭrnovo and a number of other towns.

There were other protests against Greek bishops. In 1846 the Bulgarians in Rusé demanded that they should choose their own bishop, have a bishop who spoke their language, and be allowed to expel bishops who were excessive in their monetary exactions. In the same year a long battle began between the Greek bishop of Samokov and his flock; the bishop was chased out of the town but returned, a procedure which was repeated three times before his death in 1862. By the end of the 1840s there had been moves against Greek bishops in Ohrid, Syar (Seres), Lovech, Sofia, Samokov, Tŭrnovo, Lyaskovets, Svishtov, Tryavna, Vratsa, and Vidin. The nature of the struggle had changed by the end of the decade; the Bulgarians' protest had become quite clearly one not against corrupt Greek bishops because they were corrupt, but against Greek bishops because they were Greek: 'The Bulgarian people no longer wanted Greek bishops, good or bad.'[26]

Neofit Bozveli had played a major role in igniting the national consciousness of the Bulgarian intelligentsia in Constantinople, and in this he had been helped to some degree by the hatt-i-sherif of 1839. The decree declared that all religions should be equal. The intention was to proclaim equality between Christianity and Islam but some Bulgarians also interpreted this to mean equality between groups within each faith. The effect of the reform, however, was muted as far as the Bulgarians were concerned because implementation of it was left to the separate millet leaders, and the Bulgarians could not expect concessions to their national demands from the leader of the Church they seemed to be wanting to divide. Nevertheless, encouraged by the hatt-i-sherif and by the growing strength of feeling within the Bulgarian congregations, in 1844 Neofit Bozveli, now returned from exile, and Ilarion Makariopolski, a leading figure in the Bulgarian religious community in Constantinople, presented a set of wide-ranging demands which amounted to 'the first request for the official recognition of the Bulgarian nation now in the process of formation'.[27] The demands, in which religious ones were prominent, included the appointment of Bulgarian bishops in Bulgarians sees, the election and payment of bishops, the formation of a four-man representative body at the Porte, separation from the Patriarchate, the building of

---

[26] Petŭr Nikov, *Vŭzrazhdanie na bŭlgarskiya narod; tsŭrkovno-natsionalni borbi i pos-tizheniya* (Sofia: Strashimir Slavchev, no date cited but before 1931; republished, Sofia: Nauka i izkustvo, 1971), original edition, 67–75, 75.

[27] Genchev, *Vŭzrazhdane*, 204.

a Bulgarian church in Constantinople, full freedom both to open Bulgarian schools and to publish Bulgarian books and newspapers, and the founding of mixed Bulgarian and Turkish courts. In the following year Bozveli and Makariopolski were empowered by the *aba*-makers guild in Constantinople to present to the Porte and the Patriarchate the wishes of the Bulgarians with regard to the Church; 'thus was created the first representation of the Bulgarian nation.'[28] Both the Porte and the Patriarchate rejected these demands and, with the encouragement of the Russian ambassador, Bozveli and Makariopolski were exiled to Athos, where Bozveli died in 1848.

Such action did not stem the tide, the Bulgarians of Constantinople intensifying their demand for a Bulgarian church in the city. In 1848 twenty-four *esnafs* asked the head of the *aba*-makers guild to take up the cause; he agreed and was helped by Aleksandŭr Eksarh, who had arrived from Russia in 1847, and by Stefan Bogoridi, a Bulgarian who had attained wealth and high office in the Ottoman administration. Their demand was almost immediately granted.

The creation of a specifically Bulgarian church in Constantinople was a huge advance for the Bulgarians. The church, St Stefan's, was built on land donated by Bogoridi and was declared the property of the Bulgarian people. It opened in October 1849 and was under the judicial and doctrinal authority of the Patriarch who would also approve the appointment of priests, but it was to be administered by a church council which consisted initially of twenty and later seventeen members; it was the first officially recognized Bulgarian institution since 1393, with its seal having Bulgarian letters and the emblem of the lion which was later to be the symbol of the independent Bulgarian state. The church's first priest, however, was a Serb, Stefan Kovačević, an unfortunate choice made because the Patriarchate refused to accept Makariopolski or Neofit Rilski for the post; Greek pressure was soon overcome and Kovačević was replaced by Ilarion Makariopolski, who had by then returned from exile.

The events of 1848 and 1849 provided a massive stimulus to the Bulgarian demand for a national church. Encouragement also came from further reforms in the Ottoman administration. In 1850 the Porte acknowledged the Protestants as a separate religious group within the Ottoman empire; in the following year the Armenian Catholics were

---

[28] Genchev, *Vŭzrazhdane*, 204.

recognized as an independent church and in 1852 were given their own patriarch and all the rights and privileges enjoyed by other independent religious communities. In the following year the Patriarchate reluctantly recognized the Greek autocephalous church in the Hellenic Kingdom. These concessions to other churches intensified Bulgarian demands that the same right be granted to them. The Bulgarian communities outside the empire gave full support to the campaign. In 1851 that in Bucharest issued 'to all our compatriots in the various towns throughout all Bulgaria' a letter which ended with the statement that 'Without a national church there is no salvation'.[29] Similar sentiments were expressed by the Bulgarians in a number of Russian towns. In a few cases Bulgarian enthusiasts took matters into their own hands. Until 1850 services in the church in Sliven were in Greek. On 8 November 1850 a group of youths entered the church during the service and demanded that the priest read the gospel in Slavonic. He refused, left the church, and fled to Adrianople never to return. From that day 'Sliven ceased to be a Greek and became a Bulgarian town.'[30]

A major advance in the Bulgarian cause came in February 1856 with the hatt-i-houmayan, the most important reforming measure the Ottoman state had yet taken. It went much further than the enactment of 1839 by promising equality of rights and privileges to all Christian sects and communities. It also ordered the Patriarchate to hold an assembly which was to work out the new constitution which all millets were required to adopt and which would shift power to mixed lay-clerical councils. The mixed council for the Patriarchate met from October 1858 to February 1860. It consisted of representatives of the priesthood, prominent laymen, and elected representatives of the guilds of the capital and of each vilayet.

The hatt-i-houmayan prompted the Bulgarian church in Constantinople to present a petition to the sultan on behalf of the 6.5 million Bulgarians in the empire asking for an independent Bulgarian Church. And in the same year it sent a letter to all major Bulgarian towns and villages asking them to elect delegates to attend a meeting in Constantinople to lobby for a separate Church. When it convened the meeting, though not large—it had sixty members, forty of whom were from Constantinople—was the first modern, Bulgarian, elected, national assembly.

The demand for a separate Church was central to the development of Bulgarian national consciousness not only in the major urban centres but

---

[29] Nikov, *Vŭzrazhdanie*, 64–7.   [30] Tabakov, *Chintulov*, 173.

also in the villages. Here the Church not only presided over the great events of individual lives—birth, confirmation, marriage, and burial— but was also crucial in the control of local schools and charitable institutions. In some instances the churches even fulfilled the functions of the banks, the local Christians not trusting the official, Ottoman institutions, and there are records of Muslims lodging funds from the local mosques with the local church for safe-keeping.[31]

With the promulgation of the hatti-i-houmayan the discussion of Bulgarian ecclesiastic independence had moved into official channels. But there it made little progress. The mixed council in the Patriarchate, which was to prove the first of seven major conferences between 1858 and 1872, made no concessions to the Bulgarians, whose demands greatly alarmed the leadership of the Orthodox Church. The Bulgarians wanted to reverse the order by which religious affiliation in the Ottoman empire was regulated: instead of cultural identity being a consequence of religious affiliation they wished religious affiliation to be a result of cultural identity, and if this notion were to be applied throughout the empire Orthodoxy would dissolve into separate Bulgarian, Romanian, Serbian, Albanian, Vlach, and Greek organizations. The Patriarchate naturally feared a change which would diminish its extent, its influence, and its income; it also argued that the Bulgarians did not have enough trained clerics to administer a Church of their own. At the international level Russia shared the fears of fracturing Orthodoxy mainly because its treaty rights to protect 'Orthodox Christians' within the Ottoman empire would be diminished were any group to secede from the Patriarchate. The western powers were also suspicious of moves towards an independent Bulgarian Church because, conversely and perversely, they believed that it would prove to be a vehicle of Russian influence in the heart of the Balkans.

Lack of progress in the mixed council persuaded some Bulgarians to follow the example of their compatriots in Sliven almost a decade before. In the church of the Holy Virgin in Plovdiv on Sunday 29 November 1859, a pupil read the Gospel in Bulgarian. Most of the Bulgarians in the congregation were delighted but the Greeks were enraged and disorders followed. The following day, in St Andrew's church, the same happened and this time the disorders spilled out into the streets. The Ottoman

---

[31] Toma Nikolov, *Spomeni iz moeto minalo* (Sofia: Otechestven Front, 1989), 40.

authorities, fearful for public order, commanded the Patriarchate to find some solution which would satisfy the Bulgarians. It was decided that in the two churches services would be alternately in Greek and Bulgarian.

These events were a major advance for the Bulgarians but they were soon overshadowed by others in the imperial capital. On Easter Sunday, 3 April 1860, the congregation interrupted the priest, Ilarion Makariopolski, at the point in the service where he was to pray for the Patriarch. The Patriarch's name was omitted, Ilarion praying directly for the sultan's welfare. This was an explicit rejection of the millet system which made the Patriarch, as Orthodoxy's *milletbashi*, the link between ruler and ruled. In the evening service, for which the customary patriarchal permission had not been secured, the Gospels were read in eleven different languages; Greek was not one of them.

To this virtual declaration of ecclesiastical independence the Bulgarians responded deliriously. Georgi Rakovski was so excited that he wanted to make 3 April a national holiday whilst thirty-three Bulgarian communities petitioned the Porte with their support for the declaration, as did 734 merchants from thirty-two towns who had met at the Uzundjovo trade fair, one of the biggest in the Balkans.

The Patriarchate responded, through the Porte, by arresting three major Bulgarian clerics: Makariopolski, Avksentii of Veles, and Paisiĭ, the bulgarophile Albanian bishop of Plovdiv; they were exiled in 1861. This only intensified the determination of Bulgarian communities throughout the empire to adopt Bulgarian bishops and align themselves with the Bulgarian Church in Constantinople and, with very few exceptions, between 1860 and 1869 all towns and dioceses in Moesia, Thrace, and Macedonia cut themselves off from the Patriarchate. Sliven was the first to do so in 1861. The dioceses of Veles, Lovech, Samokov, Shumen, Preslav, and Vidin, refused to accept bishops who, though Bulgarian, had been appointed by the Patriarch. The same happened in Sofia and when a new bishop arrived to take up his place his flock blockaded his house and had to be dispersed by troops, whilst the local guilds declared a strike, shutting their stalls and closing the market, after which the hapless cleric was persuaded by the Ottoman authorities to withdraw to Adrianople. In Rusé the Bulgarians made it clear that they no longer wished to have the Greek Sinesiĭ as their bishop and he was withdrawn, but when, in 1864, they were asked to pay his salary for the last three years riots broke out, the bishop's residence was ransacked by enraged women, and here too the market was closed by striking guildsmen. In Plovdiv there had been tension since the riots of 1859 and when, two years later, their bulgarophile bishop Paisiĭ was sent into exile the Bulgarians in the city elected Stoyan Chomakov to represent the Plovdiv bishopric in Constantinople; he did so for the next ten years and in that he was paid for doing so, he may lay claim to the perhaps dubious privilege of being considered modern Bulgaria's first professional politician.

Yet there were setbacks as well as gains for the Bulgarians. In the 1850s a division had emerged between some Bulgarian bishops and their flocks, the former not wishing to split the Church. In Vratsa the Bulgarian bishop supported the metropolitan of Tŭrnovo against his flock, and the bishop of Lovech was so committed to the unity of Orthodoxy that he was to refuse a see when the separate Bulgarian Church had been created. The great monastery of Rila, under the renowned Neofit Rilski, remained steadfastly loyal to the Patriarchate despite numerous pleas and petitions urging it to join the Bulgarian Church.

More distressing for advocates of a separate Church was the fact that despite the advance of 1860 and the enthusiasm with which it was greeted, there was no sign that the separate Church would receive official recognition. On the contrary, the Porte, rather than welcoming the new Church as a device which would weaken the Patriarchate, as the Bulgarians had hoped and expected, urged them to kiss the hand of the new Patriarch when he was elected soon after Easter 1860. Nor had the Porte done anything to frustrate the Patriarchate's decision after 3 April to exile the three leading Bulgarian clerics. The question of how recognition of ecclesiastical independence might be secured now became the subject of an intense debate in the newly emerging Bulgarian press.

There were two main factions. Again Bulgarians used the terms 'old' and 'young' for the moderates and radicals respectively. Both factions had newspapers, *Vreme* (Time) for the former, and *Gaĭda* (a Bulgarian musical instrument somewhat akin to the bagpipes) and *Makedoniya* (Macedonia) for the latter. The moderates were led by Gavril Krŭstevich, by now a high-ranking Ottoman civil servant, and Todor Burmov. They wanted an independent Bulgarian Church without breaking away from the Oecumenical Patriarchate and preferred to concentrate on negotiations with rather than public pressure on the Porte and the Patriarchate. The extremists were led by Petko Slaveĭkov and Stoyan Chomakov; the latter, between leaving school in Koprivshtitsa and being appointed Plovdiv's representative in Constantinople, had studied medicine in Pisa, Florence, and Paris. The radicals did not shy away from a schism, not least because that would intensify Bulgarian national consciousness. They laid great stress on the need to include all Bulgarians in the Bulgarian Church, and here their special concern was Macedonia. They also urged Bulgarians to act alone and not to be too dependent on outside factors, their main anxiety being the possible over-mighty influence of Russia. They had strong support amongst the guilds, within the Bulgarian community in Constantinople, and, as their nickname indicated, amongst the young. They were also greatly influenced by the examples of Romanian and Italian unification; if the Italian nationalists could proclaim that *Italia fara da sè*, then the Bulgarians too should consider acting independently of external sponsors.

The events of the early 1860s exposed the emptiness of both old and young arguments. The Porte did not respond to the diplomacy with which the old were trying to woo it, whilst independent action on Easter Sunday 1860 had failed to budge either Porte or Patriarchate in the direction of recognition. The only conclusion seemed to be that the Bulgarians would have to seek help from external factors. The question was, which one? The traditional champion of the Slav Christians, Russia, had lost credibility in the eyes of many Bulgarians. In the past it had supported the Patriarchate and in the war of 1828–9 it had abandoned the Bulgarians once tsarist objectives in Greece had been achieved. It had also lost a great deal of international influence following its recent defeat in the Crimean war, after which it offended many Bulgarians by its sponsorship of the settlement of Bulgarians in the Crimea and its support for the related Ottoman policy of settling Circassians in the Danubian plain. And democrats had no taste for tsarist autocracy.

A possible alternative was seen by some, for example a number of eminent Bulgarians in Plovdiv, in a possible alignment with the Serbian Church. Others, following a meeting of Bulgarian prominenti in Constantinople on 13 January 1861, decided to turn to the Evangelical Union and seek support from Britain, Prussia, and the Protestant world.

These suggestions made little headway but there was much greater support for the idea of joining the Uniate Church. Founded in the late sixteenth century the Uniate Church allowed local churches to follow their own liturgy, in their own language, as long as they recognized the Pope as the head of the Church and accepted the western *filoque* clause in the creed. The great political advantage of Uniatism was that it allowed local churches to seek the diplomatic support of the Catholic powers which in the 1850s and 1860s meant primarily France and the Habsburg empire. The chief Bulgarian advocate of Uniatism was Dragan Tsankov. Born of wealthy parents in Svishtov in 1828, he had abandoned his given name of Dimitŭr because it was Greek. He received his first schooling in his native town and then went to the seminary in Odessa. After a year there he continued to Kiev and by 1848 had moved to Galați in Wallachia to become a teacher. By 1850 he had joined his elder brother in Vienna where they published their Bulgarian grammar in German. He soon moved again, this time to Svishtov, and in 1853 to Constantinople. His reception into the Catholic Church in 1855, Russia's defeat in the Crimea, and his links with Polish refugees in Constantinople all strength-ened his view that the Bulgarians should seek support in the west; if Khan Boris I at the opening of a new era had been prepared to deal with Rome, he suggested, there was no reason why contemporary Bulgarians, hoping they too were approaching the dawn of a new era, should not do likewise.

The Uniate option had already been raised in the 1840s in parts of Macedonia and in dioceses such as Vratsa and Tryavna where pressure for the appointment of Bulgarian clerics was intense, but its main focus was around Kukush (Kilkis), where local Bulgarians had been raging against their bishop for over a decade. On 12 June 1859 they addressed a letter to the Pope asking to be taken under his protection. The document was sophisticated and written in faultless diplomatic language, so was probably prepared with outside help. After Easter Sunday 1860 and the need to secure recognition of the independent Bulgarian Church in Constantinople, the argument in favour of Uniatism gained greater currency, the more so with the arrest of the three clerics—would, the supporters of Uniatism asked, the Catholic powers have tolerated such goings on?

It was an issue of ecclesiastic discipline which precipitated the decisive move towards Uniatism. A Bulgarian priest from the Varna diocese had been sent to Constantinople for punishment by the Patriarch, his crime being his refusal to kiss the hand of his Greek bishop. On 18 December 1860 Tsankov led a delegation to Makariopolski's residence to demand union with Rome. When this was refused Tsankov took his men to the home of the papal representative where an agreement was signed after the Bulgarians had stated that they would accept Catholic dogma in all its aspects. In March 1861 Tsankov, accompanied by Dr Georgi Mirković, the Montenegrin deacon Rafael, and Ĭosif Sokolski, abbot of the Sokolski monastery near Gabrovo, went to Rome where they were received by the Pope and welcomed into the Catholic fraternity. Ĭosif came back bearing the title of Archbishop and Vicar of all the Bulgarians and was immediately recognized by the Porte as a *milletbashi*. The Uniates proclaimed that the Bulgarians had secured their own Church and cultural autonomy which was all they had asked for; Uniatism had given the Bulgarians complete victory.

The Uniates' triumph was short-lived. They had always faced strong opposition, not least from Rakovski, who in 1860 was in Belgrade. He made his *Dunavski Lebed* (Danubian Swan) a mouthpiece for anti-uniatism, even though this meant a vicious exchange of insults with his former friend Tsankov. Rakovski, 'the only great Bulgarian figure of the last [nineteenth] century not to give himself over to either the west or the east',[32] feared Uniatism would split the Bulgarian nation just when unity was essential. He also believed the Bulgarian Uniates were being used by the western powers as an anti-Russian, anti-Pan Slav tool. And why, he asked, risk latinization just after escaping hellenization? Many less prominent Bulgarians agreed, considering the new Church too fundamental a breach with tradition. For them faith was still far more important than ethnicity or nationality; and they were prepared to wait until recognition came to realize their dream of a separate Bulgarian Church within the Orthodox community. Nor was the promise of ecclesiastical autonomy under Uniatism completely honoured. In January 1861 Todor Ikonomov, a young, highly intelligent, and totally destitute writer arrived in Constantinople. He became involved in Uniatism because of its apparent success but soon after March he experienced doubts, principally because the Catholics in Constantinople began to interfere in Bulgarian communal affairs, chiefly to promote Catholic ritual and liturgy.

A few months later the Uniate adventure collapsed in total farce. In June 1861 Ĭosif, with the help of Petko Slaveĭkov, went to see the Russian ambassador, Prince Alexeĭ Lobanov-Rostovski. He told him he wished to revert to Orthodoxy, whereupon the ambassador obligingly arranged for him and Slaveĭkov to leave for Odessa on a ship used for carrying the

---

[32] Naĭden Sheĭtanov, 'Duhŭt', 266.

Russian diplomatic bag. Neither passenger had a passport, but this was not to say that Ĭosif lacked papers; he was taking with him all the documents of investment he had received from the Pope and the Porte. He was to spend the rest of his life in a seminary in Odessa, a weird, sad figure chiefly interested in natural science.

Uniatism in the imperial heartlands could not recover from such a blow. Soon afterwards most Uniate clergy left the Uniate church in Galata and issued a public statement that they were returning to Orthodoxy. A successor to Ĭosif was appointed in 1863. He was Raphael Popov, then aged 33.[33] In 1872 he petitioned the President of France for funds to build a Uniate church in Constantinople. The petition was granted and construction on the new church began in 1874 but after 1861 Uniatism had no standing in the Bulgarian community in the capital. Though it remained a source of concern to Russian diplomacy it survived in any strength only in the Kukush, Doiran, Enidje-Vadar, and Voden regions of Macedonia where it had been established before 1861.

After the collapse of Uniatism the Bulgarian Church cause, despite grass-roots pressure throughout the Bulgarian areas, made little or no progress towards recognition. Bulgarians ruefully contrasted their own position with that of the Romanians when, in 1865, the bishoprics in Moldavia and Wallachia united in a single Romanian Orthodox Church without the approval of the Patriarchate. In the same year another church council met in Constantinople to consider the question of the Bulgarian Church, but it brought only minimal gains to the Bulgarians. It agreed to increase the number of bishops who would take part in the election of the Patriarch from twenty-eight to fifty-eight but it rejected the Bulgarians' request that they should have half the seats on the Synod. The Patriarchate did accept, however, that when nominating bishops it would choose ones who knew the local language. It had taken virtually twenty years for the Bulgarians to secure acceptance of this notion.

Agitation in the Bulgarian communities continued apace but the log jam was broken by external rather than internal factors. The second half of the 1860s was a time of growing international instability. The Austro-Prussia war altered the balance of power in north-central Europe and the subsequent Austro-Hungarian *Ausgleich* of 1867 provided a model of

---

[33] Christopher Walter, 'Raphael Popov, Bulgarian Uniate Bishop: Problems of Uniatism and Autocephaly', *Sobornost*, 6/1 (1984), 46–60.

imperial devolution which could have relevance in the Ottoman domains. At the same time slavophiles in Russia looked away from Poland and towards the Orthodox Balkans where they favoured the Slavs rather than the Greeks. In Serbia Michael Obrenović was promoting the idea of a Balkan alliance and an agreement was signed in May 1867 by the Serbian government and Bulgarian representatives who were in Belgrade. This came after an alliance between Serbia and Montenegro in September 1866, and was itself followed by a Greek-Serbian treaty in the summer of 1867, and by an agreement between Serbia and Romania in January 1868. Most worrying of all for the Porte, however, was an insurrection in Crete in 1866 which threatened to bring about intervention by the great powers which would in turn greatly increase the risk of mass unrest amongst the Christians of Ottoman Europe.

If the Cretan emergency was the most dangerous development for the Porte, perhaps the most surprising was the incursion of two armed Bulgarian bands into Ottoman territory in 1867. More were to follow in 1868.

The sudden manifestation of an armed threat from the Bulgarians, however minuscule, persuaded the Porte to put pressure on the Patriarchate. In March 1867, Gregory VI, who had become Patriarch in the preceding month, therefore produced a plan for creating a separate Bulgarian Church. The scheme was unacceptable to the Bulgarians because it said nothing about the status of the Bulgarian church in Constantinople and did not include the dioceses of Thrace or Macedonia. Nevertheless, 'for the first time the Patriarch had recognized the right of the Bulgarians to their own separate Church'.[34]

In February 1870 the sultan issued a ferman, or declaration of intent, for the setting up of a separate Bulgarian Church. The new model was based on Gregory VI's proposals of 1867 and on a scheme submitted to the Porte by Gavril Krŭstevich in 1869. Under it the Bulgarian Church was not to be completely independent. It was still to mention the Patriarch in its prayers, and it was to be subordinate to him in matters of doctrine and in the procurement of Holy Oil. It was to be headed by an exarch, (originally an exarch had been the head of a monastic house but by the mid-nineteenth century the word was used to denote an ecclesiastical rank between patriarch and metropolitan), and in all matters of internal

---

[34] Nikov, *Vŭzrazhdanie*, 233.

administration the Exarchate was to be completely free of the Patriarchate. The ferman said nothing on where the new Church should have its headquarters. The Porte's acceptance of the separate Bulgarian church in Constantinople in 1849 had been the first official recognition of a specifically Bulgarian institution since 1393; the ferman of 1870 went further in that it was the first official recognition given by the Ottoman or any other state of the existence of a Bulgarian nation.

On the critical question of the extent of the new Church Krŭstevich had suggested that it should have twenty-five dioceses, including most of those in Macedonia, and the Patriarchate forty-one, with the remaining eight to be divided between the two. The ferman was not so generous. Article 10 divided dioceses with a predominantly Bulgarian population into three groups: those totally included in the Exarchate; those which were partially incorporated; and those not specifically named in the ferman but which had the right to decide by a two-thirds majority in a plebiscite whether they wished to join the Exarchate. Those fully incorporated were Rusé, Silistra, Shumen, Tŭrnovo, Sofia, Vratsa, Lovech, Vidin, Nish, Pirot, Kyustendil, Samokov, and Veles. The partially incorporated were Varna, where the city and twenty coastal villages with a non-Bulgarian population remained in the Patriarchate; the district of Sliven minus Anhialo (Pomorie) and Mesemvria (Nesebŭr); the county of Sozopol excluding the coastal villages; and Plovdiv without the city itself, Stanimaka, and a number of named villages, though four monasteries, including the famous foundation at Bachkovo, and the Virgin Mary district of Plovdiv were to be part of the Exarchate; those citizens of the Virgin Mary district who did not wish to join the Exarchate would not be required to do so.[35] In effect, the Bulgarians were to have all the dioceses of northern Bulgaria, including

---

[35] This from the English language version of the ferman in M. Voinov and L. Panayotov, *Documents and Materials on the History of the Bulgarian People* (Sofia: BAN, 1969), 157–9. Slightly different distributions are given in Markova, *Ekzarhiya*, 30 and appendix 4, 328–9 and Nikov, *Vŭzrazhdanie*, 272–3. The latter, also seemingly quoting the ferman itself gives the following sees: Rusé; Silistra; Shumen; Tŭrnovo; Sofia; Vratsa; Lovech, Vidin, Nish, Pirot, Kyustendil, Samokov, Veles, Varna (minus the city itself and twelve villages which had non-Bulgarian populations), Sliven (without Anhialo and Pomorie); the sanjak of Sozopol (without the coastal villages), and the see of Plovdiv without the city and the Stanimaka district, though the four important monasteries and the Virgin Mary district of Plovdiv were to be part of the Exarchate. Skopje and Ohrid joined in 1874. The Rusé and Silistra sees were combined in 1872, as were Varna and Preslav in the same year.

the Morava valley and the Dobrudja, but south of the Balkan range it was to have only a small part of Thrace and the Veles district of Macedonia. Most of the other Macedonian dioceses were to decide their affiliation by plebiscite.

The ferman pleased neither side. The Patriarchate declared that the Exarchate was in contravention of canon law, and the Bulgarians could scarcely rejoice over the territorial provisions. Once again there was stalemate. It lasted for two years.

The final breach between the Patriarchate and the Exarchate began in St Stefan's, Constantinople, in January 1872. By this time the three exiled Bulgarian bishops had been allowed to return on condition that they did not make life difficult for the Patriarchate. For this reason they did not officiate in St Stefan's until 5 January when the Bulgarian guilds in the city demanded that Bulgarian clerics should preside over the Epiphany service on the following day. This they did and after the service offered prayers both for the sultan and for the implementation of the ferman of 1870. This was a final provocation for the Patriarchate which had just come under the leadership of Antim VI, Gregory having resigned. Antim felt slighted and was easily influenced by the more extreme hellenists who urged him to condemn the Bulgarians as schismatic, the first step towards which was the convening of a yet another Patriarchal assembly. For their part the Bulgarians responded by moving closer to outright rebellion; they decided to go ahead and, notwithstanding the lack of consent by the Patriarch, elected Antim of Vidin as their first Exarch. In April he declared that the suspension of the three Bulgarian bishops had been illegal and was therefore abrogated, and in May, having celebrated the liturgy in St Stefan's, read a long proclamation of independence for the Bulgarian Church. The Patriarchal council immediately declared the Bulgarian Church schismatic, as did an Oecumenical council in September. The breach was not to be repaired until after the second world war.

After the promulgation of the ferman of 1870 the Bulgarians had to consider how their new Church was to be governed. A provisional council was formed in Constantinople which in October 1870 sent a circular to Bulgarian communities telling them to elect representatives for a national church council which was to meet in the city in January 1871. Each village was to choose three representatives to send to the chief town of the diocese where they would elect, in secret, the number of representatives appropriate for that diocese. The council convened on 23 February 1871 and was to have thirty-seven meetings before closing on 24 July. Its president was Ilarion Lovchanski. It had fifty members, eleven of whom were priests and thirty-nine laymen. The council's task was to devise a constitution for the Exarchate and this it completed on 14 May. The most notable feature of the constitution was that 'no-one, from the highest to the lowest, was nominated; everyone was elected, including the officials of the Exarchate.'[36]

The church council was seen by many Bulgarians as a virtual national parliament. Newspapers of the day frequently referred to it as 'the Bulgarian National Council' and Krŭstevich, a moderate and still an Ottoman government official, had to remind it that 'We are organizing a Church, not a government.'[37]

The campaign for a separate Church had provided an enormous stimulus in developing Bulgarian national consciousness. In Macedonia the appearance of Slaveĭkov's *Makedoniya* in 1866 played a huge part in persuading many Slavs to think of themselves as Bulgarians. The clause of the 1870 ferman allowing for plebiscites mobilized opinion even more. A petition signed by over two-thirds of the adult population asking for inclusion in the Exarchate was sent from Ohrid as early as May 1870, and similar documents were prepared in many other Macedonian sees and parishes. Official plebiscites were held in 1874 in the Ohrid and Skopje dioceses, both of which voted for inclusion in the Exarchate. In fact, it was in the church campaign that the modern Bulgarian nation was created. It was a campaign in which the Bulgarians had broken away from the hellenizing influence of the Patriarchate; yet they had retained their essential Orthodoxy and had rejected the westernizing pressures inherent in Uniatism; the Bulgarians had also found methods for the articulation of their national aspirations which were political in form but religious in content. The campaign had been one for a recognized place within rather than one against the existing Ottoman institutional framework.

[36] Markova, *Eksarhiya*, 44.   [37] Zhechev, *Velikden*, 267.

5. THE REVOLUTIONARY AND POLITICAL
MOVEMENTS

The creation of a separate Bulgarian Church had huge political implications. Gregory VI recognized this; when he presented his plan for a Bulgarian Church to the Russian ambassador in 1867 he remarked, 'With my own hands I have built a bridge to the political independence of the Bulgarians.'[38] But Bulgarians could be pushed towards political demands by the frustrations as well as by the successes of the church campaign. In 1872 Ikonomov stated that the Bulgarian cause had regressed rather than advanced since Easter 1860; two years earlier he had written in *Makedoniya*, 'Many nations have their own church but those churches are very far from furthering national progress. On the contrary, they work against it.'[39] Furthermore, the attainment of the Exarchate meant that religious objectives had been achieved; nationalist passions therefore now had only one real outlet: in the demand for political concessions, a demand which in the Ottoman context was virtually a statement of revolutionary intent. Nor had it escaped the notice of many Bulgarians that, however insignificant the incursions of 1867 and 1868 may have been in military terms, they had portentous political implications; shortly after the 1870 ferman had been issued a friend of Pandeli Kisimov, who was close to the Porte, told him, 'Thanks to the bands which appeared in Bulgaria and to the impression they had on thinking both inside and outside Bulgaria, we were granted the Exarchate.'[40] By the mid-1870s therefore the focus of the Bulgarian national movement had shifted to the military struggle for political independence.

Until the 1870s there had been little revolutionary activity, that is conspiracy and the use of armed force for defined political objectives, during the *vŭzrazhdane*. A few proponents of armed struggle took inspiration and encouragement from the unifications of Italy and the Principalities of Wallachia and Moldavia, from the rising in Crete, from

---

[38] Nikov, *Vŭzrazhdanie*, 230.

[39] *Makedoniya*, 7 April 1870 quoted in Zhechev, *Velikden*, 257.

[40] Zhechev, *Velikden*, 241 quoting from Pandeli Kisimov, *Istoricheski Raboti*, 3/1 (1901), 62.

Serbian ideas of Balkan cooperation, and from Serbian attacks on the Ottoman garrison in Belgrade in 1862. It was in that year in Belgrade that Georgi Rakovski formed his Legion on the model of Garibaldi, and in 1868, in his 'Gorski Pŭtnik', Rakovski declared, 'The Turkish yoke, four centuries endured | Let us smash heroically',[41] but such calls for action were rare and had little effect. When revolutionary activity did occur it was usually sporadic, ill-organized, and, notwithstanding the impact of the 1867 incursions, largely ineffective. And whilst during the church campaign external influences, though important, had by and large been subordinate to internal ones in securing any advance, in the armed, political struggle the reverse was the case.

There were many reasons for the relative lack of political and revolutionary activity. The Bulgarian historian Petŭr Mutafchiev argued that the Slavs were not, from the earliest days, natural state formers.[42] The Russians, Ukrainians, Serbs, and other Slav groups, he asserted, did not form states until late in their histories and if the Bulgarians were an exception this was because of the Proto-Bulgars, and even then the Bulgarian empires did not develop many of the usual features of the state including, as has been noted, the construction of a navy or the minting of coins.

Ethnic psyche, however, is a dubious concept. Geography is not. Bulgaria was not, like Romania, Greece, or Serbia, at the periphery of the Ottoman empire but close to its heart. This had two major effects: it meant that the Porte would not concede any form of meaningful political devolution, and it made military opposition to the empire virtually impossible.

The absence of a strong political movement was also, of course, a result of the Bulgarians' concentration on the cultural and ecclesiastical campaigns. But even in these campaigns the proximity of the Ottoman capital was an important factor. The nearness of Constantinople meant that large numbers of Bulgarians settled there and the size, wealth, and power of this community meant that the locus of the church struggle was in Constantinople, which therefore became more important than the large sees and historic centres such as Tŭrnovo, Plovdiv, and Ohrid with their predominantly Slav populations. The Bulgarian national cause was therefore located precisely where it would be most difficult to make any

---

[41] Cited Firkatian, *Forest Traveler*, 113.   [42] Petŭr Mutafchiev, *Kniga*, 99.

realistic claim to political devolution, and émigré organizations based in Belgrade, Bucharest, or Odessa could not by geographic definition be the locus of a new, Bulgarian, political centre. This meant that when it did emerge Bulgarian nationalism had an unusually weak sense of territorial nationalism. The impossibility of a political solution and the power of the émigré communities combined to ensure that Bulgarian nationalism was primarily cultural rather than political and territorial.

Despite the virtual impossibility of successful armed resistance to the Ottoman regime there were revolts. In 1408 there was a rising in western Bulgaria. In 1598 there was a large revolt around Tŭrnovo when it was hoped the Habsburg armies would move south of the Danube. A century later Habsburg forces did move south and as a result the Bulgarian Catholics of Chiprovets staged their ill-fated rebellion. The Bulgarian lands, however, were always too near the centre of Ottoman power for the sultan to allow them to escape his grasp. If outright revolt were impossible there remained the possibility of disobedience and banditry, and groups of 'haiduts' were formed in the mountains from where they harried travellers and government representatives. Later nationalists would glorify the deeds and laud the motives of the haiduts but the latter, like the English pirates who roamed the Spanish main, acted out of greed at least as much as patriotism; nor were the haiduts ever a serious military force, most bands consisting of fewer than fifteen men.

From the early eighteenth century onwards Bulgarians found a more effective means of military opposition in joining the Christian armies which, with increasing frequency and effect, invaded the Ottoman empire from the north. A number of armed Bulgarian units joined the Russians in the war of 1735 to 1739 and there were Bulgarian groups fighting in Suvorov's army in the 1790s. Bulgarian bands led by the haidut Velko Petrovich appeared in 1807 during the Serbian war of independence, and in 1808 a Bulgarian merchant in Bucharest, Pinalov, raised a 486-man cavalry unit headed by Georgi Guzen. Bulgarian engagement in the war of 1806–12 was greater than in all previous conflicts. A volunteer cavalry squadron of almost a thousand men fought under the command of one Nikich, whose qualities Kutuzov thought made him worthy of officer status, and according to two Russian diplomats almost 10,000 Christians had entered Wallachia from Bulgaria hoping to fight as volunteers. In 1811 in Wallachia the 'Bulgarian Land Army' (Bŭlgarska zemska voĭska) was formed, whilst in northern Bulgaria a secret network was established to supply intelligence to the Russians. When the tsar's forces entered Bulgaria large numbers of locals joined them, some no doubt responding to Sofroniĭ Vrachanski's call to welcome the Russian soldiers as liberators; at the same time, in the mountains around Gabrovo almost the entire population was mobilized, and Bulgarian units showed conspicuous gallantry during the attack on the fortress at Silistra. Bulgarians also helped the Greeks in their war against the Ottoman authorities, and there were hundreds, perhaps thousands, of Bulgarians in the forces of Ipsilantis and Tudor Vladimirescu. When the Russian army invaded the Ottoman empire in 1828–9 the Bulgarians again tried to help them, particularly in the Sliven area, though in this instance the Russians did not welcome such help and did much to frustrate it.

Military organization on their own soil, however, remained too dangerous for Bulgarians. When the first military groups were formed they were therefore based outside the Bulgarian lands. And when they did eventually emerge the Bulgarians' lack of recent experience in the organization and direction of military units was apparent. The first appeared in Belgrade in 1862 when Georgi Rakovski formed the Bulgarian Legion, hoping that it would take part in the forthcoming Serbian attack on the Ottoman garrison in the city and then form the core of a larger Bulgarian armed force. The Legion, however, was soon abandoned amidst accusations of peculation and incompetence. Military action was to be contemplated again, and was to achieve indirect success when the band incursions of 1867 hastened concessions in the church dispute, but there were still serious divisions on strategy between the advocates of armed action. Some argued that the Bulgarians should rely on the incursion of armed bands, others thought they must send apostles to agitate and prepare leadership cadres within the Bulgarian lands, another group called for a general rising, and others believed they should institute a partial rebellion in the hope that the great powers would then intervene and force the Porte to make concessions. Not until the early 1870s was sufficient consensus found to undertake serious military operations.

That it took so long for a political movement and an armed insurrectionary movement to appear was in part because of the concentration of efforts and energies on the cultural and ecclesiastical campaigns. But it was also because after the mid-1820s a new symbiosis between the

Bulgarians and the Ottoman state had appeared. The economic and social base of the vŭzrazhdane was the wealth created from the late 1820s onwards, and that wealth depended on the continued existence of the Ottoman state, and especially its army. Furthermore, with some regional exceptions, the years from the 1820s to the 1870s were ones of relative economic prosperity. The guildsmen and merchants were to some extent pushed into being traditionalists, wishing, for their own economic well-being, to preserve the state, albeit a reformed version of it. Whilst the merchants and handicraft producers found themselves as de facto supporters of the status quo, the clerics and teachers became the modernizers.

The relative prosperity of the era also meant that there was not the dispossessed tenantry or hand-worker who formed the backbone of early protest movements in the centre and west of Europe. Nor were there serious outbursts of hunger similar to those which afflicted western and central Europe and above all Ireland in the mid-1840s.

During the initial stages of the vŭzrazhdane the state itself was not the main instrument of oppression in most Bulgarians' eyes. That was either the corrupt, and coincidentally Greek-dominated Church, or the local landowner or his representative. It was not until 1832 that the collection of state taxes became the responsibility not of the local landlord but of a state official, and therefore it was not until then that the personification of the exploiting agency became a political figure, representing the state, rather than a social or an ecclesiastical figure. Furthermore, the liquidation of the old system was gradual. In these circumstances a call for revolutionary action against the state would have little appeal and would in all probability alarm or alienate the wealthy without whose backing any action was doomed.

A final cause for the lack of a strong political movement was the lack of interest amongst the great powers. The Russians' conduct in the critical years of the 1850s was ambiguous and neither they nor the western powers were yet ready to sacrifice their interests in the Ottoman empire as a whole for the sake of the Bulgarians.

Despite all these impediments a political movement did finally emerge in the 1870s. The central figure in its creation was Georgi Rakovski. Born in Kotel in 1821 he had been educated at the local cell school before moving to Raĭno Popovich's school in Karlovo and then to the Greek gymnasium in Constantinople. After completing his education he travelled widely, spending time in Athens, Marseilles, and Braila. By the time he returned to Constantinople in the mid-1840s he knew Turkish, Greek, French, Serbian, Russian, Romanian, and German, and had studied Latin, Arabic, and Persian. He had also become a practised conspirator. In Athens he had set up a 'Macedonian Society' and in Braila he played a prominent part in organizing a revolutionary group amongst the local Bulgarians; for this he was sentenced to death. He escaped but was jailed in Constantinople from 1843 to 1845. During the Crimean war he led a small group of armed men into Bulgaria to try and link up with Russian troops. After the failure of this expedition he moved restlessly through the Balkans until settling in Belgrade in 1860. Here he drew up 'A Plan for the Liberation of Bulgaria' and 'The Statute of the Provisional Bulgarian Command in Belgrade'. He had now come to the conclusion that a revolutionary army command should be established to unite all armed Bulgarians in exile and to establish secret committees within Bulgaria itself. The first Bulgarian Legion of 1862 implemented these ideas. Unfortunately for him they also alarmed the Serbian authorities and in 1863 he was forced to leave Belgrade for Bucharest.

Here Rakovski again turned to conspiracy, this time with more lasting consequences. He was mainly responsible for setting up the Secret Central Bulgarian Committee (SCBC) in 1867. The SCBC performed two important functions. It brought the Bulgarian question to the attention of a wider audience, and it organized the armed bands which went into Bulgaria in 1867 and 1868.

Rakovski had always appreciated the need for publicity. Throughout his life he was a prolific writer both of prose and poetry. He was also one of the most accomplished and influential journalists of his time, contributing to and editing a number of newspapers. He aimed his journalism at readers outside as well as within the Bulgarian lands; his *Dunavski Lebed* for example was modelled on *The Times* and Rakovski on occasions had copies of it translated into English and sent to London. The SCBC also ensured it made itself heard in central and western Europe by circulating a 'Memorandum to the Sultan' and then by issuing a pamphlet, 'Bulgaria before Europe', which was printed in Bulgarian and French. The Memorandum proposed a Turkish-Bulgarian dualism—this was the year of the Austro-Hungarian Ausgleich—with the sultan becoming king of the Bulgarians and with the Bulgarians having full autonomy within their ethnic frontiers, together with their own capital, parliament, and Church. The empire, said the Memorandum, was collapsing and there was a veiled threat that if it did not make concessions to the Bulgarians they would take to arms to hasten its demise.

Having made this veiled threat the SCBC moved to implement it by financing and equipping the bands of Filip Totyu and Panaĭot Hitov which crossed into Bulgaria in 1867. Hitov's band, or 'cheta', emerged unscathed but Totyu's was destroyed. The SCBC and the bands owed much to the intrigues of the Russian ambassador to Constantinople, Count Nikolaĭ Ignatiev, who wanted to dispel the prevalent notion that the Bulgarians never had and never would take to arms. The Committee also received support from the Romanian authorities because in the mid-1860s the Ottoman government had concentrated troops on the Danube. When they were withdrawn so too were the subsidies the Romanian authorities had given to the SCBC which then collapsed. Shortly afterwards Rakovski died of tuberculosis.

Further incursions by Bulgarian bands, led this time by Stefan Karadja and Hadji Dimitŭr Asenov, took place in 1868 but they lacked the financial and logistical support the SCBC and the Russian embassy had given to those of 1867 and the Ottoman authorities, now on their guard against such units, quickly defeated them.

The ideas of the Memorandum and the SCBC, however, lived on and evolved. Rakovski had been an inspiration to many, particularly through his poetry, but his thinking had not been consistent; by the time the cheti entered Bulgaria in 1867, for example, he had concluded that because the Cretan revolt had been contained, such military action could no longer be effective. Nor had Rakovski realized the importance of careful, detailed preparation for a rising within Bulgaria itself.

These deficiencies were remedied by Bulgarian nationalism's greatest ideologist and greatest practitioner, Lyuben Karavelov and Vasil Levski.

Karavelov was born in Koprivshtitsa in 1834 and educated there and in Plovdiv. In 1857 he went to Russia, where he attended classes in history in Moscow University and became acquainted with a number of revolutionary figures, including Nechaev. In 1864 he returned to the Balkans, where he acted as correspondent for two influential Russian newspapers. After spending some time in Belgrade he moved to Novi Sad, where he was arrested on charges connected with the murder of Michael Obrenović of Serbia. After a short while in the fortresses of Peterwardein and Buda he was released and went to Bucharest, where he met both Vasil

Levski and the poet and future revolutionary activist, Hristo Botev. Karavelov, like Rakovski, was a prolific writer and, again like Rakovski, was an active journalist and editor. In Bucharest he began publishing *Svoboda* (Freedom) which was banned only to reappear shortly after as *Nezavisimost* (Independence). Karavelov favoured the form of civic nationalism advocated by Young Italy and Young France and was more distant from the church struggle than Rakovski. He rejected the notion of an Ottoman-Bulgarian Ausgleich, arguing instead for the creation of a federation of liberated Balkan states. In Bucharest he took part in the foundation of the Bulgarian Revolutionary Secret Committee which welcomed all who shared its views, 'irrespective of creed or nationality'.[43] He also continued his journalistic activities but his morale was severely dented after setbacks suffered by the nationalist cause in Bulgaria itself in 1873. By 1875 he was sufficiently recovered to begin a new paper, *Znanie* (Knowledge). In the Serbo-Turkish war of 1876 he organized bands of Bulgarian volunteers and in the war between Russia and the Ottoman empire in 1877–8 he aided the Russian forces. He returned to Bulgaria in the second half of 1878 but died shortly thereafter. He was the only one of the major political activists in the pre-liberation revolutionary movement who lived to see the new Bulgarian state.

In his 'Programme' published in 1870 Karavelov had stressed the need for cooperation with Bulgaria's neighbours, recommending the setting up of a Danubian or Yugoslav federation, but in general he tended to overestimate both the ease with which such cooperation could be achieved and its military effectiveness should it ever come about. His major contribution to the strategic thinking of the revolutionary movement was with regard to the methodology of the struggle within Bulgaria itself; it was to insist that before the bands could be effective 'apostles' must be sent into Bulgaria to prepare the people for an armed uprising when the cheti did appear.

In political terms Karavelov was a radical. He was an atheist and like Rakovski before him and Botev after him regarded the *chorbadjii* as hostile and an impediment to the national movement. In *Svoboda* he had written that 'the chief enemy of the Bulgarian nation is the Bulgarians

[43] Konstantin Kosev, 'Ideĭno-politicheski i organizatsionni predpostavki', in Konstantin Kosev, Nikolaĭ Zhechev, and Doĭno Doĭnov, *Istoriya na aprilskoto vŭstanie 1876*, 2nd edition (Sofia: Partizdat, 1986), 120–56, 139.

themselves, i. e. our *chorbadjiĭ*,[44] and in *Nezavisimost* he made his famous statement that 'Bulgaria will only be saved when the Turk, the *chorbadjiya*, and the bishop are hung from the same tree'.[45]

The third most prominent of the revolutionaries, Vasil Kunchev, or Vasil Levski as he was later known, was born in 1837 in Karlovo. He was educated there and in Stara Zagora, where he trained for the priesthood, entering a monastery in 1858. He remained there for only two years and by 1862 was in Belgrade, where he became a member of Rakovski's Legion, taking part in the action against the Ottoman garrison in the city. His skill and bravery in this action earned him the nickname 'Levski', or 'lion-hearted'. After the dissolution of the Legion Levski spent a little time in a monastery and for a while worked as a teacher near Karlovo and then in the Dobrudja. In 1867 he went to Romania. He acted as a standard bearer in Hitov's cheta and was also a member of the second Bulgarian Legion which entered Bulgaria in 1868; he was frustrated in a further attempt to enter Bulgaria when he was arrested by the Serbian authorities at Zaĭchar. He was a founder member of the Bulgarian Revolutionary Central Committee (BRCC) in Bucharest in 1869 but by then the failure of the cheti had convinced him that the centre of revolutionary activity must be moved into the Bulgarian lands; accordingly, in 1869 he established a number of revolutionary committees in Bulgaria and by the mid-1870s his Internal Organization consisted of around 200 such committees ready and willing to take part in an armed uprising. He was again in the Bulgarian lands between 1870 and 1872, where he concentrated on uniting the local committees under a Provisional Government of Bulgaria in Lovech. The committees were dominated by the intelligentsia and the merchants. Of the 1,001 members of the committees identified in the early 1870s, the occupation of 214 was unknown and of the remainder 271 were peasants, 191 teachers and priests, 159 merchants, 134 craftsmen, 17 officials, 15 apprentices and journeymen, and 7 came from the ranks of the very wealthy.[46]

In 1872, without Levski's consent, a group of activists staged a robbery in Arabakonak. They were captured. One of them attempted to argue that their action had been political rather than purely criminal and this

[44] Konstantinova, *Dŭrzhavaost*, 118.   [45] Ibid.

[46] Figures in Konstantin Kosev, 'Sotsialno-ikonomicheski predpostavki', in Konstantin Kosev et al., *Aprilskoto vŭstanie 1876*, 15–119, 81–2.

led to the exposure of the committees and to the arrest of Levski, who was on his way to Lovech to try and save the Internal Organization's archives. He was executed in Sofia in February 1873. Levski became Bulgaria's most revered nationalist martyr, his immortal phrase, 'If I succeed the whole nation succeeds: if I fail, then I perish alone', is carved in huge letters on his monument outside the National Palace of Culture (NDK) erected in Sofia in the 1980s.

Levski had believed that it was hopeless to dream of foreign sponsorship or assistance: Bulgaria's liberation, he insisted, could be achieved only by the Bulgarians themselves. That did not turn out to be the case. In 1875 the Balkan peninsula was thrown into turmoil by a rebellion, sparked primarily by social discontent, in Bosnia. The tensions could not be contained and in the following year Serbia went to war with the Ottoman empire. These events were followed with mounting excitement by the Bulgarian intelligentsia and the revolutionaries believed this was their chance, the more so after Prince Milan of Serbia promised them 2,000 rifles. Atanas Uzunov, whom the BRCC had nominated to succeed Levski, wrote to Hristo Botev,

I can only say that Bulgaria is dissatisfied, that it is in a terrible condition, that it is ready to take up arms to decide between life and death. I can assure you that in our homeland there is not a single Bulgarian who is not thinking of the fate of the Bulgarian nation and of its political liberation. Even the government officials and the *chorbadjii* who at the moment are carrying out their loathsome obligations are not that loyal to the authorities. I can *assure you* that the majority of these Turkish officials and the *chorbadjii* are members of the revolutionary committees.[47]

Other reports came in of a willingness and preparedness for an armed uprising. The apostle in Stara Zagora wrote to the BRCC in August 1875 that, 'Everyone is buying arms and supplies'.[48] There were also attempts at action. There was a wild scheme to set fire to Constantinople and, more seriously, the BRCC in Bucharest attempted to stage an insurrection in the autumn in the Stara Zagora region. Despite the defeat of the attempted rising the Russian consul in Rusé reported in October that 'It seems to me that the time is not far off when the whole of Bulgaria will rise up',[49] and

[47] Kosev et al., *Aprilskoto vŭstanie 1876*, 87–8.
[48] Cited in Doĭno Doĭnov, 'Iztochnata krisa i revolyutsionniyat podem na Balkanite— 1875g', in Konstantin Kosev et al., *Aprilskoto vŭstanie 1876*, 157–215, 180.
[49] Ibid. 205.

Nikolaĭ Obretenov wrote that despite the failure in Stara Zagora, 'Whatever happens we won't leave Turkey in peace. Either we shall all perish or we shall free Bulgaria.'[50]

Enthusiasm was clearly in the ascendant and the Bulgarian lands had already been divided by the BRCC in Bucharest into four revolutionary districts based on Tŭrnovo, Sliven, Vratsa, and Panagyurishte, and a number of apostles and deputy apostles had been nominated. Furthermore, arms had been purchased with money donated by wealthy Bulgarians such as Evlogi Georgiev. Leaders of the fourth revolutionary district met in Oborishte near Panagyurishte in April 1876 and agreed to declare an uprising against the Ottomans in May. Tragically the authorities discovered what was afoot and sent a regiment to the town on 19 April. Following a prearranged agreement of what to do in such circumstances the rising was declared immediately in Koprivshtitsa. The April uprising had begun.

The April uprising was the beginning of the birth of the modern Bulgarian state. The midwife was Russia. After the Koprivshtitsa declaration a number of cheti moved into Bulgaria, the most dramatic incident being when a band led by Hristo Botev seized an Austrian steamer on the Danube and landed at the Bulgarian port of Lom. They marched southwards but were soon surrounded and destroyed. Many others died as the authorities suppressed the rising with relative ease.

The April uprising suffered from a number of weaknesses. Coordination between local committees and those in exile was weak, particularly in the crucial years from 1872 to 1876, and when it was decided to act the final preparations were too rushed, being completed in only four months. Help from Serbia, or anywhere outside the Bulgarian lands, failed to materialize. The Ottoman authorities had learned that a revolt was being considered and from the late autumn of 1875 had taken appropriate measures, increasing their patrols on the Danube to prevent bands crossing from Romania, and also sending more spies and agents provocateurs into Bulgarian areas. These did considerable damage to the infrastructure of the revolutionary organization and on the eve of the rising itself scores of activists, particularly teachers and priests, were arrested. The revolutionaries also

---

[50] Ibid. 206.

wildly overestimated the degree of support they would receive from the population at large. Uzunov's optimism had been widely shared by those organizing the uprising in the Plovdiv area who had expected more than 70,000 to join the revolt, but in the event throughout the Bulgarian lands no more than 10,000 took to arms.[51] Hopes that the *chorbadjii* and Ottoman officials of Bulgarian extraction would rally to the rebel cause were also misplaced, and in Koprivshtitsa they even fed information on the uprising to the police.

Those who did take up arms found that there were no carefully prepared plans or methods of communication between rebels and their immediate commanders, and links between the latter and the émigré organizations were as bad if not worse than before. The rebels were insufficiently armed. In the north they were affected by the refusal of boatmen to transport across the Danube weapons bought and stored in Romania, and although they famously fashioned some forty cannons out of wood these were useless in the military sense. The local leaders were equally lacking, initially at least, in military knowledge, both of strategy and of how to use what weapons were at their disposal. This meant that the rebels were no match for the Ottoman forces. Units of the regular army armed with artillery were deployed, as were groups of irregular *bashibozuks* who were also well armed.

Nevertheless, whatever its weaknesses the April uprising had shown to the outside world that there existed in Bulgaria a desire for political freedom for which many were prepared to sacrifice their lives.

The rising was accompanied by appalling savagery. In some areas the revolutionaries attacked Muslims, thus provoking massive reprisals. The main instruments of these reprisals were not regular soldiers but local Circassians and *bashibozuks*, many of whom were Muslim Bulgarians. It was they who were mainly responsible for the terrible massacres in Bratsigovo, Perushtitsa, and above all Batak, where 5,000 Bulgarian Christians, mostly women and children, were said to have been killed, many of them being herded into the local church and burned alive.

The massacres revolutionized the Bulgarian revolution. The revolutionaries had never anticipated such appalling events but they had always intended to publicize their cause to the maximum degree; that way 'the strategic reserve of the revolution—decisive Russian military

[51] Kosev, 'Sotsialno-ikonomicheski predpostavki', 98.

intervention'[52]—might be brought into action. As Ignatiev had told the young revolutionary Stefan Stambolov in 1876, 'Russia cannot do anything for Bulgaria if the Bulgarians do not give us a reason to do so'.[53]

The supporters of the rising were well aware of the need for and the value of publicity. When the rising began there were three centres from which its supporters fed information to the outside world: Bucharest, Plovdiv, and Constantinople. To spread their message more widely a number of Bulgarian newspapers published material in foreign languages, especially French and Romanian, whilst from Plovdiv Ivan Evstratiev Geshov sent material in English to *The Times*. The deputy commander of the Panagyurishte revolutionary district, Todor Kableshkov, wrote during the April uprising, 'It is not in the musket ball that I place my hope, but in the noise of its discharge, which surely must be heard in Europe, in fraternal Russia...'[54] The massacres ensured it was.

If the massacres revolutionized the Bulgarian revolution, they also Europeanized it. The horrors produced not only Gladstone's famous pamphlet but also an international conference in Constantinople at the end of 1876. The conference devised a series of reforms to ensure that such atrocities against the Christians of the Ottoman empire would not happen again, but the Russians were not satisfied with the guarantees given for the implementation of the reforms and in June 1877 declared war. Bulgarians from throughout the Balkans rushed to join volunteer detachments to fight alongside the tsar's soldiers and they performed valuable services, particularly during the battle of the Shipka Pass in August 1877.

Russia's victory in the war of 1877–8 was more hard won than had been expected but it was complete and allowed the Russians to dictate preliminaries of peace at San Stefano, just outside Constantinople, in February 1878. The peace of San Stefano provided the Bulgarians with all they could dare hope for, uniting the three historic areas of Moesia, Thrace, and Macedonia in one Church and one state which was to stretch from the Black Sea and the Danube to the Aegean. Over 23,000 grateful Bulgarians signed a petition of thanks to Tsar Alexander II. But if the peace was all that the Bulgarians dared hope for, it was also all that Britain

---

[52] Konstantin Kosev, 'Politicheski rezultati i znachenie', in Konstantin Kosev et al., *Aprilskoto vŭstanie*, 528–52, 532.

[53] Cited in Encho Mateev, *Dŭrzhavnikŭt Stefan Stambolov* (Sofia: Letopisi, 1992), 111.

[54] Konstantinova, *Dŭrzhavnost*, 218.

and Austria-Hungary feared. These two powers suspected the new Bulgarian state would be a centre of Russian influence in the near east; the British were concerned for the safety of the route to Suez and India, and the Dual Monarchy did not want so large a Slav state established in the Balkans. London and Vienna therefore refused to endorse the agreement concluded at San Stefano and insisted on its revision. This was carried out in the Congress of Berlin in July 1878. There the Bulgaria of San Stefano was reduced to a rump state confined to the area between the Danube and the Balkan mountains; it was only a little over a third of the size of the San Stefano variant. Even north of the Balkan mountains the new state was truncated, the Morava valley being given to Serbia, and the northern Dobrudja to Romania. Thrace, under the name Eastern Rumelia, was to become an autonomous province of the Ottoman empire with an administration located in Plovdiv, but the most cruel blow of all was that Macedonia was to be handed back to the Porte with no brighter prospect for its future than a promise that misrule in the area would cease.

Just as no neighbouring state had come to the aid of the uprising in 1876, so at Berlin no power took up the Bulgarian cause. Bismarck stood aloof to play the role of honest broker, and the Russians were too exhausted to oppose Britain and Austria. Serbia was not distressed that its new neighbour was to be reduced in size, particularly because the treaty of Berlin placed Bosnia and Hercegovina under Habsburg administration and therefore forced Serbia to look southwards towards Albania or Macedonia for expansion. Nor was Greece displeased not to have so large a Slav state on its northern border, particularly because the Hellenic Kingdom had not yet itself received any significant territorial gain from the redrawing of the Balkan frontiers. And not even a deputation of Bulgarians themselves turned up in Berlin to plead their cause. The new state therefore began life with a ready-made irredentist programme and a bitter resentment at its treatment by the great powers.

Both San Stefano and Berlin stipulated that the new Bulgarian state was to be a principality whose Christian ruler was to be elected by the Bulgarians and confirmed by the powers signatory to the Berlin treaty. The elected prince was not to be a member of any major ruling European dynasty. Before he was chosen an elected assembly was to convene in Tŭrnovo to draw up a constitution for the principality. The new state was to remain a vassal of the sultan whose suzerainty it had to acknowledge and to whom it was required to pay tribute; it was also to assume a due proportion of all the international obligations already undertaken by its suzerain, and this meant paying a share of the Ottoman Public Debt, abiding by existing tariff agreements, retaining the Capitulations under which subjects of various European powers had the right to trial in their own consular courts, and building its sections of international railway lines which the Ottoman government had agreed to construct. In Eastern Rumelia the sultan was to exercise direct political and military authority, although *bashibozuks* were to be banished from the province and no Ottoman troops were to be quartered on its population. Order was to be maintained by a gendarmerie whose ethnic composition was to mirror that of the locality. The province was to have a militia but was not to construct forstresses. The senior administrator in Eastern Rumelia was to be a governor-general appointed by the sultan for a five-year period and approved by the signatory powers.

4

The Tŭrnovo Constitution and the Reign of Prince Alexander, 1878–1886

Before the convocation of the assembly of notables in Tŭrnovo Bulgaria and Eastern Rumelia were to be governed by a Russian Provisional administration. It made one important executive decision, nominating Sofia as the capital of the principality, primarily because it lay at the crossroads of the main north-east to south-west and north-west to south-east routes across the Balkans, the old Bulgarian name for the city having been *Sredets*, or 'central point'. Sofia was also within relatively easy reach of Macedonia.

1. THE TŬRNOVO CONSTITUTION AND POLITICAL INSTABILITY, 1879–1881

The assembly of notables met in the Nadezhda (Hope) *chitalishte* in Tŭrnovo on 10 February 1879. The forces which had shaped the vŭzrazhdane were discernible throughout its deliberations. Of the 231 delegates 89 had been elected, 116 appeared ex officio, 21 were appointed, 5 represented associations and societies, added to which there were two who were present both ex officio and as elected members. The central role of the Church in bringing about the national renaissance and liberation was recognized by the inclusion amongst the ex officio members of thirteen bishops, whilst amongst those representing associations and societies there were five deputies nominated by monasteries. The assembly also contained a rabbi and a mufti. The head of the Russian provisional administration, Prince Aleksandr Dondukov-Korsakov, nominated a further nineteen members, some of whom were important figures who had not otherwise secured admittance to the assembly; half of them were ethnic Turks. The Turks were the largest group in the sixteen members who were non-Bulgarian, the others being Greek or Jewish. The largest occupational group were teachers, who numbered sixty, but there were also fifty-three who were engaged in trade or in manufacturing, most of these being prominent figures within their guilds. The assembly was overwhelmingly urban, only a small proportion of its members coming from the small villages in which most Bulgarians lived. The important Bulgarian communities in Constantinople, Braila, Odessa, and Vienna were also represented as, most importantly, were the Bulgarians from the now alienated territories of Eastern Rumelia, Thrace, Macedonia, the Dobrudja, and the Morava valley.

Inevitably the issue uppermost in the minds of the representatives was that of national unity, or rather the lack of it. So enraged were some that they urged a boycott of the assembly, arguing that it was better to remain united as one nation under Ottoman rule than to be dismembered on the lines of the treaty of Berlin, and so strong was this strand of opinion that St Petersburg ordered the head of the Russian provisional administration to open the assembly before its members melted away. When the deliberations did begin there was no way the issue of national unity could be avoided and before discussion of constitutional issues were undertaken the assembly undertook a week-long, intense, and cathartic debate on this question. The irreconcilables were led by Dragan Tsankov, Petko Slaveĭkov, and Petko Karavelov, brother of Lyuben. They wanted to postpone the constituent assembly whilst a delegation toured the European capitals arguing the Bulgarian nationalist case. The pragmatists' leaders, who were later to dominate the Bulgarian conservative party, were Dimitŭr Grekov, Marko Balabanov, Grigor Nachovich, and Konstantin Stoilov. They believed that to postpone the assembly would only make matters worse and that therefore the best course was to begin the debate on the constitution whilst addressing a petition on the national issue to the powers. This view was supported by the powers themselves, including Russia. In the meantime it was decided to establish a commission of the assembly to report on the question, the debate on the report of that commission raging from 27 February until 6 March. The commission itself had recommended the pragmatist line but the irreconcilables were not won over. The emotional intensity of the debate reached its apogee when the Exarch Ĭosif I spoke and quoted Jeremiah 31: 16–17:

Thus saith the Lord; refrain thy voice from weeping and thine eyes from tears: for thy work shall be rewarded, said the Lord; and they shall come again from the land of the enemy.

And there is hope in thine end, said the Lord, that thy children shall come again into their own home.

There were few eyes which could refrain from weeping at the Exarch's peroration but tears do not make policy and after a series of defeats the irreconcilables forced their last, unsuccessful vote on 6 March.

The lines of division mapped out in the debate on the national question were for the most part seen again during discussion of the new constitution, and they resembled closely the divisions seen between old and young in the period of the vŭzrazhdane. Although the terms were little used at the time, the two tendencies have become known as liberals and conservatives. The latter adopted an essentially paternalist attitude to the peasant mass of the nation. The peasants, they argued, were unsophisticated, inexperienced, and, after five centuries of Ottoman domination too distrustful of state power to be entrusted with full control of it. For the most part the conservatives came from the wealthier ranks of the guilds and the trading communities. For the liberals, however, the peasant was the embodiment of a nation which was essentially egalitarian in composition and disposition; and they dismissed the notion that the peasant was inexperienced by reference to the functioning of communal councils. The differences between the two factions came to a head in the debate over a second chamber. The conservatives wanted a senate to act as a check upon the excessive enthusiasms of the masses and to prevent the new prince being pushed into policies which would cause constitutional crises at home and thus discredit Bulgaria abroad; this, they said, would make even more difficult the quest for full national unification. For the liberals this was nonsense. The nation was socially homogeneous, they argued, and if it was undivided socially there was no need to divide it politically by creating a second chamber; why escape from the domination of the Turks, Slaveĭkov asked in a question somewhat destructive of his own argument on social unity, to hand power to the *chorbadjii*? The liberals prevailed, though the debates ended in scenes of violent confrontation which did not set an encouraging precedent for the political life of the new state.

Liberal views prevailed in other debates on the constitution. The new prince, they insisted, was to be appointed 'By the Grace of God and the Will of the People'; he was not to levy emergency taxation nor was he to bestow titles or decorations for anything other than bravery on the field of battle. The prince nevertheless retained considerable powers. He was to represent the country abroad, subject to the limitations of Bulgaria's vassal status; he was to be commander-in-chief of the armed forces; he could appoint and dismiss ministers and name the chairman of the council of ministers, or minister president; he could convene, prorogue, and dissolve the assembly, and his consent had to be given before any legislation could come into effect.

The unicameral parliament or 'sŭbranie' was to have two forms, the ordinary and the grand national assembly (GNA). The ordinary national assembly was to sit for no longer than three years and was to convene every autumn after the harvest. It was to be elected by all sane males aged 21 or over, and there was to be one representative for every 10,000 of the population; all literate males over 30 were eligible for election. Similar rules were to apply for elections to the councils in the regions and districts into which the country was to be divided. The parliamentary deputies were to be paid, a fact which helped persuade the liberals to limit the extent of each session to two months. The parliament was accorded the usual rights of reviewing and amending legislation and of vetting the accounts of the six ministries which were to be established: the interior, justice, education, finance, war, and finally foreign and religious affairs. The grand national assembly, a device copied from the Serbian constitution, was to have twice as many elected delegates as an ordinary sŭbranie, to whom were to be added representatives of the ecclesiastical, judicial, and local government hierarchies. The GNA was to elect regents and a new prince if necessary, to sanction the loss or acquisition of territory, and to amend the constitution. It therefore did not meet regularly but only when the occasion arose.

Executive power was to lie with the prince but was to be exercised through a council of ministers. Legislation could be initiated by either the executive or the legislature but had to be approved by both.

The Bulgarian constitution granted a wide range of individual liberties, at the same time requiring that all Bulgarians obey the law, pay their taxes, send their sons to the army for a two-year period, and educate their children, girls as well as boys, to primary level.

Relations between state and Church are always a potential zone of conflict and complexity but in the Bulgarian case the complexity was greatly increased by the national question. There was no controversy over the notion that Orthodoxy should be the official religion of the country which must be professed by all but the first prince. The complications arose because so many Bulgarians remained outside Bulgaria and because for the majority of them the most obvious indication of their nationality was their allegiance, actual or desired, to the Bulgarian Exarchate. It was because the national identity and the religious affiliations of the Bulgarians outside Bulgaria were so closely associated that the ministry dealing with external relations was named the ministry for foreign and religious affairs. There was a further difficulty over the question of where the head of the Bulgarian Church should reside. The Orthodox world tended to practise the principle of 'One State, One Church', and in anticipation of setting himself up in the newly liberated state the Exarch in 1878 had established a temporary headquarters in Plovdiv before moving to Sofia. But if the Exarch were to set up shop in Sofia it would be much more difficult for him to act as the defender of Bulgarian interests in those areas such as Macedonia and Thrace still under full Ottoman rule; even Eastern Rumelia might be beyond his reach. After all, as Bulgarian nationalists were quick to point out, the exarchist flock in the Ottoman empire outnumbered that in the principality; furthermore, were the Exarch to leave Constantinople the Bulgarians beyond Bulgaria would be subject to increasing pressures from the Patriarchate, pressures which an Exarch in Sofia would be able to do little to parry. The Russians would have liked the Exarch to move to the principality because this, they believed, might facilitate a reconciliation between Exarch and Patriarch and end the schism of 1872, besides which they feared that an Exarch in Constantinople would be subjected to overbearing influence from the Porte. Russian advice had no effect. Article 39 of the Tŭrnovo constitution declared that the principality was to be part of the Bulgarian Exarchate whose highest body, the Holy Synod, would have its seat in Sofia, but the senior figure in the Church, the Exarch, was to remain in Constantinople. It was a nimble compromise which lasted until 1915.

The Tŭrnovo constitution had a number of weaknesses. The major one was that it contained no provision to ensure that it was observed or that it could not be suspended. Nor was there any provision to guarantee the independence of the judiciary or to limit electoral corruption. And, as was to become obvious in the first years of Bulgaria's independence, the boundaries delimiting the powers of the executive and legislature were still not clear enough to prevent serious confrontation between those two arms of the state.

When the main outlines of the constitution had been drawn the deputies in Tŭrnovo had then to elect a prince whose name they would submit to the sultan and the Berlin powers for their approval. The choice fell upon Prince Alexander of Battenberg. He was young and had served with the Russian army in the war of 1877–8, a fact which pleased the Russians and delighted the Bulgarians. As no other power had any objection to his candidature he was duly elected and arrived in his new principality on 24 June 1879. He landed at Varna and went via Tŭrnovo to Sofia.

It was to be little more than two years before Alexander's attempt to accommodate his temperament to the rules of the Tŭrnovo constitution game failed and he carried out a coup d'état. His instincts, if not authoritarian, were paternalistic, and it was not surprising therefore that he spent much time in the company of conservatives such as Konstantin Stoilov, whom he made his personal secretary, and Todor Burmov. Alexander did not compensate this bias by any gestures, social or political, towards the liberals. The prince suffered from this because at Tŭrnovo the conservatives had been branded as wealthy *chorbadjii*, in addition to which many of them had been educated in the west which meant they were much less attuned to the popular mood than the liberals whose education had usually been in Bulgaria itself or in Russia. More damaging to the prince's immediate position was that he also found it extremely difficult to work with the Russians.

The Russians were a major factor in the political life of the new principality. Tsarist Russia tolerated the liberal Tŭrnovo constitution because it wanted pro-Russian popular opinion to dominate the assembly, and because it did not want the principality to have a constitution less liberal than that of Rumelia; that might mean the absorption of Bulgaria into Rumelia which was the creation of Russia's diplomatic opponents and was more closely integrated into the Ottoman empire than was the principality. The Russians tended to regard Bulgaria as their own creation in which they had a natural right to exercise influence. Most officers, and all the 300 or so senior officers, in the new Bulgarian army were Russian, as was the minister of war. Furthermore, the vast majority of the nation still held the tsar and the Russians in almost mystical awe. In these circumstances any major political decision would be difficult, and any depending on the use of the army impossible without Russian approval.

The most powerful political element in the country was the liberals, who soon organized themselves into a national Liberal Party, thanks in no small measure to the efforts of Stefan Stambolov from Tŭrnovo. Stambolov, who had been an apostle in the Stara Zagora region in 1875, stood on the left wing of the new party, having had links with the Russian nihilists before becoming active as an apostle. (His marching song as an apostle had been 'We don't want riches, | We don't want money, | We want liberty | And human rights'.)[1] The dominant figures in the party, however, were the moderates, Petko Slaveĭkov and Petko Karavelov. The latter had a diploma in law from Moscow and had served as deputy governor of the Vidin province under the Russian provisional administration before becoming one of the most powerful and influential voices in the constituent assembly. Slaveĭkov was less experienced in administration than Karavelov but his literary gifts enabled him to present political ideas in the homely form easily understood by the peasant masses of the nation. The titular head of the Liberal Party was Dragan Tsankov. Although his views were to the right of most other major figures he had so long served the national cause that all regarded him with respect and his long years as an Ottoman civil servant had given him a great deal of experience in the arts of negotiation, intrigue, and compromise.

The strength of the liberals made them the obvious choice to form the first government, but with this the prince did not agree. Under Russian pressure he attempted to construct a coalition but when he failed he turned happily to the conservatives, appointing Todor Burmov as his first minister president or prime minister. The new government faced a number of serious problems. One was that of brigandage. After the defeat of the sultan's armies a number of Bulgarian Muslims had taken to the hills and woods much in imitation of the Bulgarian haiduts; so troublesome were these bands that parts of north-eastern Bulgaria had to be placed under martial law. This strained relations between Bulgaria and the Ottoman empire, these tensions being exacerbated when many Muslims who had fled during the recent war returned to find their properties had been taken over by Bulgarians.

---

[1] Doĭno Doĭnov, 'Iztochnata krisa', in Kosev et al., *Aprilskoto vŭstanie 1876*, 157–215, 187.

A much more difficult problem for the new ministry arose with the liberals. Essentially this was a continuation of the debates at Tŭrnovo with conservative, patrician, and paternalist ideas clashing with the liberals' veneration for the new constitution which for them represented, in the absence of a united Bulgaria, the achievements and attainments of the nationalist movement. Thus the liberals protested vigorously when the prince decided to use the title *visochestvo* rather than *svetlost* prescribed by the constitution; the former implies a higher ranking than the latter. Another dispute arose when Alexander expressed the wish to appoint 500 German officers for the army, a move which was opposed as much by the Russian minister of war, General Pyotr Parensov, as by the liberals; Alexander was eventually persuaded that the sŭbranie would never agree to this and had to content himself with two German officers for his personal staff. Equal anger was caused when Alexander issued a decree giving him the right to appoint half the members of city councils; this was a direct affront to one of the great pillars of the national movement and when in August 1879 he dismissed the municipal council of Sofia the liberals raged that not even the Turks had dared to interfere with the system of local, elected, self-government which, they said, had saved 'our faith, our nation and our language'.[2]

Such policies aroused the anger of a population which was already discontented because of problems on the economic front. A rise in the salt tax had been unpopular and the government was blamed for this and for the ruinous currency speculation which arose from the fact that the rouble, still the main unit of currency in Bulgaria, was worth less in the principality than in Romania. To make matters worse, the harvest of 1879 was poor and food prices rose accordingly. Protest was voiced in the liberal press, in large public meetings, and even in popular songs.

The government's response to these protests did little to calm the waters, particularly when it was decided to remove liberal supporters from the ranks of government employees. Most of these were at local level and had little or no national profile, but an exception to this was Petko Slaveĭkov, who was sacked as prefect of the Tŭrnovo region. This was to prove a most damaging precedent.

[2] Petŭr Mirchev, *Kipezhŭt. Kniga za Sofiya 1878–1884* (Sofia: Otechestven Front, 1971), 69.

Alexander would have liked to go much further and postpone the elections which were due to be held in September 1879, but so drastic a deviation from the constitutional rules could be made only with Russian consent and this was not forthcoming. Russian prestige abroad would be impaired if its constitutional creation was so soon disrupted, and within Bulgaria it would be hugely damaged if the Russian-officered army were to be deployed to contain the unrest which might follow the postponement of the elections.

The elections deepened the rift between the prince and his government on one side and the liberals on the other. The liberals had been alarmed when, during the polls, the government had posted troops in a number of constituencies, and alarm turned to rage when the government followed this by trying to exclude Stambolov from parliament because he was too young, and then by annulling the votes in Svishtov and announcing that a by-election would be held at some unspecified time in the future. The government also exerted pressure on the voters; electoral corruption began early in Bulgaria's modern history and was to last long into its life.

Despite these measures the massive popular support for the liberals secured them an easy victory. Once parliament had assembled the liberals lost no time in pressing for the removal of the Burmov government, immediately excluding the conservative deputies from the assembly and passing a motion of censure on Burmov who thereupon resigned. A caretaker government under Metropolitan Kliment of Tŭrnovo was formed and new elections called in January 1880.

In the meantime the prince travelled to Petersburg, where he attempted to secure Tsar Alexander II's approval for a change in the Bulgarian constitution. The tsar refused. Such a change would damage Russian prestige, he said, and certainly should not be undertaken until the liberals had been given an opportunity to govern, though Alexander II did agree to recall Parensov, who was replaced as minister of war by General Kazimir Ehrenroth, who was a Finn and therefore not prone to Pan-Slav enthusiasms. He was also a tough-minded political conservative who soon after his arrival in Bulgaria had those convicted of committing atrocities against the Turkish minority hanged in public.[3] Having failed

---

[3] Karel Durman, *Lost Illusions: Russian Policies towards Bulgaria in 1877–1887*, Upsala Studies on the Soviet Union and Eastern Europe, no. 1 (Stockholm: Acta Universitatis Upsaliensis, distributed by Almqvist & Wiksell International, 1988), 74.

to secure Russian approval for constitutional changes the prince had to abide by the Tŭrnovo rules which insisted that the sŭbranie must meet within two months of the elections. The new assembly therefore convened on 22 March.

A liberal government under Dragan Tsankov was immediately formed. It now set about the much-needed task of building a new state apparatus. In this a leading part was played by Karavelov, who became minister of finance. One of his first measures was to introduce a new national currency, the lev (plural leva), based on the French franc.[4] Karavelov also did what he could to prune government expenditure, lowering official salaries and reforming the tax system, though in the latter sector his measures were cautious; rather than rationalizing the multiplicity of different levies inherited from the Ottoman empire he attempted to make their collection more efficient, and rather than implement a liberal promise to abolish the tithe he arranged for it to be collected in cash rather than kind. The tithe issue was to remain important in Bulgarian politics for two decades. The liberal administration also took energetic, ruthless, and successful steps to liquidate brigandage, a problem thrown into sharp focus by the murder in June 1880 of the wife of the great Slav hero, the Russian General Mikhaïl Skobelev.

Such successes did nothing to diminish the tension between the liberals and their opponents. There were still disagreements over the title Alexander should use and there were skirmishes over the financing of the prince's residence in Sofia. The conservatives were alarmed by the rigorous use the liberals made of the established practice of the sŭbranie vetting the returns of all deputies and excluding those where suspicions of electoral irregularity were found. Tsankov then angered the Church by attempting, unsuccessfully, to reduce both the number of bishops and the power they could exercise, the hierarchy being, he argued, an alien feature foisted onto the democratic Slav Church by the Greeks. But the major confrontations came over the liberals' planned militia bill and over attitudes to Russia.

Supporters of the militia bill claimed that it was part of the move towards the *Gleichschaltung* of Bulgarian and Rumelian institutions in that it would replicate in the principality a feature of the autonomous

---

[4] Lev means 'lion' and was chosen because this had been the symbol of the Bulgarian nationalists before 1878 and since liberation had been the state emblem.

province. But Alexander and the conservatives saw immediately that it would provide an alternative military force. It would also be a predominantly liberal one because its officers were to be elected by their men and supreme command was to be vested not in the prince but in a commission of six elected from the sŭbranie; it was, as Alexander said, 'ideal for a revolutionary army'.[5] For the liberals the militia would provide the protection they needed against the coup which they suspected, rightly, Alexander wished to carry out. The debate over the bill was intense, and the longest yet seen in the assembly. The prince and the conservatives were saved not by their own ingenuity but by divisions within the liberals over procedural matters.

The radicalism of the liberals rang alarm bells in Russian ears. Ehrenroth had seen parallels between the militia bill and the Paris Commune and the attempt to interfere in ecclesiastical affairs had been extremely unpopular in conservative St Petersburg, where the distinction between liberal and nihilist was not always made. The Russians took further offence at Tsankov's approach to the vitally important question of railways in Bulgaria, a question which was to be at the top of the political agenda for a further two years.

The treaty of Berlin required the Bulgarian principality to purchase the British-owned and bankrupt Rusé to Varna railway and to complete that section of the international Vienna to Constantinople line which lay within its territory. With regard to the latter the Austrians favoured the shortest route, which was from Sofia to Nish via Tsaribrod; the Bulgarians pressed that the line should run from Sofia via Kumanovo and Skopje and thence to Nish. The latter would have brought a direct rail link between Bulgaria and northern Macedonia and thus the railway issue, like so many others, could not be divorced from the national one. The matter was further complicated by the Russians who wanted the Bulgarians to build a line from the Danube southwards to Sofia and the Maritsa valley, a line which would have obvious strategic significance in any Russian military advance into the Balkans. When the Bulgarians insisted that they did not have enough money to complete the international trunk line and to construct one across the Balkans, the Russians urged that if the Bulgarian National Bank (BNB), created during the Russian provisional

---

[5] Ilcho Dimitrov, *Knyaz, Konstitutsiyata i Narodŭt. Iz istoriyata na politicheskite borbi v Bŭlgariya prez pŭrvite godini sled osvobozhdenieto* (Sofia: Otechestven Front, 1972), 30.

administration, were opened to foreign investors Russian money would be forthcoming via that channel. Again the national question interposed itself because the Bulgarians wanted the bank to be a state-owned institution and therefore one less prone to external influences and manipulation.

In one international debate, however, Tsankov did defend Russian interests. The treaty of Berlin had stipulated that the European Danube Commission, set up in 1856, should regulate traffic on the river, but when discussions were held to organize this Tsankov's representative in the negotiations, who was also his nephew, departed from his instructions and opposed an Austro-Hungarian plan which would have given the Dual Monarchy a preponderant interest on the Commission; this was done with the connivance of his uncle and despite the fact that Prince Alexander had already given his approval to the plan. Tsankov's scheming may have aided the Russians but it did him little good, giving the prince the excuse to remove him in November 1880. He was succeeded as minister president by Karavelov.

2. PRINCE ALEXANDER'S ATTEMPTED AUTHORITARIAN RULE, 1881–1883

Within six months of Karavelov's taking office the political scene in Bulgaria was transformed, but it was transformed by a change not of minister president in Sofia but of the ruler in Russia. The assassination of Tsar Alexander II on 1 March 1881 appalled all Bulgarians but it also emboldened the anti-liberals, most of whom thought the Bulgarian liberals were little more than nihilist wolves in sheep's clothing. Ehrenroth now insisted that something had to be done to prevent Bulgaria from falling into anarchy. The prince needed little encouragement. When he returned from the funeral of the tsar he dismissed Karavelov, made Ehrenroth minister president, and announced that elections would be held for a grand national assembly which was to meet in Svishtov.

The new tsar, Alexander III, although not enthusiastic, gave official sanction to the coup. The Russian diplomatic agent in Sofia made it clear that his government approved of Alexander's action and expected the Bulgarian liberals to do likewise. Shortly afterwards the tsar himself gave public endorsement to the coup, prompting Tsankov to retort that this would force the Bulgarians to direct to their liberators 'the words with which an ancient sage addressed a bee, "I want neither your honey nor your sting".'[6] The liberals' disappointment at Russian attitudes was compensated by their confidence that they would secure victory in the elections for the GNA. This confidence was misplaced. The liberals had been caught by a contradiction in their own position. Their intense devotion to Russia had never led them seriously to ponder on what to do if Russia ceased to champion their national cause and defend their beloved Tŭrnovo constitution. Furthermore, their domestic political base, the peasantry, was insecure. The liberals had lost some political credit because they could do nothing to defend the peasant against rising taxation and the social difficulties that were growing in post-liberation Bulgaria. Furthermore, the peasants were devoted to the Russians, Tsankov once remarking that if the tsar stuck a *kalpak* (the traditional Bulgarian fur hat) on a pole and told the peasants to elect it as prince, they would do so, and thus it followed that if the tsar approved of Battenberg's coup, then the Bulgarian peasant would not oppose it.

Immediately after the coup the prince divided the country into five administrative districts, each of which was ruled by an 'extraordinary commissioner' who, with his equally powerful officials, was to purge the local bureaucracy of its liberal supporters. Liberal meetings, offices, and newspapers were subjected to intimidation, frequently violent, and constituencies were given the right to elect their member of parliament by 'collective declaration' if they so wished. If they did not so wish then elections were to be held but in every polling booth there was to be a Russian officer 'to prevent fraud' and 'to aid illiterates'. On the polling days themselves, 14 and 21 June, military units and gangs of *shaĭkadjii* (men armed with clubs etc.) were on hand to ensure the desired result; that the *shaĭkadjii* were used was indicated by a remark of the minister of education, Constantin Jireček, who confided to his diary that matters must have proceeded reasonably well in Samokov because 'only three people were badly beaten'.[7] In the event only two constituencies, Gabrovo and Tŭrnovo, elected liberal deputies and of these the two from

[6] Ilcho Dimitrov, *Knyaz, Konstitutsiyata i Narodŭt. Iz istoriyata na politicheskite borbi v Bŭlgariya prez pŭrvite godini sled osvobozhdenieto*, 76.

[7] Konstantin Irechek (Constantin Jireček), *Bŭlgarski Dnevnik, 30 Okt 1879–26 Okt 1884g*, 2 vols. (Plovdiv: H. G. Danov, 1930–2), i. 441–2.

Gabrovo were stopped en route to Svishtov whilst the four from Tŭrnovo, who included Slaveĭkov, Karavelov, and Tsankov, were subjected to such harassment that they left Svishtov without attending the assembly. When it convened the assembly met for less than two hours and passed all the constitutional modifications which the prince required.

The Svishtov constitution created the paternalist system which Alexander and the conservatives had always wanted. The prince was to be given full powers for seven years and was to create a new body, the state council, which was to exercise executive authority. The sŭbranie was to be reduced to seventy members elected on an indirect franchise and civil liberties were to be reduced. After seven years another GNA was to be elected to review the working of the new system.

Alexander's attempt at authoritarian rule lasted little more than two years. He had planned to create an unchallenged executive but although he went a considerable way to doing so he did not secure personal control over it. He failed to use the state council to control individual ministers, some of whom became over-mighty. Alexander, like Frankenstein, was to become the prisoner of his own creation.

Alexander intended to rule in cooperation with the conservatives, to whose cloth the 1881 system had been tailored. The prospects seemed favourable. The liberals were demoralized and disorganized. Slaveĭkov, Karavelov, and other extreme liberals had fled to Eastern Rumelia and did not share Tsankov's view that it was better to stay in the principality and influence the new rulers from within and gradually bring about a restoration of the Tŭrnovo constitution; 'You cannot dig wells with needles' was Slaveĭkov's response to this argument.[8] But Tsankov persisted. Early in 1882 he launched a campaign for the restoration of the constitution, insisting as he did so that the campaign must employ only legal means. There was an encouraging response as public meetings, petitions, and above all the liberal press attacked the coup and the new, paternalist system. The government played into the liberals' hands by placing further restrictions on their newspapers, banning meetings, detaining some of their provincial leaders, and putting Tsankov under house arrest in Vratsa. This only intensified public anger and the expression of it. The conservatives needed an ally in government and turned therefore to the Russians.

---

[8] Dimitrov, *Knyaz*, 180.

This made political sense. The years 1879 to 1881 had shown that Alexander could not rule with the liberals, but by the spring of 1882 it was clear that the nation would not tolerate rule by the conservatives. But the conservatives and the Russians did not make easy bedfellows. They had already fallen out when the Russian minister of the interior, General Arnold Remlingen, had closed a leading conservative newspaper which, in the wake of disturbances in Gabrovo and Sofia, had accused him of being unable to maintain order. He resigned. The prince also had disagreements with the other Russian member of the cabinet, Colonel Vladimir Krilov, the minister of war; Alexander sacked him when he refused to implement the prince's order forbidding officers, most of whom were Russian, to take part in politics. In April 1882 a new beginning was made when the Russian generals Leonid Sobolev and Aleksandr Kaulbars became respectively minister of the interior and of war, with Sobolev also serving as minister president. Both generals came with excellent credentials; they were young, both had fought in the war of 1877–8, and they had both served in the Russian provisional administration. The hope that these qualifications would endear them to the Bulgarian political establishment and the Bulgarian nation were not to be fulfilled.

The experiment began well. The conservatives were given the remaining cabinet posts and the state council was dominated by hard-line members of the same party. They were pleased when Sobolev sanctioned legislation passed in 1881 which reduced the size of the sŭbranie to fifty-six, all of whom were to be indirectly elected on a new franchise which limited voting rights to those with certain educational and property qualifications. When a new sŭbranie was elected in the autumn of 1882 the conservatives' hold on the assembly was secured when the few liberals who had squeezed through the electoral net resigned their seats in protest at the new franchise.

Although they seemed to have neutralized the liberals the conservatives were soon to discover that working with the Russians was far from easy. Sobolev was patronizing and seemed intent on making Bulgaria 'just another khanate', similar to the one he had previously ruled in Bukhara.[9]

---

[9] Karel Durman, *The Time of the Thunderer: Mikhail Katkov, Russian Nationalist Extremism and the Failure of the Bismarckian System, 1871–1887* (Boulder, Colo.: East European Monographs no. 237, distributed by Columbia University Press, 1988), 340.

Given such attitudes he clearly had no liking for parliaments which he considered unsuitable to the Slav temperament and this inevitably led to tension with the sŭbranie which, though elected on the restricted franchise, contained a high proportion of wealthy merchants, professional men, and members of the intelligentsia, all of whom had been part of the national movement and who were not prepared to see their newly liberated country become a Russian satrapy.

As soon as the sŭbranie met the deputies were offended by Sobolev's heavy-handed and patronizing attempts to bribe them; he even had sweets put in their desks. There was a much more substantial disagreement over the military. In 1881 a new Russian-officered armed force, the Dragoons, had been created by Remlingen as part of the general increase in the machinery of control imposed on the country. The force was as unpopular as it was efficient and the conservatives managed to direct popular dislike of it against the Russians who created and led it. The Russian response was to suggest incorporating the force into the army, a suggestion warmly welcomed by the prince, who was ever keen to see the size of the army increased. The conservatives in both the sŭbranie and the state council disagreed and successfully insisted that the force be disbanded.

In addition to the spat over the Dragoons there was continuing and increasingly bitter debate on the railway question. Here again the conservatives and the Russians were soon at loggerheads. One of the first acts of the new sŭbranie was to dismiss a young Russian whom Sobolev had appointed as director of railways in Bulgaria and fuel was added to the growing fire when Nachovich presented a bill to the assembly granting a conservative-backed rather than the Russian-favoured consortium the right to survey the line from the Danube to Sofia and then on to the Macedonian border. The Russians suffered another setback in April 1883 when it was announced that Bulgaria was to sign a convention with Austria-Hungary, Serbia, and the Ottoman empire for the completion of the international trunk line, the Bulgarian section of which was to be built by an Austrian concern headed by Baron Hirsch, who had close connections with a number of leading Bulgarian conservatives.

By the time the announcement of this convention *à quatre* was made the conservatives were no longer in office. The Russians had found the means for their removal in a worldly cleric, Metropolitan Mileti of Sofia. Mileti had joined the Russians in the war of 1877 but this had alarmed the Exarch, who feared that the Ottoman authorities might take reprisals against his flock, and Mileti had therefore been exiled to Vratsa. After the liberation he had been released and was soon elected metropolitan of Sofia. Mileti was a conservative as well as a russophile but when these allegiances clashed he sided with the Russians and for this the conservatives took their revenge by persuading the ecclesiastical authorities to reimpose his sentence of exile. This Sobolev contested and demanded the resignation of Konstantin Stoilov who, as minister for foreign and religious affairs, was responsible for dealings with the Church. Both Sobolev and Kaulbars threatened to leave Bulgaria if Stoilov remained in office. He did not. He resigned, but the two other prominent conservatives in the government, Nachovich and Grekov, went with him.

The resignation of the leading conservatives produced a state of complete fluidity in Bulgarian politics. The generals turned to the liberals for support, Sobolev having come to the conclusion that the Tŭrnovo constitution had to be restored if the country was to be made governable. His colleague Kaulbars, meanwhile, showed scant regard for the spirit of that constitution by illegally dismissing over a hundred pro-Battenberg army officers and civil servants. This helped convince Tsankov that the Russians had now become a greater obstacle than the conservatives to the restoration of the Tŭrnovo constitution and therefore he responded by spurning Russian overtures and accepting approaches from the conservatives who, with the prince's blessing, offered to convene a new grand national assembly to discuss the issue of restoration. The new Russian diplomatic representative in Sofia then made a better offer: a joint Russian-liberal campaign for the full restoration of the Tŭrnovo system. It gave the liberals all they wanted without them having to make any sacrifices and they accepted immediately. Tsankov informed Alexander that if he were to make the same offer the liberals would probably accept because some of them, like Tsankov himself, were becoming restive at excessive Russian interference in Bulgaria; for this reason, he said, they might also endorse the *à quatre* agreement, the non-implementation of which was causing the prince great embarrassment in Vienna.

Events moved swiftly. The sŭbranie was recalled in emergency session. It endorsed the *à quatre* agreement and then petitioned the prince to turn the emergency session into a full legislative assembly, in effect a restoration of the Tŭrnovo constitution because under the 1881 arrangements the sŭbranie had no legislative function. The liberals had secured all they wanted; and the conservatives and the prince could rejoice in the endorsement of the *à quatre* agreement. They rejoiced even more at the discomfiture of the Russians who had stormed out of the sŭbranie after the vote. The generals had been completely outflanked and on 7 September they resigned. A new government was formed with Tsankov as minister president and minister of the interior; the majority of his cabinet colleagues were conservatives. A coalition of liberals and conservatives, in cooperation with the prince, had asserted Bulgarian national interests against the Russians.

3. THE RESTORATION OF THE TŬRNOVO CONSTITUTION AND THE RULE OF THE LIBERALS, 1883–1885

The settlement of September 1883 produced an uneasy truce rather than a peace. The new cabinet had no Russian but neither did it have a minister of war, the convention being that this post should be held by a Russian officer. The vacancy reflected continuing tensions between the prince and the Russians over the army. There were still no Bulgarian officers above the rank of captain, all senior posts being held by Russians. The political turmoil of the summer of 1883, when rumours of military plots against the prince had been rife, increased Alexander's determination to hedge the power of these Russian officers. Eventually St Petersburg acquiesced and signed an agreement which reaffirmed the 1882 ruling that Russian officers in the Bulgarian army were not to take any part in local political affairs. Even when this question was settled, however, there were tensions between the prince and the Russians over the former's plans to marry a German princess. It was not surprising that the tsar instructed his representative in Sofia and the newly nominated minister of war that Russia's interests in Bulgaria were to be secured by cooperation with the liberals whose strength and unity were to be promoted.

This was far from easy. There was serious disquiet in the party at Tsankov's cooperation with the conservatives and there were reservations about the constitutional situation; there had been no guarantee that the Tŭrnovo system would not be changed and indeed the composition of the cabinet together with the continued existence both of a sŭbranie elected on the 1881 franchise and of the state council made alterations to the system likely. These fears were confirmed at the end of the year when a commission under Grekov and Stoilov, good conservatives both, reported on constitutional change. What was proposed was little different from the 1881 system and legislation to impose these changes was rammed through the sŭbranie in secret session for fear of popular protests. The Tŭrnovo constitution had been restored by those who wished to destroy it, the prince and the conservatives. The proposed changes were never to be implemented because they were repealed a little over a year later but they had a profound effect on the Liberal Party.

After the constitutional bill had been pushed through the assembly the conservatives, having secured all their constitutional needs, resigned from the government, leaving Tsankov to form a cabinet dominated by the liberals. But the administration was drawn from only one faction of an increasingly divided Liberal Party. The left, led by Karavelov and Slaveĭkov who were both still in Plovdiv, found two major faults in Tsankov. On the constitutional question he had compromised with and then, by forcing the December 1883 bill through the sŭbranie, done the bidding of the conservatives. And secondly, he had moved too close to the prince and the conservatives on the question of relations with Russia. Whereas Tsankov had come to have serious doubts about Russian policies in Bulgaria, many rank and file liberals still held to the view that Bulgaria owed a debt of gratitude to the liberating power which should be allowed to determine the broad outlines of Bulgarian foreign policy; when it was proposed to appoint a Bulgarian representative in St Petersburg some liberals protested on the grounds that relations between the two states should be so close as to make Bulgarian representation in the Russian capital otiose. By the beginning of 1884 the left had formed a distinct faction under the leadership of Karavelov, whose programme was summed up in the slogan, 'Neither a people without a prince, nor a prince without a people; neither a prince without power, nor a people without rights.'[10]

There was a further bone of contention between Tsankov and the extreme liberals, the Rusé to Varna railway. Built in the 1860s to shorten the journey from central Europe to Constantinople by cutting out the long, final, north-east running section of the Danube, the line had soon been deprived of its economic rationale by the improvement to Danubian ports and by the announcement of the building of the direct

[10] Georgi Borushkov, *Istoriya na bŭlgarskata zhurnalistika, 1844–1877, 1878–1883* (Sofia: Nauka i izkustvo, 1976), 500.

Vienna–Constantinople trunk railway. By 1883 the British were pressing for fulfilment of the obligation imposed on the Bulgarian principality at Berlin to purchase the Rusé–Varna line, and finally in February 1884 Tsankov's government announced it was ready to pay 50 million francs for it. Both the conservatives and the karavelist liberals were enraged, Karavelov's newspaper denouncing the agreement as 'daylight robbery'.[11]

The questions of the December 1883 constitutional bill and the Rusé–Varna railway dominated the elections held in May 1884. They returned a majority of liberal deputies but when Tsankov met with them after the elections they immediately rejected the railway deal and demanded the repeal of the December 1883 bill. The karavelists had clearly triumphed and Tsankov resigned. Karavelov, who had mended his fences with the prince by assuring him that 'There is no dynastic question in Bulgaria',[12] was made minister president. Slaveĭkov became minister of the interior with the remainder of the cabinet, the minister of war excepted, being left liberals. The Liberal Party now split. The tsankovists retained the old party machine, and name, and found press backing in the recently founded *Sredets*. The karavelist wing later reconstituted itself as the Democratic Party.

Predictably Karavelov began his period in office by repealing the December 1883 law. He then cut the Gordian knot of the railway problem. The *à quatre* agreement had decided that the international trunk line would follow the *tracé* via Tsaribrod rather than the liberals' preferred route via Kumanovo, and it also decided that the Bulgarian section of the line would be built by the Hirsch consortium. What it had not decided was who would operate the Bulgarian section of the line when completed. Karavelov announced that institutions of such economic, social, and strategic importance as railways could only be owned and operated by the state, and in December 1884 his government passed the railway act. It stated that control of the trunk line within Bulgaria would be in the hands of the government and that in future only the government would have the right to construct railways, all of which would be state property and would be operated by the nationalized Bulgarian State Railways (BDZh). Karavelov's administration also brought about the nationalization of the Bulgarian National Bank. Like

[11] Todor Girginov, *Istoricheski razvoĭ na sŭvremenna Bŭlgariya ot vŭzrazhdaneto do balkanskata voĭna 1912 godina*, 2 vols. (Sofia: 1934, 1935), i. 159.

[12] Simeon Radev, *Stroiteli na sŭvremenna Bŭlgariya*, 2 vols. (Sofia: Bŭlgarski Pisatel, 1973), vol. i, *Tsaruvaneto na kn. Aleksandra, 1879–1886*, 441–2.

the railways, the BNB had been the object of much speculation on the part of foreign investors and again Karavelov insisted that so important an institution had to be in state ownership.

That Karavelov was able to pass such important acts was in large measure due to the fact that the settlement of the constitutional disputes had at last brought relative stability to Bulgarian politics. But the four years of factional fighting and instability had damaged the body politic. All contestants in the Bulgarian political arena had been weakened. Alexander had failed to find supporters who would be loyal without attempting to secure supremacy for themselves, and his confrontations with the Russians had puzzled ordinary Bulgarians. The conservatives had been discredited by the failure of their ideals which were enshrined in the 1881 system. The Russians had been weakened because the overbearing behaviour of the generals had dented the respect held for Russia by many Bulgarians, particularly those in the politically active elements. The liberals appeared to have emerged victorious in 1883 as they had done in 1879 but in fact Tsankov's readiness to compromise with the prince and the conservatives had strained the unity of his party almost to breaking point, and many rank and file liberals were perplexed by the disagreements with the Russians. At the same time, internal instability had diminished Bulgaria's prestige abroad. Most damaging of all was the fact that the politicking at the highest level of the state had opened a rift between the political establishment and the body of the nation. Incomprehension at the political intrigues and puzzlement over the breach with the tsar and the liberating power bred alienation or indifference. In the long run, both were to provide fertile ground for the growth of political clientelism and authoritarianism, but in the meantime the national question could provide a means to re-engage and reunite the nation.

4. THE NATIONAL QUESTION, AND THE UNIFICATION OF BULGARIA AND EASTERN RUMELIA, 1878–1885

Though the constitutional conflicts had overshadowed it, the national question had never been forgotten. The determination to bring Rumelia into union with Bulgaria was as strong as ever; there was a deep bitterness that the area where the revolution had been best supported and where the worst atrocities had been committed should have been separated from the principality. There had been a number of quiet and sometimes covert moves to bring Bulgaria and Rumelia closer together. In the spring of 1880 a central committee to coordinate Bulgarian and Rumelian policies and institutions was founded. This involved secret meetings between leading political figures in the principality—Stambolov was one of them—and in Rumelia, and a closed session of the sŭbranie agreed to defray 8,000 leva to support the Rumelians. For their part the Rumelians did all they could to align their institutions with those of the principality. Thus their school system was similar to that used in Bulgaria, Rumelian militia officers were trained in the Sofia Military Academy, the press of province and principality circulated freely in both, the Bulgarian foreign ministry communicated with Plovdiv not in French or Russian but in Bulgarian, and the Rumelians used the same national anthem as the Bulgarians.

Such policies were easily adopted but they did little to address the fundamental problems of unification. There was no dispute as to what was desired, the union of the principality with Rumelia, Thrace, Macedonia, the Dobrudja, and the Morava valley, and for most Bulgarians the most important of these lost territories were Rumelia and Macedonia. But if there was general agreement on the ends, there were deep divisions over the means. Some believed that the major effort must be directed towards the redemption of Macedonia because that would be more difficult to secure than Rumelia; the latter was already separated from Constantinople and given time should fall like a ripe plum into Bulgaria's lap. Others rejected this, arguing that the unification of Bulgaria and Rumelia would produce a stronger Bulgarian state and would provide the momentum to go on to the next step of incorporating Thrace and Macedonia. This strategy was criticized on the ground that a union of Bulgaria and Rumelia would alarm the great powers and the other Balkan states who would be put on their guard against further Bulgarian expansion, which would make the acquisition of Thrace and Macedonia much more difficult. A third opinion was that the first step should be to unite Rumelia and Macedonia.

Views on the tactics for achieving unification were as varied as those on strategy, and sometimes distinctly bizarre. Sobolev, for example, had a mad idea of selling his estates in Russia, moving to Bulgaria, and there using the money to finance a Slav 'liberation crusade', the first step of which would be to drive into Rumelia or Macedonia thus reopening the eastern question and, he hoped, forcing Russia to intervene. In 1880 another impracticable scheme surfaced when Prince Alexander proposed that the Bulgarian army should be mobilized for pretended manoeuvres and then march through the Ihtiman pass into Rumelia; this, it was argued, would make the union a *fait accompli* which no power would dare contest. The plan embarrassed the liberals because they knew Russia, which wanted stability in the Balkans whilst it pursued its goals in Asia, would oppose it; the liberals torpedoed it by revealing all to St Petersburg.

In reality in the first half-decade of its existence the Bulgarian principality was not strong enough to pursue a forward policy in the Balkans, the more so because of its internal political difficulties. Whilst the principality was absorbed in its constitutional crises Eastern Rumelia developed its own political structures.

The first governor-general was Aleko (Aleksandйr) Bogoridi Pasha, a Greek-educated, Ottoman civil servant whose father had donated the land on which St Stefan's church in Constantinople had been built. Bogoridi spoke no Bulgarian but this disadvantage was balanced by his appointing as his deputy the well-known vйzrazhdane activist and author of a history of the Bulgarians, Gavril Krйstevich. The new administration was to consist of six directorates or ministries. There was also to be a regional assembly. This was less democratic an organization than the sйbranie in Bulgaria in that of its fifty-six members ten were appointed ex officio, ten were nominated by the governor-general, and the franchise for electing the remainder was to have a small property qualification. This the conservatives to the north would have liked and they would have been even happier with Rumelia's standing committee; this ten-man body was to be elected from within the regional assembly and was to enjoy many of the powers the northern conservatives were to give to the state council in 1881. Rumelia had large Turkish and Greek minorities and the great powers who had drawn up the province's organic statute, or constitution, intended that the governmental system should reflect this. They were not entirely successful. In the first assembly all but five of the elected deputies were Bulgarian as were eight of the ten members of the standing committee; in the latter case the powers had devised a system of proportional representation (PR) so that four of the members of the committee would be non-Bulgarian, but this had been frustrated by Ivan Salabashev, a Bulgarian deputy who had a Ph.D. in mathematics and who arranged the voting of his compatriots to ensure the return of the maximum number of Bulgarians.[13]

Initially, internal Rumelian politics bore some similarity to those of the principality. There was a running contest between the governor-general and the Russians, the former fearing overbearing Russian influence in the militia. The contest was to reach its most intense point when Aleko Pasha refused to allow the construction of a war memorial at Shipka on the grounds that it was too like a fortress, the treaty of Berlin having prohibited the construction of fortresses in the province. In retaliation, in 1884 St Petersburg vetoed Aleko's reappointment and his deputy, Krŭstevich, was nominated in his place. Rumelia also saw a political division between conservative and liberal, though here it was the former rather than the latter who were initially the stronger faction, exercising power through the Nationalist Party, which was dominated by the two wealthy Geshov cousins, Ivan Evlogi and Ivan Evstratiev. Their dominance was shaken in 1881 by the arrival in Rumelia of the liberal refugees from the north and in October of that year the liberals won every one of eighteen assembly seats which had to be re-elected; five of the ten members of the standing committee chosen immediately afterwards were also liberals. When the other eighteen seats in the assembly were contested in 1883 the liberals achieved an absolute majority. The conservative response was to play the nationalist card, even renaming their party the Unionist Party; in elections in 1884 they reversed many of the recent liberal gains.

At this point union did not seem a realizable objective, not least because of the attitude of the great powers. Initially Britain and Austria-Hungary would have resisted it because it would have been seen as an extension of Russian influence; when Prince Alexander fell out with the Russians the latter would block it because it would increase the prince's power. And by the mid-1880s the Russians, who were turning their interest ever more towards Asia, wanted only stability and the status quo in the Balkans.

Nevertheless, pressure for union was mounting in both Rumelia and the principality. The Rumelians were becoming more conscious of the limitations on their freedom, particularly when the Porte used its power of veto to block the formation of a Rumelian bank or to build a railway

---

[13] This, at least, is the contention stated in his far from modest memoirs, Ivan Salabashev, *Spomeni* (Sofia: Knipegraf, 1943), 8–17.

from Yambol to the port of Burgas, a line which would have allowed Rumelian traders to avoid paying Ottoman customs dues; Constantinople also refused to sanction a Bulgarian-Rumelian agreement to lessen tariffs on trade between the province and the principality. And the Rumelians complained, justifiably, that their bureaucracy was over-extended and too expensive, and that the tithe in kind, calculated on the ten years before the war of 1877 when agricultural prices were high, was more exacting than the cash levy in Bulgaria which was assessed on the three years before the war.

These frustrations gave greater impetus to the nationalist movement, as did the publication in Plovdiv in 1884 of the memoirs of the revolutionary hero, Zahari Stoyanov. For many Rumelians the nobility of the struggle he described contrasted sharply with what they saw as the cynical manipulation of nationalist passions by their own leaders. In 1884 a number of committees were formed throughout Bulgaria and Rumelia, that in Plovdiv, the Bulgarian Secret Revolutionary Committee, being led by Stoyanov himself. The initial objective of these organizations was the full national programme of the liberation of Macedonia and Thrace and the union of Bulgaria and Rumelia. The failure of attempted incursions from Bulgaria into Macedonia, however, persuaded Stoyanov and his allies to concentrate on Rumelia alone; in July 1885 they renamed their organization the Committee for Union. Agitation intensified. In March 1885 the guilds in Plovdiv had called on the powers to bring about unification and this call was echoed by guild meetings throughout Rumelia and Bulgaria. In May the Bulgarians in Plovdiv defied an official prohibition and celebrated Botev's crossing of the Danube in 1876, and in July there was a highly emotional meeting at the spot where in 1868 Hadji Dimitŭr Asenov and his twenty-five revolutionary colleagues had died in an encounter with Ottoman troops.

When Stoyanov's committee was renamed and reorganized in July 1885 it included two members from north of the border, Captain Kosta Panitsa and Dimitŭr Rizov. It redefined its aims not only to limit action to unification but also to state that that unification should come about under Prince Alexander. It also made an important tactical decision: it was no longer to attempt to organize a popular uprising but was to concentrate on recruiting followers in the militia who were then to engineer a coup d'état. An uprising, it was feared, might be prolonged and bring about intervention by Ottoman forces, whereas if a coup were expeditiously carried out no external power, not even the Ottoman empire, would intervene to reverse a *fait accompli*.

It was intended that the coup would be effected in the second half of September after the harvest had been taken in and when the Bulgarian army would be mobilized for its autumn exercises. In fact, action began early and though not entirely coordinated was overwhelmingly successful, the incumbent authorities having no desire to resist so popular a movement. On 6 September union with Bulgaria was proclaimed.

This presented Alexander Battenberg and his government with a dilemma. It was one born of the complexity of Bulgaria's national problem. Whilst pressure for unification had been growing in Rumelia the pressure inside Bulgaria for action in Macedonia had also been mounting. This pressure was exercised primarily by the thousands of Macedonians who had fled to the principality after Macedonia had been restored to Ottoman rule by the treaty of Berlin. By 1884, with the constitutional disputes now settled, they became both more organized and more vociferous, the newly founded society Makedonski Glas (Macedonian Voice) being a particularly effective mouthpiece. The Macedonians and their many supporters amongst native-born Bulgarians expressed growing concern at the failure of the Ottoman regime to implement both article 23 of the treaty of Berlin which promised reforms for Macedonia, and the assurances given to the Exarchate with regard to bishoprics in Macedonia which had opted for the Bulgarian Church. They were also concerned at Russian policy in Constantinople which was pressing for an end to the schism in Orthodoxy; were the Exarchate to be forced back into union with the Patriarchate the Bulgarian cause in Macedonia would be lost. At the same time the situation in Macedonia itself was becoming less stable as Slavs protested at the non-fulfilment of article 23 and the Ottoman authorities punished them for doing so. To complicate matters even further, there were increasing signs that Bulgarian claims for the allegiance of the Macedonian Christians would be contested by the Serbs as well as the Greeks. By the end of 1884 there had been a series of meetings in Sofia and elsewhere to protest against the mistreatment of Christians in Macedonia, and the temper of the protesters had not been sweetened by a government statement that nothing could be done but care for the refugees.

Many Macedonians and their supporters disagreed and here the argument over means became serious. By the spring of 1885 Makedonski

Glas was calling for 'forceful and desperate' deeds to awaken the Berlin powers to their moral obligation to insist that reforms be introduced in Macedonia. But there was action as well as words. In imitation of the cheta campaign of the 1860s bands entered Macedonia. The most serious incursion was in May when a Russian adventurer, Kalmykov, led between sixty and seventy men into Macedonia with arms taken, with the obvious complicity of its commanding officers, from the garrison in Kyustendil.

The bands had little impact on the situation in Macedonia but their effect in Bulgaria was considerable. Karavelov insisted that nothing could be achieved by the use of force and ordered all known Macedonian activists to be removed from border areas. They were, often with considerable brutality, and this only fuelled Macedonian anger and strengthened the Macedonian faction which was becoming a threatening element on the left flank of Karavelov's party. The bands also complicated Karavelov's relations with the Russians, whose continued preoccupation with central Asia made them even more desirous of stability in the Balkans. Karavelov's failure to control the Macedonians seemed to be threatening that stability.

If the cavortings of Kalmykov and his band were embarrassing to Alexander and Karavelov, the declaration of union in Plovdiv in September posed immensely greater difficulties. The prince had recently assured the Russians that there would be no dramatic developments in Bulgaria or Rumelia, an assurance given in good faith because although he had heard rumours of what was afoot they were little different from many previous rumours. For Alexander now to accept the union would gravely compromise his position in Russia and he therefore dithered.

Karavelov was even more hesitant. He had always believed that Bulgaria should not, and could not pursue an independent foreign policy; 'we leave that to those who gave us our political life', he once wrote in his newspaper, *Tŭrnovska Konstitutsiya* (Tŭrnovo Constitution),[14] and he now hid behind the risible argument that Bulgaria could not afford the costs of unification or to assume responsibility for the Rumelian debt. The president of the sŭbranie, Stambolov, was made of sterner stuff. He met the prince in Tŭrnovo and told him that if he did not accept the union his reign would be over, and also, more tellingly, that if he attempted to undo the union it would cause a popular uprising which

---

[14] Cited in Mateev, *Stambolov*, 15.

could easily spread to Macedonia and Thrace and thus plunge the Balkans into even greater disorders; in effect, though the Russians might not like the union they would like its alternative even less. Alexander was persuaded and on 8 September he arrived in Plovdiv to an ecstatic welcome.

Two days after Alexander's entry into Plovdiv an extraordinary and secret session of the sŭbranie voted a war credit of 10 million leva. Only one deputy voted against the bill; it was Dragan Tsankov, whose suspicions of Russia had dissipated to such an extent that he was now prepared to support a Russian occupation. This was not entirely unconnected with the fact that, being heavily in debt, he had become dependent upon the Russians for money.[15]

5. WAR WITH SERBIA AND THE DEPOSITION OF PRINCE ALEXANDER, 1885–1886

Given the danger of Ottoman resistance to the coup the prince, when he reached Plovdiv, ordered that as many militiamen and volunteers as possible should be moved to the border with the Ottoman empire. At the same time he also telegraphed to the tsar expressing the hope that the latter would give his blessing to the union. He did not. Not only did he denounce it, but he ordered all Russian officers serving in the Bulgarian army and the Rumelian militia to return home immediately; those forces were therefore left without any officer above the rank of captain. The Russians had turned all the blame for their discomfiture over the union on Alexander Battenberg. In fact, it was partly their own fault. That they were not well informed about the situation in Eastern Rumelia was because their representative, Sorokin, was on holiday and reluctant to believe the news of the union. And nor did St Petersburg really try to find out if the Bulgarian government had deceived it or had been faced with a *fait accompli* brought about by events in Plovdiv over which it had no control.

It soon became apparent that Bulgaria and its seemingly enfeebled forces were facing the danger of war, but the danger came not from the Ottoman empire in the south-east but from the north-west. King Milan of Serbia had always insisted that if unification took place Serbia would

[15] Durman, *Thunderer*, 404–5.

demand territorial compensation. As a ruler who looked towards Vienna for patronage, however, that compensation could not come in Bosnia, then under Habsburg administration, nor would the Austrians permit Serbian expansion into Macedonia. The only alternative was to demand territory from Bulgaria itself. And it seemed an easy way out. The Bulgarians were torn between joy at the union and concern at having offended Russia, whilst their small, almost officer-less army was at the far end of the country with few means of moving to the Serbian border. On 2 November Milan ordered his army to set out on what he thought would be a 'stroll to Sofia'.

They did not get very far. Three days later the First Serbian Army reached Slivnitsa, a pass 30 kilometres from Sofia which offered direct access to the Bulgarian capital; but it was also an excellent defensive position. This the Bulgarians knew and had dug in and were soon strengthened by the arrival of more troops from the south. By 7 November the Serbian attack had broken and, after an audacious but unauthorized sally by Captain Atanas Benderev, the Serbs began to retreat. After their Second Army had been repulsed near Vidin the retreat became a rout; the Bulgarians were soon on Serbian soil and their advance towards Belgrade was halted only by Austro-Hungarian diplomatic intervention.

The Bulgarian victory had been amazing. It was true that the Serbian army was ill-supplied and lacking in motivation, but that could not diminish the sense of achievement on the part of the Bulgarian nation. The army's march from south to north was little short of an epic; there was no complete railway line and on what track that did exist there were only five functioning locomotives. Despite this, and despite the lack of senior officers, the army moved prodigious distances in a short time, mostly on foot; 40 and 60 kilometres per day were routine and the Third Haskovo Company marched 110 kilometres in 37 hours.[16] There was no organized commissariat and the troops had therefore to rely on the local peasantry for food, shelter, and frequently for footwear. The necessary support was readily given and it was given by Turkish and Pomak as well as Bulgarian peasants; all minority groups except the Greeks volunteered to fight. Immediately after the liberation there had been some feeling that the Bulgarians were too immature to assume the full responsibilities of

---

[16] Stiliyan Kovachev, *Zapiski na generala ot pehotata 1876–1918* (Sofia: Georgi Pobedonosets, 1992), 11.

statehood, this feeling being expressed by some Bulgarian conservatives as well as Russian advisers. There could be no such feelings after 1885. On the other hand, the great victory perhaps did too much to encourage the idea that the most effective solution to national problems lay in the use of the sword, even if it had not been the Bulgarians who first unsheathed it.

In the event, the Bulgarians gained relatively little from their victory. On 19 February 1886, the anniversary of San Stefano, the treaty of Bucharest restored the status quo ante between Bulgaria and Serbia, the latter having been protected by Austria. In April the Constantinople agreement settled the unification crisis, but the settlement was not one which pleased many Bulgarians. In effect it was agreed that the Rumelian administration and military establishment should be absorbed into those of the principality and that all customs barriers should be abolished. Bulgaria was also to cede to the Ottoman empire the Kŭrdjali and Tŭmrŭsh areas which were populated overwhelmingly by Muslims and which had never been brought under Christian control. The critical condition, however, was that the prince of Bulgaria should become the governor-general of Rumelia. The governor-general was still to be reappointed every five years and had to secure the consent of the sultan and the Berlin powers, thus giving the Russians the opportunity to veto Battenberg's reappointment; he would then have to abdicate because Bulgaria would never tolerate a prince who was forced to cease being governor-general of Rumelia.

Alexander's position in Bulgaria had already been weakened. He had been with his troops as lines were drawn for the great battle at Slivnitsa but his own interventions in the planning for it had been inept. More damaging still was the fact that he left for Sofia on the morning of what he knew would be the decisive day. He had intended that his presence with the troops would encourage the army and augment his own political prestige; if the former had been achieved the latter had not. His conduct at Slivnitsa had discredited him in the eyes of most of the officer corps whilst the unification and the war with Serbia had enraged Alexander III in St Petersburg.

The prince did what he could to repair relations with Russia but the tsar remained implacable, and his attitude hardened rather than softened in the months after the Constantinople agreement. The Russians in Sofia made little secret of their policy: if the Bulgarians wanted full unification they could have it only if Battenberg were removed. This, the Russians knew, would not happen immediately and in the meantime they supported those in Bulgaria who were not opposed to the removal of the prince.

There were a goodly number of these. Most karavelists and tsankovists still believed Russia should control Bulgarian foreign policy, and Tsankov himself had raised his voice in the sŭbranie against the union because it had been carried out without the consent of the tsar. Others resented that in becoming governor-general of Rumelia Alexander had become an Ottoman official. A more substantial concern was that in accepting the union Alexander had made even more difficult the liberation of Macedonia and Thrace. As many Bulgarians had feared, the union had put the powers and the other Balkan states on their guard against further Bulgarian expansion, and as a result there had been a significant increase in hellenist and Serb propaganda in Macedonia. The prince also had critics in Rumelia. Here too there was concern that the links with Russia had been severed whilst those with the Ottoman empire had been preserved. Others were angered at the savage paring of the Rumelian bureaucracy; however necessary that may have been it could not be welcomed by those who lost their jobs, whilst those who expected a pruning of the administrative machine to be followed by a reduction in taxes were soon disillusioned. Much worse was Karavelov's insistence that because the Bulgarian budget made no provision for such expenditure Rumelians who fought in the 1885 war could not be paid; the Rumelians took matters, and the cash, into their own hands by helping themselves to the deposits in a Plovdiv bank.

These growing discontents were seen in May 1886 when the elections for the first united sŭbranie were held. In the north the government used strong-arm tactics at the polls and secured a majority of pliant deputies, but those elected in Rumelia were by no means so biddable; the south Bulgarian lobby had arrived in the Sofia assembly and it was to be present at least until the first world war. The government came under criticism for the alienation of the Kŭrdjali and Tŭmrŭsh areas, the opposition arguing, correctly, that the constitution stated that only a grand national assembly could alienate territory.

The prince's ministers rode this storm but they faced even more turbulent waters when the question of the Rusé–Varna railway once again came before the assembly. In July the government introduced a bill authorizing purchase of the line for 44.5 million francs. The government's case was easily undermined. Many saw the sale as a quid pro quo for British support in the unification crisis; the price, they said, was too high, not only in cash but because it would further alienate Russia. Why not, they suggested, purchase renewed Russian support for Bulgaria, for which a much lower price was being asked, namely, the abdication of a German prince from the throne of Slav Bulgaria? Opposition to the bill came from many who two years previously had proposed paying more than 44.5 million francs. It also came from the southern Bulgarians who had no desire to pay anything for a clapped-out line in the north of the country when the government would not even pay Rumelians who had fought in the war. The debate produced scenes of utter chaos. At one point a crowd burst into the chamber which had to be cleared by a specially summoned detachment of militiamen; Karavelov collapsed in a state of nervous disorder; his minister of justice, the tough Vasil Radoslavov who had overseen the application of government pressure during the elections, defected to the opposition, and the bill was passed only when the president of the sŭbranie, Stambolov, called for a vote by a show of hands which, he said, produced a majority in favour of the bill. Few of those present shared his opinion.

Disorder was not confined to the assembly. In the spring a Russian officer, Captain Nabokov, who had served in the Rumelian militia, attempted to raise a pro-Russian rebellion near Burgas. He failed but was saved from punishment by the Capitulations, under which he had the right to be tried by Russian law in a Russian consular court.

It seemed as if the country, so soon after its great triumph, was becoming ungovernable. The instrument of that great triumph now decided to intervene. It was not to be the last time the army played a crucial role in Bulgaria's political life. The senior officers, all of them Russian trained, tended to be pro-Russian and therefore increasingly critical of the prince. Relations had not improved during the war when the prince and these senior officers had frequently disagreed over tactics, Alexander even rebuking Benderev for the unauthorized action which did so much to secure victory at Slivnitsa. After the war Alexander lost support among the more junior officers, most of whom had previously backed him in his efforts to check Russian influence. Now many of them found that their promotion prospects, so much encouraged by the departure of the Russian officers, were not as bright as had been anticipated, partly because Rumelian officers had to be given their share of higher posts. By May a vague conspiracy had begun, the chief plotters being Major Radko Dimitriev and Benderev who, astonishingly, had not been promoted. On the night of 8 to 9 August they entered Alexander's palace and demanded his abdication. The prince had always said that he would not remain if the Bulgarian people wished him to leave and therefore he offered no resistance. He signed a deed of abdication and crossed the Danube into Romania.

His intended destination was Darmstadt but he had journeyed only as far as Lemberg (Lviv) when word reached him that opposition to the coup had been organized by Stambolov. The latter had excellent connections with European diplomacy and from these he learned that other powers would oppose any Russian measures to prevent Alexander from returning to Bulgaria. Stambolov also had excellent connections within the Bulgarian military, not least through his brother-in-law, Sava Mutkurov, who commanded the Plovdiv garrison; from this source he learned that a number of military units were opposed to the August putsch and these he concentrated around Sofia. The plotters had not envisioned opposition to their action and, with civil war facing the nation, they gave way. On 17 August Alexander recrossed the Danube to Rusé, where he received a tumultuous welcome.

Alexander now committed a political blunder of stupendous proportions. He sent to the tsar a telegram saying that he would not return to Bulgaria permanently unless the tsar approved, and that, 'As Russia gave me my crown, I am prepared to give it back into the hands of its sovereign'. The tsar could hardly have asked for anything more; here was a chance to secure the departure of Battenberg without having to pay any price for it. He seized it with alacrity, immediately publishing the prince's message and his own reply which stated that he did not approve of Battenberg's return and that he was sure, under the circumstances, Battenberg would 'understand what devolves upon you'. Alexander had boxed himself into a corner. He had offered to leave Bulgaria of his own free will and the offer had been accepted. He left for Darmstadt on 26 August. Later he was to join the Austro-Hungarian army and to marry an opera singer before dying in December 1893, aged only 36.

6. THE ELECTION OF PRINCE FERDINAND

With the departure of Prince Alexander a regency was formed under Stambolov, Mutkurov, and Karavelov. Radoslavov was made minister president and constructed a cabinet in which all factions but the extreme russophiles were represented, though the latter were given support and encouragement by General Nikolaĭ Kaulbars, brother of the former minister of war, who arrived as the tsar's special commissioner. The regency's primary objective was to convene a grand national assembly which would elect a new prince and return the country to stability, and elections were therefore called for September. Before they were held Stambolov and his allies encouraged the establishment of new Patriotic Associations throughout the country. They were to be a powerful local arm of the central authorities and eventually an important basis for Stambolov's new political party, the National Liberal Party.

Whilst the regency prepared for the elections Kaulbars insisted that they be postponed because the consent of the Porte, which was technically necessary, had not been secured; he also demanded the lifting of the state of siege imposed in August, and the release of all those arrested for complicity in the overthrow of Alexander Battenberg. Stambolov gave way on the question of the siege but not on the other demands whilst Kaulbars, for his part, accepted that the elections would take place and therefore set about doing all he could, including touring around the country to speak on the hustings, to secure the return of pro-Russian deputies.

He had little success. In the elections of 28 September the government secured a massive majority. It was true that it had used a considerable degree of force during the voting and had declared martial law on the eve of the polls, but such measures were hardly necessary. Kaulbars had overplayed his hand and his hectoring tone was much resented. The deposition of Alexander Battenberg had also angered many voters but most important of all was the russophiles' failure to answer two questions: what conditions would Russia insist upon for the full recognition of the union of 1885, and who was Russia's candidate for the vacant Bulgarian throne?

Despite the genuinely popular result Kaulbars continued to denounce the election results as manufactured by government thuggery. He also made increasingly loud and frequent complaint about the alleged mistreatment of Russian subjects in Bulgaria. Tensions reached their height in the middle of October when it was announced in St Petersburg that two Russian warships would sail to Varna to protect Russian interests. Stambolov then agreed to release the officers arrested after the August putsch.

Stambolov's overriding aim was to secure the election of a prince before the country descended into chaos. That there was a danger of this was illustrated when Nabokov once more attempted to raise a revolt near Burgas; he was again captured and once more escaped punishment via the Capitulations, but not before his captor, Captain Panitsa, had insisted he be put before a Bulgarian military tribunal which found him guilty before handing him over to the Russians. A more serious threat to stability appeared in the guise of a mutiny in three southern Bulgarian garrisons, the leader of the revolt being Radko Dimitriev.[17] Neither attempted rising attracted much popular sympathy nor, more significantly, did they provoke any attempt by the Russians to land troops from their two warships.

This provided the regency with some breathing space. By this time Karavelov had left its ranks, having decided that Bulgaria must accept whatever terms the Russians dictated. He was little missed by the massively russophobe GNA, which nominated Georgi Zhivkov, a prominent defender of the Bulgarians in Macedonia, as his replacement. Two days later, on 8 November, Kaulbars decided that he could make no further headway in Bulgaria and left the country. Diplomatic relations between Bulgaria and its liberator were thus severed. They were not to be restored for almost a decade.

Relations between Russians and Bulgarians had never been simple. Despite the ties of religion and language the Russians had not always endeared themselves to the Bulgarians. The behaviour of the Russian troops and administrators in 1877–9 caused some alienation. The soldiers looted, rampaged, and raped, and the administrators behaved with a cruelty which though customary in their homeland was unknown in Bulgaria. Bulgaria, said one Russian administrator, was 'a miserable nation that has to be treated harshly'; another, speaking at an official banquet at which Bulgarians were present, derided them and said that it was 'a shame the Turks did not annihilate them to the very last one'.

---

[17] Dimitriev remained a committed russophile. In the first world war he asked Ferdinand to be allowed to join the Russians 'to whom we are obligated as our liberators and for whom in this difficult time I consider myself obligated to serve however I can'. Permission was granted and he rose to command the III and later the XII Russian armies. In the civil war he was taken hostage by the Bolsheviks who later shot him. Richard C. Hall, *Bulgaria's Road to the First World War* (Boulder, Colo.: East European Monographs no. 560, distributed by Columbia University Press, 1996), 312 n. 39.

Another official ordered that if the mayor of a community failed to deliver a thousand loaves for the Russian army he was to be beaten with a hazel-rod; he had little sympathy when told that such a punishment had not been used even under Ottoman rule.[18] After liberation Russian ministers in Bulgaria had often appeared patronizing, overbearing, or even contemptuous. In June 1885, in a report to St Petersburg, the Russian diplomatic agent in Sofia referred to the Bulgarians as 'semi-illiterate savages' for whom, 'The best solution would be our occupation of the principality, the appointment of a Russian governor general and the introduction of our laws.'[19] No matter how devoted the liberals were to the Russians, attitudes such as these, and the actions they fostered, inevitably affected Bulgarian opinion.

With the departure of Kaulbars Bulgaria had reached a crossroads. Even its russophiles had been forced to recognize that absolute faith could not be placed in the liberating power. Bulgaria therefore had to prove that it could exist independently of Russia as well as of the Ottoman empire. At the same time, there was the danger that without a prince the country would descend into anarchy, and the longer there was no prince the greater was that danger; but at the same time the greater the danger the less likely it was that any candidate would accept the Bulgarian throne. This was the main problem facing the three-man delegation which the GNA appointed to visit the European capitals, St Petersburg excepted, in search of a new prince.

As the delegation moved around Europe Stambolov was forced to use tough methods at home to prove that the country was still governable. In Constantinople the exiled Tsankov supported all opposition to the regency, but a greater danger appeared when, once again, there were attempts to provoke the army into rebellion. The focal point in this instance was Silistra. Once again the attempted revolt came to nothing but savage punishment was meted out to those involved, with some units having one in twenty of their number, chosen at random, executed by their comrades. In fact in early 1887 Stambolov, with the help of the local Patriotic Associations, imposed a virtual reign of terror over the civilian population as well as the military establishment. The most prominent civilian victim of this tough regime was Karavelov who had now joined

---

[18] Durman, *Thunderer*, 235–6, 530 n.51.   [19] Durman, *Lost Illusions*, 109.

with his old liberal adversary Tsankov in a new russophile alliance. Karavelov was put in jail where he was mistreated by another old enemy, Captain Panitsa. Karavelov's sufferings gained considerable coverage in the European press, mainly because of the efforts of his wife, Ekaterina, one of the most formidable women ever to appear on the Bulgarian political stage. But the tough methods adopted by Stambolov did not end the disorders. An attempt was made to kill the Bulgarian representative in Bucharest, where a number of military dissidents had taken up residence, and in Sofia in April the supporters of Alexander Battenberg exploded a bomb in front of the house of Major Popov, one of Stambolov's most ardent supporters.

The battenbergists had been encouraged by the departure of Kaulbars and by March 1887 even the minister president, Radoslavov, had joined their ranks. Stambolov, however, knew that the Russians would prevent a restoration and he began therefore to think in dualist terms. His first approach was to the sultan. Stambolov's plan was for the sultan to become prince of Bulgaria but of a Bulgaria which would include not only Bulgaria and Rumelia but also Macedonia and Thrace. The plan was much discussed in Bulgaria and the sultan did not veto it. But the Russians did. A similar approach to King Carol of Romania, under which a new Romano-Bulgarian state would become the starting point of a new Balkan federation, received a decidedly cold shoulder.

The answer to the question of a prince finally appeared when it was learned in Vienna that Prince Ferdinand of Saxe-Coburg-Gotha might be willing to consider moving to Sofia. He claimed to have the support of the Habsburg emperor and to be a friend of the tsar. The latter claim was definitely not justified but Russian hostility was now irrelevant: any candidate appointed by the GNA would be rejected by St Petersburg, where the assembly was still regarded as illegitimate. By the summer of 1887, with no other candidate in sight, Stambolov arranged for the election of another GNA, which was to meet in the pro-stambolovist bastion of Tŭrnovo, and a dependable pro-regency majority was secured. It offered the throne to Prince Ferdinand who accepted. On 14 August he took his oath of allegiance before the GNA; he was to remain head of the Bulgarian state for thirty-one years.

5

Stefan Stambolov, Prince Ferdinand, and the Quest for Recognition, 1887–1896

For the half-dozen years after 1887 Bulgarian political life was to be dominated by the new prince and the man who had brought him to the throne, Stefan Stambolov. They were unlikely and uncomfortable partners. A member of the European nobility—his mother was a daughter of King Louis Philippe of France and had witnessed the fall of the Orléanist dynasty in 1848—Ferdinand came from a background of privilege, wealth, culture, and sophistication. He himself was not comfortable with the equestrian and military preoccupations of many of the nobility but he had a passionate interest in science and technology, though, paradoxically, he was preternaturally superstitious. Stambolov was the son of an innkeeper. Born near Tŭrnovo he had been apprenticed to a tailor in that city but soon enrolled in a school run by a dedicated nationalist who rapidly recognized the ability of his new pupil. Stambolov won a scholarship, endowed by the Russian empress, to study at the theological seminary in Odessa. Once there he soon forsook the prophets for the populists. This led to his expulsion from Russia. He went next to Bucharest where he became involved in Lyuben Karavelov's revolutionary committee and in 1876 went into Bulgaria as one of the revolutionary apostles. His energy, intelligence, and fortitude made him one of the most notable figures of the revolutionary movement and assured him prominence in the politics of the liberated state.

Though there was no personal liking between the two men, Ferdinand and Stambolov depended on one another. Their policies were directed towards the interlinked objectives of securing stability at home and external recognition of Ferdinand as the legitimate prince of Bulgaria. Before those objectives were attained relations between the prince and his minister president collapsed.

1. STAMBOLOV ASCENDANT, 1887–1890

After Ferdinand's arrival in Bulgaria in August 1887 Stambolov was made minister president. He constructed a ministry dominated by his own close supporters and the conservatives, and this was backed by a compliant sŭbranie.

The problems faced by the Stambolov government and the prince were considerable. The Russians remained adamant that Ferdinand's election had been ultra vires. They conducted a rigorous diplomatic campaign against him, registering a significant gain in March 1888 when they persuaded the sultan to declare, for the first time, that Ferdinand's election had been illegal. This was a serious blow for Ferdinand and Stambolov, but the internal implications of Russia's attitude were even more threatening. If, as the Russians insisted, Ferdinand was not the legitimate ruler, then any action taken to unseat him was not revolutionary; at the same time, anyone taking forcible action against Ferdinand and Stambolov might reasonably assume this action would be condoned and perhaps approved by the tsar and his ministers. This threat had been made apparent soon after Ferdinand arrived in Bulgaria when Nabokov once again crossed into Bulgaria with the intention of raising a revolt against the regime. As during his previous incursions Nabokov found no enthusiasm amongst the local population; but this time the authorities made sure that he, and most of his band, were killed before they could be handed over to the Russians and the consular court.

Adventurers such as Nabokov were relatively easily dealt with; Ferdinand and Stambolov would face much greater dangers if the Bulgarian army were enlisted in the struggle against them. Stambolov moved rapidly to avert this danger, increasing the standing army by 50 per cent in order to increase the promotion prospects within the officer corps. But this did not remove the threat. Many officers remained pro-Russian, others resented the government's apparent indifference to the Macedonians, and some remained loyal to Alexander Battenberg. Captain Panitsa belonged to all three categories: he was a Macedonian, a close associate of Battenberg, and he believed fervently that no progress in Macedonia could be made without Russian help which would not be forthcoming as long as Ferdinand was on the throne; therefore he had to be removed. In 1889 Panitsa began to plot against Ferdinand. The plan was to arrest or assassinate the prince at a court ball in January 1890, but so widespread a conspiracy could not remain secret and the plotters were arrested before they could act. In June Panitsa was tied to a tree in front of the Sofia garrison, many of whom had been involved in the conspiracy, and shot by a firing squad made up of Macedonians. The clinical brutality of his death showed the determination of Stambolov, but it also pointed to the drastic measures he was to use to secure stability and order.

Ferdinand and Stambolov faced many plots and conspiracies but that hatched by Panitsa was the most dangerous of them all. The conspiracy proved to be far more extensive than had at first been thought, and its links with the army would have been dangerous even without the precedent of the military coup against Alexander in 1886. Panitsa had also had links with exiled politicians such as Tsankov and Karavelov, and with a number of Russian diplomats. He had based his plot on the fact that Ferdinand's presence in Bulgaria made impossible any progress in the sacred cause of Macedonia. The conspiracy threw Stambolov's self-reinforcing problems into stark relief: as long as the prince remained unrecognized Bulgaria would be vulnerable to plots, conspiracies, and disorders; the prince was likely to remain unrecognized as long as there were plots, conspiracies, and disorders. There would be no recognition of Ferdinand without stability and good order in Bulgaria. This was more likely to come about if the regime could secure some significant gain to put before the public.

At his trial Panitsa's defence lawyers had argued that Panitsa's actions were justified because they were intended to advance the Bulgarian cause in Macedonia. Stambolov therefore concentrated on achieving success in the same cause. His efforts met with stunning success, the Exarch Ĭosif, who disliked Stambolov, later telling Tsankov that whatever he, Ĭosif, had achieved, 'was due solely to our late and great statesman, Stefan Stambolov'.[1]

Any sober analysis of the Macedonian question indicated that military action was impossible in that it would provoke intervention by the other

---

[1] Mateev, *Stambolov*, 94.

Balkan states and the Ottoman empire, and possibly by the great powers. On the other hand, the Bulgarian position there could be strengthened by increasing Bulgarian national consciousness via the Church, just as had happened during the vŭzrazhdane. This would have to be done through the Exarchate, a manoeuvre which would also improve relations between the regime and one of its main institutional opponents, the Bulgarian Church.

Stambolov had never enjoyed good relations with the Church and especially with its hierarchy which he, like many Bulgarian liberals, regarded as a foreign, Greek, imposition on an egalitarian, Slav body. In 1886 and 1887 relations deteriorated when Stambolov reduced the bishops' salaries and refused to allow the Holy Synod to meet. The arrival of Ferdinand made matters much worse. The prince initially made a public display of his Catholicism, a mistake he did not repeat, and in retaliation the senior cleric in Bulgaria, Metropolitan Kliment of Tŭrnovo, refused both to celebrate a Te Deum for Ferdinand, or to allow prayers to be said for him in Orthodox churches. The Exarch in Constantinople approved of this, in retaliation for which Stambolov suspended subsidies paid by the Bulgarian government to exarchist schools and publications in Macedonia. The minister president also forced Kliment to leave Sofia and return to Tŭrnovo. He reappeared in Sofia briefly in January 1889 to attend the Synod which Stambolov had at last allowed to meet, though it was not long before the bishops were escorted back to their dioceses by the police. Stambolov seemed implacably opposed to any compromise with the clergy unless they made some gesture towards the recognition of the prince.

It was the Panitsa plot which changed his mind. The regime could not afford to have so powerful an enemy as the Church. And for his part, the Exarch was by now desperate for an arrangement with the Bulgarian government, primarily because the position of the Exarchate in Macedonia was weakening. Since the union of Bulgaria and Rumelia, Greek and Serbian propaganda had increased in Macedonia and the rupture of relations between Sofia and St Petersburg meant that Russia backed Greece and Serbia, especially after a coup in Belgrade had replaced the pro-Habsburg King Milan with a pro-Russian regency and government. In addition to this, the Porte had delayed implementing berats, or letters of intent, for the transfer to the Exarchate of those Macedonian dioceses which had voted by plebiscite to leave the Patriarchate. In the spring of 1890 the Exarch responded positively to unofficial and secret overtures from Sofia which promised to restore government subsidies if Exarch Ĭosif would make some acknowledgement, even privately, of Ferdinand's position as prince of Bulgaria.

It now remained for Stambolov to convince the Porte. Stambolov's case was that Bulgaria and the Ottoman empire were in a state of symbiotic interdependence. Bulgaria wanted the continuation of Ottoman power in Macedonia because if it were removed or even weakened there would be a massive, popular demand for Bulgarian intervention: if the Sofia regime did not intervene it would be swept away by popular pressure; if it did intervene it would provoke the Greeks and Serbs to do the same and they, with Russian backing, would outweigh Bulgaria, who would therefore lose Macedonia. But this would be an equal disaster for the Ottoman empire because if the present Bulgarian regime were deposed its successor would not only be more aggressive over Macedonia but, more importantly, it would be backed by Russia. The Porte therefore stood to gain by Stambolov and Ferdinand remaining in power but this, as the Panitsa plot had indicated, they were unlikely to do unless they gained concessions in Macedonia which would disarm the Macedonian lobby which had been so important in the formation of the Panitsa conspiracy.

Stambolov placed his arguments before the Porte immediately after the Panitsa trial had ended. The Porte responded positively, agreeing to send a representative to Sofia. He was nominally to supervise the fate of the Muslim religious properties in Bulgaria, but it was the first time since 1887 that an official of the sultan had travelled to Sofia and this had to be seen as a move towards recognition de facto if not de jure. The Exarch was also to have the right to establish contact with Bulgarian communities in the Adrianople vilayet, but the most dramatic concession was that berats were promised for the Skopje, Ohrid, and Bitola dioceses. The vŭzrazhdane in Macedonia, all but frozen since the early 1870s, could resume.

Relations between the Church and the government in Bulgaria improved immediately. A meeting of the Holy Synod in Rusé agreed that prayers for Ferdinand should become part of the liturgy of the Church in Bulgaria and in August the government announced it would provide 3 million leva a year to support exarchist schools in Macedonia. By the end of the year all major differences between Church and state seemed settled. All the political parties in Bulgaria, even the tsankovists, now accepted Ferdinand as head of state and in elections held in the autumn there was little need to coerce the country into voting for a government which had proved it could preserve order and secure, without the use of force, major concessions for the national cause in Macedonia.

2. THE DECLINE AND FALL OF STAMBOLOV, 1890–1894

The triumph of the summer of 1890 benefited Ferdinand more than Stambolov; it was not long before the flower of his victory disseminated the seed of his defeat. Simply stated, the more Stambolov succeeded in entrenching Ferdinand the less necessary he became; he was, and would always remain, a kingmaker without an alternative king whilst Ferdinand, if secure on his throne, could consider dispensing with the kingmaker. Stambolov also faced a long-term difficulty in that the crises of 1887 to 1890 had forced him to rely on tough methods. The press was restricted, police spies were widely used, army units were billeted in villages which refused to pay their taxes, and electoral management was very widely practised. This meant that if the opposition lost a major platform by accepting Ferdinand they could easily find another by denouncing the anti-democratic and frequently unconstitutional methods used by Stambolov. There was a further danger for Stambolov. His success in 1890 had delighted the nationalists but his long-term strategy for Macedonia demanded more patience than many Macedonians could muster. They would soon demand further concessions but this would in all probability alarm the Porte and therefore Stambolov intended to keep the Macedonians under tight control. It was a danger-ous tactic and one which would eventually cost him his life. And there was still the danger which both Stambolov and Ferdinand faced: if, as seemed to be the case, successes such as those of 1890 did nothing to make recognition by the great powers more likely, was there any future for Ferdinand in Bulgaria at all?

The need for recognition was underlined by two murders; the minister of finance was killed in Sofia on 15 March 1891 as he was walking along-side Stambolov, the intended target being Stambolov himself, and just under a year later Georgi Vŭlkovich, the Bulgarian representative in Constantinople, was mortally wounded. The government in Sofia was convinced, partly on the evidence of some supposedly official documents, that Russia was behind these atrocities. Stambolov's immediate reaction was to impose what was a virtual reign of terror in which over 300 leading russophiles, including Karavelov, were thrown into prison. But the government also knew that political violence would cease only if Ferdinand could secure recognition. Both Stambolov and the prince believed that if they could persuade the sultan to recognize Ferdinand the other powers, even Russia, would follow suit. After the murder of Vŭlkovich Bulgaria therefore presented a note to the Porte arguing once more the symbiosis between Bulgaria and the Ottoman empire and suggesting that disorders such as the recent murder would cease only if Ferdinand were recognized. The Porte was not prepared to risk Russian displeasure.

One possible way to break out of the difficulty was for Ferdinand to marry and establish a dynasty; to overthrow one prince and replace him with a Russian-backed alternative would not be easy, but to remove a prince and a legitimate heir would be infinitely more difficult. A suitable candidate was found in Princess Marie Louise of Bourbon-Parma. Her family, however, insisted that any children of the marriage must be brought up as Roman Catholics. This would contravene article 38 of the Tŭrnovo constitution which stated that all but the first prince of Bulgaria must be of the Orthodox faith. In 1887 it had been decided that because Alexander had abdicated Ferdinand could be counted as the first prince, but that indulgence could not be stretched to any offspring.

Stambolov had in fact already decided that article 38 had to be revised. Only an Orthodox family would agree to the conditions stipulated therein, but the only Orthodox dynasties with brides to offer were the Russian and the Montenegrin; and Russia would veto the latter as firmly as it would oppose the former as long as Stambolov and Ferdinand remained in power. The bride therefore had to be either Catholic or Protestant and article 38 would have to be amended to make this possible. This was unpopular with the Church and Russian threats became so menacing that Stambolov told foreign representatives in Sofia that there was a danger of a Russian invasion, though the sŭbranie remained undaunted, dutifully enacting changes to article 38 which now allowed the first prince and his heir to be non-Orthodox. The change was ratified by a grand national assembly in May 1893. Ferdinand and Marie Louise had married in the previous month. The marriage was welcomed by the general population and when the unreconciled Metropolitan Kliment denounced the prince in a sermon in May the enraged congregation drove him out of his cathedral. There was an even greater national display of solidarity with the new princely couple when, nine months after the wedding, Princess Marie Louise gave birth to a son, the first to be born to a reigning Bulgarian monarch for 500 years. Ferdinand decided that the child should be called Boris after the great Bulgarian monarch of the tenth century. It was a hugely popular decision.

The beneficiary of this advance was once again Ferdinand rather than Stambolov. The birth and naming of the heir were Ferdinand's responsibility and for this he received popular support. The other preoccupation of most Bulgarians, their declining standard of living, was, most people believed, entirely the fault of Stambolov. The problem of social unrest was one of which Stambolov had neither experience nor knowledge. Government expenditure was rising as loan obligations had to be met and a number of development projects financed. But there were few extra sources of revenue except the peasantry and in 1892 the government decided to revert to tithe payments in cash; payment in kind had been restored in 1888 but by the early 1890s falling world prices for grain were depressing government returns. The peasants were dismayed. Many of them were facing increasing debt payments to private usurers and there was great anger that whilst the peasants were forced to pay more the well-paid civil servants were not. This enraged a number of younger members of the intelligentsia already alienated by Stambolov's strong-arm tactics and limitations upon individual liberties. They looked to the radical ideas of the socialists, rural or urban. Radicalism also took hold amongst a number of Macedonians who disliked Stambolov's policy of cooperation with the Porte and who felt frustrated by the long delays it involved; they had begun to question the linkage with the Exarchate and were looking towards the much more radical notions of socialism and a Balkan federation.

This was a long-term threat and in the summer of 1893 Stambolov was more concerned with a new challenge from within the constitutional framework. It came from a recently formed coalition which grouped around the newspaper it had founded, *Svobodno Slovo* (Free Speech). The coalition included a number of former ministers, a southern liberal faction, Radoslavov's northern liberal group, and the conservatives under Konstantin Stoilov. Their policy was based upon acceptance of Ferdinand as prince but rejection of Stambolov's method of rule. Those methods were amply displayed in July. In the elections of that month Stambolov and his National Liberal Party campaigned on their success in bringing about the royal wedding. They also used what had by now become the customary methods of bullying, intimidation, and manipulation to secure a parliamentary majority. It was grist to *Svobodno Slovo*'s mill.

The new opposition was also anxious to mend the breach with Russia, arguing that this could be achieved not, as the former opposition had asserted up to 1893, by the sacrifice of Ferdinand, but by the removal of Stambolov. For the latter there was now the increased danger that in the *Svobodno Slovo* group the prince had at last found an alternative government. The growing strength of the opposition only intensified Stambolov's determination to hold on to power and when supplementary elections were held early in 1894 he resorted to even greater measures of restraint with over twenty people being killed in one village near Razgrad. There were furious protests in many towns and petitions and letters of complaint poured in to the prince.

Ferdinand needed little encouragement to break with Stambolov. Relations between the two men had never been good, Stambolov once telling friends that he knew within two or three days of Ferdinand's arrival that he would bring suffering and hardship to Bulgaria, whilst the prince told his close associates that in his palace he preferred to have servants rather than advisers.[2] After 1890 relations between them deteriorated steadily but Ferdinand would not make a decisive move against Stambolov until he was certain he could rely on the support of the army. This he secured when the press broke a story that Stambolov had had an affair with the wife of General Mihail Savov, the minister of war. This was untrue but the two men could no longer work together and when the minister of war resigned his replacement was, at Ferdinand's insistence, entirely the prince's man. He was also already chief of the general staff and therefore had greater control over the army than his predecessors in either post. On the day on which Savov resigned, the Porte, sensing the danger Stambolov was in, granted further concessions to the Bulgarians in Macedonia, including berats for the appointment of exarchist bishops to the sees of Nevrokop (Gotse Delchev) and Veles. These were huge concessions but so devalued was Stambolov's political stock that they made almost no impact in Sofia. In May Ferdinand left for Vienna and

---

[2] Mateev, *Stambolov*, 67, 69.

whilst he was away *Svobodno Slovo* published a number of doctored letters between himself and his minister president; in self-defence Stambolov published the original versions in his own paper, *Svoboda* (Freedom), but one of these letters the prince regarded as private and he vented his rage in a telegram to his private secretary, Dimitŭr Stanchov,[3] who leaked the prince's message to *Svobodno Slovo*. It was an unseemly business indicative of the tortuous nature of Bulgarian politics and of the quality of the Bulgarian political press, but it destroyed Stambolov, who resigned a few days later on 18 May. Stoilov formed a new administration which was a coalition of northern and southern conservatives with Dimitŭr Tonchev's southern and Radoslavov's northern liberal groups.

Stambolov, and more particularly his methods, had outlived their purpose. After holding the country together in 1886 without resorting to the military dictatorship which many, including his minister president Radoslavov, wished to impose,[4] he had brought Ferdinand to Bulgaria, installed and kept him upon the throne, and provided him with a loyal and dependable government. Above all he had successfully defended the principality against the machinations of those, many of them backed by Russia, who would have compromised its independence. And he had secured major advances for the Bulgarian cause in Macedonia. He had had by necessity recourse to unsavoury methods to keep Ferdinand in power and these had been accepted as unavoidable by most of the population when there was a perceived danger. But that danger was less visible after 1892 and Stambolov's tough methods had therefore become more and more unpopular, as had his policies over the tithe. Yet despite all his successes he had not made recognition more likely. His tough methods had been justified by the argument that order must be preserved to secure recognition, but if, as seemed the case in 1894, there was no prospect for recognition there was therefore no longer any justification for Stambolov's violent methods.

Violence accompanied Stambolov into retirement, and to and even beyond the grave. The opposition press vilified him and one newspaper

---

[3] This is the transliteration of his name, but in later years when a biography of him was published in English, the name and the transliteration appeared as Dimitri Stancioff. The book was Nadejda Muir, *Dimitri Stancioff, Patriot and Cosmopolitan, 1864–1940* (London: John Murray, 1957).

[4] Radoslav Popov, 'Stefan Stambolov i Vasil Radoslavov v borba za politicheskata vlast v perioda na regentstvoto (1886–1887g)', *Istoricheski Pregled*, 37/1 (1991), 13–28.

declared that the flesh of such people should be 'torn from their bones'. The following day Stambolov was so viciously attacked that his hands had to be amputated and he died a few days later. His funeral procession was interrupted because one of the wheels on the gun carriage had been sabotaged and when it stopped at the point where the assault on Stambolov had taken place it was attacked by an angry mob; at the graveside obscenities were screamed into the face of Stambolov's widow, Polikseniya, the grave was desecrated even before the mourners had dispersed, and a year later the memorial tablet erected over it was demolished by a bomb. Some of Stambolov's supporters blamed the prince for these outrages but this was unlikely; he abhorred bloodshed, and shied away from major decisions, besides which he could scarcely gain from events which shamed Bulgaria on the international stage where he wished to play a major role. In fact, the culprits were almost certainly disaffected Macedonians, one of whose brothers had died under torture in a stambolovist jail.

3. THE RECOGNITION OF PRINCE FERDINAND, 1894–1896

Ferdinand had dropped his pilot in 1894, but he was not to reach the safe haven of recognition for another two years. Recognition was brought about by Stoilov's need to consolidate his regime at home, by changes in the personnel directing Russian foreign policy, and by growing international concern that the Ottoman empire was on the brink of collapse.

Stoilov's position was far from secure. His coalition was not well cemented and the prince regarded him as little more than a stopgap. Stoilov began his search for greater security by forming a new party, the National Party, which consisted of the northern conservatives and the southern unionist faction under Grigor Nachovich; the party's slogan was 'Freedom and Legality, Order and Recognition'. Stoilov's next step was to dissolve the stambolovist parliament and hold elections in September 1894. Despite his party's programme, Stoilov did not abjure the use of those methods of electoral management which he had condemned in Stambolov, and so firm was the government's hand at the polls that one of his ministers resigned in protest.

Despite the use of electoral management, the sŭbranie was less amenable than expected and Stoilov remained in office primarily because he had the support not only of the coalition parties but also of the tsanko-vists and other russophiles who had been won over by Stoilov's attitude towards Russia. Bulgaria, said the new minister president, did not wish to provoke Russia: 'If Germany and Austria and the other great powers are well disposed to Russia', he told the *Frankfurter Zeitung*, 'why should we, a small state, play the role of the dog which barks at her?'[5]

But still there was no thaw between St Petersburg and Sofia. There was growing concern in Russia at the state of the Ottoman empire, a concern prompted chiefly by a series of massacres in Armenia, and it was realized in the Russian capital that if the sultan's rule collapsed the Balkans would be massively destabilized and that in those circumstances Russia would have to come to some accommodation with Bulgaria. But the Russians were not confident that Stoilov had complete control over the sŭbranie or his cab-inet, and for its part the Bulgarian government was unwilling to commit itself to a new initiative in view of the illness of the tsar, besides which they knew if they took the initiative the Russians would drive a hard bargain.

The situation changed when the tsar died on 20 October. Ferdinand ordered requiem services to be held, and in his own name and that of the Bulgarian people sent telegrams of condolence to the new tsar, Nicholas II. Nicholas replied thanking Ferdinand for his message but he refused to allow a delegation from Bulgaria to come to Russia for his father's funeral. The Russians then let it be known that were a delegation to come from Bulgaria, perhaps to lay a wreath on Alexander III's grave, then it must be a delegation from the sŭbranie, not from Ferdinand or from any govern-ment appointed by him, because Russia still regarded both Ferdinand and his administration as illegal. It was also said that Russia would insist that Bulgaria take the initiative and that if recognition were to come about Prince Boris must first be received into the Orthodox Church.

There was clearly little prospect of an early reconciliation and Stoilov therefore undertook a series of measures intended to show his good intent towards Russia. These included the exclusion from the cabinet of the pro-Austrian Radoslavov, the release from prison of a number of russophiles, Karavelov included, and limitations on the stambolovist

---

[5] Quoted in Ivan Panaĭotov, *Rusiya, velikite sili i bŭlgarskiyat ŭupros sled izbora na knyaz Ferdinanda, (1887–1896)* (Sofia: Universitetska Biblioteka No. 247, 1941), 203.

press. None of these measures seemed to soften Russian attitudes and therefore Stoilov eventually accepted that Bulgaria would have to take the initiative and it was agreed in May 1895 that a delegation from the sŭbranie should go to Russia to lay a wreath on the grave of the late tsar. The delegation was to be headed by Metropolitan Kliment and included such prominent figures as the poet and novelist Ivan Vazov. It left Bulgaria in June.

It returned the following month with little to report other than that Russian terms were unlikely to be any easier than those already hinted at, and that prominent amongst them would be the conversion of Prince Boris. This was something on which the prince alone could make a final decision and Ferdinand therefore undertook a series of consultations with his relatives and with Pope Leo XIII, who told him bluntly that abdication would be preferable to the conversion of Boris. Ferdinand was genuinely torn between his faith and his duty to his adopted nation. The latter told him that conversion would take away the anti-dynasts last weapon. It was also known that should the Armenian massacres bring about the collapse of the Ottoman empire Bulgaria could only secure a reasonable share of the spoils in European Turkey with Russia's blessing. By the autumn the pressure on Ferdinand was growing with calls in the sŭbranie for conversion, to which Stoilov finally added his voice, threatening that the government would resign by the end of the parliamentary session in January if Ferdinand did not come to a decision. Were Stoilov to go the only alternative administration seemed to be one under Radoslavov which would not favour reconciliation with Russia; whether the nation, whose hopes of reconciliation with Russia had been raised, would accept this was doubtful and the prince was presented with the choice between the conversion of Boris and probable anarchy in the country. Ferdinand, after once more consulting with his relations and with the Pope, with much the same result, finally gave way and on 22 January announced that Boris would be received into the Orthodox Church on 2 February. The tsar was asked to stand as godfather and this he agreed to do *in absentia*.

With that the last obstacle to Boris's conversion was removed and the ceremony was performed on the appointed day by the Exarch. Ferdinand was recognized by Russia on 19 February, the anniversary of San Stefano, and the other powers rapidly followed suit. At a celebratory dinner in the palace in Sofia the Exarch underlined the pivotal role the Church had played and was still playing in the evolution of the Bulgarian nation; he told the prince, 'For the Bulgarian people its faith, the Eastern Orthodox faith, is inseparable from its nationality. For it the true Bulgarian is the Orthodox Bulgarian.'[6]

4. PARTIES, PARTIZANSTVO, AND THE POLITICAL SYSTEM

In the years between liberation and the recognition of Ferdinand the mould of the Bulgarian political system was cast. It was to last, with some interruptions, until the end of the second world war, and was to be based on the instability of the political parties, the manipulation of those parties and their leaders by the prince, and by *partizanstvo*, the system of clientelism and political jobbery which made that manipulation possible. So complex, convoluted, and confusing were the changes in party structure after 1894 that a full description of them has been confined to a separate appendix. It is sufficient to note here that the effects of the frequent divisions within the parties were that Bulgaria was denied the stability which solid party organization can offer, that no strong political personality emerged or remained long enough in office to challenge the growing power of the prince, and that the very multiplicity of parties enabled the latter to play one off against another. The frequent splintering of the parties enabled power to slip steadily from the assembly to the palace.

Stambolov's great achievement had been to show that Bulgaria could exist as an independent state, even if it was treated as an international pariah. But the manner in which he exercised power did considerable damage to the Bulgarian political system. He did not introduce any new method of electoral management and he was not the only one to use force; anti-stambolovists in Dupnitsa in the elections to the 1887 GNA savagely killed two government deputies and a teacher. But Stambolov made such persistent and effective use of electoral management and manipulation that they became entrenched in the Bulgarian political system and political psyche; from 1886 until the 1990s only two national

---

[6] Hristo Dermendjiev, *Tsar Boris III. Zhivot i deli v dati i dokumenti* (Sofia: Istoricheska Biblioteka Tsarstvo Bŭlgariya, 1990), 25.

elections were relatively free and open. One consequence of this was that the majority of the population showed little interest in the established political process or the parties within it. Turnout figures in the late nineteenth century were generally very low and when the majority of the peasantry became politically active at the end of that century they turned to a radical alternative rather than to the established, parliamentary parties.

The methodology of electoral control was relatively simple. The first priority was to ensure control of the all-powerful electoral bureaux. These usually consisted of the first voters to appear at the polls and they rapidly became the mechanism by which opponents could be excluded, opposition votes discarded, multiple and illegal votes cast for the required party, and a host of other devices used to secure the desired result. And if oppositionists survived the election they could always be expelled from the assembly when it reviewed all electoral returns and annulled those where irregularities were deemed to have occurred.

Stambolov also entrenched rather than initiated the Bulgarian system of clientelism known as *partizanstvo*. Immediately after the liberation the new government in Sofia had needed to recruit a large number of civil servants to run the new administration, and it attracted qualified men to these posts by offering high salaries. The demand for civil servants was soon satiated but by then the expectation had been created amongst the suitably qualified that they could reasonably anticipate employment at high salary in the government machine, and those that did not find such employment refused to take any other. At the same time the commercial bourgeoisie was not sufficiently developed to absorb these out-of-work would-be civil servants; this produced a form of civil service or white collar proletariat. Once the monolithic Liberal Party had fractured opposition parties found it easy to promise employment to these unemployed, potential administrators, and if such a party were included in government one of its first tasks would be to clear out the existing civil servants to make room for its own followers; those affected ranged from regional prefects at the top down through sub-prefects, mayors, appointed town and village officials, school inspectors, and even, at the lower levels, policemen. When Stoilov came to power in 1894 all but three of the twenty-four regional prefects were replaced within a month as were seventy of the eighty-four rural magistrates and police inspectors; by the end of 1895 almost the entire complement of the civil service and the police force had been changed.

The evil of *partizanstvo* poisoned much of the political system. Any attempt by a government, however well intentioned, to expand the sphere of civil service responsibility, be it to introduce a rudimentary district health service, advisory councils for farmers, government-sponsored veterinary supervision, or a factory inspectorate, were immediately viewed with suspicion as merely a device to increase the number of jobs at the disposal of the incumbent ministry. The proliferation of parties bred *partizanstvo*, *partizanstvo* produced patronage, and patronage provided political power.

The system had also so evolved that ministerial changes took place before rather than after a general election. Therefore the latter was not, as in many western democracies, a device to test popular opinion and secure a legitimate government, but a means to provide a pre-chosen ministry with a dependable majority in parliament. This meant that once a new ministry had been installed one of its first tasks was to organize the elections to give it that dependable majority; as a conservative commentator later wrote, 'consulting the electorate does not take place so that the rulers can find out what is the will of the masses, but so that that the masses can be told what is the will of the rulers.'[7] In this process the recently installed office holders would turn to local figures who controlled blocks of votes, be they moneylenders, merchants, or employers. Those who controlled these votes seldom had any party loyalty but sold their votes to the highest bidder; and the office holder was almost always able to outbid anyone else by offering cash, contracts, bribes, minor offices, licences to cut forests, or other favours at the disposal of the local or national civil servant. Not all central and local government posts were involved in this process but many were and they were essential to the functioning of *partizanstvo*.

The manipulation of the political process was made much easier by the proliferation of parties, smaller and weaker parties being much easier to dominate than larger ones. Until the Liberal Party began to disintegrate in the mid-1880s *partizanstvo* was less common, but by the turn of the century it had become much more prevalent because the increasing number of parties allowed the prince to play one off against the others. It also meant that should he wish to displace a government there would be a larger pool of alternative leaders. And should he consider a change of administration

---

[7] Stoyan Mihaĭlovski, 'Kak zapadat i se provalyat dŭrzhavite', in Elenkov and Daskalov, *Zashto sme takira?*, 102–16, 115.

desirable, the head of state simply had to manufacture a crisis, internal or external, then dismiss the incumbent ministry and appoint a new one which would then call a general election to secure a majority in the parliament. Tellingly, when informed in May 1916 that there were rising concerns at food shortages, the minister president of the day's first reaction was, 'Probably the king wants to provoke a ministerial crisis.'[8]

Ferdinand was to become a master of *partizanstvo*. In this he was aided by his possession and skilful use of compendious, secretly collected files on individual politicians. Ferdinand exercised particularly tight control over the vital ministries of war and of foreign affairs, the first giving him internal security and the second allowing him to fulfil his ambition of becoming a decisive figure in Balkan and perhaps European affairs. The contest between executive and legislature, begun in the early days of the new principality, had been decided in favour of the prince. Ferdinand had created a 'personal regime'.

His use of political power to create a personal regime was to be copied with varying degrees of success by other holders of the supreme executive post, though not necessarily with the same identity of the personal and the national interest. Ferdinand, true to Saxe-Coburg tradition, became a generous benefactor to his adopted country, particularly in the arena of science and technology, but he saw himself as a monarch whose function was to play as large a part as possible on the European stage. He was to dream in 1912 of a triumphal coronation in Constantinople and in the following year he seriously considered asking the great powers to grant the island of Samothrace not to Bulgaria but to him personally. When the first world war ended in defeat for Bulgaria Ferdinand went to Berlin where he returned all his medals and decorations to the Kaiser Wilhelm II on the ground that the Bulgarian army had not been worthy of them.[9] In the words of one Bulgarian historian 'Ferdinand was neither a russophobe nor a germanophile, nor even a bulgarophile—he was solely and simply a ferdinandophile.' He used Bulgaria 'as a trampoline to achieve his own maniacal egocentric desires'.[10]

In the years after recognition in 1896 those desires were one of the factors which were to take Bulgaria twice to war, though on the first occasion his own and the national interest were in harmony.

[8] Ilchev, *Radoslavov*, 184.   [9] Kovachev, *Zapiski*, 162.
[10] Mateev, *Stambolov*, 214. And for the Samothrace idea, ibid. 196.

6

Prince Ferdinand's Personal Rule, 1896–1912

1. THE MACEDONIAN QUESTION, 1894–1898

The restoration of relations with Russia in 1896 meant that at last Bulgarian political life could return to some form of normality and stability. Politicians exiled for their opposition to Ferdinand and Stambolov were allowed to return and in 1898 the contentious issue of the pro-Russian Bulgarian officers who had left the country in 1886–7 was at last solved.[1] Their return was greeted by the population at large but resented by many army officers who had remained in Bulgaria and who regarded their former colleagues as little more than deserters, nor could they be unaware that because many of those who had left held senior ranks their return would produce promotion congestion.

The return of almost all the officers—Benderev remained one of a handful of exceptions—pleased the Russians but there were other questions which remained at issue between St Petersburg and Sofia. One of them was Macedonia. The Russians still hankered for a reconciliation between the Exarchist and Patriarchist Churches, something which the Bulgarians could not contemplate, not least because it would have weakened their position in Macedonia.

When he became minister president Stoilov had neither the will nor the desire to restrain the Macedonians as Stambolov had done. With the Ottoman empire apparently in fragile condition there seemed little point in pursuing the stambolovist policy of cooperation with Constantinople,

[1] For this issue, see A. K. Martynenko, *Russko-Bogarskiye otnosheniya v 1894–1902gg* (Kiev: Kiev University Press, 1967), *passim*; Kovachev, *Zapiski*, 72–80.

besides which Stoilov needed Macedonian support on the domestic front. He had done little therefore to oppose the formation either of a new Macedonian central committee late in 1894 or of armed cheti in the mountains along the border with the Ottoman empire in 1895; one of the latter, to great popular rejoicing, captured and held the town of Melnik for a number of days. By the end of 1895 the Macedonian movement in Bulgaria had strengthened considerably and in its second congress the central committee renamed itself the Supreme Macedonian Committee; this was a reaction to the foundation in 1893 of what was later to become the Internal Macedonian-Adrianople Revolutionary Organization (IMRO)[2] which aimed for Macedonian autonomy rather than union with Bulgaria and which was soon to be in bitter rivalry with the Bulgarian 'supremacists'.

If Stoilov did not intervene to prevent these activities he could not afford to endorse them openly. Even after recognition his government wanted good relations with Russia; to foster disturbances in Turkey-in-Europe would only alienate the Russians whose attention was still focused on Asia and who in 1897 were to conclude an agreement with Vienna to keep the Balkans 'on ice'. Both powers exercised pressure in the Balkan capitals to ensure that the status quo was not disturbed. Rather than openly encourage the Macedonian activists Stoilov put forward proposals for widespread reforms of the administration in European Turkey. These the Porte accepted but failed to implement.

In putting pressure on the Ottoman government the Stoilov administration sought the cooperation of the other Balkan states. When the Greeks rejected the idea of a joint approach to Constantinople the Bulgarians turned to the Serbs, with whom a secret agreement on peaceful collaboration in Macedonia was concluded; it was an implicit recognition that Serbia had a legitimate claim to part of Macedonia and therefore a rejection of the stambolovist concept that Bulgaria should one day inherit all of it.

In 1897 the Bulgarians, taking advantage of the outbreak of war between the Ottoman empire and Greece over the future of Crete, secured berats for the dioceses of Kukush, Strumitsa, and Melnik,

---

[2] Though it came into common usage, IMRO is not an entirely accurate acronym. The full title of the organization was The Internal Macedonian and Adrianople Revolutionary Organization. The acronym derived from its Slavonic name, VMORO, is sometimes used by historians and appears in the titles of some post-Yugoslav Macedonian political parties.

together with the right to appoint Bulgarian commercial agents in Salonika, Skopje, Bitola, Dedeagach (Alexandroupolis), and Adrianople, but any further advances were prevented by Russia and Austria-Hungary's decision to freeze the situation in the Balkans. It was therefore a matter of considerable embarrassment to Stoilov when, in November 1897, a large arms cache was discovered after a Turkish landowner had been murdered in Vinitsa in Macedonia. Other caches were revealed after those arrested for the murder had been tortured. There was a good deal of irony in this because although the Bulgarian government was held responsible for secreting the weapons the latter belonged not to the supremacists but to IMRO.

Relations between the supremacists and IMRO were deteriorating and were soon to become an issue of critical importance. Both groups saw autonomy as the immediate objective but for IMRO the ultimate goal was the inclusion of Macedonia in a Balkan federation; the supremacists intended that Macedonia should follow the Rumelian example and move through autonomy to unification with the principality. IMRO also criticized the supremacists for allowing Bulgarian political considerations to affect their campaign, alleging that Ferdinand and the government in Sofia turned support for the Macedonian cause on and off according to their own political calculations or because of pressure from the great powers. This accusation could not be denied. Bulgarian government support for the Macedonians had been reined in when Ferdinand wished to secure recognition and after Russian and Austro-Hungarian diplomatic intervention had insisted that the Balkan status quo must not be disturbed. The outcome of the disagreements between IMRO and the supremacists had been that IMRO formed its own cheti for whose activities, as the Vinitsa incident had shown, the Sofia administration could, mistakenly, be held responsible. Meanwhile, within Macedonia itself IMRO rapidly increased its strength and established a sophisticated system of local self-government in the area. In 1900 its leadership, based in Salonika, successfully organized a takeover of the Sofia supreme committee. For over a year the government in Sofia had little or no control over either branch of the Macedonian movement.

By the end of the 1890s the Bulgarian position in Macedonia had worsened considerably both because of advancing IMRO activity inside Macedonia and because of setbacks on the diplomatic front. After recognition Russia had given little or no support to the Bulgarians and had continued to press for an end to the schism with the Patriarchate. The Bulgarian position in Macedonia had benefited from the berats at the beginning of the Graeco-Turkish war but had worsened after it because the Greek government, in order to re-establish its position in Macedonia, had opted to cooperate with the Porte against the Exarchists. At the same time, the Porte had driven a wedge between the Bulgarians and the Serbs. Despite the agreement of 1897 between Sofia and Belgrade there was a series of disputes in Macedonia itself. In Kumanovo there was a long-running tussle over the ownership of the town's major Orthodox church and there was fierce competition for ecclesiastical supremacy in Skopje, the key to domination over northern Macedonia. It was a competition which, thanks in no small measure to Russian help, was won by the Serbs when one of their priests, Firmilian, was nominated as administrator to the metropolitan of Skopje in 1897.

Bulgaria in fact appeared to be almost isolated internationally. After the war of 1897 and the apparent rejuvenation of the Ottoman empire Russia had turned its attention once more to Asia, reinforcing its desire for stability in the Balkans. Austria-Hungary, the major European Roman Catholic power, was still affronted by the conversion of Boris; Germany also wanted stability in the Balkans because it was consolidating its close relations with the Ottoman empire, whilst Britain and France were preoccupied by colonial issues. Within the Balkans the Macedonian question prevented close relations with Serbia and Greece and there was little to be gained from friendship with Montenegro or Romania, though Ferdinand visited both countries. He also paid two visits in the late 1890s to Constantinople but the Porte suspected him and his government of fomenting unrest in Macedonia and the visits produced no significant gains for the Bulgarians. Both Ferdinand and his ministers were conscious of the dangers of this apparent isolation. And their awareness of these dangers was greatly sharpened by rapidly intensifying political, financial, and social crises within Bulgaria.

2. THE ORC FIASCO, 1894–1899

The recognition of Ferdinand earned Stoilov some political credit and this, plus the liberal use of government influence, brought him a comfortable majority in the elections he called in the autumn of 1896.

Recognition and the return to relative political normality had also allowed Stoilov to place greater emphasis on one of his main political objectives, the modernization of Bulgaria; he wished, he said, to make Bulgaria the 'Belgium of the Balkans'. He had made a significant step in this direction in 1894 with his encouragement of industry act which protected home manufacturing through tariffs and encouraged it by a variety of subsidies. Recognition also made it easier to secure external loans for capital projects such as railway construction. Not for the first time railway development was to be the cause of a major domestic political crisis.

In 1878 the railways in Rumelia were owned and operated by the Oriental Railway Company (ORC) whose headquarters were in Vienna. The most important of the ORC's lines was the Rumelian portion of the international trunk line and when that was completed in the summer of 1888 it was agreed that the BDZh should operate the section between the Serbian border and the exchange facilities at Saranbeĭ (Septemvri) where the ORC would assume responsibility. It was obviously irksome to the Bulgarian regime that a large proportion of the country's most important line should be beyond its control, but this was much more than a question of national pride or administrative convenience. It was one of vital economic importance, especially for the southern Bulgarians who had a powerful voice in Stoilov's cabinet. Their main complaint was over the ORC's pricing policies. The BDZh kept its rates at the same level as those in Austria-Hungary and Serbia, but the ORC charged far more; for example, it levied 7.5 cents per ton per kilometre for carrying grain, a major export commodity in southern Bulgaria, whereas the rate on the rest of the international line was three cents per ton per kilometre. The ORC also attempted to prevent Stambolov constructing a line from Yambol to Burgas because that would offer southern Bulgarian exporters access to a port not under ORC control, and when these attempts failed the ORC tried to force traffic to use the line to Dedeagach which it did control. There was a further complication. Stoilov's encouragement of industry act had stipulated that raw materials for, and the products of Bulgarian manufactories would be carried on the state railways at preferential rates. These rates could not be enforced on the ORC and thus manufacturers in southern Bulgaria were placed at an unfair disadvantage.

The southern lobby in Stoilov's cabinet demanded redress. Stoilov dared not nationalize the ORC line because this would antagonize the

European financial markets to which Bulgaria was looking with increasing appetite. Furthermore, the owners of the ORC by the second half of the 1890s included the Deutsche Bank which was becoming interested in railway projects in Asia Minor; this would eventually become part of the fabled Berlin to Baghdad railway and therefore there was little likelihood that the ORC lines would be offered for sale, even if the Bulgarian government could afford to purchase them, which it could not. The only alternative was to build another line which would bypass the ORC tracks. This in the summer of 1896 Stoilov reluctantly agreed to do. The so-called parallel line would run from the BDZh-ORC junction at Saranbeĭ to Plovdiv and then northwards to Nova Zagora where it would join with a second new line which was to link it with the Yambol–Burgas line. Burgas would thereby be joined to the rest of the BDZh network and some at least of the disadvantages suffered by the southern Bulgarians would be alleviated.

The problem was that the parallel line had to be paid for. Governmental revenues were obviously insufficient, the more so since 1894 when, as part of his modernizing programme, Stoilov had replaced the tithe with a land tax which produced less revenue; so too did customs and excise after the encouragement of industry act exempted from all tariffs the raw materials for specified manufactured items. Stoilov borrowed some money from the Agricultural Savings Bank but was thwarted when he tried to take out the second part of an international loan granted in 1892; the Deutsche Bank vetoed the idea. To make matters worse there was a dearth of capital in the European markets because of the emergency in South Africa. Finally, in December 1898, a Franco-Austrian-German consortium agreed to lend the Bulgarian government 290 million francs. Much of the loan was to be spent converting existing loans, on terms not advantageous to Bulgaria, but the rest was to go not to building the parallel line but to purchasing the operating rights of the ORC in southern Bulgaria. There was outrage. When the sŭbranie debated the loan proposal in December the galleries were packed and the vote was allegedly carried in scenes almost as chaotic as those of 1883 when the government had agreed to the purchase of the Rusé–Varna line; but this time it did not much matter because in the event the Ottoman authorities, bowed by pressure from the Deutsche Bank and the German embassy in Constantinople, refused to sanction the sale of the ORC's operating rights.

Since 1896 Stoilov had been losing the confidence of the political classes of Bulgaria. The opposition had shown signs of greater cohesion in 1897, alleging, after the elections of the previous year, that the Stoilov regime, which had promised to cleanse the Bulgarian political machine, was every bit as dictatorial as that of Stambolov. There was also widespread anger at the failure of Stoilov to make further progress in Macedonia, and at the isolation of Bulgaria in European affairs. The prince, too, had begun to distance himself from his first minister. Stoilov, whose political problems had been compounded by his own declining health, resigned on 13 January 1899.

Following Stoilov's departure a new administration was formed under Dimitŭr Grekov who was close to the stambolovist National Liberal Party, though his cabinet also included members of other liberal groups, a conservative, and three independents. The elections following the formation of the new administration were more open than any since 1886, thanks in part to minor electoral reforms enacted by Stoilov. They were, however, more violent; in five constituencies the disorders were such that the voting had to be postponed and in those constituencies where voting did take place five people were killed and twenty wounded.

The new government was soon under vicious verbal assault on the question of the ORC. At a conference in March 1899 the company dictated a victor's peace to the Bulgarian government. The ORC was to retain all its existing privileges and the government had to agree not to build any new line which might compete with those of the company, to exempt the company from stamp duty, and to rent to the company that part of the parallel line which had been built, the latter concession being a clear infringement of the 1884 railway act; the ORC was to be allowed to claim compensation from the government for any losses incurred as a result of war; it was not even required to recognize Bulgarian as an official language in its administration, and in some circumstances it had the right to compensation from the revenues of the BDZh. The ORC's only concessions were a slight reduction in its general rates, an agreement to abide by the preferential rates proscribed in the encouragement of industry act, and the setting up of a new administrative zone based on Plovdiv, the existing ones being outside Bulgaria in Constantinople, Adrianople, and Salonika. The sŭbranie endorsed the agreement but only after fierce debate in which one deputy stated that foreign interests now had such power in the country that this was 'the beginning of the end of the state as an independent entity'.[3]

Grekov could offer little to sweeten the bitter pill of national humiliation. St Petersburg had again ruled out any prospect of action in Macedonia and the Bulgarian minister president therefore had to tell his nation that the great powers alone could bring about any significant change in that area; the only grain of comfort was that Grekov persuaded the Porte not to issue the berat on Firmilian's appointment as administrator of the Skopje archdiocese. Grekov's immediate problem, however, was not with public opinion at large or in the assembly, but within his own cabinet where the most destructive tensions were those between the stambolovists and radoslavists. In October 1899 these tensions drove Grekov to resignation. His successor was the minister of education, Todor Ivanchov, a non-party man who had the backing of the radoslavists.

3. THE AGRARIAN CRISIS AND THE BIRTH OF BANU, 1899–1901

Ivanchov's most pressing immediate problem was finance. The government needed money for capital projects to develop the country's infrastructure, for the army, and not least for the servicing of its newly acquired loan. A small loan from a consortium dominated by the Banque de Paris et de Pays Bas (Paribas) went some way to cover an impending budget deficit of 26.3 million leva but it involved a pledge by the government to assign revenue from the banderolle, a tax on processed tobacco, to Paribas for the years 1901 to 1904, this being the first time that any item of national income had been specifically earmarked for the repayment of a loan. It was also the beginning of a decade of French domination of Bulgarian loans. But if railways and harbours were to be built and the army strengthened, the government needed greater sums than those Paribas or anyone else was prepared to lend. That money therefore would have to be raised internally, an exercise which, it was hoped, would also enhance Bulgaria's reputation in the capital markets and avoid the humiliating earmarking

---

[3] Tsvetana Todorova, *Diplomaticheska Istoriya na vŭnshnite zaemi na Bŭlgariya, 1888–1912* (Sofia: Nauka i izkustvo, 1971), 252.

of specific revenues for loan servicing. Unfortunately, this policy did not work, and rather than enhancing Bulgaria's external standing it helped precipitate the most serious crisis since 1878, a crisis which, unlike those of 1881–3 and 1886–7, involved not the small politically active elite but most of the peasant masses of the nation; at its height it was a struggle against the entire political system not merely one for control of it.

Some sources of internal revenue were easily tapped. Ferdinand's decision to forgo half his civil list for 1900 was welcomed and there was little or no objection to a 7 per cent reduction in officers' and officials' pay, or to a cut in the military budget in 1900. But these were drops in the financial ocean. The government needed large sums and with industry and commerce relatively little developed, and with the treaty of Berlin pegging tariff levels, there was only one source of such moneys: the country's agrarian base, that is the peasantry.

In October 1899 the government announced that for the years 1900 to 1904 the land tax would be replaced by a tithe in kind on arable land. This, it was believed, would raise more revenue than the land tax. But the decision indicated ignorance of or indifference to conditions amongst the peasant mass of the nation. There had been a series of bad harvests, the worst of which was that of 1899 itself; by the end of the year the Agricultural Savings Bank was distributing relief, most of it in the form of grain, to no fewer than 60,000 families. By 1901, 301 villagers were listed as being completely ruined by debt and in the hands of the usurers, and a further 470 were on the verge of ruin. A major cause of the problem was that whilst incomes were depressed by poor harvests expenditure was rising, primarily through indebtedness. In an economy where banks were almost unknown outside the largest towns the usurer was king. In some cases the peasant agreed to sell his crop to the creditor before it was harvested and at a price set by the creditor. This price was frequently far below the market value and the peasant's return so low that he was forced back into debt later in the year. This selling of crops 'on the stalk' had been banned by a law of 1880 and there had been efforts to limit the powers of the usurer, but these enactments were seldom implemented. As was so often the case, legislation for the good of the many was ineffective because its implementation depended on the few who gained from the malpractices that law was designed to eliminate.

Taxation was another problem. By 1897 average taxation per capita was 29.52 leva compared to 15.31 leva a decade earlier. One of the main reasons for the rise in the tax burden was the increases in indirect taxation. In 1879, 19 per cent of total tax revenue had come from indirect taxation whilst in 1900 the figure was 37 per cent; and between 1903 and 1907 revenue from indirect exceeded that from direct taxation for the first time since 1879. The tax system also discriminated against those on the land. In 1901 it was calculated that an income of 5,400 leva per annum from one of the professions would require a tax payment of 162 leva whilst the same income derived from working the land would incur taxes of 2,565 leva. In addition to this disparity, there was also that between facilities in the towns and those in the villages. In the latter roads and postal services were poor and telephones virtually unknown; few villages had secondary schools, and in 1901 of Bulgaria's 504 doctors only 12 had rural practices, and only 2 of the 102 pharmacies were in non-urban communities, and they were seasonal facilities in spa resorts. To the peasant it seemed that those who paid the most received the least.

The increasing financial pressure on the peasantry and the growing disparity between urban and rural life not only widened the gap between the peasant and the urban professional but also produced a widespread feeling of malaise, pithily expressed in the contemporary saying, 'ot tursko po-losho' (things are worse than under the Turks). They also helped to give rise to the most original political phenomenon to appear in modern Bulgaria: the Bulgarian Agrarian National Union (BANU).

The impetus for the formation of an agrarian organization came from a populism derived ideologically from the narodniks of tsarist Russia and applied by the native intelligentsia, in particular the teachers. It was a recreation of the alliance which had driven the vŭzrazhdane. Narodnik ideas had influenced Bulgarian activists even before the liberation and afterwards they continued to be expressed through writers such as Todor Vlaĭkov. The teachers were particularly susceptible to such ideas, their susceptibility being considerably increased by their poor pay and working conditions. They called for the formation of agrarian societies, the first of which appeared in the Varna and Tŭrnovo regions. The societies were greatly encouraged by *Selski Vestnik* (Village Herald), which was first published in the summer of 1893 with a print run of 4,000, and which was produced by the youth section of the *chitalishte* in the village of Musina in the Tŭrnovo region. In 1896, again in the Varna region, Nikola Holevich founded the first Bulgarian agrarian society; Holevich soon began publishing a series of newspapers, the most influential of which was *Zemedelska Zashtita* (Agrarian Defence) which first appeared in September 1899. Most of these publications were relatively short-lived but their cumulative effect was to spur peasants and their supporters within the intelligentsia to found societies in their own localities. The tithe announcement accelerated this process; in the three years up to the announcement on the tithe about 150 local peasant associations had been founded, but after it they were being set up at the rate of thirty per month.

The mobilization of the peasantry was strongest in the north-eastern centres of Varna, Tŭrnovo, and Pleven but it remained uncoordinated until a congress met in Pleven in December 1899. The Pleven congress had 845 delegates from 45 of Bulgaria's 71 districts. It was here that BANU was founded.

BANU emphatically denied any party affiliation or association. It was, it said, a lobby or pressure group. Its programme was intensely practical. It called for commassation, or the consolidation of separate strips into compact holdings; it wanted to find the means to provide the peasant with cheap credit and so release him from the grip of the usurer; it demanded cheap and reliable legal advice for the peasant, the lawyer being near the usurer in the agrarians' list of demons; and it intended to conduct propaganda on behalf of the peasant and of the agricultural sector. It was avowedly non-party political, hostility to the established sŭbranie parties being strongly felt amongst the delegates; one delegate described the political parties as 'the gangrene which will destroy beautiful Bulgaria'[4] and the congress changed the name of the local associations from 'druzhini' (battalions), because this word was used by the stambolovists for their party units, to 'druzhbi' (friendly associations).

The centrepiece of its campaign, however, was the demand for an immediate abandonment of tithe in kind. This was loathed by the peasants. It involved inspection and evaluation by government officials, always an opportunity for corruption, and the delays this caused could deprive Bulgarian sellers of the advantage of being in the market before their competitors from further north. In many cases the delays meant that the crops declined in quality or even rotted. The peasants assumed that the government had restored the tithe in kind because world prices in

⁴ Vladislav Topalov, 'Politicheska deinost na bŭlgarskiya zemedelski sŭyuz prez 1900–1901g', *Izvestiya na Instituta za Istoriya*, 10 (1962), 61–119, 79.

grain had been rising since the mid-1890s and that the government would impose whatever form of taxation brought it the most return, whatever the interests or condition of those who paid it.

After the sŭbranie had agreed to the reversion to the tithe in kind in January 1900 BANU concentrated on trying to persuade the prince not to sign the bill. Petitions were sent to the palace and again public meetings were organized, some of them being enormous by Bulgarian standards; one in Tŭrnovo was attended by an estimated 20,000 people. In March Ferdinand said he would receive no more petitions and could not understand why people would not accept a decision made by the elected assembly. The BANU leadership still wanted to keep the campaign within lawful channels, though there was a sharper edge to their general propaganda which now called not only for the end of the tithe in kind but also for an end to Ferdinand's personal regime. The campaign also became violent, the major confrontation between protesters and the authorities occurring in Darankulak in the Bulgarian Dobrudja. In clashes between troops and protesters in the village on 19 May between 120 and 150 people were killed, including two officers and a number of soldiers; over 800 demonstrators were wounded. The government had already invoked extraordinary powers and it clearly had the strength and the support of the army. BANU therefore recognized that it could not prevail against the authorities and once again did all it could to confine the discontent to legal channels; it arranged two large rallies to demand the end of the tithe in kind and the formation of a non-party government which must organize free elections; if it did not BANU was ready to go to extremes to end the present dictatorial rule. In an impressive show of strength BANU also participated in the local elections of August 1900, after which some 120 communes were under agrarian control.

By the elections the agitation had passed its peak with the peasants now concentrating on bringing in the harvest, but the political establishment had been rudely shaken and the long-term effects of the crisis were profound. BANU had not achieved its objectives but it had shown an elemental if as yet unrefined power, and a deep hatred had been sown between it and the crown. Subsequent inquiries into the disorders showed that the problems had been aggravated by the poor quality of local officials, many of whom owed their appointment to *partizanstvo*. The army too had been bruised. Many officers were still embittered by the reduction in their salaries and now they were having to perform police duties which they and their men hated, whilst nothing was being done to advance Bulgarian interests in Macedonia. The teachers, too, were offended. The government had decreed that they must take part in the evaluation of the tithe; thereafter Bulgaria's teachers were almost always to be found in the ranks of the most radical political movements; not only had they access, through their education, to radical ideas, but their poor working conditions, irregular and low pay, and unhygienic school buildings—the death rate from TB amongst teachers was twice as high as that for the population as a whole—bred anger and resentment. The most important result of the crisis, however, was that the peasants, already alienated from the established or sŭbranie political parties, now had a new focus for their loyalty. *Partizanstvo* and political corruption would ensure that the potential of BANU was not immediately realized but, as Stoilov perceived, the parties in the national assembly no longer had any representative function or significance for the peasant whose real defender was BANU, which, as Stoilov also saw, was already the strongest political force in the country.

4. MONEY AND MACEDONIA, 1900–1903

Gravely weakened by the agrarian crisis the Ivanchov cabinet resigned in December 1900, though Ivanchov himself remained in office until elections were held in January. In 1903 members of his cabinet became the first in Bulgarian history to be arraigned before the State Court, the charge being infringement of the constitution.

The 1901 elections were uncharacteristically free of government interference and no party secured an overall majority; BANU had thirteen deputies in the new assembly and there were three socialists. A coalition was formed in which Petko Karavelov, the leader of the Democratic Party (the tsankovists) became minister president and Stoyan Danev of the Progressive Liberal Party minister for foreign affairs. The minister of war, who was, as always, Ferdinand's nominee, was General Stefan Paprikov; he had close connections with the Macedonian activists and his appointment indicated that it would be Ferdinand who controlled policy with regard to Macedonia.

Danev was a russophile and his nomination showed that the new administration would lean towards a pro-Russian policy but the fact that it was Karavelov who became minister president proved that the new cabinet's chief priority was finance rather than foreign affairs. Bulgaria now had foreign debts of over 200 million leva and 30 per cent of government revenue was being absorbed by charges on them. To make matters worse heavy rain had damaged the harvest and the yields from the tithe in kind were about a quarter below expectations. The new government, which wanted to boost its standing in the sŭbranie, abolished the hated levy and at the same time made the vainglorious promise that it would never in future allow the hypothecation of a particular source of government revenue for the servicing of foreign loans.

That did not make it any easier to find the new loan which was desperately needed. Danev predictably sought help in St Petersburg but was told only that Russia did not have money enough to lend to Bulgaria and that even if it did the 50 million francs Sofia was asking for 'would, for your ailing and ruined finances, be like a glass of champagne for a dying man; it would give him a strength which would last but a few minutes'.[5] The Russians did give a small loan of 4 million francs but this was only short term and merely added to the desperate need for a substantial borrowing. That was secured from Paribas which agreed to lend Bulgaria 125 million francs but the conditions were tough: the revenues from the taxes on both raw and processed tobacco would be earmarked for servicing the loan; the government would introduce a state monopoly over the manufacture and sale of tobacco products; and the government would need the consent of Paribas to any change in Bulgaria's financial structures. In December Karavelov submitted the loan plan to the sŭbranie which rejected it; the following month Karavelov handed the minister presidency to Danev. The latter then went to St Petersburg where it was agreed that Paribas should loan 92 million francs and the Russians 14 million, but the conditions were hardly less onerous. Nevertheless, Danev accepted them and in July persuaded the sŭbranie to do likewise. When they agreed to the loan both the Russians and the French had made it known that they did not want Bulgaria to follow a forward policy in Macedonia.

By now it was as difficult to solve the Macedonian problem as it was to balance the budget. All the powers, not only France and Russia, wanted the Balkans to remain stable but with Greek, Serbian, and Bulgarian

[5] Simeon Damyanov, *Frenskoto ikonomichesko pronikvane v Bŭlgariya ot osvobozhdenieto do pŭrvata svetovna voina (1878–1914)* (Sofia: BAN, 1971), 121.

nationalist propaganda intensifying peace in the Balkans was becoming more and more threatened. Ferdinand, for his part, wanted to work with the Macedonian activists, partly in order to control them, but also because he feared that if he did not they would kill him, as they had Stambolov. The prince's hope was that diplomacy would secure in Macedonia reform radical enough to placate the activists, at least for a while. If this did not happen there was the danger that IMRO might so increase in strength that it would dictate the course of events and instigate a rising which, if successful, could lead to the absorption of Bulgaria into Macedonia rather than vice versa. If this were to happen Ferdinand might well lose his throne; both the son and the brother of Alexander Battenberg were being talked of as the possible governor-general of an autonomous Macedonia, and Ferdinand was realist enough to know that a majority of his subjects would be more attracted to a Battenberg than to him. For Ferdinand, therefore, control of the Macedonian activists was a matter of life and death.

In 1900 he had not had that control. The dangers this caused were soon apparent. The supremacists caused Bulgaria great embarrassment by kidnapping and ransoming Ellen Stone, an American missionary in Macedonia, and murdering a prominent Romanian opponent of the Slav cause in Macedonia, whilst within the principality their supporters raised large sums of money and were not afraid to use tough methods in the process. Russia soon began to demand that the activists be brought under control. The Ivanchov government, exhausted and discredited by its confrontation with the peasants, dared not move against the Macedonians, not least because support for them was deeply entrenched in the army. Karavelov and Danev, russophile by instinct, were prepared to act and had to do so if Bulgaria were to receive financial help from St Petersburg. In April 1901 therefore Bulgarian army officers were forbidden to belong to the Macedonian committees, a small number of leading activists were arrested and, though soon acquitted by a court, were detained long enough for Ferdinand to place two trusted officers in charge of the Supreme Committee. Their tactic, however, was to begin preparing for a rising, despite the displeasure this would cause in Russia.

It also caused great displeasure amongst the internalists, or supporters of IMRO. They feared the rising would be premature and that its inevitable defeat would mean the destruction of IMRO's carefully nurtured organization in Macedonia. IMRO therefore once more dissociated itself from the Supreme Committee. The internalists argued strongly that autonomy was the only feasible solution for the Macedonian problem; it alone would guarantee protection to all the ethnic groups through a Swiss-style devolved form of local government, and the alternatives were either partition by the surrounding states, which was undesirable, or absorption by one of them, which the great powers would not permit. The supremacists disagreed and in the spring of 1902 sent large numbers of *comitadji* (literally 'committee men' but by implication agitators or members of armed gangs) into Macedonia.

Despite knowing that it would cause anger in St Petersburg Danev had accepted this policy which he was persuaded would force the Porte to grant reforms in Macedonia. He was compelled to change his mind when he went to Russia in April 1902. Here he was told that if he were to secure a loan and a military convention, both of which he had asked for, then he would have to accept Firmilian as administrator in the Skopje archdiocese, and put an end to the incursions of the *comitadji*. The first condition was a national disaster for Bulgaria because it handed northern Macedonia to the Serbs, and the public was outraged. The suppression of the *comitadji* was less unpopular and relatively easily achieved by tighter control of arms sales, the transfer of some officers from border regions, and the setting up of a new force to guard the frontier; civil servants were now also forbidden membership of the Macedonian committees. The suppression of the armed bands also made political sense. If unrest in Macedonia appeared to be more the result of incursions from Bulgaria than of genuine, internal discontent, the Porte could claim that there was no need for fundamental reform and the problem would best be addressed by disciplining Bulgaria. The Russians were pleased by the measures introduced in Sofia and provided the necessary help in the loan negotiations with Paribas. They also agreed to draw up a military convention but this never came into effect because the tsar would not sign an agreement with a ruler who was still technically a vassal of the sultan.

Ferdinand may have been a vassal, but he was a wily one. Despite the measures introduced in the spring the supremacists were still being encouraged to take action, not least to prevent IMRO seizing control of events in Macedonia. In September the supremacists therefore staged a rising around Gorna Djumaya, the present-day Blagoevgrad. It was carefully timed. Not only was the Bulgarian army mobilized for its autumn manoeuvres but national emotions were charged by celebrations to mark the twenty-fifth anniversary of the battle at the Shipka Pass in 1877. The Gorna Djumaya rising received little local support and was easily suppressed by the Ottoman forces. It did, however, indicate that the supremacists rather than the internalists were the dominant force amongst the Macedonian dissidents. It also galvanized European diplomacy which in the spring produced a reform scheme for Macedonia. But before that, in December 1902, the Russian minister for foreign affairs, Count Vladimir Lamsdorff, had visited the Balkans and delivered a stern message in Belgrade and Sofia to the effect that all links with the Macedonian revolutionaries must be severed.

This time there was no room for wily manoeuvre, the more so because the king of Serbia quickly announced that he would not assist the insurgents; if Ferdinand did not do likewise Russia would favour Serbia at the expense of Bulgaria. In February 1903 Danev dissolved the Macedonian committees in Bulgaria and arrested their leaders; after a three-day debate, the sŭbranie approved his action.

Danev did not long survive the debate. His concession over Firmilian had alienated a large section of public opinion; the prince resented the government's intrusion into foreign policy, which he regarded as his own preserve, and believed that now the Paribas loan had been secured and the *comitadji* suppressed, Danev had fulfilled his purpose. In addition to this, there had been a series of unseemly confrontations between the prince and a number of his cabinet ministers. The Russians, too, lost faith in Danev when a number of bomb outrages took place in Salonika for which most foreign observers believed the Bulgarians were responsible, though in fact the explosions were the work of anarchists. In May, after yet another unseemly, and this time public row between Ferdinand and a cabinet minister, Danev resigned.

5. THE ILINDEN RISING AND THE SECOND STAMBOLOVIST GOVERNMENT, 1903–1908

Danev's successor as minister president was a non-party soldier, General Racho Petrov, but the government was dominated by the national liberals under the firebrand journalist Dimitŭr Petkov who was made minister of the interior. Petkov was the cabinet's strong man. He had lost an arm in the war of 1877–8, had proved his administrative toughness when he drove through schemes for the modernization of Sofia of which he was elected mayor in 1878, and in the recent elections of October 1903 had used the usual machinery of electoral control with Stambolov-like thoroughness.

The administration's first task was to reassure the Russians that the russophobia of the old National Liberal Party of Stambolov was a thing of the past. This was done through a series of press articles. Traditional national liberal policies were followed, however, with regard to the Ottoman empire, but before any real progress could be made in improving relations between Sofia and Constantinople, Macedonia once more erupted.

The Gorna Djumaya rising and its suppression had borne out the worst fears of the internalists. They now decided that they must stage a rising of their own before the supremacists acted again and inflicted even more damage on IMRO's organization. There was also the danger that the reforms to be introduced in Macedonia might so improve conditions that there would no longer be any popular support for a rising. In January 1903 the IMRO leadership decided that the revolt should take place in the summer and arms were therefore procured and Macedonia divided into a number of revolutionary districts. The rising began in the Bitola district on 2 August 1903, St Elijah's day, or Ilinden in Slavonic. It soon spread throughout most of Macedonia and into the Adrianople vilayet, a republic being declared with Krushevo as its temporary headquarters. But the revolt was doomed. It received no help from outside Macedonia and by the end of September large numbers of Ottoman troops had been moved into the area. By the end of October the Ilinden uprising was over.

In the principality itself tension had been mounting throughout the summer. When the Ilinden rising began the calls for intervention reached fever pitch and some extremists took violent measures to try and force the government to send the Bulgarian army into Macedonia. The worst outrage was the placing of a bomb in the first-class saloon of a Bulgarian ferry boat; twenty-seven people died as a result of the explosion and the minister president admitted privately that the government would soon have to choose between intervention in Macedonia or revolution at home. But intervention was not an option. Russia and Austria-Hungary were totally against it, and Bulgaria could not afford to act alone; it would antagonize the powers and the Balkan states and, given the Greek experience in 1897, it might end in defeat. The Bulgarian army therefore remained inactive and the insurgents in Macedonia were left to their miserable fate. A large number emigrated to Bulgaria or further afield, whilst many of those who remained were forced by deprivation or physical intimidation to join the Greek or Serbian Churches. The Bulgarian cause in Macedonia never really recovered from the joint blows of the appointment of Firmilian and the Ilinden uprising.

The Ilinden emergency paralysed the Petrov government whose stambolovist inclinations meant it sought improvement in Macedonia via cooperation with the Porte. By March 1904, however, tensions had subsided enough for the Bulgarian government to sign a treaty with the Ottoman empire. Both parties undertook to police their common borders more effectively, whilst the Porte agreed to apply the reform programme decided upon by Austria-Hungary and Russia at Mürzsteg late in 1903, and to release the majority of those detained after the recent rising. The agreement also contained clauses promising cooperation on railway policies, extradition procedures, and posts and telegraphs. In subsequent years there was occasional friction over the application of the treaty but in general it helped to stabilize the situation in the Balkans.

Shortly after the conclusion of the treaty with the Ottoman empire the stambolovist government also signed a series of agreements with Serbia. These, like the treaty with the Porte, were partly prompted by the fear that Austria-Hungary might take advantage of Russia's increasing preoccupation with the far east and Japan to advance into the Balkans. Amongst the agreements was one to establish a customs union but this supposedly secret arrangement the Bulgarian government placed before the sŭbranie; this enabled the Habsburg empire, which had long known of the proposed union, to denounce the proposal and to place a trade embargo on Serbia's main export, pigs.

This wrecked the scheme for closer Bulgarian-Serbian ties, but these were in all probability already doomed by growing tensions in Macedonia. The Mürzsteg agreement had provided for the drawing up of new administrative boundaries in Macedonia to give each new unit a more homogeneous ethnic character. The competing Christian factions immediately strove to persuade as many communities as possible to join their schools, churches, etc. After 1903 the Macedonian question became as much, if not more, a contest between the separate Christian groups than one between the Christian population and their Ottoman rulers. By 1906 there was fierce competition between the Bulgarians and Serbs around Kumanovo and Skopje. Relations between Bulgarian and Greek in Macedonia were even worse. The first armed Greek band had appeared in Macedonia in September 1904; this and later bands were sponsored by the Greek government and the Bulgarians were furious that the Greek state was now following the strategy Bulgaria had employed in 1902 and 1903 but which had since been prohibited by the Russians. Both the Greeks and the Serbs were helped in Macedonia by the post-Ilinden weakness of their Christian opponents. Not only had the internalists lost their arms, money, and infrastructure, but they had become bitterly divided whilst their antagonism towards the supremacists remained undiminished. Between 1903 and 1908 a number of spectacular murders were carried out by the various Macedonian factions, most of the victims being leaders of various IMRO groups.

This internecine strife affected the Macedonian cause inside Bulgaria. The popularity of the Macedonian leaders declined not only because of their squabbling but because a number of them were now living in luxury, a luxury financed by the often enforced donations of their supporters. The decline in the popularity of the Macedonian cause was registered by the closure of a number of pro-Macedonian newspapers but was to be seen most dramatically in the sharp decrease in the number of Bulgarian soldiers deserting the army to join the *comitadji*; in 1907 only three NCOs and thirty men did so, a tiny fraction of the numbers who had deserted in previous years.

The Petrov administration was not concerned by this development. Its strategy for Macedonia had been to cooperate with the Porte for short-term gain but in the long run to rely on the Bulgarian army for the attainment of an ultimate, maximalist victory in Macedonia. At present, however, the army was considered to be ill-equipped and underfunded and time and resources would have to be defrayed in order to modernize and strengthen it. By 1907 spending on the military was 50 per cent higher than in 1902. Some of the costs of this augmented spending were met from further loans but some increases in taxation, most noticeably a new and steep excise duty on spirits, were also introduced.

The increases in taxation occasioned some discontent but a series of excellent harvests meant that there was little unrest in rural areas, a fact which did much to blunt BANU's cutting edge. There was, however, unrest in the towns. In 1905 compositors in Sofia struck for higher wages and students at Sofia university became active. The latter resented what they regarded as excessive restrictions within the university, and their political consciousness was raised by events in Russia. In January 1905 the university authorities banned student political associations or discussions, a move which only inflamed the situation. In April the university was closed. It did not reopen until the autumn, but when it did so the students were given a number of concessions. There was also a growing concern in some quarters over the prince; Danev's newspaper, *Den* (Day), never a friend to Ferdinand, criticizing him for his long absences from the country.

The Petrov government also faced a new problem: widespread and violent action against Bulgaria's Greek minority. There were protests in 1905 in Varna when a new Greek bishop arrived in the city. He was not a Bulgarian citizen and therefore technically not eligible to assume his duties, but the government relented in his case; enraged local Bulgarians attacked a number of Greek churches, schools, and a hospital. In 1906 the agitation intensified. It was orchestrated by the stambolovist party Patriotic Associations and reached its climax in attacks on the Greeks in Plovdiv and in the Black Sea town of Anhialo, or Pomorie in Bulgarian. The Greeks in the town were prepared to hand over to the Exarchate local schools and churches but not a large monastery near the town. In the resulting struggle much of the town of Anhialo was destroyed. The anti-Greek outbursts had originally been directed against patriarchist institutions not individuals; after Anhialo they were more like racist pogroms.

There had been occasional outbreaks of tension between Greek and Bulgarian before the mid-1900s, including violent confrontations in Plovdiv in April 1885. In general, however, relations were good. In some areas the general populace made little distinction between Exarchist and Patriarchist Churches and intermarriage was not uncommon. Even by the beginning of the twentieth century most of the guilds in Plovdiv were still multi-ethnic and the wealthy Greeks were not the hellenists Bulgarian nationalist propaganda made them out to be; what such Greeks wanted was autonomy on the millet model not assimilation in the Hellenic kingdom which would threaten the peace, prosperity, and social pre-eminence they presently enjoyed. If in cities such as Plovdiv Bulgarian merchants were jealous of the Greeks' commercial prowess and power and therefore joined one of the many nationalist groups, and if the Greeks favoured Greek clothes and customs, the tensions were defused in the mixed social gatherings at plays, concerts, and balls.[6] The situation was changed by Macedonia. Bulgarians were angered by the appearance of Greek bands in the region in the mid- 1900s, but it was the collapse of the Ilinden rising which radically altered relations between Bulgarian and Greek. A large proportion of those who attacked the Greeks in 1905 and 1906 were Macedonians who had fled from their homes in 1903.

When the Anhialo outrage took place the minister of the interior was taking the cure in Karlsbad. Once back in Bulgaria Petkov organized relief for the homeless and destitute, and ordered local officials to prevent further outbreaks and to punish those responsible for recent ones. He also agreed to restore a small number of churches to the Greek communities. This did not happen and after 1906 all Greek communities were dissolved and the primary schools they had been responsible for were merged with Bulgarian ones. The Sofia government also decreed that the affairs of the Greek Church in Bulgaria were to be placed alongside those of the Bulgarian Orthodox Church. This meant that the ordination of Greek priests had to be sanctioned by the relevant Bulgarian department of state rather than by the Patriarch in Constantinople; it also meant that the Bulgarian authorities would not recognize the validity of marriages and baptisms performed by Greek priests, though the Greek Orthodox bishoprics remained until they were abolished in June 1914. By then a large number of Greeks had decided that emigration was preferable to the assimilation which seemed to be the only alternative. The government in Athens, however, did not forget the events of 1905 and 1906 and was still demanding compensation for them in the early 1930s.[7]

The Anhialo affair had discredited the minister president who had also been implicated in a financial scandal, and in October he was replaced by Petkov. Petkov's immediate task was to deal with another but much more serious outbreak of urban unrest. The tax increases introduced by the Petrov government had been acutely felt by the small number of urban workers in Bulgaria whose wages did not keep pace either with the rises in taxation or in the cost of living; the cost of maintaining two adults and

---

[6] Spyridon Ploumidis, 'Symbiosis and Friction in Multiethnic Plovdiv/Philippoupolis: The Case of the Greek Orthodox and the Bulgarians (1878–1906)' Ph.D. thesis (London, 2004).

[7] Vasil A. Vasilev, 'Bŭlgaro-britanski finansovi i tŭrgovski otnosheniya po vreme na svetovnata ikonomicheska kriza ot 1929–1933g', in V. A. Vasilev et al. (eds.), *Bŭlgaro-angliĭskite otnosheniya v novo i naĭ-novo vreme*, Izsledvaniya po bŭlgarska; istoriya, no. 9, (Sofia: BAN, 1987), 45–103, 54.

two children per month leapt from 71.04 leva in 1895 to 103.44 leva in 1912. The increasing gap between prices and income caused a number of strikes to which the government responded in 1906 with legislation to increase the power of the old guilds as a counterweight to the trade unions, the first of which had been formed by compositors in Sofia in 1882 and which since then had been growing rapidly in strength. The legislation also gave the employer the right to claim compensation from strikers for losses caused by stoppages of work. This provoked a demonstration in front of the sŭbranie in December 1906.

By this point a new industrial problem had emerged. Over 2,000 poorly paid public servants had petitioned the minister president for an increase in wages. Petkov retaliated by fining those who had signed the petition a month's salary, and warning that any further complaint could lead to dismissal. The railway workers were public servants and they threatened to strike in protest. Petkov then rushed through legislation which provided for the immediate dismissal of any civil servant who refused to work and even enabled the government to strip any striking public employee who had not been in employment for fifteen years of his or her pension rights. Petkov also said that if the railway workers struck he would send in the army to keep the trains running. He was as good as his word, and when the railwaymen did strike on 21 December 1906, soldiers were immediately sent to replace them. Four days later the heightened tension in the capital was shown when students and striking railwaymen bombarded the prince with insults and lumps of ice when he opened the new National Theatre; it was the first time that Ferdinand had been openly and directly reviled. The government's response was savage. The university was closed, its teachers sacked, and those students of military age called up for service in the army; a demonstration against these measures was dispersed by soldiers with whips. Petkov told the sŭbranie that the demonstration outside the National Theatre had been 'a grave crime and the punishment has to be correspondingly severe'.[8] He followed this statement by introducing further legislation to restrict the power of the press and then, under pressure from Ferdinand, took steps to cleanse the education system at all levels of anti-government elements.

---

[8] *Doklad na izpitatelna komisiya po upravlenieto na stranata prez period ot 5 Maĭ 1903 do 16 Yanuariĭ 1908*, (Sofia: Narodno Sŭbranie, 1910), 23.

The situation was clearly serious. In addition to the tensions created by the government's tough stance the population of the cities, and of Sofia in particular, were suffering hardship because the stoppage on the railways had created fuel shortages in what was an abnormally severe winter. The opposition parties responded by forming a united bloc and organizing large demonstrations in all major towns and cities. At the same time the non-government press, despite the increased restrictions on it, lambasted the authorities with many papers declaring that the fundamental problem in Bulgaria was the personal regime of the prince; the Democratic Party's newspaper, *Pryaporets* (Banner or Standard), declared that the political status of the country was 'constitutional absolutism'.

There was much in the observation. The government had an unassailable and entirely obedient majority in the assembly, yet it was not the sŭbranie but the prince who decided when cabinets should come and go. And with the alternative to the stambolovists being a fragile coalition stretching from the conservatives to the moderate socialists Ferdinand was unlikely to dispense with Petkov, even though his extreme measures had alarmed the prince. In any event, tensions eased in early February when the railwaymen went back to work in return for higher wages and a promise of no victimization.

Petkov, however, was victimized. On 27 February 1907 he was assassinated in the streets of Sofia. He was succeeded by Petŭr Gudev, the president of the sŭbranie, whose policies differed little in content though were softer in form. He remained in office until January 1908. Ferdinand did not wish to remove him as long as the alternative remained the exotic coalition of oppositionists, and he wanted stability during 1907 when he would celebrate the twentieth anniversary of his accession. Those celebrations, which included the unveiling of Zocchi's statue of Tsar Alexander II opposite the sŭbranie building, went off without incident, but the mood of the nation was once more turning sour. The harvest had been poor and the junketings for Ferdinand's anniversary contrasted starkly with the plight of many small farmers. There was also anger at the government's refusal to reinstate sacked teachers, whilst the attempt to recruit replacements for the dismissed university faculty proved farcical. Resentment at the continued harsh treatment of the teachers was increased by the obvious indulgence the authorities showed to Macedonian activists guilty of killing their opponents. And finally the Gudev government showed an appetite for self-enrichment which was unprecedented; its leader amassed a huge fortune in a matter of months. When it was discovered that 14 million of the 20 million leva allocated for the construction of an un-needed royal palace in Plovdiv were to be siphoned off for the use of ministers, the prince decided it was time to replace them. A new administration was formed in January 1908 with Aleksandŭr Malinov as minister president; born in the Bulgarian community in Bessarabia he had been educated in Kiev and had succeeded Karavelov in 1903 as the leader of the Democratic Party. Six months after taking office Malinov staged a general election in which the stambolovists were eliminated and as a result of which the Democratic Party's representation rose from three to 128. Despite widespread electoral management, however, BANU now had twenty-four deputies.

6. THE GOVERNMENT OF MALINOV AND THE DECLARATION OF INDEPENDENCE, 1907–1911

Malinov's major achievement was the declaration of independence for Bulgaria in September 1908. Bulgaria's vassal status had restricted its sovereignty in matters such as tariffs or in the exercise of jurisdiction within Bulgaria because many foreign subjects could still invoke the Capitulations and demand trial in their own consular courts. By the middle of the first decade of the twentieth century there was hope of a change in Bulgaria's status but sharp disabusal of this hope came in 1907 when the Ottoman government objected to Bulgaria's participation in The Hague Peace Conference on the grounds that Ferdinand was a vassal of the sultan, and at the end of the following year the Capitulations were invoked by European diplomats in Sofia to prevent the passing of a law which would have made it almost impossible for foreign insurance companies to do business in Bulgaria.[9] The prince had long desired to secure full independence, now he was determined upon it.

The opportunity for securing this was presented by the Young Turk revolution of July 1908. The Young Turks were set upon creating in the Ottoman empire a new sense of Ottoman nationalism which, temporarily,

---

[9] See Buchanan to Grey, 9 May 1909, National Archives, Kew, FO 371/605.

persuaded most factions in Macedonia to cooperate with the new rulers in Constantinople. The new rulers were also determined to reassert Ottoman authority in all parts of the empire. One area affected by this was Bosnia and Hercegovina which, though under Habsburg administration since 1878, was still part of the sultan's domains; its Habsburg rulers were therefore greatly disconcerted when the Young Turks announced that Bosnia and Hercegovina, like all other Ottoman territories, would be entitled to elect deputies to the parliament which was to assemble in Constantinople. The Habsburgs had not allowed the Bosnians and Hercegovinians any rights of representation and to prevent further embarrassment they decided to annex the province. This gave Austria-Hungary and Bulgaria a common cause.

Like Bosnia, southern Bulgaria, the former Eastern Rumelia, was also still technically part of the Ottoman empire, and Ferdinand was still nominally governor-general of the province as well as prince of Bulgaria. This in itself was cause enough for concern in Sofia, but then the Young Turks declined to invite the Bulgarian representative in Constantinople, Ivan Stefanov Geshov, to the annual dinner to honour the sultan's birthday, insisting that he should appear instead with those of equal rank: the heads of the Ottoman vilayets.

The Young Turks apologized for this insult, but very soon after the Geshov incident another, and much more serious dispute arose. Early in September workers in the Constantinople depot of the ORC had struck for higher wages and their action was immediately copied by ORC workers in southern Bulgaria. The Young Turks decided to send Ottoman army officers to negotiate with the strikers. Were these officers to enter Bulgaria it could be seen as a reassertion of Ottoman sovereignty in southern Bulgaria, and the Bulgarians therefore refused to allow them to cross the border. The ORC, with its network in Bulgaria paralysed, then asked the Bulgaria government to take over the running of the company's lines in southern Bulgaria, a proposal which the government accepted with alacrity. The arrival of BDZh locomotives and crews in southern Bulgaria was enthusiastically welcomed, but there was now the problem of what to do when the strike ended. The Malinov government knew that if it handed control back to the ORC this would be seen as a recognition of ORC, and indirectly of Ottoman authority in southern Bulgaria; not to return the system to the ORC and to nationalize its property in southern Bulgaria, on the other hand, would be a clear breach of the treaty of

Berlin. And if Bulgaria committed this relatively minor infringement of the sacred Berlin text why should it not go further and declare full independence? This was dangerous in that it would be opposed not merely by the Young Turks but by a number of great powers, especially Great Britain which championed the new regime in Constantinople. Only if Bulgaria could act in tandem with a great power would it be possible to infringe the treaty. With its common interest in wishing to see the treaty changed, Austria-Hungary secretly gave its consent to bold action by Bulgaria.

As soon as he knew this Malinov was able to persuade Ferdinand to agree to the nationalization of the ORC lines in southern Bulgaria. After that it was easy to secure the prince's consent for the second and more significant infringement of the Berlin treaty. Ferdinand, who was in Vienna during the negotiations, hurried back to Bulgaria and on 22 September full independence was declared. On the following day Austria-Hungary annexed Bosnia and Hercegovina. The latter action angered the Russians far more than the Bulgarian declaration of independence, and because of mounting tension between the two great powers all the Balkan states, the Ottoman empire included, were warned that the peace of south-eastern Europe must not be disturbed. This ended any danger that the Young Turks might contest Bulgaria's action.

In April 1909 the Constantinople convention settled detailed financial and other issues arising from Bulgarian actions in 1908. The agreement had been brokered by the Russians and was an astute piece of diplomacy. The Bulgarians were to pay 82 million francs to the Porte, 40 million for amortization of the Eastern Rumelian tribute, and 42 million as compensation for the ORC. The Turks had originally asked for 125 million but the Russians persuaded them to write this off in return for Russia's agreement to forgo the unpaid indemnities owed to it by the Ottoman empire since the war of 1877–8. To complete the circle Russia agreed to lend Bulgaria at a very favourable rate the 82 million francs it needed. Uncharacteristically for such agreements, all parties seemed content and with the financial disputes settled Bulgaria's declaration of independence was soon accepted by all other states. By 1912 Bulgaria had secured the abolition of all signs of its former vassal status.

The changes of 1908 did not meet with universal rejoicing in the domestic arena. Ferdinand's decision to adopt the title of 'tsar' (king) was not universally welcomed; the forceful leader of the agrarians, Aleksandŭr Stamboliĭski, even went so far as to declare that the attainment of independence had been ruined because it was associated with the prince/king. The Macedonians feared that the action might indicate that the Bulgarian government and monarch were satisfied with the existing territorial settlement in the Balkans, though this was a mistake in that Ferdinand was to take the title 'King of the Bulgarians' not 'King of Bulgaria'. There were even signs of a recrudescence of the intense russophilia of the immediate post-liberation period for a number of Bulgarians criticized the declaration of independence as a betrayal of the Slav cause because it had been achieved through cooperation with Austria-Hungary rather than Russia.

The changes to Ferdinand's title had to be endorsed by a grand national assembly but before that convened the Malinov government introduced a number of other reforms. The university question was addressed, the few foreign teachers who had accepted posts in it being dismissed and the original faculty restored. The stringent press laws brought in by the second stambolovist administration were relaxed and Malinov allowed the cabinet to be overruled by Democratic Party deputies in the sŭbranie who wanted commissions of inquiry set up to investigate the activities of members of the previous government who were then to be arraigned before the State Court. Another change was the implementation of party promises to reform the taxation system. The Democratic Party had also promised to move towards greater democracy. This it did by introducing referenda for certain issues of local government expenditure and by arranging for local elections to be conducted under proportional representation which it also planned to implement at a national level, an experiment being introduced in the Tŭrnovo and Plovdiv regions.

In the national political debate the position and personality of the monarch could not be avoided. Ferdinand had never courted popularity and with the relaxation of press controls the attacks upon him intensified. Particular criticism came from the National Party for whose leader, Ivan Geshov, Ferdinand had an almost pathological dislike. A party conference in February 1910 criticized his personal regime. This, it was said, created government by placemen whose rapacity and lack of concern for the public at large was undermining the constitution and ruining the nation and its political system; 'for many years, and especially since 1903', the conference concluded, 'we have seen at the helm "People without Party or Parties without People", whilst the stronger parties are made to keep their distance.'[10] The party conference also complained that there had as yet been no grand national assembly to confirm or reject the changes of 1908. But the National Party was by no means the only source of criticism. When Sultan Abdul Hamid II was deposed and exiled in 1909 the socialist newspaper, *Kambana* (Bell), thought this an admirable precedent.

The agrarians were particularly vehement in their criticism of Ferdinand, never missing an opportunity to demand, for example, a reduction in the civil list. They also criticized the army; it was, they said, expensive and the placement of orders for military equipment provided too much scope for graft and corruption. The army was also criticized from the political right. Here there were concerns that the army was an expensive item which was not being used, even as a threat, to secure concessions in Macedonia. The army was further damaged in December 1908 when an officer administered a public thrashing to a journalist who had offended him. Earlier that year both the king and the army had been embarrassed after troops had killed between fifteen and twenty people in Rusé during riots following the return to her father of a Muslim girl who had eloped with a Christian boy; the authorities in Rusé had been told to take any necessary measures to prevent an anti-Muslim outbreak because the king was shortly to visit Constantinople. The incident provoked demonstrations throughout the country and was still being debated in the sŭbranie in 1914 with the army and/or the king being held chiefly responsible for the outrage.

Although the Rusé incident was one of the causes which brought about the resignation of the Malinov government in March 1911, the main reasons for its demise were to be found in foreign affairs. Malinov had hoped to secure concessions, above all a rail link from Kyustendil to Kumanovo, by cooperation with the Porte. He failed. The main reason for this was that the Young Turk policy of Ottoman nationalism soon alienated the subject peoples of European Turkey and Macedonia was once more destabilized. By 1910 the *comitadji* were active again and Malinov's hopes for good relations with Constantinople dwindled.

The events of 1908–9 had transformed the diplomatic situation in south-eastern Europe. After its defeat by Japan in 1904–5 Russia had

[10] Giska to Aerenthal, 13D, 24 February 1910, Vienna: Haus-Hof- und Staatsarchiv, PA XV/70.

turned once more to the Balkans, but only to face humiliation when Austria-Hungary annexed Bosnia and Hercegovina without any compensating gain for Russia. Russia was determined to prevent further Habsburg encroachment but itself was too weak to think of military action; an alternative means of containing Austria-Hungary would be to bring the Balkan states closer together. Serbia needed little encouragement in this direction because it too emerged from the crisis of 1908–9 with a deep sense of grievance because it had harboured designs on Bosnia and Hercegovina which now seemed permanently locked in the Habsburg embrace. The Serbian government, however, had no liking for its counterpart in Sofia which had collaborated with the Habsburgs in 1908, but it had little choice but to look to its Balkan neighbour for help.

Malinov's attitude was not encouraging. He resented Serbian actions and successes in Macedonia, the most notable of the latter coming in 1910 when the Serbs were given the bishopric of Dibra, which he regarded as an exarchist see. He cited the differences in Macedonia as justification for rejecting a Serbian approach in 1910. Yet Malinov's attitude had become outdated. Growing instability in Macedonia made the collapse of Ottoman authority a probability and should that occur Bulgaria had to be in a position to stake its claim if it were not to lose out to Greece and Serbia. Malinov's strategy of cooperation with the Ottoman empire and his reluctance to sign agreements with the other Balkan states would not now advance Bulgarian interests and he was therefore removed in March 1911. After some negotiation Ferdinand decided Geshov should be appointed minister president.

7. THE GROWTH OF POLITICAL RADICALISM

From the beginning of the new state's existence in 1878 there had been a gap between the peasants and the intelligentsia, the alliance between whom had produced the national revival. After 1879 the peasant took relatively little interest in national political affairs and general elections seldom produced a turnout of even half the eligible electorate. The peasant was puzzled by the alienation between Bulgaria and Russia and was angered by the growing power and arrogance of the new class of highly paid civil servants to which many of the intelligentsia gravitated.

The growth of *partizanstvo* deepened peasant disillusionment. The political machine was more and more manipulated by the few and the quality of the lowest ranks of the administration, those with whom the peasant had most contact, was abysmal. A discontented element within the intelligentsia saw this problem and it did much to reproduce the peasant–intelligentsia alliance which had underlain the vŭzrazhdane, not least by helping in the birth of BANU.

The intelligentsia itself was changing. The original intelligentsia had achieved its prime objective, the creation of a nation state; the new one faced the task of bringing about full national reunion within the San Stefano boundaries, but the political dynamics of Europe made that impossible. The new intelligentsia therefore did not have a national purpose comparable to that of the old. As a result, not only did it gravitate towards the civil service but it was also attempting to differentiate itself from folk culture and present itself as part of a higher, 'European' culture.[11] Influenced by the narodniks, members of the new intelligentsia fell into the trap of thinking that they could catch up with the west in one leap. Not wishing to live or work in the villages themselves they sold their properties and migrated to the towns, thus separating themselves physically as well as mentally from their roots. In the towns, not least because of *partizanstvo*, they were easy prey to the rentier mentality which believes that wealth can be created without work, the converse of the Bulgarian peasant outlook. The new intelligentsia had made two critical errors. It had failed to realize that the society from which it emerged, and on which it still depended for the creation of the wealth it wished to consume, did not have the same material base as the western models it was desperately trying to emulate. And, secondly, it attacked and denigrated the traditions of the people without, as yet, giving it any alternative set of values. The intelligentsia in the city, particularly that part of it associated with office via *partizanstvo*, was the antithesis of the Bulgarian peasant with his intense attachment to the land and his strong work ethic.

These developments did not go unchallenged, and the reaction to them would greatly help the agrarian movement. In 1893 Dimitŭr Rizov had stated that Bulgaria's intelligentsia concerned itself with everything except that which was most important, 'the establishment of some form

[11] Daskalov, *Mezhdu*, 37.

of political morality'.[12] In 1898 the respected scholar and commentator, Krŭstyu Krŭstev, delivered a blistering attack. The new intelligentsia, he said, was 'either a constituent part of the state bureaucracy, or revolved around it, drawn to it as if it were the sole source of life and creative energy'. There was a new generation, he continued, which, unlike the old, had no glorious past and sought any future glory in careers and in wealth; it had 'sold its soul to the devil';[13] a later writer, the historian Petŭr Mutafchiev, referred to the new generation as a 'semi-intelligentsia'.[14] The novelist and short-story writer, Elin Pelin, also made much of the growing alienation of the Bulgarian peasant from the 'foreign' bureaucracy.[15] In these circumstances, political parties seemed to have no purpose. Their fragmentation, together with popular indifference and intelligentsia avarice, meant that they easily became enmeshed in *partizanstvo*.

Despite the strictures of Krŭstev and others, the intelligentsia was not entirely the creature of the new establishment. Some writers did call for attempts to improve the lot of the average Bulgarian and the moral quality of its leadership, intellectual and political. The influence of the Russian populists was again strong in this respect and one organized attempt by disaffected Bulgarian intelligentsia appeared in the *Sirohmahomilstvo* (Pauperophilia) movement which borrowed much from Chernyshevki and other Russian thinkers; the movement was developed enough for the stambolovist police to break it up. Others followed Russian populists such as Mikhaïlovski and Lavrov in arguing that the backwardness of the peasantry was the key to the country's problems and that this backwardness could be overcome only by the education of the peasantry in modern methods of production; this would eventually bring prosperity and with it the political maturity needed for the functioning of a truly democratic system.

A number of populist-inspired activists attempted in the 1890s to put these ideas into action. Yanko Zabunov, the director of the State Viticulture Institute in Pleven, published a journal, *Zemedelets* (Farmer),

---

[12] Eli Velinova, 'Iz korespondentsiyata na bŭlgarski politicheski i obshtestveni deĭtsi do Konstantin Velichkov (1887–1896g)', *Izvestiya na Dŭrzhavnite Arhivi*, 9 (1965), 79–112, no. 15.

[13] K. Krŭstev, 'Bŭlgarskata inteligentsiya', *Misŭl*, 8/1 (15 January 1898), 1–3.

[14] Petŭr Mutafchiev, 'Za kulturnata kriza u nas', originally published in *Prosveta*, 1/4 (1935), 385–97, and included in Elenkov and Daskalov, *Zashto sme takiva?* 370–9.

[15] See for example his 'Andreshko'.

which though mainly technical in content did include some political material. It did not last long but was followed by others whilst in 1898 another activist, Ĭordan Pekarev, established a network of over sixty local groups in the Varna region. Pekarev and fifteen associates also set up the 'First Constituent Committee' of an agrarian organization and launched a newspaper, *Zemedelska Borba* (Agrarian Struggle) which had the motto, 'The moral and material improvement of the peasants is the business of the peasants themselves'. This was a rejection of the populist notion that the peasant had to be led by the committed intelligent, but it had a powerful appeal and in 1899 the authorities conscripted Pekarev into the army before he could do more damage. But then the situation was transformed by the announcement of the tithe in kind.

Even before this announcement the socialist Tsanko Bakalov, better known under his pseudonym Tserkovski, became so concerned at the plight of the peasants that early in 1899 he issued an *Appeal to the Peasants of Bulgaria* in which he urged them to establish an organization similar to a trades union or a benevolent society. He quite deliberately did not suggest a political party because this would compete with the socialists. In April a meeting in the Tŭrnovo district endorsed this appeal and urged all communities to send delegates to the congress which had been called in Pleven in December and which was to establish BANU. Most delegates in Pleven were peasants but there were also a number of teachers, priests, and agricultural advisers. Their influence was imprinted on the new organization. One of its stated aims was 'to raise the intellectual and moral standing of the peasant and to improve agriculture in all its branches'.

The intelligentsia was always to have a role to play in the affairs of BANU but the organization was soon preoccupied with immediate, practical concerns rather than with ideology. For two years the question of how far BANU should involve itself in the political arena was hotly debated. The decision to introduce the tithe was a political one and opposition to it could hardly be non-political, and the use of troops to suppress discontent in Darankulak was a highly contentious political issue. The second congress of the Union, held in December 1900, continued to insist that the movement was non-political but it was already making overtly political demands such as those for a return to constitutional rule and for a reduction in official salaries. Furthermore, the political potential of the agrarian organization had already been seen, above all in its successful promotion of pro-agrarian candidates in the local elections of August 1900. The national election of February 1901 underlined this lesson in that, despite the youth, poverty, and lack of experience of the movement, twenty-three agrarians were elected. When all but seven of these defected to other parties after joining the sŭbranie the argument for making agrarianism a political organization was strengthened, because without some form of party political organization and discipline there would be constant seepage of elected deputies to other parties. At the third congress, held in Sofia in October 1901, it was finally decided to redefine the organization as a political one. It was now that it adopted the name, the Bulgarian Agrarian National Union. It elected Zabunov as its leader.

The agrarians, however, were still riding on the wave of the tithe protest. After 1901 their fortunes declined. The fourth congress, in Shumen in October 1902, was told that of the 400 druzhbi created during the tithe struggle only about forty remained and a year later only a handful of delegates appeared for the fifth congress in Stara Zagora. In the elections of 1903 not a single Agrarian was returned to the sŭbranie. There were a number of reasons for this. The debate over whether the movement should become a political party had divided and weakened the leadership and by 1903 the founding fathers had mostly resigned and the future leader, Aleksandŭr Stamboliĭski, had not yet established himself. Harvests were good; the cooperative movement was spreading, organizing the marketing of agricultural products and relieving some of the debt pressures on peasants; public attention was focused more on Macedonia; and after 1903 the stambolovists used tough measures of political control. *Partizanstvo*, too, had had a baleful effect. Most local agrarian druzhbi had been infiltrated by members of other parties who often placed the local BANU vote at the disposal of those parties.

BANU's fortunes revived after 1907. In the elections of the following year the agrarians again won twenty-three seats and they polled an impressive 11.2 per cent of the poll, some 100,000 votes. In local elections in the same year BANU captured control of almost 300 communes, and there were 1,123 local druzhbi. In the 1911 GNA there were fifty-three Agrarians, the party had over 14,000 members, and the number of druzhbi had risen to 1,421. The poor harvest of 1907 was one reason for the revival, and another was the general disgust at the corruption of the Petrov/Petkov administration. But structural changes within

BANU also contributed to the revival. Tighter internal discipline made defection to other parties almost impossible and the transfer of party headquarters from Stara Zagora to Sofia in 1907 increased the party's effectiveness and raised its national profile. The party had also made a considerable difference to the daily lives of many peasants. It had become fully involved in the burgeoning cooperative movement; it had set up an insurance scheme for local party organizations; and it had established the 'National Store', a nationwide retail cooperative. Its political impact was heightened when the two main agrarian newspapers merged in 1902 to form the new *Zemedelsko Zname* (Agrarian Banner). In 1906 Aleksandŭr Stamboliĭski was made editor. He had a huge and immediate impact on the paper and within the leadership of the party itself. By 1908 he was its dominant personality and was a major cause of its regeneration.

Born in 1879 in Slavovitsa in the Pazardjik region, Stamboliĭski had studied at the State Viticulture Institute in Pleven where he had been much influenced by Zabunov. Stamboliĭski, more than anyone else, codified the ideology of agrarianism which he expounded in the party newspaper and then in two major books, *Political Parties or Estate Organizations*, published in 1909, and *The Principles of the Bulgarian Agrarian National Union*, which appeared a decade later. Stamboliĭski did not accept the socialist notion that private property was evil. There were two sides to human nature, he argued: the individual and the communal. Private property satisfied the needs of the former but as productive relationships became more complex a communal consciousness developed because the good of one individual became dependent on the good of all the others. A further consequence of the development of complex relationships would be that all individuals would cooperate to achieve the most efficient form of production; work would therefore become collective but ownership would remain individual. Stamboliĭski rejected the socialist concept that society was divided into classes with the relationship to the means of production determining in which class a person belonged; to this he opposed the notion of 'labour property', or the ownership of the means of production by those who worked them. And he saw society as divided not into mutually hostile and irreconcilable classes, but into seven 'estates': the agrarian, the artisanal, the wage-labouring, the entrepreneurial, the commercial, and the bureaucratic. What determined membership of an estate was less ownership than activity, and thus a small peasant farmer was of the same estate as the larger landowner. But Stamboliĭski was also an egalitarian. The dictates of the communal good required that no individual own too much or too little private property; it was from inequalities in property holding that injustice arose. These theoretical arguments led to the practical demand that property must be taken from those who had too much, including the Church, the crown, and the state, and redistributed to those who had too little.

The most important of the seven estates was the agrarian, not merely because it produced the basic necessities of life, but also because it provided the means to the greatest self-fulfilment of the individual. The peasant, Stamboliĭski argued, was not confined to the repetitive performing of one task, as was the factory worker, but had direct contact with and knowledge of the natural world. For Stamboliĭski the village was the only place where this fundamental alliance of man and nature could function properly and he therefore abominated urban life and what he saw as the parasitic appurtenances of it. These included the bureaucracy, the legal profession, the political parties, the military, and the crown.

Individual ownership in the agrarian estate was not to mean cut-throat competition because cooperation, which was at the core of agrarian ideology, would meet the needs for communal credit, the storage of harvested crops, and the marketing of the individual producers' goods. The functioning of the cooperatives would in the long run help to promote a new communal consciousness and produce a new political and social morality. At an international level a number of agrarian states would evolve a similar cooperative mentality which would lead to peace, stability, and a new form of state relationships in a peasant international.

The immediate application of these ideas was seen in Stamboliĭski's call for government subsidies for agriculture and the peasantry. These subsidies should take the form of help for the cooperatives, and especially for the credit cooperatives, mass health and insurance schemes, and better educational facilities in rural areas. The money for these projects could easily be found, he argued, if the state cut its expenditure on the royal family, the bureaucracy, and above all the army. Stamboliĭski argued that Bulgaria would not need an army if it pursued a peaceful policy abroad and aimed for a Balkan federation, preferably of agrarian regimes, in which an autonomous Macedonia would be one of the constituents.

In practical, domestic policy the agrarians demanded the election of all officials, much greater autonomy in local government, the repeal of the anti-trade union legislation of the Petrov/Petkov administration, a ban on private usury, the reform of the Agricultural Credit Bank, protection for the credit cooperatives, female suffrage, proportional representation, a progressive income tax, and an end to the government monopoly on the sale of necessities such as salt and matches. BANU also called for the redistribution of Church property and the enactment of a maximum size for landholdings. These policies appealed most strongly to the poorer peasants and in 1919 those holding less than 50 dekars of land—the smallest category—formed 51 per cent of BANU's membership, with membership rates declining as the average size of holding increased. With the small peasants being by far the most numerous social group in the country it was little surprise that it was their political representatives who stepped into the vacuum when the Tŭrnovo system almost collapsed.

Like the agrarians the socialists offered an alternative to the Tŭrnovo system. Socialist ideas had been current in the 1880s though they had made few converts and those who did espouse the new creed were shown little tolerance; in 1890 Stambolov's police broke up the first attempt in Bulgaria to celebrate May Day. The most noted radical socialist was G. A. Kŭrdjiev who later joined Tsankov's Progressive Liberal Party.[16] Marxism was introduced by Dimitŭr Blagoev, a Macedonian who had been expelled from Russia. In 1891 a small group of intellectuals met at Buzludja in the Balkan mountains and established the Bulgarian Workers' Social Democratic Party (BRSDP) on marxist principles. The new party contested the election of 1893 but only 531 people voted for it. In the following year, with stambolovist controls decreased if not dismantled, the party secured four sŭbranie seats, though one deputy was disqualified for electoral irregularities.

The main practical difficulty facing the workers' movement in Bulgaria was that there were so few workers, the vast majority of those espousing socialist ideas being teachers, lawyers, students, or other members of the intelligentsia. Some factories did appear but the proportion of the population employed in them was minute and production remained concentrated in the small workshop. Even in 1910 only 5.1 per cent of Bulgarian manufacturing concerns employed more than ten workers, only about half of the latter had no property, and 35 per cent

---

[16] Kiril Lambrev, *Nachenki na rabotnicheskoto i profsŭyuznoto dvizhenie v Bŭlgariya 1878–1891* (Sofia: BAN, 1960), 155.

had both a home and some arable land; just as Bulgaria had a semi-intelligentsia it also had a semi-proletariat.[17]

This posed theoretical and practical problems. Blagoev, in his *What is Socialism and is there the BASIS for It in this Country*, published in 1891, attempted to surmount the former by arguing that the small peasant was destined to disappear as agriculture inevitably moved towards capitalization and larger units worked by wage-labourers; today's small peasants were therefore tomorrow's rural proletariat and should be approached as such. Others argued that in the absence of a developed working class the party should concentrate on improving the living standards of the peasant masses and, if necessary, cooperate with the bourgeois parties to bring this about.

By 1903 the party had registered some gains, most noticeably in the elections of 1897 and 1901 when it returned six and eight deputies respectively, though not all of them survived the scrutiny of electoral returns when the sŭbranie met. In 1903 they received no seats at all and were not represented in the assembly again until 1912. This was in part the result of changes in the electoral system, particularly a law of 1903 which meant that each constituency could return only one deputy; the established parties already had a stranglehold on urban seats and after 1908 the agrarians dominated those rural ones not in the pocket of one of the establishment parties. But the socialists' weakness was also very much the result of a split in the movement of 1903.

This was the culmination of the disputes of the 1890s and divided the purist marxists, led by Blagoev, from the pragmaticists who argued that political democracy had to be secured before socialism could be built, and therefore it was legitimate to cooperate with the agrarians and the existing left-wing parties in the sŭbranie. The pragmaticists, led by Yanko Sakŭzov, published their ideas in *Obshto Delo* (General or Joint Affairs) and became known, because of their willingness to operate on a less exclusivist basis, as the 'broad socialists' or the 'broads'; they stated they were 'the party of the present as well as the future, of reform as well as of revolution'.[18] Blagoev's marxists were given the antonymic nickname the 'narrows'. They rejected cooperation even with the agrarians. The split

---

[17] Even in 1946 only 6,586, or 5.7 per cent of Bulgaria's 115,720 workshops had more than five workers. Genchev, *Ochertsi*, 188–9.

[18] Dimitŭr Sazdov, *Mnogo-partiĭnata sistema i monarhicheskiyat institut v Bŭlgariya 1879–1918* (Sofia: Stopanstvo, 1993), 117.

was replicated in the trade union movement and in all socialist bodies, even those which provided the urban workers with much-needed facilities such as libraries or baths.

The two groups remained distant, mutually hostile, and uncompromising, and they showed little willingness to suspend hostilities even during the unrest of 1907. The railway workers were mostly broads and the ambivalent attitude adopted by the narrows caused deep and lasting bitterness. There were attempts to repair the split, including some made by the Socialist International, but they came to nothing. The broads were to become the social democrats and the narrows the Bulgarian Communist Party which took great pride in the fact that, like its Russian counterpart, it had split in 1903. The narrows doubled their membership between 1903 and 1912 and were able to boast that nearly three-quarters of that membership, much in contrast to that of the broads, was of proletarian origin.

The bifurcation of 1903 and thereafter weakened Bulgaria's socialist movement but it nevertheless remained the strongest in the Balkans.

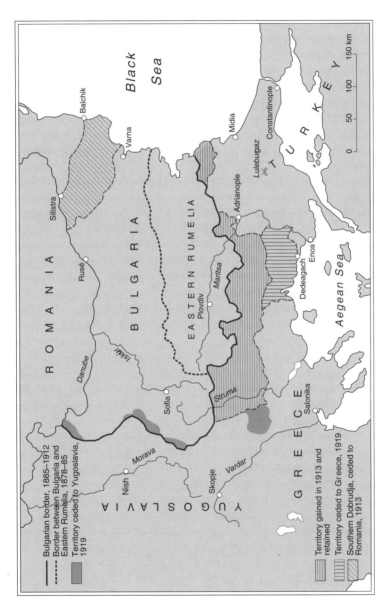

Map 4. Bulgaria's frontiers, 1878–1919

7

Bulgaria at War, 1912–1918

1. CONSTITUTIONAL CHANGE AND THE FORMATION OF THE BALKAN LEAGUE

The constitutional changes implicit in the 1908 declaration of independence demanded ratification by a grand national assembly. This did not meet until the summer of 1911, after Geshov had taken office.

The assembly, which met in Tŭrnovo, contained over fifty opposition deputies, most of them agrarians. It enacted a number of constitutional amendments unconnected with the changes of 1908, such as the provisions that the sŭbranie was now to be re-elected every four rather than every five years, and its annual sessions were to be four rather than two months long.

The central issue at Tŭrnovo, however, was not the parliament but the monarchy. And behind the sometimes fierce debates lay fears that Ferdinand's personal regime had become too powerful. The agrarians immediately made their displeasure known by insisting that Ferdinand had had no right to open the assembly before it had decided whether or not to accept his change of title, and therefore when he started his speech Stamboliĭski also rose and began to speak; this was a symbolic protest which the pro-government majority in the GNA easily brushed aside to endorse Ferdinand as 'King of the Bulgarians'. There were other changes affecting the crown. Article 38 was again changed, this time to state unequivocally that all Bulgarian monarchs with the exception of Ferdinand must belong to the Orthodox Church. It was also decided, despite fierce agrarian complaint, that the Bulgarian monarchy was to be based on male primogeniture in the Saxe-Coburg-Gotha family.

The most important proposed change was that in article 17 of the Tŭrnovo constitution, which was the subject of a ten-day debate.

The original article gave the prince, as he then was, the right to conclude treaties with neighbouring states, the restrictions of vassaldom and the treaty of Berlin confining Bulgaria's relations to those states alone, but after the declaration of independence Bulgaria had no need or intent to limit its agreements to its neighbours alone. The first proposed amendment gave to the monarch the sole right to negotiate and conclude treaties with foreign states and also stated that 'The king ratifies those treaties and informs his ministers of them if the interests and the security of the country allow it.' The justification for giving the monarch such wide-ranging powers was that the complex relations of the Balkans, or even of loan negotiations, put a premium on secrecy. The argument did not carry. The amendment was rejected and the power to negotiate treaties vested in the government. Nevertheless, even the modified amendment stated that the ministers would inform the sŭbranie of any treaties 'if the interests and the security of the state allow it', and given Ferdinand's power over foreign policy formulation, and the ease with which he could dispense with ministers, he would have little difficulty in persuading his government not to reveal agreements they had concluded. Not much more than a year after these amendments to the constitution were passed they were applied with radical and ultimately disastrous effect.

The rejection of the first proposed amendment in article 17 and the insistence that it must be the government rather than the monarch who negotiated treaties reflected the opinion of the National Party deputies who dominated the GNA, that party being fiercely opposed to Ferdinand's personal regime. This was again seen when an ordinary sŭbranie, elected with a predictable National Party majority after the GNA had closed, extended the experiment in proportional representation to cover the entire country. The government calculated that this would limit the king's power by making it more difficult for incoming administrations to secure a dependable majority. Ferdinand was of another mind; he believed that PR would lead to an even greater fragmentation of the political parties and therefore make it even easier for him to play off one against another.

The fact that Ferdinand had installed an administration headed by a man he loathed had obvious political implications. It was clearly not Geshov's domestic policies which had overcome the king's distaste for the man because the National Party was amongst the most critical of the personal regime. It could only be that Ferdinand considered Geshov would follow an acceptable foreign policy, and one different from that of Malinov who had colluded with Austria in 1908 and cold-shouldered advances from Serbia two years later.

Ferdinand clearly intended Bulgaria should become more willing to cooperate with its Balkan neighbours and improve its relations with Russia. The latter process was under way by the summer of 1911 with Prince Boris travelling to St Petersburg to see his imperial godfather and a squadron of Russian warships paying a courtesy visit to Varna.

By this time Russia's main foreign policy objective was the formation of a Balkan alliance to resist further Habsburg advances into the Balkans. Bulgarian attitudes to the Balkans were somewhat different. They were determined less by fear of Austria-Hungary than by concern at the fate of Turkey-in-Europe. The centralizing policies of the Young Turks had by 1910 alienated most groups in the area, including the Albanians who in that and the subsequent year had staged revolts against the regime in Constantinople. This raised a twofold danger for Bulgaria and the other states bordering on Turkey-in-Europe. The first was that the great powers might intervene diplomatically to enforce on Constantinople effective reform of its administration in the Macedonian and the Albanian vilayets; were this to happen the indigenous populations might become contented as a result of which the surrounding Balkan states would be deprived of any excuse for intervention and the acquisition of territory. The second danger was that the great powers themselves would decide to take over Turkey-in-Europe, either as some form of protectorate or by partitioning it amongst themselves. The danger of intervention by the powers seemed to increase significantly in 1911 when Italy went to war with the Ottoman empire over Tripolitania. The Italians denied any intention to intervene elsewhere in the Ottoman domains but the Balkan governments were alarmed.

In the meantime, Bulgarian public opinion had been mobilized by the deterioration of the condition of the Bulgarians in Macedonia, and by the appointment of Serbian bishops in Dibra and Veles. In December 1911 between fifteen and twenty Christians were killed in riots occasioned by the blowing up of railway facilities in the Macedonian town of Shtip, and a wave of protest meetings was staged throughout Bulgaria. There was a strong head of steam building up over the Macedonian issue and Radoslavov, now the leader of the national liberals, remarked pointedly, 'We have not spent 950 million leva on the army just to look at it in parades'.[1] He was not alone in this implied criticism of the government for its inactivity.

In fact Geshov's government had not been inactive but had been working secretly. Its original policy with regard to Macedonia had been, like that of so many of its predecessors, to try and work with Constantinople to secure effective reforms and concessions for the Exarchate. This had not worked, and Geshov and the king therefore decided that Bulgaria's objectives must be sought not by soft but by hard methods, that is by the use of force. Bulgaria was still not strong enough militarily or diplomatically to act alone and therefore it had to have an ally and here the obvious candidate was Serbia, the more so as Russia was pushing hard for a Serbo-Bulgarian rapprochement.

That this would not be easily achieved was shown when Geshov opened negotiations with Belgrade. The minister president began by adopting the traditional Bulgarian position that Macedonia should become autonomous, the idea clearly being that it would then follow the example of Rumelia and join Bulgaria. The Serbs insisted on partition, and this was a price Geshov had to pay. It was not a low one. After some hard negotiating it was agreed that Bulgaria's sphere of interest should be south of a line from Lake Ohrid in the south-west to Mount Golem in the north-east; Serbia was to have the area north of the Shar mountains, which gave it Old Serbia and most of the Albanian-inhabited Scutari vilayet; between the two areas was the so-called 'contested zone' whose fate was to be determined by future negotiations or, if these proved fruitless, by the arbitration of the tsar. Even without the contested zone Geshov had had to sacrifice Kumanovo and Skopje, though Bitola, Veles, and Shtip were included in the Bulgarian sector. On the basis of this division a Serbian-Bulgarian treaty was signed in February 1912 and was followed by a military convention in April. Both agreements were secret.

The February agreement formed the core of a loose system of agreements which became known, for convenience rather than accuracy, as the Balkan alliance or the Balkan league. Bulgaria's participation in the 'organization' was complemented first by a treaty and a military convention with Greece signed in May and September respectively. Neither agreement mentioned any territorial settlement, largely because the Bulgarians did

---

[1] Andreï Pantev et al., 'Vŭnshnata politika i opozitsionite partii (1900–1914)', *Izvestiya na Instituta za Istoriya*, 23 (1974), 105–48, 134, n. 130.

not believe that the Greek army would be able to contest a Bulgarian occupation of Macedonia; after tough negotiations both Sofia and Athens accepted the idea of autonomy for the region. In August the league was completed by verbal agreements concluded with Montenegro. Bulgaria had been largely responsible for the construction of the league and it had the largest army within it: 'Bulgaria', concluded an American scholar, 'had not exercised such a predominance in the Balkan peninsula since the time of Tsar Ivan Asen II in the thirteenth century.'[2]

Whilst the diplomats worked in secret public opinion in Bulgaria was becoming ever more vociferous. In May 1912 a large meeting in Sofia demanding action to save the Christians of Macedonia was graced by luminaries such as the poet Ivan Vazov.

One reason for public concern was growing unease over the position of the Exarch and the Exarchate. Until 1908 all exarchist areas, even the vassal principality of Bulgaria, had been technically part of the Ottoman empire. After the declaration of independence in 1908 and the Porte's recognition of it in 1909 this was no longer the case, and a second synod had been established in Constantinople. This and its counterpart in Sofia were soon in dispute over matters of liturgy, administration, and property. The discomfort so caused was intensified by pressure from the Russians who, as keen as ever to end the schism in the Orthodox Church, urged that the Exarch should move to Sofia. Another difficulty was the question of what was to be done when the present Exarch, who was already old and infirm, died. The statutes of the Church stated that all bishops must take part in the election of the Exarch but whilst the Porte would have accepted this when Bulgaria was still a vassal state, the nationalist Young Turks were unlikely to agree to what were now foreign bishops taking part in the election of what was still an Ottoman official. If, on the other hand, no bishops from the Bulgarian state took part in the election the candidate chosen was certain to be one on whom the Young Turks could count and who would *ipso facto* be unacceptable in Bulgaria. There were fears in 1912 that the russophiles, who dominated the government and who had great power in the synod in Sofia because its chairman was now the extreme russophile Metropolitan Simeon of Varna, would solve the issue by declaring the Church in Bulgaria a separate, autocephalous body. This would please the Russians but it could be a disaster for the Bulgarians; it would sever the links between the Macedonian Slavs and the Bulgarian Church; and it would fragment the institution upon which the national revival had been founded. A special conference on the question could decide only to leave matters where they stood.

By August 1912 the situation in Macedonia had deteriorated noticeably. Another Albanian rising had been so successful that Skopje had fallen into rebel hands and the Young Turks had resigned as a consequence. The new government was less centralist and agreed to an Austro-Hungarian proposal for thoroughgoing reforms in European Turkey. This intensified the danger that action by one or more of the great powers would exclude the Balkan states from Macedonia. The extremists in Bulgaria therefore redoubled their calls for military intervention, the more so after Christians were killed in bomb outrages and rioting in Kochane and Berana. The demands for action rose to a fever pitch. A huge meeting in Sofia on 24 August was the largest of many which called for war whilst Radoslavov repeated his demand for military action, announcing that 'the Macedonian question is to be solved not by the bluffing of the Bulgarian government or by the bombs of the *comitadji*. It can be decided only by the Bulgarian army.'[3] By this time neither Ferdinand nor Geshov disagreed. One reason why they had signed the alliance with Serbia was because they wished to take the initiative out of the hands of the committee-men just, as Geshov was to comment, 'as Cavour took the question of Italian unity out of the hands of the Italian revolutionists'.[4]

In late August the cabinet decided unanimously in favour of military action. The king did not oppose them. Approaches were therefore made to Belgrade with a view to declaring war. Before this could happen the two states had to determine what action to take should Austria-Hungary threaten Serbia in the north, and these discussions took up most of September. By the end of that month the Ottoman government had helped the allies by a series of hostile gestures, including firing on a Greek steamer and refusing to allow war matériel destined for Serbia to pass through Salonika. On 11 September the Ottoman government mobilized a number of reserve divisions, to which the Balkan allies

---

[3] Pantev et al. 135, n. 134.
[4] Ivan Ev. Geshov, *The Balkan League*, trans. by C. C. Mincoff (London: John Murray, 1915), 19.

responded with full mobilization on 17 September. A week later Montenegro invoked a long-standing frontier dispute with the Ottoman empire as an excuse for declaring war. Ten days later, on 4 October, Bulgaria, Greece, and Serbia did likewise.

2. THE FIRST BALKAN WAR

The campaign of the autumn of 1912 was short and decisive. Bulgaria mobilized almost 600,000 men, who were divided into three armies. They were helped by the Macedonian-Adrianople militia, which consisted of almost 15,000 volunteers, mostly from exiles from those areas living in Bulgaria. A further 2,000 volunteers came from the ranks of the *comitadji*. The bulk of the Bulgarian forces were deployed in Thrace, though two divisions, the 2nd (Thracian) and 7th (Rila) were sent into the Struma valley to help the Serbs. The II Army moved towards Adrianople from the west whilst the I Army advanced upon it from the north. Within ten days the city was under siege. The Ottoman army dug in along a defensive line from Luleburgaz to Bunar Hissar but in a five-day battle around Luleburgaz the Bulgarian III Army had smashed its way through the defences and the Turks were forced back to the complex system of fortifications at Chatalja which defended Constantinople. Within weeks the Ottoman empire in Europe was reduced to the area within the Chatalja perimeter and the besieged cities of Scutari, Ioanina, and Adrianople.

Were an attack to be launched on the Chatalja lines a Bulgarian entry into the Ottoman capital might be possible. King Ferdinand favoured this policy and was rumoured to have ordered the necessary regalia[5] for a parade through the city. Geshov too was in favour of an attack, this time on the grounds that 'the temporary occupation of Constantinople would give us the most important and effective guarantee for the conclusion of a peace treaty favourable to us'.[6] The generals were less enthusiastic. Their men had fought hard and moved a great distance. They needed time to rest, recoup, and solidify their supply lines, besides which there had been

[5] The sumptuous robes are described in Georgi Markov, *Bŭlgariya v balkanskiya sŭyuz sreshtu osmanskata imperiya, 1912–1913* (Sofia: Nauka i izkustvo, 1989), 130.

[6] Al. Girginov, *Narodnata katastrofa: voĭnite 1912/13* (Sofia: Armeĭskiya voenno-izdatelski fond, 1926), 49–50.

outbreaks of cholera amongst them. The generals therefore were in favour of accepting the armistice offered by the enemy and General Radko Dimitriev, commander of the III Army, said he would not order an attack unless he received written orders to do so. These were issued and the attack began on 4 November. After two days it was clear it had failed and it was now the Bulgarians who requested an armistice. To this the Ottomans agreed; it was signed on 20 November.

Whilst the III Army had been engaged in Thrace another Bulgarian force had raced towards Salonika, hoping to reach the city before the Greeks. This was a highly prized goal for the Bulgarians. It was the nearest port to Sofia; without being linked to its natural, Bulgarian, hinterland it would, said Bulgarian propaganda, turn into nothing more than a large village; but the dependence was mutual, a popular slogan of the time stating, 'Bulgaria cannot survive without Salonika'.[7] The largest element in the port's population was neither Bulgarian nor Greek, but the Ladino-speaking Jews,[8] and the Bulgarians therefore put as many Jewish soldiers as possible in their advance units. It was to no avail; Greek forces entered the city only hours before the Bulgarian army reached it. This did not prevent Ferdinand, together with his two sons, Princes Boris and Kiril, paying a visit to the city early in December; but the Greek king was also present and Ferdinand claimed at the time that his days in Salonika were the most tense of his life.[9]

A few days after the armistice a peace conference began in London, the great powers having decided that the status quo ante could not be restored and that the belligerents were to be left to redraw the boundaries with the proviso that a new, independent, Albanian state be created. The Bulgarian delegation was headed by the russophile Stoyan Danev who, not wishing to take a subordinate ministry in Geshov's cabinet, had become chairman of the sŭbranie in 1911. No progress was made in the peace conference in the early months of 1913 because in January a coup in Constantinople had brought the Young Turks back to power with a specific pledge not to surrender Adrianople. Fighting therefore began again. The Ottoman army was reinforced by 35,000 troops brought over from Asia Minor. They were contained by a new Bulgarian IV Army formed from the 2nd and 7th Divisions and the Macedonian-Adrianople

[7] Ilchev, *D Radoslavov*, 11–12.
[8] See Mark Mazower, *Salonica, City of Ghosts; Christians, Muslims and Jews 1430–1950* (London: Harper/Collins, 2004).   [9] Kovachev, *Zapiski*, 93–7.

militia units. The siege of Adrianople continued with the Bulgarians, who received help from two Serbian divisions, dropping bombs from aircraft, the first time this weapon had been used in Europe. This had little effect and on 10 March, their concerns after the experiences at Chatalja notwithstanding, the Bulgarian generals committed their men to a direct assault on the city and its 70,000 armed defenders who surrendered two days later. The Balkan peace conference reassembled in London.

3. THE SECOND BALKAN WAR: THE FIRST 'NATIONAL CATASTROPHE'

The London conference could not devise a peaceful division of the spoils. Romania, which had remained inactive in the autumn of 1912, complicated the process by demanding territorial compensation; Romania, said the Bucharest government, had obeyed the orders of the great powers whilst those who had disobeyed them had secured considerable territorial gains. Romania needed an increase in territory both to reward it for its good behaviour and to compensate it for the aggrandizement of its neighbours. The only source of such aggrandizement could be Bulgaria, which immediately came under intense diplomatic pressure to give way, and in April was forced to agree that the southern Dobrudja up to a line from Silistra to Balchik should be ceded to Romania. This made Bulgaria all the more determined to hold on to as many as possible of its gains in Thrace and Macedonia. Yet this was made difficult by the powers' insistence that a new Albanian state be created. Its existence blocked Serbian expansion south-westwards and at the same time made unrealizable one of Serbia's main war aims: the possession of a port on the Adriatic. Therefore Serbia too was all the more determined to hold on to as many of its gains in Macedonia as possible.

The Bulgarians were by now wary of Serbian intentions, and rumours had been rife that Belgrade was already laying claim to towns such as Ohrid and Prilep which were in the Bulgarian zone as defined by the February 1912 treaty. By the early spring there were suspicions in Sofia that both the Greeks and the Serbs were prevaricating in the peace negotiations with the Ottomans: as long as those talks were continuing the Bulgarians would be forced to concentrate their troops in the east and would not be able to move them towards Macedonia. Eventually the

British foreign secretary, Sir Edward Grey, told the Balkan delegates to sign or get out of London. They signed. But the peace treaty of 17 May with the Ottoman empire did nothing to ease the problem of Macedonia; in fact it made it worse.

The Bulgarians argued that each belligerent should be compensated according to the effort they had made, a convenient doctrine in that Bulgaria had mobilized far more men and had suffered a much higher rate of casualties than its allies. The Serbs and the Greeks countered this by saying that the final settlement must preserve a basic balance of power in the Balkans.

Between Bulgaria and Greece the main bone of contention in Macedonia was Salonika. The Bulgarians, assuming that the Jews would opt for Bulgaria rather than Greece, suggested that a plebiscite should decide the town's fate. The Greek response was that the area and the town were Greek, even if much of it was occupied by 'Bulgarian-speaking Hellenes'. Salonika was not the only locus of conflict and on 9–10 May a serious clash between Bulgarian and Greek troops took place near Angista. After the clash Tsar Nicholas II sent a sharp warning to Ferdinand not to take military action against Bulgaria's former allies.

The Serbs, meanwhile, had made confidential approaches to Sofia, suggesting a redefinition of the agreed zones in Macedonia. Geshov was not to be drawn; he expressed regret that Serbia would not now be able to expand into Albania but that was not of Bulgaria's doing, he said, and if Bulgaria's gains were greater than those of Serbia then this merely reflected the greater sacrifices it had made, besides which Bulgaria alone amongst the allies had been forced to cede territory to Romania. The two states then explored the possibility of referring the question to St Petersburg for the tsar to arbitrate, but they could not agree on the terms of such arbitration, Serbia insisting that they must include an enlargement of the Serbian zone. A further attempt at direct negotiation between Geshov and the Serbian premier, Nikola Pašić, also failed.

By then two developments had fundamentally changed the situation. The Serbs and the Greeks had concluded a secret treaty and military agreement under which they agreed to exclude Bulgaria from Macedonia west of the Vardar, whilst the boundaries to the east of it were to be drawn on the basis of effective occupation. The second development showed the worst aspects of Ferdinand's personal regime.

By May the demand in Bulgaria for military action against Greece and Serbia had grown considerably and Ferdinand had learned from a 'close friend' in Vienna that the Serbs were preparing to attack Bulgaria.[10] At the same time, the extremists amongst the Macedonian exiles were demanding intervention and threatened to murder anyone who opposed it, not an idle threat given the record of the past decade. Many more sober minds believed that a pre-emptive strike was necessary before the two former allies consolidated their hold on too much of Macedonia; others thought more in terms of a short, sharp action which would force the Greeks and Serbs to the negotiation table in a suitably chastened and accommodating frame of mind. Initially there had been a widespread confidence that the Bulgarian army, larger than that of both the Serbs and the Greeks, would be able to carry out a successful operation against them; the memory of Slivnitsa was still fresh in the minds of many. After the fall of Adrianople large numbers of Bulgarian troops were moved from Thrace into Macedonia to confront the Serb and Greek forces which were also concentrating along the line of division with the Bulgarians; the latter also increased the number of men with the colours from 592,000 to 600,000. By May Bulgarian confidence was waning. The army was becoming restless; desertion and disobedience were increasingly common, and there was virtual mutiny in the 9th (Pleven) Division which was out of control for three days. Most of the army had been inactive since November 1912 and many of the conscripted soldiers were asking why, if they were not required to fight, they could not leave their cold, uncomfortable dugouts and return home, particularly as the sowing season had arrived. There was a fear that a second war would keep them away from their fields until harvest time. By the middle of May the king, who had originally agreed with Geshov that a negotiated settlement must be found, had aligned with the war party. On 16 May, whilst Geshov was in Tsaribrod for his last, unproductive conversation with Pašić, Ferdinand called a crown council with the leaders of all the major political parties, all of whom had declared in favour of war. Geshov was dumbfounded that he, as minister president and leader of the largest party in the sŭbranie, should not have been consulted, and he resigned. This, under the workings of the personal regime, was what he was

---

[10] Hall, *Bulgaria's Road*, 198. The information is taken from the archives of King Ferdinand in the Hoover Institution, Stanford, Calif..

expected to do. His successor was Danev, but no public announcement of the change could be made until 24 May when the new minister president returned from the London peace talks.

With tension mounting rapidly the tsar appealed to the kings of Serbia and Bulgaria to keep their swords sheathed, but also warning them that if either unleashed a war they would 'be held responsible before the Slav cause'.[11] The kings' replies were polite but non-committal, and both were then asked to submit a statement of their claims to Russia so that arbitration might begin. The Bulgarian government was now facing its ultimate dilemma. If arbitration began there could be no thought of war, but the chief of the general staff, General Mihail Savov, had issued a virtual ultimatum: the Serbs and Greeks, he said, had concluded an alliance and were concentrating their forces against the Bulgarians; in face of this danger, and with unrest in the ranks increasing, the army had to be sent into action or demobilized within ten days. When the cabinet discussed the question on 9 June Danev declared in favour of war. For such an inveterate russophile to reject the tsar's arbitration was an extraordinary step, but Danev was by now convinced that the Serbs would not be satisfied unless Bulgaria made concessions outside the contested zone. And this, he said, Bulgaria could not and should not do. The Russians were therefore told that Bulgaria would agree to arbitration only on condition that it be confined to the contested zone, that the Serbs began to demobilize, and that a decision be reached within eight days. If these conditions were not met, the Russian minister for foreign affairs was told, Bulgaria would go to war. The Russians, unaccustomed to receiving ultimata from small Balkan states, were astounded and enraged. They condemned Bulgaria and left it to its fate.

Savov reluctantly ordered the Bulgarian army to advance on 16 June. This was done without the knowledge of the cabinet and Danev tried to reverse the order, only to be overruled by the king, who was commander-in-chief of the armed forces. The king also sacked Savov, who had initially obeyed Danev's order. The confusion was in part the result of personality clashes between the king, the minister president, and the chief of the general staff, but many concluded that such things could not have happened but for the personal regime.

---

[11] G. P. Gooch and Harold Temperley (eds.), *British Documents on the Origins of the War, 1898–1914*, 11 vols., vol. ix, part ii, no. 1055 enclosure; and 'Balkanicus' (Stojan M. Protić), *The Aspirations of Bulgaria*, (London: Simpkin, Marshall, 1915), 22.

The second Balkan, or inter-allied war had begun. It was to be shorter but far more bloody than the fighting against the Ottomans. For Bulgaria it proved to be a national catastrophe. Its forces were concentrated in Macedonia, leaving the borders with Romania and the Ottoman empire virtually undefended. Both states took advantage of this, the Romanians moving towards an undefended Sofia and the Turks retaking Adrianople. Danev's desperate appeals for help from St Petersburg fell on deaf ears, and on 4 July he resigned; Malinov refused to pick up the poisoned chalice and a new government of a number of liberal factions was constructed with Radoslavov as minister president. There was nothing he could do but capitulate. Fighting ended almost immediately and the treaty of Bucharest, with Serbia, Greece, Montenegro, and Romania, was signed on 28 July; peace with the Ottoman empire was signed in Constantinople on 30 September. All that remained of Bulgaria's gains from the first Balkan war were part of Pirin Macedonia to a point between Melnik and Syar in the Struma valley; the Kŭrdjali and Gyumyurdjina areas in Thrace; and a stretch of the Aegean coastline which included the port of Dedeagach.

The result of the second Balkan war was nothing less than a second partition of Bulgaria. But in some respects it was worse than that at Berlin in 1878. This time the lost territories were not restored to an enfeebled, multinational empire which granted considerable autonomy to its separate religious communities, but to modern nation-states which, if they did not attempt to assimilate the Bulgarians, were far less tolerant of ethnic or religious diversity. There were many protests against this. A powerful new organization, Dobrudja, was formed to bring attention to the plight of the Bulgarians in this now alienated area; there were constant complaints against the serbianization of the areas of Macedonia which passed into Belgrade's hands; and in June 1914 troops had to be deployed in Burgas and Asenovgrad (Stanimaka) where rioters, enraged at the treatment of Exarchists in Greek Macedonia, wanted to attack local Greeks and their property.

In Macedonia itself the Bulgarian cause suffered losses which it was never able to regain. The aged Exarch admitted that 'Under the Turks we had ideals and hopes, now even these are lost.'[12] In the second half of 1913 a number of exarchist communities in Macedonia were reported to

---

[12] Richard von Mach, *Aus bewegter Balkanzeit, 1879–1918: Erinnerungen* (Berlin: E. S. Mittler, 1928) 218.

have sought Austro-Hungarian diplomatic protection and had talked of turning once again to Uniatism. In December 1913 the Exarch travelled to Sofia; his responsibilities in the Ottoman empire were now reduced to the Bulgarians of Constantinople and the surrounding area. There was little point in him returning to the Ottoman capital and he therefore remained in Sofia until his death in 1915.

The economic impact of the second Balkan war was enormous. In the years since independence grain had been a principal export, with the most productive area being the Dobrudja, the one area of Bulgaria where there were large, modernized agricultural holdings. Railways had been built to carry grain and other exports to Varna, whose port had been developed at great expense; in 1912 it handled more goods than Salonika. Now its hinterland had been lost and the frontier with Romania was only 15 kilometres away. The new lands gained in the south were much poorer than those lost in the Dobrudja; even the port at Dedeagach could hardly be considered a substitute for Varna because the railway to it wound in and out of Ottoman territory. The Bulgarian government therefore decided to construct a new harbour at Porto Lagos and to build a railway to it. These were costly enterprises which could not be financed without borrowing from abroad.

The defeat of 1913, the first of Bulgaria's two national catastrophes, had been caused not by the inadequacies of the Bulgarian army which held its own in the western theatre but by the failings of the politicians. When he had signed the order authorizing the beginning of the first Balkan war, King Ferdinand had said to General Ivan Fichev, 'General, I don't know anything about military affairs; all my hopes rest on you,'[13] yet within weeks Ferdinand was interfering in the military conduct of the war and bearing his usual grudges against those who attempted to question his judgement or his decisions. He had soon reverted to the personal rule which had suborned the constitutional system and without which more authority and responsibility would have resided in the cabinet where there were ultimately doubts over the unprovoked attack of 16 June. Meanwhile, there had been a series of diplomatic miscalculations. It had been supposed, wrongly, that the great powers would stand by the convention established in the nineteenth century that Christian territory, once liberated from Ottoman rule, would not be returned to it. Therefore,

[13] Cited in Markov, *Bŭlgariya v balkanskiya sŭyuz*, 41.

it was assumed, the Turks would not be allowed to regain, let alone retain, Adrianople and Thrace. Most serious of all, however, was the assumption that in the last resort Russia and the triple entente powers would back Bulgaria against the other Balkan states. This was perhaps the result of historical russophilia and of Russian actions in 1877–8. But 1908 had altered the Balkan political system more than most Bulgarians seemed to realize. In that year Bulgaria had cooperated with Russia's rival, Austria-Hungary, whilst the Serbia which emerged from the annexation crisis was an implacable opponent of the Habsburgs. And that was the crucial issue: Serbia was always a more reliable lever against Austria-Hungary than was Bulgaria, and as such would always be prized more highly by Russia. In addition to that, in 1913 the Bulgarians angered Russia by breaking up the Balkan league which St Petersburg had welcomed on the false assumption that it was primarily a defensive mechanism against Austria-Hungary. Nor did Bulgaria's policy makers fully realize that were Bulgaria to expand too much it would be seen in St Petersburg not as a potential partner or protégé but as a possible threat to Russian interests and ambitions.

That the catastrophe was the responsibility of the country's political establishment was not lost on the masses of the population. They knew too that the mass parties, BANU and both socialist factions, had opposed military action against Serbia and Greece. The alienation of the majority of the population would be seen whenever it was allowed a free voice in political affairs.

The second Balkan war was the most important turning point in modern Bulgarian history, the first world war being in many respects a repeat of that of 1913. The second Balkan war determined that in the two great crises of the twentieth century Bulgaria would align with those whom it thought most likely to return the lost territories, and in both cases that proved to be Germany. Therefore both world wars ended for Bulgaria with defeat; after each defeat radical forces took control of the country, in the first case the agrarians and in the second the socialists. Both radical regimes were eventually dismantled, the first after a short period and with great violence, the second peacefully after almost half a century.

4. FROM BALKAN TO EUROPEAN WAR

That the second Balkan war had changed the nature of Bulgarian political life was soon seen. The Radoslavov coalition faced the daunting tasks of rebuilding the country and of integrating the new territories, limited in extent as they were. The government could not work with the sŭbranie elected in 1911 to serve Geshov's regime, and a general election was called in November 1913, though it was confined to the pre-Balkan wars kingdom.

The vote was the first to be held under nationwide proportional representation and the results were astounding. The government parties polled almost 50,000 fewer votes than their opponents and secured 97 seats to the opposition's 109; of the latter 47 were agrarians and 37 sat for the various socialist groups. In March 1914 Radoslavov went to the polls again. This time the newly acquired territories were allowed to participate, though their acquisition had not yet been sanctioned by a grand national assembly, and many of those who were given the franchise had not yet received the Bulgarian citizenship without which they were not legally entitled to vote. The government indulged in other measures of persuasion. Officials from the Ottoman legation in Sofia visited every constituency in Thrace urging the local Muslims to vote for the government, though opposition spokesmen were excluded from the area on the grounds that Muslim discontent had rendered it unsafe. The government also created in the newly acquired territories more constituencies than the population warranted, and soaked the area with privileges. Despite these measures the poll produced 116 government deputies and precisely the same number of oppositionists, their ranks including 50 agrarians and 21 socialists. The verification process deprived the opposition of 16 seats, all of which went to the government. Radoslavov's actions in the new territories was said to have earned him a 'Turkish' majority. With it he was to govern for five turbulent years.

Having secured a dependable sŭbranie Radoslavov made it known that his chief objective was to procure the loan necessary to integrate the new territories and develop harbour facilities at Porto Lagos. The sum required was 250 million leva, by far the largest loan ever sought by a Bulgarian government. In the context of the deepening European crisis of 1914 the Bulgarian loan was inevitably affected by great power politics. The French were not sure they had enough money to lend such a sum, and the Russians insisted that if they did Bulgaria should be required to commit itself to the entente diplomatic camp. This the Germans exploited and offered the sums required. Radoslavov put the proposal before the sŭbranie in July. The debate was probably the most chaotic and unruly in the assembly's history. There were numerous fist fights whilst the minister president was seen to wave a revolver above his head, and when the vote was finally taken it was by show of hands. It resulted in a majority of seven for the government but few were convinced; there were accusations that many deputies had voted with both hands and that even the policemen introduced into the chamber to restore order had raised their hands for the government.

The loan was disliked because it seemed to commit Bulgaria to a pro-German position. It was also criticized because, in contradiction to the railway act of 1884, it required the Sofia administration to grant the contract for the construction of the railway to Porto Lagos to a German consortium, and because the state-owned coal mines in Pernik and Bobovdol were to be placed under the control of a German company. The agreement stated that the first instalment of the loan would be given to Bulgaria in September unless war broke out before then. The Germans invoked this clause and insisted that the loan be renegotiated, and when a second agreement was reached in February 1915 it was for 150 rather than the original 250 million gold francs. The concessions on the railway to Porto Lagos and on the state-owned coal mines were not changed, though the Bulgarian authorities were able to frustrate the implementation of the latter.

5. BULGARIA AND THE FIRST WORLD WAR: THE COMMITMENT TO THE CENTRAL POWERS

From the summer of 1914 foreign affairs were inevitably dominated by the war in Europe. Bulgaria had declared 'strict and loyal' neutrality when the war began. The country and the army were exhausted after the Balkan wars, and neither side in the great conflict appeared likely to emerge rapidly as the winner. Ferdinand and Radoslavov were temperamentally inclined towards the central powers, but with the German army stuck on the Marne and the Austrian unable to take Belgrade they did not seem a good bet. Fighting alongside the Russians and their allies, on the other hand, did not seem a good option, not least because after the Ottoman empire had joined the central powers Bulgaria would have been too distant from the entente countries to receive the help it would need if it joined them. Bulgaria could afford to wait until approached by both sides and then choose the one which offered the most and/or which appeared the more likely victor. And there was little doubt Bulgaria would be approached because it was, in the words of Winston Churchill, 'the dominant factor in the Balkans in 1914 and 1915'.[14] Bulgaria controlled the links between the Ottoman empire and the central powers; its army, despite the exertions of 1912–13, remained a large and impressive fighting force, and were it to commit itself to one side or the other Romania and Greece would probably follow suit. Bulgaria's freedom of manoeuvre was increased by the fact that, given its military strength and strategic location, both sides in the European war would be prepared to tolerate its neutrality for fear of driving it into their opponents' camp.

Between the autumn of 1914 and the summer of 1915 the Bulgarians were courted by both sides, but eventually Ferdinand and his minister president were to follow their instinctive preferences, and in September 1915 decided to join forces with Germany, Austria-Hungary, and the Ottoman empire.

The main reason for their decision was that diplomatic exchanges had shown that whatever gains in Macedonia the allies would offer Bulgaria would be dependent on what the Serbs would be prepared to allow. This did not offer much hope. Even after their defeat in 1915 the Serbs remained determined not to surrender a square centimetre of what they had previously held, or of what they had been promised in Macedonia; and their determination was reinforced after the entente powers had promised Italy territory on the eastern Adriatic. And in all this the Serbs had the full support of the Russians. The triple alliance, on the other hand, was not bound by obligations to Serbia and could therefore offer far more in Macedonia; in the summer of 1915 the central powers made it known that if it cooperated with them Bulgaria could have both its own and the contested zone. Then the Ottoman government was persuaded to promise that should Bulgaria enter the war on the side of the central powers it would receive eastern Thrace up to the Enos-Midia line and be given full control of the Maritsa valley with its railway to Dedeagach.

These were tempting offers but what finally decided the Sofia government to commit itself to the triple alliance was the apparent weakness of the entente. British and French forces had made no progress on the deadlocked western front, Italy's entry into the war seemed to have brought no benefit, the Russians were in headlong retreat from Russian

[14] Winston S. Churchill, *The World Crisis 1911–18* (London: Four Square Books, 1960), 317.

Poland, and the Commonwealth forces were pinned down on the beaches of Gallipoli. Not only could the central powers offer more, they appeared to be more likely to win.

In late August and early September 1915 Bulgaria concluded a series of secret agreements with Germany, Austria-Hungary, and the Ottoman empire. The core of these agreements was that Bulgaria would participate in the forthcoming attack upon Serbia and would, upon Serbia's defeat, receive both zones in Macedonia and a slice of Serbian territory on the eastern bank of the river Morava. Full mobilization was declared in Bulgaria on 8 September and soon 800,000 men were with the colours. On 28 September the Bulgarian army joined the war against Serbia. Within a week the entente states had declared war on Bulgaria.

In Bulgaria itself the decision was far from being universally welcomed. The agrarians had always been against participation in the war. In September 1914 *Zemedelsko Zname* had stated that the agrarians were 'not against the unification of Bulgaria . . . but to us the blood of Bulgaria's sons is more dear and more precious than any form of unification or expansion.'[15] Other groups argued that if Bulgaria must participate then it should be on the side of the entente. In the spring of 1915 Malinov had tried to put together an alliance of opposition parties dedicated to resisting any further moves towards cooperation with the central powers, but it came to nothing, partly because of the entente's declining military position and, in secret, to the fact that the central powers were in a position to make offers the entente could not equal.

The entente had placed its hope in Malinov and other opposition groups but its diplomacy in Sofia was not always coordinated, and in some respects perhaps lacked commitment. More important was the fact that it chose to concentrate on working through the opposition parties rather than the king and the minister president, despite all the evidence of the personal regime and its nature. Another problem for the entente was that some of their most prominent protégés were tainted by scandal, or worse. One of the entente's favoured sons, the former stambolovist minister Nikola Genadiev, was compromised by his alleged involvement in a Macedonian bomb outrage in Sofia in which the son of the minister of

---

[15] Cited in *Raĭko Daskalov—Politicheska i dŭrzhavna deĭnost. Privetstviya i dokladi, izneseni na natsionalnoto tŭrzhestveno sŭbranie i na nauchnata sesiya po sluchaĭ 100 godini ot rozhdeneto na Raĭko Daskalov*, no editor named (Sofia: BANU, 1988), 77.

war was killed—the main culprits were hanged before an invited audience in Sofia central prison—whilst a good deal of public opprobrium followed from the des Closières affair, an attempt by a pro-entente consortium to buy up the entire 1915 grain harvest so that it would be denied to the Germans. The consortium used unsavoury methods and in any case German purchasing agencies beat them to it and bought up most of the crop on the stalk. Nor was that the only money the Germans disbursed. Ferdinand received a personal loan of a million leva from the Discontogesellschaft and Radoslavov was given 'pocket money' of 100,000 leva. Western diplomacy, by contrast, was as parsimonious as it was misdirected.

As commitment to the triple alliance appeared ever more likely the opposition attempted to limit rather than prevent Bulgaria's involvement in the war, and in August 1915 all the non-government parties apart from the narrows came together in a united bloc. When the decision to commit Bulgaria to the German side had secretly been made Radoslavov sought to defuse potential trouble by offering the opposition two cabinet posts, the ministries of the interior and of railways. Stamboliĭski was in favour of accepting on the grounds that control of these ministries could frustrate mobilization were it to be declared. The other parties would not agree but they were reunited over the demand that the king grant them an interview. When it took place the opposition leaders demanded that the sŭbranie be recalled before any decision on war be made and that a coalition of all major parties be created; they also warned the king that the people would never tolerate war against Russia. The interview ended with an exchange of insults between the king and the agrarian leader. Stamboliĭski then published the exchange and called upon the people to resist mobilization. He was sentenced to life imprisonment for *lèse-majesté* and treason.

Other opposition leaders continued to press for the calling of the assembly but instead Radoslavov convened a meeting consisting only of pro-government deputies and explained to them that the country had to seize the opportunity to undo the 1913 settlement in the Balkans. He further insulted the other parties by then calling and immediately postponing the sŭbranie. Despite these dubious tricks most of the opposition parties were prepared to suspend political hostilities for the duration and when the assembly finally met in December all of them except the narrows voted for a 55 million leva credit to meet the costs of the war and of supporting the soldiers' families. By this time Bulgaria was already in the war and had occupied much of Macedonia; to deny credits at this stage would have seemed close to treason.

6. BULGARIA IN THE FIRST WORLD WAR: THE SECOND 'NATIONAL CATASTROPHE'

Bulgaria was the last country to join the grouping of the central powers and was to be the first to leave it. When Bulgaria did withdraw from the war it was partly because of doubts as to whether its war aims could be fulfilled but mainly because the war had reduced the army and the population to the verge of destitution.

The war began with success on the battlefield and after the defeat of Serbia there were calls for an attack on Greece. This the Germans prevented until the spring of 1916 on the grounds that if the allied troops were driven out of Salonika they would be redeployed on the western front. In August of that year the allies attacked from Salonika and at the same time Romania entered the war on their side. The attack in Macedonia was easily repulsed and Bulgarian troops advanced there and in western Thrace, taking Drama, Syar, and Kavalla. In the north they joined Ottoman units which took the southern Dobrudja and then crossed the Danube into Romania proper. Later in 1916 the Bulgarians suffered some setbacks in what was for them the main theatre of war, Macedonia, and by the end of the year the Serbs had repossessed Bitola. From then until the Bulgarian collapse of September 1918 the Macedonian front was almost as immobile as that in France.

Like most belligerents Bulgaria did not immediately define its war aims. In January 1916 Radoslavov told the sŭbranie that war was being fought to unite the Bulgarian nation within its historic and ethnographic borders, by which he meant the acquisition of Macedonia, Thrace west of the Maritsa, the Dobrudja, and the Morava valley. This was a maximalist programme and by the middle of 1916 there were some doubts as to whether the Morava valley should be included in the list if a stable peace were ever to be established in the Balkans.

Even before September 1915 the government had done much to prepare the country for war. When neutrality had been declared a state of emergency had been proclaimed, giving the government powers to close newspapers and restrict political gatherings. It was a wise precaution. Since August 1914 the population had shown no enthusiasm for war, and none whatever for war against Russia; when the tsar's forces had taken Przemyśl early in 1915 there had been boisterous pro-Russian demonstrations and church bells were rung throughout Bulgaria. When Bulgaria did join the war, the authorities in Sofia sought to counteract this resilient russophilia by promoting closer ties between Germans and Bulgarians. Not surprisingly these included newspaper articles and films showing fraternal cooperation between troops of both nations, there were predictable exchanges of parliamentary delegations, and Ferdinand, one of the least military of monarchs, was made an honorary field marshal in the German army. The government propaganda machine also put great stress on the ethnic solidarity of Bulgarians, Turks, and Hungarians, and emphasized the advantages to Bulgaria of the notion of Mitteleuropa.

It was partly in order to bring Bulgaria and Germany closer together that the government decided that the country should switch to the Gregorian calendar on 14 April 1916, with religious festivals henceforth being celebrated on the day in the western calendar which corresponded with the festival in the Julian, so that Christmas would be on 7th January rather than 25th December. Stoilov had attempted to make this change as part of his modernizing policies in the 1890s and had been defeated by clerical opposition, but in 1916 the alignment with Germany offered an excellent opportunity to bring about the change. It would make dealings with Bulgaria's allies less complicated and conveniently it was one of the rare years in which the dates of Easter, Whitsuntide, and Ascension coincided in both calendars.

These efforts to stress the affinity of Bulgarian and German cultures failed to overcome Bulgaria's traditional russophilia, especially after the revolution of February 1917 had dismantled the Russian autocracy.

By the time of the Russian revolution considerable tension had developed between the Radoslavov government and the army. Early in the war a number of senior, pro-Russian officers had been retired and their places taken by younger men, many of whom were supporters of the Democratic Party, the party which more than any other represented the intelligentsia, military as well as civilian. Radoslavov attempted to neutralize any criticisms they raised as politicking on behalf of the Democratic Party but this was patently not the case, particularly when the soldiers highlighted the problems in the supply of essential commodities both to the civilian population, especially in the occupied territories, and to the army. This was to be one of the crucial problems of the war and was to precipitate Bulgaria's withdrawal from the conflict in September 1918. The civilian problem was by no means confined to the occupied territories.

The war brought inflation. An index measuring a number of necessities at a base of 100 in 1914 rose to 122 in late 1915, 200 in 1916, and 505 early in 1918; in July 1918, with a disastrous harvest impending, it was 847. And these were official prices; those on the black market, often the only source of supply, were considerably higher; that of sugar, for example, was ten times the official level in 1918. There were serious shortages of a number of essential commodities. Clothing was one, partly because the army requisitioned more than it was eventually to need. Food was an even more serious problem. The peasants could escape the worst of the food shortages but they had no relief from those of salt, nor could they evade the exactions of the requisitioning authorities who took meat, eggs, and dairy produce. In the towns the suffering was greater and by 1918 bread was being manufactured from a mixture of wheat and maize so injurious to the digestive system that it caused a number of deaths.

In March 1915, in another of its measures to anticipate possible entry into the war, the government had given itself the right to extend its control into many areas of the economy. This did not prevent confusion in September when the usual channels for food distribution were disrupted by mobilization, by the tendency of food purchasing agencies to overestimate their needs, and by the fact that there were separate requisitioning authorities for military and civilian food supplies.

These difficulties were ironed out but more sinister and intractable ones remained. Chief amongst them was that the Germans and Austrians took increasingly large quantities of food for themselves and their ever more hungry families at home. Allied soldiers had been given the right to send home 5 kilograms of food per week but there was widespread suspicion that, abetted by their extensive powers over the Bulgarian rail and telephone networks, the Germans were abusing this privilege. The suspicions were far from groundless. German and Austrian troops stationed in Serbia were crossing into Bulgarian-occupied areas to avail themselves of the food purchasing privilege. This was made easier for them by the fact that German and Austrian currency had become legal tender in Bulgaria, and because the German and Austrian troops were better paid they were able to take greater advantage of the flourishing black market. By early 1916 even bread, rationed since the beginning of the war in Bulgaria, was in short supply and so bad was the problem in the occupied territories that a number of deaths from starvation were reported in Ohrid. By the end of the year the amount of food being sent to Germany and Austria would have been sufficient, had the 5-kilo ration been observed, for about 200,000 troops rather than the 16,000 who were involved. Later in the war the right to send food parcels was limited to a small number of national or religious holidays.

Public resentment at increasing food shortages was intensified by universal suspicions, all too frequently justified, that the problem was compounded by the involvement of corrupt Bulgarian officials. Train loads of food were leaving the country for Germany in wagons labelled 'war matériel', because Bulgarian customs had no right to inspect such cargoes. There were also spectacular individual instances of malfeasance; the brother of a former minister made a million leva from the illegal export of 30,000 sheep that were embarked at Burgas during a fake air-raid.

Rising public anger was expressed both by the army high command and in the sŭbranie. In the spring of 1916 the former demanded the suspension of food exports and even posted guards on the frontiers and on railway wagons to prevent food from leaving the country. In the assembly there was fierce criticism of the organization of supplies, to which the government responded by forming the central committee for economic and social welfare which was to include sŭbranie deputies from all the major parties.

Radoslavov's government rode out this storm because the opposition was divided and because he was able to argue that the acquisition of the fertile Dobrudja would ease the situation. It did not, not least because so relentless were the German food requisitioning agents that as soon as it was acquired the area was stripped not only of food but of seed corn too. In 1917 the supply problem was much worse. Official sources spoke of 'thousands' of deaths from hunger, a fifth of Sofia's children were reported to find most of their food by begging in taverns, and in Plovdiv there were demonstrations against the government. Again the situation in the occupied territories was worse. By April 1917 the Morava valley was in a state of virtual revolt, the problem of food shortages having been greatly exacerbated by an attempt to conscript the young men of the area; they had no wish to fight their fathers who had been enlisted into the Serbian army in 1914.

The hardships suffered on the domestic front inevitably affected military morale, particularly in units raised in urban centres; in May 1917 the men of one company of the 1st (Sofia) Infantry Regiment had refused to fight until they had been promised that their families would be better cared for. By the middle of the summer there were 500 soldiers detained in Sofia's central prison for agitating amongst the troops. Discontent amongst the troops was aggravated by the knowledge that their German and Austrian allies were better fed, better clothed and shod, better armed, and better protected because their supplies of cement were more reliable. Many politicians who had reluctantly supported the war became more critical whilst those who had always opposed it campaigned openly against it. Stamboliĭski liaised with many soldiers home on leave until September 1917 when he was moved from the political section of Sofia prison and sent to the fortress in Vidin.

The army high command had by this stage established virtual control over all supplies. Relations between it and the civilian powers were by now at a low ebb. The military regarded the central committee for economic and social welfare, which had been created by and was dominated by the politicians, as incompetent. The politicians, for their part, held the military responsible for many of the problems, particularly in the occupied territories. In April 1917, when the civilian authorities secretly admitted that they could do nothing to improve the supply problem, the high command seized its chance. The generals easily persuaded the government of the need for a complete reappraisal of the administrative system and the committee was replaced by a directorate for economic and social welfare which was in reality little more than a department of the general staff.

The military's assumption of control over supplies took place against the background of shifts in the disposition of political forces. The main factor responsible for this was the Russian revolution. This had raised hopes of a separate peace and, with the consent of Berlin, various approaches were made to Petrograd. They came to nothing, but the revolution did increase the politicians' willingness to question the conduct and even the purpose of the war, the more so when students released by the Russians in 1917 returned home saying they had been told by the new minister for foreign affairs in Petrograd that Russia would be willing to sign a separate peace once the present Bulgarian government and monarch had been removed. Stamboliĭski, still in Sofia, added another arrow to the opposition quiver; now tsarism had fallen, he argued, the United States would enter the war on the side of the entente and this would end all hope of victory for the central powers, and therefore Bulgaria should pull out of the war immediately. On the Romanian front soldiers in the III Army seemed to be doing precisely this because there were many instances of fraternization with the Russian troops in the opposing lines.

Radoslavov continued in office because he was still able to buy enough support in the sŭbranie, particularly from the stambolovist factions, and because there was still force in his oft-repeated argument that despite all the hardships the war had at least achieved national unification. When this argument was undermined his position became very precarious. The first serious questioning of his argument came when Bulgarian troops crossed the Danube into Romania. This was not fighting for national unification, said Naĭcho Tsanov, leader of the russophile Radical Party, but naked aggression. His assertion gained considerably in strength in July when the German Reichstag approved a resolution calling for a peace without annexations or indemnities, although the mover of the resolution hastened to assure the Bulgarians that they would not be denied their justifiable right to national unification.

In a stormy sŭbranie session in late October Radoslavov still had enough political backing to survive, but to an increasing degree opposition to him was shifting away from the constitutional arena, and once again the motivating forces were desperation at food and other shortages, and increasing political radicalism inspired by events in Russia and the United States. By the beginning of 1918 the Germans had extended their control over the Bulgarian railways and telephone system and were taking more food than ever from the country. In December 1917 10,000 protesters in Sofia heard narrow socialist leader Dimitŭr Blagoev demand peace and revolution; in the following month rioting in Gabrovo lasted for three full days. By May disturbances by semi-starved housewives had become endemic throughout the country, and commentators were talking of the 'Women's Revolt'. In the same month an angry crowd near Plovdiv broke the windows of the train carrying Emperor Karl and the Empress Zita who were visiting Bulgaria. The country was facing famine; the Bolsheviks were offering a radical alternative to the existing political structure; and, after President Wilson had announced his fourteen points in January 1918, the United States was proposing a peace settlement as good as any Bulgaria was likely to find.

The fourteen points did much to weaken Radoslavov's hold on power. Until January 1918 he could also argue that Bulgaria had to remain in the war because Germany would strip it of its gains if it threw in the towel. The eleventh of Wilson's fourteen points, however, offered the Balkan states borders based on historically determined lines of nationality with guarantees for future independence and territorial integrity. This, most Bulgarians believed, would guarantee the retention of their recent gains, and given that Bulgaria had not gone to war with the USA, there was every likelihood that Washington would back Bulgaria's claims. To make matters worse for Radoslavov, it then transpired that the Germans, whom he had cited as the guarantors of national unity, would not live up to their allotted role. The Bulgarians considered the Dobrudja as one of their legitimate historic claims. But this their allies refused to accept. In May 1918, after three months of negotiations between Sofia, Vienna, Berlin, and Constantinople, the treaty of Bucharest partitioned the food-rich area. The northern part was placed under joint central-powers administration and full Bulgarian control confined to the southern Dobrudja. To make matters worse, Austria-Hungary demanded the Vranya triangle in Serbia, and the Ottoman empire the return of much of Thrace. Even Radoslavov admitted that Bulgaria had been treated not as an ally but as a vanquished foe. The Dobrudja was seen as the least contentious of Bulgaria's national claims and if it were not conceded the prospects in Macedonia, Thrace, and the Morava valley were bleak indeed. Radoslavov's credibility was totally destroyed and on 20 June he resigned.

His successor was the Democratic Party leader Malinov. He wanted to create a wide coalition and even brought Stamboliĭski back to Sofia prison in the hope that he might persuade BANU to join the government, but Stamboliĭski would agree only if the government pledged itself to withdraw from the war, and this the king would not contemplate. Malinov did achieve a minor victory in July when the Germans agreed to revise the treaty of Bucharest and grant Bulgaria sovereignty over northern Dobrudja, but it was too late for territorial gains to win over a population totally demoralized by prolonged deprivation and the prospect of even worse to come.

It was by now obvious that the authorities could not find more food, despite the increasingly ruthless and therefore unpopular activities of the food procurement agencies. Furthermore, the 1918 harvest was going to be even worse than those of the immediately preceding years. Part of the reason for this had been the widespread mobilization not only of men— the women could take their place in the fields—but of draught animals; the figures for the production of grain in quintals per hundred of population tell their own stark story:

1911	653.1
1912	589.2
1913	539.6
1914	407.6
1915	482.0
1916	368.1
1917	348.4
1918	241.0[16]

Soldiers home on harvest leave saw the plight of their families and were enraged, not least because the hated requisition authorities, usually with the connivance of local officials, took not only food but other scarce commodities such as salt, soap, matches, and fuel; although they usually paid for these items the requisitioning units frequently resold them on the black market for huge profits. If the soldiers were appalled and enraged at the condition of their families, the reverse was also true. The soldiers, too, were short of food but they were also badly clothed and even more badly shod. Many were starving in trenches near German troops who were well fed on Bulgarian food. Civilian and soldier alike in the summer of 1918 saw the other as deprived and duped by devious politicians who had taken the country to war for the benefit not of Bulgaria but of Germany. Radical feelings inevitably rose rapidly with soldiers establishing links with the anti-war parties, particularly BANU and the socialist factions. Desertions multiplied, councils, or 'soviets', were formed in many units, and scores of meetings along the front demanded an end to the war. There were similar protests throughout the country which seemed now to be on the verge of collapse.

The final collapse was not civilian but military. It came with an entente attack on Bulgarian positions in Macedonia in the middle of September. By 25 September French and British troops had entered Bulgaria proper

---

[16] Hristo Hristov, *Revolyutsionnata Kriza v Bŭlgariya, 1918–1919* (Sofia: BAN, 1957), 37.

and the Bulgarian army had virtually dissolved, many units being more intent on entering Sofia and punishing those responsible for the war than in resisting the entente forces. A crown council decided to seek an armistice and a delegation, which included the US consul in Sofia, was sent to Salonika to secure it.

Before the delegation left Stamboliĭski had been released from prison and asked to do all he could to calm the army; this he agreed to do on condition that Bulgaria must immediately accept whatever peace terms the enemy chose to dictate. Stamboliĭski then set off for general staff headquarters in Kyustendil. By the time he arrived his agrarian colleague, Raĭko Daskalov, who was in Radomir, had decided that the radical forces in the army were strong enough to take Sofia, and he therefore suggested to Stamboliĭski that they march on the capital. Stamboliĭski's reply was non-committal but it did not deter Daskalov who, having declared a republic, set off from Radomir for Sofia. He did not reach it. The government had rallied some loyal troops and Macedonians who were strengthened by German units rushed from the Crimea, and these units repulsed the republican attack on Sofia. Stamboliĭski declared that he had had no connection with the Radomir rebellion which, he said, had been forced on Daskalov by the mutinous soldiery. He was not believed and therefore tried to enlist the support of the narrows for a full-scale revolution. The narrows' leader in Sofia, Georgi Dimitrov, refused; he did not wish to cooperate with a petit bourgeois party when he was convinced a socialist revolution was about to take place. Stamboliĭski then went into hiding.

The Radomir rebellion failed primarily because the main objective of the mutineers, an end to the war, was achieved with the signature of an armistice in Salonika on 29 September. The terms were announced early in October. The first required Ferdinand to leave the country and he therefore abdicated in favour of his son, who became King Boris III. When Ferdinand left Bulgaria Radoslavov went with him, to live on a German state pension until his death in Berlin in 1929. The armistice also made it clear that Bulgaria would have to withdraw from virtually all the territory it had acquired during the war.

Malinov continued in office with an expanded coalition for only a few weeks when Todor Todorov, the deputy leader of the National Party, reconstructed a government which included the broad socialists and the agrarians. The main purpose of the coalition was to prepare the country for a general election in August 1919 and to await the definitive terms of peace which would be dictated by the allies in Paris. In the interim food shortages were not greatly alleviated.

The first world war was the second national catastrophe; it had made San Stefano Bulgaria an even more distant prospect, and it had reduced the majority of the population to the verge of starvation. The prospects for the established political parties seemed slim and the real question seemed to be whether radical forces would be strong enough to destroy the Tŭrnovo system altogether.

8

Between Two Wars, 1919–1941

The first world war severely damaged but it did not destroy the established political system in Bulgaria. Immediately after the war that system was overwhelmed by radical forces on the left, but within half a decade extreme forces on the right had seized hold of the state apparatus. Both the left and the right tolerated, albeit grudgingly, the established order and in the second half of the 1920s something akin to the pre-war system was restored. Many of the pre-war parties revived, and *partizanstvo* continued to flourish, though a number of ministers deemed responsible for the national catastrophe of 1918 were arraigned before the courts. The major difference was that after the abdication of Ferdinand the personal regime of the monarch was not re-established until the middle of the 1930s. This threw the disadvantages of *partizanstvo* and the multi-party system into even sharper focus, and in the 1920s and early 1930s produced increasing criticism of and intensifying demands for the eradication of these features of the political establishment. These demands were welcomed by certain sections of the army and the intelligentsia, though those who turned towards fascism were relatively few. The forces which contested for political supremacy were therefore: the radicals, agrarian and socialist; the old political parties; the military; and, in the 1930s, the crown.

The end of the fighting in September 1918 did little to ease the appalling food shortages caused by the war, and the larger towns survived thanks mainly to imports of American wheat. To the problem of food supplies were added the social and economic stresses of demobilization in a country which had called to the colours a greater proportion of its male population than any other belligerent.

Despite the unpopularity of the old regime and the parties which had sustained it, only 60 per cent of the votes cast in the elections of August

1919 were for the radical parties. Electoral management had not disappeared. The 60 per cent was more or less evenly divided between BANU who had 31.02 per cent of the votes, and the socialists, though the latters' vote was split between the narrows, who had become the Bulgarian Communist Party (BCP) in May, with 18.20 per cent, and the broads, who now constituted the Social Democratic Party (SDP), with 12.83 per cent. The BCP's leap of 176 per cent compared with the votes polled by the narrows in 1914, was thanks in no small measure to the recent gains made by the Bolsheviks in Russia. The agrarian vote had increased by 38 per cent, though from a much higher base. The agrarians' 85 seats in the sŭbranie did not give them an absolute majority, the communists having 47, the social democrats 38, the Democratic Party 28, the National Party 19, with the remaining 19 seats being divided between three liberal parties. Despite the presence in the new sŭbranie of 66 deputies from the old parties the driving force in the assembly was on the left; the major issue was which of them would be the more powerful.

It was to take until October to construct a cabinet. One reason for the delay was that Stamboliĭski, as the minister president elect, had to journey to Paris to learn details of the peace treaty to be imposed on Bulgaria. Another reason was that his preferred coalition partners, the communists, rejected him; still believing that a proletarian revolution was imminent and that the future therefore lay with them; they were not prepared to enter into a misalliance with the Bulgarian Kerensky and his petit bourgeois party. Reluctantly Stamboliĭski turned to the old political establishment and concocted a cabinet of five agrarians, two nationalists, and Danev, who led the progressive liberals.

1. THE TREATY OF NEUILLY-SUR-SEINE

The immediate political issue was the impending peace settlement. Stamboliĭski had been in Paris at the beginnings of the negotiations and had made a number of moves intended to show the victorious allies that Bulgaria had put its old ways behind it and had relinquished the aggressive nationalism of the past. To this end, and to appease the widespread thirst for a scapegoat at home, a number of leading Macedonian extremists, including General Aleksandŭr Protogerov who had organized the defence of Sofia against the Radomir rebels, were arrested as were members of the Radoslavov administration. By 1923 twenty-nine of the latter had been sent to prison.

The attempts to soften allied attitudes had little effect. The treaty of Neuilly-sur-Seine, signed on 27 November 1919, required Bulgaria to relinquish all territory occupied during the war. In addition it was to cede to the new Triune Kingdom of the Serbs, Croats, and Slovenes (Yugoslavia) three small Bulgarian-inhabited but strategically important enclaves on its western border. It was also to cede to Greece Bulgarian Thrace, though article 48 of the treaty allowed Bulgaria economic access to the Aegean; how or where that access was to be provided was not defined, and in the event it was never given. The lost territories contained some 90,000 ethnic Bulgarians; if the Slavs of Macedonia were accounted Bulgarian, as they were in most Bulgarian minds, the number of Bulgarians left outside the national state was in the region of one million.

The treaty also limited the Bulgarian army to 20,000 volunteers and restricted the number and type of weapons it might use. Reparations in items such as coal, livestock, and railway equipment were to be paid to Yugoslavia, Romania, and Greece, and massive financial reparations of 2.25 billion gold francs were to be paid to the allies within thirty-seven years. This sum was reduced in 1923 and the payments abolished by the convention on reparations in Lausanne in 1932 by which time Bulgaria had paid over 40 million gold francs.

The terms of the peace were harsh but, at least in its territorial provisions, not as crippling as those imposed on Germany, Austria, and Hungary. Stamboliĭski's view was that the worst terms of the treaty, like the division between Bulgaria and Eastern Rumelia in 1878, would be alleviated when it was seen they were unworkable. Only in terms of reparations payments did this prove to be the case.

2. THE AGRARIANS VERSUS THE COMMUNISTS, 1919–1920

The signing of the peace treaty cleared the decks for action on the domestic political front where the critical issue was which radical faction was to fill the vacuum created by the discrediting of the former political establishment. Having rejected Stamboliĭski's offer of cooperation in government the BCP had shown that it regarded itself as the rightful heir. Its confidence was boosted by the fact that Lenin and his Bolsheviks were surviving all attempts to dislodge them, and by the BCP's strength in the cities. After the war food prices rose and the peasants, whilst not becoming wealthy, were no worse off than before the war. This could not be said of the towns. Since 1914 the cost of living had risen twelvefold with wage increases running at only half that level, and tensions were aggravated by the stresses of demobilization and the consequent unemployment. This did not affect industrial workers alone and civil servants, pensioners, and former army officers swelled the ranks of the urban discontented. In July 1919 there had been a huge protest demonstration in Sofia, the violent repression of which by the SDP minister of the interior had boosted the BCP in the August elections. The communists were also increasingly dominant in the trade union movement, their General Workers' Trade Union having ten times more members than its SDP equivalent.

The major confrontation came at the end of the year. A day of action was called on Christmas Eve and for the first time since 1903 both major factions of the socialist movement worked together. The government reacted swiftly and harshly, banning public meetings and arresting a number of activists. This did not prevent thousands taking to the streets and presenting a petition demanding concessions to the workers. After these were rejected at the end of December a general strike was declared. This time the government reacted even more fiercely. All the forces at its disposal were turned against the strikers. Not only did the government use its power of arrest to the full, it also resorted to such devices as depriving strikers' families of their ration cards or evicting them from their homes. This was too much for the strikers. On 5 January 1920 the general strike was abandoned although the miners in Pernik stayed out for another six weeks. In fact, the strikers had never been fully united, the SDP having joined less from conviction than from the fear that if it stayed out it would lose ground to the communists. And even a number of communists had had their doubts; they knew the state was still a powerful machine and the recent repression of the Béla Kun regime in Hungary had shown that a resolute leader could defeat bolshevism however successful Lenin might be in Russia.

In resisting the strike Stamboliĭski had used the police, the army, and the Orange Guard. The latter had been formed soon after the protests of July 1919, partly to counteract the armed groups formed by other parties; in Bulgaria, as in much of the rest of Europe immediately after the first world war, most radical political parties set up their own armed formations. For Stamboliĭski there was a further consideration. After the peace treaty the Bulgarian army was too small to preserve order throughout the country; furthermore, Stamboliĭski feared that a volunteer army would be recruited primarily from the discontented urban elements, and would turn into an armed subsidiary of the BCP. Stamboliĭski therefore created the Orange Guard as an armed subsidiary of BANU. It was to become a powerful and important institution, particularly towards the end of agrarian rule.

Having gained victory over the communists on the industrial front, Stamboliĭski took the battle into the political arena and called a general election on 28 March 1920. The communists had been strengthened by their contest with the government, membership rising by 70 per cent to 36,000, and their vote increased by almost 60 per cent on the 1919 figures; they now held 51 seats in the sŭbranie. The agrarian vote went up even more, by over 90 per cent, mainly because Stamboliĭski had passed a law making voting compulsory in general elections. The agrarians had 110 seats in the sŭbranie. The Democratic Party was the largest of the old parties with 23 seats, the main losers in 1920 being the SDP whose vote fell by a third and who ended with only seven deputies. However, the new assembly still did not give Stamboliĭski an absolute majority, and he therefore annulled the election of thirteen deputies, nine of whom were from the BCP, to give the agrarians a slender absolute majority of two. This, plus the fact that the agrarians had not been averse to the use of pressure during the elections, showed that however much Stamboliĭski might rail against the iniquities of the old system he was not averse to borrowing some of its more dubious methods.

3. BANU IN POWER, 1920–1923

BANU now had control of the constitutional machinery. It seemed the party was free to rebuild Bulgaria on the basis of agrarian ideology.

The new government, however, did not have complete freedom of action. The victorious allies kept a watchful eye out for any developments which they felt might threaten their influence and were occasionally to intervene to frustrate BANU plans. And they had ample means to enforce their views. The application of the Neuilly terms was supervised by the inter-allied commission and by the reparations commission; and if the allies' will needed to be enforced then they could call upon their occupation troops who were to remain in the country until January 1928. The inter-allied commission was an active body. It frustrated Stamboliĭski's intention to establish diplomatic relations with Lenin's Russia, and later interfered to amend his policies with regard to the setting up of a grain consortium, the imposition of a property tax, and the punishment of former ministers.

A less obvious restraint upon the agrarian ministers was the peace treaty's requirement that fuel and draught animals be handed to former enemies. This slowed the return to economic stability and therefore put a brake on the drive for radical reform.

The Macedonian question also inhibited the Stamboliĭski regime. There was still powerful support for the idea of retaking Macedonia when conditions allowed, and to strengthen this feeling there were nearly half a million new refugees from the area who, at the same time, placed yet another burden on the state's finances because most of them had to be housed and fed at the public expense. A further potential restraint on the regime's freedom of action came from another group of refugees, the 30,000 veterans of General Wrangel's defeated White Russian army; many of them were still armed and were they to align with dissident groups they might, after the reductions in the regular army, prove a decisive force. Nor had the agrarians' victory and the post-electoral doctoring of the sŭbranie eliminated the opposition parties who could also act as a restraint upon the new government. The old parties still had a vibrant press, and many of them had direct links with the allies and their occupying forces. The communists, too, could still commandeer considerable political muscle.

Despite these restraints, there were areas in which the new government could act to impose its ideology. One of its first reforms, and it was one which the communists welcomed, was to bring in legislation aimed at reducing the power of the professional lawyer. Lawyers were now banned from sitting in the sŭbranie or on local councils, nor could they hold major public office. The agrarian ideology was again seen in a further reform of the legal system which created new first level courts which were to deal with such basic issues as boundary disputes, and in which peasants were frequently to present their own cases and to elect the judges; it was an attempt to de-professionalize and to democratize the legal process at its lowest level. There was also a general welcome on the left for legislation which required the banks to make funds available on favourable terms to the credit cooperatives. Nor did the communists or other radical groups object to the setting up of grain depots run by a government-backed consortium. The objective here was to store surplus grain until world prices favoured selling it, after which the profits would be divided between the producer and the consortium. The idea was designed to help Bulgaria's grain trade re-establish itself after the dislocation of the war, but it had the added attraction for the agrarians of limiting the activities and the profits of the grain merchants. This alarmed the allies who feared it was a restriction upon trade and in 1921 they intervened, forcing the government to abandon the scheme.

The allies were also concerned at one of Stamboliĭski's two major legislative innovations, the compulsory labour service (CLS). This was an attempt to apply the agrarian ideal of cooperative work within and for the community. The system, introduced in June 1920, initially required all males on reaching 20 to perform a year's work; unmarried women over 16 were required to serve for half that time. The CLS was to help improve the infrastructure, particularly in rural areas, and was also responsible for the production of its uniforms and much of its own equipment. The scheme was unpopular with the old parties, particularly because initially it was impossible to purchase exemption. For the allies, the scheme seemed too much like a subterfuge army; the new service was headed by a former general, was uniformed, and was organized into units which bore military names. Once again the allies intervened and in October 1921 forced the government to modify the scheme. After the fall of the agrarian government labour conscription for women, but not for men, was abolished.

The other major legislative initative was less controversial in allied eyes. It aimed to redistribute agrarian property. Bulgaria had long been a land dominated by the small peasant producer, but BANU believed that some redistribution was still necessary. In June 1920 a law provided for the setting up of a state land fund. Into this fund would be transferred land held in excess of what was considered the proper maximum of 30 hectares, though larger areas were permitted for woodland and in mountainous areas, and the allowances were to be increased in proportion to the number of persons in a household. The fund would also receive the property of absentee landlords who would be deprived of all holdings above the

4 hectares minimum which was to be guaranteed to all owners. The assets acquired by the state land fund were to be redistributed to those who did not have sufficient land. Compensation was to be paid to former owners in state bonds, though payments were to be on a sliding scale which discriminated against the wealthy. In April 1921 further legislation made it more difficult to bribe officials to escape the legislation, and also made monastic property not worked by monks eligible for redistribution. The agrarians hoped to redistribute nearly a quarter of a million hectares of land, but when they fell from power in 1923 only 82,000 hectares had been transferred via the state land fund to the smaller landowners. Nevertheless, the legislation was not unpopular and was retained by subsequent regimes, albeit with more generous allowances for individual holders.

Much less popular was the BANU's attempt to apply the principle of equality of holdings in the urban sector. Urban accommodation, particularly in Sofia, was in extremely short supply after the war, not least because of the influx of refugees, and a law was passed limiting each family to two rooms and a kitchen, with more space being allowed for larger households. The ministry of the interior appointed inspectors who had wide powers to enforce the new regulations which were to apply to office as well as domestic properties. The inspectors were hated by almost all whom they visited and a more successful response to the housing crisis, but one which still conformed to agrarian ideology, was the building of new blocks of flats which were cooperatively financed but in which the separate apartments were privately owned. This legislation also survived the fall of the BANU government and the building of cooperatively owned blocks continued throughout the inter-war years.

Stamboliĭski's main interest was in rural rather than urban change. Like other European agrarian leaders such as Wincenty Witos in Poland, he kept in close touch with the land, tending, as often as state business allowed, his own vineyards in his home village of Slavovitsa—and to good effect according to a number of visitors. Whilst in office he made tours of villages as frequently as possible, wanting to hear at first hand the concerns and aspirations of the peasants.

These aspirations were reflected in a number of other reforms introduced by Stamboliĭski's government, including a progressive income tax, a company tax, laws to promote commassation, the raising of the school leaving age to 14, and measures to encourage crop diversification and the breeding of better strains of animals and seeds. New regulations made it profitable for peasants to join cooperatives and most did so, though this was never made compulsory.

The agrarians had always seen education as having a central role in improving the life of the peasants and their villages. The Stamboliĭski government therefore introduced compulsory secondary education and built 800 new pro-gymnasia, as well as 300 new elementary schools. It also set up faculties of veterinary science at Sofia University, and founded higher education institutions for forestry and commerce. The agrarian government also increased the time allotted to vocational subjects, and did what it could to eliminate jingoistic nationalism and the marxist theorizing which had been so common in pre-first world war schools; all teachers who were known to be communists were sacked at the beginning of BANU rule after which, in another application of agrarian local democracy, all teachers' posts were to be subject to review by plebiscite every four years.

Perhaps Stamboliĭski's most radical actions were not in domestic but foreign policy. He was the first Bulgarian leader publicly to renounce the notion of national reunification. It was this, the agrarians argued, which had persuaded Bulgaria to subordinate itself to foreign patrons, which had necessitated the spending of vast sums of money on the army, conscription, and the monarchy, and which had created and perpetuated the social domination of the officer caste. This did not mean that Stamboliĭski was an out-and-out pacifist, or was lacking in patriotism. When, in 1922, there were rumours that Yugoslavia might occupy the Pernik mining complex in retaliation for incursions into Yugoslavia by Macedonian activists based in Bulgaria, Stamboliĭski told the king that if the mines were occupied he would lead the fight against such an infringement of Bulgarian sovereignty, adding that, 'A nation which does not defend its territorial integrity does not deserve to live in freedom.'[1]

In 1920 Stamboliĭski sought to plead Bulgaria's cause and further its needs in a tour of the major European capitals. As a result Bulgaria became the first defeated state to be admitted to the League of Nations and it was in this arena, rather than on the battlefield, said Stamboliĭski, that Bulgaria should press its case for the implementation of article 48

[1] Konstantin Muraviev, *Sŭbitiya i hora: Spomeni*, ed. Ilcho Dimitrov (Sofia: Bŭlgarski Pisatel, 1992), 78.

and for steps to be taken under the League's minority protection treaties to defend the Bulgarians in Macedonia from serbianization. Another means to helping the Macedonians in Yugoslavia, Stamboliĭski believed, was to establish good relations with Belgrade.

This would also be the essential first step along the long road to the agrarians' goal of a Balkan federation. But this first step was more difficult than most. The Macedonian exiles were even more embittered than before the war, and in Petrich in south-west Bulgaria they established a virtual state within the state. From here they launched raids into Greek and Yugoslav Macedonia. The Yugoslavs would not consider improving relations with Sofia until the Bulgarians took measures to control the Macedonian extremists. This was a price which Stamboliĭski was prepared to pay. He purged the army and the frontier police of many IMRO supporters, and when he was at last allowed to visit Belgrade in November 1922 he openly denounced the Macedonian extremists as the cause of most of Bulgaria's misfortunes, including the calamitous second Balkan war. In March 1923 Bulgaria and Yugoslavia signed the Nish convention in which they agreed to cooperate against extremism. In the following month the Bulgarian government banned all terrorist organizations, shut down their newspapers and periodicals, and confined most of their leaders to camps in eastern Bulgaria.

The Macedonians were powerful enemies who operated just as much at home as abroad. In their Petrich enclave they levied taxes on the already hard-pressed peasants and especially upon the tobacco growers and dealers, and few voices in Sofia, in the government or the media, were raised against these practices. This was hardly surprising. The Macedonians frequently exacted swift and pitiless revenge on those who opposed them, and they seemed particularly determined to sow fear and terror amongst the agrarians; they killed a number of them, most notably Aleksandŭr Dimitrov, the minister of war and a close associate of Stamboliĭski. The problem with the Macedonians was worsened by struggles between their various factions, struggles which were even more violent than those immediately after the Ilinden rising. The main division was between the 'autonomists', who included those based in Petrich, and the 'federalists'. The disputes between the factions led to a number of murders and, in October 1922, to the occupation of Nevrokop by an IMRO unit which wished to liquidate a rival band of federalists based in the town. So widespread did the actions of the Macedonians become that Metropolitan

Stefan suggested privately that the government should pay the autonomists 50 million leva to cease their attacks.[2]

The Macedonians were not Stamboliĭski's only enemies. There was general distaste and anger over the corruption of the agrarian regime. Stamboliĭski attempted to excuse this on the grounds that the party had not had time to train a large enough leadership cadre to fill all the posts which, because of the workings of *partizanstvo*, were there to be filled when BANU took office. Separate groups had more specific grievances. The communists were still nursing the wounds inflicted on them in 1919–20 and they remained strong in the cities where unchecked inflation had reduced the 1919 value of the leva sevenfold by 1923. The BCP also complained that the agrarians had done little for the working class apart from introducing the eight-hour day, and the communists continued to demand further reforms such as a wealth tax. Professional civil servants resented the tendency of the government to replace the established administrative machinery with agrarian party bodies, as when the government employed the Orange Guard rather than the police or army, or when local party druzhbi rather than organs of local government were made responsible for carrying out land redistribution. The teachers were also smarting over the dismissal of so many of their profession and the need to submit themselves to re-election every four years, whilst the lawyers were just as resentful over the new limitations placed upon their activities. Even the medical profession was uneasy over rumours that doctors and other medical personnel were to be sent from the towns and cities to the villages and the more remote areas of the country. The small but influential group of university teachers also had cause for complaint, particularly over the government's measures to limit socialist influence in the profession; this was seen as an infringement of academic freedom and of the university's autonomy. The Church, meanwhile, was unhappy at the projected redistribution of some church and monastic lands, and at the actual allotment of some of Rila's properties to an Italian commercial concern. It also resented the decrease in the time allowed in schools for religious education, and was furious when the Holy Synod was transferred to Rila; it also disliked Stamboliĭski's overt free thinking and complained of his alleged sexual licence.

---

[2] Stamboliĭski told Stefan, ' "With your plan, my lord, you would send the government to hell." ' Ibid. 67.

Before the first world war the army's officer corps had been one of the most influential and prestigious forces in the land. Now it was greatly reduced in status as well as size. Thousand of officers had lost their jobs and were understandably resentful. Those who were lucky enough to retain their commissions disliked Stamboliĭski's use of the Orange Guard which, together with the police in Sofia, outnumbered the military. Equally distasteful to the serving officers was Stamboliĭski's pacific foreign policy, as was the fact that his government did not maintain the army even at the modest levels set in the treaty of Neuilly; by the end of the agrarian government the army had munitions enough only for eight days of fighting. Many officers had close links with members of Wrangel's army and they were angered when Stamboliĭski succeeded in disbanding that force in May 1922, whilst others were offended by the agrarians' hostility to the Macedonians, many soldiers regarding the latter as some form of super-patriots prepared to cock a snook at the treaty of Neuilly.

In 1919–20 Stamboliĭski had defeated the left; by moving against the wrangelists he appeared to have weakened the right. BANU's seventeenth congress in May 1922 gave him a triumphal reception, but serious opposition was beginning to form, and it was soon to find a crystallization point.

In 1922 Stamboliĭski had lifted the state of siege imposed in 1919, as a result of which a number of old parties formed the Constitutional Bloc and launched a new newspaper, *Slovo* (Word). The old parties had little appeal for the electorate and therefore the leaders of the Constitutional Bloc aligned themselves with another new organization, the National Alliance (Naroden Sgovor), an elitist and exclusive association of professionals, especially academics and members of the Military League. The latter had been established in 1914 and by 1919 was led by General Protogerov. It had at its disposal the training, organizational skills, and discipline of the officer corps; it was an enemy qualitatively different from the other groups of disgruntled professionals.

The National Alliance did not initially believe it needed the organizational skills of the military, and intended to defeat the agrarians by constitutional, parliamentary means. To that end it arranged three large meetings, the first of which was to take place in the home of constitutionalism in Bulgaria, Tŭrnovo, and the largest of which, with Mussolini's recent antics in Rome in view, was to take the form of a march on Sofia. The Alliance's leaders set out for the first meeting on 16 September.

Shortly before they reached their destination they were taken from the train and, but for the intervention of the prominent agrarian Raĭko Daskalov, who was also on board, they might well have been thrown over the Stambolov bridge to their deaths.[3] The threatened politicians were placed in Shumen jail for their own protection, the Orange Guard took control of Tŭrnovo, and the government banned all public meetings. The road to constitutional change seemed closed.

Supporters of the Alliance soon began to fear that not only was constitutional change impossible but that Stamboliĭski was moving towards a party or even a personal dictatorship. One indication of this was the decision by the sŭbranie in November 1922 to institute legal proceedings against members of the Geshov, Danev, and Malinov cabinets. Few had shed tears in 1919 when members of the Radoslavov government had been sentenced to varying terms of imprisonment for taking Bulgaria into the first world war, but the new action was on a much larger scale. No fewer than thirty-four men were tried and were soon convicted, a development which threatened to neutralize what remained of the pre-war 'bourgeois' political establishment. The convictions were annulled after the fall of the agrarians but in the interim they provided yet another reason for the non-agrarian parties to take defensive measures.

The National Alliance also feared that BANU was usurping the proper machinery of the state. When, in December 1922 Macedonian activists, furious at Stamboliĭski's denunciation of them in Belgrade, occupied Kyustendil where they passed death sentences on the minister president and a number of his colleagues, it was not the army but the Orange Guard which was used to restore central control. The Macedonians retreated to their stronghold in Petrich and the Guard then returned to Sofia, where it launched a savage attack on the offices of the bourgeois parties and their newspapers.

Opposition fears intensified in the new year. In February 1923 the Macedonians made an unsuccessful attempt on the life of Stamboliĭski. He immediately took steps to entrench his power, first removing dissident agrarians from his cabinet, and then calling a general election for 22 April. But before the vote was held he abolished proportional representation. BANU romped home with 212 seats to the communists' 16, and the National Alliance's 15. The agrarians had not scorned the use

---

[3] *Raĭko Daskalov*, 153.

of pressure during the election campaign, particularly against the communists who in local elections in February had taken control of a number of important municipalities. Soon after the elections Stamboliĭski carried out another purge of the administration, after which came a series of mass BANU meetings at which members swore on religious relics and the party flag to give their lives for BANU. Stamboliĭski's increasing personal ambition seemed confirmed a few weeks later when he reviewed an Orange Guard parade seated upon a white charger.

Perhaps Stamboliĭski's government had hit the rock that lies in the path of many radical, reforming regimes. He had achieved virtually everything he could without breaking out of the Tŭrnovo system and establishing an agrarian republic on an entirely new constitutional basis. That Stamboliĭski wished to do this is questionable. He distanced himself from and publicly argued against those in the party who called for 'a peasant dictatorship'; but if Stamboliĭski himself had no intention of changing the constitution some of his opponents feared his party was less moderate and that the extremists might push him aside. After the elections of April 1923 important elements of the opposition moved from complaint to conspiracy.

This was not the first plot against the agrarian minister president. In 1919 the Military League had wanted to take action and in 1921 Protogerov constructed a wide-ranging conspiracy, many of whose members were linked through the masonic lodges which had flourished in Bulgaria since the end of the war. The 1921 plot came to nothing, primarily because the Democratic Party refused to take part in it. Their growing fears of Stamboliĭski's constitutional intentions had changed their minds by 1923.

The conspiracy of that year was hatched by members of the Military League, the National Alliance, IMRO, and a few social democrats. Once again, a high proportion of those involved were members of masonic lodges.[4] There is little doubt that the king knew what was afoot and his voice was not raised against the planned coup. Nor were the allies likely to be much concerned at Stamboliĭski's removal, and the same could be said for the communists. The coup was carried out on 9 June 1923. There was little resistance except in the Pleven area where local communists

---

[4] For details on the masonic lodges, see Velichko Georgiev, *Masonstvo v Bŭlgariya. Pronikvane, organizatsiya, razvitie i rolya do sredata na tridecette godini na xx vek* (Sofia: Nauka i izkustvo, 1986). For the statement with regard to the coup of 1923, 116.

cooperated with the agrarians until told by BCP headquarters in Sofia to cease doing so. Stamboliĭski went into hiding and was not captured until 14 June when he was brutally mutilated before being murdered—in a grim repetition of Stambolov's killing the Macedonians sliced off 'the hands that had signed the Nish treaty' before sending Stamboliĭski's head to Sofia in a biscuit tin. By then over 3,000 agrarians were in detention. The violence and the killings in 1923 were the work primarily of 'the convention', as the inner guiding circles of the Military League were known.

Stamboliĭski, who was on holiday in Slavovitsa when the coup took place, had been an easy target. He had always disdained the need for personal protection. In Geneva he had rejected a suggestion by the police that they provide a guard because they had information of a Macedonian plot to kill him, and in Bulgaria he refused to set foot in a bullet-proof car procured by one of his ministers. He seemed to have adopted the attitude of 'I would rather be killed than kill'. One reason for this could well have been his belief that popular support for the agrarians was so strong that even a coup could not keep them out of power for more than a few weeks.

The ease with which a government enjoying such strong support was defeated illustrated a number of key features of the Bulgarian political system. It showed that the Stamboliĭski regime had not succeeded in bringing about any significant shift in the centre of power from the old, centralized, state institutions to the villages. A small number of urban-based, armed, organized, and above all disciplined conspirators could still defeat the diffused peasant masses. The lack of popular resistance reflected a common thread of Bulgarian history seen since bogomil times: that retreat into the enclosed, private world of the self was preferable to a probably hopeless struggle with the forces of evil represented by the authorities. The more immediate explanations for Stamboliĭski's defeat were that he had alienated virtually all possible allies, and therefore no group would come to his aid. The communists persisted in regarding the agrarians as petit bourgeois; the western powers would not be concerned at the removal of a radical regime, even if it was anti-communist and had tried to preserve Balkan stability by containing the disruptive Macedonians. Nor would any other Balkan state have the interest or capability to intervene on his behalf.

The king's part in the coup remains obscure. Stamboliĭski himself did not believe that 'tsarche', or 'little king' as he called Boris, would raise a hand against him and in subsequent years Boris certainly showed a retrospective admiration for the martyred minister. But it has to be asked whether the army would have dared to involve itself in so dramatic a deed without royal consent, and according to one agrarian source Boris personally phoned and told the doubting commander of the Shumen garrison and the commander of a unit in Pirin to back the 1923 coup.[5]

The agrarian government had been Bulgaria's most radical to date. Its achievements, given the constraints upon its freedom of manoeuvre and the relatively short period it spent in office, were considerable, the fact that succeeding administrations retained many of the reforms attesting to the relevance and effectiveness of agrarian policy. The government's most obvious weakness had been corruption, caused partly by the lack of a trained administrative cadre. It had also shown too great a suspicion of the existing administrative machinery and too little willingness to work with it. The government had failed to contain political violence which resulted in the killings carried out by the Macedonians and by anarchists, the latter being responsible for the assassination of Aleksandŭr Grekov, the first leader of the National Alliance, in May 1922. BANU itself had developed serious divisions founded on differences of policy and personality. The administration had also been at times uncoordinated: just before Stamboliĭski left for his crucial tour of the European capitals his minister for agriculture and public properties wrote to the king suggesting he abdicate in order to make Stamboliĭski's task easier; neither Stamboliĭski nor any of his colleagues in the cabinet was consulted before the letter was sent.

Bulgaria and its political system paid a terrible price for the coup. Some conspirators had been motivated originally by concern that the Tŭrnovo system might be overthrown, but the governments which came immediately after that of Stamboliĭski saw constitutional abnormalities and infringements of personal liberties greater than anything yet experienced in modern Bulgarian history. The old sŭbranie parties which were brought back into the centre of affairs by the coup soon proved little changed from those which had debased the political system before the first world war. The army moved nearer to the centre of political power whilst the Macedonian extremists were given a new lease of life. The damage the latter inflicted on Bulgarian public affairs and on Bulgaria's

[5] Muraviev, *Sŭbitiya*, 91.

standing abroad was enormous, and it was to continue for over a decade until brought abruptly to an end by, ironically, their military allies of 1923. The communists lost a great deal of popular support and the tragedy of their stance in June was turned to farce when they changed their minds and attempted a ludicrous, doomed uprising in September. One lasting result of this was that the non-agrarian elements of the intelligentsia, the professions, and the old political parties tended to write the communists off as bumbling amateurs; at the end of the second world war they therefore underestimated the communists and were even prepared to work with them to neutralize the agrarians whom they continued to regard as the greater danger.

This was a misjudgement of tragic dimensions because after 1923, with many of its surviving leaders in exile, BANU did not so much split as fragment. The two major factions were Dimitŭr Gichev's more moderate Vrabcha (sparrow) group which in later years was prepared to accommodate with the existing political establishment, and the Pladne (Noon) Agrarians who rejected such moderation. The two main camps sustained a bitter enmity which absorbed much of their time and energy until after the second world war. This was perhaps the most tragic of the consequences of the coup. The agrarian party which, despite its faults in office, had produced the most original of all responses to Bulgaria's social and economic problems and had proved one of the most powerful of agrarian movements in Europe, was mortally wounded. Nevertheless, from the end of 1918 to the spring of 1990, with the exception of the years 1923 to 1931, there was scarcely an administration in Bulgaria which did not contain a representative of the agrarian movement.

4. THE TSANKOVIST TERROR, 1923–1926

In the two months after the 9 June coup the National Alliance was expanded and reformed into a united political bloc, the Democratic Alliance. It had two broad wings: that led by figures such as Atanas Burov and Andreĭ Lyapchev which favoured a parliamentary, constitutional system; and that with more authoritarian inclinations, led by Aleksandŭr Tsankov, a professor of economics, and General Ivan Vŭlkov of the Military League. The Military League, not trusting the old political parties and their constitutional-parliamentary methods, backed the authoritarians and made Aleksandŭr Tsankov minister president and minister of the interior.

The first months of Tsankov's rule gave few indications of what was to follow. The new government moved rapidly to arrange elections in November to produce a dependable sŭbranie, but having done so it then adopted seemingly conciliatory policies; it modified but did not end the agrarians' programme for the redistribution of agrarian property, though it increased the minimum holdings for larger families; ironically the Democratic Alliance redistributed more property than BANU. The Tsankov regime also encouraged the banks to lend to the cooperatives, retained social legislation such as the eight-hour day, increased civil service salaries, allowed workers to form trade unions, and even reinstated some of those sacked during and after the 1919–20 strike.

The peace was shattered by the communists. The passivity of the BCP in June had not been well received by the Comintern in Moscow, which ordered the Bulgarian party to redress its error. Accordingly the BCP ordered its members to stage a revolt on 23 September. There was insufficient time to prepare a nationwide outbreak, the party's supporters were poorly armed, and many of them still regarded the agrarians with whom they were now urged to cooperate as the doomed petit bourgeois producers which BCP propaganda had for so long painted them. Worst of all, the government learned of the plot and imposed martial law before 23 September. The uprising had some successes in the Plovdiv, Vratsa, and Stara Zagora areas where there was cooperation between the communists and the agrarians, but even here the uprising lasted no longer than five days. Tsankov took advantage of the rising and in November passed the defence of the realm act which conveniently enabled him to use massive government influence in the elections. In April 1924 the BCP was banned, its property confiscated, and its trade unions disbanded.

The defeat of the 1923 uprisings and its consequences discredited the BCP leadership under Blagoev to the advantage of Georgi Dimitrov and Vasil Kolarov who escaped via Serbia to Moscow. By 1925 they had decided that the armed struggle was no longer justified in view of the changed conditions within Bulgaria, but a small group within the party in Sofia refused to follow this line. This faction's campaign of violence culminated on 16 April 1925 with the detonation of a huge bomb in the roof of Sofia's Sveta Nedelya cathedral during a funeral service attended by the king and most of the government and military leaders.

None of these eminent personages was amongst the 130 or so who died. The advocates of violence had argued that a dramatic gesture such as the cathedral bombing would persuade Boris to ditch Tsankov and introduce a democratic regime. They could not have been more mistaken.

The government, having declared martial law, unleashed a reign of terror in which thousands were arrested, hundreds disappeared without trace, and some were executed in public. It was the most savage official violence yet seen in Bulgaria and it earned the country widespread international opprobrium.

More international condemnation was to come as a result of violence from another quarter, the Macedonians. In August 1923 in Prague they had murdered Raĭko Daskalov, the prominent agrarian and leader of the Radomir rebellion in 1918, and in October they killed the former stambolovist minister and entente protégé, Nikola Genadiev, but although Bulgarian political *prominenti* continued to be targets more violence now arose from another split within the Macedonian movement, one faction of which had opted in 1924 for cooperation with the communists. Two of those who had signed the declaration calling for such cooperation were murdered in 1924 and a third in 1927. Many lesser known figures also fell victim to these feuds; between 1924 and 1934 the Macedonian organizations were believed to have been responsible for over 800 murders in Bulgaria.

These internecine disputes, many of them acted out in the streets and cafés of Sofia and other Bulgarian cities, did not mean any cessation of incursions from Petrich into Yugoslavia and Greece, and in October 1925 a division of the Greek army occupied areas of south-western Bulgaria for a few days in retaliation for yet another raid into Greek territory. It retreated at the insistence of the League of Nations and Greece later paid Bulgaria 20 million leva in compensation for the intrusion.[6]

By 1925 the severity of the Tsankov regime was the cause of domestic and foreign concern. In September the king expressed the view that a relaxation of controls would be welcome but he was as yet in no position to make such a change. International financiers were much more powerful. The Tsankov government was in need of a loan and astutely argued in the League that the money would be used to settle Macedonian refugees

---

[6] Panaĭot Panaĭotov, *Vŭnshnata politika na Bŭlgariya, 1919–1945* (Sofia: Agres, 1990, first published, Rio de Janeiro, Svoboden bŭlgarski tsentŭr, 1986), 31.

and thereby lessen the likelihood that they, and the communists who also bred on social deprivation, would threaten the stability of the Balkans. The League was persuaded but the London money-merchants who would provide most of the funds were more hard-headed. They declared they would not lend a penny to so unsavoury a crew as Tsankov's cabinet. In January 1926 the minister president therefore resigned in favour of Andreĭ Lyapchev of the Democratic Party and the refugee loan was raised.

5. THE GOVERNMENT OF THE DEMOCRATIC ALLIANCE, 1926–1931

The resignation of Tsankov had not been the only condition of the refugee loan. It required that all beneficiaries from the loan had to be Bulgarian citizens. This meant that those in receipt of lands drained or improved with funds from the loan had to renounce their citizenship in non-Bulgarian territories, i.e. primarily Yugoslavia and Greece. By the end of the decade over 650 communes had agreed to such conditions and a little had been done to ease the refugee problem in Bulgaria. Lyapchev also raised a large stabilization loan which was used to alleviate the growing problems arising from reparations payments.

Lyapchev had fulfilled expectations that he would moderate the terror by decreeing a large number of amnesties and releasing many of the detainees. He also relaxed the censorship, ended many of the restrictions on the trade unions, and allowed the BCP to reconstitute itself under the name the Bulgarian Workers' Party (BWP). It rapidly re-established the communists' youth and trade union organizations.

Lyapchev was a Macedonian by birth and he showed no sign of intending to limit the activities of his more extreme co-Macedonians. The incursions from Petrich continued, as did the deadly vendettas between the Macedonian factions. The general public had perhaps become immune or indifferent to these events but there was anger at the number of jobs which the government was giving to Macedonians; that there were one hundred in the Pernik mines alone showed the scale of the process. Much worse was the Marinopolski affair in 1930 in which the eponymous officer confessed that after terrible tortures at the hands of the Macedonians he had given false evidence against a senior officer who was critical of Macedonian excesses; on the basis of that evidence the officer had been condemned to death as a spy. The army felt humiliated that its officers, both Marinopolski and his victim, could be treated in such a fashion.

By 1930 the effects of the great depression were beginning to be felt. For Bulgaria the impact of the disaster was made worse by the fact that in 1928 international financiers had persuaded a reluctant Bulgarian government to return to the gold standard. It did so at an unrealistically high level which forced the administration to cut back on government expenditure to support an overvalued currency, and therefore when the great crisis broke there was less scope for retrenchment. When the impact of the depression began to be felt it occasioned strikes and demonstrations.

Lyapchev's position was undermined by these protests and by his weakening control over the Democratic Alliance. Malinov, the leader of Lyapchev's own party, had never joined the Alliance and he remained critical of it, as did Aleksadŭr Tsankov. A further difficulty in the mid-1920s was the increasing fragmentation of the political parties. Lyapchev attempted to counter this by enacting a law based on the Italian fascists' practice by which the party securing the largest share of the vote in a general election was guaranteed an absolute majority in the assembly. This was applied in elections held in May 1927 but one of the effects of the new law was to precipitate a scramble to form electoral alliances or blocs, a scramble which produced a massive amount of unseemly horse-trading and even more fragmentation amongst the parties. The latter seemed to be little more than irrelevant coteries of job-seekers and the fact that the budget of 1930 was sanctioned by an inquorate assembly under-lined the seeming futility of the national parliament and the electoral system at a time when the global economic catastrophe demanded effective and selfless leadership from the nation's political masters.

6. THE PEOPLE'S BLOC AND THE GREAT DEPRESSION, 1931–1934

In the spring of 1931 Lyapchev lost control of the sŭbranie following a typically degrading squabble over the distribution of cabinet posts. He called a general election for June for which proportional representation was restored. The election of 1931, like the one thirty years before, was one of the two between 1879 and 1990, which could be described as entirely open. And it was unusual in that it took place before rather than after a change of government and was therefore an exercise to assess the popular mood rather than a device to manufacture a reliable parliament for a pre-chosen government. The group which now took power was the so-called People's Bloc, which included some agrarians and which was led by Malinov. He was soon forced to resign because of ill health, his place as minister president being taken by Nikola Mushanov.

Having kept its distance from the Democratic Alliance the Malinov/Mushanov wing of the Democratic Party was therefore one of the few old parties with a claim to respectability. The fact that prominent agrarians such as Dimitŭr Gichev were in the new administration also increased its legitimacy and there was some hope that national confidence in the country's rulers might at last be restored. It was not.

The beginning, however, was encouraging. Not only had the new administration come to power by a free election, after gaining office it declined to play the *partizanstvo* game. The most important posts, the chief regional and local officials, were placed in reliable hands but only fifty-six policemen were removed, an astonishingly small number. This was due less to respect for constitutional niceties than to fear. In the summer of 1931 the strikes and protests at the worsening economic situation intensified; these made Mushanov ask himself 'whether this was the most opportune moment for a total change of the police apparatus'.[7]

The effects of the great depression were profound. When agricultural prices began to fall peasants assumed this was part of the natural trade cycle and held on to their produce until prices rose again. The fact that they did not rise caused food shortages in the towns which could be alleviated only by the import, at great cost, of grain from Yugoslavia. The continued low price levels and the withholding of crops from the market meant that many peasants had insufficient income to service their debts, and creditors therefore began to refuse new loans and to call in existing ones. This again had a knock-on effect in the towns. With the peasants earning less their purchasing power declined and the market for manufactured produce fell. This, together with the new tough attitudes to credit, hit the manufacturers, who began to cut wages and then to lay

[7] Rositsa Stoyanova, 'Demokraticheskata partiya i nachaloto na blokovoto upravlenie (yuni–oktomvri 1931g)', *Istoricheski Pregled*, 47/2 (1991), 21–35, 23.

off workers. Between 1929 and 1933 peasant income per capita fell by 50 per cent and industrial wages by 27 per cent.

Both the National Alliance and the People's Bloc administrations made efforts to soften the impact of the depression. In 1930 a state grain purchasing agency, Hranoiznos, was established which guaranteed the peasant would have a purchaser for his surplus grain, but it was difficult for the new agency to sell the grain and even if it did prices remained at rock bottom; Hranoiznos was later to increase in power and importance but initially it made little impact on the plight of the peasantry. A further attempt to relieve rural distress was made in September 1931 with the introduction of legislation regulating the industrial and commercial cartels. These had been a powerful factor in Bulgarian industry since the end of the nineteenth century and were regarded with deep, and not entirely misplaced suspicion by the peasants. The new legislation established a government commission to supervise the cartels and in October the commission ordered a normalization of prices for certain items of prime necessity, including soap, sugar, cement, cotton goods, and gas. In the same month the BNB was given near monopoly control over commercial transactions in foreign currency.[8] In December 1932, following pressure from the League of Nations' financial committee, 10,000 civil service posts were axed to reduce government spending. Other measures were aimed directly to alleviate the suffering of the individual. These ranged from the provision, twice a month, of free performances for the poor at the National Theatre, to tax cuts, and legislation to reduce debts and to extend repayment periods. These measures eased the symptoms of the problem whilst its causes were tackled by efforts to encourage the production of high-price export commodities such as wine, fruit, vegetables, and hazelnuts, the latter acquired not entirely legally from Turkey. Whatever the government did, however, could not have any great ameliorative effect until the international market had recovered, and in the meantime many Bulgarian peasants retreated into self-sufficiency.

This was not possible in the towns and cities where protests continued throughout 1931 with the communists playing a leading role in the organization of a number of strikes. The government attempted to mediate but the strikers were seldom minded to participate in talks.

[8] Vasilev, 'Bulgaro-britanski', loc. cit., 50.

In retaliation the government ordered the closure of BWP clubs in Sofia, Sliven, Yambol, Plovdiv, and other industrial centres, and forbade meetings or assemblies called by the party. This did not prevent the communists from registering significant gains in local elections in November, and in February 1932 they secured an absolute majority on Sofia city council. In an act which would have been deemed unthinkable by the founding fathers of the Tŭrnovo constitution, the People's Bloc government dissolved the council; in April 1933 it ejected from the sŭbranie fifteen of its twenty-nine BWP deputies.

That the People's Bloc had as little respect for the constitution as other governments was most blatantly illustrated in the enthusiasm with which it resorted to the ancient practice of self-enrichment. And the worst offenders, despite BANU's continual denunciation of this evil, were the agrarians. If the masses of the peasantry had had any hopes that the presence of BANU representatives might rebuild the alliance between rulers and ruled, these hopes were disabused by the effects of the depression and by the cupidity of the agrarian members of the People's Bloc government.

If that government brought little change to domestic politics it was equally lacking in innovation in foreign affairs. Here the advent of the Nazis was to question the established practice of relying on the League of Nations as the means by which foreign policy objectives were to be achieved. In regional terms, too, Bulgaria's position deteriorated. In July 1933 an agreement signed in London had defined international aggression and had included in the category of aggressor a country which supported or failed to take effective measures against armed subversive groups which used its territory as a base for operations in another state. With the Macedonians still operating unhindered from Petrich this placed Bulgaria in considerable danger. In February of the following year Yugoslavia, Turkey, Romania, and Greece signed the Balkan entente. This recreated the alignment of 1913 and emphasized Bulgaria's isolation; the entente states made it clear that they would not include Bulgaria in any collective security arrangement unless Sofia accepted the permanence of the post-first world war frontiers, a step which no Bulgarian government dared to take.

The People's Bloc had failed expectations of an improvement in the quality of government, it had failed to shield the population from the effects of the great depression, and it had allowed the country to become more isolated and endangered. But what was the alternative? The old parties were discredited, and the agrarians seemed little better; the communists were strong in the towns but with full-scale collectivization in the Soviet Union they were unlikely to attract peasant support and even if they did they were likely to be suppressed by the authorities; and the social democrats were by now almost a *quantité négligeable*. On the right a few small fascist movements raised their ugly heads in the 1920s and a more substantial one appeared in 1930 when Aleksandŭr Tsankov established the National Social Movement (NSM). The rise of Hitler and the impact of the depression helped the NSM gain public attention but it faced severe disabilities: though he had been forced to resign his chair, Tsankov was a professor not a demagogue; the theatricality of fascism was alien to Bulgarian political and cultural traditions; and anyone seeking a violent extreme nationalist cause would in all likelihood already have found it in one of the Macedonian organizations.

The paucity of alternatives to the People's Bloc enhanced the significance of Zveno (Link). Founded in 1927 this supra-party pressure group had two main platforms: it wanted an end to the petty squabbling and corruption of the political parties which, it maintained, put party before country; and it wanted better relations with Yugoslavia. That these were strained was clear, but some improvement was possible, as had been shown by the Pirot agreements of 1929–30 over minor issues such as railway connections and access to properties divided by the border.[9] But no real improvement could be achieved without reining in the Macedonians and Zveno's wish for better relations with Yugoslavia inevitably put it on a collision course with them. Zveno was a small organization which was self-avowedly elitist, étatist, and authoritarian. Its supporters, the zvenari, were to be found amongst the disillusioned professional and intelligentsia elites and amongst sections of the Military League, although the royalist elements of the latter had some doubts because initially the king and his advisers were wary of Zveno's anti-Macedonian stance. The latter consideration indicated that the king had become a more powerful factor in politics, as had the army.

---

[9] Dimitŭr I. Mitev, 'Velikobritaniya i bŭlgaro-yugoslavskite sporazumeniya ot 1929–1930g', in Vasilev et al. (eds.), *Bŭlgaro-angliĭskite otnosheniya*, 23–44.

7. THE ZVENARI GOVERNMENT, 19 MAY 1934–JANUARY 1935

In November 1933 zvenari elements within the army decided to act. The plan to replace the existing regime was drawn up by Colonels Damyan Velchev and Kimon Georgiev, both of whom were connected to the republican faction within Zveno. The decision to implement their plan was prompted by yet another degrading squabble over the distribution of cabinet posts, by fears that the king might use his newly nominated minister of war, Atanas Vatev, to limit the anti-monarchist lobby in the army, and not least by a massive rally which Tsankov, whose NSM was to do surprisingly well in local elections in February, was planning to hold on 21 May 1934 when Hermann Göring would be in Bulgaria on a private visit. The putsch was swiftly executed on 19 May and within hours the entire country had been taken over. Georgiev became minister president.

The 19 May regime, like Piłsudski's *sanacja* in Poland, attempted to cleanse the political system. This meant in the first instance the elimination of party rule and the restructuring of the sŭbranie. In one of its first acts the new government abolished all political parties and closed their newspapers. The sŭbranie was also dissolved and its powers transferred to the executive. The assembly was to be reorganized with only one-quarter of the deputies representing 'the political element'. The remainder would represent the estates into which the 19 May regime, mixing agrarian and fascist ideas, divided society; the estates were workers, peasants, craftsmen, merchants, intelligentsia, civil servants, and the free professions. The estates were also used as the basis for the reconstructed trade union system which was introduced in 1935. A new Bulgarian Workers' Union was to be the only permitted labour organization; membership was voluntary and it soon attracted large numbers.

Centralization and rationalization were at the core of the new regime's programme. The sixteen regions were replaced by seven provinces run by prefects nominated by the government, and all elected mayors were replaced by centrally appointed officials who were required to be educated to at least secondary level and to have some legal training. Local councils were reorganized so that henceforth only half their members were to be elected and were also to be divided into the seven estates; the other half were to be selected by senior officials. Centralization also affected the provincial banks, nineteen of which were amalgamated into the Bulgarian Credit Bank based in Sofia. Rationalization meant a reduction in the number of government ministries and therefore in the number of civil servants, about of a third of whom were dismissed. Many of those sacked were replaced by supporters of the government thus proving that *partizanstvo* was not dead. The dismissal of civil servants was not an unpopular move, but the reorganization of local government was. The elected communal councils were still seen by many as the historic bedrock of Bulgarian democracy and the new, appointed officials, many of whom had been prominent during the Tsankov reign of terror, were frequently career administrators who had few links with the locality and who seldom stayed long enough to form them; they became known as 'Flying Dutchmen' and were much disliked.

If the new rulers were centralizers and authoritarians they were not fascists. They did not form a political party but instead established the directorate for social renewal. This centrally appointed and hierarchical body was intended 'to direct the cultural and intellectual life of the country towards unity and renewal', and was given wide powers over the press, the arts, and on questions such as public meetings. It aimed its propaganda particularly at the nation's youth, for which it began to set up a national organization, and presented its new policies in a series of public meetings and lectures; but these attempts to generate enthusiasm amongst the masses for their new masters met with little success.

Far more successful and popular was the 19 May administration's foreign policy. In July 1934 most Bulgarians welcomed the opening of diplomatic relations with the Soviet Union, though the event was marred somewhat by the fact that on the day the new Soviet representative arrived in Bulgaria two men were executed in Plovdiv for alleged communist conspiracies.[10] Following the lead of Zveno the new government advocated closer relations with Yugoslavia. There had already been an increase in sporting contents and cultural exchanges, and in October 1933 King Alexander of Yugoslavia visited Bulgaria.

These were minor advances and if the new government was really to improve relations with Yugoslavia it had to grasp the Macedonian nettle.

---

[10] Panaĭotov, *Vŭnshnata politika*, 48.

The Zveno government knew that the Macedonian issue was poisoning relations between Bulgaria and Yugoslavia, was threatening the internal stability of Bulgaria itself, and was exposing the country to the dangers inherent in the 1933 London convention. It therefore sent the army into the Petrich enclave and at the same time took action against Macedonian extremists elsewhere in the country. The operation was swift and effective; the Macedonian organizations were not destroyed and they could still command support for public demonstrations, but they were hugely weakened. They ceased to launch major raids into Greece and Yugoslavia, the internecine strife which had produced so many murders decreased, and the Macedonian question was no longer a major constraint in the formulation of Bulgarian foreign policy. The action against the Macedonians was popular as well as effective. The murders, and particularly the Marinopolski affair, had alienated many moderate nationalists as well as army officers, and the dangers posed by Macedonian activities had created fears for Bulgaria's international standing and even security; moreover, in areas under their control the Macedonians had exacted heavy taxation which seemed to produce little result and which with the impact of the depression became more than usually onerous.

The suppression of the Macedonian enclave in Petrich did not mean that the zvenari lacked nationalist sentiment. They were in fact extremely Bulgaro-centric. They strengthened the authority of the Bulgarian Church and restricted the spread of foreign sects. They also enforced a large number of place-name changes, the previous Turkish variants being replaced by Bulgarian ones.

Like many military regimes, that of 19 May proved very skilful in taking power but less adept at retaining it. The regime had an extremely limited social base, its support coming primarily from the officer corps and senior civil servants who had been less affected by job losses than the lower ranks of the administration. Nor did it have a secure political base, not least because both the military and the political wings of Zveno were divided within themselves as what form any such base should take, the major issue being whether a new, mass party should be formed. An even more serious division arose over the relationship between the army and the crown. Velchev denied any wish to do away with the monarchy but he was known to lean towards republicanism, though most officers, having taken their oath of allegiance to the king, would support the latter should he enter openly into the political arena.

In that sense, Zveno's power would last only as long as the king chose to stay neutral. In January 1935 it became known that he was no longer prepared to do so.

As soon as the king had made plain his intention to appear on the political stage the pro-monarchist officers turned against Georgiev and Velchev, who were easily outmanoeuvred, Georgiev being replaced as minister president by Petko Zlatev. Zlatev was merely a stopgap and was himself replaced in April by Andreĭ Toshev. Civilian rule had been restored.

The 19 May regime had been short-lived and had alienated many of its subjects, but a number of its reforms remained in place until the emergency of the second world war and afterwards. Political parties were not reconstituted, though because most of them were so closely associated with individual leaders they continued to have a form of twilight semi-existence; the Bulgarian Workers' Union remained in being as the only permitted labour organization; the new arrangements for local government and the reconstituted form of sŭbranie were unaltered; the rationalization of the central government was not revoked; diplomatic relations with the Soviet Union remained; and there was no retreat either from the pro-Yugoslav foreign policy or from the concomitant containment of the Macedonians. The directorate of social renewal was, however, abolished.

8. THE PERSONAL REGIME OF KING BORIS, 1935–1941

In a proclamation issued on 21 April 1935, the day the new cabinet was formed, Toshev and the king promised to return the country to a stable life with a constitution adapted to modern needs; the intention was to fuse the democratic traditions of the nation with the discipline of the 19 May system.

This proved hard to accomplish. Toshev himself produced two draft constitutions but neither found favour with his ministerial colleagues or with the king. Nor could the cabinet and the palace agree on the question of whether or not to found a mass political movement to provide support for the new government. Toshev was against the notion, which he feared might rekindle party politics, but the monarchists in the Military League, who still exercised considerable influence, pressed for a Bulgarian National Front of agrarians and the NSM, which they saw as a fusing of the radical, left-wing past and the radical, right-wing future. These and other less important differences within the new leadership persuaded Toshev to resign in November. His had not been an entirely appropriate appointment. He was too long in the tooth to pose convincingly as the person who would restructure Bulgaria on modern lines, and his past links with IMRO made it difficult for Boris to pursue the better relations with Yugoslavia which had now become the cornerstone of Bulgarian foreign policy. Toshev was replaced by Georgi Kyoseivanov, a bridge-playing diplomat who was so much the king's man that he asked Boris for advice as to whom he should include in his cabinet; nevertheless, most of those who were included came from the old political parties which Boris despised.

By the beginning of 1936 domestic politics centred on the relationship between the king and his government on the one hand and the army on the other, Kyoseivanov telling a Greek newspaper that the central task of his administration would be to remove the army from politics. In this Kyoseivanov was blessed by good fortune. Velchev had gone into exile in 1935 but in October of that year had returned illegally and was soon captured; in government circles it was assumed that the Military League was again planning to act and, if necessary, declare a republic. In February 1936 Velchev was tried and sentenced to death, though this was soon commuted to life imprisonment by the king. Political capital was easily made out of Velchev's alleged attempt to depose the government and in March Boris dissolved the Military League and dismissed or moved anti-monarchist officers. Thereafter he did all he could to provide the army with new, modern equipment; his view, as reported by the British minister in Sofia, was that, 'So long as they had not enough "toys" to keep them occupied, the soldiers were apt to meddle in political affairs.'[11]

The dissolution of the Military League, however, did not remove the danger of the army's renewed meddling. In the summer of 1936 officers in the Plovdiv garrison threatened to support striking tobacco workers in the city. A combination of disaffected army officers and discontented urban workers was a strange concept but it did not appear an impossible

---

[11] Bentinck to Eden, 149 confidential, 23 May 1936, National Archives, Kew, FO 371/20370.

one. There were more working days lost through strikes in Bulgaria in 1936 than in any other year in the inter-war period, and the communists had made the chilling claim that they had established cells in almost every garrison in the country. The communists were an increasingly real danger. Their prestige had rocketed when their leader, Georgi Dimitrov, had ridiculed his Nazi prosecutors during the Reichstag fire trial in 1933, and the Comintern's adoption of the 'Popular front from below' strategy in 1935 threatened the creation of a network of apparently innocent but communist-dominated organizations. There were other threats to the Kyoseivanov government. Gichev's Vrabcha agrarians were pressing hard for an alliance of all political parties to confront and overturn the government. There seemed to be a rising danger on the right too. The successes of the fascist powers encouraged Tsankov and his supporters and at its congress in the summer of 1936 the NSM agreed upon a restructuring of the movement's organization to make it more like fascist parties elsewhere in Europe.

The activities of the extremes of left and right made it more difficult for Boris to find the middle ground on which he wished to base his new system. His search was complicated by the fact that it was hard to establish where the middle ground was; there had been no general election since 1931 and the limitations placed on the freedom of the press made it difficult to establish the popular mood, and therefore to know what could be regarded as an acceptable constitutional compromise. For what remained of the old parties the answer was the restoration of the Tŭrnovo system which would at least limit royal power, and five of the shadow parties came together in May 1936 to form the Petorka (Five) to press for that solution; it was later expanded into the People's Constitutional Bloc which included the Pladne agrarians and even the BWP.

Boris rejected the idea of a full restoration of the Tŭrnovo system and fell back upon a policy of gradually amending the constitution and in particular the rules regarding the franchise. The objective was to create 'a tidy and disciplined democracy imbued with the idea of social democracy'; Bulgaria was heading for authoritarian but not totalitarian rule. When a general election was finally held in March 1938 candidates had to confirm in writing that they had never been communists; rural voters were required to have primary, and urban voters secondary education; proportional representation was again to be abandoned in favour of single-member constituencies; constituency boundaries were to be redrawn by government officials; the minimum age for election to the assembly was to be 30 rather than 25; and voting was to be staged on three separate Sundays so that if necessary sufficient numbers of police and troops would be available in areas where they might be needed. For the first time the franchise was to be extended to women, but only those who were married or widowed, and for them voting was not compulsory as it was for men. The new sŭbranie was to be smaller than its predecessor, but when eventually elected it proved to be more independent and critical of the government than expected. Kyoseivanov therefore dismissed it in December 1939, and in the elections for its successor tightened yet further the restrictions on non-government candidates. Kyoseivanov was then dismissed by the king.

Kyoseivanov had lost credit by his inability to redefine the constitution and produce an entirely docile sŭbranie, but his most damaging failings had been in foreign policy which by the end of the 1930s naturally dominated political affairs.

Stamboliĭski had hoped to defend and further Bulgaria's interests by cooperation with its neighbours and with the League of Nations. The concept of peaceful revisionism via the League was retained after the coup of 1923, but it was thought preferable to find a patron amongst the larger powers rather than to rely on cooperation with the other Balkan states. Italy seemed to offer the best prospects, particularly because Mussolini's ambitions on the eastern shore of the Adriatic gave him and Bulgaria a common cause against Yugoslavia. The pro-Italian orientation of Bulgarian policy was reflected in King Boris's marriage in 1930 to the Italian Princess Giovanna of Italy. But by then the law of diminishing returns seemed to apply to reliance on Italy, and Bulgaria's rulers therefore moved back towards Stamboliĭski's idea of working with the other Balkan states.

Agreements were concluded with Romania on the teaching of Bulgarian and Romanian as minority languages. Relations with Greece in the early 1920s had been dominated by the consequences of an agreement signed in 1919 for an exchange of populations; agreement on some other issues was reached in 1925 though difficulties remained over property claims on both sides until a further agreement in 1931. In 1925 an agreement had also been concluded with Turkey which in the early 1930s made approaches for a mutual pact with Bulgaria. The critical relationship, however, was that with Yugoslavia and the suppression of the Petrich enclave at last allowed real progress to be made towards closer ties between Sofia and Belgrade. The Yugoslavs responded sympathetically to approaches both from the 19 May regime and from Zlatev, but it was not until January 1937 that a treaty of friendship was concluded between the two countries. In that following year all Balkan states signed the Salonika agreements by which they renounced the use of war and, somewhat paradoxically, condoned massive rearmament.[12]

The move away from Italy and towards an accommodation with the neighbouring states had begun in the early 1930s but was intensified in the mid-1930s by changes in the general international situation. The Abyssinian crisis and the Spanish civil war indicated that too close a relationship with Italy would be unpopular in London and Paris. In the increasingly unstable and belligerent atmosphere of the second half of the 1930s Bulgaria could not risk diplomatic isolation. The altered international climate also meant that Bulgaria could not risk continued military unpreparedness. In 1935 therefore, despite the terms of the treaty of Neuilly, it began to rearm. In 1934 Bulgaria had no military aircraft yet by 1939 it had 258 of them. The military hardware, which had the domestic political advantage of pleasing the army, came mostly from Germany. This did not necessarily indicate a leaning towards Hitler's Reich. German armaments were modern and of high quality and the blocked marks agreements provided the means to pay for them; under these agreements Germany purchased primary produce from Bulgaria and other East European states but the money for it was deposited in a German bank and could be used only for the purchase of German manufactured goods. Germany was also one of the few countries willing to train Bulgarian officers.[13]

Rearmament, the Bulgarian-Yugoslav treaty, and the Salonika agreements were integral parts of the attempt by the states concerned to create some form of regional security in face of the growing crisis in Europe, a crisis soon to be made infinitely more grave by the Munich settlement and the first Vienna award. The former had wrecked the little entente of Romania, Czechoslovakia, and Yugoslavia and thereby deprived the latter of its chief diplomatic shield; as a result Yugoslavia

[12] For Bulgaria's relations with its Balkan neighbours in the 1930s, see Krŭstyu Manchev and Velerian Bistritski, *Bŭlgariya i neĭnite sŭsedi 1931–1939; Politicheski i diplomaticheski otnosheniya* (Sofia: Nauka i izkustvo, 1978).
[13] Lyudmil Petrov, *Problemi na voennata politika na Bŭlgariya 1934–1939g* (Sofia: Voenno Izdatelstvo, 1990).

moved closer to Bulgaria, offering a customs union, a military alliance, and frontier rectifications if Bulgaria would renounce all claims upon Macedonia. Boris was receptive to the Yugoslav approaches; when asked where Bulgaria stood, he once replied, 'Wherever Yugoslavia is',[14] but the difficulties over Macedonia were still enormous, and the Yugoslav condition with regard to it highlighted a problem which Bulgaria alone faced. The redrawing of the map of central Europe left Bulgaria as the only revisionist state which had not benefited from the recent territorial changes; it was hardly likely to give up its claims on Macedonia when the tide was running in favour of revision. Yet this did not mean that Bulgaria wished to fight for territorial expansion.

In the late 1930s Boris had visited the European capitals in an attempt to prevent war between the great powers and when it came he immediately declared neutrality, believing that this was the best, or the least harmful policy for Bulgaria. He rejected pressure from all lobbies, famously remarking, 'My army is pro-German, my wife is Italian, my people are pro-Russian, I alone am pro-Bulgarian.'[15] Despite this there were powerful factors pushing Bulgaria towards the Axis.

Germany had established a strong trading presence in Bulgaria through the blocked marks agreements, the first of which was signed in the summer of 1932[16] and which were continued by the Nazis. But the blocked mark agreements were not solely responsible for drawing Bulgaria towards Germany, because similar agreements had been concluded between Germany and other Balkan states. Much more important was the fact that Germany was a revisionist state, and an increasingly successful one, above all at Munich. Then the Nazi-Soviet pact in August 1939 made association with Germany easier; Bulgarians could happily support a grouping which included Russia and which was also in favour of revising the 1919 peace settlement. The Nazi-Soviet pact enabled Bulgaria to combine business with pleasure.

The direction in which Bulgarian policy was moving was indicated in February 1940 when Boris replaced the pro-western, anglophile Kyoseivanov with Bogdan Filov, an academic archaeologist with very strong pro-German inclinations. Filov, whose father had been shot for involvement in the pro-Russian Rusé rising of 1887, immediately proved

---

[14] Manchev and Bistritski, *Bŭlgariya*, 292 n. 55.
[15] Marshall Lee Miller, *Bulgaria during the Second World War* (Stanford, Calif.: Stanford University Press, 1975), 1.   [16] Panaǐotov, *Vŭnshnata politika*, 43.

his pro-Nazi credentials by decreasing cultural links with the west, closing the masonic lodges to which most prominent Bulgarian politicians belonged, forming a new nationalist youth organization, and nominating one of Bulgaria's few anti-semites as minister of the interior.

Boris intended by these gestures to buy off the Germans and to preserve Bulgaria's neutrality, a point also indicated by his appointment of the pro-western Ivan Popov as minister for foreign affairs. He also intended to resist further pressure from both the Germans and the western allies. In February 1940 Bulgaria had rejected overtures from the Balkan entente because that grouping was believed to be too pro-western, but the king's calculations had to be remade after the sweeping German victory over France in May and the entry of Italy into the war on the German side, a development which the Bulgarians believed would exclude the British navy from the eastern Mediterranean.

With war appearing more likely the government gathered unto itself greater economic powers. In 1939 Kyoseivanov's government had passed the law of requisitions, and in the following year laws on civil mobilization and on the regulation of supplies and prices gave the central authorities wide-ranging powers, including the right to take over industrial enterprises. In 1940 the CLS was placed under army control and in December a new defence of the nation act placed further restrictions on the communists. The defence of the nation act also extended anti-semitic legislation introduced earlier in the year; Jews were no longer allowed to have Bulgarian names or Jewish ones with Bulgarian suffixes, they were required to wear the yellow star, and restrictions were placed on their freedom of movement. This provoked a number of protests from, amongst others, Kimon Georgiev. In the same year a new purity of the nation act forbade mixed marriages. This applied not only to unions between Bulgarians and non-Bulgarians but also to those between Turks and Jews, partly because the incidence of Turkish-Jewish marriages had been increasing as Jews saw this as a means to hide their racial origins and escape the effects of the anti-semitic laws;[17] in the event the law had little effect on these marriages but it was another indication that the government was leaning more towards the Nazi camp.

---

[17] Mary Neuburger, *The Orient Within: Muslim Minorities and the Negotiation of Nationhood in Modern Bulgaria* (Ithaca, NY: Cornell University Press, 2004), 51–2.

Before the passing of the defence of the nation act Bulgaria had received its first territorial concession when the treaty of Craiova, signed on 7 September 1940 and brokered by the Nazis with Soviet approval, had returned the southern Dobrudja to Bulgaria. In celebration a number of Sofia's prominent thoroughfares were renamed after prominent Germans, but still Boris refused to commit himself to the Axis, rejecting an offer from Mussolini by which Bulgaria would gain access to the Aegean if it joined the forthcoming Italian attack on Greece. He was equally dismissive of a Soviet proposal for a non-aggression pact under which Bulgaria would offer the USSR use of Bulgarian naval bases and would join in a descent on Turkey from which it would receive Thrace and the Soviets the Dardanelles. The Soviet offer, though made in secret, was soon well known in Bulgaria and produced a rash of pro-Soviet posters and graffiti. Boris, however, knew that the Soviets had used different language in Berlin where they referred to Bulgaria as a 'Soviet security zone'; the Baltic states had recently been declared a Soviet security zone and the precedent was hardly encouraging.

Boris had played the neutrality game long and hard but the final whistle was about to blow. German-Soviet relations had been deteriorating steadily in the autumn of 1940 and by the end of the year Hitler had decided upon his fateful attack upon the Soviet Union, in preparation for which large numbers of German troops had been moving into Romania. If, as seemed increasingly probable, Bulgaria had to choose between friendship with either Germany or the USSR neither Boris nor his ministers had any doubts that the former would be safer and more profitable.

Before Hitler's assault on the Soviet Union could be launched Germany was forced to come to the aid of Mussolini whose attack on Greece in October had ground to a halt. This aid could be delivered most easily by moving German troops from Romania into Bulgaria. When Boris visited the Berghof on 17 November Hitler told him he had decided to attack Greece. On 8 December German staff officers arrived in Bulgaria and Luftwaffe units began deploying in the country; on 20 January 1941 a meeting was held in Varna between Boris, Filov, Popov, the minister of the interior Petŭr Gabrovski, and General Teodosi Daskalov. For Boris and his ministers the fear was that the German army advancing from the north would be opposed by Anglo-Greek forces, probably with Turkish backing, and that the crucial battles would take place on Bulgarian soil. If, as they were determined to do, the Germans were to pass through Bulgaria, 'It is better', said Daskalov, 'they pass through as friends rather than as enemies.'[18] Throughout the discussions Boris had been indecisive, the real driving force determining Bulgarian policy being Filov.

Later in the month Filov went to Berlin to decide further details of the German operation. German troops were to enter Bulgaria on 2 March and from there would launch their land assault upon Greece. On 1 March Filov went to Vienna to sign the tripartite pact. The sŭbranie approved the deed by acclamation, despite vociferous protests from the opposition. British diplomatic representation was immediately withdrawn. Bulgaria was effectively a member of the Axis although a formal state of hostilities did not exist until Bulgaria declared war on both Britain and the United States immediately after the Japanese attack on Pearl Harbor in December 1941. War was never to be declared on the Soviet Union.

---

[18] Cited in Dimitŭr Ïonchev, *Bŭlgariya i Belomorieto (Oktomvri 1940–9 Septemvri 1944); Voennopoliticheski aspekti* (Sofia: Dirum, 1993), 25.

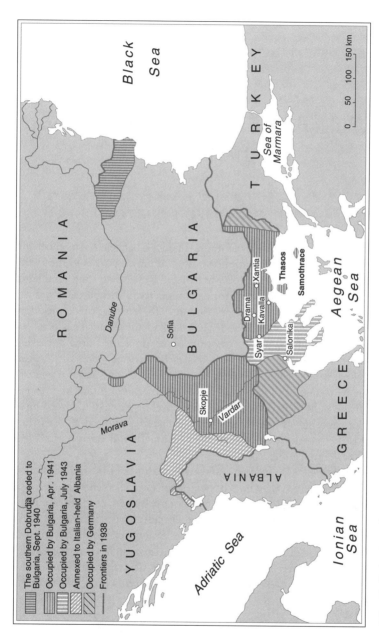

Map 5. Bulgaria in the second world war

The southern Dobrudja ceded to Bulgaria, Sept. 1940

Occupied by Bulgaria, Apr. 1941

Occupied by Bulgaria, July 1943

Annexed to Italian-held Albania

Occupied by Germany

Frontiers in 1938

0   50   100   150 km

Black Sea

ROMANIA

Danube

Sofia

BULGARIA

YUGOSLAVIA

Morava

Skopje

Vardar

ALBANIA

GREECE

Syar

Drama

Kavalla

Salonika

Xantia

Thasos

Samothrace

T U R K E Y

Sea of Marmara

Aegean Sea

Adriatic Sea

Ionian Sea

9

Bulgaria and the Second World War,
1941–1944

1. THE OCCUPIED TERRITORIES

Before the German invasion of Greece Yugoslavia had rejected membership of the tripartite pact and had shown signs of moving closer to the Soviet Union. For these reasons it too was invaded by Germany and its allies in April 1941. Bulgaria's reward for its complicity in these attacks was the restoration of the western territories lost in 1918, western Thrace, including the islands of Samothrace and Thassos, and the acquisition of all of Yugoslav Macedonia with exception of an undefined area bordering Italian-held Albania in the west. Bulgaria was not given the Aegean coastline, which remained under German control, and as yet it was not given ownership of Thrace and Macedonia; these it occupied 'to preserve order and stability in the territories taken over by Germany', a wording of Boris's choosing.[1] Nevertheless, most Bulgarians rejoiced at what they saw as the reunification of their historical lands and Boris himself was dubbed, 'King Unifier'.

Initially most Macedonian Slavs saw no reason to object to inclusion in Bulgaria; it would, they hoped, be a relief from the centralization and serbianization imposed by Yugoslavia. For the Bulgarians the first priority was to re-establish and to entrench their cultural domination of these areas. There was much to be done. Since 1918 in the acquired territories of Macedonia and Thrace over 1,700 Bulgarian churches and monasteries had been taken over by the Greek or Serbian Churches, and over 1,450 Bulgarian schools had closed. There had also been a prohibition on the

---

[1] Ivan Paunovski, *Vŭzmezdieto* (Varna: Georgi Bakalov, 1982), 287, 302.

public use of Bulgarian, though other languages were not proscribed. The need to establish or restore Bulgarian cultural predominance in these areas was enhanced by the fact that Bulgarian sovereignty there had not been recognized in any international agreement, not even with the Third Reich; if they were to be awarded to Bulgaria the Bulgarian nature of the territories had to be incontrovertible by the end of the war.

Education was a first priority. The ministry of education in Sofia organized crash courses in Bulgarian for Macedonian teachers, and set about integrating Macedonian schools into the Bulgarian educational system. Over 800 new schools were built between 1941 and 1944, and Macedonia's first institute of higher learning, the King Boris University in Skopje, was established.

Inevitably, the Bulgarian Church was to play a major cultural role, and there were moves to integrate Macedonia into the Exarchate. In 1941 a Bulgarian priest officiated at the Easter service in Skopje cathedral and efforts were made to restore exarchist control in all churches, with former priests in Bulgaria being urged to come out of retirement and take control of parishes in Macedonia. The leaders of the Bulgarian Church hoped that national reunification would bring about the restoration of the Bulgarian Patriarchate, the plan being that all Bulgarian communities should take part in electing a religious leader who would remain head of the national Church whatever the political system or even the territorial extent of the state. The king, however, was not willing to see the creation of another focal point for national loyalty. The government in Sofia also interfered heavy-handedly in the appointment of exarchist bishops to Macedonian sees, showing a marked preference for clerics from Bulgaria rather than from Macedonia itself; this caused both disappointment amongst Bulgarian nationalists and resentment amongst many ordinary Macedonians. The Bulgarian authorities were repeating the Serbian mistake of over-centralization, and by 1944 rule from Sofia was as unwelcome to most Macedonians as domination from Belgrade had been before 1941.

The situation in Thrace was more complicated and more difficult and here the Bulgarian government was to meet with serious opposition. Until the signature of a German-Turkish treaty of friendship and non-aggression in June 1941, the Germans were anxious not to annoy or alienate the Turks by allowing the Bulgarians a permanent position in Thrace, and until August there were German, Bulgarian, and Greek jurisdictions, sometimes with farcical results. Only after the signature of the German-Turkish treaty was Bulgarian civilian administration permitted.

Since it had been lost to Bulgaria at the end of the first world war the ethnic composition of the area had been changed by the population exchanges following the Greek-Turkish war in Anatolia which involved the departure of many Turks and the arrival of far more Greeks from eastern Thrace and Asia Minor. Bulgarian policies in Thrace followed traditional means, both hard and soft. Considerable pressure was put upon the local Turks to leave, occasioning constant complaint from Turkish consular officials in the region.[2] At the same time, there were measures to bolster Bulgarian culture via the Church and education. Most of the villages were incorporated into the Nevrokop diocese of the Bulgarian Orthodox Church, though in some areas local priests tried, with a good deal of success, to promote cooperation between incoming Bulgarian priests and resident Greek ones.

In education the Bulgarian school system was introduced for the school year beginning in September 1941. As in Macedonia, considerable energy was devoted to improving existing and building new schools; in the academic year 1941–2 189 new primary schools and 30 gymnasia were opened. By the end of 1942 there were 6 kindergarten, 200 primary schools, and 34 gymnasia, all for Bulgarians. There were also schools for non-Bulgarians, some of them private; in 1942 and 1943, 25 private primary schools were opened, 20 for Turkish children, four for Armenians, and one for Italians. But there were also assimilationist pressures. Children were classified by ethnic group which meant that the Pomaks were included in Bulgarian, Christian schools. When some hodjas (Muslim religious instructors) inveighed against this and attempted to prevent Pomak children attending Christian schools the local teachers invoked the help of the local Patriotic Associations.

As a result of these policies between the summer of 1941, when the Bulgarian authorities made a hurried and not entirely accurate assessment of the population, the Christian Bulgarians increased from 6.74 to 15.91 per cent of the total and the Pomaks from 0.95 to 4.32 per cent, whilst the Turks declined from 11.24 to 10.84 per cent and the Greeks from 71.11 to 65.11 per cent. In absolute terms the number of Bulgarian Christians rose by 57,787, and that of Pomaks by 21,414, whilst the Greeks decreased by 46,387.

[2] Neuburger, *Orient Within*, 184.

The main thrust of Bulgarian policy was to remove those Greeks who had arrived in Thrace after 1918, a commission of inquiry insisting that of the 460,000 Greeks in western Thrace in 1941 only 150,000 had been born there. The Bulgarian government wanted to restore the ethnic balance to its 1918 position when Bulgarians were predominant, and planned to replace the departing Greeks with Bulgarians from southern Macedonia. In June 1941 the law on internal migration and consolidation was enacted to encourage this process and thereafter, particularly after Thrace had been placed under Bulgarian civilian administration, great pressure was placed on the newly arrived Greeks to leave. Soon the Germans were complaining that the expellees could not be accommodated in Salonika and south-west Macedonia, and there were also complaints from the Bulgarian army who said that most of the displaced families were settling in areas which had majority Bulgarian populations, but where that majority might disappear because of the newly arrived Greeks.

The most serious complaint, however, came from the afflicted Greeks themselves. On the night of 28–9 September they staged an uprising in Drama which had echoes elsewhere. Both Bulgarians and Greeks acted with great brutality before the rising was crushed. Greek sources later put the number of killed at between 45,000 and 65,000, and claimed the rising was provoked by the Bulgarians in order to justify a policy of wholesale expulsions. The Bulgarian authorities, however, appear to have been taken by surprise and according to archival sources the estimated number of killed in Drama was 1,600.[3]

The rising did not end the resettlement drive. In February 1942 the Bulgarians established a land directorate to encourage settlement, and grants of land were made to officials, the property becoming fully theirs after three years. After February 1942 there were stronger moves to create areas of compact Bulgarian population which usually meant moving Greek families to other parts of a village or out of the village altogether. By the end of March, 18,925 resettlement permits had been granted in Thrace, most of them to former inhabitants of the area or their descendants, but the most rapid increase in the pace of resettlement came in the second half of 1942. Thereafter it declined. After Alamein and Stalingrad the number of Bulgarians wishing to move to Thrace fell, not least because both the

[3] Ïonchev, *Belomorieto*, 85.

Turks and the Greeks threatened retribution when they resumed control of the area, an eventuality made much more probable by the allied victories. In August 1944 the Sofia government issued a desperate but largely ineffective order forbidding civil servants to move their possessions out of Thrace.

Compared to the rest of Bulgaria and Greece, western Thrace was backward and impoverished. There was a low percentage of land use, a high incidence of malaria, the roads and the rail network were primitive, and water supplies were not reliable. Bulgarian rule at least brought some improvements. Institutions such as the Cooperative Bank were intended to help local farmers, albeit with a bias to the Bulgarians amongst them. The Bulgarians also improved the roads and, most importantly perhaps, western Thrace was spared the horrific starvation visited upon German- and Italian-occupied Greece, because food was brought in from the rest of Bulgaria.

2. DOMESTIC POLITICS DURING THE WAR

Bulgaria's commitment to the Axis had profound effects on the domestic political scene. The defence of the realm act and other legislation in the summer of 1940 had shown official favour to the political right and nationalist, fascist, and proto-fascist groups had taken encouragement from this. Prominent amongst the nationalist organizations was 'Otets Paisiĭ' (Father Paisiĭ), which saw national salvation in the rediscovery of the ideals of the vŭzrazhdane, whilst in the more extreme categories were the youth movement *Brannik* (Defender), established by government decree in 1941, the Bulgarian National Union 'Kubrat', and the semi-military Legionaries. Another active organization was Rodina (Kinsman). Formed in 1937, its purpose was to inculcate a greater Bulgarian consciousness amongst Pomaks; it had arranged for the Koran to be translated into Bulgarian and in 1942 pioneered legislation which required all newborn children to be given Bulgarian names and abolished legal fees for anyone wishing to adopt Christian or Slav names.[4]

---

[4] Valeriĭ Rusanov (compiler) and Lilyana Aleksandrieva (ed.), *Aspekti na etnokulturnata situatsiya v Bŭlgariya i na Balkanite*, vol. ii, the proceedings of a seminar held in Sofia, 21–3 February 1992 (Sofia; Fumi Press for the Friedrich Naumann Foundation, 1992), 39–40.

The strengthening of the organized political right was not welcome to Boris who, as ever, was sensitive to any threat from other centres of power within his kingdom. He was even more suspicious of the military, his fear that a victorious general might return from the eastern front and depose him being one reason why he had ruled out Bulgarian participation in the German-Soviet war. But neutrality in that conflict did not isolate Boris from danger. The German victories in 1941 and 1942 gave rise to the anxiety that Bulgaria would soon be restructured to make it conform to the Nazis' New Order in Europe; there was no guarantee there would be any place within that order for a monarch, least of all one who could exercise real power. From early 1941 therefore the king placed severe restraints upon the activities of the extreme right.

The most dangerous figure on the right was General Hristo Lukov, one of the founders of the Military League. During the second half of the 1930s he, like Tsankov, had been forbidden to hold public meetings, but he enjoyed great respect amongst the officer corps, was a friend of Göring, and commanded the Legionaries. In September 1942 the king refused to allow him and another right-wing officer, Colonel Atanas Pantev, to go to Berlin. Lukov was not perturbed and by early 1943 was confident that his hour would soon come. In this he was mistaken because he was assassinated in February.

Boris's fears of a German-backed move to dethrone him were misplaced. As long as he remained committed to the Axis the Germans were hardly likely to remove him themselves. Nor would they be likely to find powerful internal forces which would do this for them. There was no significant German minority through which the Nazis could work, and Bulgaria's right-wing forces were splintered, poorly led, and lacking in mass support. Nevertheless, Boris was by nature insecure and feared that the assassination of Lukov might spark another series of political assassinations similar to those carried out before the suppression of the Petrich enclave and that he might himself be a victim; it was reported that at Lukov's funeral his hands shook so much that he had difficulty lighting a candle.[5]

Lukov's assassination was the work of the communists. Until the Nazi attack upon the Soviet Union they had been allowed some political liberty, and they had mounted a vigorous campaign in favour of the Soviet

[5] Vitka Toshkova (compiler), *Dnevnik na Bekerle, Iz dnevnika na Bekerle—pŭlnomoshten ministŭr na tretiya raĭh v Bŭlgariya* (Sofia: Hristo Botev, 1992), 72–3.

proposal for a non-aggression pact in November 1940. After June 1941 they were repressed. The nine sitting deputies who were known communists, together with 282 other leading members of the party, trade unionists, and veterans of the Spanish civil war, were interned. This did not end communist activities. Soon after the opening of the German-Soviet war a number of communist agents were landed by parachute and submarine in an effort to rally the Bulgarians against the Germans, but they had little success. The government rounded them up together with a number of returned communist émigrés; 700 more party members and anti-government activists were sent to detention camps. More repression followed the discovery in April 1942 of communist conspiracies in two regiments of the Bulgarian army. General Vladimir Zaĭmov, who had been involved in the 1934 coup, was executed after the Gestapo provided information that he had been colluding with the Soviets,[6] and by the summer of 1942 the police had virtually liquidated communist organizations in the country, real and suspected. Over 6,000 were sent to labour battalions and 11,000 were incarcerated in camps. The few that remained at liberty were still under observation, a former royalist police officer revealing in 1991 that, 'In the whole of Bulgaria about five to six hundred people went underground. We knew them all by name—even their partisan names';[7] and so disrupted had the communist organization become that from midsummer 1942 until September 1944 there was no direct radio link between the few communists left at large in Bulgaria and their leadership in the Soviet Union.

With Bulgaria firmly ensconced in the New Order it was inevitably subjected to Nazi pressure on the Jewish question. The anti-semitic legislation of 1940 and early 1941 did not satisfy Nazi ideologues such as Adolf-Heinz Beckerle, who was made German minister in Sofia in October 1941. In an attempt to placate the Nazis further restrictions were placed on the Bulgarian Jews; their businesses were subject to compulsory purchase by the state, Jewish organizations were dissolved, and Jews were deprived of their civil rights. And in August 1942 the sŭbranie passed a law which deprived Jews in Bulgarian-occupied territory of

[6] For his activities on behalf of the Soviets see Luiza Revyakina, 'Sŭvetskata legatsiya v Bŭlgariya (22 yuni 1941–9 septemvri 1944g)', in Maj. Gen. Prof. Dr V. Zolotaryov et al. (eds.), *Bŭlgaro-sŭvetski politicheski i voenni otnosheniya (1941–1947). (Statii i dokumenti)* (Sofia: Voenno Izdatelstvo, 1999), 24–41, 28–30.

[7] Interview with Boris Dimitrov in *Anteni* (Sofia), 24, 12 June 1991, and 25, 19 July 1991.

their Bulgarian citizenship. This was a fateful decision which cost most of those Jews their lives. In March 1943 they were deported to the death camps.

By a sleight of hand the head of the Bulgarian commissariat for Jewish affairs, Aleksandŭr Belev, arranged for 6,000 Jews from the pre-war kingdom to be included in the deportations; they were to be put on trains in Kyustendil. This soon became public knowledge because a four-person delegation from Kyustendil came to Sofia to express its concern and because Belev's mistress, appalled at the scheme, leaked the news to the press. She was not alone in feeling revolted, and there was immediate and widespread outrage with protests pouring in from all sections of society. Professional groups such as the doctors' union, the association of Bulgarian writers, the bar association, and the painters' union voiced their opposition, as did students at the pedagogic institute; the Church at all levels denounced the plan; so too did railway workers, tobacco workers, shoemakers, bakers, petty traders, and tailors; communist cells organized some of the protests but most came spontaneously from ordinary citizens, including illiterate peasants who signed petitions with their thumb-prints; amongst the many prominent individuals who raised their voices were Aleksandŭr Tsankov and, on the other side of the political spectrum, Ekaterina Karavelova, widow of the former minister president;[8] even Ivan Mihaĭlov, leader of IMRO's most powerful faction, intervened, sending a seminary student based in Salzburg to the general staff in Sofia to warn them that if one Jew were deported the wrath of IMRO would fall upon those responsible.[9]

The most important focus of institutional resistance was the sŭbranie. The cabinet had known what was afoot and had raised no objections but, unusually, the pro-government sŭbranie deputies refused to be obedient. The deputy speaker, Dimitŭr Peshev, who was also one of the two members for Kyustendil, organized a petition which, he said, would be more powerful if it were signed only by deputies from the majority pro-government faction. Despite pressure from the administration

---

[8] Michael Bar-Zohar, letter to the *New York Times*, 28 May 2001. For a full account, see Dr Bar-Zohar's, *Beyond Hitler's Grasp: The Heroic Rescue of Bulgaria's Jews* (Holbrook, Mass.: Adams Media Corporation, 1998).

[9] This information from an email of 23 February 2001 from George Lebamoff to Roy Freed; the message was posted on the Bulgarian Studies Group Website, Bulgarian_Studies@yahoogroups.com, on 21 February 2001.

forty-three deputies did sign the petition which was then submitted to the king who immediately vetoed the deportations. In May the anti-semites, with German backing, made a second attempt to deport Jews from the old kingdom. Again they failed, the opposition being led this time by Metropolitan Stefan, although the communists also organized a demonstration in Sofia. The Jews were saved but their lives were not made easy. Most were deported to camps in the interior of Bulgaria where they were put to work on the roads and building sites.

Boris had shown disquiet over the measures against the Jews and in March 1943 had received the Chief Rabbi to warn him of the impending tightening of anti-semitic measures. But he had shown little resolve to oppose German intentions, although he had intervened to save a small number of Jews he knew personally;[10] his wife saved more, including a handful from the occupied territories, by securing them transit visas enabling them to travel via Italy to Argentina.[11] The king followed rather than led opinion on the Jewish question, but once he had been persuaded to forbid the deportations from Bulgaria proper he stuck to his decision. The critical issue was citizenship. Boris argued, as did others opposed to the deportations, that any decision affecting Bulgarian citizens could only be made by the Bulgarian authorities; it was a matter of national sovereignty as well as human decency. No doubt another consideration was that after Stalingrad it appeared ever more likely that the Germans would lose the war, and the United States had already made it known that after the war anyone guilty of persecuting the Jews would be punished. Beckerle eventually recognized that the Jewish question in Bulgaria and the Balkans was different from in other areas; the Bulgarians, he said, had grown up with Greeks, Armenians, and Turks, and therefore did not have the antipathy to Jews found in northern Europe, and he concluded eventually that Berlin should not endanger its political standing in Sofia by pursuing the matter any further.[12]

---

[10] Sharlanov and Meshkova (eds.), *Süvetnitsite*, 210–11.

[11] Stephane Groueff, *Crown of Thorns: The Reign of King Boris III of Bulgaria, 1918–1943* (Lanham, Md.: Madison Books, 1987), 320–2, and Pashanko Dimitroff, *Boris III of Bulgaria (1894–1943): Toiler, Citizen, King* (Lewes: The Book Guild Ltd., 1986), 182.   [12] Groueff, *Crown of Thorns*, 331.

3. BULGARIA'S MILITARY PARTICIPATION IN THE WAR

When Bulgaria joined the tripartite pact it had been agreed that it would not offer military assistance to Germany and no military convention had been signed. The determination to stay out of the war was increased by the German attack upon the Soviet Union, after which Bulgaria represented German interests in the USSR. Bulgaria's contribution to the war in the east would go no further than allowing Bulgarian charitable foundations to equip a Red Cross train which was to be for the use of both sides.

Boris argued that the Bulgarian army was not equipped for a war such as that on the eastern front, and that the country's peasant conscripts would never be fully committed to fighting on foreign soil, especially against the Russians. He also argued that if his army were kept in the Balkans it could deter Turkey from entering the war on the allied side, and could also deter, or if necessary resist, allied landings in the Balkans, an increasingly forceful argument after the Italo-German defeat in north Africa. So determined were the authorities in Sofia to avoid any form of military commitment to the German war effort that when the Germans suggested that fifteen Bulgarian pilots trained in Germany might fly with the Luftwaffe, Boris's ministers insisted that they must not wear German uniforms or take the oath of allegiance to Hitler, and were to serve only in the north African theatre; and even this permission was withdrawn in May 1942.[13]

In the early stages of the war the Bulgarian position caused no tension between Berlin and Sofia. Filov had been given an assurance by Hitler in March 1941 that the Germans 'would not in any event wish us to do anything which we ourselves did not wish to do'.[14] The Bulgarians were helped by the fact that Hitler held their monarch in high regard, later telling the Hungarian prime minister, Count Kállay, that he 'had never met politician as intelligent and shrewd' as King Boris.[15] The Germans

---

[13] See R. Rumelin, 'Za bŭlgarsko-germanskite voennopoliticheski otnosheniya v navecherieto na 9 Septemvri 1944', in V. Hadjinikolov (editor in chief), *Bŭlgarsko-Germanski Otnosheniya i Vrŭzki*, vol. ii (Sofia: BAN, 1981), 383–9.

[14] Ilcho Dimitrov (ed. in chief), *Bogdan Filov, Dnevnik* (Sofia: Otechestven Front, 1990), 270.   [15] Ibid. 521.

were also in full agreement at this stage with Boris's assessment of the capabilities and function of the Bulgarian army.

Bulgaria's line of non-commitment, however, was a difficult one to hold. In December 1941 Bulgaria bowed to German pressure and declared war on Britain and the United States. The war, insisted the Bulgarian government, was merely 'symbolic', but the declaration of war had a deep psychological impact. Bulgaria, it was widely, and correctly, assumed had succumbed to the German will; and few could understand why Bulgaria should pit itself against the USA with which it had remained at peace during the first world war. Boris himself seems to have shared these anxieties; after the declaration in December 1941 he was absent for hours until finally discovered in fervent prayer in a remote corner of the Aleksandŭr Nevski cathedral. December 1941 also saw another important development.

The German failure to take Moscow meant that the Wehrmacht had to call upon German troops from occupation duties in the Balkans, and to replace them a new Bulgarian army corps of three divisions was formed and placed under German command. The new Bulgarian army helped to guard railways, mines, ammunition dumps, and other strategic installations in Serbia. Bulgarian troops had not been deployed outside the Balkans but they had been used outside areas under Bulgarian political control in support of a non-Bulgarian authority.

The German request for help in Serbia had embarrassed the Bulgarian government, which was further discomforted by German pressure for the closure of the Soviet consulates in Varna and Burgas on the ground that they were nests of spies. The Bulgarians denied this, but nevertheless raided the consulate in Varna in September, though this was more because of its known connections with communist subversion than its alleged espionage activities.

Having failed to secure its expected rapid victory in the war against the Soviet Union, and facing a resurgent British army in north Africa, the German high command had to consider the prospect of a Soviet, or more probably an Anglo-American landing in the Balkans. This led to the promulgation in December 1942 of Directive No. 47 stating that in this eventuality the Bulgarian forces involved would be under the German Süd-Ost high command.[16] In the same month a senior Wehrmacht

---

[16] Kiril Vasilev et al. (eds.), *Otechestven Front; dokumenti i materiali*, vol. i, part i, *22 yuni 1941–april 1944* (Sofia: Otechestven Front, 1987), 180 n. 1.

officer arrived in Sofia to suggest that the Bulgarian army take part in operations against the partisans in Bosnia and Greece. This question was taken up again when Boris visited Hitler in April 1943. By this time the military situation had been transformed by El Alamein and Stalingrad. Boris resisted the calls for the wider deployment of Bulgarian forces in German-occupied areas, insisting once again both that the Bulgarian army had to be kept in Macedonia, not least to combat Italian intrigues, and that the Bulgarian peasant conscript would not be suited to fighting far away from his native soil.

Boris was 'neither intoxicated nor intimidated by Hitler',[17] but when the two met again in June 1943 the king acceded to Hitler's request that the Bulgarians take over an area in north-eastern Serbia to release the German troops stationed there for duty on the eastern front; previous deployments by the Bulgarian army in Serbia had been to assist the German forces; now they were to replace them. Hitler also wanted the Bulgarians to take over most of Greek Macedonia. Boris declined to accept all of the latter on the grounds that for Bulgaria to take Salonika would be too much of a provocation to the Turks and the Italians, though he did agree that the Bulgarian 7th Division be placed under German command around Salonika itself. The request with regard to Serbia was accepted on the grounds that the German troops so released might prevent a Soviet landing in Bulgaria, an eventuality which would bring about what Boris and Filov feared most: full Bulgarian involvement in the German-Soviet war. As a result of the June meeting Bulgarian soldiers assumed guard duties along the Belgrade-Salonika railway and replaced the Germans in northern Serbia and along much of the Aegean coast of Thrace.

Although Boris had successfully resisted pressure to sign a military convention with Germany, the use of Bulgarian troops to replace German forces in northern Serbia and in much of Aegean Thrace meant that Bulgaria had become part of the German sphere of military operations and that military assistance to Germany was being provided indirectly. There was further integration of Bulgarian forces into the Wehrmacht's Balkan operations when the Bulgarian Second Army Corps, formed in Thrace in December 1943, was placed under German command. The Germans also influenced the appointment of senior officers in the Bulgarian army.

It has to be presumed that the question of the further deployment of Bulgarian troops was one of the items discussed by Hitler and King Boris when the two met in East Prussia in August 1943; there can be no definite knowledge because the most important conversations were *à deux* with no interpreters present and no records taken. Two weeks after he returned to Bulgaria Boris became ill and on 28 August died, aged only 49. Rumours spread immediately that he had been murdered, but if this were the case it would be difficult to say who would have been responsible. No one knew who would replace him as the director of Bulgaria's foreign policy, and all the major suspects, the Germans, the British, and the Soviets, stood to lose as much as they would gain by removing him. In the early 1990s an examination of his remains revealed that an infarction of the heart's left chamber had been the direct cause of death.[18]

Boris's death occasioned widespread national grief. He was the leader who had brought about national reunification and, probably more importantly, had kept Bulgaria out of the murderous war on the eastern front. His rule had been firm but not totalitarian. Restrictions were placed on the press but even in the war one formerly pro-allied newspaper, *Mir* (World or Peace), was allowed to continue publication; even May Day parades were permitted until 1941. Boris had also curbed the party political warfare which had produced ineffective government and he had contained the extremes of right as well as left.

4. THE REGENCY AND THE END OF THE 'SYMBOLIC' WAR

As Boris had hovered between life and death an observer in the German foreign service commented,

In the eyes of the Bulgarian people the king is less a monarch than a leader. He is a symbol of national unity and his disappearance could certainly transform the internal situation. The nation would be leaderless and insecure and would to an increasing degree fall under the influence of communists and anglophiles. In conclusion one can say that under King Boris there was no reason to fear political

---

[18] Georgi Markov, *Kambanite biyat sami. Nasilie i politika v Bŭlgariya, 1919–1947* (Sofia: Georgi Pobedonosets, 1994), 145.

developments unfavourable to us, but his disappearance could lead both to an internal crisis and to external realignments.[19]

It was an accurate assessment. After Boris's death the extremes of both right and left were less restrained, and were more likely to find popular support now that the paternal hand of the king had been removed. At the same time the wisdom of Bulgaria's continued commitment to the Axis would be increasingly questioned.

Boris's successor, Simeon II, was a minor and a regency was formed consisting of a soldier, General Nikola Mihov, Boris's younger brother Prince Kiril, and Filov, who was the dominant personality. Filov's former position of minister president was given to Dobri Bozhilov who was a creature of Filov. The new regency did not receive the endorsement of a grand national assembly, as the strict letter of the constitutional law required and as the political opposition, legal and illegal, demanded; the government feared unrest if elections were to be held and it therefore stated that the stresses of the war made the calling of a GNA impossible but promised that once the fighting had stopped one would be convened to sanction both the regency and the acquisition of the new territories. The regency and its governments would face two main problems: the rise of opposition within the country itself, and the increasing likelihood of Bulgaria's full involvement in the European war.

In March 1943 Boris himself had admitted to Filov that he had lost faith in a German victory.[20] By the summer of 1943 that victory was even more improbable. With the turn in the tide of war Bulgaria's diplomatic and strategic position shifted. Stalingrad had seen the destruction of the better part of the Romanian army, thus making Bulgaria the strongest military power in the Balkans. By the summer of 1943 the German withdrawal from the Caucasus was releasing pressure on Turkey's Asiatic flank which made it more likely that the latter would join the allies, in which event Bulgaria would be the essential first line of Axis defence in south-eastern Europe; at the same time, Italy's collapse had increased the expectation of an Anglo-American descent upon the Balkans. This fear, together with the beginning of the Soviet advance in the east, prompted many Bulgarians to think of an accommodation with the western allies.

[19] Helmut Heiber, 'Der Tod des Zaren Boris', *Vierteljahreshefte für Zeitgeschichte* (Munich), 9 (1961), 384–416, see 390–1.   [20] Dimitrov (ed.), *Filov, Dnevnik*, 565.

These thoughts were made stronger by the intensifying activity of the partisans. Bulgarian troops in Serbia and Macedonia came under increasing attack and in October 1943 a huge unit of over 200 launched an assault on Pirot, then garrisoned by the Bulgarian army. Bulgaria was in an increasingly dangerous position. Not only was it threatened by the prospect of a war on two fronts, against the partisans in the west and an allied/Turkish force in the south-east, but these threats made it ever more dependent on Germany for military supplies. This closer dependence upon Germany increased the likelihood of Anglo-American action against Bulgaria, and worst of all for Filov and his supporters it could lead to a Soviet declaration of war against Bulgaria. This added force to the arguments of those who wanted to come to an agreement with the western allies.

Unofficial feelers for such a deal had been put out in May 1943 but the response had not been encouraging. In the summer approaches were received from Bucharest and from Washington but Filov spurned them. By October he had become more pliant. He allowed one of his associates to try and establish contact with the Americans with the object of discovering what peace terms the allies might offer. The response was discouraging: unconditional surrender, the evacuation of all recently acquired territory, and an allied occupation of Bulgaria. Bulgaria was not near enough defeat to accept such terms which might in any case have provoked an angry reaction in nationalist circles.

Soon there was even greater cause to seek a peace as Bulgaria's war ceased being 'symbolic' and became very real. Small air raids had been carried out on Bulgarian targets from the beginning of the war but they had had little effect. This changed in November 1943 when Sofia was subjected to its first heavy dose of bombing, with what Filov called 'the first large terror raid'[21] being carried out on 10 January 1944. The raids continued intermittently until another massive assault, chiefly with incendiary bombs, in March. The raids were intended to disrupt civilian life, to alienate the population from the authorities, and to force a withdrawal of Bulgarian troops from Serbia and Greece. The raids did indeed disrupt civilian life. Thousands of Sofiotes fled the city and for more than a week the country was virtually without a functioning government or civil service. The raids also affected public opinion.

[21] Dimitrov (ed.), *Filov, Dnevnik*, 655.

The clandestine opposition made much of the government's inability to protect Sofia, and the same allegation was levelled against the Germans. At a service for victims of the January bombing the bishop of Sofia delivered a sermon strongly critical of the government and of its pro-German orientation; if, he noted, the government was serious in its assertions that its prime objective was to defend the nation from the ravages of war it had clearly failed. The bond of trust between citizen and government was severed and was never restored, particularly amongst the intelligentsia.[22] The third aim of the bombing was not achieved; the Bulgarian government made no moves to withdraw its forces from occupation duties in Serbia and Greece. It did, however, resume its approaches to the allies only to be told that the latter's terms were unchanged; so too was the Bulgarian government's unwillingness to accept them.

The approach to the allies had been prompted by the bombing offensive and also by growing pressure from the Soviet Union. The Bulgarians had turned to Moscow with requests that it intercede with the allies to suspend the bombing but the answer had been discouraging. The Soviets soon assumed a more menacing tone, complaining that Bulgaria was not observing strict neutrality in the Soviet-German war. In a note of 22 January 1944 the Soviet Union requested an immediate end to the construction in Varna of vessels for use by the German navy in the Black Sea. On 1 March the request turned into a demand for an end to this and other infringements of Bulgarian neutrality. The Bulgarian government immediately promised to restrict the German use of Bulgarian ports and, as a further sign of good will, refused a German request that the Bulgarian railway system be used to transfer German troops and equipment westwards. This was not enough to placate Moscow, which dispatched a series of missives culminating in a note of 18 May tougher than any of its predecessors. It stated that despite previous Bulgarian assurances there were still fifty to sixty German naval vessels, including submarines, in Varna harbour, where barges for use by the German army were also under construction; if Bulgaria's promise to abide strictly by the laws of neutrality were not implemented immediately, the note concluded, the Soviets would break off diplomatic relations.

---

[22] For a brilliant exposition of this theme see Irina Dimitrova Gigova, 'Writers of the Nation: Intellectual Identity in Bulgaria, 1939–1953', Ph.D. thesis (University of Illinois at Urbana-Champaign, 2004), especially 73–109.

The allied bombing and the Soviet diplomatic offensive unnerved Filov and his government. Like Boris, Filov believed that the greatest danger facing Bulgaria was that it might find itself at war with the Soviet Union; public opinion would never tolerate it, particularly now the Red Army was advancing, and if it came about the present political order would collapse and the national reunification of 1941 would be undone as Berlin had once undone San Stefano. On the other hand, Filov exploited recent German action in Hungary to argue that attempted withdrawal from the Axis would result in a full-scale German takeover. Bulgaria seemed to be facing its ultimate nightmare: the Soviets would declare war on and eventually occupy Bulgaria if it did not abandon the Germans; the Germans would declare war on it and occupy it if it did. In reality the Bulgarian and Hungarian situations were not the same, the Germans not having sufficient troops available to occupy Bulgaria, but the analogy was nevertheless seized upon by Filov to justify procrastination. His policy was now to balance Moscow against Berlin for long enough for him to seek an accommodation with the western allies.

5. INTERNAL OPPOSITION: THE FATHERLAND FRONT, AND THE PARTISAN MOVEMENT

By the late spring of 1944 the regency and the government were also facing mounting internal pressures as well as threats from the allies. Disenchantment had never been entirely absent and was, as in the first world war, in part a result of problems with food supplies, and for many of the same reasons. In 1941 the government had attempted to avoid these problems by passing laws to stimulate agricultural production, to remit the peasants' petty debts, to protect workshops, and to regulate war profits. But these laws had little long-term effect. As in the first world war German soldiers in Bulgaria sent home more food than they were allowed to, the army confiscated more food than it needed, the peasants refused to hand over to the requisitioning agencies as much food as they should have done because it would fetch more on the black market, the distribution of goods was slower because the transport system had been disrupted by mobilization, and everywhere corruption enabled the unscrupulous to circumvent the regulations. By the middle of 1944 official food prices were five and a half times higher than in 1939, whilst those on the black market, again frequently the only source of many commodities, were almost seven and a half times higher. The deleterious effects of this were felt most acutely in the larger urban centres. The opposition, meanwhile, insisted that the shortages were being accentuated because the Germans took Bulgarian food and paid for it not with cash or useful manufactured items, but with fripperies such as 'children's toys, chandeliers, gramophone records and eau de cologne'.[23]

A legal opposition had been established in the spring of 1943 but there was also illegal action. There were a number of assassinations and occasional acts of terrorism but a more coordinated threat to the government's authority was presented by the Fatherland Front (FF). The first FF had been formed by a number of leftist factions in 1941, but it had collapsed because the communists demanded virtually total control. It was reconstituted in February 1942 and consisted of the communists, the zvenari, left-wing agrarians under Nikola Petkov, and a social democrat faction headed by Grigor Chesmedjiev. In the following year a central committee was set up consisting of Petkov, Kimon Georgiev from the zvenari, a communist, and two social democrats. The FF declared that it was 'not a party organization, either of the Workers' or of any other party. It is a mass organization of all the people which on the basis of its programme unites the widest spectrum of the popular masses irrespective of their political allegiance.'[24] The movement also went out of its way, as did the BWP, to stress that an FF government would not be Soviet rule; said a statement in February 1944, 'This is not Soviet rule. Do not be frightened! This is the precondition for the establishment of real, popular, democratic power.'[25]

The FF programme demanded withdrawal from the war, the evacuation of Bulgarian troops from Yugoslavia and Greece, the end of Bulgarian membership of the Axis, a ban on food exports, friendly relations with the allied powers, the release of all those detained for anti-fascist activities, the removal of the army from royal control, the full restoration of civil liberties, the guarantee of a decent standard of living for all, and the dissolution of all 'fascist' organizations. By the spring of 1944 the FF was calling upon peasants to refuse to hand over food or other items to the

---

[23] Kiril Vasilev et al. (eds.), *Otechestven Front; dokumenti i materiali*, vol. i, part ii, *1 maĭ 1944–11 septemvri 1944*, (Sofia: Otechestven Front, 1987), 61.
[24] Quoted ibid i. 360.   [25] Ibid. 583.

requisitioning authorities and even to refuse to pay taxes, and the government had become concerned enough to set up the New Social Force to unite the village populations against the revolutionary movement. The FF was undeterred. A proclamation from its national committee in June insisted that only an FF government could save the country and called on all 'citizens, workers, peasants and intellectuals' to come out onto the streets to demand peace, the withdrawal of Bulgarian troops from occupation duties, 'fraternal union with the Soviet Union and our neighbours, [and] a peoples-democratic government for Bulgaria.'[26] The FF's increasingly confident and aggressive messages reached far greater numbers through the popular Hristo Botev radio station operated from the Soviet Union since July 1941.[27]

The FF's hand was strengthened by the partisan movement which increased as German military fortunes declined. It was dominated by the communists who in August 1943 had declared 'mass mobilization', as a result of which some 200 people from Sofia took to the mountains. In September 1943 the head of the police reported that, 'The problem of liquidating these bands is at present the central problem in Bulgarian internal affairs',[28] whilst in the following month came reports that in Turkey and other countries the Soviets were buying up Bulgarian currency, a sure sign, it was feared, of impending action in Bulgaria. In October and November 400 partisans were killed and half that number captured. These losses were rapidly replenished, particularly after the allied bombing. The partisans continued to increase in strength and in March–April 1944 they were reorganized by the BWP Central Committee (CC) into a united National Liberation Revolutionary Army. Communist historical sources speak of the forces at the disposal of the FF by the late summer of 1944 as consisting of 1 division, 9 brigades, 36 companies, a number of independent bands, hundreds of armed groups, and 200,000 sympathizers and helpers.[29]

The Bulgarian partisans were stronger than those in Hungary, Romania, and Finland but Bulgaria, not being a defeated or occupied nation, did not produce a resistance movement comparable to those in Greece or Yugoslavia. Even in the summer of 1944, when the movement

[26] Vasilev et al. (eds.), *Otechestven Front*, ii. 75.

[27] E. Valeva and Nina Vasil'eva, 'K istorii otnoshenii SSSR, Kominterna i bolgarskogo antifashistskogo dvizeheniya (1941–1943gg)', in Zolotaryov et al. (eds.), 7–23, 19.

[28] Vasilev et al. (eds.), *Otechestven Front*, i/i, 414.   [29] Ibid. 45.

was nearing its peak, a British intelligence report concluded that the partisans 'had a negligible influence on the military configuration in the Balkans' and were incapable of grappling with either the German or the Bulgarian forces.[30] They lacked equipment, they were still weak numerically compared to the movements in Greece and Yugoslavia, and, most importantly, they made a serious tactical error when they set up a 'free zone', an intended base for the future general rising, in the Plovdiv area rather than in the west near the Yugoslav partisan forces. This policy was adopted in part because it was what Moscow wanted, but it had the disastrous consequence of splitting partisan forces; when they advanced towards Plovdiv they did so in two separate rather than one compact unit and both were destroyed by the police. It was in this operation that the British SOE officer, Frank Thompson, was captured and executed.

Despite these setbacks, however, the partisans were of increasing concern to the government. In April 1944 it ordered all security and police organizations to cooperate with the army in combating the insurgents and in the summer it was forced to conduct the large-scale Operation Bogdan against partisan units in the Sredna Gora.

6. BULGARIA'S EXIT FROM THE WAR

On 1 June 1944, in an attempt to placate the internal opposition and the allies, Filov sacked his minister president, Bozhilov, who was replaced by Ivan Bagryanov. Bagryanov had been prominent in the agrarian cooperative movement as well as a close associate of King Boris, and although he had served in the German army during the first world war he was considered to be pro-western and had been involved in the secret approaches to the allies earlier in the year. He came to office insisting that 'The nation must take its own fate into its own hands.'[31] Bagryanov was to remain minister president for three critical months during which he made frenetic and frequently confused attempts to stave off the approach of war and to placate the internal opposition. The frenzy and confusion were to continue in intensified form after he left office until, on 9 September 1944, a coup d'état was carried out.

[30] Marieta Stankova, 'Bulgaria in British Foreign Policy, 1943–1949', Ph.D. thesis (London, 1999), 70.   [31] Vasilev et al. (eds.), *Otechestven Front*, i/ii, 94.

When Bagryanov assumed office Filov still exercised great influence and although he had come reluctantly to the conclusion that Bulgaria had to escape from the alliance with Germany, he insisted that the change should come later rather than sooner. He argued that popular opinion still would not tolerate the loss of the occupied territories and that unconditional surrender was not an option whilst allied troops were still too distant to protect Bulgaria against the German occupation it would precipitate; Bulgaria would join the allies, he said, when the allies joined Bulgaria by invading the Balkans. The Normandy landings on 6 June put paid to that dream. They also ended hopes that Sofia could continue its balancing act between Moscow and Berlin long enough to find agreement with the western allies who would then prevent a Soviet occupation. By landing in Normandy the allies had in effect declared that they would not intervene in the Balkans. With the Red Army moving rapidly through Ukraine and with the Germans beginning to withdraw from Greece, Bulgaria had little if any military significance for the western allies; conciliation of the USSR therefore became even more necessary.

Surprisingly, the Normandy landings seemed to moderate the attitude of the western allies. When Bagryanov approached them they responded that although their terms for an armistice were unchanged they now conceded that the requirement that Bulgaria must evacuate the occupied territories did not prejudice any decisions as to the future of those territories. Bagryanov also met with some success in his initial dealings with the Germans. They agreed to withdraw their military and naval equipment, particularly two hydroplanes,[32] from Varna, accepting Bagryanov's argument that their presence might cause the opening of another front in the east. Thereafter the Sofia government insisted that on no account might the Germans bring any more troops into the country and even those retreating from the east were to be denied entry.

On the domestic front Bagryanov set about abolishing the apparatus of authoritarian rule, and on 17 August granted an amnesty to all political prisoners and repealed all anti-Jewish legislation. He had hoped this would bring him support from all groups, even the communists, but he was to be disappointed. His government was still mistrusted by both the

---

[32] Georgi Mishkov (ed.), compiled by Georgi Mishkov and Todor Dobriyanov, *Dnevnik na Pŭrvan Draganov, bivsh ministŭr na vŭnshnite raboti ot 12 yuni do 1 septemvri 1944 godina* (Sofia: Georgi Pobedonosets, 1993), 11 *et seq.*

communists and the agrarians, the latter being alienated by the fact that Bagryanov had included in his cabinet Slaveĭko Vasilev who was said to have been the killer of Stamboliĭski. In any event, the FF would now have no truck with any administration unless it declared full neutrality. This Bagryanov did on 27 August, at the same time placing 8,000 railway wagons at the disposal of the Germans to expedite their withdrawal from the country. The FF denounced the move as one which merely allowed the Germans to plunder more food.

The decision to declare neutrality had been hastened first by Turkey which, after pouring armament into eastern Thrace, had broken off diplomatic relations with Germany at the beginning of August, and secondly, and more importantly, by the Red Army's crashing through the German defences in Romania so that there was now nothing to stop the Soviets reaching the Bulgarian border. Bagryanov assured Moscow that all foreign troops in Bulgaria would be disarmed and that the sŭbranie would be dissolved. The Soviets were not impressed and insisted that Bulgaria declare war on Germany. This Bagryanov would not do on the grounds that it would infringe the neutrality Bulgaria had recently declared. He did, however, demand the evacuation of German troops from Bulgaria and the disarming of those arriving in the country from the Dobrudja. He also intensified the negotiations he had opened with the western allies; were he to reach a settlement with them the Soviets would have no reason to intervene in Bulgaria and little say in the determination of its future. Stalin clearly realized this and on 30 August said he would no longer respect Bulgarian neutrality. Bagryanov gave up and resigned.

The new minister president was Konstantin Muraviev, another agrarian and a nephew of Stamboliĭski. Muraviev immediately sought to include the illegal opposition in the new government, but the FF refused; it now wanted power for itself, not as part of a coalition. In any case, Muraviev had made cooperation impossible by refusing to declare war on Germany. He did, however, maintain pressure for the withdrawal of German forces, whilst those who remained were disarmed and interned. But he would go no further. He feared that if Bulgaria did break with Germany the Soviets would use this as an excuse to come to Bulgaria's aid and occupy the country. His attitude increased popular discontent and on 4 September the FF organized widespread strikes; at the same time it did nothing to discourage the increasing number of desertions from the army to the partisans. On 5 September therefore Muraviev at last decided to sever relations with Germany but his minister of war, Lt. Gen. Ivan Marinov, persuaded him to delay announcing this for two days so that Bulgarian troops might be withdrawn from Macedonia without German interference. Not until the last German troops had left Bulgaria at around 15.00 hours on 7 September did Bulgaria declare war on Germany. It was too late: 'history had allowed only three days for the solution of questions which could not be decided in the previous three years.'[33] A few hours before that the Soviet Union had declared war on Bulgaria and on the following day Soviet troops began crossing the Danube. The Soviet declaration was made 'to liberate Bulgaria' but it was also made without consultation with or the consent of Britain and the USA.

During the night of 8–9 September the old political order in Bulgaria, though still intact and with the army still at its disposal, collapsed. With the connivance of Marinov partisan detachments entered Sofia and took control of the city. The FF formed an administration on 9 September, the new cabinet containing five zvenari, four agrarians, three social democrats, and four communists; the minister president was Kimon Georgiev.

In the final days there had been some skirmishes between the police and the FF with three demonstrators being killed in Silistra on 7 September. Fighting took place on the same day in Knyazhevo and in Sofia where some deaths were reported. But opposition to the FF was rare and that to the Red Army virtually non-existent.

In later years the regime in Sofia was to create the myth of partisan resistance, of a communist-inspired heroic victory on 9 September, and of a country already won over by the FF. In fact, the communists were as surprised as anyone else when they were catapulted into power. Government troops in Sofia outnumbered pro-FF units by four to one but, not least because of the presence of the Red Army in the country, they did not think it worth resisting the coup; and not until after the ministries of the interior and justice were in communist hands did the partisan units dare to approach most larger towns. In many areas the takeover took the form not of a heroic armed struggle but rather of a telephone conversation between a partisan leader and terrified local civil servants, policemen, or army officers. Nor was it the communists who masterminded the

---

[33] Valentin Aleksandrov, *Atanas Burov: banker, politik, diplomat; politicheska biografiya* (Sofia: Anteni, 1992), 96.

seizure of power by the FF. That was brought about chiefly by Damyan Velchev and Kimon Georgiev who had proved their ability in carrying out coups ten years previously. Nor had the FF established itself throughout the country; in three-quarters of localities the local FF committees were set up after not before 9 September.

10

Social and Economic Factors, 1878–1944

From the liberation to the end of the second world war Bulgaria saw, in Gershenkron's classic analysis, growth without structural change, whilst a more recent study has referred to the entire period from the early nineteenth century to the first world war as 'evolution without development'.[1] From 1878 to 1944 a number of traditional practices disappeared but the fundamental nature of both society and the economy were little altered: Bulgaria remained predominantly rural, its society rested on the village and the family, its agriculture was almost entirely the preserve of the small peasant proprietor, and its exports, at least in times of peace, were dominated by grain. Its industries grew but they remained closely linked to agriculture, and they continued to be dominated not by large factories but by small workshops which employed only a handful of workers. There was slow but organic change. From 1944 to the early 1990s there was to be rapid but artificial change as socialist planning transformed both society and the economy through the collectivization of the land, rapid urbanization, and the development of a heavy industrial base.

1. DEMOGRAPHY

At the beginning of the 1880s the total population of Bulgaria and Eastern Rumelia was 2.8 million. It rose steadily in the succeeding

---

[1] For the Gerschenkron thesis, see Alexander Gerschenkron, 'Some Aspects of Industrialization in Bulgaria, 1878–1939', in Alexander Gerschenkron (ed.), *Economic Backwardness in Historical Perspective* (New York: Praeger, 1965), 233–98; the more recent study is Michael Palairet, *The Balkan Economies, c.1802–1914: Evolution without Development* (Cambridge: Cambridge University Press), 1997.

Table 10.1 Total population

Census year	Total population
1880/1	2,823,865
1887	3,154,375
1892	3,310,713
1900	3,744,283
1905	4,035,575
1910	4,337,513
1920	4,846,971
1926	5,528,741
1934	6,077,939
1946	7,029,349

Sources: Figures for 1880/1 are from the censuses taken in Eastern Rumelia in 1880 and in Bulgaria on 1 January 1881, and given in Spiridion Gopčević, *Bulgarien und Ostrumelien, mit besonderer Berücksichtigung des Zeitraumes von 1878–1886, nebst militärischer Würdigung des serbo-bulgarischen Krieges* (Leipzig: Elischer, 1886), 18–22. These figures are less reliable than those for later censuses, and slightly different statistics are given in Franz Josef Prinz von Battenberg, *Die volkswirschaftliche Entwicklung Bulgariens von 1879 bis zur Gegenwart* (Leipzig: Veit & Co., 1891), 6–8; for the remaining figures, see www.nsi.bg/Census_e/Census_e.thm.

Table 10.2 Rural and urban populations

Census year	Rural population		Urban population	
	Total	%	Total	%
1880/4	2,390,392	81.01	560,207	18.99
1887	2,560,828	81.18	593,547	18.82
1892	2,658,385	80.30	652,328	19.70
1900	3,001,848	80.17	742,435	19.83
1905	3,245,886	80.43	789,689	19.57
1910	3,507,991	80.88	829,522	19.12
1920	3,880,596	80.06	966,375	19.94
1926	4,398,610	79.56	1,130,131	20.44
1934	4,775,388	78.57	1,302,551	21.43
1946	5,294,161	75.32	1,735,188	24.68

Sources: www.nsi.bg/Census_e/Census_e.thm. Figures for 1880/4 are a combination of the records taken in the principality in 1880 and in Rumelia in 1884 and are given in *Statisticheski Godishnik na Tsarstvo Bŭlgariya, godina xxxi* (Sofia: Glavna Direktsiya na Statistikata, 1939), 20, table 1. Gopčević, the source used for 1880/1 in Table 10.1, does not give figures for rural and urban population distribution.

decades to 3.53 million in 1910, 4.85 million in 1920, and in 1934, the last census before the second world war, it was 6.08 million. In the first post-war count it was 7.03 million (see table 10.1).

From 1878 to 1944 the proportion of the total defined as urban changed relatively little, rising from 18.99 per cent in 1880/4 to 24.68 per cent in 1946 (see table 10.2).

2. STABILITY AND CHANGE

The basically static ratio between urban and rural population until the end of the 1940s did not mean that the liberation of 1878 brought no changes to the country and its people. A number of traditional practices and institutions could not survive for long in the altered political and economic climate, though in some cases their demise would have occurred without the emergence of a separate Bulgarian state. Before the liberation there had been over 300 fasting days of one sort or another for the Christian communities, but by the mid-1880s the observance of them, particularly in the larger settlements, was in rapid decline. The fairs, above all that at Uzundjovo, which had for centuries been a major trading point, also rapidly disappeared, the government-sponsored Plovdiv International Exhibition of 1892 symbolizing the replacement of the traditional by the modern.

Transhumance, which in the early nineteenth century had made a number of towns rich, also declined. From 1878 to 1885 the border between Bulgaria and Rumelia divided many summer from winter pastures, and more importantly the sheep tax was levied in both jurisdictions. After 1885 southern Bulgarian drovers found a new frontier between them and their traditional markets in Adrianople and Constantinople, and their trade contracted. It also suffered from brigandage along the Macedonian and Thracian borders but its decline was caused above all by the railways and then by refrigeration.

An institution which also declined after the liberation and which attracted much attention from both contemporary and later anthropologists and sociologists, was the 'zadruga', or communal family. The zadruga, though that term was seldom used in Bulgarian, has been described 'tentatively, as a household consisting of two or more biological or small families, closely related by blood or adoption, owning its means of production communally, producing and consuming the means of its livelihood jointly, and regulating the control of its property, labour and livelihood communally.'[2] The origins and the customs of the zadruga were varied,[3] some having been founded to clear forest or mountain land for the plough, others being set up when and where defence was needed against disorders, as in the *kŭrdjalĭĭstvo* or when Circassians or Tatars were settled along nearby.

Some survived the changed conditions after the liberation. In the 1880s there was a zadruga near Pernik which consisted of forty-one members; its head had at one time been a director of a bank in Sofia and had arranged zadrugal affairs whilst at home during the weekends and had paid his salary into the communal, zadrugal coffer.[4] In general, however, the zadrugas declined. There was no further need for defence; the Tatars and Circassians had for the most part departed, and if the Turks remained they were no longer regarded as a threat. And where the original function of clearing land had been achieved the extended households lost their cohesion and tended to split into separate nuclear families. Furthermore, after the liberation the availability of large areas of cheap land encouraged nuclear families to leave the zadruga to set up on their own, and in general the expansion of the money economy and the individualistic enterprise encouraged by the market conflicted with the traditionalist, communal ethos of the zadruga.

Some zadrugas were weakened by female inheritance. The inheritance law of 1889 allowed daughters to inherit land, albeit only half the amount inherited by sons, and even if the law were honoured as much in the breach as in the observance and was revised in 1906 to limit female inheritance even further, some damage had been done, particularly amongst the more intelligent of young women who wanted to escape from the restrictions of the collective family. Female secession was also encouraged by the fact that households where there was no male head or where he was over 50 were exempt from conscription; this led to a number of cases of widows or older men with children leaving the zadruga and establishing a separate household where the young males would be free from military service.

---

[2] Philip E. Mosely, 'The Peasant Family: The Zadruga, or Communal Joint-Family in the Balkans, and its Recent Evolution', in C. F. Ware (ed.), *The Cultural Approach to History* (New York: Columbia University Press, 1940), 95–108, 95.

[3] Crampton, *Bulgaria 1878–1918*, 197–204.

[4] Iv. Ev. Geshov, *Zadrugite v zapadna Bŭlgariya* (Sofia: 1887), 10–11.

After 1900, and even more so after the first world war, the gradual increase in land prices meant that it was more difficult for zadrugas to acquire additional land as their numbers grew; in such cases it often proved easier to split the zadruga and to establish separate households. Universal primary and expanding secondary education brought fresh ideas into the communal families, more especially because in many cases children were forced to leave the zadruga to receive their schooling. Even more disruptive was conscription. Many of the young men who returned from their time in the army, which frequently provided their first experience of town life, felt frustrated by the traditional patterns of life in the zadruga. But despite these factors some zadrugas survived well into the twentieth century.

If many zadrugas disappeared other features of the Bulgarian country-side were more permanent. The traditional arrangement of each village having two, or more usually three large fields in all of which individual families held a number of strips, often some distance from each other, persisted. In the two-field system a grain crop alternated with a year of fallow, and where a third field existed it was usually given over perma-nently to the cultivation of maize. The villages themselves changed little in appearance, usually consisting of long, frequently twisting streets with a few communal buildings in the larger settlements. There was a large degree of self-sufficiency. Cloth was home-spun, though factory produced materials did become more common after the beginning of the twentieth century, and houses were built with the use of few imported articles, mostly nails and window frames. The homes tended to be dark, damp, and ill-ventilated with very little in the way of furniture. The diet, almost all of which was home produced, was frugal but healthy with adequate supplies of fruit and vegetables in addition to the staples; meat was generally a luxury but eggs, poultry, and, in the appropriate areas, fish were plentiful. Improvements in facilities were made after the liberation. The railways and, to a lesser degree, improvements in the roads, expanded contacts with the outside world, as, after the first world war, did, for those who could afford it, the radio. Agrarian rule in the early 1920s saw improvements in drainage and water supply, the straightening of many streets, and the erection of new communal buildings, not least the cinemas. But even by the end of the 1930s most villages remained without electricity.

3. THE PERSISTENCE AND DOMINANCE OF THE SMALL PEASANT PROPRIETOR

The most enduring feature of the Bulgarian village was that it remained the bastion of the small peasant proprietor (see table 10.3).

In general holdings of less than 2 hectares were insufficient to maintain the average peasant household; those in the small category were large enough to support such a family; medium holdings could provide a surplus for sale in the market and might require occasional labour from outside the family; and those classified as large needed full-time wage labour if they were not, as many of them were, subdivided and rented.

From the figures in Table 10.3 it would appear that before the first world war just under half of the population did not have enough land to feed itself. This was not the case. The census returns on landownership were based on returns by villages but there was a widespread practice of families owning small plots of land, usually acquired by marriage or inheritance, in other villages, such plots frequently being used to cultivate specialized crops such as vines. In 1908 almost half the holdings in the very small category were of this type. In addition to this, almost all peasants had the use of village communal land for grazing. Very few of Bulgaria's rural dwellers in fact were forced to rely on hiring themselves out as labourers. In the inter-war years the percentage of the rural population living on properties of less than 10 hectares increased yet

Table 10.3 Distribution of landholdings by size, percentage of total

Size of holding	1897	1908	1926	1934	1946
Very small, under 2 hectares	45.48	45.52	24.3	27.0	29.8
Small, 2 to 10 hectares	41.82	41.43	60.7	62.3	63.3
Medium, 10 to 30 hectares	11.57	11.96	14.7	10.3	6.8
Large, over 30 hectares	1.13	1.09	0.6	0.4	0.1

Sources: For 1897 and 1908, *Statisticheski Godishnik na bŭlgarskoto Tsarstvo*, vols. v–xiv (1913–1922) (Sofia: Dŭrzhavna pechatnitsa, 1924), table 4, section vi, 4; for 1926 and 1934, *Statisticheski Godishnik na bŭlgarskoto Tsarstvo*, vol. xxxi (Sofia: Glavna Direktsiya na Statistikata, 1939), Table VIIA, 181; figures for 1946 based on those in Joseph Rothschild, *East Central Europe between the Two World Wars*, A History of East Central Europe, vol. ix (Seattle: University of Washington Press, 1974), 330.

further; in 1908 it had been 86.95 but by 1946 was 93.1. At the same time the increase in population and the fact that the proportion of the total population living in rural areas did not fall meant that the average size of each holding fell; in 1926 it had been 5.73 hectares but in 1946 was 4.31 hectares. By the end of the second world war holdings of over 20 hectares made up only 1 per cent of the total agricultural area. Before the first world war there had been few incentives to modernize holdings and the loss of the Dobrudja in 1913 deprived Bulgaria of most of its larger, commercialized farms.

In the 1880s the Tsankov government had banned the selling of land in plots of over 4 hectares and the purchase of plots of more than 16 hectares. But the continuing domination of the small and medium holding was less the result of government fiat than the operation of profound social and economic forces which combined to make land plentiful. During and immediately after the war of 1877–8 the departure of large numbers of Muslims had left a great deal of land untended and in the subsequent years much of this was taken over by Bulgarians. Within a decade of the liberation an estimated 50,000 hectares, or approximately a quarter of the total arable area, had been transferred by legal means. Most of the transfers were from Muslim to Christian ownership, the proportion of land owned by Turks in Rumelia falling from around 50 per cent in 1875 to 28 per cent in 1885. In the early 1890s so much land was available that Stambolov reportedly remarked that Bulgaria might have to import foreign labourers and settle them on it.[5]

By the end of the first decade of the twentieth century the price of land had increased but Bulgaria did not experience anything like the land hunger which afflicted some parts of Russia. This was because Turkish emigration continued, albeit at a much reduced volume, and after the upheavals in the middle of the decade a number of Greeks left Bulgaria, as did many Bulgarians who set out for the new world. And even when this source of land was exhausted extra tillage could be found in the comparatively large unworked areas of land, especially to the north of the Balkan range. A large amount of this property was acquired thanks to the pre-liberation convention which bestowed ownership on anyone who worked a piece of land for three consecutive years, a convention

---

[5] Edward Dicey, *The Peasant State: An Account of Bulgaria in 1894* (London: John Murray, 1894), 156.

which was much cited when Bulgarians took over the property of émigré Turks.

A further reason for the continuance of the small proprietor was government intervention to save him from the worst effects of debt. The National Party governments of the second half of the 1890s passed legislation which guaranteed to each family a certain amount of property which was to be inalienable, even against the claims of creditors. In the early twentieth century there was also a marked reduction in the area of land left fallow, this falling from 36.8 per cent of cultivable land in 1896 to 21.3 per cent in 1911; the cause for this was the increasing use of better ploughs and of fertilizers; the consequence was an increase in the supply of land. The decrease in fallow land had also been stimulated by the imposition of a supplementary land tax on untilled land in 1905. The most important reason for the continued domination of the small proprietor in the 1890s and 1900s, however, was the appropriation by the individual owner of communal and, more frequently, state property, much of it former forest. Between 1897 and 1908 the area of land in use increased by 7.67 per cent, whilst the area of woodland and forest in the country fell from over 3 million to 2.5 million hectares in the years 1906 to 1912. The alienation of state and communal property caused some concern and in 1909 there was an uncharacteristically lively debate in the sŭbranie on a government bill limiting the process and even allowing for the state and the local authorities to repossess some of the land taken illegally from it. Cases of such repossession, however, were rare.

In the inter-war period communal property continued to be sold and the agrarian government's reforms did bring about some redistribution of larger properties, but the supply of unused land was diminishing and for the first time since the liberation demand tended to increase more rapidly than supply with a consequent increase in prices.

4. STANDARDS OF LIVING IN RURAL AREAS

For the individual peasant proprietors conditions generally improved after the difficult years up to and through the agrarian crisis at the beginning of the twentieth century. In the first decade of that century their standard of living increased notably. If the index for national consumption is set at 100 for 1896 it had risen to 411 by 1911, as a result both of a succession of good harvests, 1907 being an exception, and of a rise in the price of grain on the world market. At home the growth of towns and the improvement in communications created new markets whilst the increasing use of modern agricultural machinery improved productivity on the land; the imported tonnage of such machinery rose more than fivefold between 1900 and 1911, and by the latter year the value of agricultural machinery in Bulgaria was seventy times greater than in 1897. Nevertheless, by 1910 only 18 per cent of Bulgarian farmers had metal ploughs.

A critical factor in improving the well-being of the peasantry was the development of the cooperatives. Like the agrarian movement, with which they were inextricably bound, the cooperatives owed much to narodnik ideas imported into Bulgaria in the 1880s. One of the many of the young intelligentsia influenced by populism was Stefan Kostov, a long-serving secretary of the Holy Synod, who in 1888 published *Sŭdruzhestva v Evropa* (Cooperation in Europe). The first agricultural credit cooperative was founded in the village of Mirkovo in the Pirdop district but, like many of its successors, it did not last long because its leaders lacked experience and, much more importantly, capital.

Much was done to rectify the latter deficiency by the transformation of the Agricultural Savings Bank into the Bulgarian Agricultural Bank in 1903 and, crucially, by an amendment to the commercial code of 1897. The code had defined cooperatives as joint stock companies whose directors were each required to guarantee up to a tenth of the company's capital. When this hurdle was reduced in 1902 to a fixed sum of 200 leva investment in cooperatives became much safer and thereafter they increased rapidly not only in number but also in longevity. A law on cooperatives passed by the stambolovist ministry in 1907 codified the regulations for the founding and administration of the cooperatives, and by granting them a legal identity did more to increase their security. By 1910 there were 931 registered cooperative societies, 721 of which were credit cooperatives of the Reiffeissen type. Concern over the financial condition of some cooperatives led in 1911 to the foundation of the Central Cooperative Bank and this, together with the setting up of the General Union of Bulgarian Agricultural Cooperatives, of whose standing committee Stamboliĭski was a member, restored the health of and confidence in a movement which had revolutionized many peasants' lives by bringing the process of borrowing under control and thus liberating them from the usurer. The cooperatives strengthened their presence in the countryside after the first world war, and by the end of the 1930s approximately 60 per cent of all rural families were included in one. Some cooperatives agreed to consolidate the members' holdings into single, compact farms and the fifty-eight which did this were the only agrarian enterprises to make a profit, legally, in the final years of the second world war.

The consolidation and spread of the cooperatives was perhaps the most important single development in the social evolution of the Bulgarian village between the liberation and the end of the second world war. The cooperatives, along with the agrarian political movement, at least in its early stages, also did something to bring back together the native intelligentsia and the peasantry because teachers and priests played as crucial a role in running the cooperatives as they had in spreading national consciousness during the vŭzrazhdane.

5. AGRICULTURAL BACKWARDNESS

The dominance of the small proprietor was a major reason for the relatively slow growth of commercialized agriculture in Bulgaria. In the years immediately after the liberation there was enough land for everyone and therefore labour to work commercialized estates was very difficult to come by. Another problem in these years was a lack of draught animals. In the war the Ottoman government had mobilized large numbers not only of horses but of oxen and water buffalo, and after the war the departing Muslims usually took with them what animals had remained after the mobilizations. This problem was repeated in more severe form in the Balkan wars and more especially in the first world war. In the latter the Bulgarian army was deployed along a huge front, most of which was in mountain areas without railways or adequate roads. In many places pack animals were therefore the only means of carrying men and equipment, and the animals came in the main from the civilian population. By the end of the war the sight of old people pulling their carts was not uncommon.

Commercialized farming was also discouraged by the backwardness and inefficiency of Bulgarian agriculture. Mechanization was not only impossibly expensive but also impracticable on the small strips so characteristic of the Bulgarian village. At the time of the liberation there was scanty knowledge of fertilizers and little money to buy them, and although government-sponsored education and improvement schemes did something to remedy the former deficiency, they could not make much impact on the latter and for most peasants fertilizers remained prohibitively expensive; in the 1930s Bulgarians used only 0.01 kg of nitrates per hectare, compared to 10.7 kg in Denmark.

The lack of capital was a major cause of agricultural backwardness. There was not an absolute lack of money for investment; the problem was rather that investment in an unmodernized, inefficient agriculture paid few dividends. It was much more profitable to lend surplus cash to the needy, who had little choice but to pay the high rates of interest the usurer insisted upon. In the two decades after the liberation there was a constant demand for loans from peasants who wished to purchase land and the animals, seed, and equipment to use upon it. Before the liberation rural credit had been available from the institutions introduced by Midhat Pasha in the 1860s, but after 1878 they collapsed and were not immediately replaced. This left the field free for the usurer and by the beginning of the twentieth century peasant indebtedness was a major social problem. The cooperatives did much to reduce this problem, as did inflation in the first world war, but escape from indebtedness did not mean the end of agricultural inefficiency and therefore the disincentive to invest in the land remained.

Another enormous impediment to improving agricultural efficiency in pre-communist times was the increasing parcellization of land, an important cause of which was divided inheritance. Between 1897 and 1908 the number of agricultural holdings increased by 16.7 per cent, yet the number of strips rose by 23.7 per cent, and from 1908 to 1926 the average number of strips per holding increased from eleven to seventeen. There were some legislative attempts to redress the problem, the most notable being the 1906 amendment to the inheritance law of 1889 which prevented female inheritance of very small strips. The Malinov government introduced a land register which, it was hoped, would make consolidation easier, and after the first world war the agrarian government and the cooperatives made efforts to promote commassation, but despite successes in some areas the parcellized holding remained the rule rather than the exception.

Parcellization caused many problems. Huge amounts of time were lost moving from strip to strip, especially when the draught animals used were the slow-moving oxen or water buffalo. The system also gave rise to frequent disputes. Some concerned allegations that one cultivator had damaged the crop of his neighbour, others arose over where the boundaries between strips should be drawn, and yet others were the result of rival claims to ownership. Some of these disputes gave rise to serious friction; one of the arguments in favour of a land registry had been that it would bring an end to the disputes or, in some cases, murders which arose from confrontations over landownership. Even if disputes could be settled by legal means the legal costs involved were so great that few peasants could afford them. The consolidation of strips obviously could not take place unless ownership was uncontested.

An inefficient agrarian system dominated by the small peasant proprietor moved only slowly towards greater diversification of crops. The main crop was grain which accounted for 77.93 per cent of production in 1897, 78.95 per cent in 1911, and 61.9 per cent in 1938. There were structural impediments to greater crop diversification, particularly before the first world war. In the traditional two- or three-field system the important decisions on when to sow and harvest were taken not by the individual farmer but by the village council, a procedure which could inhibit those who wished to grow alternative crops which required a different timetable. Indeed, some village councils insisted that all strips in the communal field had to grow the same crop if harvesting was to be efficiently carried out.

Some individuals and a few villages did try and break away from the established patterns. The emergence of local manufacturing encouraged the planting of rape-seed, flax, hemp, and sugar-beet, the area devoted to the cultivation of these industrial crops growing by 91.56 per cent in the decade after 1897. But extensive change did not come until the first world war.

Karavelov had spoken in the 1880s of the need to produce export crops whose value was stable or rising, unlike that of grain which was falling; he suggested wine and tobacco. In the subsequent decade Bulgarian economists had argued for concentration on growing crops which were not easily grown elsewhere, again citing wine and tobacco as examples. But in the 1890s and 1900s the vineyards had to contend with phylloxera, whilst tobacco was a difficult and fickle crop which was heavily dependent on the weather and which needed expert tending. Tobacco cultivation received some encouragement from the incorporation of tobacco-producing Pirin Macedonia into Bulgaria in 1913, but the major stimulus came with the first world war when Bulgarian tobacco enjoyed a virtual monopoly in the markets of central Europe. This led to soaring prices and handsome profits. In 1909 tobacco had accounted for 9.9 per cent of the total value of Bulgarian exports; in 1917 it accounted for 70 per cent, far more than grain. After the war grain again became the largest export earner, accounting for 33.7 per cent of value in 1922, but this was to be compared to the 61.2 per cent of 1912. In 1922 tobacco earned 27 per cent of the income from Bulgarian exports but in the second half of the 1920s its share rose to over a third and this despite a dip in world prices and a poor harvest in 1926.

After the depression there were further moves towards other industrial crops, and particularly those which could supply domestic manufactories. Cotton production, for example, expanded by 900 per cent between 1929 and 1939 and there was greater concentration on high-quality, high-price export commodities such as vegetables, fruit, and wine, a trend which intensified from 1941–4 partly because government interference in such crops was less than in grain and tobacco, and also because such produce was more easily sold on the black market.

From the earliest years of the new Bulgarian state the government had attempted to modernize agriculture and improve its efficiency. Efforts were made to expand knowledge with the setting up of the Model Agricultural School in Sadovo and later with the founding of special agricultural schools, of which there were fourteen by 1912. In the previous year the University of Sofia had opened an agricultural faculty. Vocational lessons in farming were also introduced into secondary schools, though the major advances in this respect came with the BANU administration in the early 1920s.

Governments also intervened directly in the agricultural sector. In 1882 a new ministry of public works, agriculture, and trade was set up, which in 1893 became the ministry of trade and agriculture. It helped organize the work of agricultural advisers who disseminated knowledge on fertilizers and alternative crops; in 1904, for example, they were instructed to encourage the planting of mulberry bushes and over 50,000 families had responded to this advice by 1911. Governments also helped by removing all duties on imported agricultural machinery, and by assisting in the search for and exploitation of new sources of water for irrigation. The BANU government naturally spent much of its administrative time and energy on attempts to improve agriculture and the well-being of its practitioners, though the efficacy of its efforts is hard to assess given its short period in office and the fact that the agrarian economies of Europe and elsewhere were shattered by the depression of the early 1930s. The setting up of the state grain purchasing agency, Hranoiznos, in December 1930, was intended to alleviate the effects of the depression. It began operations in February of the following year and was given exclusive control of grain purchase and sales. Within a few years it had similar powers over sugar-beet, flax, and hemp, and by 1943 twenty-three items were under its control, its structure having formed the skeleton of the administrative body the government set up to manage the economy in the second world war.

Government efforts to foster agricultural improvement were at times frustrated, particularly before the first world war, by *partizanstvo*, which bred suspicion that any attempt to increase governmental activity was a device to augment the number of jobs at a ministry's disposal. The setting up of agricultural councils, and the establishment of a separate ministry of trade and agriculture were both criticized as acts intended primarily to expand government patronage. Not only did *partizanstvo* breed suspicions it also impaired the efforts of the Sadovo school and other similar institutes, too many of whose graduates preferred a career in the bureaucracy where salaries were higher and opportunities for self-enrichment greater than they were in the vocation for which they had been trained at the public expense.

6. URBAN GROWTH

Although Bulgaria's urban population remained much the same percentage of the total until the 1950s, it nevertheless grew in size; between 1887 and 1946 it increased by 92.34 per cent compared to an increase of 22.64 per cent in the total population. In 1881 there had been only five towns, Plovdiv, Rusé, Shumen, Sofia, and Varna, with more than 20,000 inhabitants; in 1905 there were eight, and in 1934 twelve.

The fastest growth was in Sofia, not surprisingly in a country which, after 1885, was intensely centralized. In 1878 it was the smallest of the five towns with a population of over 20,000 with 20,248 inhabitants. By 1905 it was the largest city in the country with a population of

80,261, an increase of almost 200 per cent. In 1934 its population was 133,612.

The changes were qualitative as well as quantitative. In the years immediately after the liberation most of the town's houses were primitive and offered little protection against either the intense cold of winter, or the rampaging rodents of the summer: shortly after the liberation a young secretary at one diplomatic agency had his ear chewed by a rat whilst he slept in bed.[6] It also had something of the frontier town where, 'A chef who could cook European food was more highly esteemed than the wisdom of Solomon',[7] and where, in 1882, three people were killed by the packs of wild dogs which roamed the streets until they were liquidated in 1884; at the end of the nineteenth century wolves were still descending from the mountains to the Prince Boris gardens in the centre of town. But by then the city itself had been transformed. The maze of narrow, crooked streets of the Ottoman town with their wooden buildings had made way for a modern city based on the grid pattern with western-style housing blocks; few of its inhabitants now kept a cow or two grazing on nearby meadows as they had done in the 1870s, and cooks familiar with western foods were no longer a rarity. Before the Balkan wars water was being piped from a reservoir in the mountains and the city's rapidly growing suburbs were linked to the centre by an electric tramway system. Other towns underwent similar transformations. In the 1880s most of the population of Plovdiv drank water taken directly from the river Maritsa and sold in the streets, with the result that there were frequent epidemics; their incidence fell by more than half once clean water had been piped in from the Rhodopes.

The early growth of Sofia was due to a considerable degree to the expansion of the state administrative machine. At the end of the Russian provisional administration in 1879 there were only 2,121 native Bulgarian administrators in the country. The gap was filled partly from the ranks of the 90,000 to 95,000 Bulgarians who immigrated after 1878 or by foreign experts, but also by the graduates of the Bulgarian school system which, in the words of Ivan Geshov was 'a factory for manufacturing civil servants'.[8] The state apparatus expanded in 1885 when the administrative powers

---

[6] Irechek, *Dnevnik*, i, xviii.   [7] Georgiev, *Osuobozhdenieto*, 172.

[8] Quoted in Krŭstyo Dimitrov, *Bŭlgarskata inteligentsiya pri kapitalizma* (Sofia: Nauka i izkustvo, 1974), 76.

previously located in Plovdiv were moved to Sofia. By 1905 government officials, with army officers, formed a quarter of Sofia's working population, and were the largest occupational group in the city.[9] In the towns as a whole administrators rose from 0.9 per cent to 2.1 per cent of the economically active population in the first decade of the twentieth century.[10]

The rise in the number of officials reflected not only the concentration of administration in Sofia but also the extension of government activity. By the beginning of the Balkan wars Bulgaria had acquired the apparatus of a modern state. The Tŭrnovo constitution (article 161) had stated that there were to be six departments of state,[11] but new ministries were soon created, the first being that of public works, agriculture, and trade in 1882; by 1911 there were eleven government departments.

In addition to the ministries the state had also established and was financing, though it did not necessarily run, the National Library, founded in 1878, and the Kliment Ohridski University in Sofia established in 1888. In 1906 the Ethnographic Museum separated from the National Library to form another state-sponsored institution. The National Theatre, opened with such drama in the following year, was also a state-owned institution. In 1908 the Archaeological Museum followed the path of its Ethnographic sister body. In the reign of Alexander Battenberg the state had established the Model Agricultural School in Sadovo, and a similar institution to promote manufacturing was set up later in Knyazhevo near Sofia. The state was also responsible for the School of Drawing, established 1896, which became the School for Art and Industry on the eve of the Balkan wars. In 1912 the School of Music, established in 1904, became the State School of Music. The state was also responsible for Bulgaria's most prestigious institute of learning, the Bulgarian Academy of Sciences which was established after a reorganization of the Bulgarian Literary Society in 1911.[12]

---

[9] John R. Lampe, 'Modernization and Social Structure: The Case of the pre-1914 Balkan Capitals', *Southeastern Europe*, 5/2 (1979), 11–32, 28. For further information on the growth of Sofia, see the same author's 'Finance and Pre-1914 Industrial Stirrings in Bulgaria and Serbia', *Southeastern Europe*, 2/1 (1975), 23–52.

[10] Ljuben Berov, 'Changes in the Social Structure of the Urban Population in Bulgaria from 1878 to 1912', *Southeastern Europe*, 5/2 (1979), 105–20, 112–13.

[11] See above, p. 99.

[12] For more details on the activities of the state in the cultural sector see, Rumyana Koneva, 'Dŭrzhavnite kulturni institutsii v Bŭlgariya (1912–1918g)', *Istoricheski Pregled*, 47/3 (1991), 52–66.

7. INDUSTRIAL DEVELOPMENT

The development of modern manufacturing in Bulgaria was slow with most of the concerns which were set up being small and foreign owned; in 1904 there were only twelve enterprises with more than half a million leva capital and in 1911 there were thirty-one, with food, drink, and textiles dominating production. Despite this increase in numbers by 1911 only 19,500 persons, or 0.5 per cent of the population, were employed in factories. The situation changed little after the first world war, particularly after the onset of the great depression. When allied intelligence sources surveyed the Balkans in 1943 they recorded disparagingly, 'Bulgaria is a one-horse country with no industry of any significance.'[13]

Disparaging as this observation may have been, it was nevertheless accurate. In 1938 industry accounted for only 5.6 per cent of gross national product, not much above the 5.1 per cent of 1926. And, most significantly, although factories grew in number, in Bulgarian industry, as in agriculture, it was the traditional small enterprise which still dominated production at the end of the second world war. In 1934 only 322 of over 80,000 workshops and factories had more than 50 employees, whilst the number of employees per enterprise actually declined from 32.5 in 1931 to 26 in 1944; and the share of workshops in the total of manufactured production rose from 5 per cent to 9.3 per cent between 1926 and 1938; from 1936 to 1944 the number of workshops almost doubled, and in the latter year there were 112,966 independent workshop masters, 40 per cent more than in 1900.[14] Even in 1946 the number of persons engaged in workshop production was still twice that of those in factories, and 60 per cent of workshops had no worker apart from the owner. Nor was there great change in the goods produced. In 1937 textiles were still the major product and the vast majority of industrial output was related to agriculture.

The factories which did appear showed, at least until the eve of the first world war, the usual social problems of early industrial expansion. Taxation fell disproportionately on the urban workers whose wages could

[13]   See National Archives, Public Record Office, Kew, AIR 9/462, annex to paper 3.
[14]   Dimitŭr Ludjev, 'Sotsialna harakteristika na gradskite drebnoburzhoazni sloeve v Bŭlgariya v sredata na 40-te godini na xx.v', in Hristo Hristov (ed. in chief), *Iz istoriyata na stopanskiya i sotsialniya zhivot v bŭlgarskite zemi* (Sofia: BAN, 1984), 124–79, 127–8.

seldom keep pace with rises in the costs of living; working conditions were dangerous and unhealthy; and hours of work were long. A women and children's employment act was passed in 1905, banning the employment of children under ten and limiting the hours to be worked by those above that age; the act also granted women one month's maternity leave with a guarantee of a return to their former job at the end of it. This was a welcome advance but the enforcement procedures were cumbersome until the establishment of a factory inspectorate in 1907. The scale of the problem facing the inspectors, and an indication of the working conditions in the Bulgarian factory, was seen when they reported in 1911 that of the 375 institutions they had visited in 1910 only three were regarded as entirely satisfactory. Legislation on safety at work was enacted in 1917. This act also banned the employment in factories of anyone under 12, the minimum age being raised to 14 in 1919, when the eight-hour day was introduced.

If the small workshops remained the dominant feature of the Bulgarian industrial landscape this did not mean that they and what they produced were entirely unchanged. Those which had created the wealth that financed the Bulgarian cultural revival were hard hit by the political liberation of 1878. In Gabrovo, which weathered the post-liberation storm better than most towns, the number of workshops fell from 937 in 1880 to 601 in 1902; in Kazanlŭk the 280 workers in various workshops on the eve of the liberation had been reduced to 35 by 1885. In October 1883 the Liberal Party newspaper *Sŭedinenie* (Unification) stated that there had been a tenfold drop in the number of workshops in Pirdop, Samokov, Etropole, Vidin, Silistra, Varna, and Shumen. The chief causes of the workshops' decline were the import of cheaper, European, factory-made items, the loss of established markets, and the change in tastes and social attitudes brought about by the liberation.

Amongst the indigenous producers ruined by the import of cheaper, factory-made goods were nail makers, chandlers, and the most important of all native manufacturers, those in textiles. This so affected the towns along the Balkan foothills, many of which had been partially destroyed by *bashibozuks* in 1876, that in Sopot in 1883 employees, enraged by cheap materials imported from Britain and elsewhere, burned bales of imported cloth. The liberation also meant that the Ottoman army ceased to purchase *aba* and *gaĭtan* from the workshops of Plovdiv, Samokov, and other towns. The departure of the Turks brought about a drastic decline in demand for a number of traditional products, and thus the makers of leather belts and slippers survived only in areas such as Haskovo and Sliven where significant numbers of Turks remained. Liberation meant for most Bulgarians, and especially those in the towns, a switch to modern, European fashions. The cushions on which Bulgarians had previously slept gave way to beds, western porcelain replaced the traditional copper for tableware, and even the colours now in vogue were more easily obtained from imported cloth than from native producers. In diet the new fashions included tomatoes, potatoes, pasta, tea, kvass, lemonade, and beer. Some manufacturers managed to adapt by importing western machinery and raw materials and then reproducing western-style goods. There had been no breweries in Bulgaria before 1878 but by the mid-1890s there were twenty-nine; in Gabrovo seven new textile mills and ten new leather works were opened between 1888 and 1893, all of them using imported machinery and three of them being joint stock companies.

The decline of traditional workshop production affected the guilds, which had already been deprived of many of their judicial and administrative functions which were passed to the local authorities in 1879. That left them with responsibilities for the welfare of their members but by the mid-1880s many guilds no longer had sufficient resources to meet these obligations.

The depression in the traditional industries was reflected in the population of many manufacturing centres, negative growth rates being registered in the first decade of the twentieth century in Dryanovo, Gabrovo, Kalofer, Karlovo, Kotel, Omurtag, Shumen, Sopot, and Tryavna; the population of Koprivshtitsa fell by 5.4 per cent between 1900 and 1905 and a further 13.21 per cent between 1906 and 1910.

Successive governments made efforts to halt the decline in traditional manufacturing. In 1881 a law in the principality declared that all civil servants and all messengers employed by the government must wear uniforms produced from home-made cloth, and in December 1883 the law for the development of national small industry placed the same obligation on the police and the army. But these laws did little to help the traditional workshop because those who benefited most from the new regulations were the few employers who had switched to modern machinery and factory methods.

8. THE STATE AND INDUSTRY

The state had involved itself in the Bulgarian economy from the early 1880s. Its first major strategic intervention was Karavelov's railway act of December 1884. In addition to stating that railways should be government owned, the act also drew up a plan for future railway development, a plan intended, as far as was possible, to safeguard Bulgaria's independence and to create a rail network that served the country's best interests, political as well as economic. The backbone of the system was to be the international trunk line but other important lines were to run along the northern and southern edges of the Balkan mountains, and these were to be linked by a trans-Balkan line. The international trunk line opened in July 1888 and by the beginning of the first world war most of the lines envisaged in Karavelov's plan of the early 1880s had been completed, though not every line had been built with the best interests of Bulgaria in mind. Three *tracés* had been proposed for the important trans-Balkan line, for example, and the one chosen, that via Tryavna, was the least beneficial to the Bulgarian economy, but it was the one which took it near the Prince Boris mines owned by Paribas upon whom Bulgaria was by then dependent for loans. There were also two important unfulfilled objectives. The first was that there was no rail link with Romania across the Danube and the second was that, despite intense efforts, the line from Sofia to Pernik and Kyustendil had not been extended across the border to Kumanovo in Macedonia; the extended line would have linked the BDZh to the Athens–Nish line and so, it had been hoped, increase Bulgaria's leverage in Macedonia. A bridge across the Danube was to be constructed in the inter-war years, but the much-desired Kyustendil to Kumanovo extension was never built; but nor was it forgotten and serious discussions on building it began after the fall of the communist regime in Bulgaria in 1990.

Other government interventions to stimulate the creation of the economic infrastructure included financing the construction of harbour facilities at Burgas and Varna. The relevant legislation was taken through the sŭbranie in 1894 and the facilities were opened in 1903 and 1906 respectively. In 1893 the government had provided 90 per cent of the capital for the Bulgarian Steamship Navigation Company. The state also developed the coal mines at Pernik and the lignite mines at Radomir, and granted a number of government monopolies, including one in the early 1880s for the use of hermetically sealed cess carts in Sofia. But as yet there was no planned, organized strategy of government encouragement for industry.

This came with Stoilov's encouragement of industry act of 1894. Under the act enterprises with at least 25,000 leva of capital and employing a minimum of twenty workers were to qualify for various forms of help. These included: free grants of land; free use of publicly owned quarries and water power; preferential rates on BDZh; preferences in securing contracts to supply state or local government purchasers, even if the equivalent imported commodities were 15 per cent cheaper; and subsidies for the construction of necessary road and rail links. The act was to last ten years and was immediately renewed, for twice that period, by the stambolovist government of 1903–8; at the same time, the definition for qualification in the encouraged category was eased, and the privileges of inclusion extended. In 1909 there were further relaxations and in 1912 yet more industries were brought into the scope of the acts, the major newcomer being tobacco processing. By this stage almost all Bulgarian industry was in the encouraged sector.

The encouragement of industry remained a staple feature of Bulgarian economic life until the mid-1930s. The Stamboliĭski government extended the scope of the legislation and Lyapchev's administration broadened the concessions granted to encouraged industries and increased tariffs on imported manufactured goods. In 1936, however, enterprises accounting for almost half of industrial output were denied the privileges of state encouragement, though they still benefited from government tariff policies.

The strategy of boosting home produced goods did have some success, the proportion of these items rising from 13 per cent of total national consumption in 1896 to 43 per cent in 1911. In some areas, however, the plan to rely on the domestic product was thwarted by its poor quality when compared to the imported equivalent; in 1909 half the wool processed was imported and over two-thirds of the leather worked came from imported hides because the local ones had been ruined by the warble fly. Bulgarian industry was also inefficient; production per head of the population in 1911 was 28.3 gold leva compared to 1,128 gold leva in the USA.

Tariffs formed an integral part of the strategy to promote domestic manufactories. In 1887 a government commission on the subject had recommended a levy of 20 per cent on goods which could be produced at home. This was impossible partly because of the political insecurities in Bulgaria itself, but also because the treaty of Berlin had insisted that Bulgaria observe the trade treaties agreed between the Ottoman empire and most major European states. These meant in effect that Bulgaria had freedom to set its own tariffs only with Romania, Serbia, and the Ottoman empire. For all other states the maximum levy was 8 per cent *ad valorem;* these values had been set in the Ottoman treaties concluded in the 1860s and the depression in agricultural prices since then had meant that the tariff was often as low as 4 per cent, which provided neither effective protection against foreign imports nor adequate sources of government revenue. In 1889 Great Britain agreed to tariffs of 8 per cent on current prices and in the early 1890s Germany, Italy, Austria, Italy, and France did likewise. After the recognition of Prince Ferdinand the Sofia government felt emboldened enough to announce that it intended to introduce a 14 per cent general tariff with some articles essential for local factory production paying less and those which would compete with home industries paying more. The great powers agreed to these levies which remained in force until 1906 when a general rate of 21.5 per cent was adopted, though negotiations with the governments of individual trading partners forced a reduction in the tariffs on many items. Protectionism, which was to remain the basis of Bulgarian tariff policy until the country joined the Soviet trading system in 1949, was popular with industrialists, who exercised a good deal of influence via the chambers of commerce which appeared in most Bulgarian towns.

Neither protectionism nor the encouragement of industry acts did much to alter the pattern of Bulgaria's external trade. Grain continued to be the dominant export and the Ottoman empire remained the main market, though by the years 1908–12 Belgium had replaced Great Britain in second position. The primary source of Bulgarian imports was Austria-Hungary throughout the period up to the first world war, though towards the end of it Germany's share was increasing, as was that of France. During the first world war Bulgaria's trade was limited to that with the central powers, The Netherlands, and Switzerland; by 1918 half of Bulgaria's external trade was with the latter, the main export being tobacco.

In the inter-war period Bulgaria's external trade, like that of other south-east European states, was hugely affected by the depression and the collapse of the central European banking system. And like those other states, in the 1930s Bulgaria's trading links with Germany increased, primarily because of the German blocked mark system; in contrast

France, in the early 1930s, was still insisting on payment for its exports in convertible currencies. By 1939 Germany accounted for 67.8 per cent of Bulgarian exports and provided 65.5 per cent of its imports, whereas in 1934 the respective figures for Germany and Austria combined were 48 and 44.9 per cent.

The basis of a modern Bulgarian financial system was laid when the lev was adopted as the national currency in 1880, the minting of coins beginning the following year, though Ottoman and Russian notes and coins continued to circulate until the beginning of the twentieth century. Note issue was the sole prerogative of the Bulgarian National Bank. The second largest bank was the Agricultural Savings Bank, which began to have a major impact in the second half of the 1890s. It was also in this decade that foreign banks first became heavily involved in Bulgaria. The French Louis Dreyfus Bank had branches in most major towns by the mid-1890s and together with the Salonika-based French Alatini Bank had a near monopoly in the financing of the grain trade of southern Bulgaria, though Austrian banks tended to predominate north of the Balkans. The 1903 reform of the 1897 commercial code, in addition to helping the cooperatives, removed the previous restriction that all joint stock companies had to have a controlling committee of three Bulgarian citizens, all of whom were resident in the country. After that, foreign, and particularly German, banks increased in number. The 1903 amendments to the commercial code also encouraged foreign direct investment, mostly in the larger of the encouraged enterprises. By 1929 15 per cent of Bulgarian industry was foreign owned. Foreign capital had also led the way in the setting up of insurance companies, nine of the thirteen operating in 1911 being foreign owned.

Foreign money also played another important role in post-liberation Bulgaria, that of financing the growing gap between government expenditure and income. Until 1900 money had been raised in Vienna, Paris, or Berlin, but between 1900 and 1909 France was the sole supplier of Bulgarian government loans, after which Austria-Hungary and later Germany returned to the field. Between 1901 and 1912 Bulgaria's foreign debt increased from 354.3 million to 646 million leva. The money borrowed was spent primarily on arms, which was not a productive investment, creating at the same time the problem of debt servicing, which even by 1908 accounted for 18 per cent of government expenditure. The problem became more severe in the 1920s because of the need to pay reparations and with increased government expenditure on the welfare of refugees from Macedonia.

9. PUBLIC HEALTH

Before the first world war the government's ability to intervene in matters concerning health had been limited by lack of funds and a shortage of trained personnel. In the Balkan wars the authorities had been shocked when cholera raged first through the troops massed along the Chatalja lines, and then in 1913 through the civilian population of northern Bulgaria when the disease was reintroduced by returning prisoners of war and by the invading Romanian army. An enquiry revealed that only 900,000 of the 2,000,000 leva needed for sanitation and medical provision had been forthcoming and that only 600 doctors had been available to care for 600,000 people.[15] The military took immediate steps to safeguard the health of the army, and these seem to have been remarkably successful; when cholera broke out amongst troops in 1916 it was quickly contained with not a single life being lost. During the first world war action was also required of the civilian authorities; local communes were ordered to establish health councils whose members, to mitigate *partizanstvo*, were to be unpaid; only fifty-eight of over 2,000 local communes failed to comply with the order. The health councils did excellent work in improving water supplies, drainage, sewage disposal, and in increasing public awareness of health issues. But Bulgaria still lagged behind many other European countries in health provision and in the early 1930s had the highest tuberculosis mortality rate in Europe.

10. THE POSITION OF WOMEN IN BULGARIAN SOCIETY

After 1878 Bulgarian women, particularly in the towns, were able to enjoy a public social life, appearing with much greater freedom in mixed company in theatres, cafés, parks, etc. But they were still a long way from equality. A husband's right to beat his wife was scarcely contested and

---

[15] Markov, *Bŭlgariya v balkanskiya suĭuz*, 105.

other less offensive traditions persisted; men, for example, would carry home from the shops meat purchased for home consumption but not bread, because that was women's work.[16] Many conservatives even regarded women who read as dangerous; the holders of such attitudes retained the traditional prejudice that 'A woman who reads is a loose woman'. Such views were challenged by writers such as Spiro Gulabchev who argued that for women to be emancipated they must read. An increasing number did. In 1902 only 66 women visited or borrowed from Plovdiv's main public library; in 1907 1,552 did so. A number of translated works on women's position in society had appeared in Bulgarian translations, the first being August Bebel's *Die Frau und der Sozialismus* in 1893, and others being J. S. Mill's *On the Subjugation of Women* in 1903 and Avril de Sainte Croix's *Feminisme* in 1911.[17]

Few women took part overtly in public affairs or exercised political influence. One exception was Ekaterina Karavelova, the wife of Petko Karavelov; she defended him stoutly and publicly when he was persecuted by the Stambolov regime and survived to take part in the campaign to prevent the deportation of Bulgarian Jews in the second world war. Less public a figure was Sultane Petrova, the wife of minister president Racho Petrov and confidante of Prince Ferdinand, who in the early twentieth century exercised considerable influence through her salons. The communist movement produced a number of prominent women activists. Tsola Dragoicheva joined the party in the 1920s and, having survived the torture chambers of the Tsankov repression, became a member of the politburo.

Women at times also took direct action. The burning of bales of imported textiles in Sopot in 1883 had been the work of local women. The 1918 'Women's Revolt' began in February when around 200 women had attacked the local offices of the directorate for economic and social affairs in Asenovgrad, demanding an increase in rations and the return of their husbands and sons from the front. The protests spread to other towns. In May there were disturbances in Sofia and Sliven and on 20 May three women were killed when the mayor of Plovdiv ordered the police to fire on demonstrating women. By August protests by half-starved women were an almost daily occurrence and added greatly to the rapidly increasing tensions in the country and to the demoralization of its armed forces.

[16] Georgiev, *Etnokulturnoto razvitie*, 68.   [17] Daskalova, *Gramotnost*, 175–82.

The women borrowed the slogan of 'Bread and Peace' from the Russian revolutionaries of the previous year, but they also always demanded an immediate return of the army from the front. [18] In the second world war the authorities were sufficiently frightened of women political activists to set up a special detention centre for them at Sveti Nikola.

In Bulgaria it had always been common for women to take a significant part in work in the fields as well as to be responsible for maintaining the home. During the first world war in Bulgaria, as elsewhere in Europe, mobilization of the menfolk increased the demands for female labour. A contemporary observer reported even in the early stages of the war, 'one could see with one's own eyes that the fields contained only women who, surrounded by their numerous children, were ploughing, sowing, reaping, carrying the hay, threshing and so forth'.[19] Some females were employed in workshops specially created to provide employment for poorer women by their colleagues who were more fortunately placed; these better-off women also played a prominent role in the communal kitchens and other charitable institutions which attempted to alleviate the suffering of the poor in the latter stages of the war. One woman who broke a social barrier was the scientist Teodora Raĭkova who in February 1918 became the first woman to be appointed to the staff of Sofia University; when the medical faculty was opened in the university in April of the same year fifteen of the hundred-strong intake were female.[20]

The second world war did not produce a social crisis as severe as that of 1918, nor did it see the mobilization of a proportion of the menfolk as high as that of 1915 to 1918. Nevertheless, more women were employed in the workplace as a result of the conflict.

---

[18] Hristov, *Revolyutsionnata Kriza*, 198–206; Lyubomir Ognyanov, *Voĭnishkoto Vŭstanie 1918* (Sofia: Nauka i izkustvo, 1988), 85; G. Tsanev, 'Gladnite buntove v tŭrnovski okrŭg prez 1918g', *Izvestiya na Dŭrzhavnite Arhivi*, no. 5 (1961), 144–60.
[19] Kovachev, *Zapiski*, 166–7.   [20] Koneva, '*Dŭrzhavnite*', loc. cit., 63.

11

The Communist Acquisition of Power, 1944–1948

In the Fatherland Front government established after 9 September 1944 the communists were a forceful, and frequently the dominant element, but they did not have a monopoly of power. This they established gradually and ruthlessly, destroying first the old political system then devouring their erstwhile allies until finally eliminating or taming all other political, social, and cultural organizations. The communists' major confrontations were with the agrarians and the army, and not until the end of 1947 was communist power fully entrenched. In their assumption of power the communists were aided by external as well as domestic factors.

1. THE FIRST PURGES, SEPTEMBER 1944–MAY 1945

In the late spring and early summer of 1944 diplomatic exchanges between London and Moscow had adumbrated what later became the percentages agreement concluded by Churchill and Stalin in October. Under that agreement Bulgaria was to be subject to '75 per cent' Soviet domination whilst the west was to have a 90 per cent interest in Greece, a condition which ended Bulgarian hopes of an outlet on the Aegean. The Soviets immediately put that agreement into effect, insisting that until the end of hostilities in Europe the Soviet high command would have the deciding voice in the Allied Control Commission (ACC) which was to oversee Bulgarian affairs until the signature of a definitive peace treaty. The absence of the western powers meant there were fewer restraints on communist enthusiasms and less support for any forces which might question communist actions.

There was no effective opposition therefore when the authorities decided to dissolve the pre-September sŭbranie, leaving the FF government to rule by decree until a new assembly was elected in November 1945. In October 1944 a decree banned all parties outside the FF until those elections were held. A new regency was established consisting of Venelin Ganev, an academic, diplomat, and lawyer who was a non-party member of the national committee of the FF; Tsvyatko Boboshevski, a former progressive liberal, supporter of the 1934 coup and an opponent of partisan activity during the war, but at the same time an anti-fascist and an advocate of friendship with Britain and France; and Todor Pavlov, a communist, an academic, and a marxist philosopher. The communists also insisted that as soon as the FF government was formed they control the vital ministries of the interior and of justice. They then launched an all-out offensive against the old political establishment.

As early as December 1942 radio Hristo Botev had warned that all who served in the pro-German, 'monarcho-fascist' government would be brought to justice before 'people's courts'. This threat was rapidly implemented, the first assault taking place at the local level. By November 1944 the 700 local FF committees which had existed in September had increased tenfold, and in them the communists outnumbered the agrarians by two to one and the zvenari by thirty to one. These committees encouraged the setting up of the people's courts before which many of the former local leaders were tried. Others were dismissed from their jobs, driven from the locality, or simply murdered. Amongst the victims were teachers, priests, local civil servants, and, above all, policemen; 'There will be no place in liberated Bulgaria for the police and civil servants who have covered themselves in the people's blood', the FF local committee in Pernik had stated chillingly on 5 September.[1]

The peoples' courts often worked in tandem with another new institution, the workers' councils. These had the power to vet company accounts and to denounce anyone who had collaborated with the fascists, foreign or Bulgarian. It would have been difficult to manage any form of economic enterprise in wartime without working with the existing authorities but that argument carried little weight and a large number of

---

[1] Vasilev et al. (eds.), *Otechestven Front*, i/ii, 258.

middle-class employers were ruined by this process. So enthusiastic did many local people's courts and workers' councils become that after a few weeks party leaders in Sofia had to order restraint; '[E]fficient administration rather than the pursuit of revolution was the priority', Georgi Dimitrov informed the party on 28 September,[2] but before order had been restored some thousands of lives had been taken; the most sober estimate puts the number at 3,000[3] but some believe that six times as many were affected, most of whom simply disappeared.[4] Many had been killed without trial but even legally the toll had been high; before they ceased operating in April 1945 the people's courts had tried 11,122 individuals, sentencing 2,618 of them to death, of whom 1,046 had been executed. During what the communists called the 'fascist' era from 1923 to 1944 the courts had handed down 1,590 death sentences for political crimes, of which 199 had been carried out.

Communist power was exercised not merely through civilian bodies. On 28 October an armistice had been signed with the Soviet Union and Bulgaria had agreed to join the allied war against Germany; the majority of the regular Bulgarian army was then attached to Marshal Tolbukhin's Third Ukrainian Front and was to fight alongside its new allies all the way to Budapest and Vienna, leaving behind 32,000 dead in the process.[5] With the army away fighting in central Europe the former partisans were now the largest armed force in Bulgaria and they formed the basis of the new people's guard which was completely under communist domination. So too was the new police force, the people's militia, the old police apparatus having been dismantled immediately after 9 September. The new force was both larger and better armed than the old. A report from the American Office of Strategic Services dated 30 December 1944 stated that whereas there used to be one or two policemen in a village, there were now fifteen or sixteen militiamen.[6] A new and largely secret political police body had also been established under Soviet guidance.

---

[2] Cited in Vesselin Tzvetanov Dimitrov, 'The Failure of Democracy in Eastern Europe and the Emergence of the Cold War, 1944–1948: A Bulgarian Case Study', Ph.D. thesis (Cambridge, 1997), 148.   [3] Ibid. 141.

[4] Markov, *Kambanite*, 147.

[5] For the participation of Bulgaria in the latter stages of the war see, D. Dimitrov, 'Uchastieto na Bŭlgariya vŭv voĭnata sreshtu hitleristka Germaniya v razvŭrshvashtiya etap na vtorata svetovna voĭna (Noemvri 1944–yuli 1945)', *Istoricheski Pregled*, 51/4 (1995), 27–38.   [6] Zolotaryov et al. (eds.), *Bŭlgaro-sŭvetski politicheski*, 218–21.

After the elemental disorders of the immediate post-9 September weeks the several new police authorities, together with the people's courts and the ministry of justice, instituted a further purge of political opponents at both central and local levels. By the end of 1944 over 30,000 officials had been dismissed; it was *partizanstvo* on a massive scale. Most of those removed had been accused of collaboration in one form or another, and the proportion of Bulgarians against whom such charges were laid was to be higher than in any other state in eastern Europe, despite the fact that the country had not been fully occupied, had not sent its Jews to the death camps, and had not been involved in the savagery of the eastern front. But elsewhere in eastern Europe the Gestapo or its local equivalent had destroyed most of the independent-minded local intelligentsia and political structures. In Bulgaria the communists had to do it all themselves.

They did not find it difficult. In January the police arrested the former regents, a large number of courtiers, every minister who had served in government since 1941, and all members of the sŭbranie dissolved in September 1944. They were all tried in the following month and most were found guilty. The prosecution demanded the death penalty for fifty of them, but twice that number were shot in batches of twenty immediately after the verdicts had been given. Not even the communists could disregard Bulgaria's tradition of legal rights for the accused and in court the defence lawyers had mounted an impressive and popular case, arguing, for example, that joining the tripartite pact had been a lesser evil than the sort of occupation suffered by Greece and Yugoslavia.

But legal traditions and legal arguments were not the decisive factors. The entire process was political rather than judicial. As early as 29 September 1944 Traĭcho Kostov, an able young communist who had been in Bulgaria throughout the war, spoke to a regional party conference in Sofia of a 'national court' for which 'the legislation is already prepared'.[7] The verdicts were decided not by the judges but in the BWP politburo where Kostov had 'personally instructed the Public Prosecutors not "to measure who is guilty of what" but to "look out for the slightest thing that would prove the guilt of these bandits" '.[8] And it was his insistence on the most severe of punishments that led to the orgy of judicial killings. The victims included Prince Kiril and the other two regents; all

---

[7] Paunovski, *Vŭzmezdieto*, 14.   [8] Stankova, 'Bulgaria', 157.

members of the Filov and Bozhilov governments; half those from Bagryanov's administration; sixty-seven sŭbranie deputies, including two who had signed the petition against the deportation of the Jews in 1943, and forty-seven generals or colonels. Amongst the survivors was Ivan Marinov, the minister of war who had admitted the partisans into Sofia on the night of 8–9 September.

In addition to attacking the old political establishment the communists had already secured almost total domination over the media. Opposition newspapers could still appear but circulation outside the capital was limited and if they became too outspoken the distribution of newsprint could be managed to the disadvantage of disobedient journals, or the communists could call upon their supporters in the print unions to force editors to drop or amend undesirable articles. The radio was under total FF command and in the cinemas Soviet productions became the main bill of fare.

By the spring of 1945 the communists had destroyed the centre and the right of the Bulgarian political spectrum. But that had been a relatively easy task. These enemies were already discredited, they lacked mass support, and they had been outside the framework of the FF. The next objective was to neutralize the non-communist left, and particularly the agrarians. This would be much more difficult. The agrarians were extremely popular, they had opposed the recent war, and they were an integral part of the FF coalition. Their defeat would mean the virtual destruction of the FF. And all the time, even though the military and the agrarians had little in common, the communists would have to keep an eye on the army.

2. THE COMMUNISTS VERSUS THE AGRARIANS, MAY–NOVEMBER 1945

Agrarianism, despite its defeat in 1923, the splits which had followed it, and the behaviour of some of its leaders in office between 1931 and 1934, remained the strongest political force in the country, and in the months after 9 September 1944 agrarian membership grew even more rapidly than that of the BWP. The communists faced a further difficulty in that, unlike in most other countries in eastern Europe, there were no aristocratic or émigré estates or newly acquired territory which the communists could parcel out to the peasants and thereby win their support. There was no alternative to a direct assault on BANU, even though it was a member of the FF.

Initially the leader of the agrarians was G. M. Dimitrov, known as 'Gemeto' (the G. M.) to distinguish him from the communist leader of the same name, but he was easily compromised because of his very close links with the British before and during the war; in April 1945 he fled to escape arrest. His successor, Nikola Petkov, was a much tougher nut to crack. A son of the minister president murdered in 1907, he was a brilliant speakers and a resolute nationalist with an impeccable record of resistance in the war; he was soon the most popular politician in the country. The communists' first tactic was to engineer a split within Petkov's party, after which the ministry of justice declared that all the party's property, including its newspaper, belonged to the pro-communist faction led by Aleksandŭr Obbov, an unpleasant character 'who has been paid by almost every European government, a man who sold the Salt Commission to the Fascists and [has] lived on the profits of it ever since'.[9] Petkov immediately set up a new party, the Bulgarian Agrarian National Union–Nikola Petkov (BANU-NP). After splitting the agrarians the communists carried out a similar manoeuvre against the social democrats, Kosta Lulchev emerging to lead the anti-communist faction.

Petkov soon won a major victory over the communists. The latter, with full Soviet backing, had demanded that a general election be held in August and that all the FF parties should appear on a single list. The ratio of deputies for each party on this list was decided by an FF congress which allotted ninety-five each to the agrarians and the communists; an accurate measure of their respective popular support would have given the agrarians three times as many candidates as the communists. Petkov declared this to be anti-democratic, and in doing so he called upon the British and the Americans for support. Western influence in Bulgaria had become more powerful in that the end of the war in Europe in May 1945 meant that the two western powers began taking a full part in the ACC. They gave their backing to Petkov's resistance to the single-list project,

[9] The words are those of Maynard Barnes, the head of the US delegation on the Allied Control Commission for Bulgaria, cited in Michael Boll (ed.), *The American Military Mission in the Allied Control Commission for Bulgaria, 1944–1947, History and Transcripts* (Boulder, Colo.: East European Monographs, no. 176, distributed by Columbia University Press, 1985), 105.

and to his call for the postponement of the elections until November. Petkov and his allies secured the second of these objectives, which did much to enhance the BANU-NP leader's prestige amongst opposition politicians and increased yet further his popularity amongst the peasantry; within two months over 2,000 new petkovist local druzhbi were founded. In his call for the abandonment of the single-list, however, Petkov was unsuccessful and, against western advice, he ordered his supporters to boycott the elections when they were held on 18 November. Petkov's decision was a mistake, the result of overconfidence following his recent successes.

3. THE COMMUNIST OFFENSIVE, DECEMBER 1945–OCTOBER 1946

After the elections a new cabinet was formed under communist leader Georgi Dimitrov who had returned from Moscow on 7 November. The western powers and their protégés in Bulgaria then seemed to score another victory when, at the foreign ministers' conference in Moscow at the end of the year, they persuaded the Soviets to agree to a widening of the government coalitions in Bulgaria and Romania. This was as far as the concessions went. Petkov and Lulchev demanded that BANU-NP, as the largest party in the country, be given the minister presidency, and that the communists relinquish their hold on the ministries of the interior and justice, dissolve the sŭbranie, and hold new, free elections. The communists refused all three demands and early in 1946 went on the offensive once again. They had full Soviet backing.

This time the chief target was the army. It was not the first attack on the military. The sending of the army to fight alongside Tolbukhin's troops had had the advantage of removing it from the country whilst the basis of communist domination was being laid, but even then 800 officers had been dismissed as politically unreliable, amongst them the chief of the general staff who was replaced by Colonel Ivan Kinov, a Bulgarian who had long served in the Red Army. When Damyan Velchev, who had become minister of war after 9 September, had tried to interfere in this purge his action had prompted the first direct and overt intervention into Bulgarian domestic affairs by the head of the Soviet military mission, General Sergeĭ Biryuzov. With the end of the war in Europe most of the army had returned to Bulgaria where Velchev had been largely successful in preserving its autonomy. This the communists feared. The army now outnumbered the pro-communist militia which had no heavy weaponry and communist insecurity was increased by memory of the army's historic record and consciousness of the fact that both Georgiev and Velchev, the architects of the 1934 coup, were still in influential positions. Furthermore, as the men returned from central Europe it was the communist officers who were demobilized first. This was usually not a political move but merely because they were the least experienced, but it served to increase communist anxieties yet again. Measures had to be taken to keep the army under tight control, to prevent any repetition of June 1923 and May 1934, and to hamper any cooperation between the army and oppositionist forces.

In February 1946 a prominent social democrat had been arrested after using the columns of his party's newspaper to criticize a speech by Dimitrov. During the subsequent trial there were allegations of a military plot and in July a bill was enacted transferring control of the army from the ministry of war to the cabinet as a whole. This weakened Velchev, who resigned his post and in September became Bulgarian minister to Switzerland. Velchev was not the only victim; 2,000 so-called 'reactionary' officers were dismissed. This neutralization of the army was the most significant political development in Bulgaria since the coup of 9 September 1944.

Having clipped the army's political wings the government carried out two national polls. Early in September 1946 a referendum was held on the monarchy. Some irregularities occurred during the voting but government pressure was hardly necessary; the fond memories of Boris had faded and the monarchy seemed distant and irrelevant to most Bulgarians, many of whom also realized that the declaration of a 'people's republic', which took place on 15 September, would indicate that Bulgaria had turned its back on a dynasty which had twice taken it to war on the German side. This was an important consideration in that the Paris conference to determine the terms of the peace treaties for Germany's former allies had begun discussion of the treaty with Bulgaria in August.[10]

[10] For the peace negotiations in Paris see, Nina Vasil'eva, 'SSSR i problema podpisaniya mirnogo dogovora s Bogarieĭ posle vtoroĭ mirovoĭ voĭni', in Zolotaryov et al. (eds.), *Bŭlgaro-sŭvetski politicheski*, 129–50, 142–8.

The second poll, held on 27 October, was the election of a grand national assembly which was to draw up a new constitution fit for the new republic. This also had relevance for the Paris peace talks. The GNA would represent all parties except the monarchists and the fascists and would therefore produce a system which had the backing of the majority of the nation. Any government created by such a system would be legitimate and therefore worthy of international recognition. The western powers were not impressed, not least because Petkov and the other main opposition leaders, who had joined forces in the Federation of Urban and Rural Labour so as to be able to present a single list for the GNA elections, complained there had been widespread intimidation and fraud at the polls. The opposition took 28.35 per cent of the votes and were given 99 seats in the assembly; the FF had 70.10 per cent of the poll and 366 seats in the GNA, of which 275 were given to the communists. In December 1947, when a new constitution was adopted, the GNA transformed itself into an ordinary sŭbranie and continued sitting until elections were held in October 1949.

Immediately after the elections of October 1946 a new government was formed with Georgi Dimitrov again serving as minister president. The cabinet contained five obbovite agrarians, two zvenari, including Georgiev who was minister for foreign affairs, and two pro-communist social democrats.

4. THE COMMUNISTS EMBATTLED, OCTOBER 1946–FEBRUARY 1947

In late 1946 and the first half of 1947 the communists increased their attacks on the remaining opposition parties. In December the Democratic Party, the one respected party from the old regime, was emasculated when its newspaper, *Zname* (Banner), was shut down. In March 1947 the central committee (CC) of the BWP ordered further action to weaken the oppositionist agrarians and social democrats, as a result of which further splits were engineered in both groups.

This aggression on the part of the BWP was precipitated as much by weakness and anxiety as by strength and self-confidence. During the October 1946 election campaign over 30,000 people had turned out for an opposition rally, after which the BWP CC ordered local party committees to take control of opposition rallies with the result that anti-communist activists scarcely dared appear in public. Despite this many former supporters of the FF defected to the united opposition list which secured 30 per cent of the vote, whilst the non-communist FF parties took 18 per cent, meaning that the communists only had a slim majority of the total poll. The communists then made themselves more unpopular by manipulating the allocation of FF seats; having secured 22 per cent of the FF vote it took 27 per cent of the seats.

This manipulation of the representative system was profoundly unpopular. Petkov's party gained even more members and a significant number of local druzhbi which had previously aligned with the pro-FF agrarians now switched allegiance. Within the FF itself the non-communist parties at last realized that they had been too closely associated with the BWP and attempted to move towards a more independent position. Vasil Yurukov, leader of the pro-FF Zveno faction, condemned the 'doctrinaire marxism' of the government and transformed his newspaper into a mouthpiece for opposition views; in November 1946 even the odious Obbov made approaches to the Americans[11] and in July 1947 declared it was time to separate from the FF and the communists. The communists thereupon engineered his removal from the leadership of the FF agrarian faction.

There was also mounting disenchantment with the communists outside the political arena. The previously compliant Bulgarian Orthodox Church began to have doubts. In the summer of 1945 Metropolitan Stefan had promised the FF government the Church's full backing, even referring to Dimitrov as an 'angel';[12] now the Holy Synod rejected proposals from the FF for the democratization of the Church. Within the FF's youth organization, set up and dominated by the communists immediately after 9 September, discomfort at BWP policies was growing, as it was in the FF's women's movement. This in part reflected mounting anxieties amongst the intelligentsia and the bourgeoisie. The latter was small and, not expecting much from the communists, had accepted restrictions on capital and on commercial and industrial

---

[11] Michael M. Boll, *Cold War in the Balkans: American Foreign Policy and the Emergence of Communist Bulgaria, 1943–1947* (Lexington: University of Kentucky Press, 1984), 182 ff.

[12] Dimitŭr Sirkov (compiler and editor), *Georgi Dimitrov: Dnevnik (9 mart 1933–6 fevruari 1949)* (Sofia: Kliment Ohridski, 1997), 499.

activities. More difficult to accept, both for the bourgeoisie and the intelligentsia, were the currency reforms of March 1947. These were intended to contain inflation and create a new post-war fiscal stability; they therefore introduced a new lev but at the same time they blocked all bank accounts of over 20,000 leva, imposed a windfall tax on all other accounts, and prevented the accumulation of future savings by means of a new progressive tax on savings as well as incomes.

The BWP would not be unduly concerned by hostility from the other parties, the Church, the bourgeoisie, or even the intelligentsia. It had much greater reason to be anxious at growing hostility from both the rural and the urban masses.

Any government, communist or non-communist, in Bulgaria after the second world war would have faced enormous problems on the economic front; the country was, concluded an American diplomat in December 1944, 'in a hell of a state'.[13] The bombing had severely disrupted national life, the transport system was exhausted and overburdened, and previous trading patterns, focused on Germany, had been destroyed. These difficulties were made worse by Soviet reparations and by the west's refusal to conclude trade agreements with or grant loans to Bulgaria until it had signed a peace treaty.

The communists, however, compounded their difficulties. Since September 1944 they had kept studiously quiet about collectivization, but a series of fiscal measures had been introduced to encourage peasants to join the new socialized farms, the TKZSs, of which many peasants were deeply suspicious. These peasants saw such measures not as encouragement but rather as pressure to join the TKZSs. They also mistrusted further regulations to restrict the size of individual holdings and to impose compulsory delivery quotas at set prices.

Even more serious for the communists than the anger of the peasants was the growing alienation of the urban proletariat. And here the major problem was unemployment. After 1945 Bulgarian manufacturers, increasingly harassed by central government and the local FF committees, had to find new markets in an impoverished Europe. Their position was made worse by a lack of capital to repair existing or invest in new equipment. The consequent inability to reconstruct industry and to find

---

[13] Maynard Barnes to Secretary of State, Sofia, 1 Dec. 1944, *Foreign Relations of the United States 1944*, iii (Washington, DC: Department of State), 495–7, 497.

export markets for manufactured goods was one cause of unemployment. Others were demobilization and the return to the country of thousands of Bulgarian civilians who had gone to work in the German Reich. By the beginning of 1947 there were some 38,000 unemployed in Bulgaria, around a fifth of the workforce, and almost half of them were in the tobacco industry, a traditional communist stronghold.

A further cause of discontent amongst the urban masses was that food exports to the Soviet Union were diminishing supplies, thus triggering price rises which quickly outstripped increases in wages. In 1947 the short story writer and humorist, 'Chudomir', confided to his diary, 'Our country has never been as poor as it is now. After this unprecedented war, after these years of drought, we have become so ragged and famished that I cannot imagine how things might get better.'[14] The sense of grievance over this was aggravated by the 'voluntary' 'Freedom Loans' organized by the local FF committees. Much of the money raised from these loans went to pay the increasing occupation costs demanded by the Soviet Union for the upkeep of the Red Army in Bulgaria, costs which accounted for almost half of the entire expenditure of the Bulgarian government.

The growing discontent in the towns caused strikes and the return of many workers to their villages where their families still owned land; mining was particularly severely affected by this development and the consequent fall in coal production inevitably added to the urban tensions both by increasing the cost of fuel and, because of the lack of coal for the railways, slowing food distribution and pushing prices up even further. The miners were not the only workers who were deserting industrial complexes for the villages. After the bombing many manufacturers had moved out of the larger towns whilst new enterprises founded after 9 September also favoured the smaller communities where housing shortages were not a serious problem. These new enterprises tended to be small; between 1944 and 1947, whilst the number of employees in plants with over twenty horsepower rose by just under a third, those employed in smaller plants went up by well over half.

These were hardly the conditions in which to establish socialism. If the communists did not act soon social developments and rising political opposition could make their assumption of full power much more difficult if not impossible. In May 1947 Dimitrov wrote to Stalin asking

---

[14] Cited Gigova, 'Writers of the Nation', 130.

for a credit of at least 10 million dollars, and, given the prospect of another bad harvest, 100,000 tons of maize and wheat.

In the same letter Dimitrov had advised 'the great comrade' in the Kremlin that Bulgaria's government also faced external problems because of the west's refusal to sign any form of financial or trade agreement until a peace treaty had been concluded and Bulgaria granted international recognition.

And, as ever, there were difficulties over Macedonia. Since 1941 the Yugoslav partisans had spoken of uniting all parts of Macedonia in a socialist republic which would be part of a new Yugoslav federation.[15] As they increased in strength they had begun to map out their strategy for the future of their country. In November 1943 at Jajce in Bosnia they had announced that the future federated Yugoslavia would consist of six republics, one of which would be Macedonia. The collapse of Axis power in the second half of 1944 enabled the partisans to establish the new Macedonian republic, which many Yugoslav communists, elated by their recent triumphs, began to talk of as the kernel of a new People's Republic of Macedonia (PRM) which, when a Balkan socialist federation was established, would incorporate all ethnic Macedonians, including those in Bulgaria's Pirin Macedonia.[16] The west's backing of the anti-communist forces in Greece put paid to any ideas that Greek Macedonia would join the new entity, but the situation was different in Bulgaria. In November 1944 Dimitrov informed the Yugoslav comrades that the BWP organization in Gorna Djumaya (Blagoevgrad) was to be redesignated a Macedonian party organization, local schools and other institutions were to be named after Macedonian rather than Bulgarian heroes, and a Macedonian-language newspaper was to be published; 'Our party', Dimitrov declared, 'has always stood and still stands firmly on the position that Macedonia belongs to the Macedonians.'[17] Edvard Kardelj, one of Tito's most influential advisers, immediately went to Sofia, but by the time he arrived Bulgarian enthusiasms had cooled, not least because of the opposition of powerful party figures, amongst the most outspoken

[15] Georgi Daskalov, *Bŭlgaro-yugoslavski politicheski otnosheniya, 1944–1945* (Sofia: Kliment Ohridski, 1989), 23–57.

[16] Veselin Angelov, 'Neizvestni pisma za prisŭedinyavane na pirinska Makedoniya kŭm Yugoslaviya (Avgust–Septemvri 1944 godina)', *Istoricheski Pregled*, 47/9 (1991), 91–5. He cites evidence from the Blagoevgrad regional archives.

[17] Petŭr Semerdjiev, *Bŭlgariya na balkanite sled vtorata svetovna voĭna* (Paris: no publisher cited, 1985), 37.

of whom was Kostov. The matter was put on hold to await the formation of a Balkan federation, something which could not come about until Bulgaria had signed a peace treaty.

The issue was reactivated suddenly in July 1946 by Dimitrov, who had always admired Tito. The Bulgarian leader told the Yugoslav ambassador that Pirin Macedonia would become part of the PRM, and in August a Bulgarian CC plenum was secretly informed that there were not three Macedonias but one, the PRM, and that Pirin and Aegean Macedonia would eventually become part of it. Friendship with Yugoslavia was popular in Bulgaria, but, as under Stamboliïski, the Macedonian price that was to be paid for it was not.

5. THE PEACE TREATY AND THE ELIMINATION OF PETKOV, FEBRUARY–SEPTEMBER 1947

A peace treaty between Bulgaria and its former enemies was signed in Paris in February 1947. It did not bring immediate relief to the communists. Bulgaria was to lose all the territory gained after 1 March 1941, and was to pay compensation to both Yugoslavia and Greece; there were also to be limitations on the size of the Bulgarian armed forces. And the Red Army was to leave Bulgaria within ninety days of the signature of the treaty. The peace treaty did at least allow Bulgaria to keep the southern Dobrudja but this was little consolation to those who had hoped that some of the gains in Macedonia and Thrace might be retained, a hope which had been bolstered by indications that the claim to these areas would be supported by Moscow.

The requirement that Soviet troops leave Bulgaria had a profound effect on its internal political evolution. From the very beginning Dimitrov and the communists had relied enormously on Soviet backing and had often allowed Stalin to dictate policy at critical junctures. In the spring of 1945 Moscow had chided the Bulgarian communists for their caution: 'We are amazed', Molotov told Dimitrov on 18 March, 'by your moderation . . .'[18] and just over a year later, in June 1946, before the attack upon the military, the Bulgarian party boss was told that Biryuzov was returning to Sofia 'with new instructions from Moscow concerning

---

[18] Sirkov (ed.), *Dimitrov. Dnevnik*, 523.

the situation of the Bulgarian army.'[19] The presence of the Red Army in Bulgaria was the ultimate guarantee that Moscow's orders could be enforced. Its departure, it was widely believed, would therefore weaken Dimitrov and the communists. That was Petkov's view, and his confidence was boosted by the Truman Declaration in March.

The emboldened Petkov went onto the offensive when the GNA began detailed debate on the new constitution. He denounced the BWP as a 'fascist' party which should be banned, and he ridiculed the regime by showing that it was spending far more on police and public control than the pre-9 September governments had. But Petkov had miscalculated. Even he could not imagine how ruthless the communists could be; he failed to see that the Truman Doctrine, though expressed in global terms, was aimed at Greece and Turkey, and the United States would not, and the United Kingdom could not think of committing themselves to defend the democrats of Bulgaria; nor did he take sufficiently into account the fact that although the peace treaty would mean the departure of the Red Army it would also mean the end of the ACC and the removal of this western shield against communist ruthlessness. Petkov also failed to realize that the signature of the peace treaty and the stipulation that the Red Army would leave Bulgaria nine months thereafter would force the communists into action against him; they knew that without the backing of the Soviet forces they could not be certain of defeating him and therefore, if they were to secure definitive control of the country, Petkov had to be destroyed before the Red Army left.

Petkov's arrest took place on 5 June in the sŭbranie, technically an illegal act. He was charged with conspiring to organize acts of terrorism, wishing to collaborate with 'monarcho-fascists' in Greece, plotting to destroy Bulgarian-Soviet friendship, and attempting to divide Bulgarian peasants and workers. The most important charge, however, was that of attempting to form a military league. By linking Petkov with the army Dimitrov and the BWP were delivering a final blow to their two principal enemies.

The trial was one of the most dreadful of eastern Europe's show trials. Petkov was arraigned with three soldiers and a peasant, and none of the accused was allowed a defence lawyer or to put evidence before the court, though the prosecution witnesses had been very carefully prepared and

---

[19] Sirkov (ed.), *Dimitrov. Dnevnik*, 529.

rehearsed, invariably in the torture chambers. A verdict was reached and the death sentence passed on 16 August. The execution took place on 23 September. Petkov was hanged rather than shot and, though one of the few genuine believers in Bulgarian politics, was denied both the last rites and a religious burial. On the day of the execution the BWP bussed in thousands of obedient peasants to celebrate the event and the trade unions organized demonstrations demanding, 'To a dog, a dog's death'. Dimitrov, who had earned worldwide admiration for his conduct during the Reichstag fire trial in 1933, turned a deaf ear to pleas for clemency from leading socialists such as Edouard Herriot and Leon Blum, and from the man who had acted as his defence lawyer in Leipzig.

Petkov had placed hope and faith in the western powers but in these early stages of the cold war those powers were unable or unwilling to help him. The communists were determined that this should not go unobserved by other would-be oppositionists and the persecution of Petkov was closely linked to developments on the international stage: on 4 June the United States ratified the peace treaty with Bulgaria; on 5 June Petkov was arrested: on 20 September the peace treaty came into force; on 23 September Petkov was executed.

6. THE COMMUNISTS ASSUME TOTAL CONTROL, SEPTEMBER–DECEMBER 1947

After the arrest of Petkov the BWP liquidated his party. Deputies who had remained loyal were either deprived of their seats in the GNA or, like Asen Stamboliĭski, son of the great leader, warned that future opposition to the government would not be tolerated. In August BANU-NP was dissolved, its youth organization broken up, and its property confiscated. There was also a final cull of the army's officer corps. In October a prominent and immensely popular republican soldier, General Kiril Stanchev, was tried with thirty-eight other officers, the prosecution alleging that Stanchev and his associates had been involved in Petkov's attempt to form a military league. Stanchev had been brutally tortured and a verdict of guilty was a foregone conclusion. After the trial almost a third of serving officers in the army were sacked because of their alleged anti-FF sympathies. Velchev, who had been close to Stanchev since the 1930s, resigned his diplomatic post in Switzerland and retired from public life. The army would no longer threaten a communist regime, though almost two decades later it could still oppose its leader.

In October 1947 the BWP CC resolved that the remaining opposition parties should be liquidated entirely.[20] With the most powerful opposition personality and party removed and the army rendered politically impotent it was not a difficult task. In October the FF underwent structural changes, proposed by the BWP CC, which strengthened the so-called worker-peasant alliance, a euphemism for communist domination on the Soviet pattern. In December the agrarians formerly led by Obbov agreed that there should be a common programme with the other FF parties, i.e. the BWP, to create a 'workers' democratic and socialist society' in Bulgaria. Further consolidation of the FF followed with the merging of the separate parties' women's and youth movements into single ones dominated by the communists working through the FF apparatus. In August 1948 the social democrats within the FF merged with the BWP and the other groups, the radicals and the zvenari, were subsumed into the FF structure; only the agrarians remained as a separate organization, but they had long since sacrificed their independence. The social democrats under Lulchev had been destroyed in July; six of their nine GNA deputies had been arrested and their leader tried and sentenced to fifteen years in gaol, a virtual death sentence for such an elderly man. Most of the other groups outside the FF withdrew from political life, though the radicals survived until 1949, no doubt because they were small and powerless.

The intensification of the communist attack on the other parties was in part the result of the division of Europe, which had become much more marked in 1947. Following the Truman Doctrine had come the Marshall Plan in June and then the formation of Cominform in October. The latter had urged all communist parties in government to intensify their efforts to establish full socialist rule and to begin the reconstruction of the country on the Soviet model. The communists also calculated, correctly, that the west would not interfere. The western powers, with problems in other parts of Europe, the middle east, and Asia, would not risk further international complications for the sake of Bulgaria, not least because a war-weary public opinion would never sanction such a course; and with

---

[20] Lyubomir Ognyanov, *Dŭrzhavno-politicheska sistema na Bŭlgariya, 1944–1948* (Sofia: BAN, 1993), 191–5.

British and American aid being given to the minority royalist forces in Greece the west was in no position to take the moral high ground.

The Bulgarian communists did not need the urging of Cominform to persuade them to move towards a Soviet system; this had been in their minds since 9 September 1944.[21] The first step was to adopt a new constitution. A number of drafts, submitted by various parties, had been discussed by the GNA but when one arrived with a Moscow postmark there was deemed to be no need for discussion; the 'Dimitrov constitution', made in the Soviet Union, was adopted by acclamation on 4 December 1947.

The constitution declared Bulgaria a 'people's democracy'. The full panoply of individual rights was guaranteed, including complete emancipation and equality for women. Also guaranteed were the right to work and the right to own private property. But the constitution also contained limiting clauses. The right to work only applied to occupations which were not 'to the detriment of the public good', whilst the right to own private property was hedged by a clause which placed all the means of production in public ownership. The old system of local government was abolished, power at that level being placed in the hands of people's councils. Popular sovereignty was still to be exercised through a sŭbranie elected every four years, but the old doctrine of the separation of powers was jettisoned. The sŭbranie was to elect *inter se* a praesidium which until 1971 was to be the supreme organ of state power, fulfilling the functions of a head of state. The praesidium decreased the importance of the assembly itself, but in any event the latter became a parliament only in name; in succeeding years almost all deputies had to be approved by the communists and therefore there was no effective opposition. The sŭbranie became a rubber stamp for decisions taken by the leaders of the communist party.

The government was to include not only the minister president and an unspecified number of ministers but also the heads of the state planning commission, the commission for state control, i. e. the secret police, and the commission for science, art, and culture. The sŭbranie was also to elect the supreme court and the public prosecutor, whilst lower courts were to have lay assessors who would 'help' the professional lawyers. The assessors were to be approved by the local FF committees, in effect by the communists, as were all parliamentary candidates. This, and its

[21] Dimitrov, 'Failure of Democracy', esp. 406–10.

domination of the people's councils, ensured the communist party political authority at the local level. At the governmental level most ministers and other leading officials were members of the BWP CC, and until 1953 the minister president was also the first secretary of the CC, or party boss. Communist rule had been established, though it was not until a year later, in December 1948 at its fifth congress, that the party decided to revert to its former name, the Bulgarian Communist Party (BCP).

12

The Communists in Power, I. The Rule of Terror, the Reign of Vŭlko Chervenkov, and the Rise of Todor Zhivkov, 1948–1965

The Dimitrov constitution and the new party programme announced at the fifth congress intensified the communists' drive to remodel Bulgaria and to do away with the old regime. The process was seemingly completed with the law of 20 November 1951 which rescinded all laws and regulations deemed to contradict the Dimitrov constitution and which declared all pre-9 September 1944 legislation invalid. But communist rule in Bulgaria, as elsewhere in eastern Europe, was not simply a matter of political power or legislative monopoly. It also involved total control of the economy and of society.

1. THE TRANSFORMATION OF THE SOCIAL AND ECONOMIC ORDER

Social control was exercised partly through the FF. To it were affiliated all important social organizations such as the trades unions, the women's organizations, the youth movement, the professional associations, and powerful bodies such as the League for Large Families, which had been set up in 1943 and which by 1944 had over 80,000 members.[1] All affiliated

---

[1] For an excellent survey of this important but little-known organization, see Svetla Baloutzova, 'State Legislation on Family and Social Policy in Bulgaria, 1918–1944', Ph.D. thesis (Cambridge, 2005).

groups were controlled by the FF, which in effect meant by the communists, with the result that almost every individual in the country was subject to communist power. In addition there was the complex system of police control exercised through the party organizations. The party maintained cells in almost all places of work and all social organizations. These primary party organizations passed to the local party committee information on the conduct of the members of the workforce or the society concerned. To this apparatus of social surveillance was added the Soviet system of cadre selection and nomenklatura posts which, operating at all levels of state and society, ensured virtual total control for the party. It was to be used ruthlessly in the first years of BCP rule. The party itself, meanwhile, was organized on the authoritarian Soviet model of democratic centralism.

After the adoption of the new constitution the Dimitrov government integrated Bulgaria even further into the Soviet system. Bilateral agreements with the Soviet Union and the other states of the socialist bloc had already been signed in 1947, and in the summer of that year Bulgaria's adhesion to the coalescing Soviet bloc was emphasized when pressure from the Kremlin prevented Bulgaria joining the Marshall Plan.[2] After December 1947 the trading ties were cemented, with Bulgaria joining the newly formed Council for Economic Cooperation (Comecon) in January 1949. A series of cultural treaties was also signed.

At home the major task was to reconstruct the economy on a socialist foundation. The Dimitrov constitution followed its stalinist archetype in demanding that the economy be rigidly planned. Bulgaria, like the Soviet Union, would place the economy under state control, would build a heavy industrial base, and would promote collectivization in agriculture. A two-year plan had been introduced in April 1947 to help ease the transition to post-war economic realities, but this was a temporary expedient and did not compare in scope or intent to the first five-year plan (fyp) presented to the fifth party congress in December 1948.

The plan, which was to come into operation at the beginning of 1949, would place the economy in public ownership and set as its first objective the creation of a heavy industrial base. Under the plan industry was to receive 47 per cent of total investment in the economy, with almost half

---

[2] Gospodinka Nikova, 'Planŭt Marshal, evropeĭskite sili i Bŭlgariya', *Istoricheski Pregled*, 49/4–5, (1993), 56–74.

that sum going to the development of electricity generation and the chemical industry. New plants were to be constructed for the production of metal, fertilizers, electrical apparatus, construction materials, and agricultural machinery. Industrial production was to rise by a total of 119 per cent but within the industrial sector heavy industrial output was to increase by 220 per cent and that of light industry by only 75 per cent. The balance of the economy as a whole was to be shifted; whereas at the end of 1948 agriculture produced 70 per cent of the national output and industry 30 per cent, by the end of the first fyp it was to be 45 and 55 per cent respectively. Private trading was to disappear. A critical feature of the plan was the statement that three-fifths of the nation's food would be produced on collective farms. There would be no nationalization of the land, but, the plan stated delphicly, conditions would be created 'in which the problem of the nationalization of the land would be solved in practice'.

A number of steps had already been taken towards placing the economy in public, i.e. state, ownership. On 23 December 1947 specially trained groups had taken physical control of the 6,000 private enterprises still operating in the country. The GNA gave retrospective sanction to this and ruled that the former owners should be paid compensation in government bonds; but compensation was not to be paid to anyone who had cooperated with Bulgarian or foreign 'fascists' or post-9 September 1944 'reactionaries', a ruling which cut the final compensation bill by about 90 per cent. The liquidation of private banking followed rapidly upon the nationalization of industry, Bulgaria's thirty-two remaining banks being merged into the BNB. In February 1948 foreign trade was made a government monopoly. In the same month larger urban properties in private hands were socialized. The latter measure meant that the private landlord had ceased to exist and Bulgaria's small bourgeoisie had been all but destroyed.

The liquidation of private property in the rural sector was a much more difficult task and involved the greatest social transformation forced upon the country since the Ottoman conquest. It was nevertheless a task which the new stalinist ideology demanded should be completed and which the Bulgarian party was ruthlessly determined to carry out.

Soon after the FF came to power the communists had been able to push through legislation allowing the formation of state and collective farms (TKZSs), though very few of the former were established in

Bulgaria. To transfer landed property from individual to public or collective ownership seemed a mammoth undertaking. The continuation of divided inheritance had meant that the number of individual holdings after the second world war was greater than ever before. There were now 1.1 million landowners and the average area owned was a little over 4 hectares. Over four-fifths of the population relied on private agriculture for their livelihood. The party, in effect, was challenging the majority of the population.

The first moves towards collectivization were cautious. Membership of the new units was to be voluntary, though any peasant joining had to remain in the collective for at least three years; he was to be paid wages for work done on the collective and a ground rent in proportion to the amount of land he had contributed. In 1946 a second act strengthened the collectives. Under the new legislation those joining a TKZS were to own not actual areas of land but a percentage of the total commensurate with the land contributed. The 1946 act also laid down both maximum and minimum areas of land which any one private agricultural producer might own. The maximum was to be 20 hectares of arable land, though in the Dobrudja, where larger units were more common, the upper limit was to be 30 hectares. Any land in excess of the maximum holding could be taken by the state, as could land which the owner refused to cultivate, and the property of disbanded organizations such as foreign churches or charitable institutions. The state could also take possession of holdings smaller than the prescribed minimum. Half the land taken under the 1946 act was given to 129,000 dwarf holders, the other half going to the TKZSs. The TKZSs were also favoured in that they were given tractors and other machinery imported from the Soviet Union.

The remaining private producers on the land were discriminated against in a variety of ways. Tax regulations introduced in 1946 aimed to deprive the richer peasants of between 80 and 90 per cent of their income, and in the following year a new law closed many of the taverns owned by wealthy peasants.[3] Procurement prices and quotas under the enforced requisitioning of some crops favoured the collective producer. The two-year plan of 1947 rationed essential commodities and at the

[3] For details of the assault on the richer peasants, see Vladimir Migev, 'Borbata sreshtu kulachestvoto i negovoto likvidirane v Bŭlgariya (1944–1958)', in Hristo Hristov (ed. in chief), *Stopanskiya i sotsialniya zhivot*, 40–84.

same time divided the nation into seven orders of priority for receipt of those commodities; members of the TKZSs were in the third order of priority, the private farmer was in the last. In 1948 local party organizations began compiling and then publishing lists of 'kulaks', many of whom were no more than middle peasants, and those on the lists were denied certain commodities. A critical blow against the private farmer was an enactment in February of the same year confiscating all privately owned agricultural machinery, all of which was henceforth to be owned by the new motor tractor stations (MTSs). The MTSs' monopoly over agricultural machinery meant that these institutions, under the guidance of local communists, could discriminate savagely against the private producer. This accelerated the formation of collectives, of which there were 1,100 by the end of 1948, 300 more than the government's target, but despite this only 292,000 hectares were in the socialized sector against the government's hoped-for figure of 400,000 hectares. And those joining the TKZSs were still mainly small farmers. The middle farmers, whose voluntary conversion to the collective ideal Lenin had seen as the signal for socialism's victory in the countryside, remained infidels.

The fifth party congress launched a new crusade. Whereas the constitution had been opaque in its pronouncements on landownership, the fifth congress was unambiguous. It called for mass collectivization and as a result thousands of meetings were held throughout the country to persuade farmers to join the collectives. They largely failed. The private producers were suspicious and frightened, and furthermore they were now faced with impossible demands. The first fyp allotted 6 per cent of investment to agriculture which employed around 80 per cent of the population, and demanded an increase in production of 59 per cent. In the first half of 1950 the so-called kulaks received a series of virtual knockout blows with new targets for state deliveries of grain and pulses, revised regulations for income tax, and the trial of a number of peasants on charges of hoarding grain; from 9 September 1944 to the end of 1949 156,000 peasants had joined the socialized sector, but in the first two months of 1950 twice that number did so. After a CC plenum in October 1950 the richer peasants were excluded from the TKZSs and were denounced as collaborators with the former regime, and as racketeers and smugglers who had thrown in their lot with BANU-NP. The social and the political power of the independent peasantry had finally been destroyed.

In Bulgaria in the late 1940s and early 1950, as in the Soviet Union in the 1930s, the creation of a heavy industrial base and the collectivization of agriculture were inextricably linked to bursts of ferocious and at times seemingly irrational political persecution. The reason for this, in both cases, was that the huge economic and social upheavals produced tensions which the leadership believed could be contained only by extreme measures. The fyps demanded gargantuan economic effort but they provided inadequate investment to meet the changed social conditions created by that economic effort. Enforced industrialization combined with collectivization meant rapid urbanization but if this created the labour force needed by the new industries the plan did not allocate enough funds to provide adequate schooling, medical care, recreational facilities, and above all housing. Furthermore, the raw, young, and inexperienced management cadres drafted in to staff the new industries were, like the huge bureaucracies which ran them, frequently inadequate to their tasks, and maladministration added to the social distress felt by many.

If there were similarities between the Soviet Union in the 1930s and Bulgaria in the late 1940s there were also differences. Bulgaria did not have the resources on which a heavy industrial base could rationally be built. It had almost no deposits of ferrous ores, it did not possess any substantial reserves of fossil fuels, and its topography did not make hydro-electricity an easy alternative source of energy. It therefore became dependent on the Soviet Union for the energy.

The Soviet Union was later to be extremely generous in its energy-pricing policy to Bulgaria, but initially the Soviets were very tough financial masters. In the areas occupied by the Red Army the Kremlin insisted that it had the right to take as reparation any industrial facilities which had been used to promote the enemy war effort, an understandable claim given the damage the Axis forces had inflicted upon the Soviet Union. But Bulgaria had not participated in the war against the Soviet Union, and the definition for assessing reparations claims was so wide that almost any industrial enterprise might come within it, and many suspected that Soviet exactions had gone even beyond these extensive boundaries. Even if they had not the Soviets used this facility to its fullest extent. In September 1944 a number of German Reichsbahn locomotives and wagons had been in Bulgaria and these had passed to the Soviets as war booty; in 1946 the Soviets sold these items to Bulgaria for 2,000 million leva.[4] And although the Soviets seized German and Italian concerns, they did not take responsibilities for their liabilities. Such measures were naturally resented in Bulgaria. So too were the five Soviet-Bulgarian so-called 'joint stock companies' established for lead and zinc processing, uranium extraction, the construction industry, shipbuilding, and commercial aviation; the structure of these concerns gave real control to the Soviets. Most unpopular of all, however, were the trading practices the Soviet Union imposed on Bulgaria and the rest of eastern Europe. An agreement signed in Moscow in July 1947 placed Bulgarian foreign trade under virtual Soviet control and provided for a barter deal under which Bulgaria would trade products such as rose oil and tobacco for Soviet cotton, rubber, railway equipment, motor vehicles, and agricultural machinery. To the dismay of many Bulgarians the agreement did not end the practice, adopted by the Soviet Union in 1944, by which the goods it took from Bulgaria were valued at 1939 prices whilst those it exported were assessed at the much higher current prices. This meant that the Soviets in 1945 had purchased Bulgarian rose oil at $110 per kilo and sold it on the world market at $1,200 per kilo. Many in Bulgaria, and elsewhere in eastern Europe, thought the Soviets were pursuing policies reminiscent of those once adopted by western European states towards their colonial possessions.

2. THE TERROR AND THE STALINIST PURGES

The tensions caused by collectivization, industrialization, and urbanization, and aggravated by Soviet discriminatory financial policies, could find expression in one of three outlets: religious bodies; institutions which had connections with centres outside the Soviet bloc; and domestic political organizations, of which there was now only one with any real authority or power, the BCP. In the late 1940s and early 1950s a series of purges ensured that all three outlets for discontent were closed off.

The most powerful of the religious bodies, the Bulgarian Orthodox Church, was relatively easily muzzled. Immediately after the war the

---

[4] Magarditsch A. Hatschikjan, *Tradition und Neuorientierung in bulgarischen Aussenpolitik, 1944–1948; Die 'nationale Aussenpolitik' der bulgarischen Arbeiterpartei (Kommunisten)*, Südosteuropäische Arbeiten 86 (Munich: R. Oldenbourg, 1986), 315, n. 125.

Church had been left a considerable degree of freedom, not least because the FF government still needed the cooperation of the ecclesiastical hierarchy. It had taken advantage of this in 1945 to repair the breach with the Oecumenical Patriarchate in Istanbul; the schism of 1872 was finally overcome. The *modus vivendi* between Church and state was partly the result of the pro-regime pronouncements of the then head of the Church, Metropolitan Stefan of Sofia, and of the Church's support in the referendum on the monarchy. But there was friction as well as cooperation. The Church bitterly resented a decree of May 1945 making civil marriage obligatory, and from January 1946 it joined battle with the government over the ever sensitive question of religious education. In May 1947, on the thousandth anniversary of the death of Ivan Rilski, however, Dimitrov told the Church that it had to be a progressive, republican church, fully supportive of the civilian power; it should, he said, learn from the example of the Russian Church.

The government's attitude hardened further after the referendum on the monarchy, the peace treaty, and the elimination of Petkov. The Dimitrov constitution enacted the separation of Church and state and there were further encroachments on the Church's right to raise revenue and to train priests. On 18 November 1948 the BCP politburo resolved to remove Metropolitan Stefan to Banya in the Blagoevgrad region, also deciding that if he refused 'he would be taken there with the assistance of the appropriate administrative organs'.[5] Stefan resigned in December and was sent to a monastery. He was accused of being a British spy, one of his sins in the eyes of the authorities being that he had wished to attend the Lambeth conference. After Stefan's removal priests were 'invited' to join a newly formed Union of Bulgarian Priests; most of those who declined were sent to a labour camp. In February 1949 a new law on religious denominations completely subjugated all religious bodies to the civil power. The Bulgarian Orthodox Church was recognized as 'the traditional church of the Bulgarian people' but church finances and appointments were now to be subjected to lay scrutiny, the pulpit was not to be used for political purposes, and the Church was to be subordinated to 'the will of the people'. In 1951 the status of the Church was raised to that of a Patriarchate but if this enhanced the status of the head of the Bulgarian Orthodox Church it also severed

---

[5] Daniela Kalkandjieva, *Bŭlgarskata pravoslavna tsŭrkva i dŭrzhavata, 1944–1953* (Sofia: Albatros, 1997), 236.

the last remaining link between that Church and the Oecumenical Patriarchate in Istanbul. In 1953 Metropolitan Kiril of Plovdiv was elected Bulgarian Patriarch and further reforms were introduced to strengthen the power of the lay elements within the ecclesiastical administration.

The chief target of the February 1949 law on religious denominations had been the non-Orthodox Churches. They were by now the most influential organizations which still had connections with the non-Soviet world, and as such they were the most important of the second of the three possible outlets for internal discontent. With the cold war entering one of its most intense phases and with eastern Europe convulsed by the sudden expulsion of Yugoslavia from the communist fold in June 1948, Dimitrov and his colleagues were more than ever wary of such links to the world outside the Soviet bloc. Accordingly, the Roman Catholic Church in Bulgaria was greatly weakened by the communists' refusal to allow the newly appointed apostolic delegate to take up his office. In the early 1950s further pressure was exerted. In September 1952 the leading Catholic prelate in Bulgaria, the bishop of Nevrokop, was put on trial accused of spying for the Vatican and for France; with him in the dock were twenty-seven Catholic priests and twelve prominent Catholic lay figures. The bishop and three others were sentenced to death. Roman Catholicism in Bulgaria had been completely emasculated.

The charitable institutions of the Protestant Churches had been sequestrated in 1948 and after the legislation of February 1949 the churches themselves were dissolved. Those churches, though never strong numerically, had made a significant contribution to the Bulgarian nation, particularly in education, and Georgi Dimitrov himself had been brought up in a Protestant village. These Churches therefore had to be discredited as well as disabled. To achieve this fifteen prominent Protestant pastors were arrested early in 1949 and subjected to show trials in which they confessed pitifully to having conspired with Petkov and to being agents of Britain, the United States, or the renegade and revisionist Tito.

The show trial was about to become a prominent feature of Bulgarian public life as the regime turned its attention to the third and by far the most important and powerful of the three possible outlets for popular discontent: the communist party itself. By 1948 the communists had effectively rendered all other political parties impotent. If unrest were to find a political outlet it could therefore find it only through the communist party. Furthermore, the party had been founded by those who wished to end inequalities and social suffering and its older members at least might be expected to turn a sympathetic ear to the cries of those enduring social pain. The party, however, had the historic task of pushing through the policies which were causing that pain and in these circumstances the party had to be hardened to a new task; if there were elements in the party which were not tough enough for that new task they would have to be removed. And to justify so unthinkable a policy as the removal of established, long-time party members it had to be shown that even the most trusted elements were liable to corruption and susceptible to the wiles of the enemy. Eastern Europe was entering the grotesque era of the purges.

The chief victim of the Bulgarian purges was Traĭcho Kostov. Kostov had been a communist *aktiv* before the war and had been imprisoned during it; he had jumped out of his cell window in an attempt to avoid further torture but had been recaptured and then sentenced to death; his sentence was commuted to life imprisonment by King Boris. Kostov had therefore spent relatively little time in the Soviet Union, which helped to make him more popular than a number of those who had, among them Dimitrov himself, his heir apparent Vasil Kolarov, and his son-in-law, Vŭlko Chervenkov. Kostov's relative inexperience of Moscow mores also made him less inhibited when it came to assessing Soviet conduct, and he had voiced criticism of Soviet economic policies towards Bulgaria. This the Soviets knew and it was their influence which prevented Kostov from being elected to the politburo. He was, however, appointed as deputy minister president and chairman of the CC's economic and financial secretariat. From these posts he was suddenly removed in March 1949 to be made director of the National Library. In December of the same year he, together with ten other prominent party figures, was brought to trial on a number of wide-ranging and improbable charges. The trial was broadcast live on state radio, until, that is, Kostov withdrew his confession claiming that it had been extracted under torture. He was taken away for further treatment and the following day restated his confession. He was sentenced to death on 14 December and executed two days later.

The Kostov trial was a defining moment in the entrenchment of the BCP's power. In part it helped solve what had become an embarrassing problem over the succession to the party leadership. Dimitrov, for long in poor health, had died in Moscow on 2 July and his assumed successor,

Kolarov, was also far from well and was to die in January 1950. Kostov would be a popular successor at home but would not be acceptable in Moscow, whose wishes in such matters could not be gainsaid. The removal of Kostov therefore avoided complications with Stalin and left the way open for Dimitrov to be succeeded by Chervenkov. The timing of the trial was also determined by the fact that on 18 December 1949 Bulgaria was to hold its first elections since the adoption of the Dimitrov constitution. Perhaps the trial was meant to remind the doubters that if the mightiest in the land could be humiliated and degraded there was little point in raising an opposing voice in the polling booth, though such a message was hardly necessary; 97.66 per cent of the 98.89 per cent of the electorate who cast their votes did so for the FF.

There were more important factors than the bogus election behind Kostov's trial. Amongst the charges laid against him was that of conspiring with the external enemies of the Bulgarian regime. These included, as with the Protestant pastors, the American and British intelligence services, and Tito; for a prominent communist association with the heretic was far more compromising than conspiring with the infidel. Behind this lay the complicated problem of the BCP leadership's policy over Macedonia.

After the signature of the Paris peace treaty Bulgaria enjoyed greater freedom of diplomatic action and in August in the Slovene town of Bled signed an agreement on cooperation with Yugoslavia. The Bled agreement provided for the abolition of customs dues, closer economic cooperation, and the reduction in formalities at the borders between the two states. There was also to be cooperation to prevent incursions by anti-communist forces from Greece, and Belgrade agreed to forgo the $24 million reparations from Bulgaria awarded it by the Paris treaty. In the same month that the Bled agreement was signed the Bulgarian parliament enacted a law which seemed to settle the question of Pirin Macedonia. The Macedonian language and Macedonian history were now to be taught in the area's schools, and the Bulgarian government was to pay for eighty-seven teachers from the PRM to come to Pirin for three years to provide the teaching for the new language classes. A Macedonian Theatre was also to be opened in Gorna Djumaya with the help of the National Theatre in Skopje. The new theatre opened in November, the month in which Tito paid a visit to Bulgaria to sign the final treaty of friendship and cooperation between Bulgaria and Yugoslavia.

Friendship and cooperation did not last long. They were one of the first victims of the split between Tito and Stalin in 1948. The split meant that Bulgaria was now isolated from all other Balkan states except Albania, but for most Bulgarians this disadvantage was more than offset by the fact that the breach between Moscow and Belgrade enabled the Bulgarian communists to reverse their policy on Macedonia.

The Macedonian question had been one reason for the Tito–Stalin split. Perhaps because he was ill Dimitrov had not kept Stalin fully informed of the developing ties between Bulgaria and Yugoslavia. In January 1948 he complicated the situation further by speaking to a journalist of a future federation which would include not merely Bulgaria and Yugoslavia, but also all the other states of Soviet-dominated Europe and Greece. Stalin was furious. He intended to abide by the percentage agreements and leave Greece in western hands, and feared that any suggestion that he might not do so would intensify anti-Soviet sentiment in the United States and western Europe. And the United States must not be provoked whilst it enjoyed a nuclear monopoly. The Bulgarian and Yugoslav leaders were summoned to Moscow, and though Tito himself refused to go Dimitrov attended and meekly accepted Stalin's demand that no foreign policy initiative could be undertaken without first consulting the Kremlin.

The breach between Tito and Stalin served the Bulgarian communists well. In the first place it enabled them to abandon their intensely unpopular policy over Pirin Macedonia. It also enabled them to argue that closer relations with the Soviet Union were more than ever necessary to defend Bulgaria from Yugoslavia's reckless and assertive young leaders; old-fashioned nationalism could now be married to the new proletarian ideology. Nevertheless, the party had been embarrassed by the fiasco over Yugoslavia and Pirin Macedonia, and was therefore on the lookout for a scapegoat. Kostov, who enjoyed some popularity even outside the party, could be blamed for policies which had sanctioned the alienation of Bulgarian territory. It was a common feature of the stalinist show trials that the victims would be blamed for policies they had opposed and which had been espoused by those who were about to destroy them.

If the accusations levied against Kostov made much of his alleged foreign links his trial, like all show trials, was intended mainly to influence domestic affairs. It was meant to stiffen party discipline and was one of the principal justifications for the thoroughgoing purge of the party ranks which had already been set in train. The number of people sent to labour camps per month reached a record high of 4,500 in September, that is *before* the Kostov trial had begun. After the trial a CC plenum in January 1950 ordered the party to learn the lessons of the dangers of 'the enemy with a party card' and 'the enemy in a communist mask'; it also ordered that party activists had to be 'as pure as the lakes at Rila'.[6] Between December 1948 and the end of 1951 the party shed some 100,000 men and women, or around 22 per cent of its former membership of 460,000.

As with all communist parties in the Soviet bloc, that in Bulgaria had grown rapidly since the end of the war. Before September 1944 there had been around 15,000 party members in Bulgaria but with the accession of the FF to power numbers increased exponentially. In the process the communists' characteristic tight discipline and organization were diluted, the Plovdiv party secretary admitting in the spring of 1945, for example, that he did not know whether his branch had 5,000 or 15,000 members.[7] Ideological purity could not be maintained in these circumstances, nor could careerists be excluded. But it was not merely the Johnny-come-lately communists who suffered in the purges. Those not tough enough to push through the new policies whatever their social consequences had to go, because what the party now demanded was not loyalty to leninist ideals but obedience to stalinist practices. Many old party members could not pass this test and suffered accordingly; amongst those who fell were six members of the politburo, thirteen of the CC, and ten ministers. Two groups much at risk were those who had been associated with the extreme left of the party in the 1930s, and, reflecting Stalin's fear of the outside world, those who had extensive experience of life beyond Bulgaria or the Soviet Union, be it in the Spanish civil war, via domicile abroad, or even through marriage to a foreigner. The forces of law and order had to be made reliable and therefore in October 1949 the upper echelons of the army were purged and in May of the following year the security police were subjected to similar treatment. The purges, at least at the upper level, were managed by Soviet advisers attached to the ministry of the interior and the relevant police organizations.

Whilst the BCP was deprived of more than one in five of its members the institutions of state and society experienced purges every bit as savage, with non-party members suffering equally with those associated with

---

[6] Niko Yahiel, *Todor Zhivkov i lichnata vlast; spomeni, dokumenti, analizi* (Sofia: M 8 M, 1997), 28. [7] Dimitrov, 'Failure of Democracy', 154.

the BCP. In 1948 there had been a call for increased vigilance and the authorities soon began deporting entire families from the larger towns and the frontier regions; the deported were accused of being 'betrayers of their country', 'enemies of the people's power', or 'helpers of bandits'; by September 1953 when the practice was ended 6,626 families had been 'resettled'.[8] The victims were former activists in non-communist parties or the inter-war right-wing organizations, members of the industrial and commercial bourgeoisie, and the small, anti-socialist intelligentsia. Again amongst the most vulnerable were those with connections with the outside world. Association with the western embassies was particularly dangerous, particularly after February 1950 when a former translator at the US embassy in Sofia confessed in court to espionage for the Americans; as a result of allegations he made against the US minister in Sofia, Washington broke off diplomatic relations with Bulgaria. In 1953 draconian laws were introduced for the punishment of those attempting to flee abroad; these laws included provision for exacting revenge on the relatives of anyone who succeeded in escaping.

3. VŬLKO CHERVENKOV AND THE SOVIETIZATION OF BULGARIA, 1949–1953

During the purges the domination over the party of Chervenkov, 'Bulgaria's little Stalin', was unchallenged, and he used his power to fashion Bulgaria even more closely after the Soviet model. Dimitrov had once proclaimed that 'for the Bulgarian people friendship with the Soviet Union is just as necessary for life as the air and sun is for any living creature',[9] and his successor was no less fulsome in his devotion to the motherland of socialism and its masters referring to 'the gratitude, love and boundless devotion felt by the Bulgarian party and the entire Bulgarian people for the fraternal Soviet peoples, the party of Lenin and Stalin, great in wisdom and strength—and the teacher and inspired leader, Comrade Stalin.'[10]

---

[8] Evgeniya Kalinova and Iskra Baeva, *Bŭlgarskite prehodi 1944–1999* (Sofia: Tilia, 2000), 55.

[9] Cited in L. A. D. Dellin (ed.), *Bulgaria*, published for the Mid-European Studies Center of the Free Europe Committee, Inc. (New York: Frederick A. Praeger 1957), 227.

[10] Cited in François Fejtö, *A History of the People's Democracies: Eastern Europe Since Stalin*, trans. Daniel Weissbort (London: Pall Mall, 1971), 4.

Under Chervenkov's rule almost all national institutions were reformed to bring them closer to their parallels in the Soviet Union. The army, in a situation reminiscent of that after 1878, had over 400 foreign officers attached to it, but there was no Alexander of Battenberg or Stambolov to resist russianization in Chervenkov's brave new world; the army's command structure, its methods of training, its weapons, and its uniforms were all thoroughly sovietized. In education and culture there was rapid and sometimes brutal progress towards fulfilling the fifth congress's demand that marxism-leninism must dominate all spheres of science and culture, the controlling body here being the committee for science, art, and culture established in 1948 and headed by Chervenkov himself. 'You have to understand', he told members of the artists' associations, 'that the party will lead on the cultural front, as it will on all the other fronts...'[11] Thus socialist realism reigned supreme, stalinist architecture dominated the rebuilding and expansion of the cities, Soviet films and books swamped the market, and even the alphabet was brought closer to the Russian by the elimination of two purely Bulgarian letters. In scientific research the new attitudes meant that genetics and cybernetics were written off as 'reactionary' whilst the concentration on applied science led to a neglect of fundamental research.

Higher education had been under communist pressure since late 1944 when decrees were passed allowing for the sacking of teachers at all levels if they were suspected of political unreliability. In 1947 a law on higher education required all students, whatever their speciality, to study Russian, one western language, and philosophy, the latter meaning dialectical and historical materialism. The law also required the annual election of deans and rectors, and much to the concern of the opposition in the sŭbranie, allowed for the expulsion of staff and the exclusion of students for 'fascist' and 'anti-popular' activities. Higher education was then included in the remit of the committee for science, art, and culture, thus placing it directly under the control of the party boss. In September 1948 the GNA passed a second law on higher education which 'completely eliminated the autonomy of higher educational institutions and placed their activity under state control'. All such institutions were told that they had 'to develop Bulgarian national culture in the spirit of

[11] Dellin, *Bulgaria*, 65.

socialism'.[12] This went to such lengths that soon students would sit their examinations under slogans such as 'Every examination taken a blow against fascism!' From the beginning of the 1950 academic year the number of students from proletarian and peasant backgrounds was also increased substantially; as is usual in such exercises this was done irrespective of ability.

Between 1952 and 1954 all stages of education were reformed to follow the Soviet pattern. Soviet textbooks were used for many subjects, the school year was divided into four terms, medals and rewards were introduced for conspicuous success, and the five-grade Soviet marking system was introduced.

Soviet practices also became widespread in the economy. In the burgeoning factories and construction sites payment by piecework was introduced as was the system of work norms with much-publicized rewards for those who conspicuously over-fulfilled them. These practices were not popular amongst the workers but they were not as hated as another Soviet import, the 'voluntary shifts', 'Lenin Saturdays', and other devices by which men and women were virtually forced to work for no pay. Some use was also made of forced labour by which prisoners, many of them purge victims, were required to work as virtual slaves, though in Bulgaria there were no grandiose projects similar to the Danube–Black Sea canal in Romania.

In trading relations the Soviet Union and the other socialist states assumed a position of total dominance. By 1951 the Soviet bloc provided 92.92 per cent of Bulgaria's imports and accounted for 93.11 per cent of its exports. Bulgaria also copied the Soviet example by declaring that its first fyp had been completed one year ahead of schedule, Bulgaria being the only east European state to make this claim. In the industrial sector the claim had some justification with probably four-fifths of the planned targets being achieved.

In agriculture it was a very different story. Here the actual increase in production was a mere 11 per cent compared with a plan target of 59 per cent with returns declining by an average of 0.9 per cent per annum between 1949 and 1952. The problem lay in collectivization and the resistance to it. Although more households had joined the TKZSs in

---

[12] Bozhidar Doĭchinov, 'Promeni v strukturata na visheto obrazovanie v Bŭlgariya (9 Septemvri 1944–1948g)', *Istoricheski Pregled*, 47/1 (1991), 43–55, quotations on 55.

1949 than in any previous year, by the end of that year the collectives included only 11.3 per cent of the total arable area, and this despite increased legal pressures on the independent peasantry. Further pressure was applied in the early 1950s. In 1950 sale of land from one private farmer to another was banned; the only legal transfer was now from the individual holder to the collective. These measures, together with continuing financial pressure on the independent farmer, forced a million households into the collectives in both 1950 and 1951. Collectivization had become inescapable but the inevitable was not always accepted passively. The peasants resisted in every way they could. Many slaughtered their cattle and burnt their crops rather than hand them over to the collectives or to the state requisitioning authorities. In some areas the peasants resorted to armed resistance, the most serious clashes taking place in the Vidin and Kula regions of north-western Bulgaria. The resistance was repressed in savage fashion but it nevertheless had a huge impact on agricultural production.

4. THE 'NEW COURSE' IN BULGARIA, 1953–1956

In the early 1950s discontent was not confined to the rural areas. The death of Stalin on 3 March 1953 produced expectations of change and less fear of expressing discontent. Amongst the first workers in the Soviet bloc to demonstrate openly were those in Plovdiv's tobacco industry who came out onto the streets in May with demands that new work schedules be rescinded. Spontaneous action by workers could not be tolerated but in Moscow Stalin's heirs were insisting that all ruling parties adopt the so-called 'new course' which would relax the terror, separate the party from the state, institute 'collective leadership' in the party, allow more investment in consumer industry and agriculture, increase social and welfare benefits, and adopt a more accommodating attitude in some matters of foreign policy.

In one respect of the latter Bulgaria was already leading the way and the death of Stalin enabled it to secure Soviet approval of its plan to seek a restoration of relations with Greece, broken off in 1941 and made tense in 1952 by an exchange of artillery fire. By the end of 1953 the two Balkan states had settled a number of border disputes and signed a limited commercial agreement but plans to open full diplomatic relations were frustrated by financial questions arising from Bulgaria's obligation to pay reparations after the second world war and by its counter-claims for property and equipment left in Greece after the Bulgarian withdrawal from the country in 1944. Not until 1964 were these issues solved and diplomatic relations resumed. In a speech on 9 September 1953 Chervenkov stated that he wished to secure better relations not only with Greece but also with the United States, though progress was again slow and it was not until March 1959 that diplomatic relations with Washington were restored.

On the domestic front Chervenkov signalled his acceptance of the new course and promised to increase the production of consumer goods; he also made a number of concessions to agriculture, but to the collectivized sector not the independent farmers. The new course also brought about the recall of most of the Soviet advisers who had dominated much of the Bulgarian administration since 1948 if not before, and in 1954 the five joint-stock companies were transferred to Bulgarian ownership. The new course also involved scaling down the terror and in June 1953 all but 'those most dangerous to the social order' were released from the camps, the last and largest of which, that at Belene, was closed in September.

When it came to the distribution of political power Chervenkov was more reluctant to follow the new course. The latter required that the leadership of the party and government should be separated. At the BCP's sixth congress in March 1954 Chervenkov therefore announced that he would relinquish his post as head of the BCP, choosing to retain leadership of the government rather than the party. Chervenkov's former post of secretary-general of the CC was abolished and replaced by a secretariat of three, though of these the first secretary was in effect the leader of the party. The post of first secretary went to a self-effacing but efficient apparatchik named Todor Zhivkov. He was to remain in that post until 1989, outlasting all other contemporary heads of party. As Zhivkov later admitted, however, until April 1956 he was head of the party in name only as Chervenkov continued to take all major decisions.

Chervenkov's authority was undermined by the Soviet leaders, and more specifically by Nikita Khrushchev. Although Chervenkov had expressed a willingness to improve relations with Yugoslavia he had not expected the admission by the Soviet leader in May 1955 that the breach of 1948 had been the fault of the Soviet Union. Chervenkov, like most other east European leaders of the day, owed his power to the elimination of alleged titoists such as Kostov; if Tito had been innocent, Kostov had not been guilty, and Chervenkov's legitimacy was thereby diminished if not destroyed. In February 1956 came another blow when Khrushchev revealed to the twentieth congress of the Communist Party of the Soviet Union (CPSU) that Stalin had committed a number of 'errors', one of which had been to allow the 'cult of personality' to dominate the party.

5. THE APRIL PLENUM 1956

When a BCP CC plenum met from 2 to 6 April 1956 to consider party strategy in the light of the twentieth party congress in Moscow, it was soon clear that Chervenkov's position was threatened by Khrushchev's assault upon Stalin and stalinism. The Bulgarian plenum dutifully condemned the cult of personality which, it decided, had grown up around Chervenkov, and called for collective leadership in the future. On 17 April Chervenkov submitted his resignation as minister president.

After the plenum delegates were ordered to explain matters to the local organizations. It was a lively affair with 'questions and criticism raining down'[13] with most of them focusing on the cult of personality and the distortions it caused; in one meeting in the Academy of Sciences a leading academician compared Stalin's regime to that of Mussolini. Closely allied to the question of the cult was that of the purges. In a speech to Sofia party activists a few days after the plenum Zhivkov admitted that 'innocent comrades were accused and unjustly punished', but the question was not resolved until another plenum was convened in September 1956. It met in some tension because it brought together the purgers and some of their victims who had recently been released from the labour camps. The latter wanted full rehabilitation for all, but this far the leadership, so many of whose members were themselves purgers, would not go. The charges against Kostov and the other prominenti were dropped and the sentences annulled, but they were still held to have committed errors, particularly on the national question. Other victims, including the veterans of the Spanish civil war, were fully and immediately rehabilitated.

[13] Yahiel, *Lichnata vlast*, 75.

The report and the protocols of the April plenum were kept in a safe which needed nine keys to open it and not even a summary of the proceedings was made public until 1981 with the full details not being revealed to the general public until after the collapse of the communist regime. But if its proceedings were kept secret the April meeting was nevertheless a turning point in post-war Bulgarian history. It opened the way, for a while at least, towards a relaxation in the arts, for open discussion of marxist theories, and for objective science—Lysenko, for example, was ditched. And even if the scope for discussion and free expression would later fluctuate according to the political climate, there was never a return to the reign of terror, political arrests became reactive rather than proactive, and if Todor Zhivkov was to establish, like Ferdinand before him, a 'personal regime', it fell short of the cult of personality which Chervenkov had attempted to build around himself. Its rejection of the cult of personality and of departures from the party's 'traditional and tried methods of work' were the core of the so-called 'April line' which was to remain the BCP's basic strategy from April 1956 until the summer of 1987.

The April line meant the relaxation but not the end of party control. This was a lesson soon learned by the Bulgarian intelligentsia. Even before the twentieth congress of the CPSU there had been stirrings. After February 1956 a new generation of poets, the so-called 'second mobilization' emerged, and satirical journalism was reborn, particularly in the weekly *Stürshel* (Hornet). Even staid, establishment journals such as *Literaturen Front* (Literary Front) and *Otechestven Front* (Fatherland Front) became more lively, the former at one point even advocating that education should have a religious component.[14] But there were limits to what could be allowed. In May 1956 Vladimir Topencharov, editor of *Otechestven Front* and a brother-in-law of Traïcho Kostov, was forced to resign as editor and as president of the Bulgarian Union of Journalists after publishing an editorial arguing that Bulgarian journalism had been made lacklustre through fear. The Polish and Hungarian upheavals of the second half of 1956 then brought an all-round tightening of discipline. In November over 500 party members were arrested whilst in the following month the police were given the power to detain 'politically dangerous

---

[14] Dimitǔr Dimitrov (ed.), *Sǔvetska Bǔlgariya prez tri britanski mandata* (London: BBC, 1994), 13.

figures' and the camp at Belene was reopened. In February 1957 Chervenkov was brought back into the government as minister for education and culture. The 'thaw' in Bulgarian literature had ended.

There had been little danger of 'Hungarian events' in Bulgaria where there was no equivalent of the fierce anti-russianism which fired many Hungarians; nevertheless, the tough measures taken against the intelligentsia and the 'Hungarian prisoners' showed Moscow that the Bulgarian leadership was determined to maintain order.

6. ZHIVKOV VERSUS YUGOV, 1956–1962

Collective leadership in eastern Europe's ruling communist parties quickly developed into a struggle between the individuals involved. In Bulgaria Zhivkov's growing strength was based on his tightening hold on the party apparatus and his increasingly close ties with the man who was to emerge on top in the Kremlin, Nikita Khrushchev.

In 1957 Zhivkov removed from the Bulgarian leadership three potential rivals in what was obviously an imitation of Khrushchev's attack on the 'anti-party group' in Moscow. This increased Zhivkov's power but that power was not yet uncontested. In the summer of 1960 seven party members who had been *aktiv* before 1944 wrote to the CC criticizing the leadership's economic and political policies. There were also, they said, deformations in the political sector. At a plenum on 3 March 1961 the seven were accused of titoist revisionism, vilified, deprived of their jobs and their residences, and sent to settlements for anti-social, criminal recidivists. Zhivkov was still enraged when the letter was made public in 1994. The removal of the offending seven, however, still did not leave Zhivkov without rivals.

The principal one was Anton Yugov, Chervenkov's successor as minister president. Zhivkov had greater influence in the party, an influence which he bolstered in 1959 when he founded the committee for active fighters against fascism and capitalism in Bulgaria, a relatively small and highly privileged group devoted to Zhivkov. On the other hand, Yugov had far more experience of the non-agrarian sector of the economy, and the increasingly authoritarian direction the party was moving in after the suppression of the Hungarian revolution appeared to strengthen Yugov rather than Zhivkov. Yugov had earned a reputation for toughness in the period 1944 to 1948 and although he retreated into the shadows during and after the Kostov trial he had been brought back into the limelight to deal with the Plovdiv tobacco workers in 1953. The contest between Zhivkov and Yugov was to last from 1957 to 1962.

These years were dominated by economic issues. At the end of 1957 Zhivkov told the fifth national congress of TKZSs that full collectivization had been achieved, making Bulgaria the first state after the Soviet Union to reach this goal. In the same year Bulgaria also became the first state in eastern Europe to grant pensions and other welfare benefits to collective farmworkers. At the same time agricultural wages were increased. But the Bulgarian countryside was not to be allowed to rest undisturbed in its newly collectivized state. Late in 1958 a further upheaval began when it was decided that the country's 3,400 TKZSs should be merged into 932 units. These huge new units—their average size was 4,200 hectares—were created in order to bring about economies of scale. A further part of the 1958 reforms insisted that all bureaucrats, both in the party and the state, must spend forty days per year working in field or factory to prevent them from losing touch with the working masses.

The amalgamation of the collectives was intended to help facilitate the programme put forward in the so-called 'Zhivkov Theses' published in January 1959. This extraordinary scheme called for a fourfold increase in industrial production by 1965 and a trebling of agricultural output within a year. It also planned to create 400,000 new jobs by the end of 1962 and thus put an end to the prevailing practice by which Bulgaria's surplus labour was absorbed by migration to the Soviet Union. Only in the latter objective was the scheme successful. Its projected increases in production were little short of lunatic. Neither Bulgarian industry nor agriculture had the technology for such rapid expansion, and credit to finance it was either unavailable or hopelessly expensive. By the end of 1960 Zhivkov was insisting that the projected increases were to be not in the volume of production but in the rate of increase; by 1961 the scheme had been virtually abandoned and the third fyp, introduced in 1958, restored. Some commentators believed that Zhivkov had been influenced by contemporary Chinese ideas and the policies of 1959 were therefore sometimes referred to as Bulgaria's 'great leap forward', but in fact most of the ideas in the 'Zhivkov Theses' came from the USSR, not the People's Republic of China.

The influence of the Soviet Union was also felt after October 1961 when, at the twenty-second congress of the CPSU, Khrushchev delivered his second and much fiercer attack upon Stalin. This produced another thaw in Bulgarian literature which allowed the publication of previously banned foreign and dissident writers, including Kafka, T. S. Eliot, and Solzhenytsin, and allowed innovative or critical native writers such as Georgi Markov, Nikola Lankov, and Radoï Ralin more freedom of expression. There was also a noticeable relaxation in censorship of the theatre and the cinema, particularly animated films. Symbolic of the new relaxation was the journal *Literaturni Novini* (Literary News), in which appeared works no one else would publish; it ceased publication in 1964.

Any gain which relaxation on the cultural front might have brought Zhivkov was counterbalanced by food shortages which had become so pressing by the second half of 1962 that the eighth party congress, scheduled for August, had to be postponed. In October rationing of some foodstuffs had to be introduced, and to keep the towns and the army fed an agreement was signed by which Bulgaria was to import 100,000 tons of wheat per annum from Canada for the next three years. That the harvests of 1961 and 1962 had been extremely poor, with production scarcely reaching the level of 1939, was no fault of Zhivkov's but the disruptions brought about by the *folies de grandeur* of his 1959 theses, particularly with regard to agriculture, were. These had so angered the agricultural sector that they had to be balanced by concessions such as increases in purchase prices for a wide range of products, a decrease in the prices of fertilizers, fuel, and other commodities used by the TKZSs, and the introduction of eastern Europe's first minimum wage for collective farm workers. Socialized agriculture in a traditionally agrarian country could not, it seemed, feed the country. And the measures taken to overcome the food crisis were extremely expensive as well as ideologically demeaning. Also, as the party leadership admitted, the concessions to the farmers had to be paid for by 'temporary sacrifices on the part of the urban population and the working class'. The latter was not pleased and there was considerable unrest in the towns where the authorities sought to re-establish their prestige by such measures as clamping down on the black market, not an entirely placatory measure as this was, once again, the only place certain items could be found.

The food crisis embarrassed Zhivkov. He was further weakened, it seemed, when Yugov voiced strong criticism over Khrushchev's policies towards China and Cuba, and over a twenty-year plan for Bulgarian economic development drawn up by Zhivkov with Soviet cooperation. Yugov did not pull his punches when the politburo met before the eighth congress, which was now to convene in November. In the middle of the politburo meeting Zhivkov flew to Moscow to be briefed by Khrushchev on the Cuban crisis. Zhivkov used the meeting to secure Khrushchev's backing against Yugov and when the politburo resumed Yugov was removed and sacked as minister president. At the same time Chervenkov was expelled from the party. The congress accepted the changes without a murmur and Yugov retired into an obscurity from which he emerged in 1984 to be rehabilitated and made a 'hero of socialist labour'.

Before the November events Zhivkov had removed the political police, the *Dŭrzhavna Sigurnost* (DS), from the ministry of the interior, a Yugov stronghold, and had made it an autonomous institution, all of whose important posts were filled with men loyal to him; during the critical politburo meeting which ousted Yugov, one of them sat in an adjacent room holding a pistol and ready to intervene if necessary. After the eighth congress Zhivkov brought two trusted supporters into the politburo and in 1964 sought to extend his power-base, particularly in the countryside, by enhancing the status of BANU. In 1964 Zhivkov made its leader, Georgi Traĭkov, head of state and on 9 September, on the twentieth anniversary of the FF takeover, amnestied a number of petkovists. For the remainder of communist rule in Bulgaria the practice, which had become common by 1964, continued that when the politburo was discussing agricultural questions the head of BANU should attend and members of the BANU leadership frequently appeared in the BCP CC. But, on the other hand, all important matters regarding BANU, even internal ones, were decided by the BCP politburo.

The removal of Yugov meant that when Khrushchev fell Zhivkov had no internal rival who might capitalize on the eclipse of his erstwhile patron. Zhivkov, however, had one more threat to face before his power was absolutely uncontested, and it was one well within Bulgarian historical tradition. A small group of army officers, grouped around General Ivan Todorov, or 'Gorunya' (an old Bulgarian word meaning a strong or resilient tree), decided to stage a coup, believing that after the recent events in the Kremlin Bulgaria too needed a change of leadership; they were perhaps also encouraged by the belief that with Khrushchev out of power Zhivkov was less secure. Gorunya was a humble, former partisan who had been imprisoned before 9 September 1944, and who, like a number of those who joined him, felt dissatisfied both at his own lack of advancement and at the nature of communist party rule under Zhivkov. The conspirators' main political aspiration seems to have been to wean Bulgaria from its overdependence on the Soviet Union. In the context of the early 1960s this led many to assume that the plotters were therefore pro-Chinese, but in fact their objective seems to have been to make Bulgaria into a more independent and individualistic communist state on the lines of Yugoslavia or Romania. Their intention was, like the conspirators of 1886, to use the Sofia garrison as their main base of operations, but whatever plans they had were doomed. The secret police were soon aware of what was afoot and once they had placed a microphone in Gorunya's cap badge they knew every step the plotters were taking. The latter were rounded up on the eve of their intended coup. It was the last serious attempt by the Bulgarian military to intervene in the political arena and was therefore the end of a long and unwholesome tradition. If the attempted coup had many historical precedents, the leniency with which the conspirators were treated did not. Gorunya himself committed suicide to avoid arrest but most of the hundred or more officers sent to prison were released within a few years.

13

The Communists in Power, II. The Rule of Todor Zhivkov, 1965–1989

1. TODOR ZHIVKOV

For almost a quarter of a century after the army plot of 1965 Bulgarian public life was dominated by Todor Zhivkov. Born in Pravets, 100 kilometres from Sofia, on 7 September 1911 in a peasant household which was neither obviously rich nor conspicuously poor, Zhivkov went to Sofia in his early teens where, like Georgi Dimitrov before him, he became a printer. He was soon involved in trade union activities. From 1943 he acted as a liaison officer between the Sofia party cell and the Chavdar partisan brigade, but there have also been accusations that he was a police informer or even a British agent. In 1945 he became a candidate member and in 1949 a full member of the CC. At this time he was also party boss and chairman of the FF and people's committees in Sofia, where his responsibilities included supplying leading party figures with furniture and other properties confiscated from the bourgeoisie. In July 1951 he became a member of the politburo where he specialized in agricultural affairs.

His appointment as first secretary of the CC, or party boss, in 1954 owed much to the fact that he had been Chervenkov's right-hand man in the purges, not least in the persecution of Kostov, and had played the leading role in constructing the 'cult of personality' around 'Bulgaria's little Stalin'. In the long run, another of his strengths was that he was the one person at the highest level of the party for whom no other leading figure felt fear or animosity; no doubt his activities in redistributing the properties of the Sofia bourgeoisie had helped him in this respect. Zhivkov was a dull but efficient apparatchik. In later years he displayed considerable peasant cunning in his management of the party and of its personalities, but he was scarcely considered a giant amongst European communist leaders. A leading Bulgarian communist, Dobri Terpeshev, noted that he was so unremarkable that even in the small Bulgarian party of the past 'there were at least a thousand who were his equal', and Chervenkov dismissed him as 'vapid and stupid'.[1] The British minister in Sofia ended his annual report for 1960 by remarking that Bulgaria had not produced one figure comparable to the leaders of other socialist countries;[2] Enver Hoxha thought Zhivkov 'a worthless person, a third-rate cadre' and 'the prototype of political mediocrity',[3] whilst the Czechoslovak communist Zdenek Mlynář, who moved in the upper echelons of the communist world in the 1960s, thought Zhivkov 'outstanding for his quite exceptional dullness. My years of close contact with many high functionaries had taught me not to have high standards, but observing a living Zhivkov from close up was shocking all the same.'[4]

If no intellectual, Zhivkov knew instinctively how to use and to retain power, though he had no taste for the brutalism of the stalinist terror. For Bulgaria's experience of this he blamed Georgi Dimitrov, whose birthplace he never visited. In 1962 he received alarming reports of conditions in a labour camp set up outside Lovech in 1959; he had that and all other such institutions closed. Those in the upper echelons of the party who fell out of favour were seldom imprisoned, most being given posts abroad or in the trade unions, and the families of those demoted, disgraced, or detained were usually cared for. He was not personally corrupt on the scale of Ceaușescu, Brezhnev, and others, he never acquired his own car, apartment or villa, and the many palaces built for him around the country were built for the leader of the party not Zhivkov personally. He had an easy rapport with ordinary Bulgarians and unlike many of the post-liberation intelligentsia, he knew, valued, and exploited the Bulgarians' love of peasant wit and down-to-earth pragmatism. As party leader he also established a separate office in the CC to deal with the thousands of letters which poured in to him, dealing with the most difficult

---

[1] Petŭr Semerdjiev, *Nishtozhestvo v dospehite na velichie* (Paris: no publisher cited, 1985), 21, 25.   [2] Dimitrov, *Sŭvetska Bŭlgariya*, 88.
[3] Jon Halliday (ed.), *The Artful Albanian: The Memoirs of Enver Hoxha* (London: Chatto & Windus, 1986), 168 and 362, n.19, respectively.
[4] Zdenek Mlynář, *Night Frost in Prague: The End of Humane Socialism*, trans. Paul Wilson (London: Hurst & Co., 1980), 156.

of them himself. His wife, a doctor on whom he greatly relied until her premature death in 1971, also received and answered scores of letters.

If Zhivkov was prepared to listen to the views of ordinary people and party members, he was not prepared to allow nonconformity, at least in public. A poet was expelled from the Writers' Union in 1970 because he refused to sign a telegram condemning the awarding of the Nobel Prize for Literature to Solzhenytsin, and for most of Zhivkov's period in office literature and the arts were required to support the April line and laud its creator.

Zhivkov's rule was consistently authoritarian, frequently unimaginative, and ultimately stultifying, but it was not a rule of terror and until its final stages brought a steady improvement in the standard of living of most Bulgarians.

2. BUILDING SOCIALISM

Increases in material well-being were indicators of progress towards what was the purpose of Zhivkov's and the BCP's power: to build socialism and to progress through 'real existing' or 'mature' socialism to the first stages of communism. This required sustained increases in national wealth which were regularly achieved until the early 1980s. The average annual growth rate in net material product (NMP) for the years 1950 to 1953 was 12.3 per cent; in subsequent five-year periods production continued to increase, though at a lower rate (see table 13.1).

Table 13.1 Percentage average annual growth rate of Net Material Product, 1950–1970

1950–55	12.3
1955–60	9.7
1960–65	6.7
1965–70	8.2
1970–75	7.9
1975–80	6.2
1980–85	3.7
1985–89	3.0

Source: John A. Bristow, *The Bulgarian Economy in Transition*, Studies in Communism in Transition, series editor Ronald J. Hill (Cheltenham: Edward Elgar, 1996), 19.

In terms of increasing the provision of consumer goods and services for the individual citizen there was considerable advance.[5] This was accelerated by a CC plenum in December 1972 which promised more investment in consumer goods and in social services such as education, health, and accommodation. From 1948 to 1952 agricultural production was still only 91 per cent of that for the years 1932–8, in part reflecting the turmoil of collectivization, but by 1956–60 the figure was 119 per cent, in 1966–70 169 per cent, in 1971–5 183 per cent, and for 1976–80 199 per cent. Meat consumption increased from 27 kg per capita in 1956 to 70 kg in 1983; in 1965 there were 8 television sets per 100 households and in 1983 87, whilst in the same years the incidence of private car ownership rose from 2 to 34 per 100 households. In 1956 there were 5.0 hospital beds and 4.8 university students per thousand of the population, figures which had increased to 9.0 and 9.6 respectively by 1983.

The construction of socialism demanded not merely increases in production and in material well-being but a transformation of economic structures and a social reconstruction which would leave industry, the towns, and the proletariat in a dominating position. By the end of the 1960s the Bulgarian regime decided that the economy and society had been sufficiently changed to justify claiming that Bulgaria had entered the socialist stage. The collectivization of agriculture had been completed in the late 1950s and by 1960 the proportion of the labour force involved in agriculture had fallen from the 82.1 per cent of 1948 to 35.6 per cent; and by 1970 the percentage of NMP originating in the industrial sector was 55; in 1948 it had been 23. In the same period the proportion of NMP derived from agriculture had declined from 59 to 17 per cent.

A further indication of the social revolution was the growth in the urban population. In the census of 1946 24.68 per cent of Bulgaria's population had been classified as urban dwellers; by 1965 it had risen to 46.46, and by the next census in 1975 more than half of the country's inhabitants, 57.99 per cent, were living in towns. In 2001 the figure was 69.05 per cent. Between 1946 and 1987 the urban population increased by just over 240 per cent. In 1934 there had been seven towns with more than 30,000 inhabitants; in 1988 there were twenty-eight with more than

---

[5] Figures taken from tables in John R. Lampe, *The Bulgarian Economy in the Twentieth Century* (London: Croom Helm, 1986), 170, 194.

50,000 inhabitants. The population of Sofia had passed the million mark in the 1980s and by 2001 stood at 1,009,507.

Bulgaria's economic reconstruction was not free of some of the failings of the stalinist model. Zhivkov and his advisers still believed that a heavy metallurgical industry was essential for a modern economy and therefore a massive iron and steel complex was built at Kremikovtsi near Sofia despite expert advice that the adjacent deposits of iron ore were inadequate in quality and not suitable for processing in a plant of the type which was being constructed. It opened in November 1963. When the plant did open ore had to be imported from the Soviet Union via Burgas, thus costing huge amounts of money and causing congestion at the port and on the railway between it and the capital.

3. 'MATURE' OR 'REAL EXISTING SOCIALISM' IN BULGARIA

The failings of Kremikovtsi were not admitted in public and in 1971, to mark the attainment of the socialist stage, Bulgaria adopted a new constitution and the BCP a new party programme. The preamble to the constitution stated that it was based on the 1944 socialist revolution and the subsequent development of a socialist society and a people's democracy. Article 1 declared Bulgaria to be 'a socialist state of the working people in town and countryside headed by the working class'. The constitution also guaranteed all citizens the rights to holidays, insurance, free education, and medical care.

The 1971 party programme had little new to say in terms of party discipline or organization, and it reaffirmed that the 'April line' was its guiding principle, but the party had now to adapt to the new stage of 'mature socialism' which was described as 'the highest and concluding development of socialism as a phase in the building of communism'. The party was to create 'a unified socialist society'. This was interpreted to mean bringing about the end of the differences between rural and urban life and physical and mental labour. This would produce a nation entirely working class in its composition and thus the party of the working class, the BCP, would become the party of the entire nation. Perfecting the mature socialist society would require further increases in material wealth but, now that the infrastructure of an industrial society had been built, further development would be intensive rather than extensive, and would concentrate on improving productivity. To achieve this the party and the state would exploit the opportunities offered by 'the scientific-technological revolution' which would be the key to enhanced productivity and greater wealth. Zhivkov had for some time been aware of the importance of advancing technology and for this reason had incorporated into the government both the president of BAN and the head of the Agricultural Academy.

Another aid to increasing productivity was to be more intense specialization within the Soviet bloc. Bulgaria, unlike Romania, had warmly welcomed Comecon plans in the early 1960s for economic specialization within the socialist world. In 1965 an agreement was signed with the Soviet Union by which Bulgaria was to assemble cars and lorries manufactured in the USSR. In the following years similar agreements led to Bulgaria developing shipbuilding, the manufacturing of railway rolling stock, and the construction of commercial vehicles such as fork-lift trucks; by 1975 a third of Bulgaria's industrial output was in transport goods. By the late 1970s country-by-country specialization was also developing in the most modern branches of industry. Under these arrangements Bulgaria began to supply magnetic disks for computers and by the end of the decade was manufacturing computers themselves. In 1981 a Soviet space satellite carried Bulgarian equipment designed not only to measure the ionosphere and the magnetosphere but also to search for archaeological sites in Bulgaria itself.

The close economic links with Comecon, and particularly with the Soviet Union, gave Bulgaria secure markets for its exports which on the open market faced two severe disadvantages. Bulgaria's agricultural produce, despite its generally high quality, was not needed and was therefore discriminated against in the hard-currency markets of the European Economic Community (EEC) and north America, and its industrial exports were of such poor quality that only a regulated, ideologically determined market such as Comecon would accept them. The links with Comecon also gave Bulgaria secure supplies of raw materials and energy. The latter was a crucial factor, making up for Bulgaria's lack of indigenous sources of energy. This the Soviet Union supplied on the most generous of terms until the second half of the 1980s.

Close ties to Comecon did not rule out trade with the west which, as Zhivkov knew, was developing modern technology more rapidly than the socialist bloc. This had been brought home to him in particularly stark fashion when he visited Expo70 in Japan in 1970, that visit being itself part of the reason why the regime laid such emphasis on the scientific-technological revolution.

4. ZHIVKOV ASCENDANT, 1965–1975

Whilst these economic and social changes were being brought about the political system in Bulgaria remained little changed, and Zhivkov's hold on the levers of power did not slacken. Zhivkov, however much he disliked stalinist terror, was an absolute believer in the leninist maxim of the leading role of the party. He was the first east European leader to visit Budapest after the 1956 revolution where he advised the newly installed János Kádár to adopt tough policies, and he was a very early advocate of the use of military force against the Dubček regime in Czechoslovakia in 1968, though in this case mainly because he did not want to lose his position as a close associate of Brezhnev. As the Czechoslovak party moved towards greater relaxation of control the BCP moved in the opposite direction. The FF incorporated the few remaining and utterly innocuous social organizations such as the committee for sobriety into its organization, whilst the party told its members to ensure that they had domination in all committees running blocks of flats or other residences, and in all those concerned with the supply and distribution of food and other essential commodities. Within the party itself a plenum called for 'iron discipline'.

The party had not been mentioned in the Dimitrov constitution but article 1 of that of 1971 recognized it as the 'leading force in society and the state', its task being to mastermind 'the building of a mature socialist society in close cooperation with the Bulgarian Agrarian National Union'. After the twelfth congress in 1981 official statements continued to refer to the 'April line' as the basic strategy of the party but thereafter it was commonplace to add that this line 'was inseparable from the personality and the actions of Comrade Todor Zhivkov'.

The new constitution of 1971 also enhanced Zhivkov's personal authority. It created a new body, the state council, which was to replace the praesidium of the national assembly as the supreme organ of state power. The state council exercised the standard functions of a head of state such as signing treaties, declaring war, etc., but it also had responsibilities for overseeing the administration, responsibilities which in many communist states were left largely in the hands of the party. The state council could also issue decrees when the sŭbranie was not sitting, which was for most of the year. The chairman of the state council was the official head of state and inevitably this post went to Zhivkov. Between 1962 and 1971 the centre of state power had been the ministerial council; after 1971 it was the state council.

Within the upper echelons of the party Zhivkov tolerated little opposition, particularly in his earlier years in power. After the army plot he tightened his grip. He reverted to the practice of the Chervenkov years whereby the affairs of the State Security or DS were dealt with by the politburo and by the party leader in particular. The DS was also told to keep a close watch on all those associated with the CC and, given the misplaced fears of the 1965 plotters' pro-Beijing inclinations, a new unit was created to watch over Chinese and Albanian diplomats. A little later another new department within the DS, the sixth directorate, was established to monitor foreign intelligence activity amongst the intellectuals; its responsibilities soon widened and it became the main body of the political police. Its information went directly to Zhivkov and to Zhivkov alone.

After 1965 Zhivkov further safeguarded his position by ensuring that no potential rival held the same post long enough to build up a solid and dependable body of support, and for this reason he frequently shifted ministers and party leaders from one post to another. This did not preclude occasional purges. In 1977 Boris Velchev was removed from the politburo because he had developed ideas which were too liberal. His removal was followed by a purge in which 38,500 party members were expelled. This was the largest of the purges carried out by Zhivkov but it was not one which included show trials, wide scale imprisonment, or political executions. There was another extensive round of sackings at the top level of the party in 1988.

Zhivkov's domination of the BCP acquired many of the characteristics of the 'personal rule' of Ferdinand earlier in the century. His total control of the armed forces and the police was one, and his frequent moving of ministers and other higher officials served much the same function as Ferdinand's changing of ministers and cabinets. Zhivkov, like Ferdinand, conducted policy on an individual basis or with a few hand-picked cronies and officials. The decision to join in the Warsaw pact invasion of Czechoslovakia in 1968, for example, was taken without reference to the politburo, and discussion of the fatal policy of the attempted assimilation of the Turkish minority in the 1980s was confined to a small coterie of top officials. Many of the major issues in Zhivkov's time were in fact debated not so much in the politburo or the CC, but in meetings over coffee with a few trusted officials or colleagues.

A notable feature of socialism as practised by the BCP under Zhivkov was frequent and often radical experimentation in the economy. The Zhivkov Theses and the chaos they caused in the early 1960s did not act as a deterrent. Zhivkov had followed Khrushchev in drawing up a twenty-year economic strategy which was to usher the country through socialism into the first stages of the transition to communism, and in 1963 discussions began on a set of reforms which were endorsed by a CC plenum in April 1966. These aimed to establish 'a new system of planning and management', to decentralize much of the economy, and to allow greater scope to the profit motive, the lack of the latter being, in Zhivkov's view, one of the main impediments to faster economic growth. Profit was to be encouraged by tying wages and capital accumulation to the performance of the individual enterprise, and enterprises, once they had fulfilled the requirements laid down by the economic plan, were to be allowed to produce what they liked and sell where they wished. Enterprises were also to take a greater role in drawing up their own projects which would then be coordinated with other enterprises in the same economic sector and with the central planning authorities. This 'planning from below' was to be accompanied by a greater degree of democracy in that directors of enterprises were to consult with 'production committees' elected by workers. This latter move smacked of Yugoslav self-management ideas but what wrecked the Bulgarian reform scheme was not this analogy but its closeness to current Czechoslovak practices. In July 1968 a CC plenum called for the 'perfection of centralized planning' and by 1969 most of the reforms had been abandoned.

The 1965 reform scheme had concentrated upon industry but whilst it was being run down far-reaching and much more long-lasting changes were being introduced in agriculture. In 1968 new statutes regulating the TKZSs were introduced. The ground-rent previously paid to farmers for the land they had contributed to the collective was abolished and workers were now to be grouped into permanent brigades which would have some autonomy and would be responsible for assigned plots of land. A much more important reform began in the Vratsa area in 1969. Here seven collectives were amalgamated into a loose federation of 38,700 hectares. In April 1970 this policy was applied throughout Bulgaria and by the end of 1971 the thousand or so TKZSs had been amalgamated into 170 units covering 90 per cent of the country's arable area. They each had at least 6,000 workers and covered between 20,000 and 40,000 hectares incorporating half a dozen or so villages, one of which was designated the administrative headquarters and which was to acquire the features and amenities of a small town.

The purpose of the new units was to bring about specialization in a small number of crops and animals which local conditions particularly favoured, and each unit was expected to produce no more than three major items. There were also plans to link the units with manufacturing industries, or even to site certain processing plants within the new units, hence their name: agro-industrial complexes (AICs). This would help stem the drift to the towns which was placing considerable strain on the housing sector, frequently the Cinderella of communist planning. Not only would the AICs ease social difficulties and bring about economies of scale, the joining of agricultural and industrial activities within the same unit would also foster the amalgamation of town and countryside, of rural and urban labour, and would therefore help bring about 'a unified socialist society'. This was also promoted by the fact that the amalgamation of units into the AICs meant the disappearance of the previous difference between two types of property: the collective and the state farm. The latter were never numerous in Bulgaria but the elimination of the difference between the two forms of property removed an ideological embarrassment, a not unimportant consideration in a socialist society. By the end of the 1970s it was clear the AICs had created as many problems as they had solved and the process of redivision began; by March 1979 the 170 units of 1971 had increased to 338.[6]

Part of the difficulty with the AICs was that the initial increases in production had not been maintained. They were not the only part of Bulgaria's economy showing signs of stagnation by the 1970s, and a new bout of radical reforms was soon introduced, this time under the general title of the new economic mechanism, the NEM. Approved by a CC

[6] Kalinova and Baeva, *Bŭlgarskite prehodi, 1944–1999* (Sofia: Tilia, 2000), 95.

plenum in March 1979 the NEM came into operation at the beginning of 1982. Its purpose was to provide 'a new approach to the management of the economy in the scientific-technological revolution'. Its intention was to increase productivity, improve the lamentable quality of Bulgarian goods and services, and to expand exports and thereby decrease the trade deficit and contain mounting hard-currency indebtedness. The NEM revisited some of the reformist ideas of the 1960s. Decentralization was to be brought about by reducing the scope of the central economic plan, which was now to become much more general, whilst the central economic ministries were to lose the power to supervise individual enterprises, a reform which had the additional advantage of slimming down the economic bureaucracy. A further reduction in the apparatus of economic administration came with the ending of a number of trading monopolies. The NEM also decided that if any higher institution caused economic damage to a lower one the offending body would have to use its own wages fund to compensate the injured party. Further decentralization was to be achieved by the fact that under the new system each enterprise was to receive from the central planning authorities a general guideline rather than a set quota for production and that enterprise was to decide itself, in consultation with its constituent brigades, how the plan could best be fulfilled. The brigades were to be given much more responsibility in both the ordering of the necessary raw materials and in the disposal of the finished product, and they were to retain the profits for investment or for distribution amongst their members. The brigades were to be 'the chief organs of self-management' and through them was to be applied Zhivkov's doctrine that the state was the owner of socialist property but the workers were its managers.

The NEM introduced more democracy into the workplace by making all important posts in the enterprise elected; this was 'mobilization from below'. The NEM was to introduce competition by making enterprises and units within them compete for investment funds and equipment, and those which did not adopt the most up-to-date production methods brought about by the scientific-technological revolution were to be penalized. The profit motive was emphasized by allowing direct links between producer and consumer both at home and abroad; this, it was hoped, would, together with the abolition of the trading monopolies, force Bulgarian producers to have more regard for the quality of their goods. Enterprises which could not satisfy the consumers' demands would face the consequences and they were no longer to count upon government subsidies which under the NEM would be given only in exceptional circumstances and then for a limited period of two years. The NEM also involved a retreat from the big-unit mentality which had pervaded much of Bulgarian economic planning in the Zhivkov era; now the emphasis was to be on the promotion of small and medium-sized enterprises which could more easily adapt to the scientific-technological revolution and to consumer demand, and find western partners for joint enterprise ventures.

The NEM promised much but achieved little, and in the mid- to late 1980s was to give way to a frenetic wave of reforms.

5. ZHIVKOV'S EXTERNAL POLICIES

'What' a Bulgarian teacher asked the class, 'is two plus two': answer, 'three, but with the help of the Soviet Union, four.' As was frequently the case in communist times popular humour encapsulated political reality which could not be expressed explicitly, for dependence on and obedience to Moscow were the most obvious features of Zhivkov's rule.

He had become a close associate of the Soviet ambassador in Sofia in the early 1950s and this had helped him establish a good working relationship with Khrushchev. After the latter's fall Zhivkov was on equally good terms with Brezhnev. This was in no small measure due to Milka Kalinova, who worked in the Bulgarian embassy in Moscow and who became close to both Brezhnev's daughter Galina and his son Yuri, mainly by showering them with expensive presents bought on the budget of the Bulgarian intelligence services. Zhivkov and Brezhnev met frequently, often on the hunting expeditions so beloved of most communist leaders.

In September 1973 Zhivkov stated in public that Bulgaria and the Soviet Union would 'act as a single body, breathing with the same lungs and nourished by the same bloodstream'. Behind the scenes he went even further. In the early 1960s ideas of Comecon specialization and ever greater integration inspired Zhivkov to propose to Khrushchev that Bulgaria should eventually be incorporated into the USSR. The BCP hierarchy expressed some doubts over the scheme, but when Zhivkov insisted that Khrushchev had approved the idea, both the politburo and the CC in Sofia accepted it. Khrushchev's commitment to the scheme was dubious and after his fall from power in October 1964 it receded into the background until revived in modified form by Zhivkov in 1973. His motive for doing this seems to have been to deflect Soviet and internal Bulgarian party criticism from steps Bulgaria had recently taken to achieve closer economic ties with the west. This time Moscow was more receptive. Once again nothing came of the plan, not least because publication of it would have complicated the process of détente which was moving towards its culmination in the Helsinki accords of 1975.

In the conduct of general foreign policy Bulgaria could almost always be relied upon to support the Soviet position, particularly in the important issues such as arms control, Vietnam, the middle east, and Latin America. There were instances where divergences did appear, for example over Zhivkov's proposal that the Balkans should become a nuclear free zone, an idea current in the late 1970s and early 1980s when the ailing Soviet leaders were unable to exert their usual dominance.

For many Bulgarians, not least Zhivkov's own daughter, the closeness of Soviet–Bulgarian relations was demeaning, but it also had its political rationale. For the Soviet Union Bulgaria served a useful purpose. For Moscow the Balkans were of secondary strategic importance when compared to the Warsaw pact's 'northern tier' of the GDR and Poland, but the Soviet Union still needed a reliable partner in the peninsula, and with Greece and Turkey in NATO and the other Balkan socialist states hostile or seemingly unreliable, Bulgaria alone could fulfil this role, in addition to which in the event of war Bulgaria's proximity to the Straits would give it considerable strategic importance. Also, Bulgaria was the only Warsaw pact state, apart from the Soviet Union itself, which had two NATO states as neighbours. In diplomatic terms Bulgaria benefited from the close relationship with and patronage of Moscow, but its main gain was economic. The Soviet Union provided a secure market for goods which would otherwise find no buyers but much more importantly, until the mid-1980s, Bulgaria received Soviet oil and gas at discounted prices. Nor did Moscow object when Bulgaria sold some of this on the world market at current prices in hard currency. This was the lifeline which kept the Bulgarian economy functioning.

Closeness to the Soviet Union did not prevent Bulgaria developing relations with the west. In 1966 Zhivkov paid his first visit to a non-communist European state, de Gaulle's France being suitably anti-American for such an enterprise. Economic links with federal Germany had been developing since the 1950s and full diplomatic relations were established with Bonn in December 1973. Trading ties with Germany, it was hoped, would provide hard currency and the know-how essential for the scientific-technological revolution, and similar considerations had been behind the expansion of trading links with Japan after Zhivkov's visit to the country in 1970. A notable departure in foreign policy came in June 1975 when the Bulgarian party boss was received by Pope Paul VI in the Vatican. Later that year the Sofia regime sanctioned the appointment of a number of Roman Catholic, including Uniate, bishops in Bulgaria and by 1979, for the first time since the 1940s, no Catholic see in Bulgaria was without a bishop.

By the late 1970s the third world had assumed a notable role in Bulgarian foreign policy. Students from Africa, the middle east, and Asia had been attending higher educational institutions in the country since the 1960s, though they were not always well received and in 1965 had staged angry demonstrations in Sofia to protest at their treatment by the authorities and by the population at large. These tensions subsided in later years and there was a growing traffic in the opposite direction. In the early 1980s many Bulgarian doctors, nurses, engineers, and other specialists were working in the third world with over 2,000 Bulgarian doctors and nurses in Libya alone. Zhivkov himself underlined these developing relationships by visiting, between 1978 and 1983, Nigeria, Mozambique, Angola, South Yemen, Vietnam, Laos, Kampuchea, Mexico, Cuba, Iraq, Syria, and Libya. In addition to these visits, he received the heads of state of Iran, Ethiopia, Zambia, Afghanistan, Grenada, the Congo, Guinea, and Algeria.

As the cold war eased after the Cuban crisis, the Zhivkov regime maintained good relations with all the other Balkan states with the exception of pro-China Albania, where distance and indifference rather than hostility characterized the links. Tensions with Greece eased in the 1960s particularly during the rule of the colonels who sought better relations with their communist neighbours, though Sofia did follow the Moscow line in the mid-1970s and frustrate Greek efforts to create a nuclear-free zone in the peninsula, a step which made Zhivkov's later espousal of such a policy all the more remarkable. Relations with Turkey also improved, thanks in part to an agreement in 1969 on the emigration of limited numbers of ethnic Turks from Bulgaria. In 1976 Zhivkov became the first

Bulgarian leader since the second world war to visit Turkey. With Ceauşescu he regularly exchanged visits but there was little else which brought their two countries closer together or drove them further apart; a number of joint economic projects were agreed upon but little came of any of them. With Yugoslavia there was always the Macedonian question to complicate relations. In the 1960s Bulgarian attitudes on this issue hardened with the elimination of 'Macedonian' as an ethnic category in the census of 1965, and with revived and intensified campaigns to insist that two-thirds of the population of Yugoslav Macedonia were ethnic Bulgarians. In the 1970s Bulgaria made propaganda over a series of historic anniversaries concerning Macedonia, and in 1979 the long-serving communist and member of the politburo, Tsola Dragoicheva, angered the Macedonian establishment by claiming in her memoirs that the Yugoslavs had reneged on a promise made during the second world war that no decisions on the future of Macedonia would be made until the end of the conflict. In the 1980s there were further academic disputes and historical celebrations, Yugoslav hackles being raised particularly in 1985 when officers inducted into the Bulgarian army were dubbed 'the Slivnitsa generation'. Despite these spats, however, Zhivkov never allowed the Macedonian issue seriously to threaten his relations with Yugoslavia which in general were correct if not cordial; and he made no attempt to exploit Belgrade's difficulties in Kosovo in 1968 or 1981.

Bulgaria's attempts to increase its links with the west received a number of setbacks in the late 1970s and early 1980s when Bulgaria was implicated in a series of scandals. The most notorious was the killing of Georgi Markov in London in 1977. Markov had once been close to the Bulgarian political hierarchy but had then gone into exile, from where he used western broadcasting stations to spill the beans on the high life enjoyed by those close to Zhivkov. Two weeks after the attack on Markov a similar attempt, using pellets of ricin shot from an umbrella or fountain pen, was made upon another exile, Vladimir Kostov, this time in Paris. Kostov, who survived, had embarrassed the Sofia regime by revealing how close the Bulgarian intelligence services and political police were to their Soviet counterparts. After these incidents came the allegation that the Bulgarian secret service had been involved in the attempt to assassinate Pope John Paul II in May 1981. The post-communist governments of Bulgaria have accepted responsibility for the Markov and Kostov incidents, but have vehemently denied culpability in the case of

John Paul II; their protestations would seem reasonable on the grounds that an organization which could operate with such sophistication when dealing with Markov and Kostov would hardly rely on a volatile Turk armed with a small handgun amidst a crowd of thousands. Other allegations were less easily dismissed. Bulgaria was said to be manufacturing counterfeit whisky and, more seriously, evading sanctions upon South Africa. Even more seriously, the Bulgarian export agency, Kintex, was widely believed to have been involved in the smuggling of drugs and with the money gained thereby purchasing arms for subversive movements in central America, Turkey, and Africa. In July 1982 the United States placed Bulgaria on its list of countries engaging in 'state-sponsored terrorism'.

If conformity with the Soviet Union was the dominant feature of Zhivkov's external policy this did not mean that he was completely without national feelings or pride. In his, albeit self-justificatory memoirs he wrote, 'Everything I have done has been based on the feeling that it was for the good of Bulgaria', and that 'I am proud of my own honest and uncomplicated love for Bulgaria'. For him, he said, 'The voice of the nation is the voice of God.'[7] He also claimed, with some justification, that he had opposed the Soviet Union on educational reform, on economic restructuring, and over Macedonia. He also allowed the making of overtly nationalist films on Khan Asparukh and Boris I, and sanctioned the publication of some works which criticized Russia, including Simeon Radev's great work on the years 1879–86[8] which had long been blacklisted; and in private Zhivkov admitted to an admiration of Stambolov, about whom official historiography was largely silent. Zhivkov's nationalism, however, paled into insignificance beside that of his daughter.

6. THE AMAZING CAREER OF LYUDMILA ZHIVKOVA

Lyudmila Zhivkova was born in 1942 and was therefore a young teenager when her father was made first secretary of the BCP CC. Her ability combined with her privileged status to produce an extraordinary

---

[7] Todor Zhivkov, *Memoari* (Sofia: Abagar, 1997), 650, 696, and 671.
[8] Simeon Radev, *Stroitelite na süvremenna Bülgariya, 1878–1886*, 2 vols. Originally published in 1911 and republished, to the astonishment of Bulgarian historians of the day, in 1973 by Bülgarski pisateli.

personality, and a meteoric rise into the stratosphere of Bulgarian politics. After attending Sofia and Moscow universities she went to St Antony's, Oxford, for a year as a graduate student, and upon her return to Bulgaria rapidly assembled around herself a coterie of admiring intellectuals, artists, and literary figures, most of whom were regular attendees at the meetings she held each Friday evening in her home on Boulevard Tolbukhin, now Boulevard Vasil Levski. In 1971 she was appointed deputy chairperson of the committee for art and culture and four years later became its head. In 1976 she was given extensive power over the press, radio, and television, and in 1980 was put in charge of the CC secretariat for science, culture, and art. She became a member of the politburo in 1979.

Her main concerns were to promote a sense of Bulgarian separateness, to bolster Bulgarian culture, and to increase national self-confidence in that culture. She poured money into the arts and by the early 1980s there was scarcely a regional town without a theatre or an opera company. She saw religion as part of the nation's cultural heritage and therefore she not only wanted to restore Bulgarian churches, monasteries, and shrines, but also drew up plans to train religious activists in lay educational institutions. Her concern for Bulgaria's cultural heritage was not confined to Bulgaria itself. She was anxious to protect and to promote Bulgarian culture abroad, once upbraiding Nicolae Ceauşescu to his face for the neglect of Bulgarian cultural monuments in Romania. More importantly, one of her early successes was to help send the great Thracian treasures from Sofia's Museum of National History for exhibition in Paris, Moscow, Leningrad, Vienna, and London. At home, her emphasis on Bulgarian cultural identity brought about in 1981 a huge celebration of the 1,300th anniversary of the foundation of the first Bulgarian state, and also resulted in the construction, at enormous cost, of the massive NDK in Sofia which, until the late 1980s, bore her name.

Zhivkova also did a great deal of work with and on behalf of children, both in Bulgaria and in the underdeveloped world. This and her championship of Bulgarian separateness made her hugely popular, as was attested by the amount of mail she received, far more than any other member of the politburo.

Yet it was to the intelligentsia that Zhivkova made an especial appeal. Many of them revelled in her assertion of Bulgarian individuality, not least because it balanced what they considered the excessively pro-Soviet attitudes of her father. Also, the 1,300th anniversary celebrations and similar events presented a different image of Bulgaria to that portrayed in the recent international scandals. But for the intelligentsia there was more to Lyudmila than that. She protected those around her who might otherwise have fallen foul of the system; had Zhivkova not protected him, for example, her close adviser Aleksandŭr Fol would have suffered because his father had been an associate of King Boris. Furthermore, she was known to espouse ideas which were unusual in most contexts and utterly bizarre in the communist world. By 1975 she was turning increasingly to mysticism and asceticism, and even the mortification of the flesh. Much to the embarrassment of the party establishment, she visited Baba Vanga, an aged, blind soothsayer in Petrich who enjoyed a huge popular following. In 1978 she went on a long trip to India and Nepal where it was said she went alone into the mountains to live for a few days like Ivan Rilski as a hermit in a cave. There, she told an assistant of her father's, she had learned to meditate and to levitate, and had been in contact with unearthly powers—in other words she had been ' "sanctified" '.[9] Some of her notions were plainly absurd. She believed that Bulgaria would become the cultural centre of the world, and that by 1990 the world would be speaking Bulgarian. As her fascination with mysticism intensified so her language became more opaque; 'think of me as fire' she told her associates. And her behaviour became even more peculiar. She came to believe that her mission in life could best be accomplished with assistance from the great 'enlightened' figures of the past; these included Alexander of Macedon, Napoleon, and Christ himself, and these pre-existing beings were invoked in seances.

Leading figures in the party knew much of this and were naturally suspicious of Zhivkova and questioned her commitment to the party, its policies, and its ideology. They had every reason to be suspicious. In public she did not criticize the Soviet Union but under her influence academic works critical at least of Russia did see the light of day, one of them being an examination of Russian diplomacy in the period from 1879 to 1886.[10] In private she was much less restrained, telling a confidant that, ' "We made a terrible historical mistake when we aligned ourselves with the most uncivilized country in the world" ', and she

---

[9] Kostadin Chakŭrov, *Vtoriya Etazh* (Sofia: Plamŭk, 1990), 154.

[10] It was Elena Statelova, *Diplomatsiyata na knyazhestvo Bŭlgariya 1879–1886* (Sofia: BAN, 1979).

thought Hitler was ' "the offspring of Stalin and his system" '.[11] As for the party, that, in her private words, was no more than 'a funereal procession of people dragging themselves after the catafalque of a moribund political teaching'.[12]

Zhivkova died in July 1981, aged only 39. The official cause of death was cerebral haemorrhage and there seems little reason to disbelieve this, despite widespread suspicion that she had been murdered. Her health had been undermined by a serious car accident in the Soviet Union and by years of an extremely ascetic diet, in addition to which she had been greatly agitated by a scandal in her office as a result of which she felt forced to sack her long-serving private secretary. Whatever the cause of her demise, her funeral saw the greatest expression of grief for any political figure since the death of Boris III in 1943.

For many in Bulgaria the death of Zhivkova destroyed hope that Bulgaria might be moving towards a more self-confident future, freer from the previous sycophantic relationship with the Soviet Union and freer too of the arid dogma of marxism-leninism. Her death was to be followed by a series of crises at home over the economy and policies adopted toward the Turkish minority. These both contributed to a decline in the authority of the party. In the late 1980s the environment became a prominent issue and abroad the advent of Gorbachev funda-mentally altered the relationships between Bulgaria and the Soviet Union and between the BCP and the CPSU. At the end of the decade these accumulated tensions, resentments, and frustrations would destroy first Todor Zhivkov and then the apparatus of communist party rule itself.

7. THE DECLINE OF COMMUNIST POWER; THE COLLAPSE OF THE ECONOMIC STRATEGY

By the late 1970s the communists had in effect brought Bulgaria into the modern era. Over three-fifths of the population lived in towns and the economy was no longer dominated by agriculture or the processing of agricultural products; in 1983 the percentage of industrial production based on food processing, which had been 51.2 per cent in 1939, had declined to 26.9 per cent, whilst in the same years textiles declined from

---

[11] Chakŭrov, *Vtoriya Etazh*, 160.   [12] Ibid. 157.

19.8 to 5.5 per cent and machinery rose from 2.4 to 14.2 per cent. As a proportion of exports machinery had risen from 8.2 per cent in 1955–7 to 53.8 per cent in 1981–3.

The communists had brought social modernization too. During their time in office it became the norm rather than the exception for women to have paid employment outside the family. By 1987 49.8 per cent of the total labour force was female. In 1947 42.0 per cent of the pupils in secondary schools were girls, whereas in 1988 the figure was 49.0 per cent; in tertiary education the increase was from 28.73 per cent in 1958 to 54.0 per cent in 1988. The advance of women into the labour market and higher education did not mean the entire disappearance of traditional prejudices against women, particularly against women in positions of power and authority in the work unit, but at least the opportunities for advancement had been created.

Education had also become more widely available, the number of teachers in primary and secondary schools rising from 34,073 in 1948 to 92,083 in 1988, an increase of 170.25 per cent. In 1958 there had been 40,053 pupils in tertiary education; thirty years later the number was 150,517. The communists had also fought an impressive campaign against illiteracy. Shortly after September 1944 the FF had introduced night schools for adults unable to read or write; although laced with political propaganda the campaign drove the illiteracy rate down rapidly; by 1983 only 4.5 per cent of over 15-year-olds could not read or write.

Health provision had also improved under communist rule. In 1946 infant mortality had been 125.1 per thousand, but this figure fell steadily to 14.4 in 1989 and at the end of the 1970s life expectancy was 68.35 years for males and 73.55 years for females, compared to 52.56 and 50.98 years respectively in the years 1935–9. The number of doctors increased from 1,800 in 1951 to 24,718 in 1984, which meant, for the same years, a decline in the number of inhabitants per physician from 4,032 to 363. The number of hospital beds per one hundred households went up from 5 to 9 between 1956 and 1983.[13]

These were official statistics and they hide the fact that the benefits were not evenly distributed and that the party *priviligentsia* enjoyed access to better facilities than ordinary mortals. And in the late 1970s ordinary mortals were becoming more conscious of these disparities.

[13] Figures from UN Yearbooks and Lampe, *Bulgarian Economy*, 194.

Table 13.2 Average annual growth in Net
Material Product in percentages, 1950–1989

1950–55	12.3
1955–60	9.7
1960–65	6.7
1965–70	8.2
1970–75	7.9
1975–80	6.2
1980–85	3.7
1985–89	3.0

Source: John A. Bristow, *The Bulgarian Economy in Transition*,
Studies in Communism in Transition, series editor Ronald J.
Hill (Cheltenham: Edward Elgar, 1996) 19.

The communists could bring Bulgaria into the modern age but they were to find it much more difficult to adapt it to the post-modern era. Intensive was to prove far more elusive than extensive development. The slow down in growth became apparent in the late 1970s and is illustrated in table 13.2.

By the late 1970s the party leadership was increasingly conscious of the difficulties posed by the switch from extensive to intensive development, and of the fact that previous estimates of growth had been overenthusiastic. The seventh fyp of 1976–81 had predicted growth in national income of 45 per cent and in industrial output of 55 per cent; the eighth fyp, for 1981–5, was much more modest with figures of 20 per cent and 28 per cent respectively. The NEM was then introduced to stimulate the economy. But the results were disappointing.

The reasons for this were varied. One was that the Bulgarian managerial cadres were unprepared for the new market conditions which the NEM hoped to create. Managers who for decades had been accustomed to have their production quotas decided by a central ministry and had their plant subsidized if they failed to make a profit, were frequently incapable of finding their own suppliers and their own customers, to say nothing of balancing their books. Some feared political reprisals if they purchased western goods when Soviet or east European ones were available, even if the latter were demonstrably inferior. At times local party officials of the older generation even obstructed the adoption of new techniques.

Another serious impediment to the NEM's desired economic regeneration was that the scientific-technological revolution had not proved the hoped-for *deus ex machina* to save the socialist economy from its woes. One problem was that the pace of change had become so rapid that no planned system could cope with the galloping advances in computer technology and fibre optics. A second problem was that from the very beginning Bulgaria had depended on western know-how to modernize its economy. The Bulgarian computer industry relied heavily on the import of western manufactured components, a process which began after Zhivkov's visit to Japan in 1970. A number of agreements were concluded with western companies for the manufacture of their products under licence in Bulgaria, and an important ten-year trade deal with federal Germany was intended to introduce modern methods into Bulgaria. However, the acquisition of western technical know-how became more difficult in the 1980s when the United States insisted that its trading partners observe the restrictions the coordinating committee for multilateral export controls had placed upon the export to communist states of any items which might assist the latter's military programmes.

A major weakness in the strategy of relying on the west for material and technical expertise was that Bulgaria was buying with hard currency but selling primarily in the communist bloc for soft. This was because of the poor quality of Bulgarian manufactured goods and the discrimination in western markets against its agricultural output. The difficulty of covering hard currency imports with hard currency exports became much greater after western prices rose following the oil crises of 1973 and 1979. This exacerbated the already mounting debt problem. By the mid-1980s the regime was admitting to an accumulated foreign debt of $3 billion, and servicing the debt was absorbing 38 per cent of hard currency earnings. By 1989 the debt had reached $10 billion. Although Zhivkov did not go to the extremes of a Ceaușescu, the need to service the debt did force a number of the better quality Bulgarian products, especially in the agricultural and vinicultural sectors, into the export markets and thereby deprived domestic purchasers of high-quality items.

This emphasized the problem of the quality of Bulgarian goods in general. The NEM had made it one of its tasks to improve quality but this proved perhaps its most conspicuous failure. So serious was the problem that in May 1983 Zhivkov spoke live on radio and television and, without his customary touches of humour, harangued his audience about the lamentable quality of many products. In March 1984 the party held a special national conference to discuss the issue.

The failure of the NEM to improve the standard of goods was a prime reason for the growing sense of disillusionment with the party in the mid-1980s. Another was the unreliability of electricity supplies. In most large towns a regime of three hours on and three hours off for at least six days a week became normal, but even these supplies could not be guaranteed and power was frequently suspended without warning. This seriously affected public morale: 'The dark nights played a prominent role in the demoralization of society and in the draining away of faith in a system which after forty years of socialism was not able to guarantee a normal daily life.'[14] The disruption in energy supplies was one of the main causes of a sharply worded samizdat letter of complaint organized by workers at the Dimitrov locomotive shops in May 1986. This fragility in electricity supplies was not entirely the fault of the government. There were severe droughts in 1984 and 1985, the latter being the worst for a century, and these diminished generation in the hydro-electric plants. On the other hand, the authorities were held responsible for the delays both in planned repairs to the existing nuclear power plant at Kozloduǐ and in the construction of a second complex at Belene. By the mid-1980s Kozloduǐ, which opened in 1974, was producing up to a quarter of the nation's electricity and interruptions in its output were immediately felt.

Zhivkov's response to increasing economic frustration was predictable. He launched yet more reform schemes. Central Committee plena were convoked in February 1985 and January 1986 where it was argued that there must be a shift from 'bureaucratic to economic' planning. In December 1986 yet another plenum intensified the reforming drive and signalled a move towards more 'self-management' and more competition. The plans for this were presented at a CC plenum at the end of July 1987. At it Zhivkov stated that Bulgaria had to create new hierarchies but on an economic not an administrative basis, and the key was competition, internal and external, because that was what had enabled capitalism to flourish. He also denounced in very forthright terms the middle ranks of the bureaucracy in both party and government, which he said had sabotaged previous attempts at reform and must now be removed to allow for worker self-management. The party, Zhivkov insisted, must withdraw

[14] Kalinova and Baeva, *Bŭlgarskite prehodi*, 132.

from certain areas of social and economic life and leave individuals and working groups free to make their own decisions. So radical were the changes intended that the long-serving April line was abandoned as the party's guiding principle to be replaced by 'the July concept'. In August 1987 parliament sanctioned a series of reforms, including an extensive restructuring of local government and the abolition of a number of central ministries; these reforms were intended to begin the new era. For the most part the latest batch of reforms meant little more than dislocative reorganizations in the administration of the economy.

In the second half of the 1980s some attention was diverted from the economic and social discontents by the so-called 'regenerative process' which, in the end, was to become a massive, self-inflicted wound on the Zhivkovian body politic.

8. THE DECLINE OF COMMUNIST POWER: THE 'REGENERATIVE PROCESS'

In 1958 the party and government had set about implementing a decision taken at the April 1956 plenum to assimilate the minorities. In the late 1950s and early 1960s there was pressure on the Roma and Tatars to adopt Bulgarian names, Bulgarian and Turkish elementary schools were merged, and, by the mid-1970s, Turkish language publications had all but disappeared. There was also pressure on the Pomaks, the party considering a series of 'voluntary' name changes in Pomak areas. In 1964 in the Blagoevgrad region the imposition of these changes by force provoked violent resistance, as a result of which the party retreated, reversing the enforced name changes, only to perform another about turn in the 1970s. This time name changes were enforced on Pomaks through-out the country. Again there was widespread resistance followed by repression–there were 500 Pomaks in the labour camp at Belene in 1974—but the regime did not budge.

There was no similar pressure on the Turks who at this point were being offered the chance to leave Bulgaria under the ten-year agreement between Sofia and Ankara signed in 1969; 130,000 Bulgarian Turks took advantage of the offer in the years up to 1978. Late in 1983 it was decided that assimilationist pressures would be applied in areas of compact Turkish population; on 19 June 1984 the party resolved to integrate the

Bulgarian Turks 'in the cause of socialism and the policy of the BCP' which was to accelerate the economic development of the Turkish areas.[15] A full-scale assault on Turkish ethnic identity was then launched. In some localities speaking Turkish in public was banned, the one remaining newspaper published partly in Turkish was closed down, broadcasts in Turkish ceased, and, most importantly, all Turks were required to adopt a Slav name. Those refusing had a name assigned to them, the changes being effected through the introduction of new identity cards, without which salaries could not be paid, travel tickets purchased, medical services received, or bank accounts accessed.

The regime's propagandists announced that the Turks were not in reality ethnic Turks but Bulgarians who had been Turkified in the years since the Ottoman conquest; their Bulgarian consciousness was being 'regenerated'. The Bulgarian word used was a cognate of vǔzrazhdane and thus 'As Bulgarians had been "reborn" through their national awakening in the nineteenth century, so too, according to the Communist Party, were Muslims now "reborn" as Bulgarians.'[16] There was in fact little if any similarity between the two processes and the twentieth century phrase was a euphemism for the attempted assimilation of Bulgaria's ethnic Turkish minority.

The regenerative process was a foolhardy venture. When the southern Dobrudja had been returned to Bulgaria in 1940 Turkish place names had been replaced with Bulgarian ones, but it had been considered too dangerous to attempt to force individuals to change theirs. What led the Bulgarian regime to take the risk in the 1980s cannot be stated with certitude. There was indubitably a fear of growing Islamic assertiveness as registered in the Iranian revolution of 1979 and the Kosovo disturbances two years later, after which came the emphasis placed on Pan-Turkism by Turgut Yozal, who became prime minister of Turkey in 1983. Another fear was no doubt the difference in birth rates between Bulgarians and Turks; in December 1975 the average live birth for every married woman in Bulgaria was 1.95, but in the Kǔrdjali region it was 2.95,[17] and other

---

[15]   Kalinova and Baeva, *Bǔlgarskite prehodi 1944–1999*, 201 n. 10.

[16]   Neuburger, *Orient Within*, 58.

[17]   Nikolai Michev, 'The Demographic Transition and Regional Variations in Birth and Death Rates in Bulgaria', in James H. Johnson (ed.), *Geography and Regional Planning*, Proceedings of the second British-Bulgarian Geographical Seminar, Sofia 22–9 September 1980 (Norwich: Geo, 1983), 113–21.

evidence showed that whereas from the 1940s to the 1960s the average number of children in an ethnic Turkish family was between two and three, in the early 1980s it was between five and six.[18] After 1965, for the first time since 1878, the percentage of Turks within the total population of the country began to increase.

Another probable factor was that ever since the enforced name changes of the early 1970s Pomaks had been showing an increasing inclination to see themselves not as Bulgarians but as Turks. Since 1878 it had been assumed that because the Pomaks, unlike the other Muslims, were ethnically originally Bulgarian they would one day be reincorporated into the main body of the nation; the new trend, itself largely the consequence of the enforced assimilationist attempts a decade before, was a psychological blow to Bulgarian national feeling. In more practical terms it was seen as a danger in that it would artificially increase the size of the Turkish minority.

Others have argued that the real motive for the regenerative process was the belief that Islam was too conservative a religion to adapt to the changes required by the scientific-technological revolution and the development of real, existing socialism. The campaign was directed, therefore, not merely at the Bulgarian Turks but at Islam in general. This argument is given strength by the facts that not only is the adoption of a name an important part of the maturation of the Muslim, but also according to Islamic teaching Muslims who do not have their proper name face eternal damnation. There were also other restrictions on or affronts to Islamic practices. Since the 1960s party officials had been keen to ensure that Muslims on the collective farms took their part in the rearing of pigs; circumcision by anyone but a qualified surgeon had been banned for hygienic reasons since December 1959 and the washing of the dead had been proscribed, again on health grounds; it had also become very difficult for Bulgarian Muslims to make the *hadj*, and a number of Muslim shrines and buildings within Bulgaria had been allowed to decay or had even been destroyed.

The regenerative process might also have been seen as a mechanism to crank up the regime's waning support by beating the nationalist drum, and there is no doubt that the regenerative process was popular in

---

[18] Valeri Stoyanov, *Turskoto naselenie v Bŭlgariya mezhdu polyusite na etnicheskata politika*, (Sofia: LIK, 1998) 153.

populist circles. There were also fears that, given the higher Turkish birth rate and the fact that a national intelligentsia was beginning to emerge within the ethnic Turks, this could pose a future threat to Bulgaria. The composition of its conscript army would in the long run be affected by the differential birth rates, and there were fears that increasingly self-confident Turks, living in compact areas of the country, might demand autonomy, which would be the prelude to the incorporation of those areas into Turkey. And if anyone questioned the probability of this Eastern Rumelia in reverse, they would be told to look at the example of northern Cyprus; Zhivkov is reported to have stated that, 'We have to get rid of at least 200,000 Muslims or in a few years Bulgaria will become another Cyprus.'[19]

Whatever its causes the regenerative process provoked intense resistance. On 30 August bombs exploded in the railway station in Plovdiv and at the airport in Varna; Zhivkov was scheduled to visit both towns that day. Shortly after the explosions fly-sheets appeared in the streets threatening, 'Forty years, forty bombs', it being near the fortieth anniversary of 9 September 1944. It is not improbable that the explosions were part of the protest at the regenerative process. The leadership was prepared for protests, and had threatened that 'Anyone who resists will be killed like a dog.'[20] Scores were, particularly in Momchilgrad and Benkovski near the Turkish border, after troops, including tanks and crack parachute units, had been deployed in what was the largest operation conducted by the Bulgarian army since the second world war. Hundreds of protesters were arrested. An illegal opposition group, the Turkish National Liberation Movement in Bulgaria, was created under the leadership of a philosopher, Medi Doganov, who was later to become better known under his Turkish name of Ahmed Dogan. The organization conducted propaganda on behalf of the Turks and indulged in economic and political sabotage. The regenerative process also brought Bulgaria condemnation from a number of prominent international organizations, including the United Nations (UN), the Islamic Conference Organization, the Council of Europe, and the European Court of Justice, whilst the EEC suspended all negotiations with Bulgaria in protest.

[19] Valeri Stoyanov, *Turskoto naselenie v Bŭlgariya mezhdu polyusite na etnicheskata politika*, 204.

[20] Hugh Poulton, *The Balkans: Minorities and States in Conflict* (London: Minority Rights Publications, 1991), 144.

9. THE DECLINE OF PARTY AUTHORITY,
1975–1985

Not all Bulgarians had disagreed with the regenerative process, despite its unfortunate international consequences, but there were few who did not feel aggrieved at the poor performance of the economy, and for this they quite naturally blamed the all-powerful, monolithic party.

Even before the 1980s dissatisfaction had been on the increase. In 1977 a tendency in the party itself to flirt with euro-communism had led to the Velchev purge. In December of the same year Zhivkov made his first public reference to dissidence in Bulgaria, and in March 1978 a clandestine publication, 'Declaration 78', copied from the Czech charter of that year, appeared, a noteworthy event in a country where samizdat was rare. The Bulgarian leadership was frightened enough of Solidarity to take steps to ensure that the contagion did not spread to Bulgaria. The shops were filled with food and consumer goods, though the danger facing the Bulgarian party was not at this stage serious, not least because Bulgaria had no equivalent of the Roman Catholic Church to offer an alternative source of loyalty to its inhabitants.

A much greater threat was posed by the influx of western culture. By the late 1970s restrictions on Bulgarians travelling abroad had been eased, though by no means entirely removed, and for those who could accumulate enough hard currency visits to the west were now much easier. There was also increased traffic in the opposite direction, more especially to the ghastly tourist complexes which had mushroomed along the Black Sea coast. The increase in visitors to and from the west coincided with greater ease in communication. The Helsinki agreements had brought about the end of the jamming of western radio and television broadcasts but more important still was the rapid increase in the circulation of audio and then video tapes. At first the regime attempted to stem the incoming tide but it proved a hopeless task and there were few young Bulgarians who were not familiar with the latest western fashions in music and clothing. Many films and TV programmes were also imported. The differences between the affluent, care-free, colourful, libertarian west and the dour, grey, unimaginative world of communist Bulgaria did not have to be stated to be perceived.

A persistently unpopular feature of the system for most Bulgarians was the almost universal corruption in public life. Petty corruption was endemic, and no worse than in many other societies, but it led to proposals such as that in 1979 that official petrol should be dyed a different colour to help prevent its resale on the black market. Large-scale corruption at the higher levels of party and government was widely suspected, the suspicions being fed by a series of exposures of illegal dealing. One area where malpractice was rife was in sport, and so bad was the situation in the world of soccer that in 1985 two of Sofia's oldest and most popular clubs were dissolved, reorganized, and renamed. The venality of organized sport was to survive all communist efforts to eradicate it, and was still extant in 2004 when the BBC exposed the president of the Bulgarian Olympic Committee, Ivan Slavkov, showing him discussing how votes could be bought in the campaign to host the 2012 summer games. The general public's distaste for corruption was increased by resentment at the privileges offered to party members in almost all aspects of life. Corruption and privilege were distancing the party from the population.

Party members made up 9.3 per cent of the total population when the twelfth BCP congress met in 1981. Just over two-fifths (42.7 per cent) of the membership were of working-class origin but in 1981, in a departure from previous practice, the social origins of the remaining three-fifths was not revealed. What was obvious, however, was that the higher echelons of the party were dominated by males from the administrative and managerial cadres. Of the 173 central committee members only nine were workers; the others consisted of one industrial and one agricultural manager, thirteen functionaries of the mass organizations, seventy full-time party employees, and seventy-nine government officials. Only eleven of the 173 were women. There were three Jews, one Turk, and one Pomak.

Such an organization had little appeal for a youth increasingly saturated with western mores. This the party had long recognized but its efforts to remedy the situation had only made it worse. In 1975 a special party conference was held to discuss problems such as football hooliganism and anti-social behaviour by minors. At the eleventh party congress in 1976 there was severe criticism of the attitudes and conduct of the nation's youth which was accused of being too interested in material acquisitions, pop music, drugs, and alcohol, and too little concerned with party ideology. The remedies offered indicated how little hope the party had of finding a solution; in 1982 the head of the Dimitrov League of Communist Youth, Bulgaria's komsomol, suggested that current political and cultural information be announced in discos.

Disaffection with or simply lack of interest in the party and its ideas led to widespread cynicism and a precipitate decline in ideological belief. According to one close adviser this was felt even by Zhivkov himself. The party leader frequently asked such questions as, ' "Why did we abolish private property? What have we replaced it with? We can't find anything to replace it," ' or ' "What were we doing when we abolished religion? What have we given to the people? Religion at least taught them not to steal; we can't even do that." '[21] After he had fallen from power, no doubt helped by hindsight, Zhivkov glibly declared to western reporters that he had long since relinquished socialism as an idea or an ideal.[22] Only with the advent of Gorbachev did interest in the party, particularly amongst the young and in the ranks of the intelligentsia, revive, but Zhivkov was not prepared to accommodate to the changes suggested by Moscow.

By the mid-1980s the Bulgarians were facing a crisis. It was not the first since the second world war but no previous one had combined such totally different elements. And nor could the regime any longer hide behind the pretence that the rest of the world was equally badly or worse off; the increasing contacts with the west showed plainly that it was not.

10. THE COLLAPSE OF THE ZHIVKOV REGIME, 1985–1989

When introducing the July concept Zhivkov had quoted the words of Vasil Levski, 'Either we live up to our times, or they will destroy us.' Zhivkov, it was soon clear, could not live up to his times. If the regenerative process was intended to deflect attention from Bulgaria's crumbling economy, its erratic electricity supply system, and its other manifold woes, it failed. Nor could it lessen the impact of two other factors which fundamentally altered the political situation: the mobilization of the masses over the question of environmental degradation, and the reforming agenda being pursued by the new Soviet leadership.

Concern over the environment had been growing for years and by the mid-1980s this concern was being articulated more powerfully, more

---

[21] Chakŭrov, *Vtoriya Etazh*, 98–9.

[22] In his memoirs Zhivkov denied he ever made this remark. The interpreter who was present has confirmed to the present author that he did.

openly, and more frequently. The concerns ranged from the disappearance of the eagles from Mount Vitosha near Sofia, to the appalling pollution of the Black Sea, and to the morality of a system under which a factory manager who had polluted a river could be acquitted in court because he pleaded that his actions had been necessary to fulfil his plan targets. As elsewhere in eastern Europe, however, anxieties over pollution were hugely augmented by the Chernobyl disaster in April 1986. Radioactive clouds drifted over Bulgaria from the stricken reactor and immediately there were rumours that special, guaranteed safe food was being flown in from places such as Egypt for use by the party and government *priviligentsia*. The rumours were not without foundation. The minister of defence, an old partisan comrade of Zhivkov, had arranged for the army to receive safe food and that for the higher echelons of the establishment was subjected to special laboratory tests. Privilege, it seemed, could even purchase greater immunity from environmental danger.

The environmental issue posed enormous difficulties for communist administrations throughout eastern Europe, not least because their fyps made no provision either for making production cleaner or for repairing the ravages already caused. The environmental issue also presented the regimes with unprecedented ideological problems. The environmental protesters could not be written off, as many other complainers had been, as 'class enemies' or acolytes of some outmoded or obscurantist religion. They were mainly young people who had grown up under the socialist system, and they were complaining at what that system was doing to the world they were soon to inherit. That their complaints were justified was obvious to all who could see or smell.

The party and its leaders were held responsible for the damage their policies were inflicting upon the nation, and this severely weakened Zhivkov, but of all the factors undermining his regime in the second half of the 1980s the most important was the appointment of 54-year-old Mikhaïl Gorbachev as leader of the CPSU in March 1985. Zhivkov was 73 and after the death of Enver Hoxha in April 1985 was the longest-serving party boss in any ruling communist party; for reformers like Gorbachev Zhivkov was an unwelcome survival of the brezhnevite 'years of stagnation'. Zhivkov made the situation worse by appearing to patronize the new Soviet leader, sending Gorbachev his *Considerations of some Basic Problems in the Development of Real Socialism*, in which Zhivkov tried to set out the ways in which socialism could be revivified.

The differences between the two leaders were soon apparent. When Zhivkov paid his first visit to Gorbachev he was kept waiting until the second day before seeing him, an unprecedented snub, and in July 1985 the Soviet ambassador in Sofia said to a Bulgarian journal that Gorbachev had told Zhivkov that although the roots of friendship between the two parties were deep and strong, the plant needed tendering if it were to bear fruit. When Gorbachev attended a meeting of the Warsaw pact political consultative committee in October 1985 at Boyana, Zhivkov's palace on the outskirts of Sofia, Zhivkov made noises about closer association with the USSR, but these Gorbachev dismissed, making it clear instead that he wanted to introduce realistic pricing into Soviet-Bulgarian economic relations: 'Friendship for friendship: cheese for money', he said; this was the first warning of the serious blow which was to fall on Bulgaria when the Soviet Union insisted in August 1986 that in economic relations between the Soviet Union and the other Comecon states, market forces would prevail; most critically this meant that the USSR would charge world prices for its oil and gas exports.

Relations deteriorated rapidly after the Boyana encounter, and in his speech to the thirteenth BCP congress in April 1986 Zhivkov did not mention Gorbachev. In October of the following year Zhivkov was summoned to the Kremlin, where Gorbachev expressed considerable doubts over the July concept and other aspects of Bulgarian policy. He thought Zhivkov was trying to make his country into a 'mini-west Germany or Japan', he said Zhivkov's plans to withdraw the party from some sectors of social and economic life went too far and were a departure from leninism, and he accused the Bulgarian leader of having too much perestroika and too little glasnost. Zhivkov went on the offensive. The purpose of glasnost, he riposted, was to show the need for perestroika, but as Bulgaria had already introduced perestroika via the July concept it did not need more glasnost. In fact, Bulgaria was receiving glasnost whether Zhivkov liked it or not. For the first time in decades queues formed at news kiosks to buy the latest Soviet newspapers, subscriptions to Soviet journals rocketed, and every Friday Bulgarian television relayed a Soviet channel live. This it had done for years but now what was flowing in was not rigid conservatism but exciting radicalism.

The ageing Zhivkov floundered. He refused to contemplate abdication, which was what many were now demanding, and he failed to see that his credibility as a reformer was exhausted and that he and those around him were now seen as the origin of not the solution to the nation's problems. Most damaging of all for Zhivkov was that this was the view not merely of the public but of the party; in 1986 a leading publishing house published a book which discussed Bulgarian and foreign marxist philosophers and did not contain a single reference to Bulgaria's 'son of the people' either in the text or the bibliography.[23] And when it came to opposition in the party Zhivkov could do no more than fall back on the old methods which Gorbachev and the reformers were condemning. In June 1987 Georgi Tambuev, who had published four articles on corruption, was expelled from the party on Zhivkov's insistence. In July of the following year a plenum was electrified by the removal of a number of leading reformers, including politburo member and minister president Chudomir Aleksandrov. By this time Zhivkov was so embattled that he began showing signs of paranoia. He sacked a number of long-time advisers and absurd accusations of spying were made against some of them. This only intensified dissatisfaction in the party.

Communist regimes stay in power either by convincing the ruled that their power is legitimate, or by instilling such fear that protest is silenced; communist rulers remain in office as long as they can command respect or obedience in the party itself. By the middle of the 1980s few people regarded Zhivkov's regime as legitimate, and, tellingly, many of those who openly opposed it said, in a phrase popular at the time, that 'the fear has gone'. This was to be made manifest in 1989, as was Zhivkov's loss of control within the party.

In January 1989 President Mitterand visited Bulgaria. When he spoke in BAN the discussions were purely academic, but when he addressed university students they insisted on raising contemporary political issues, after which Mitterand invited twelve prominent dissidents to breakfast in the French embassy, an unthinkable occurrence even a few years earlier. Equally extraordinary, and indicative of how far the body of the party had distanced itself from the leadership, was the fact that in March the president of the trade unions, Petŭr Dyulgerov, presented a report which argued that a fully independent trade union movement was essential, and in speeches on Lenin's birthday and on 1 May, he omitted to mention Zhivkov. Another indication of the collapse in respect for the old leader

[23] The book was Aleksandŭr Lilov, *Vŭobrazhenie i tvorchestvo* (Sofia: Nauka i izkustvo, 1986).

was the mood in the two most important of the creative artists' unions, those of the writers and the film makers. At meetings of both in March the fiercest criticism of the regime was voiced by party activists.

The creative artists were leading the revolt of the intellectuals which had begun in earnest in 1988, fired by the example of the liberation of their colleagues in the Soviet Union. There had been occasional signs of nonconformity earlier in the 1980s, as when the book *Fashizmŭt* (Fascism) pointed to the similarities between fascist and socialist dictatorships; this earned its author, an academic philosopher named Zhelyu Zhelev, who had been expelled from the party in the 1960s, a sentence of internal exile. He was soon to return. Another notable example was Blaga Dimitrova's novel *Litse* (Face), which drew another parallel, that between the aspirations of the anti-fascist struggle and the realities of real existing socialism. By the late 1980s the pressure for even greater relaxation in all the arts had become all but irresistible.

In the late 1980s there were also, for the first time since the end of the 1940s, non-official, self-created organizations. These were not political parties, Zhivkov having made it clear that he did not believe Bulgaria had the social base for political pluralism; the new organizations, Bulgaria's civil society, therefore concentrated on the human rights, and religion. The new groups included the Independent Society for the Defence of Human Rights in Bulgaria, established early in 1988 by Iliya Minev, a member of the pre-1944 Legionaries. It attracted little support because its leaders were generally old and virtually unknown, and a similar fate befell the Committee for the Defence of Religious Rights, led by the better-known egregious cleric and nuclear scientist, Father Hristofor Sŭbev. More lasting and more forceful was the independent trade union 'Podkrepa' (Support).

Most of these new associations were small, relatively little known, and, because they lacked a unifying, common cause, disparate. The issue which was to provide Bulgaria's discontented elements with a common cause was the environment. The authorities had kept silent about the special provision made for the privileged after Chernobyl but they were prepared to admit to the problems afflicting Rusé. The city was subjected to periodic poisoning by a malfunctioning Romanian chemical plant on the other side of the Danube. In the autumn of 1987 mothers in Rusé began regular protest demonstrations, and at the end of the year the party allowed an art exhibition in the city, one item of which was a simple table of statistics taken from official publications. They revealed that in 1975 the incidence of lung disease in the city had been 969 per 100,000 of the population; in 1985 it was 17,386 per 100,000. The Rusé problem galvanized the nation. The Union of Bulgarian Artists published an appeal for the saving of Rusé, and was supported by a host of organizations, including the Institute for Nuclear Research, the Office of Young Writers, the Union of Teachers, and the Institute for Molecular Biology, whilst the film director Yuri Zhirov made a documentary, 'Dishai' (the imperative singular of the verb 'to breathe'), about Rusé's mothers and children. The film's premiere on 8 March 1988 was the occasion for the formation of the first proper dissident organization in Bulgaria, the Civil Committee for the Ecological Defence of Rusé.[24] Its elected leadership included popular figures such as the writer Georgi Mishev, the artist Svetlin Rusev, and the journalist Sonya Bakish; her husband was Stanko Todorov the president of the sŭbranie and a member of the politburo. She was expelled from the party and the committee was subjected to considerable police pressure. As a result it did little after its foundation but from it emerged, early in 1989, Ekoglasnost, which rapidly attracted widespread popular support.

At much the same time there emerged the Club for the Support of Preustroistvo (the Bulgarian equivalent of Perestroika) and Glasnost, the first non-communist overtly political group to be established in Bulgaria since 1949. Its origins lay in the University of Sofia whose party conference in the autumn of 1987 had expressed severe criticism of the regime, after which four lecturers had been expelled. All the organizers of the original club were long-standing party members, and some were even 'active fighters against fascism', but it rapidly attracted support from prominent and long-standing critics of the regime such as Zhelyu Zhelev, Blaga Dimitrova, and Radoï Ralin. The club insisted it was not acting outside the law, but in the spirit of the July concept which, in addition to introducing economic reform, had promised that pluralism would replace monopoly in all strands of life. The club also supported every movement of protest against the authorities.

These protest movements were becoming more numerous and more extreme. Those who had been non-communists were turning into

[24] Details of the formation and title of the committee are taken with due acknowledgement and appreciation from the work of my former graduate student, Matthew Tejada of St Antony's College, Oxford.

anti-communists who were against the system per se, whilst the communist reformers, above all the anti-zhivkovites, wanted not the dismantling of the system but its democratization on gorbachevite lines.

Both groups were equally determined that Zhivkov's rule should end and there seemed little that the beleaguered 'Bai Tosho' could do to stem the tide of opposition. But there were still many things he could do to swell it. His refusal to contemplate stepping down was one, and his conduct over the regenerative process was another. By the late spring of 1989 the beleaguered Turks had found support amongst sections of the Bulgarian intelligentsia. These, and particularly those in the Club for the Support of Preustroistvo and Glasnost encouraged a number of Turks to go on hunger strike just before a meeting of the Commission on Security and Cooperation in Europe (CSCE) in Paris in May. Tension mounted rapidly, especially in the Razgrad and Haskovo regions, and within a few days a number of clashes had taken place. So serious had the situation become by the end of the month that a politburo meeting was called on a Sunday. It decided that Zhivkov should appear on television and announce that any Turks who really believed that life would be better in capitalist Turkey than in socialist Bulgaria were free to leave. Zhivkov was convinced that few would do so, and even suggested that the few who did go should be seen off by brass bands. He was wrong. By August, when the Turkish Republic closed its borders, 370,000 ethnic Turks had fled.

Although between 40,000 and 60,000 returned in the succeeding three months, complaining that 'In Bulgaria we are Turks, and in Turkey we are Bulgarians', the economic impact of the exodus was devastating. Crops were left unharvested, animals died through lack of care, and in many areas the distribution system collapsed because the majority of its employees had been Turks. The political impact was almost as severe. President George Bush gave overt support to Turkey whilst there was no support for Bulgaria from Moscow.

Bulgaria was totally isolated and Zhivkov was held responsible. On 17 June 1989 Stanko Todorov wrote to the politburo protesting at the humiliating role the assembly had been reduced to in the exodus of the Turks. Todorov's action showed that the power structure in Bulgaria was beginning to crumble. It finally came apart in November, but not without resistance from Zhivkov. On 24 October Petŭr Mladenov, the long-serving minister for foreign affairs and a member of the politburo, wrote to both the politburo and the CC denouncing Zhivkov's method of rule and his policies. Mladenov then resigned. The politburo met on 26 October, a day when police clashed violently with protesters at an Ekoglasnost demonstration in Sofia, but still Zhivkov refused to resign. On 8 November, however, he suffered an irreversible setback when the minister of defence, Dobri Djurov, abandoned him. Djurov controlled the army and was a former wartime colleague; together with two other old partisan colleagues from the Chavdar Brigade he went to Zhivkov to tell him he must go. Zhivkov then agreed to call a special meeting of the politburo on 10 November at which he would step down.

Bulgaria's long-time party boss had been removed not by people power deployed on the streets, but by a palace coup. And, in a fine irony, the chief opponents of this erstwhile favoured son of the Soviet Union were those leading party figures who had the closest links to the Kremlin and the Soviet embassy.

14

Post-Communist Bulgaria, 1989–2005

The seven years following the fall of Todor Zhivkov, like the seven decades after the liberation of 1878, saw political development without effective structural change. For both internal and external reasons, the new Bulgaria failed to make the deep, macroeconomic adjustments which the new ruling ideology of the market demanded. It was the financial collapse of 1996–7 which brought about real structural change just as it had been the communist assumption of power in the late 1940s which forced Bulgaria into its modernizing phase. After 1997 a succession of governments pushed a not-always-willing population towards membership of the Euro-Atlantic structures, and thus provided another answer to the age-old question of which way Bulgaria should face, east or west.

1. DEVISING A NEW CONSTITUTION, DECEMBER 1989–JULY 1991

The political escape from communist authoritarianism was relatively easily effected. Zhivkov had been replaced as leader of the party and head of state in November 1989 by Petŭr Mladenov. He and his reforming, gorbachevite colleagues called a CC plenum in mid-December which promised more democracy within the party and greater powers for the sŭbranie. The plenum also apologized for previous mistakes, including the regenerative policy, and to show its commitment to glasnost admitted that the country's foreign debt was not $3 billion, as had previously been stated, but $12 billion, and $15 billion if interest were added. Another indication of its reforming credentials was that the new leadership made no move to check the mushrooming growth of other political groups. By November 1989 a number of non-communist organizations had appeared, including new political parties and reborn versions of ones suppressed after 1944. A number of these had come together on 14 November to form the Union of Democratic Forces (UDF).

Precisely one month later, the day after the end of the special CC plenum, the UDF organized a massive demonstration in Sofia to demand the amendment of clause 1 of the 1971 constitution which gave the BCP the leading role in society; the plenum had not indicated that the party would go as far along the reforming road as to abandon its leading role. The power of the UDF to mobilize the streets, the crumbling of the one-party system elsewhere in eastern Europe, and, in the near future, the tragic turmoil in Romania, together with its own reforming inclinations, persuaded the BCP to agree to round table discussions on clause 1 and on the future political structure of the country. The round table held its first meeting on 3 January and its last on 15 May 1990. Though not an elected body it became the most important political organ in the country with virtual legislative powers, and in it the country's new political personalities found their legitimization.

The demonstrations of 14 December were followed on successive Sundays in early January 1990 by protests over the Turkish question. On 29 December Mladenov had followed his apology for the regenerative policy with a decree abolishing it. On 7 January thousands poured into Sofia to protest at this decree, with counter-demonstrations in favour of it being staged the following Sunday. Given the public passions generated by this issue it was agreed that representatives of the Turkish minority and the Bulgarian nationalists should be included in the round table discussions.

When the round table talks began the problem of article 1 of the constitution was resolved with surprising ease. A number of professional organizations, acting on their own initiative, banned party cells and on 24 January the politburo proscribed them in the army and in places of work. The party also withdrew, or was ejected from other positions from which it had exercised social and political power. In February reform of the trade unions separated them from the BCP and established a new national organization, the Confederation of Independent Trade Unions in Bulgaria (CITUB). Those other bastions of the party's social influence, the youth organizations and the Fatherland Front, also underwent rapid change and all were neutered politically, the FF reappearing as the anodyne and largely ineffectual Fatherland Union. There were other steps towards the dismantling of communist power, notably the abolition of the sixth department, or secret police, early in 1990. In March strikes were legalized, after compulsory mediation, for all workers except those in the army, the police, the ports, the medical services, and the power industry. A further rejection of the regenerative process came with a law in March allowing all Bulgarian citizens a free choice of name; within twelve months around 600,000 applications to revert to former names had been filed.[1]

The party itself underwent radical change. At the fourteenth congress in January 1990 the BCP abolished the politburo and the central committee, both being replaced by larger bodies which, it was stated, would allow party members greater control over the leadership; the Zhivkov era had been a dictatorship over the party as well as over the country, said Mladenov. Zhivkov himself, it was announced, was to be tried on charges of embezzlement, abuse of power, and incitement to racial hatred, though Mladenov seemed unconscious of the irony that even in an era of supposed perestroika this decision should be announced by a party organization rather than the proper, judicial authorities. The congress also recognized that the party's political monopoly was finished, promised that multi-party democracy would be promoted and respected, and that party and state would be completely separated. In recognition of the latter Mladenov resigned as leader of the party, though he remained head of state. Aleksandŭr Lilov was elected head of the party and a new government was formed under the reformist communist, Andreĭ Lukanov. Once again there seemed little consciousness of the fact that government appointments were being decided by a party body. In April the BCP decided to change its name to the Bulgarian Socialist Party (BSP). It was to be some years before most Bulgarians and foreign observers were convinced that the change of nomenclature meant a change in nature.

The fourteenth congress promised an end to monopoly not only in the political but also in the economic sector. The new economic system was to be based on privatization, decentralization, and demonopolization. In the early months of 1990 private agriculture was legalized and restrictions on the employment of labour were removed in retailing, the service industries, and tourism.

---

[1] Rusanov and Aleksandrieva, *Aspekti*, 19.

Whilst these reforms were being put into effect the round table had continued its work of redesigning the country's political structure. By the end of March it had been agreed that a new constitution should be introduced and that, as after the liberation of 1878, the most appropriate body to define that new constitution would be a grand national assembly (GNA). There was disagreement as to how this body should be elected. The UDF pressed for elections to be held under PR to ensure representation of the smaller parties, whilst the BSP wanted a first past the post system which favoured prominent figures such as those communists who had engineered the fall of Zhivkov. It was eventually decided that half of the 400 deputies should be elected by proportional representation and half by a simple majority vote. Bulgaria was to be the only country in eastern Europe which linked its first post-communist election to the drawing up of a new constitution.

The voting took place on 10 and 17 June. Four parties were represented in the assembly. The largest was the BSP with 211 seats, the second largest being the UDF with 144. There were 23 representatives of the mainly Turkish Movement for Rights and Freedoms (MRF). The agrarians had 16 seats and there were 6 non-party members. The agrarians, fearing that their forty years of subservience to the communists would strip them of all respect in the public eye, had left the government when it was reshaped earlier in the year, thus making Lukanov's gorbachevite cabinet the first purely communist administration in Bulgaria's history.

The GNA provided Bulgaria with the chance for radical change; not for the last time in Bulgaria's post-communist history, that chance was not fully taken. Rather than being the occasion for national consolidation through the search for a new political structure, in its early months the GNA provoked division and controversy. Its opening in Tŭrnovo was marred by demonstrations against the presence of the MRF, and when it moved to Sofia it was soon dominated by demands, particularly from a student 'tent city' in the centre of town, for an investigation into alleged electoral irregularities. The protesters' demands grew in direct proportion to their numbers and soon included the resignation of Mladenov, the sacking of the director of Bulgarian Television, and the punishment of those responsible for the regenerative process, for the death of Georgi Markov, for the attack on the pope, and for the illicit sale of arms.

The first of these objectives was achieved early in July when the students discovered a video tape which, they insisted, showed Mladenov calling for the use of tanks against demonstrators in the previous December; Mladenov denied the allegation but resigned. He was replaced by Zhelyu Zhelev. His election was a welcome example of mature politics in that he, the leader of the UDF, had been elected by a socialist-dominated assembly and the UDF had agreed in return that his deputy should be the socialist, Atanas Semerdjiev. This did not mean, however, that peace had broken out everywhere. At the end of August the disturbances in the centre of Sofia reached their apogee when part of the BSP headquarters was set on fire. Despite assertions by some more extreme elements in the UDF that this was the work of the BSP which wanted to light its own Reichstag fire, the incident at last seemed to induce a realization that some form of cooperation had to replace the confrontation of the summer.

The need for this was made all the greater by the appalling economic crisis and serious shortages of food. The reasons for this will be discussed below, but its political effect was that Lukanov argued that the remedies were so severe that they would be accepted by the whole nation only if they were enacted by a coalition government. The UDF would have none of it; you made the mess, you clear it up was the pith of their response. This produced a political stalemate whilst the economic crises deepened. Once again anger spilled onto the streets and in November both CITUB and the independent trade union, Podkrepa, called for strike action. On 19 November Lukanov resigned. By now food shortages had become so severe that further all-party discussions on the model of the round table were held; they concluded that a coalition government had to be formed. A month after his resignation Lukanov was therefore replaced by a non-party lawyer, Dimitŭr Popov. Bulgaria's first post-communist government had been deposed by revolutionary action on the streets, but once again sufficient consensus had been found to avoid disaster.

Popov's administration called itself 'a government to guarantee the peaceful transition to a democratic society', and before taking office the new minister president had extracted from the major parties a promise to cooperate to bring about a peaceful and orderly transition to a democratic system; Bulgarian politics, all now recognized, had to be rescued from the streets and a new, effective constitution devised.

There was also a pressing need to secure social peace and economic reform. These were brought a step nearer on 8 January 1991 when the employers/managers, the government, and the trade unions signed a tripartite agreement under which the unions accepted a 200-day moratorium on strikes, whilst the government and the employers promised to handle the economic transition with as much concern as possible for those who would be affected by the changes. The first of those changes was soon introduced with the lifting of price controls on a wide range of goods. So unaccustomed were the Bulgarians to free prices that the minister president himself went on television to explain that the goods were not in short supply, they would still be there the next day, and that the way to force prices down was not to rush into the sort of panic purchasing which had characterized the days of shortages under the communists, but to refuse to buy until prices were lowered.

The need to tackle the economic problem diverted the attention of the government and the GNA from constitutional reform. So, too, did a brief resurgence of ethnic tensions. In February the government announced that in schools in Turkish areas there was to be four hours of teaching per week in Turkish if local opinion desired it. There were immediate protests from teachers in the areas potentially involved, especially Kŭrdjali, Razgrad, and Shumen, and some Bulgarian parents withheld their children from school. The government backed down and postponed the scheme until the beginning of the new school year in September.

There were further distractions from the constitutional debate when controversy arose over the relationship between some members of the GNA and the former security services, a debate linked to the contentious question of what to do about access to the files of the former secret police. Constructive debate was further delayed when a group of UDF deputies declared that no constitution devised by a communist dominated assembly could be truly democratic, and they staged a hunger strike to drive home their point. Their fears were that an undemocratic, communist devised constitution might entrench the BSP as the leading force in the process of transition, thus leaving the UDF without an obvious purpose. Another diversion arose from a demand that a referendum be held on the nature of the Bulgarian state, this being a euphemism for whether it should remain a republic or whether the monarchy should be restored. Debate on this question absorbed the GNA for two weeks before the idea of a referendum was dropped. Not until 12 July 1991 was the GNA able to agree upon the basic principles of a new constitution. Bulgaria was to be 'a republic with a parliamentary government'; the president was to be elected directly for a five-year term of office and had to have been resident in the country for the last five years, a restriction introduced to prevent the exiled King Simeon II standing as a candidate. There was to be a legislature of 240 members, elected by proportional representation with a threshold of 4 per cent of the national vote before parties could be represented. There was to be complete separation of powers, and a new body, the constitutional court, was to be created. Bulgaria, said the preamble, aspired to be a democratic state under the rule of the law.

2. TREADING WATER, OCTOBER 1991–JANUARY 1995

The first elections under the new constitution were held on 13 October 1991. Thirty-eight parties entered the contest but only three of them secured seats in the sŭbranie and in the region of a quarter of the votes cast were for parties which failed to pass the 4 per cent barrier; in effect the new system had left a quarter of the electorate without representation.

The elections had also been affected by a controversy over the MRF. There were protests that it contravened article 11 (4) of the constitution which banned the formation of parties on a religious, racial, or ethnic basis, though the MRF was able to argue, legitimately and successfully, that it did not represent only Turkish interests. The MRF in fact gained 24 seats and held the balance in parliament, the UDF having 110 seats and the BSP 106. The latter had suffered through its failure to condemn the attempted coup in Moscow in August; its excuse had been that it did not have sufficient information to make a judgement but its opponents derided this, insisting that the party was indecisive and, true to the communist past which it had not shaken off, wanted the coup to succeed.

The new minister president was Filip Dimitrov of the Green Party who had been elected head of the UDF earlier in the year. Dimitrov's government received the backing of the MRF, which declined to enter the cabinet on the grounds that this might compromise the government and might also limit the MRF's freedom of action. Early in 1992 presidential elections confirmed Zhelev in office for a further five years. This was expected though surprisingly his main opponent, the BSP-backed Velko Vŭlkanov, forced him into a second round. Even more surprising was that 17 per cent of the electorate voted in the first round for Georgi Ganchev, a maverick candidate who had once been a fencing coach at Eton, and who, like Stanisław Timinski in Poland, used a mixture of populism and nationalism to attract support from marginal elements in society. Unlike Timinski he remained to fight another day.

Somewhat surprisingly, the fact that both minister president and president were from the UDF did not mean that relations between them were good, the tension between the two men being one reason why the Dimitrov government achieved little in its one year in office. The elevation of Zhelev to the presidency had removed a moderating element from the leadership of the UDF, which was now in the hands of the more energetic of anti-communists, one of whom was Dimitrov himself. The new minister president's enthusiasms led him to institute large-scale changes in the foreign service, replacing former diplomats with younger men and women who were not always the dedicated anti-communists he had hoped they would be, whilst his determined non-interventionism meant he did nothing when fivefold increases in prices and soaring unemployment forced the trade unions to withdraw from the tripartite agreement of 1991. Dimitrov and the UDF enragés insisted upon the restitution of property seized by the communist regimes after 1948. The anti-communist extremists also pressed for lustration, or the punishment of former communist activists, in the military and in the universities. The lust for lustration brought about the sentencing of Zhivkov to seven years' imprisonment on charges of corruption; he was the first of eastern Europe's former rulers to be sentenced, though he was allowed to serve his time under house arrest rather than in jail. Lustration was also visited upon the Bulgarian Church. In March 1992 its head, Patriarch Maxim, was sacked after a parliamentary commission had reported that his election in 1971 had been irregular; in May Metropolitan Pimen was appointed acting chairman of the Holy Synod but in the following month the constitutional court decided that it was the election of Pimen rather than Maxim that had been ultra vires; it was, implied the court, the right end but the wrong means. The dispute led to unseemly scenes, including even fights between supporters of the rival factions on the steps of the Aleksandŭr Nevski cathedral.

Anti-communist ideology drove the Dimitrov government's economic and social policies. Foreign ownership of Bulgarian firms and the repatriation of profits were permitted by a bill passed in February 1992, there were two acts reforming the banking system, albeit in minor ways, and privatization was encouraged by the setting up of the privatization agency in April. The major act on the economic front, however, was the law of March 1992 which insisted that all agricultural collectives be dissolved by November of that year. Though a major enactment it had not been well prepared. As with the process of commassation before the second world war, decollectivization was bedevilled by competing claims to land.

Before Dimitrov came to office Bulgarian foreign policy had undergone considerable revision. A greater distance had been put between Bulgaria and the Soviet Union, and shortly before the attempted coup in Moscow in August 1991 Bulgaria had become the first east European state formally to dissolve its alliance with the Soviet Union. Diplomatic relations had in the meantime been opened with previous pariahs such as Israel, South Africa, and Chile. Dimitrov continued the process of realignment with the west, and succeeded in having Bulgaria admitted to the Council of Europe in May 1992. His administration also prepared the ground for the association agreement signed with the European Union (EU) in December of that year, although by then Dimitrov himself had left office. Dimitrov in general leaned more towards the United States than to Europe, two of his closest advisers being of American origin. His enthusiasm was reciprocated, Lawrence Eagleburger declaring that the USA was more supportive of Bulgaria than of any other east European government.[2]

Bulgaria's association agreement with the EU had been made easier to achieve by the attempted coup in Moscow in August 1991 which had raised fears in Brussels of a resurgent Soviet Union and thus made the EU more willing to deal with the states of the former communist bloc. Another factor promoting the need for consolidation amongst these states was the former Yugoslavia's rapid and alarming descent into war. This meant the dissolution of the Yugoslav People's Army, until then the largest military force in the Balkans, thus leaving Turkey as the region's major power. This, too, frightened Brussels, but it affected Bulgaria more directly. The collapse of the Warsaw pact had left Bulgaria without allies or a patron, and though the UDF was extravagantly pro-American in its attitudes and utterances, the USA, whatever Eagleburger might say, would not become Bulgaria's protector. Nor would NATO step into the

---

[2] Quoted in the UDF newspaper, *Demokratsiya*, 4 March 1992. See Evgeniya Kalinova and Iskra Baeva, *Bŭlgarskite prehodi 1944–1999*, 174 and 217 n.128.

breach. When Bulgaria approached that organization in 1990 it was brusquely told that its first step must be to secure better relations with Turkey. In March 1992 Dimitŭr Ludjev became the first Bulgarian minister of defence to visit Turkey since 1917, and in May a treaty of friendship was signed between the two countries.

The Dimitrov administration's most prominent and provocative measure in external affairs was its decision in January 1992 to recognize the independent state of Macedonia, Bulgaria being the first country to do this. The recognition was of the Macedonian state but not of the Macedonian nation. The recognition greatly angered Greece and, to a lesser extent, Serbia. The decision to recognize Macedonia was taken in part because President Zhelev's advisers feared that Turkey was about to do so and Bulgaria would be discredited if it had to follow Turkey. It was also taken in the hope that Bulgaria might exercise influence in the former Yugoslav republic, but the prime purpose of recognition was to ward off the very real prospect of a partition of Macedonia spearheaded by Greece and Serbia. Such a partition would be a repetition of 1913 but Bulgaria was not in a position to resist it on the battlefield. Macedonia had therefore to be bolstered by diplomatic means. Nationalist opinion in Bulgaria itself was not enthusiastic over the recognition of Macedonia, and in later years the fact that it was only the state, and not the nation or language that had been recognized, was to create complexities and embarrassments in relations between Sofia and Skopje. These persisted until an agreement in February 1999 resolved the outstanding differences. In the immediate term, however, Bulgaria's recognition of the new state was a stabilizing factor in an extremely febrile time in an extremely febrile area.

The means to achieving this notable external success illustrated a major weakness of the Dimitrov administration. The recognition of Macedonia had been primarily the work of the president and his close advisers, with little participation from either the minister president or the minister for foreign affairs, the latter being out of the country at the time. Zhelev had also attempted to redress Dimitrov's leaning towards the USA and had signed a treaty of friendship and cooperation with France in 1992, and a treaty of cooperation with Russia when President Yeltsin visited Bulgaria in August of the same year.

The lack of coordination between the president and minister president and within the administration itself was not an isolated phenomenon and it led to a series of disputes, including a number of bitter and public spats over the linked issues of arms sales and control of the intelligence services. By the late summer of 1992 hostilities between Dimitrov and Zhelev were open, with the latter accusing the minister president of immoderation which had alienated the press, the trade unions, and the non-parliamentary parties. Zhelev even held Dimitrov largely responsible for the fiasco in the Church.

Dimitrov could not afford to lose presidential support. His hold on his own party had never been secure but even more dangerous was disaffection within the MRF. The party was facing severe problems, some of which many Turks held to be the fault of the UDF administration. The Turks' main complaint was that the land privatization programme introduced by the UDF discriminated against them; this, they believed, was responsible for the progressive impoverishment of the Turkish minority. This was not entirely fair in that the Turks were also being hit by a worldwide decline in the demand for tobacco, the main product of many Turkish agriculturalists. Whatever the reason for their plight, many Turks responded to it by flight and this second wave of emigration raised the danger that the number of Turks might decrease to below that which would secure 4 per cent of the vote in the next election. In October the MRF finally withdrew its parliamentary backing from Dimitrov, whose government collapsed immediately.

Dimitrov's successor was Lyuben Berov, an academic and former economic adviser to the president. Berov formed a ministry of so-called experts. Its stated objectives were to privatize state property and to attract foreign capital, but it remained in office only until September 1994 and achieved virtually nothing. It introduced little in the way of much-needed economic reform and did less to tackle the growing problem of organized crime. Its most prominent piece of legislation was a bill which in effect restricted the highest ranks of the judiciary to those who had been trained under the communists. This, together with changes in the management of Bulgarian TV and the official news agency, raised fears that under Berov Bulgaria was moving back towards rather than away from communist methods of governing.

This was not the case but Bulgaria was suffering from increasing political insecurity. In the spring of 1994 Berov, who had not been well since taking office, had to undergo heart surgery. At the same time the government was losing support in the sŭbranie where the parties were fragmenting with all three groups suffering from splits and defections. Not for the first time in its modern history Bulgaria needed more government and less politics.

When Berov resigned in September 1994 a caretaker administration was formed under Reneta Indjova, Bulgaria's first woman minister president. In elections held in December the BSP secured an overall majority in the sŭbranie, the voters punishing the UDF which had dominated politics since 1991 and which was therefore held accountable for economic stagnation and the social tensions to which it was giving rise.

3. THE BSP GOVERNMENT, JANUARY 1995–APRIL 1997

The governments since 1991 had been indecisive and had done little to bring about real or effective structural change. That formed in January 1995 brought the country to the brink of bankruptcy, starvation, and collapse.

The new minister president was Zhan Videnov, who had succeeded Lilov as party leader after the BSP's electoral defeat in 1991. He was 32 years of age. The government he formed included representatives of the agrarians and one from the environmental group, Ekoglasnost. His party colleagues were mainly young komsomol colleagues who gave the impression of enthusiasm and efficiency. In his first speech to the sŭbranie as minister president Videnov committed himself to economic reform, further progress towards integration with Europe, a decrease in crime, and an improvement in relations with Russia. He was to fail spectacularly in all four areas.

For a former communist improving relations with Russia seemed an easy as well as a welcome task. Initially this seemed to be the case. In April 1993 the Berov government had signed an agreement with Russia for the supply of Russian gas below world prices and in May 1995 the Videnov cabinet capitalized on this gain by concluding agreements on trade and defence. It also concluded a deal by which Russia was to construct pipelines to carry Russian oil from Burgas to Alexandroupolis in Greece and to other points in the Balkans; a new joint Bulgarian-Russian company, TopEnergy, headed by Lukanov, was created to implement the agreement. Thereafter relations cooled rapidly. In the negotiations on the implementation of the pipeline agreement Moscow proved massively uncooperative and aggressive. The Russians then perplexed the Bulgarian government by demanding that the latter declare that it would not join NATO. Videnov had no inclination to join that organization but he could not make such a declaration on what seemed to be the orders of a foreign government. Perplexity turned to anger in April 1996 when President Yeltsin stated that Bulgaria, like Belarus and other former Soviet republics, might sign an agreement on eventual integration with Russia. Bulgaria, even under the socialists, had moved a long way from the attitudes of Zhivkov in the 1960s or early 1970s, and Yeltsin's remarks were seen as an insult to an independent state.

In economic terms the Videnov administration had much to do. Since 1989 the Bulgarian economy had suffered a catastrophic decline, with GDP dropping by a quarter between that year and 1994. This had a variety of causes. In the immediate term the departure of the Turks in the summer of 1989 had so dislocated production and distribution that there were severe shortages. In the first seven months of 1990 production was 10 per cent below even the poor levels of the previous year. The eventual return of over 40 per cent of the Turks who had fled in 1989 added to the number of mouths to be fed. This was at a time when many vendors, expecting prices to be liberated, held on to their stocks until that happy day. In September 1990 food rationing was introduced in some areas. With supplies so limited even rationing could not prevent many people having to queue for half the night for items of prime necessity such as milk. Another factor causing the economic crisis was the dissolution of Comecon; Bulgaria's trading dependence on that organization had been greater than any other east European state, and its disappearance left Bulgaria needing to find new markets for industrial goods which were still too low in quality for most purchasers. Those goods of high quality which Bulgaria had to offer, nearly all of them agricultural, were already in surplus in the markets Bulgaria wished to penetrate. To make matters worse, Bulgaria was owed money by both Libya and Iraq. Some of these debts were to be paid in much-needed oil. When Bulgaria agreed to observe UN sanctions on both countries the oil could no longer be delivered and Bulgaria thereby incurred a financial penalty which the outside world was slow to recognize and even slower to redress. In 1993 the observance of sanctions on Yugoslavia added to the burden because it severed Bulgaria's main trading route to its markets in the centre and west of Europe. There was also the need to service the mounting foreign currency debt. In 1990 Lukanov had suspended capital and then interest payments on Bulgarian debts which made further credit more difficult to secure. A breakthrough on this question was achieved in 1994 by the Berov government when an agreement with London Club which held most of the credits released Bulgaria from 50 per cent of its debt, but the agreement also meant that servicing and repayment of the remainder had to recommence. The same government also introduced VAT which in its first year produced 40 per cent more revenue than predicted.

Other reforms, however, were mostly injurious, ineffective, or absent. The land privatization act of 1992 had little immediate effect. By the end of the year no more than a quarter of landed property had been privatized and where it was the new owners seldom had the help of cooperatives or the banks and were frequently forced to retreat into subsistence farming, which further diminished the supply of food to the domestic market. So too did the fact that large numbers of those who received land through the reform had no wish to leave the towns and work on it; as a result large areas were left untilled. Berov's economic 'plan of action', with its proposal for Keynesian increases in government spending, merely alarmed powerful external agencies such as the International Monetary Fund (IMF). A number of acts by his and other governments aimed at encouraging privatization had little effect; the Dimitrov administration's hopes that its new privatization agency would bring about the selling of ninety-two enterprises in two months proved risible. Government attempts to increase the amount of foreign direct investment were almost as ineffective. The lack of the latter was in no small measure the result of the absence of any real programme of radical, structural economic reform. There were no effective bankruptcy laws; the state still commanded large sectors of the economy, including the banks and the communications networks; inflationary wage increases, such as that of 26 per cent for civil servants in the summer of 1991, were allowed; and above all no action was taken to liquidate the loss making enterprises which were amongst the main reasons for the consistently high budget deficits after 1992.

Videnov's administration exacerbated rather than ameliorated these problems. After his opening speech to parliament the minister president appeared to fulfil his reforming promises by introducing an action programme in May to implement his notions of the 'social-market economy'. Initially, as in relations with Russia, the auguries were promising. There was a 3 per cent increase in GDP in 1995, and in the first half of that year Bulgaria recorded a positive trade balance. In the same six months inflation fell from 59.4 per cent for the same period in 1994 to 15.2 per cent. In 1995 an encouraged BNB decreased interest rates no fewer than seven times.

But there were still structural weaknesses. The new administration's socialist leanings led it to increase the government's role in the economy by, for example, reintroducing price controls on 52 per cent of goods, and by allowing wages in the state sector to increase by almost a third. Ideology also persuaded the government to switch to the voucher system of privatization because this in theory allowed ownership to pass to the majority of the population and not to a small, wealthy section of it. But such a scheme does not guarantee that control of economic enterprises will pass to those best qualified to exercise it, nor does it encourage foreign participation in privatization, particularly, as was the case in Bulgaria, if it is the unprofitable or the virtually bankrupt concerns which are the first to be offered for privatization. There was also an increasing problem with food supplies, particularly of grain. Videnov could not be held responsible for the weaknesses of the UDF's decollectivization and land privatization policies, but his government did allow the export of large quantities of grain. This was questionable from the legal as well as the economic and social points of view, but closely involved in the export of grain were a number of large and powerful conglomerates which were widely believed to have close connections with leading members of the administration, including Videnov himself.

These conglomerates were now to play a decisive role in Bulgarian affairs. Their origins were to be found in the final days of communist rule when insiders within the system, realizing that it was doomed, diverted state funds into foreign bank accounts. After 1989 these funds were used to create trading or financial concerns staffed mainly by former communists, many of them from the ranks of the secret police. These conglomerates, or 'the mafia' as they were known in popular parlance, soon came to dominate large areas of the Bulgarian economy and were also reputed to be heavily engaged in illegal activities such as smuggling, especially after the imposition of sanctions on Yugoslavia had made this so easy and so lucrative. Another vital source of funds for the conglomerates was to mulct the system supporting the loss making enterprises; deals were allegedly done with suppliers who were paid inflated prices for raw materials and in return provided the conglomerate with a slice of the profits; the finished products were then sold, usually with a state subsidy to make good any losses, and once again the conglomerates were given a share of the takings. The enterprise managers also took a slice of the proceeds whilst the workforce was kept sweet by uneconomic wage increases. In effect, the profits were privatized and the losses nationalized. When pressure from the international financial organizations limited state subsidies to the loss making enterprises the burden was simply transferred to state owned banks. By 1995 subsidies to loss making enterprises from the banks were the equivalent of 15 per cent of GDP. But the conglomerates had huge political influence. Not only were high-ranking BSP members and cabinet ministers believed to be closely connected with them, but they could buy the votes of a number of sŭbranie deputies. This, many believed, was one of the principal reasons why Bulgaria had carried out so little effective economic reform and why, despite the political liberalization, it had retained so many debilitating elements of a communist economy. It was also feared that the conglomerates would resort to other more violent methods if necessary. The murder of Andreĭ Lukanov in October 1996 was widely believed to be the work of the mafia. A trial in Sofia at the end of 2003 confirmed these suspicions.

By the end of 1995 the need to prop up loss making enterprises had brought the banking system near to breaking point. In 1996 it broke. In January the Bank for Agricultural Credit 'Vitosha' had been forced to seek help from the BNB, which granted it a subsidy of $33 million. Not even this could save the bank, which then attempted to call in a number of outstanding loans, a hopeless effort in that most of these were owed by loss making enterprises which never could repay their loans and never had any intention of doing so. The Vitosha Bank had failed and its failure showed graphically the weakness of Bulgaria's transition from communism. It showed too the nexus between corruption, the political system, and the economy. In March President Zhelev complained that the banks were 'plundering' the nation.

The plundering was not yet over. Public and foreign confidence had been undermined and in May, on 'Black Friday', two more banks went under. Videnov attempted to restore calm and confidence by announcing that sixty-four of the largest loss making enterprises would be closed and a further seventy would be 'isolated', or denied any further subsidies.

At the same time the budget deficit was to be eased by increasing VAT from 18 to 22 per cent, by a levy on imports, and by swingeing increases in fuel and public utility prices. It was not enough. The IMF announced it would withhold further support from the country unless an entirely independent currency board was introduced to cut inflation, and when the government refused this condition confidence in the lev plunged yet further with nine more banks failing in September. By the end of the year interest rates had risen to 300 per cent and inflation had reached 578 per cent; with some salaries as much as three months in arrears this had a calamitous effect on many households and soup kitchens had to be set up in Sofia.

Tragically for Bulgaria the years of the Videnov administration came soon after the EU had decided in 1993 to consider admitting former communist states, as long as they fulfilled the Copenhagen criteria which demanded they have democratic political structures, functioning market economies, and the ability to bear the competitive pressures membership of the EU would entail. In December 1995 Videnov formally submitted Bulgaria's application to join the EU but any hope of its being included in the next round of expansion were naturally shattered by the economic collapse of 1996. Given the fact that as minister president Videnov never visited western Europe, it might be legitimate to ask whether his hopes were anything more than empty phrases for public consumption. Equally questionable, given the suspicions of his closeness to the mafia, were Videnov's assertions that he was determined to combat organized crime.

The Videnov administration had failed in all four of its main objectives and had brought the country to the edge of ruin. To make matters worse Videnov himself was as reluctant to compromise as he was to explain his government's problems and policies to the public.

The BSP had derived most of its support from the villages and small towns whilst the larger urban centres, and with them the media, were hostile. By the middle of 1996 almost the entire country was antagonistic or indifferent to the party, and its government was totally discredited. In June over a million people protested in a demonstration in Sofia, but a more lasting expression of public anger came with the presidential elections held on two days in October and November. The BSP candidate attracted a million fewer votes than the party had won in the 1994 elections. The victor was the UDF nominee, Petŭr Stoyanov, Zhelev having been removed from the party list by a primary contest earlier in the year. Discontent was soon voiced within the BSP itself with nineteen prominent party figures signing a letter demanding a change in leadership. On 21 December Videnov acquiesced, resigning both as minister president and leader of the party.

The country now entered a critical phase. Social deprivation was rising, as was the tension it generated, and the political system appeared to offer no solution; Videnov's putative successor, Nikolaĭ Dobrev, seemed to many to be little different from his predecessor, and elections were not scheduled for another two years. When he left office at the end of 1996 President Zhelev admitted that he was 'ashamed of the Bulgarian political class'. The UDF, led since its defeat in 1994 by Dimitrov's finance minister, Ivan Kostov, had already announced that it would accept the IMF's condition that a currency board be established and it now demanded that elections should be held immediately so that the nation might have a government which commanded public support.

The UDF's statement provided a realizable objective and public demonstrations to demand it began immediately, being much encouraged by the situation in Belgrade, where peaceful but persistent protest was to force Slobodan Milošević to accept local election results which gave victory to the opposition in a number of Serbian towns. The demonstrations in Sofia, though persistent, were not entirely peaceful, and on 10 January 1997 protesters entered the sŭbranie building, and in turn were attacked by police who injured over a hundred of the intruders, the former minister president Filip Dimitrov being among their number. Tensions rose again on 22 January after the incoming president, Stoyanov, was forced by constitutional convention to nominate Dobrev, the leader of the largest group in parliament, as minister president. At this juncture the country was nearer to civil war than at any point since 1989.

The impasse was broken by the political class so despised by Zhelev. On 4 February Dobrev announced that for the sake of national unity and stability he would not accept the post of minister president. On the same day the political parties met and agreed that parliament should be dissolved and that new elections should take place in April, until when a caretaker ministry under the mayor of Sofia, Stefan Sofiyanski, should hold office.

Before the elections there was some party redefinition. The UDF joined with the Political Union which had held 18 seats in the outgoing sŭbranie and was itself an amalgam of the old Democratic Party and

BANU-NP. The new grouping was known as the United Democratic Forces (UtDF), though the UDF was by far the most influential element in it. The BSP lost a discontented wing which defected to form Euro-Left, and the MRF joined with a number of smaller parties, including some monarchists, to form the Alliance for National Salvation (ANS). The elections produced an entirely predictable UtDF victory.

4. THE KOSTOV GOVERNMENT AND MOVEMENT TOWARDS THE EU AND NATO, APRIL 1997–JUNE 2001

The collapse of the Videnov government marked the most important dividing line in Bulgaria's post-communist history. To a large number of voters in 1997 the BSP seemed, as it did to many outsiders, an unreconstructed communist party: it was pro-Russian, corrupt, interventionist, incompetent, and incapable of or unwilling to accept post-1989 realities. The BSP recognized this and after 1997 shed its slavish pro-Russianism, ended its opposition to Bulgaria's joining NATO, and attempted to distance itself from the conglomerates. Its reformist attitudes made it more a European style social democratic organization than a former Soviet style communist party. On the other side of the political spectrum the UtDF had a coherent right of centre programme which enabled it to establish effective links with the European Peoples' Party in Brussels. For the country as a whole the failure of the socialist party at home meant that the only realistic future was with the west, a point reinforced by the Russian financial crisis of 1998. The west would demand effective and radical economic reform, which after the Videnov government most Bulgarians realized was inevitable. It was in this sense that the Videnov government marked the divide between ineffective and real economic transition in Bulgaria. It was also a political dividing line. Before the elections of 1997 no government in post-communist Bulgaria had lasted its full constitutional term of four years and the two socialist administrations had been driven from office by extra-parliamentary action on the streets rather than by due constitutional process. The next two governments both lasted their full constitutional term. It was not that political drama was lacking after 1997, but this was now mostly played out in its proper parliamentary and constitutional arena rather than on the streets. Bulgaria's political prestige as well as its economic stability increased and within a decade of the 1996–7 crisis the country had been admitted to NATO and the EU.

Ivan Kostov headed the first non-socialist government in post-communist Bulgaria to enjoy an absolute majority in parliament. The change in party leadership and in the presidency also meant that this administration, unlike Dimitrov's, was not hobbled by a running battle between the two major office holders. The new government's immediate target was to restore economic sanity and stability; its major objective was to move Bulgaria closer towards the western network of international organizations, above all the EU and NATO. It succeeded in both objectives but was to fail to grapple successfully with the perennial problems of crime and corruption.

Kostov's first major act was to fulfil his promise to introduce a fully independent currency board. It began operating in July 1997 and pegged the leva to the Deutschmark (DM) at a rate of a thousand to one, the euro replacing the DM in 1999. The board insisted that any increase in the money in circulation must be matched by an equal increase in the nation's reserves. The medicine was simple but tough. And it worked; the inflation rate was below double figures in 1998 and 1999.

In June 1998 Bulgaria had been admitted to the central European free trade zone and this, together with currency stability, aided Bulgarian trade, including that with the EU. This had been rising as a share of the total since 1993 but the increase was more rapid after 1997, and between 1993 and 1999 the share of the EU in Bulgaria's foreign trade almost doubled, moving up from 28 to 52 per cent. Volumes were low but on the other hand Bulgaria was one of the few east European countries to balance its trade with the EU.[3]

Integration into the EU was the ultimate goal of the new government. To this end Kostov set up the council on European integration which was intended to guide Bulgarian institutions through the maze of regulations which the *acquis communitaire* would require. There were a series of other measures, all of them intended to make Bulgaria qualify as a functioning market economy. Videnov's price controls were removed; new laws were

---

[3] Vesselin Dimitrov, 'Learning to Play the Game: Bulgaria's Relations with Multilateral Organizations', *Southeast European Politics*, 1/2 (Dec. 2000), 101–14, 105.

enacted on public procurement, standardization, and the liberalization of the communications industry; and there were, at last, effective measures to encourage privatization. By the end of 2000 around 70 per cent of Bulgarian enterprises were in private ownership, though when it sold the country's major oil refinery to the Russian LUKoil company the government retained a 'golden share' which enabled it to veto any decision which might drastically reduce production. Another significant advance was the liquidation of the loss making enterprises. The IMF had insisted that forty-one of the largest of these be sold or closed by the summer of 1999 and in July of that year the government announced that this deadline had been met; amongst the enterprises disposed of was the massive metallurgical complex at Kremikovtsi, sold to an Italian company for the princely sum of one US dollar. The IMF responded warmly to Sofia's efforts; in May a senior official had described the economic policies of the Bulgarian government as 'exemplary' and loans were forthcoming from the IMF, the World Bank, and the EU.

There were also measures in the non-economic sector which were taken, in part at least, to improve Bulgaria's chances of admission to the European club. To allay fears over the minorities question legislation was introduced in 1998 to allow Bulgarian radio and TV to relay programmes in languages other than Bulgarian for 'Bulgarian citizens whose mother tongue is not Bulgarian'. There were also steps to encourage the foundation of schools which taught in Turkish or other minority languages.

In the first years of the new government Brussels appeared a hard task master and in March 1999 a frustrated Kostov had wondered aloud whether it was worth persevering with negotiations if there was no prospect of membership of the EU for fifteen or more years. But in December of that year the Helsinki conference of the EU agreed that negotiations on the entry of Bulgaria and Romania should begin. For Bulgaria there was further encouragement at the end of 2000 when it was announced that from April 2001 Bulgarian citizens, though not those of Romania with which Bulgaria was usually coupled in European negotiations, would no longer require visas to enter the Schengen area.

Bulgaria's application to join NATO had been submitted by Sofiyanski's interim government and that of Kostov took a number of steps to advance Bulgaria's case. In 1999 the headquarters of the new Balkan peacekeeping force opened in Plovdiv. This 3,000-strong body had been created in the previous year and was to consist of units from

Italy, Albania, Bulgaria, Greece, Macedonia, Romania, and Turkey; it was welcomed by NATO, and others, as a useful factor in promoting regional stability. In the same month Kostov introduced 'Plan 2004' to refashion the Bulgarian army to make it conform to NATO requirements and practices, whilst in 2001 the Bulgarian government, without prior parliamentary approval, responded to the emergency in Macedonia, where Albanian unrest threatened civil war, by immediately promising NATO free use of its territory for the transit and, if necessary, the deployment of alliance troops. What did more than anything to advance Bulgaria's cause in NATO, however, was Sofia's conduct during the Kosovo emergency of 1998–9. Despite widespread popular disapproval the Bulgarian government allowed NATO aircraft attacking Kosovo and Serbia free use of Bulgarian air space. This privilege was then denied to the Russians who asked for permission to overfly Bulgaria to take supplies to their troops sent precipitately to Prishtina airport in June 1999. In November the United States signalled its gratitude when President Clinton became the first US head of state to visit Bulgaria.

The Kosovo crisis indirectly brought another benefit to Bulgaria. For years there had been negotiations with Romania on the construction of a second bridge across the Danube, but although there was agreement that such a bridge should be built there was no consensus on where, the Bulgarians wanting it cited near Vidin and the Romanians preferring a much more easterly route which would mean international traffic spending more time, and therefore more money, in Romania. The closure of all routes—road, rail, and river—during and after the Kosovo crisis underlined the urgent need for a second Danube crossing and the EU, which wanted the bridge as part of its pan-European transport strategy, stepped in, reaffirming its offer of funding and insisting that the bridge be built near Vidin. Construction began in 2005 with a projected completion date in 2008.

The Helsinki decision in December 1999 naturally intensified the Bulgarian government's efforts to conform to the tough demands made by Brussels. In 2000 Bulgaria abolished duties on 470 agricultural products imported from the EU, and also took drastic measures to make its food producing industry conform to European standards, these measures including the closure of 311 meat producing plants and 230 dairy farms. In another step intended to prove its pro-European credentials the Kostov government in 2001 introduced classes in EU integration into

Bulgarian high schools, the lessons covering the geography, history, economics, politics, and philosophy of contemporary Europe.

Greater transparency in public life was a valid goal in itself but it was also one which would strengthen Bulgaria's case for admission to the EU. In 1997 police files were opened for inspection by those on whom they had been compiled, and the ministry of the interior released the names of some public figures who had worked for the former communist security agencies. In February 2001 the government went further and granted more open access to the police files; this caused embarrassment to some but it served the beneficial purpose of making matters much more open; insinuations could now be disproved or confirmed by looking at the record and the unpleasant phenomenon of 'file blackmail' declined.

Neither the EU nor NATO would be prepared to admit states which had serious border problems. Ever since Bulgaria had recognized the new Macedonian state at the beginning of 1992 relations between Sofia and Skopje had been tense. The shadow of history still hung over the two states and their contemporary relations were complicated by Bulgaria's refusal to recognize the Macedonian language, and by Macedonia's insistence that all negotiations and agreements be conducted in two languages. An agreement in February 1999 finally settled these issues when both sides renounced any territorial claim upon the other, and agreed that negotiations between them should be conducted in 'the official languages of the two countries'.

As measures such as the opening of police files and the earlier steps to increase the use of minority languages indicated, Brussels' demands went beyond the economic sphere. There were three extra-economic areas which proved particularly difficult for the Bulgarians. The first was Kozloduĭ, the second the need to reform the judiciary, and the third crime and corruption.

During the Yugoslav wars of the early 1990s a European government had asked its Balkan embassies what they thought were the greatest immediate dangers in the peninsula. One ambassador returned a single-word answer: 'Kozloduĭ'.[4] It was an opinion widely shared in Brussels where fitful discussions on the problem had been taking place for years, and where at least four of the six Soviet-built reactors at Kozloduĭ were considered unsafe. As these reactors produced between 30 and 40 per cent

---

[4] Personal information.

of Bulgaria's energy needs to close them all would produce intolerable burdens, and would force Bulgaria to spend so much on imported electricity that its exports would become totally uncompetitive. Kostov resisted pressure on this point but in the end was faced with a stark choice: accept Brussels' terms or forget about entering the EU.[5] In November 1999 Kostov bowed to the inevitable, agreeing that the two oldest reactors would close by 2002, and reactors three and four in 2006; in return, the EU promised to provide 200 million dollars to help cover the costs of closure. It was a decision accepted reluctantly by the Kostov government and one confirmed by its successor, but there remained powerful sectors of public opinion and the political establishment which did not accept that the settlement was just or non-negotiable.

The problem of judicial reform was one which the Kostov government had little time to address, it being left to the next administration to tackle this extremely difficult problem. The questions of crime and corruption were hardly any easier to solve but they were very much a preoccupation of Kostov and his ministerial colleagues.

Petty crime had increased considerably immediately after the fall of communism as open contempt for the police was felt and expressed. By the end of the 1990s it seemed out of control and seemingly affected everyone; even the former king was robbed on a visit to Sofia in 1999. In the first half of 2001 there were an average of 380 offences per day. Petty crime bred more serious misdemeanours. In one ten-day period there were ten murders in Sofia, most of them arising from turf wars between gangs engaged in prostitution, drug dealing, and other lesser crimes.

Much more serious was smuggling, particularly to evade the sanctions imposed on Serbia and Montenegro; in 1998 this was estimated to be worth around $850 million, much the same as the national defence budget. Many of the smugglers were presumed to be former secret service officers who had privatized their former networks to carry out the new illegal operations. Kostov insisted that this practice must cease not only because it was immoral and damaging to the social and economic fabric, but also because all the multilateral agencies, the EU included, demanded

---

[5] For details see Matthew S. Tejada, *Bulgaria's Democratic Consolidation and the Kozloduy Nuclear Power Plant: The Unattainability of Closure*, with a foreword by Richard J. Crampton, Soviet and Post-Soviet Politics and Society, series editor Andreas Umland (Stuttgart: *Ibidem*, 2005).

it be expunged. The smuggling rings, however, were presumed to have links to the conglomerates which had not been dissolved since the fall of Videnov, and whose influence still reached into the upper echelons of the state and government structures. Kostov was damaged by his failure to tame them.

He was harmed even more by a series of scandals in the first year of the new millennium. In April a government spokesperson was forced to resign after being accused of accepting a bribe of $10,000 from a businessman. In June Bulgaria's chief negotiator with the EU, Aleksandŭr Bozhkov, left office after a judicial inquiry into his activities; he had previously been minister in charge of privatization, during which time he had earned the title of 'Mr Ten Per Cent'. Most embarrassing of all for Kostov was an allegation in the socialist newspaper, *Trud* (Labour), in September that a charity run by his wife had accepted $80,000 from the Russian mafia; to make matters worse Yelena Kostova did not deny the allegation and said she saw nothing wrong in putting bad money to good use. The Russian donors then stated that not only had they handed money to Mrs Kostova's charity but that they had also been giving nearly half a million US dollars a month to the UtDF. The businessmen concerned were expelled from Bulgaria in March 2001.

Kostov admitted that he had not been sufficiently rigorous in combating corruption and tried to retrieve some credibility by enacting a law requiring all government officials to declare their personal wealth when they entered and when they left office. It was little more than a tilt at the windmill of corruption and it did nothing to save Kostov's plummeting reputation at home and abroad.

The corruption problem impeded progress in the accession negotiations in Brussels, and at home it severely damaged the UtDF's prospects for the elections due in the first half of 2001. Those prospects had already suffered from a slackening in the pace of economic growth. This had been 18.9 per cent in early 1998, though this was against the low figures of 1997, and such a high level could not be maintained; in the first quarter of 1999 it was only 0.7 per cent. The adoption of the EU's rules on food processing plants diminished supplies and therefore exerted an upward pressure on prices; by 2000 inflation had reached 7 per cent and this at a time when the average monthly wage was declining; in May 1999 it had been $124 but by November 2000 had fallen back to $115. Whilst wages were falling unemployment was rising and by February 2000 had reached

18.4 per cent. Unemployment was particularly high amongst the Turkish and Roma minorities but was also at a worryingly high level amongst the young and particularly the educated young. One unemployed young computer expert hacked into the president's website and as a reward was offered a job, but for many the only alternative to years on public benefit seemed to be emigration. This, like unemployment, depressed public morale and lowered the UtDF's stock. So too did the widespread, and credible, conviction that many of the small number of Bulgarians who had become very rich very rapidly had done so by illegitimate means.

These factors helped to turn the popular mood against the government, a fact registered in the UtDF's disappointing performance in local elections in the autumn of 1999. Its woes were increased in 2000 and early 2001 by a series of defections from the party. But there seemed little alternative. The BSP had been regrouping since the debacle of 1996–7 and was embarrassed early in 2001 when an investigative journalist revealed details of the origin of the regenerative process; this made the seemingly sensible alliance of the BSP and the MRF improbable. The political situation was then transformed by ex-King Simeon. There had been rumours early in 2001 that he intended to run as a candidate in the presidential elections later in the year but he failed to fulfil the residence qualifications so in April announced that he would enter the parliamentary race at the head of the newly formed National Movement Simeon II (NMSS). Though not yet a political party the appearance of the NMSS meant an end to the basically bipolar post-1989 situation where the UDF and its allies had contested with the BSP and its affiliates.

The new movement was populist, but it was an inclusive not an exclusive populism; it did not denigrate or attack any group other than the corrupt. It appealed to Muslims as well as Christians and secured a high proportion of votes from the Roma and the Bulgarian Turks. It had support in rural as well as urban constituencies, and amongst the intelligentsia and professional elements as well as the working class. It made a particular effort to attract women and the young, and a large proportion of both groups figured prominently in the movement's membership. Its most well-known supporters included some television presenters and a pop star, but also a small number of young Bulgarians who had had dazzlingly successful careers in the money markets of the west.

During the elections Simeon had made the startling promise to the voters that if victorious he would institute 'a system of economic measures and partnerships which, within eight hundred days . . . will change your life.' He intended, he said, to alter the ethical base of society as well as the country's economic structures, this being a clear reference to his determination to root out corruption.

The NMSS soon established a lead in the opinion polls which was maintained until the elections of 17 June when it secured 120 seats in the 240-strong sŭbranie. The UtDF had 51 seats, the BSP-dominated Coalition for Bulgaria 48, and the MRF 21. Forty-eight of the NMSS deputies were female as were almost a quarter of the new parliament, whereas the proportion in previous assemblies had never been higher than a tenth.

The NMSS had benefited from the weakness of its main opponents but the principal reason for its victory was the hope which many voters placed in 'the king'. He had considerable personal charm and it was hoped that his connections with and business experiences in the west would benefit Bulgaria. More important was the fact that, unlike any other political leader in post-totalitarian Bulgaria, he had never been part of the communist system nor did he have any connections with either of the two main groups which had dominated the political system since 1989. Most important of all, however, was the fact that he was completely free of any suspicion of personal corruption, and it was assumed that his personal wealth, though not enormous, was enough to mean that he would remain free of contamination.

5. GOVERNMENT BY 'THE KING' AND ENTRY INTO NATO AND THE EU, JUNE 2001–JUNE 2005

When he returned to Bulgaria in 2001 Simeon had adopted the official surname of Saksekoburggotski. This cumbersome label was seldom used outside official circles and in popular usage the new minister president was simply 'tsarya', or 'the king'. It was a remarkable feat for a former king to return from exile as minister president and there were some Bulgarians who suspected that his ultimate aim was to restore the monarchy. This Simeon denied, insisting that his only aim was to reshape Bulgaria and to take it into NATO and the EU. To do this, as he had already made clear, would demand further economic restructuring, a radical reform of the judiciary, and the defeat of crime and corruption. These objectives were little different from those of the Kostov government but the ministerial team assembled to pursue them was more varied and appeared more dynamic. The majority of the new cabinet were NMSS supporters but there were also two members of the MRF and two from the BSP. The minister for foreign affairs, Solomon Pasi, was from the small Jewish community. Economic policy was to be dominated by two young financial whizz-kids, Nikolaï Vasilev, who became minister for the economy and a deputy minister president, and Milen Velchev, who became finance minister. They were aged 31 and 35 respectively. The NMSS administration was to achieve the notable successes of securing NATO membership for Bulgaria and signing an agreement with the EU which stated that, subject to certain conditions, Bulgaria would join that organization on 1 January 2007.

Entry into NATO proved easier than admission to the EU. If progress in talks with NATO had been advanced by Bulgaria's official policy during the Kosovo crisis, Sofia's conduct in the wars in Afghanistan and Iraq helped even more. During the Afghan war in 2001 US planes had been allowed use of the Bulgarian air base at Sarafovo. In the following year, in response to some criticism from the secretary-general of NATO, Bulgaria made further efforts to slim down its military establishment and transform its army into a modern, professional force. This satisfied NATO headquarters and at its conference in Prague in November 2002 the alliance issued an invitation to Bulgaria to join its ranks. In March 2003 the sŭbranie passed the legislation necessary for it to do so.

When this legislation was enacted Bulgaria was enjoying an international profile higher than at any time since the second, or perhaps even the first world war. It was then a non-permanent member of the UN Security Council and it was about to become of considerable strategic significance in the war in Iraq. Once again the Americans were offered the use of Sarafovo and this became a vital factor when Turkey refused to allow US troops to cross its territory en route to Iraq. After the war Bulgaria joined the international forces in Iraq, sending 500 soldiers to serve under Polish command in Kerbala. It was not a popular decision with the Bulgarian public, and hostility intensified after five Bulgarian soldiers were killed in December 2004. Nevertheless, the country's contribution to the American-British invasion of Iraq consolidated its membership of NATO.

On the domestic front the campaign to reshape the economy involved technical readjustments rather than dramatic restructurings. Privatization, particularly in the energy sector, was speeded up, tax changes were introduced to encourage investment, and a fund established to provide credit to small businesses. In 2001 a minimum monthly wage of 100 leva was introduced, public sector wages were raised by almost a fifth, and a doubling in child benefits announced for the beginning of 2002. To help pay for this electricity and central heating prices were to rise by 10 per cent. That these policies were far from popular was seen in the presidential election in November 2001 which produced a surprise victory for the BSP contender, Georgi Pŭrvanov. Pŭrvanov's success owed much to the fact that the incumbent Stoyanov was deserted by his own UDF supporters, but the new president's statements that he intended to use his powers to shield the poor from the effects of economic reform and to bring Bulgaria closer to Russia did not help the Bulgarian cause in Brussels.

The EU had already made discouraging remarks in October when it stated that Bulgaria still did not have a functioning market economy. It was becoming clear that the EU was now concentrating more on the non-economic demands for membership, insisting that more must be done to combat crime and corruption, to reform the judicial system, and to improve the lot of the minorities, above all the Roma. It came as little surprise to Sofia when in December 2001 the Laeken meeting of the EU excluded Bulgaria from the states to be included in the next round of expansion.

The NMSS government responded rapidly. It took steps to implement a framework programme for the integration of the Roma minority into Bulgarian society drawn up by the Kostov government in 1999. By 2003 schemes to combat adult illiteracy amongst Roma were in place as were measures to improve teaching for Roma in primary and secondary schools. In September 2003 an anti-discrimination law was passed banning all forms of discrimination based on gender, ethnicity, race, religion, age, education, property, and sexual orientation. The government also set up an anti-discrimination commission, an independent executive agency responsible only to the sŭbranie, to deal with all cases of discrimination in Bulgaria.

There was also steady progress in the economic sector. GDP grew by over 4 per cent in the five years up to 2002 and in that year Bulgaria's credit rating was raised five times. State revenue was also greater than forecast, a major reason for this being a steady increase in returns from the customs service after reforms were introduced to combat corruption in 2001. Even unemployment declined from 17.6 per cent in April 2002 to 14.9 per cent a year later. Inflation also fell and by November 2003 the annual rate was down to 2.5 per cent. There was a major success in the privatization process in August 2003 when the State Savings Bank, the second largest in the country, was sold; it was the last remaining state bank and its privatization meant that over four-fifths of the assets the government had earmarked for privatization had been sold.

These successes had their desired impact in the European corridors of power and in December 2002 the Copenhagen meeting of the EU decided that serious accession negotiations with Bulgaria, and with Romania, should begin with a target entry date of January 2007. But there were still a number of hurdles to be overcome before success in these talks could be guaranteed.

The EU remained concerned at Bulgarian attitudes over Kozloduĭ. The socialists, the president, and a substantial slice of public opinion were still opposed to the agreement reached reluctantly by Kostov, and in March 2003 their cause was bolstered by the supreme administrative court, which declared the intended closure of reactors three and four unconstitutional. This intensified the confrontation between the government and the judiciary.

That confrontation arose over a number of issues. At the end of 2002 the courts had declared illegal two vital privatizations, that of Bulgartabak and of BTK, the state telecommunications monopoly. Both privatizations had been insisted upon by Brussels but they were both complex processes, that of Bulgartabak being particularly sensitive because so many workers in the tobacco industry were Turks; a confidential report warned the government that if too many workers were laid off as a result of privatization there could be civil unrest in the tobacco growing areas. In retaliation for the courts' action over Kozloduĭ, Bulgartabak, and BTK, the government introduced a number of reforms to the judicial system which in turn provoked further resistance from the judges who effectively blocked the two privatizations for another year.

Behind the contest between government and judiciary lay an issue more important than the privatizations themselves. The action of the courts was seen in Brussels, and indeed by many in Sofia, as an example of how the Bulgarian judiciary could be manipulated by vested commercial or criminal interests. The question of the judiciary could not be dissociated from that of crime and corruption.

The NMSS government had taken energetic measures to combat these evils. In October 2001 a national anti-crime strategy was adopted and in February 2002 a national service for dealing with organized crime was established. Scotland Yard was invited to advise on how to combat corruption in the ministry of the interior and the police, and in September 2003 over 200 officials were dismissed and 700 employees from the ministry of the interior were under investigation. In 2002 Transparency International's Corruption Perception Index placed Bulgaria in 45th place; in 1998 it had been 66th and the advance was greater than any other candidate country, but two years later a public opinion survey found that 96 per cent of Bulgarians still believed they lived in a corrupt country. Another survey found that nearly 40 per cent of Bulgarians considered corruption to be the country's biggest problem and many interviewees stated that judges, policemen, politicians, doctors, and tax collectors were the most corrupt.[6]

The major problem, however, was seen to lie in the judiciary. In January 2003 General Boïko Borisov, the chief secretary of the ministry of the interior and the head of the nation's police services, asserted that his efforts to combat organized crime had been frustrated by the judiciary, and in April he told the press that his ministry had prepared a report which, backed by photographic evidence, proved that members of the criminal underworld had colluded with leading figures in both the government and the judiciary. The seriousness of these allegations was underlined by a series of murders or attempted murders, the most sensational of which was the killing in March 2003 of Ilya Pavlov, the head of the Multigroup conglomerate and one of Bulgaria's richest men; on the day before his death he had given evidence at the Andreï Lukanov murder trial.

The government seized upon Borisov's allegations and in September presented to the sŭbranie a bill to limit the judiciary's right to involve itself in political affairs and to reduce external influences on the judges. The bill was supported by 230 of the deputies. It was the first amendment to the 1991 constitution and it was of enormous significance in Bulgaria's negotiations with the EU because it brought about agreement on the justice and home affairs chapter of the *acquis communitaire*, which in turn meant that Bulgaria had completed the technical negotiations on entry.

[6] Information from Patricia Curtis, 'Problems of Economic Transition in the Balkans and EU Foreign Policy: A Case Study of Bulgaria', draft D.Phil. thesis (Oxford).

After the enactment of the judiciary bill Bulgaria's path to EU entry was relatively smooth. In November 2003 the EU at last conceded that Bulgaria, unlike Romania, had a functioning market economy and in February 2004 the European parliament gave enthusiastic endorsement to Bulgaria's case for accession. Negotiations came to an end on 14 June of that year in Luxembourg, where it was decided that accession would indeed take place on 1 January 2007, with the qualification that entry could be delayed for a year if the EU considered progress on the implementation of the agreements was not satisfactory.

6. POSTSCRIPT: THE ELECTIONS OF 2005

The government of the king achieved its strategic objective of integrating Bulgaria into the western and Atlantic structures of NATO and the EU. Its tactical successes on the domestic front were less imposing. It failed to convince the majority of the nation that life had become better. Unemployment, crime, corruption, pensioner poverty, and demographic decline weighed in the balance against the move towards the west, as did some of the concessions the government had been forced to make to the west. By the summer of 2005 popular feeling against the NMSS was intensifying and the elections on 25 June provided the opportunity to register this disenchantment. There was little surprise that the NMSS lost, or that the BSP emerged as the largest party, their respective share of the polls being 19.88 and 30.95 per cent. The MRF prospered, increasing its vote to 12.8 per cent of the total, but to the astonishment of most, and the despair of many the 'Ataka' (Attack) movement attracted almost 300,000 votes or 8.14 per cent of the total. Ataka polled more votes than the UDF. With its xenophobic and Bulgaro-centric slogans of 'give Bulgaria back to the Bulgarians' and 'stop the Gypsy terror', it marked a sinister turn towards the dark forces seen in the former Yugoslavia and Romania and previously absent from Bulgaria. The distribution of seats meant that no group could easily form a government and negotiations dragged on for eight weeks before the BSP leader, Sergeĭ Stanishev, was able to form a grand coalition which included the MRF and the NMSS. But the slowness in forming the administration, and the apparently trivial arguments used by all parties to the process, was not a good advertisement for Bulgarian political maturity. A number of doubting voices were raised in Brussels and elsewhere, and these became louder and more numerous after the murder in late October of the banker Emil Kyulev; by the end of 2005 there had been 140 mafia-related murders in fifteen years. In addition to this, the country appeared to be sinking into a mire of corruption; the expectation of increased EU subsidies stimulating not so much economic growth and investment as more refined and impenetrable mechanisms for filching money. In May 2006 the EU reacted sternly. Bulgaria, together with Romania, was in effect put on probation for a further six months, but the harsher conditions were imposed on the former. The EU announced a tightening of the conditions which Bulgaria had to fulfil if it were to enter the union on schedule. Those conditions included real evidence that the Bulgarian authorities had the will and the ability to implement the promises it had made to Brussels. There were particular demands that Bulgaria do more to ensure its judiciary was free of links with criminal elements, to combat criminality and corruption, and to contain evils such as the traffic in narcotics and human beings.

Despite these tough warnings entry into the EU was not delayed and took place on the appointed date of 1 January 2007.

15

The Minority and Demographic Questions

Vasil Levski said before the liberation that when Ottoman power had been removed 'Bulgarians, Turks, Jews, and others will be equal in all respects, irrespective of faith, nationality, or social position.'[1] The architects of the Tŭrnovo constitution intended that Levski's words should be fulfilled. They were careful to include in the members of the constituent assembly representatives of the non-Bulgarian and the non-Orthodox communities, and article 57 of the constitution promised all Bulgarian citizens equality before the law whilst article 61 gave freedom to any slave the moment he or she set foot on Bulgarian territory.

An obligation to protect minorities had been included in both the San Stefano and Berlin settlements in 1878 and were to be repeated after the first world war, article 50 of the treaty of Neuilly requiring Bulgaria to sign a minority protection treaty and, 'to assure full and complete protection of life and liberty to all inhabitants of Bulgaria without distinction of birth, nationality, language, race or religion'. The radicals of the agrarian and socialist movements rejected nationalism but Bulgaria did not remain immune from the nationalist virulence which affected Europe in the inter-war years and in the 1930s racist thinking and action increased. But there were still some who could argue for racial tolerance which, they insisted, was in the national tradition; in 1929 Kiril Hristov published a long essay preaching the benefits of racial admixtures,[2] and in

---

[1] Cited in Ĭono Mitev, *Istoriya na aprilskoto vŭstanie 1876*, vol.i, *Predpostavki i podgotovka* (Sofia: BAN, 1986), 143.

[2] 'Ot natsiya kŭm rasa', published in *Uchilishten Pregled*, 1929, no. 8 and included in Elenkov and Daskalov, *Zashto sme takiva?*, 429–53.

1934 Konstantin Gŭlŭbov's 'Psihologiya na bŭlgarina' (Psychology of the Bulgarian) argued that the tradition of ethnic tolerance was a cause for national pride.[3] By the end of the 1930s ethnic tolerance was an increasingly rare commodity but the early years of communist domination saw an equal and opposite reaction with the minorities enjoying a great deal of freedom in the second half of the 1940s. The advent of large-scale industrial units and of collectivized agriculture reversed this trend inadvertently or by intent because, as Yugov told the 7th party congress in 1958, 'In the collective farms it is easier to destroy old traditions and relations.'[4] Thirty years later Zhivkov launched the regenerative process, the most blatant rejection of the vaunted national tradition of ethnic tolerance, and a policy which, like the racism of the late 1930s and early 1940s, produced a swing in the opposite direction in the decade after 1989 when there was talk of 'Bulgaria's ethnic model' as a solution for minority problems in the former Soviet bloc.[5] In 1991 an official report to the committee on the elimination of racial discrimination stated that racial discrimination was ' "incompatible with the ideology and social practice of the Bulgarian people whose tolerance has been transmitted throughout its centuries-long history." '[6] Whether the success of Ataka in the elections of 2005 marked yet another swing of the pendulum remains to be seen.

Ever since the Ottoman conquest of the fourteenth century the largest minority group in Bulgaria has been that of the Turks. This element has declined since 1878, and the Greek minority has all but disappeared. The Jews too have largely left the country. The Roma have long been present but until the period after the fall of communism had been largely ignored, whilst the Bulgarian attitude to the Pomaks has generally been one of suppressed hostility.

---

[3] Originally published in *Bŭlgarska misŭl*, 9/1 (1934), 29–40 and 9/2: 109–99. The essays are reproduced in Elenkov and Daskalov, *Zashto sme takiva?*, 213–30.

[4] Cited in Neuburger, *Orient Within*, 190.

[5] Vladimir Chukov, 'A Pragmatical National Version of the Multiethnic Dialog', in four parts on http://members.tripod.com/crcs0/lgivl.html. These articles contain useful information and stimulating arguments but are written in appallingly bad English.

[6] Cited by Bernd Rechel, 'Minority Rights in Post-Communist Bulgaria', Ph.D. thesis, (Birmingham, 2006), 209.

Table 15.1 The population of Bulgaria by ethnic identity, 1880/4–2001[a]

Year	Total population	Bulgarians		Turks		Greeks		Jews		Roma	
		Number	%	Number	%	Number	%	Number	%	Number	%
1880/1	2,823,865	1,919,067	67.96	701,984	24.86	54,205	1.92	18,519	0.66	57,148	2.02
1887	3,154,375	2,326,250	73.75	607,331	19.25	58,326	1.85	23,571	0.75	50,291	1.60
1892	3,310,713	2,505,326	75.67	569,728	17.21	58,518	1.77	27,531	0.83	52,132	1.57
1900	3,744,283	2,887,860	77.13	539,656	14.41	70,887	1.89	32,573	0.87	89,549	2.39
1905	4,035,575	3,205,019	79.42	497,820	12.34	69,761	1.73	36,455	0.90	94,649	2.35
1910	4,337,513	3,523,311	81.23	504,560	11.63	50,886	1.17	38,554	0.89	121,573	2.80
1920	4,846,971	4,041,276	83.38	542,904	11.20	46,759	0.96	41,927	0.87	61,555	1.27
1926	5,528,741	4,455,355	80.59	577,552	10.45	10,564	0.19	41,563	0.75	81,996	1.48
1934	6,077,939	5,274,854	86.79	618,268	10.17	9,601	0.16	28,026	0.46	80,532	1.32
1946	7,029,349	6,073,124	86.40	675,500	9.61	Unknown		44,209	0.63	170,011	2.42
1956	7,613,709	6,506,541	85.46	656,025	8.62	7,437	0.10	6,027	0.08	197,865	2.60
1965	8,227,866	7,231,243	87.89	780,928	9.49	8,241	0.10	5,108	0.06	148,874	1.81
1975	8,727,771	7,930,024	90.86	730,728	8.37	Unknown		3,076	0.04	18,323	0.21
1992	8,487,317	7,271,185	85.67	800,052	9.43	4,930	0.06	3,461	0.04	313,396	3.70
2001	7,928,901	6,655,210	83.94	746,664	9.42	3,219	0.04	2,300[b]	0.03	370,908	4.68

[a] The censuses from 1880 and 1887 measured ethnicity by mother tongue, but in 1900 self-identification was allowed, and in 1926 the classification of 'language of everyday use' was introduced; those completing the census were required to answer the questions: '1. What language do you normally speak at home? 2. What are you by nationality, parentage, and race?'. In 1934 the latter was the only category allowed in determining ethnicity. In 1946 language of everyday use was combined with 'nationality', there being 39 available nationalities to choose from and four languages of everyday use: Bulgarian, Turkish, Romany, and Armenian. In 1956 Soviet practice was adopted, and 'nationality' became the sole category for determining ethnicity. In 1965 language of everyday use was reintroduced; the only change in 1975 was that the list of available 'nationality' categories was reduced to 36. In 1985 it was further reduced, to 12 with Cuban and Vietnamese being included in the list, the latter because of the number of immigrant Vietnamese workers, virtually all of whom left after 1989. (I am grateful to Dr Svetla Baloutzova for this information on census categories).

[b] Estimated number.

Sources: For 1880/1 see the censuses taken in Eastern Rumelia in 1880 and in Bulgaria on 1 January 1881, and given in Spiridion Gopčević, *Bulgarien und Ostrumelien, mit besonderer Berücksichtigung des Zeitraumes von 1878–1886, nebst militärischer Würdigung des serbo-bulgarischen Krieges* (Leipzig: Elischer, 1886), 18–22. These figures are less reliable than those for later censuses, and slightly different statistics are given in Franz Josef Prinz von Battenberg, *Die Volkswirtschaftliche Entwicklung Bulgariens von 1879 bis zur Gegenwart* (Leipzig: Veit & Co., 1891), 6–8; for 1887–1900, Direktsiya na Statistikata, *Naselenieto na Bŭlgariya spored prebroyavaniyata na 1 Januarii 1888, 1 Januarii 1893, i 31 dekemvrii 1900* (Sofia: Dŭrzhavna Pechatnitsa, 1907), for 1905–1926, see *Statisticheski Godishnik na bŭlgarskoto tsarstvo*, 25 (1933) (Sofia: Dŭrzhavna Pechatnitsa, 1933), table 15. Further information from www.nsi.bg/Census_e/Census_e.thm;http://countrystudies.us/bulgaria/25.thm. Figures for the 1975 census are clearly unreliable, with the Bulgarians being over-represented and the Roma massively under-recorded. There was a census in 1985, during the regenerative process; to my knowledge its results have never been published. The 1992 figures are from www. unhchr. ch/tbs/doc. nsf/(Symbol)/CERD. C.299. Add. 7. En?Opendocument. I wish to acknowledge the help received in drawing up this table from Dr Svetla Baloutzova and Dr Bernd Rechel.

1. THE MUSLIMS: TURKS AND POMAKS, 1878–1989

The war of 1877–8 produced a wave of Muslim emigration. Some Muslims were driven out by a fear of reprisals for the wrongs they had committed, others left rather than face the unpredictable and random violence of war and conquest. The exodus was greater in the western and central than in the eastern and south-eastern regions and involved between 130,000 and 150,000 people, of whom some 75,000–80,000 returned after hostilities. Prominent amongst those who left were the Tatars and Circassians, most of whom fled permanently. The treaty of Berlin, with its guarantees of minority rights, encouraged many Turks to return, particularly to Rumelia, and in this they received the support of the Ottoman government, but hopes that they might be able to retrieve their former political domination faded rapidly and after 1880 a second tide of emigration began, flowing strongly in the first half of the decade and thereafter as a steady but less voluminous stream. After the mid-1880s Turks began leaving even the areas of compact Turkish settlement in north-east Bulgaria, and they were joined too by a number of Pomaks who lived far from the Pomak strongholds in the Rhodopes. Their readiness to leave Bulgaria was increased by offers from the Ottoman government of free land in Thrace or Asia Minor. The Turkish population, which had been 26 per cent of the total in 1878, had declined to 14 per cent by 1900 and 11.63 per cent in 1910 (see table 15.1.)

The post-1880 emigration was more orderly than that during and immediately after the war, and in most cases the departing Muslims sold their land; by 1900, 600,000 hectares of Muslim land had been bought by Christians, and 175 Muslim villages had been abandoned, 118 of them between 1878 and 1885.

The emigrations increased the proportions of Bulgarians in the population as a whole, as did the immigration of ethnic Bulgarians from Bessarabia, the Banat, Serbia, Romania, and Russia. By the mid-1880s these newcomers, the majority of whom were members of the intelligentsia, manufacturers, or merchants, numbered between 90,000 and 95,000.

In general, Bulgarian governments worked conscientiously to observe the requirements of the treaty of Berlin and articles 40 and 42 of the Tŭrnovo constitution which guaranteed freedom of conscience and worship to all citizens of Bulgaria. A Turco-Bulgarian accord signed on

6 April 1909 amended these provisions to accommodate them to the new constitutional situation created by the declaration of Bulgarian independence in 1908. Both the 1879 constitution and the 1909 accord allowed *muftis* to administer the mosques, Muslim educational establishments, and the *vakŭfs* or endowed properties, and the *muftis*, together with the local Muslim judges or *kadis*, retained the right to decide disputes within Muslim families on questions such as marriage, divorce, and inheritance. After 1909 Bulgarian Muslims could still offer prayers to the *sheik-ul-islam* although he, as sultan, was now the head of a foreign state.

Despite the arrangements made at an official level, many Muslims, particularly in the immediate post-liberation years, were unable to adapt to the changes brought about in 1878; they found it impossible to accept the atmosphere and mores of a predominantly Christian state. The cultural pressures which they felt were exercised against them were sometimes intentional and sometimes accidental.

Some problems arose immediately after the end of the Russo-Turkish war. Muslims returning after the war suffered their first shock when they were told they had to surrender their weapons and would be guarded by armed Christians. Then it became clear that although the administration in Plovdiv was implementing safeguards on Muslim property rights, and had even evicted from Shipka Christians who had illegally taken property from Turks, in general the local arm of the law was generally less punctilious, primarily because the mixed Bulgarian-Turkish commissions which had decided property disputes under the Russian provisional administration were now dominated by Bulgarians. Another important incentive to emigration was the replacement of the tithe in Rumelia by a land tax in 1882. Theologically, Muslim teaching held that all land belonged to Allah and that its user had to pay tax only on what it produced; Muslim landowners, who had tended to keep more of their land fallow than did Christians, now found their tax burdens sharply increased; 1882 saw the highest incidence of sales of land from Muslim to Christian. If Rumelian legislation was an incentive for emigration, legislation in the principality had the effect of dissuading Muslims from returning to resume possession of their property. In October 1880 the sŭbranie enacted that land left untilled for three years should revert to state ownership, though the deadline was soon extended to 1885. Although this three-year convention was a continuation of Ottoman practice it meant that any Muslim intending to return would have to fight, and in all probability lose, lengthy and costly legal battles either with the Bulgarian state or with Christians to whom the land had been sold. Many Muslims decided it was not worth doing so.

Cultural alienation also followed changes in the names of many settlements, either spontaneously by their inhabitants or by governmental decision, some of the new names being chosen to commemorate Christian victories in the recent war.[7]

Another cause of alienation was the destruction of Muslim or Ottoman buildings or their conversion to other uses. In Sofia the Russian army used the cover of a thunderstorm to blow up seven mosques in December 1878. Famous, historic churches such as St Sophia in Sofia and the church of the Forty Martyrs in Tŭrnovo which had been turned into mosques after the Ottoman conquest, were now reconsecrated. Other mosques were turned into storehouses, museums, prisons, or barracks, whilst in Plovdiv, Lovech, Svishtov, Burgas, and other towns Muslim cemeteries were turned into public gardens, the headstones often being used as building material. In many villages the old Ottoman konak, or administrative centre, was pulled down or transformed into the base for Christian local government. The new churches built by Bulgarians after the liberation were also confident assertions of their new authority; gone were the small, low churches hunkered down in the landscape, to be replaced by new, bigger, and taller buildings which dominated the skyline. In the towns and larger villages the thrust towards modernization often meant the destruction of the *charshiya* (market place) which had been the focus of much social as well as economic interchange for Muslims. The local government reform of 1882 deprived the town districts of any real autonomy and as many of these districts had been formed on an ethnic basis the reform meant a diminution of ethnic minority rights. Some ethnic districts remained but in addition to having no political authority they also tended to become areas for the poor only, the more wealthy moving into the expanding suburbs thus producing towns segregated by economic rather than racial factors. Not all tradition died, however. In the public baths in Sofia there were still separate days for Christians, Muslims, Jews, soldiers, prisoners, and other groups.[8] But despite these

---

[7] P. Koledarov and N. Michev, *Promenite v imenata i statuta na selishtata v Bŭlgariya, 1878–1972* (Sofia: Nauka i izkustvo, 1973), 6.

[8] Bernard Lory, *Le Sort de l'héritage ottoman en Bulgarie: l'exemple des villes bulgares, 1878–1900*, (Istanbul: Isis, 1985), 69–79, 112–13.

survivals the Muslim presence in many towns declined significantly; shortly before the liberation there had been 1,334 Muslim households in Sofia, but in mid-1878 there were only 718.[9]

The changes in fashion led to the adoption of western styles of dress, furniture, and other items. These affected Muslim economic enterprises but other changes offended their religious habits and customs. Christians were now allowed to become tanners. In 1884 the Bulgarian government set the minimum legal age for marriage at 17 for girls and 18 for boys, both limits being raised by a further year in 1897; even if such laws were virtually unenforceable in the villages the remaining urban Muslims saw this as yet another restriction on their religious autonomy, the permitted minimum marriageable age according to Muslim custom being considerably lower than that set out in the legislation. Another blow was the refusal of the Plovdiv municipal authorities to accept a joint Turkish and Armenian proposal that Ottoman hours should be restored in public during Ramadan. That women should appear far more in public shocked traditional Muslims, as did the staging of balls, mixed dinner parties, outings, and picnics. Diet too became more European and less Ottoman. The consumption of potatoes increased rapidly north of the Balkans after 1878, whilst in Rumelia a decision of the Russian provisional administration to ban the planting of rice because the paddy fields were breeding grounds for malarial mosquitoes made eminently good sense on public health grounds, but rice was the staple of the Turkish diet and to Muslims restrictions on its cultivation could be seen as a covert assertion of Christian domination. The ban was lifted in 1884 but by then many rice producers had left.

A much more intrusive act by the state was conscription, which was introduced in one form or another in both Bulgaria and Rumelia. The Turks were given the right not to wear the cross on their uniforms but they had to obey Christian officers and eat non-Muslim food. In the 1880s Turks were allowed to escape military service on payment of a levy but this was set at a level few could afford. The Turks were mobilized in the war of 1885 and were reported as marching from Varna in their national, Turkish costume; in the fighting they earned the widespread respect of their officers and comrades, as well as a high number of medals

---

[9] Georgiev, *Osvobozhdenieto*, 13.

for bravery in action.[10] They were not called to the colours in 1912 for the war against the Ottoman empire but they did serve in the first world war when Bulgaria was allied with Turkey.

The gradual emigration of Turks continued until the first world war with a mass exodus in 1913 and 1914, after Bulgaria's conquest of densely populated Turkish areas in Thrace. Many of those leaving were refugees from Bosnia who had moved into Thrace after the annexation in 1908; in 1917 there were still 120,000 of them waiting for the end of the war to allow them to go to Turkey.[11]

In the territories conquered in the Balkan wars the Bulgarian authorities unleashed a fierce campaign aimed at forcing the Pomaks to convert to Christianity. Scores of priests were sent into the area to enforce conversions, and the Pomaks were required to adopt Slav Christian given and family names and to discard their Muslim clothing. As many as 200,000 were affected by this drive but it was abandoned immediately after the second Balkan war; Radoslavov, being desperate for electoral support, allowed the Pomaks to resume their Islamic faith and their former names and modes of dress.[12]

In the short period between the second Balkan war and the first world war there were a series of agreements on exchanges of population, although the outbreak of the major conflict in 1914 meant that for the most part these agreements were not implemented, if at all, until after 1918. Some transfers did take place, however, as a result of which some Turks left Bulgaria and a number of Bulgarians moved from the Ottoman empire to Bulgaria; in the spring of 1914, 6,200 of them arrived in Burgas and Varna from Asia Minor.[13]

Immediately after the first world war the Bulgarian government enacted the law on Muslim religious communities. This met the need to adapt the legal code to the complex changes brought about by the

---

[10] For the Varna episode, Ĭono Mitev, *Istoriya na srbskata-bŭlgarska voĭna, 1885* (Sofia: DVI, 1971), 121; and for earning respect and medals, Major A. Huhn, *The Struggle of the Bulgarians for National Independence under Prince Alexander. A Military and Political History of the War between Bulgaria and Servia in 1885*, trans. from the German (London: John Murray, 1886), 181–3.

[11] Staĭko Trifonov, *Antanta v Trakiya, 1919–1920* (Sofia: Kliment Ohridski, 1989), 105–6.   [12] Neuburger, *Orient Within*, 41–2.

[13] Valeriĭ Rusanov (compiler) and Lilyana Aleksandrieva (ed.), *Aspekti na etnokulturnata situatsiya v Bŭlgariya*, vol. i, the proceedings of a seminar held in Sofia, 8–10 November 1991 (Sofia: Fumi Press for the Friedrich Naumann Foundation, 1992), 61.

declaration of independence in 1908 and the Turco-Bulgarian accord of the following year. The act was to remain the basis of the legal position of the Muslims until after the second world war. The law established a system of Muslim courts, local and appellate. It also enacted that any community with more than forty Muslim families could establish a Muslim council which would be a legally recognized body with the right to own property such as schools and mosques. The councils could also administer the *vakŭfs*. The internal responsibilities of the councils extended more widely than those given to their Christian equivalents and included the rights to regulate matrimonial conflicts, disagreements between parents and children, divorce, paternity cases, and testamentary disputes. With the advent of the secularist regime in Ankara Bulgarian Turks were more free to follow traditional Islamist practices than the Turks of Turkey; Bulgarian Turks could write Turkish in the Arabic script, their women could wear the veil, and they had 2,300 mosques in which to worship and 4,000 hodjas to lead them in prayer.

The 1919 law on Muslim religious communities had aimed to promote education amongst the Turks. They had always had the right to their own schools which taught in Turkish, but attendance rates in the rural areas were low and in 1905 only 6 per cent of Turkish children were classed as literate. The 1919 law set up within the Bulgarian ministry of education an inspectorate for Turkish schools and this was one of the factors which brought about a rise in the literacy rate to 12 per cent in 1926. By that year there were 1,329 Turkish schools in Bulgaria with a total of 58,000 pupils; many of these schools had been considerably helped by grants of land from the state land fund set up by the Stambolïĭski government. Turkish students also attended Sofia University, where a lectureship in Turkish had been established in 1907. Higher religious training was offered at the Grand Medresse opened in Shumen in 1922.

In the inter-war period the Turkish press in Bulgaria continued to enjoy the same freedom as before 1915. At least sixty different newspapers were published in Turkish between the wars, including one for communists between 1920 and 1923, and there were Turkish-language publishing houses in Shumen and Plovdiv.

Despite the improvements brought about by the 1919 act Turkish emigration from Bulgaria resumed in the inter-war period, particularly after the Bulgarian-Turkish agreement of 1925. From 1927 until 1940 10,000–12,000 Turks left Bulgaria each year, the greatest outflows occurring in 1927, the first year áfter the agreement of 1925 in which emigration was allowed, and in 1935. The latter surge was partly the result of the Turkish government's efforts to boost Turkish rather than Islamic consciousness amongst Bulgaria's Turks and to encourage their emigration to Turkey. The zvenari welcomed the latter move because it allowed them the chance to reallocate the vacated plots to land-hungry Bulgarians and thus increase the Bulgarian element in the villages concerned. There were other measures in the 1930s to increase the Bulgarian at the cost of the Turkish element. Attempts were made, sometimes with the help of the military, to prevent the speaking of Turkish in public,[14] and in 1936 the Turan organization was banned; established in the late 1920s it had sought to raise Turkish ethnic consciousness, particularly amongst teachers. In 1940 the recovery of the southern Dobrudja brought another 130,000 Turks into Bulgaria; it also prompted another round of changes in the names of settlements.

A problem which further exercised the governments of the 1930s was that of Pomak emigration. Many Pomaks felt that the Bulgarian, Christian state discriminated against them, and they were also frequently exploited economically by local merchants, shopkeepers, landowners, and employers. They were therefore easy objects for Turkish propaganda and there was large-scale Pomak emigration in 1927, 1933, and 1935, though many later returned, finding that life in secular Turkey was no better than in Christian Bulgaria.[15] In an effort to increase the Bulgarian presence in Pomak villages the zvenari encouraged the settlement of non-Muslim Bulgarians in such communities.

There was renewed pressure on the Pomaks in the late 1930s and early 1940s. The census of 1934 was the last in which they were allowed to identify themselves as a separate category. It was a small group of Pomak progressive Islamists in Smolyan, the centre of the Pomak region, who formed the Rodina organization in 1937. The government welcomed the new organization because it advocated acceptance by the Pomaks of their Bulgarian nationality. Rodina therefore combined progressive Islamism and Bulgarian national consciousness, the latter being expressed primarily in the common language. In the second world war Rodina became more aggressive, putting pressure on Pomaks to abandon their Muslim dress. The association exercised considerable influence in Bulgarian occupied

---

[14] Iliev, *Spomenite*, 158–9.   [15] Rusanov and Aleksandrieva, i, *Aspekti*, 65–6.

Thrace where its power led to the banning of the fez, the turban, and the veil. It also took advantage of a law enacted in the summer of 1942 which in effect forced some 60,000 Pomaks to abandon their Muslim and assume Christian names. Official pressure was also put on Pomaks to make them change the interiors of their homes and to do away with the traditional lattice windows in their houses.[16]

After the acquisition of the southern Dobrudja no large-scale movement of Muslims into or out of Bulgaria took place until the early 1950s. In 1950 the Bulgarian government announced that it would permit the emigration of up to a quarter of a million ethnic Turks. The Turkish government protested, complaining at the condition of the emigrants and claiming that many were not ethnic Turks at all but Gypsies, and in September 1950 Ankara closed its borders. An agreement negotiated later in the year then allowed a daily egress of 650 persons until the borders were again closed in 1952, by which time 160,000 Turks had left Bulgaria. A significant number of the new émigrés were from the Dobrudja. The Chervenkov government had allowed, or indeed enforced, the exodus of 1950–2 because the first areas it wished to collectivize completely were the southern Dobrudja and the north-east of Bulgaria where the soil was best but where there were also large numbers of ethnic Turks. As the towns and industries were not yet ready to receive them in large numbers it was easier to allow them to leave for Turkey. In 1969 another agreement on the emigration of Turks was signed between Sofia and Ankara. It was to last for ten years and by the time it elapsed between 80,000 and 90,000 more ethnic Turks had left Bulgaria. There were no further developments until the upheavals of the mid-1980s.

2. THE OTHER MINORITIES, 1878–1944

Greek influence in Bulgaria was strongest south of the Balkan mountains and along the Black Sea coast. In 1880 33.98 per cent of the population of Burgas were Greek, as were 21.86 per cent of that of Varna, and, in 1884, 16.44 per cent of Plovdiv. The Greeks had adapted easily to the end of Ottoman rule but in 1891 they protested strongly against Stambolov's education act, which stated that only non-Christian children could be

---

[16] Neuburger, *Orient Within*, 46–54.

educated in their mother-tongue if that were not Bulgarian. In fact, this law had been aimed less at the Greeks themselves than the Gagauzes, the Turkish-speaking Christians amongst whom the patriarchists were trying to garner support; of the twelve Greek speaking private schools active in 1891 seven were in Gagauze villages.

The main factor which led to the decline of the Greek population in the second half of the 1900s and thereafter was disagreement between Bulgaria and Greece over Macedonia, and the anti-Greek riots of 1906 to which they gave rise. Immediately after the disorders 35,000 Greeks left Bulgaria and further bitterness and greater population movements followed the second Balkan and first world wars. In 1919 Sofia and Athens concluded a population exchange agreement under which 46,000 Greeks left Bulgaria for Greece. In 1956 there were almost 7,500 resident Greeks in Bulgaria, most of them being refugees from the Greek civil war. More Greek refugees arrived in 1960–1 when they were expelled from Poland.[17]

The Jewish population of Bulgaria suffered little persecution or discrimination in the post-liberation years. In 1880–1 there were schools for Ladino-speaking Jews in Sofia, Kyustendil, Dupnitsa, Samokov, Berkovits, Vidin, Lom, Rusé, Razgrad, Shumen, Silistra, and Provadiya. Others soon opened in Plovdiv, Yambol, Pazardjik, Varna, and Burgas, most of them with financial help from the Universal Israelite Alliance.[18] In the early 1900s a number of Russian Jews sought refuge in Bulgaria after the pogroms in their homeland, their numbers in towns such as Plovdiv, Rusé, Sofia, and Varna rising noticeably between 1900 and 1905. They were easily absorbed into the existing Jewish communities. Although these immigrants saw Bulgaria as a safe haven anti-semitism was not unknown in Bulgaria. There was an anti-semitic outburst in Lom in 1904 which threatened to spread to Vidin,[19] bombs were planted in Jewish properties in May 1928,[20] and there were attacks on Jewish shops in the centre of Sofia on 19 September 1939.[21] But for most Jews the

---

[17] Dimitrov, *Sŭvetska Bŭlgariya*, 107.

[18] Nikolaï Todorov (ed. in chief), *Prouchvaniya za istoriyata na evreïskoto neselenie v bŭlgarskite zemi, xv–xx vek* (Sofia: BAN, 1980), 56–64.

[19] Blagoï Popov, *Ot Protsesa*, footnote on 238.

[20] Dimo Kazasov, *Burni Godini, 1918–1944* (Sofia: 1949, republished, Sofia: Otechestven Front, 1987), 339–40. Citation from 1949 edition.

[21] Todorov, *Prouchvaniya*, 188.

country offered security. And if the conditions they endured from 1941–4 were harsh, most of them being confined to labour camps in the interior of the country, they suffered little of the violence heaped upon Jews in most other continental European states at the time.

The second world war and its aftermath had some impact on Bulgaria's ethnic composition. Forty thousand Jews left Bulgaria for Israel not because they felt no debt of gratitude to Bulgaria but because they were attracted by the opportunities offered by the new Jewish state after 1948; and some feared that communists devoted to Stalin would not be free of anti-semitism. In 1965 6,000 Jews were left in Bulgaria, half of whom lived in Sofia.

The treaty of Craiova had contained provisions for a compulsory exchange of the respective Bulgarian and Romanian minorities in northern and southern Dobrudja. Despite a number of difficulties in the application of the treaty over 100,000 Romanians had left Bulgaria by 1944 and almost 70,000 Bulgarians had moved from Romania into Bulgaria.[22]

The small German minority in Bulgaria disappeared during and immediately after the war. In December 1941 856 Germans living within the pre-1940 Bulgarian frontiers were repatriated to the Reich to be resettled in the Lublin area of Poland, and in the following year 500 more followed them. In 1943 there was an agreement to transfer ethnic Germans from the territories administered by Bulgaria in Macedonia and Thrace. After the bombing of Sofia arrangements were made for the remaining Germans to leave the country.[23]

It was planned to replace the departing Germans with 2,500 ethnic Bulgarians from Ukraine and southern Russia. Resettlement of these families began in 1944 but the projected total was not achieved and the resettlement process was fraught with difficulty, the Romanians declining to provide free transport and the Germans refusing to move draught animals without payment from Bulgaria. When they arrived in Bulgaria the settlers could not exchange their German or Soviet currency, whilst the few with professional training found that their Soviet qualifications were not recognized. The position of these former Soviet citizens worsened after Bulgaria changed sides in the war, especially so after November 1944 when the Soviet-run ACC declared that all

---

[22] Joseph B. Schechtman, *European Population Transfers, 1939–1945* (New York: Oxford University Press, 1946), 404–14.   [23] Ibid.

citizens of the Soviet Union in Bulgaria must register immediately for repatriation to the USSR.[24] In the following month the head of the Soviet military administration ordered that all ethnic Germans, most of whom were Bulgarian subjects, be deported to the Soviet Union for construction work.[25] Their Bulgarian citizenship did not protect them.

3. THE MINORITIES UNDER COMMUNIST RULE, 1944–1989

In the half-decade after the second world war the Bulgarian government, stressing the class unity of all groups, adopted extremely generous policies towards its minorities who were encouraged to conduct classes in their own languages, publish their own textbooks, and to develop their own culture. Cultural-educational organizations were set up for Jews, Gypsies, and Armenians. Newspapers and periodicals appeared in Turkish, Greek, Armenian, and Romany, which was spoken by about a third of Bulgaria's Gypsies. Other periodicals were produced in Bulgarian for the Jewish communities. Minority languages and schools were encouraged. In September 1944 there had been 424 private schools teaching in Turkish with 871 teachers and 37,335 pupils; in 1952 there were 1,020 basic schools and 3 pedagogic institutes, whilst in 1956 there were 1,149 schools teaching in Turkish.[26] State support was given to other cultural amenities, including Sofia's Gypsy theatre, which became famous throughout the Balkans. These too were the years in which the Bulgarian government and party were prepared to recognize and even to foster the development of a Macedonian ethnic group; A quarter of a million Bulgarians are thought to have described themselves as Macedonian in the census of 1946.[27] The authorities were also willing to allow emigration, not only of Jews. Armenians were encouraged to begin a new life in Soviet Armenia, though most of those who left went westwards rather than eastwards.

[24] Ibid. 444–5; most details are taken from Boĭka Vasileva, 'Migratsiya na naselenie ot Ukraina v Bŭlgariya prez 1943–1944', *Vekove* (Sofia), 4 (1986), 36–40.

[25] Petŭr Semerdjiev, *Narodniyat Sŭd v Bŭlgariya 1944–1945g. Komu i zashto e bil neobhodim* (Jerusalem: no publisher cited, 1997), 69.

[26] Cited in Kalinova and Baeva, *Bŭlgarskite prehodi 1944–1999*, 78 n.170.

[27] http://bulrefsite.entrewave.com/view/bulrefsite/s129p148.htm#Message521.

The emigration of the Jews continued after 1948 but the fifth party congress in that year brought the first hint of assimilationism when it called for the incorporation of all ethnic groups in the building of socialism. The Macedonians were the first to feel this. The number of Bulgarian citizens declaring themselves to be of Macedonian ethnicity was not revealed in the published versions of the 1946 census, but in 1956 they were, revealing that 187,789 had so identified themselves, but thereafter the political climate discouraged this and in the census of 1965 the number of declared Macedonians in Bulgaria had fallen to 9,632.[28] 'Macedonian' was not recognized again as an ethnic category in census returns until 1991.

For all non-Bulgarians the fifth congress's decisions led to the gradual raising of the status of the Bulgarian language from being the first non-native language to being the chief medium of instruction in all schools, thus reducing the importance of the minority languages in education. At the same time the party conducted a drive for membership amongst the minorities and those who did join the BCP tended to assimilate entirely. In 1949 the collectivization drive brought more pressure on the minorities; the movement to the towns split up some minority communities whose members found themselves culturally isolated and were therefore rapidly assimilated in the 1950s and 1960s.

The 1950s saw the assimilation of institutions as well as individuals. Most of the cultural-educational organizations which had flourished after the war were absorbed into the Fatherland Front and the number of non-Bulgarian language periodicals and newspapers declined; by 1957 only one Roma journal had survived; from 1959 it was written primarily, and after 1968 solely, in Bulgarian, and the vigorous and varied Turkish provincial journals were greatly reduced in number. In 1956 the privately run Armenian schools were taken over by the state and were incorporated into Bulgarian schools six years later. In the early 1950s the Sofia government also insisted that the small Karakachan minority of around 2,000 assume a sedentary life. The Karakachan spoke a northern Greek dialect and were shepherds whose winter quarters were in villages near Sozopol and Sliven. Many Gypsies too were put under pressure to settle in a fixed location, though many nevertheless continued to work semi-peripatetically.

[28] Stefan Troebst, 'Nationale Minderheiten', in Grothusen (ed.), *Bulgarien*, 474–89, 475.

Efforts by the communist authorities to assimilate the Roma, Pomak, and then the Turkish populations formed a major part of government policy from the early 1960s to the end of the 1980s, and have been included in the political narrative of this work.

4. THE MINORITIES SINCE 1989

When Bulgaria signed its association agreement with the EU in December 1992 the latter insisted upon the inclusion in the document of an article safeguarding the human rights of the ethnic minorities; although for the Bulgarians this continued the tradition set in Berlin and Neuilly it was the first association agreement concluded by the EU to contain such a clause. In general Bulgaria's record on minority issues since 1989 has been good, in part perhaps because the anti-Turkish regenerative policy of the 1980s had been a communist one and the reaction against communism was therefore also a reaction against assimilationism. The 1991 constitution recognized the right of minorities to maintain their specific cultural identity, to practise their religion, and to speak their mother tongue. This induced a greater willingness on the part of the minorities to identify themselves and to organize on an ethnic basis. The 1991 census listed 5,159 Vlachs; 5,144 Karakachans; 4,930 Greeks; 4,515 Tatars; 3,461 Jews; 2,491 Aromanians; and 1,478 Gagauzes. Most of these groups formed new or recreated disbanded cultural societies in the 1990s; some, for example the Armenian 'Erevan' and Jewish 'Shalom' organizations, took advantage of the restitution laws to regain the property they had lost when they were subsumed into the FF in the 1950s. The cultural and educational association of Karakachans in Bulgaria established in 1991 in Sliven grew vigorously, having 15 branches by 1995 when it was renamed a federation rather than an association. In 1989 the authorities permitted the reopening of the Armenian High School in Plovdiv and those of Armenian descent have assumed a high profile in the upper echelons of Bulgarian public life, Reneta Indjova being one of their number.

The question of the Turks remained a prominent and a painful one after the fall of Zhivkov in November 1989, the demonstrations of January 1990 proving that support could still be mustered for the anti-Turkish policies. But resentment by anti-Turkish elements did not deter the new government from its reforming path with regard to the minorities. The MRF, founded in January 1990, also gave the Turkish minority a political voice, and the fact that the MRF was either included in or was a close supporter of every government from 1991 to the mid-2000s meant that no administration dare move towards greater restriction on the Turks. The provision of education in Turkish was expanded, as was that for broadcasting, and restrictions on the publication of journals in Turkish were removed. In February 2000 Bulgarian television began relaying some programmes in Turkish and in the following month Islamic classes were introduced in elementary schools in twenty-two towns and cities.

After 1989 the issue of the Macedonian element in Bulgaria was again raised. The authorities did not object to, though they showed little enthusiasm for the assertion by some inhabitants of the Pirin region that they were Macedonians; in the 1991 census over 10,000 citizens of Bulgaria described themselves as being ethnic Macedonians. Attempts by the leaders of this group to establish political parties were frustrated by successive governments which invoked the law of 1990 forbidding the formation of parties based on ethnic identity. By the end of the decade enthusiasm for the Macedonian cause seemed to have declined, only 5,000 people registering themselves as of Macedonian ethnicity in the Bulgarian census of 2001, though reliable estimates put their numbers at around a quarter of a million.[29]

Since 1934 Bulgarian censuses have not recorded the number of Pomaks. In 2001 there were 966,978 Muslims in Bulgaria and 762,516 Bulgarian citizens whose mother tongue was Turkish, leaving a difference of 204,462 Bulgarian-speaking Muslims. In 1965, 22 per cent of Roma were Turkish-speaking Muslims. If it is presumed that much the same proportion applied in 2001 that would mean 81,600 of the total of 370,908 Roma were turcophone Muslims; this would in turn mean the Pomaks numbered 123,000, which is certainly an underestimate, the probable number being around 200,000. If their numbers are uncertain there is no doubt as to the Pomaks' social condition. They are now amongst the most deprived of all Bulgarians, unemployment in the Smolyan, Lovech, and Blagoevgrad districts where they are concentrated being significantly higher than the national average. Attempts to mobilize

---

[29] Rechel, 'Minority Rights', 67–9.

the Pomaks politically have met with little success; the Democratic Labour Party set up in 1992 made little headway amongst the Pomaks at whom it was aimed, and in the 2001 election they voted massively for 'the king'. The Pomaks have, however, asserted their difference from the Turkish Muslims. In 1993 the Pomaks demanded a separate chief mufti in Smolyan because the Turks had dominated that office in Sofia; the demand was dropped in 1998 when Mustafa Hadji, a Pomak, was appointed to the Sofia post, but was revived when he was removed from it in 2001.

By the end of the 1990s the principal minority issue in Bulgaria was not that of the Turks, the Macedonians, or the Pomaks, but the Roma. Before 1989 there was little public discussion of the Roma. Occasional action had been taken against them, as when those living in the Fakulteta district in Sofia were forcibly Christianized in 1942.[30] The collectivization of agriculture also made it much more difficult for nomadic Roma to continue their traditional way of life and after 1958 they were forced to settle on collective farms or in depressed urban areas. They were also subjected to intensive assimilationist pressures. The public use of Romany was banned, though this had little impact as many Roma spoke Bulgarian, Turkish, Romanian, obscure dialects, or any mixture of these. More damaging was the ban on their traditional Roma religious and cultural customs and regulations introduced in 1974 which forced them to give up their Romany names for Slav and Christian ones.

The Roma question was complicated by the fact that the Roma are not unified. Not only do they speak different languages but they adhere to different faiths, some being Muslim, others Christian, and many neither. Some settled Gypsies in Sofia have recently joined American-based revivalist sects, perhaps because of the allure of foreign and extrovert religious rites, or perhaps for more mundane and worldly reasons. There are also different levels of educational attainment. The Turkish-speaking 'kalaidjiĭ' are generally better educated than other groups; the kalaidjiĭ of Kŭrdjali were reported as saying they did not wish to go to the larger towns where they would be met with hostility by the local, less well-educated Gypsies.[31]

[30] Rusanov and Aleksandrieva, *Aspekti*, i, 115.
[31] Ibid. 108–16. For an excellent examination of the condition of the Roma minority, see Rechel, 'Minority Rights', 79–87.

The 2001 census recorded 370,908 Roma, but a number of observers have contested this figure, arguing that many Roma fear the social stigma and discrimination attached to being Roma; one French analyst went as far as to say that the total number of Roma was between 700,000 and 800,000.[32] Whatever their number, the Roma have real grievances. After the end of communism their 'sub-proletarian socio-economic status'[33] declined even further; they were, for example, excluded from the land restitution programme. According to the Democratic Romany Union, 92 per cent of working-age Roma living in Bulgarian cities were unemployed in 1998; and figures published by the official Bulgarian news agency show they made up 90 per cent of the prison population. Educational attainment and literacy levels are far below the national average, as is life expectancy, a group of fifteen NGOs reporting in April 2002 that only 1 per cent of Roma were over 80;[34] and the Roma are subjected to constant discrimination, police brutality, and exploitation by criminal gangs.

At times the tensions caused by such factors reached breaking point. In February 2002 hundreds of Roma rioted in the Plovdiv suburb of Stolipinovo after electricity supplies had been cut off. The riot illustrated the difficulties of the Roma problem. The Stolipinovo district was one of poverty and high unemployment and therefore many had found it difficult to pay their electricity bills, in recognition of which the electricity company had agreed the previous month that the district should pay 10 per cent of its outstanding debt; the suspension of supplies had come about because that agreement had not been honoured. The company's view was understandable in that the debt for the district was $2.7 million.

The Roma have advanced their case through their own political organizations. Soon after 10 November 1989 the Democratic Romany Union was formed. By the summer of 1990 it claimed to represent over 50,000 Roma and its leader, Manush Romanov, a prominent theatre director, was elected to the GNA on the UDF list. Thereafter the constitutional court denied it and similar organizations the right to stand

[32] J. P. Liegeois, *Romite-evropeĭsko maltsinstvo* (Sofia: Fondatsiya Mezhduetnicheska initsiativa za choveshki prava, 1998), 10.

[33] The phrase is taken from Rossen Vassilev, 'The Roma of Bulgaria: A Pariah Minority', *The Global Review of Ethnopolitics*, 3/2 (Jan. 2004), 40–51, 41.

[34] 'NGOS sound alarm on health problems of Bulgarian Roma', RFE/RL Newsline, Vol. 06, No. 80, Part II, 29 April 2002. Access to RFE/RL via newsline-request@list.rferl.org.

in elections because of the prohibition on parties founded on an ethnic or religious basis. The lower courts, however, proved more lenient and a number of Roma organizations did enter later elections. One of them, Free Bulgaria, secured 89,000 votes in the local elections of 1999 and had considerable influence on the formation of councils in the Lom, Pleven, and Tatar Pazardjik districts, but in national elections the organized Gypsy vote has had little influence. In 2001 two Roma were elected to the sŭbranie, one on the NMSS list and the other for the Citizens' Union Roma which was in coalition with the BSP, but given Bulgaria's PR system the Roma, who are at least 4.7 per cent of the population, could have expected a minimum of eleven deputies.

The Bulgarian government, prodded by Brussels, has taken a number of steps to improve the condition of the Roma. In 1999 the Kostov government adopted a framework to facilitate the greater integration of Roma into Bulgarian society. In 2003 the NMSS administration introduced a scheme to educate illiterate adult Roma, and courses were established in the universities of Stara Zagora and Tŭrnovo to train special teachers to work with Roma children, sometimes in mixed classes. By 2004 these and other measures had persuaded Brussels of Sofia's good intent.

Legislation, however, is a top-down process which satisfies outside observers and international organizations, and frequently the domestic political intelligentsia. From the bottom those policies may be viewed from a different perspective. It was easy for Sofia to legislate that the teaching of Turkish in schools should be increased, and it was relatively easy to find the textbooks and even the teachers to make this possible. What was much more difficult to find was the necessary curriculum time. In many cases Turkish could be taught only at the cost of another subject, frequently another foreign language. If, therefore, the take-up on Turkish classes was lower than intended this was quite likely not the result of structural racism but because Turkish parents decided they would prefer their children to learn English or German rather than the formal grammar of a language they already knew. Similarly, however well-intended the decision to introduce special teachers to aid Roma children in mixed classes the result was to make many Roma children, who already spoke perfectly adequate Bulgarian, second-class pupils for whom special translations had to be laid on.

These negative responses were muted and voiced by only a few, and in general it seemed that Bulgaria had made serious and largely successful efforts to prevent ethnic and minority problems becoming national issues. This was what made the success of the Ataka movement in the 2005 elections so surprising and alarming.

5. RECENT DEMOGRAPHIC DECLINE

Since 1989 the population of Bulgaria has declined. In 1990 there were 8,669,269 Bulgarians, but at the end of 2004 there were only 7,761,049, a fall of 10.48 per cent. In 1939 the natural growth rate of the total population had been 8 per thousand, after which it increased steadily to reach a height of 14.9 per thousand in 1950. After that it began to fall, not least because of poor housing provision and the wider employment of women of child-bearing age. By 1988 it had dropped to 1 and in 1989 stood at 0.8; after that it fell below zero reaching a depth

Table 15.2 Total population, 1880/4–2004

Census year	Total population	Percentage change
1880/4	2,950,599	
1887	3,154,375	6.91
1892	3,310,713	4.96
1900	3,744,283	13.10
1905	4,035,575	7.78
1910	4,337,513	7.48
1920	4,846,971	11.75
1926	5,528,741	14.07
1934	6,077,939	9.93
1946	7,029,349	15.65
1956	7,613,709	8.31
1965	8,227,866	8.07
1975	8,727,771	6.08
1985	8,948,649	2.53
1992	8,487,317	−5.16
2001	7,928,901	−6.58
2004	7,761,049	−2.12

Source: Figures for 1880/4 are a combination of the records taken in the Principality in 1880 and in Rumelia in 1884; for the remaining figures, see www.nsi.bg/Census_e/Census_e.thm; for 2004 data see www.nsi.bg/Population/Population.Thm.

of −7 in 1997.[35] In 2004 it stood at −5.2 per thousand. In 2003 the total fertility rate stood at 1.09 births per woman per lifetime, the lowest figure ever recorded for a European state in peacetime. If it remains at this level it will mean that each new generation of Bulgarians will be only half the size of its predecessor. Such a situation has been described as 'demographic death'.[36] A decline in total population of at least a third by 2050 is probable.[37]

The decline in the rate of natural growth was initially the result of a fall in the birth rate, a problem which had exercised Bulgarian governments since the 1960s. The first response had been to reward couples who had large families; by the 1980s the policy was to punish those who did not, the chief disciplinary instrument being the tax system. After 1989 the birth rate fell more rapidly, Bulgaria's becoming one of the lowest in Europe. It had been 12.1 per thousand in 1990 but by 2004 was only 9.0, having reached a low point of 8.5 in 2002.

By the end of the 1990s the fall in the rate of natural growth was being caused by not only a fall in the birth rate but also by a simultaneous rise in the number of people leaving the country. It is estimated that up to three-quarters of a million Bulgarians, most of them young and many of them highly educated, have left the country since 1989. There is little sign that this process will be reversed, and figures produced by the National Statistical Institute in 2002 indicate that between 12 and 15 per cent of Bulgarians under the age of 29 planned to emigrate from Bulgaria in the near future.

A third contributory factor to the fall in the population was a rise in the death rate which rose from 12.5 per thousand in 1990 to 14.2 per thousand in 2004. This was in part because the percentage of older people in the total population was rising but also because living standards were falling. The rise in the number of older people in the population has been startling with an estimated 1.8 million amongst the total population of 7.8 million in 2004. An increase in retirement age has done something to reduce the dependency rate but the provision of pensions and other welfare benefits is one of the most serious of all the problems facing Bulgaria in the future.

[35] Pre-1998 figures in Kalinova and Baeva, *Bŭlgarskite prehodi*, table 2.3, page 258.
[36] Rossen Vassilev, 'Bulgaria's Demographic Crisis: Underlying Causes and Some Short-Term Implications', *Southeast European Politics*, 6/1 (July 2005), 14–27.
[37] Richard Ehrman, 'The population boom won't come from Europe', *The Spectator*, 5 November 2005.

Epilogue: Bulgaria between East and West

'In the historic life of nations', wrote one of Bulgaria's most distinguished historians, 'there is one eternal and immutable factor: their geographic position which to a great degree determines their political and cultural evolution.'[1] For Bulgaria, its nodal position, between Europe and Asia, between the east and the west, has determined much of its development. 'In the middle ages', wrote another Bulgarian historian, 'the territorial instability of the Bulgarian state was due above all else to its extremely unfavourable location.'[2] That location produced uncertainty. The state could concentrate on its northern sector, protected by the Danube to the north and the Balkan mountains to the south, and become part of the world linked to central Europe by the Danube. Or it could see itself as a dominant Balkan power, in which case it must advance to the south-east and south-west into Thrace and the Vardar valley. When Khan Boris chose to adopt the eastern rather than the western variety of Christianity he made an explicit commitment to the latter orientation, but the Balkans could tolerate only one dominant power south of the Balkan mountains, and Byzantium would never be comfortable with a Bulgaria which ranged effectively across those mountains and between the Black, the Aegean, and the Adriatic Seas.

The medieval legacy lingered and 500 years of Ottoman rule suspended rather than solved Bulgaria's dilemma. It has been argued that Bulgaria after 1878 made a mistake by allowing itself to be dragged to the south-east into Thrace and towards Constantinople, rather than to the south-west where it needed to defend its position against Serbian and Greek counter-claims which did not exist in eastern Thrace; if Simeon was wrong to aim for Constantinople, so too was Ferdinand.[3] After the two catastrophes of 1913 and 1918, the peaceful routes to both

---

[1] Duǐchev, *Pŭteki*, 129.   [2] Mutafchiev, *Kniga*, 128.
[3] For a recent exposition of this argument, see Mateev, *Stambolov*.

the south-east and the south-west were closed to Bulgaria; not even the great powers could enforce article 48 of the treaty of Neuilly by which they had promised Bulgaria access to the Aegean.

Ferdinand's drive towards Constantinople contradicted the lesson of 1878, that the new, modernizing, Christian Bulgarian state was quite clearly oriented towards Europe rather than Asia. But if Bulgaria was clearly European rather than Asian in its orientation, it still had the dichotomy of choosing between the eastern or the central-western part of Europe.

As the dominant Orthodox power Russia exercised enormous attraction, an attraction hugely augmented by the debt the new Bulgaria owed to the Russian army. In addition to these attractions, there were similarities of language, a strong peasant folk tradition, and a common defining other in the Islamic Ottoman empire. Furthermore, Russia had helped the national revival, providing money, scholarships, and books. Not surprisingly, after 1878 Russian became part of the curriculum in Bulgaria's gymnasia.

If sentiment forced Bulgaria to look east, more down to earth considerations turned its head westward. In the 1880s Russia was too overbearing a patron, but even if the political climate had not soured other forces would still have inclined Bulgaria to the west. Russia, particularly after 1881, could not serve as a model for any emerging democracy, and Russia had little, if any, excess capital to invest in Bulgaria's modernizing economy or to put into state loans which would finance Bulgaria's infrastructure and its army. Nor was there any significant trade between the two countries. Central Europe, and before 1918 Germany, had far more to offer. In the four decades after liberation most of Bulgaria's bourgeoisie sent their children, if they could afford to do so, to the west, and particularly to Germany. Of the 1,500 or so Bulgarian students who graduated from foreign institutions between 1879 and 1915 more did so from German than any other universities, and Bulgarian graduates from Germany were more than those from France and Austria-Hungary combined. The University of Leipzig alone educated a total of 1,202 Bulgarians between 1879 and 1935.[4]

Western influences were by no means confined to the very few who had been educated 'in Europe', as the Bulgarians would have termed it.

---

[4] Rumen Daskalov, *Mezhdu*, 26 n. 59; and for Leipzig, Krŭstyo Dimitrov, *Bŭlgarskata inteligentsiya pri kapitalizma* (Sofia: Nauka i izkustvo, 1974), 146–7.

An inquiry into the borrowings of the National Library in Sofia in 1896 revealed that it had been used by 36,021 readers. The most popular author, by the books ordered, was Victor Hugo, followed, in descending order by Ivan Vazov, Jules Verne, Ilya Blŭskov, Alexandre Dumas, Nikolaĭ Gogol, T. H. Stanchov, Lyuben Karavelov, Schiller, and Shakespeare.[5] In the same year the Bulgarian ministry of education published a list of recommended reading for outside the classroom. Its 402 recommendations included authors from western as well as eastern Europe, and naturally from a number of Bulgarian writers. At the head of the list was Ivan Vazov with 23 recommended works, followed by 15 from Shakespeare, 9 from Samuel Smiles, 7 from Stoyan Mihaĭlovski, 6 from Turgenev, 5 from Victor Hugo, 5 from Konstantin Velichkov, and 1 each from Gogol, Tolstoi, and Mayne Reid.[6]

For some the importation of western notions was welcome: 'In terms of organization we, like all Slav nations, would do well to learn more from the Germans', wrote Boyan Penev in 1924,[7] but for others the impact of the west was too precipitate and too penetrative, another author likening it to 'a whirlwind which disturbed the bases of our national way of life', and led 'to an attempt on the impossible: the successful mixing of the western and the indigenous.'[8] By the 1930s there were attempts to distance Bulgaria from both west and east; Yanko Yanev, in an essay entitled 'East or West', argued in 1933 that Bulgaria had no sense of its own historical identity or purpose, that it was neither Slav nor western, did not assert its own distinctiveness, and had failed to discover its own historic path. With typical 1930s use of geopolitical and racial concepts he went on to argue that the Slav empire of the Soviet Union, with its factories and modernization, was turning itself into a copy of America whilst the west was morally moribund. The Bulgarians had therefore to create their own culture based on their unique racial combination of the western, the Gothic, and the classical.[9]

The advent of Soviet-style communism ended all official debate about whether Bulgaria should face east or west but the decay of that system produced an equal and opposite reaction. The influx of western culture

[5] Daskalova, *Gramotnost*, 115.   [6] Ibid. 145.

[7] Boyan Penev, 'Nashata inteligentsiya; fragmenti', in Elenkov and Daskalov, *Zashto sme takiva?*, 131–143, 137.

[8] Atanas Iliev, 'Narodnostno oboslobyavane na bŭlgarskata kultura', ibid. 309–19, 311, 313.   [9] Yanko Yanev, 'Iztok ili zapad', ibid. 337–41.

via the audio and video cassettes in the 1970s and 1980s was the twentieth century equivalent of the import of western culture after the liberation of 1878. Bulgaria's cultural face turned once again clearly to the west and the consequent whirlwind helped to disturb the basis of communist authority.

Under communist rule, particularly in its early stages, the links between Europe and Asia via Turkey lost much of the importance they had enjoyed in previous decades. Since 1989 the position has reversed and Bulgaria's nodal position has come more into prominence. Bulgaria will be at the intersection of at least two major EU transport projects: corridor eight, the road and rail link joining Albania, Macedonia, Bulgaria, and Turkey, an essential part of the planned connections between Europe and Asia; and corridor four, which will run from Turkey through Greece, Macedonia, and Bulgaria to central Europe. In addition, new international electricity grids will run through Bulgaria as will a number of vital oil and gas pipelines from the Caucasus to Europe. Strategically, Bulgaria will occupy a vital position, the more so if Russia continues to use its energy resources as a political and diplomatic lever.

If Bulgaria is once again at a nodal point it has not reverted to its previous state of indecision as to its cultural and political orientation. With the exception of the few disastrous years of the Videnov administration Bulgaria has looked resolutely to the west, and its acceptance into the EU would seem to set it in that mould for the foreseeable future. This would not have pleased the historian Petŭr Mutafchiev. Writing in 1938, on the sixtieth anniversary of the liberation, a point almost midway between that liberation and the agreement that Bulgaria should join the EU, he wrote that 'in the reckless effort to become Europeans we are promising to destroy everything on which rests our Bulgarian character . . . We have not, of course, become "Europeans", and we are hardly likely ever to do so, because this imagined "European" is a fiction.'[10]

This Oxford History began by stressing that the gulf between Bulgaria and the remainder of Europe, particularly Great Britain, was too large. Let it end with the hope that the admission of Bulgaria into the new and real 'imagined community' of modern Europe will end it for ever.

---

[10] Petŭr Mutafchiev, 'Edno ravnosmetka. Po sluchaĭ 60-godishninata ot Osvobozhdenieto ni', originally published in *Prosveta*, 3/6 (1938), and republished in Elenkov and Daskalov, *Zashto sme takiva?*, 380–90.

Bulgarian Political Parties, 1878–1934[1]

The underlying ideological assumptions of all Bulgarian political and parliamentary parties in the post-liberation period were, in the broad sense of the term, 'liberal'; all parties accepted the notions of popular representation, the rule of law, basic individual rights, and the separation of powers. But there were lines of division along how much democracy the constitution should allow, and these divisions were complicated by the tensions between northern Bulgarian and southern Bulgarian or 'Rumelian' groups; and a second complicating factor was the attitude towards foreign affairs and especially to the role Russia should or should not play in Bulgarian affairs.

After 1878 the more cautiously minded coalesced into the conservative faction, their initial unifying idea being the desire to limit popular sovereignty. There was a strong element of paternalism in conservative thinking. Writers such as Stoyan Mihaĭlovski argued that a democratic spirit was required before democratic laws could be enacted; foisting democracy upon a country was, he suggested, like throwing a man in a swimming pool and expecting him to learn to swim. This democratic spirit could only be developed through the formation of a benign and paternalist oligarchy; using a different analogy, Mihaĭlovski said the introduction of the Tŭrnovo constitution had asked the Bulgarian people 'to move directly from the first to the eighth grade'.[2] Such thinking survived in Bulgarian politics into the 1930s, and was reflected in contemporary justifications for the zvenari's banning of political parties and King Boris's assertion that by imposing direct rule he was trying to create 'a tidy and disciplined democracy imbued with the idea of social solidarity'.[3]

These ideas were represented in the Conservative Party, which was officially founded in the second half of 1880 in Sofia with local branches emerging slowly in subsequent months. The party's statutes were formulated after the collapse of the 1881 regime, and its programme was published in two tranches in 1882 and 1883. The Conservative Party took its belief in the sanctity of private property

---

[1] This appendix relies heavily on Sazdov, *Mnogo-partiĭnata sistema*.

[2] Stoyan Mihaĭlovski, 'Kak zapadat i se provalyat dŭrzhavite', in Elenkov and Daskalov, *Zashto sme takiva?*, 102–16, 111.

[3] 'Bulgaria: The Least Desirable Result', by Duncan Brown, Transitions on Line, 28 July 2005: www.tol.cz

far enough to favour giving their land back to returning émigré Turks. It wanted good relations with Russia but also to make Bulgaria an independent state. Its newspapers were *Vitosha*, named after the mountain near Sofia (1879–80), *Bŭlgarski Glas* (Bulgarian Voice) (1879–83), and *Otechestvo* (Fatherland) (1884–5).

The Liberal Party represented the more enthusiastic democratic elements. It had faith in the wisdom and political maturity of the masses. The party emerged when a number of dominant figures began publishing *Tselokupna Bŭlgariya* (Complete Bulgaria) in June 1879. Local groups were soon formed, especially in the liberal strongholds of Tŭrnovo, Gabrovo, and Dryanovo. Its ideas were set out in the first edition of *Tselokupna Bŭlgariya* and in the official programme published in January 1882. *Tselokupna Bŭlgariya* was published from 1879 to 1880, and was replaced by *Nezavisimost* (Independence) (1880–1), and *Tŭrnovskata konstitutsiya* (The Tŭrnovo Constitution) (1884–8). For the first half-decade after the liberation this two-party system survived but thereafter it fragmented rapidly.

A similar process was to affect the political groupings in Rumelia which were to retain much of their individuality and influence after the union of 1885.

After 1878 the dominant oligarchy in Rumelia did not set up a proper party organization until it lost power in the spring of 1883. It then established branches in all major centres and in the summer of 1883 called a conference in Plovdiv which worked out an official programme and adopted the name National (Unionist) Party, commonly known as 'the Whites'; at the same time the whites also began publishing *Sŭedinenie* (Union). They also had *Narodnŭ [sic] Glas* (National Voice) (1879–85) and *Maritsa* (1878–85).

The opposition faction in Rumelia, the liberals or 'Reds', also did not immediately form a definite party, nor did they establish their own newspaper until 1883 when *Yuzhna Bŭlgariya* (Southern Bulgaria) began to appear. At the same time the Liberal Party of Rumelia was formally established. The southern liberals had formalized their party relatively late because they read the northern liberal papers such as *Nezavisimost* and also because until September 1882 Rumelian officials, many of whom were liberals—they were popularly known as 'kazionite' or 'the office holders'—were not allowed to be journalists. The liberals' support was concentrated in the towns, particularly amongst the intelligentsia; they had little interest in and therefore received little backing from the peasantry. There were divisions between the moderates, especially the office holders, and the extreme liberals over relations between Rumelia and the principality.

In the principality the Liberal Party also suffered from divisions, above all the deepening rift between the Karavelov and Tsankov sections over issues such as the sale of the Rusé to Varna railway. The crisis after the unification of 1885 split the party into three rather than two factions. But even this tripartite system did not survive for long with personal rivalries, loyalties to Battenberg or the new prince, and above all the question of relations with Russia complicating previous divisions.

The first of the three factions, which did not immediately form parties, was that of the russophobes who had separated from the karavelists over relations with Russia; prominent amongst them were Zahari Stoyanov, Dimitŭr Petkov, Dimitŭr Rizov, and above all Stefan Stambolov. Their ideology, such as it was, came from the southern liberal kazionite and the extreme nationalist wing of the Karavelov party led by Radoslavov; their slogan was 'Bulgaria for itself'. On the opposite pole stood Tsankov and the southern unionists under Konstantin Velichkov; these extreme russophiles believed, 'Without Russia there can be no Bulgaria'. The third force was the Karavelov Party, which was basically also russophile. It wanted an independent internal policy and friendship with Russia and advocated what might be regarded as an early example of finlandization.

Stambolov's tough policies after the arrival of Prince Ferdinand brought about a virtual cessation of party politics; the leading tsankovists were in exile and the leading karavelists in jail. Stambolov's support in the country at large was consolidated by the newly formed 'Bulgaria for Itself', or 'Patriotic Associations', upon which Stambolov's own National Liberal Party (NLP) was built. Its statutes were adopted and a programme published in 1892, though there was further reorganization in 1895. The historian Simeon Radev was a major figure in working out its ideology. Its papers were *Svoboda* (Freedom) (1886–99) and *Nov Vek* (New Century) (1899–1912). After the death of Stambolov the party was led by Dimitŭr Petkov, and after his assassination by Nikola Genadiev. Genadiev himself was murdered in 1923 by Macedonian extremists, but by that time he had abandoned the National Liberal Party.

In 1887 Vasil Radoslavov distanced himself from Stambolov and went on to form his own wing of the National Liberal Party. Its papers were *Glas* (Voice) and *Narodna Volya* (National Will); it also published *Narodna Prava* (National Right/Truth) which ran, with some short breaks, from 1888 to 1932. Radoslavov's group attracted the discontented from a wide variety of social groups and its local support was particularly strong in the north-eastern centres such as Shumen, Razgrad, Preslav, and Varna. In the spring of 1899 the stambolovists and radoslavists came together to form the United Liberal Party, but in the autumn they separated again. In 1908 Ivan Andonov and T. Gashev and their adherents split away from the radoslavist faction; they published a new *Svoboda* and *6i septemvri* (6 September).

In 1893, with the encouragement of Prince Ferdinand, Radoslavov had been instrumental in establishing the United Legal Opposition, of which another prominent member was Konstantin Stoilov. It proved to be an ephemeral body but its formation signalled the rebirth of party political life and ushered in a decade of extreme instability in the structure of Bulgaria's sŭbranie groupings. By the end of the nineteenth century many parties were little more than coffee house parties, being concentrated in the capital and being dominated by one or two personalities rather than by an easily identifiable political platform.

In June 1894 Stoilov, with the help of Mincho Tsachev and Grigor Nachovich from the now more or less defunct northern Conservative Party, formed the National (Narodna) Party. The new party wanted to unite all who were opposed to Stambolov. Their aims were to restore the constitutional process, create a firm, two-party system, stabilize the economy, and cooperate to secure the recognition of the Coburg dynasty. The base of the party was a combination of the former conservatives in the north and the southern National (Unionist) Party, though it initially included some radoslavists, tsankovists, and a few stambolovists, and was soon joined by Velichkov's large Rumelian Unionist group. Despite its desire to establish a strong, two-party system, and notwithstanding its strong internal discipline, so eclectic a group could not survive for long. By the end of the 1890s the tsankovists, karavelists, and the Velichkov Unionists had all defected, leaving the party once again as primarily a combination of northern conservatives and Rumelian National (Unionist) Party adherents. Stoilov remained leader until his death in 1901. His successor was Ivan Evstratiev Geshov, though he was something of a figurehead and the real authority lay with Todor Teodorov. The party was strongly pro-Russian and was closely linked to the Bulgarian Commercial Bank. It was discredited because it was held responsible for the disasters of 1913. Its newspaper was *Mir* (World or Peace) which was published continually between 1894 and 1944.

The tsankovists had not been natural members of the National Party. Tsankov's willingness to accept both constitutional change and some increase in the powers of the prince had made it possible for him to agree with the conservatives in 1883, but after 1886 his intrigues and the incursion of tsankovist bands meant that his party in effect ceased to exist. His demoralized followers found a billet with Stoilov for the lack of anything more congenial. When Tsankov was allowed to return to Bulgaria in December 1894 life was breathed back into his party and his followers quit the National Party to return to their old leader. In 1899 the tsankovists were joined by the Velichkov faction of the National Party and they jointly established the Progressive Liberal Party in December of that year. By this time Tsankov himself had resigned as leader of the party to be succeeded by Stoyan Danev. There were two groups within the party. One centred on Danev, and the other, the *Sŭglasie* (Agreement) group, so called because of its newspaper. The *Sŭglasie* group was led by Aleksandŭr Lyudskanov. This division did not lead to a rupture in the Progressive Liberal Party, Tsankov remaining its leader until his death in 1911. The party was strongly pro-Russian, Danev having broken with Stoilov in 1894 because he believed the latter had been too dilatory in re-establishing relations with Russia. The tsankovist papers were *Svetlina* (Light) (1882–3), *Bratstvo* (Fraternity) (1884), *Sredets* (the old name for Sofia) (1884–6), *Süglasie* (1894–6), and *Bŭlgariya* (Bulgaria) (1898–1921).

The tsankovists' chief rivals in the old Liberal Party, the karavelists, also adopted a new name. In August 1894 Karavelov and his associates, then interned in the Black Mosque in Sofia, worked out the principles of what in the autumn of 1896 was to become the Democratic Party (DP). Its ideas were expounded in *Zname* (Banner), the karavelist newspaper which began to appear in late 1894, replacing *Tŭrnovskata konstitutsiya* which had been proscribed by the Stambolov regime. Like the tsankovists, the karavelists were able to resume their independent political activities in December 1894, in their case because their leader had been released from detention. The party had strong support amongst the civilian and military intellectual elite, amongst the peasantry, and amongst those engaged in the workshops. This meant that its support was substantial in areas of traditional production such as the towns on the Balkan foothills. It also had strong backing amongst senior administrators, both in Sofia and in the larger provincial towns. The party was a fierce opponent of Ferdinand and when he first arrived argued for his expulsion. It recognized him in 1893 and after the settlement with Russia its attitude moderated and in the early twentieth century it was even one of the parties which called for a strengthening of the powers of the monarchy. Nevertheless, Ferdinand regarded the DP with particular distaste and suspicion. The party believed that national reunification could be achieved solely by military means, but this could only be undertaken with Russian approval. Aleksandŭr Malinov succeeded Karavelov upon the latter's death in 1903.

The Democratic Party, the National Party, and the Progressive Liberal Party were the three largest in the country in the first decade of the twentieth century, though the latter was less financially secure than the other two. In terms of popular support, of course, all 'sŭbranie' parties were being challenged by the Bulgarian Agrarian National Union, and the need to adapt to the presence of this new, popular, and entirely different force was one of the reasons for further instability in the established parties in the first five years after the turn of the century.

In 1901 a radical faction under Naĭcho Tsanov and Todor Vlaĭkov was formed within the DP. The origins of this split went back to the mid-1890s. In July 1894 in Rusé a radical group was formed which began publishing *Signal* (Signal) and in Plovdiv in March a similar radical group had begun publishing *Borba* (Struggle). The Rusé group worked out ideas for the democratization of the constitution and for the formation of a Balkan union but there was as yet no intention to form a political party. The rise of the agrarian movement persuaded them that more radical policies were needed and they called for a progressive income tax and for the replacement of the army by a people's militia. In 1905 the radicals seceded from the DP to form the Radical Democratic Party (RDP) under the leadership of Tsanov. The RDP was heavily influenced by narodnik ideas and favoured autonomy for Macedonia and Thrace, but as a prelude to the formation of a Balkan federation rather than as the precursor of unification with Bulgaria. The party therefore opposed a large army and the preparation for war in the Balkans. Its publications were the journal *Demokraticheski Pregled* (Democratic Review) (from 1902), and the newspapers *Demokrat* (Democrat) (1905–10) and *Radikal* (Radical) (from 1910).

True to Bulgarian tradition, before the split of 1905 the radical faction within the Democratic Party was known as the 'young'. By the late 1890s a similar group had emerged within the radoslavist party and in 1899–1900 had attempted a putsch to remove Radoslavov from the leadership. They failed and were expelled and in 1904, under the leadership of Dimitŭr Tonchev, established the Young Liberal Party. Its newspaper was *Svobodno Slovo* (Free Speech) (1904–13). The paper ceased publication when the Young Liberals joined the Radoslavov cabinet in July 1913, and the party suspended its activities when Bulgaria became engaged in the first world war.

The wars of 1912–18 produced further realignment amongst the Bulgarian parliamentary parties. The national liberals had by tradition been pro-Austrian and pro-German and the catastrophe of 1913 brought Genadiev of the NLP, Radoslavov, and Tonchev together to sign a letter to King Ferdinand in which they blamed the national disaster on the russophiles and Russia, and demanded a reorientation of Bulgarian foreign policy which should now be aligned with Russia's opponents. In 1915 Genadiev changed his mind. In that year he had been sent by the king to tour Europe and assess the prospects of both sides in the war. He came back convinced that the entente powers would win and therefore switched to become a champion of joining the western powers and Russia. This his russophobe party could not swallow and the NLP fell apart, with one faction following Genadiev and the other remaining with Dobri Petrov, who continued to serve in Radoslavov's pro-central powers administration. The Democratic Party also performed an about turn in 1915, abandoning its former devotion to Russia and becoming an enthusiastic supporter of war on the side of the central powers.

After the end of the war the two former non-sŭbranie parties, the agrarians and the communists, dominated the polls but this did not prevent further realignments between the older parties. In 1920 Stoilov's National Party joined with the Progressive Liberals to form the United National Liberal Party. In the same year Genadiev founded the Nationalist Liberal Party.[4] Genadiev, who had come to

[4] The Slav languages do not distinguish between 'nation' and 'people', using *narod* or a cognate for both terms. The stambolovist party was the *Narodnoliberalna partiya* which I have translated as National Liberal Party but which could also be rendered as People's or Popular Liberal Party. The party founded by Genadiev in 1920 was the *Natsionalliberalna partiya* which I chose to translate as Nationalist Liberal Party.

know Stamboliĭski when both were in prison during the war, pushed for an alliance between his new party and the agrarians but the latter were not interested. In September 1923 Genadiev left his own Nationalist Liberal Party because his colleagues insisted on joining the anti-agrarian National Alliance. Genadiev then established yet another party, National Unity, but neither it nor he lived long thereafter, Genadiev being killed by Macedonian extremists in October.

There was further fragmentation of the parties in the 1920s, nineteen being represented in the sŭbranie elected in 1926, a number which had increased to twenty-five by 1934. The inter-war period also saw splits within the agrarian movement and factionalism even inside the Communist Party but for the old parties the trend was not now towards the redefinition of parties but towards the formation of varying alliances of existing parties. Groups such as the National Alliance, the Democratic Alliance, the Constitutional Bloc, and the People's Bloc superseded the kaleidoscopic changes in parliamentary alignments. The new situation was no clearer than the old.

Bibliographical Notes

This is not an attempt at an exhaustive bibliography of Bulgarian history. The aim is to isolate those works which the author has found valuable, significant, and/or interesting. It includes only a few of the many volumes of documents published since Bulgaria became a separate political entity in 1878, nor are many memoirs mentioned, though this is not to imply either that they do not exist or that they are not of value; they are simply too legion to list in their entirety. The bibliography does not deal with the years before the Bulgarian national revival, as those years form only the introduction to the main body of the text. Historical writing in Bulgaria has inevitably had to adapt to the changing political climate in the country. This has produced a number of violent swings, none more so than when the communists firmly established their hold at the end of the 1940s, and when that grip was relaxed and finally broken forty years later; between 1990 and 1999 the leading Bulgarian journal for academic history, *Istoricheski Pregled*, issued twelve rather than its previous six editions per year, so much was there to say and so many were the issues that had to be revised in the new, uncontrolled atmosphere. This is not to say that the intervening period produced nothing of value. Investigations into the decline of the Ottoman system of landholding and of government produced vitally important material, as did research into the early years of the labour movement in Bulgaria. Work produced under the communists was, of course, intended to serve a political purpose, but so too was much of the work produced both before and after communist rule. Few writers in any period remained uninfluenced by nationalist feelings, whilst the determination of some post-1989 historians to condemn the communists was as intense as the latter's insistence that their predecessors were little less than devils incarnate. Objectivity is a noble aspiration but few, communist or non-communist, western or eastern, can achieve it.

The following notes follow roughly but not exactly the chapters in the foregoing text.

GENERAL HISTORIES

There is no general, convenient, and satisfactory survey of the entire course of Bulgarian history. Under communist rule BAN produced the three-volume *Istoriya na Bŭlgariya*, D. Kosev, Zh. Natan, and Al. Burmov (eds. in chief) (Sofia: Nauka i izkustvo, 1961–4) which, though packed with detail on some themes, is an exemplar of the less adventurous side of marxist historiography. Towards the end of the communist years a new venture, encouraged before her death by Lyudmila Zhivkova, was launched under which BAN was to publish a lavishly illustrated, fourteen-volume history. The costly exercise was incomplete in 1989 but the published volumes were qualitatively as well as quantitatively much superior to the three-volume history. That three-volume work was summarized and presented in more sophisticated fashion by Dimitŭr Kosev, Hristo Hristov, and Dimitŭr Angelov (eds.), *Kratka Istoriya na Bŭlgariya* (Sofia: Nauka i izkustvo, 1969). The communist period saw the production of a six-volume study of Bulgaria's economic history, *Ikonomika na Bŭlgariya*, whose initial editor-in-chief was Zhak Natan and which was published in Sofia by Nauka i izkustvo, the first volume appearing in 1969 and the last in 1980. Since 1980 reassessment has been made by, amongst others, Kostadin Paleshutski and Milen Kumanov, *681–1948: iz istoriyata na bŭlgarskata narodnost i durzhava: izsledvaniya, analizi, preotsenki* (Sofia: Pelikan Alfa, 1993); Elena Statelova and Stoĭcho Grŭncharov, *Istoriya na nova Bŭlgariya, 1878–1944* (Sofia: Anubis, 1999); and Ivan Bozhilov, Vera Mutafchieva, Andreĭ Pantev, Konstantin Kosev, and Stoĭcho Grŭncharov, *Istoriya na Bŭlgariya* (Sofia: Abagar, 1998); an important recent collection of documents is Velichko Georgiev and Staĭko Trifonov, *Istoriya na bŭlgarite 1878–1944 v dokumenti: v tri toma*, 3 vols. (Sofia: Prosveta, 1994–5).

English writing on Bulgaria has produced some egregious titles. *Caitiff Bulgaria*, written by P. Pipinelis, a pseudonym for Nikolaou Panagiotes (London: Hutchinson, 1944), and published under the authority of the Greek ministry of information, reflected wartime passion and bitterness. A title which has attained individuality through the changes in English usage was chosen by Stowers Johnson for his *Gay Bulgaria* (London: The Travel Book Club, 1964). There are few English-language surveys of Bulgarian history. Nikolaĭ Todorov's *A Short History of Bulgaria* (Sofia: Sofia Press, 1977) toed the party line. Hristo Hristov, *Bulgaria, 1,300 Years* (Sofia: Sofia Press, 1980) was produced to accompany the anniversary of Bulgarian statehood, and has value only as an exemplar of how appalling such celebratory writing can become. Mercia Macdermott's *A History of Bulgaria, 1393–1885* (London: George Allen & Unwin, 1962), is a product of the socialist-nationalist school of historiography, recounting the horrors of Ottoman rule and revelling in the glories of the renaissance, but it is readable and full of information. A similar viewpoint, but with emphasis more on socialism than nationalism, can be found in Stanley G. Evans, *A Short History of Bulgaria* (London: Lawrence & Wishart, 1960). This is an extraordinary work in that its author, though an Anglican priest, clearly believed that, along with the Almighty, the propaganda organs of the Bulgarian Communist Party were the fount of all truth. A different perspective is adopted in R. J. Crampton, *A Concise History of Bulgaria*, 2nd edition (Cambridge: Cambridge University Press, 2005).

For general surveys covering parts of the modern period a new work appeared just as this current volume was being prepared for submission to the press. It is Rumen Daskalov, *Bŭlgarskoto Obshtestvo 1878–1939*, 2 vols. (Sofia: Gutenberg, 2005). The first volume covers 'The State, Politics, and the Economy', and the second 'Population, Society, and Culture'. It provides the first major synthesis by a Bulgarian scholar of pre-communist, communist, and post-communist historiography and should rapidly become and long remain an essential text for all serious students of Bulgaria in these years. There is a great deal of incisive and intelligent commentary in Nikolaĭ Genchev, *Ochertsi: sotsialno-psihologicheski tipove v bŭlgarskata istoriya* (Sofia: Septemvri, 1987).

The attempt to define what it is to be Bulgarian is part of Genchev's purpose, and is also at the centre of an extremely valuable volume of extracts of Bulgarian writing on the same theme compiled by Ivan Elenkov and Rumen Daskalov, *Zashto sme takiva? V tŭrsene na bŭlgarskata kulturna identichnost* (Sofia: Prosveta, 1994). Recent general works on Bulgarian history include Petŭr Angelov and Mito Isusov, *Stranitsi ot bŭlgarskata istoriya; sŭbitiya, razmisli, lichnosti*, 2 vols. (Sofia: Prosveta, 1993).

A concise but still thoughtful treatment of pre-socialist Bulgarian history is to be found in Tatiana Kostadinova, *Bulgaria 1879–1946: The Challenge of Choice* (Boulder, Colo.: East European Monographs no. 429, distributed by Columbia University Press, 1995). A survey of political, social, and economic evolution is provided in Richard J. Crampton, *Bulgaria 1878–1918: A History* (Boulder, Colo.: East European Monographs no. 138, distributed by Columbia University Press, 1983). See also, N. Stanev, *Naĭ-nova Istoriya na Bŭlgariya, 1878–1912*, 2 vols. (Sofia, 1925). Another pre-second world war author worth consulting is Aleksandŭr Girginov, see his *Narodnata katastrofa: voĭnite 1912/13* (Sofia: Armeĭskiya voenno-izdatelski fond, 1926), and *Bŭlgariya pred Velikata Voĭna* (Plovdiv: H. G. Danov, 1932). See also Todor Girginov, *Istoricheski Razboi na Sŭvremenna Bŭlgariya ot Vŭzrazhdaneto do Balkanskata Voĭna 1912 godina*, 2 vols. (Sofia: 1934, 1935). Foreign policy in the pre-socialist era is surveyed in Vasil Vasilev (ed. in chief), *Vŭnshnata Politika na Bŭlgariya, 1878–1944*, Izsledvaniya po bŭlgarska istoriya, no. 3 (Sofia: BAN, 1978). There is an excellent short introduction to recent economic history in John R. Lampe, *The Bulgarian Economy in the Twentieth Century* (London: Croom Helm, 1986). A long essay which provides a useful summary of the traditional Bulgarian nationalist view of the subject is Marin V. Pundeff, 'Bulgarian Nationalism', in Peter Sugar and Ivo J. Lederer, *Nationalism in Eastern Europe*, Far Eastern and Russian Institute Publications on Russia and Eastern Europe, no. 1 (Seattle: University of Washington Press, 1971), 93–165. There is an outline, introductory history of Bulgarian literature, which includes a chapter on the renaissance, in Charles A. Moser, *A History of Bulgarian Literature 865–1944* (The Hague: Mouton, 1972).

THE BULGARIAN NATIONAL REVIVAL

The Bulgarian national renaissance has not yet found an English-language author who has done justice to this important, fascinating, and frequently moving story. A critical bibliography is available in English: Rumen Daskalov, *The Making of a Nation in the Balkans: Historiography of the Bulgarian Revival* (Budapest: Central European University Press, 2004). In Bulgarian there are numerous studies. The earliest stages of the revival are well treated in Hristo Gandev, *Faktori na bŭlgarskoto vŭzrazhdane, 1600–1830* (Sofia: Bŭlgarska kniga, 1943), and the same writer continued his analysis into the 1870s in his *Problemi na bŭlgarskoto Vŭzrazhdane: trudove vŭrhu obshtestveno-ikonomicheskoto razvitie na Bŭlgariya ot sredata na XVII do 70-te g. na XIX v.* (Sofia: Nauka i izkustvo, 1976). Any work by Nikolaĭ Genchev repays reading; his *Bŭlgarsko vŭzrazhdane*, 3rd, revised edition (Sofia: Otechestven Front, 1988) is, to my mind, the best single-volume treatment of the subject. From an earlier generation there is the excellent Mihaĭl Arnaudov, *Bŭlgarskoto vŭzrazhdane* (Sofia: Ministerstvo na narodnoto prosveshtenie, 1944). More recent studies were published by Vera Boneva, *Istoricheski etyudi po bŭlgarsko vŭzrazhdane* (Tŭrnovo: Sredets, 1997); Ivan Stoyanov, *Istoriya na bŭlgarskoto vŭzrazhdane* (Tŭrnovo: Evtimiĭ Patriarh Tŭrnovski, 1999); Raĭna Gavrilova, *Vekŭt na bŭlgarskoto vŭzrazhdane* (Sofia: Slov-D, 1992); Kontantin Kosev, *Kratka istoriya na bŭlgarskoto vŭzrazhdane* (Sofia: Marin Drinov, 2001); Plamen Mitev, *Bŭlgarskoto vŭzrazhdane. Lektsionen kurs* (Sofia: Polis, 1999); Iliya Todev, *Novi ochertsi po bŭlgarska istoriya. Vŭzrazhdane* (Sofia: Vek 22, 1995), and the same author's, *Kŭm drugo minalo ili prenebregvani aspekti na bŭlgarskoto vŭzrazhdane* (Sofia: Vigal, 1999); Kiril Topalov, *Vŭzrozhdentsi* (Sofia: Kliment Ohridski, 1999); and Kiril Topalov and Nikolaĭ Chernokozhev, *Bŭlgarskata literatura prez Vŭzrazhdaneto* (Sofia: Prosveta, 1998). There are some useful essays in D. Kosev, Al. Burmov, H. Hristov et al., *Paisiĭ Hilendarski i negovata epoha (1762–1962)* (Sofia: BAN, 1962), and also of value is Virzhiniya Paskaleva, 'Za nyakoĭ osobenosti i faktori v obrazuvaneto na bŭlgarskata natsiya prez pŭrvata polovina na xix v.', *Izvestiya na Instituta za Istoriya*, 16–17 (1966), 423–52.

There is a mountain of sound scholarship on specific aspects of the vŭzrazhdane. For the Janissaries see Tsvetana Georgieva, *Enicharite v bŭlgarskite zemi* (Sofia: Nauka i izkustvo, 1988). For the communal councils during Ottoman rule see Hristo Hristov *Bŭlgarskite obshtini prez Vŭzrazhdaneto* (Sofia: BAN, 1973), and Elena Grozdanova, *Bŭlgarskata selska obshtina prez XV–XVIII vek* (Sofia: BAN, 1979). The upheavals and effects of the *kŭrdjaliĭstvo* are described in Vera P. Mutafchieva, *Kŭrdzhaliĭsko vreme* (Sofia: BAN, 2nd edn., 1993), and Virzhiniya Paskaleva, 'Za samoupravlenieto na Bŭlgarite prez Vŭzrazhdane', *Izvestiya na Instituta za Istoriya*, 14–15 (1964), 69–84. For the contribution of the Bulgarian communities in Romania, see Maksim Slavchev Mladenov, Nikolaĭ Zhechev, and Blagovest Nyagulov (compilers), *Bŭlgarite v Rumŭniya, XVII–XX v.; dokumenti i materiali* (Sofia: Marin Drinov, 1994), and the Bulgarian community in Braila, Nikolaĭ Zhechev, *Braila i bŭlgarskoto kulturno-natsionalno vŭzrazhdane* (Sofia: BAN, 1970). The French revolutionary wars had their impact on the Bulgarians on both sides of the Danube, and this is examined in Stefan Doĭnov, *Bŭlgarskoto natsionalno-osvoboditelno dvizhenie 1800–1812* (Sofia: BAN, 1979). For the evolution of the guilds, see Nikolaĭ Todorov, 'Za nyakoĭ promeni v haraktera na tsehovata organizatsiya u nas prez pŭrvata polovina na xix v.', *Istoricheski Pregled*, 14/4 (1958), 44–76.

The emergence of the Bulgarian intelligentsia is treated in Nikolaĭ Genchev, *Bŭlgarska vŭzrozhdenska inteligentsiya* (Sofia: Kliment Ohridski, 1991); and Thomas A. Meininger, *The Formation of a Nationalist Bulgarian Intelligentsia, 1835–1878* (New York: Garland, 1987). See also, Miglen Kyumdjieva, *Intelektualniyat elit prez vŭzrazhdaneto* (Sofia: Kliment Ohridski, 1997); Ramyana Radkova, *Inteligentsiyata i nravstvenostta prez vŭzrazhdaneto* (Sofia: Marin Drinov, 1995). For the *chitalishta* the best work remains, Stiliyan Chilingirov, *Bŭlgarskite chitalista predi osvobozhdenieto. Prinos vŭrhu istoriyata na bŭlgarskoto vŭzrazhdane* (Sofia: Ministerstvoto na narodnoto prosveshtenie, 1930). For the role of teachers see, Krasimira Daskalova, *Bŭlgarskiyat uchitel prez vŭzrazhdaneto* (Sofia: Kliment Ohridski, 1997).

All major participants in the vŭzrazhdane, and many minor ones, have been the subject of biographies. A work which deals with three specific members of the intelligentsia is Steven Ashley, 'Bulgarian Nationalism (1830–1876): The Ideals and Careers of Ivan Bogorov, Georgi Rakovski, and Pencho Slaveikov', D.Phil. thesis (Oxford, 1984). The most recent biography of Paisiĭ is Nadezhda Dragova, *Otets Paisiĭ. Patriarh na bŭlgarskoto vŭzrazhdane* (Stara Zagora: Znanie, 1994). For a biography of Dragan Tsankov see Margarita Kovacheva, *Dragan Tsankov. Obshtestvenik, Politik, Diplomat do 1878* (Sofia: Nauka i izkustvo, 1982). There is a well-researched if hagiographic biography of Vasil Levski in English: Mercia Macdermott, *The Apostle of Freedom: A Portrait of Vasil Levsky against a Background of Nineteenth Century Bulgaria* (London: George Allen & Unwin, 1967). Later lives were written by Nikolaĭ Genchev, *Vasil Levski* (Sofia: Voenno izdatelstvo, 1987), and Ivan Undjiev, *Vasil Levski: biografiya* (Sofia: BAN, 1993); Levski's contribution to the national movement is analysed in Hristo Ĭonkov, *Vasil Levski i bŭlgarskata natsionalna revolyutsiya* (Sofia: BAN, 1987); Tsvetana Pavlovska, *Vasil Levski i vŭtreshnata revolyutsionna organizatsiya* (Sofia: Georgi Pobedonosets, 1993) and the same author's, *Vasil Levski: nachelo na Bŭlgarskiya revolyutsionen tsentralen komitet v Bŭlgarsko* (Sofia: GoreksPres, 2001). Georgi Rakovski has attracted fewer biographies, but a recent work in English provides a very good introduction to his life and work: Mari A. Firkatian, *The Forest*

Traveler: Georgi Stoikov Rakovski and Bulgarian Nationalism, Balkan Studies no. 5, general editor Eran Fraenkel (New York: Peter Lang, 1996). The standard biography of Lyuben Karavelov is Mihaïl Arnaudov, *Lyuben Karavelov: zhivot, delo, epoha, 1834–1879* (Sofia: Nauka i izkustvo, 1972). The most recent biography of Botev is Ivan Undjiev, *Hristo Botev zhivot i tvorchestvo* (Sofia: Otechestven Front, 1983).

There are a number of superb books on the Bulgarian Church during the revival period: Petŭr Nikov, *Vŭzrazhdanie na bŭlgarskiya narod; tsŭrkovno-natsionalni borbi i postizheniya* (Sofia: Strashimir Slavchev, no date cited but before 1931, republished, Sofia: Nauka i izkustvo, 1971); Zina Markova, *Bŭlgarskoto tsŭrkovno-natsionalno dvizhenie do krimskata voĭna*, Izsledvaniya po bŭlgarska istoriya no. 1 (Sofia: BAN, 1976); and the same author's *Bŭlgarskata Ekzarhiya, 1870–1879* (Sofia: BAN, 1989). The declaration of Easter Sunday 1860 is the focus of Nikolaĭ Zhechev, *Bŭlgarskiyat Velikden ili strastite bŭlgarski*, 6th celebratory edition (Sofia: Marin Drinov, 1995). The external implications of the church movement are analysed in Thomas A. Meininger, *Ignatiev and the Establishment of the Bulgarian Exarchate, 1864–1872: A Study in Personal Diplomacy* (Madison: University of Wisconsin Press, 1970). Also, Mihaïl Arnaudov, *Ekzarh Josif i bŭlgarskata kulturna borba sled sŭzdavaneto na ekzarhiyata (1840–1915)* (Sofia: Sveti Sinod, 1915). For the unfortunate episode of the Uniates in Constantinople, see Christopher Walter, 'Raphael Popov, Bulgarian Uniate Bishop: Problems of Uniatism and Autocephaly', *Sobornost*, 6/1 (1984), 46–60.

There is excellent discussion of the press during the Bulgarian renaissance in Zdravka Konstantinova, *Dŭrzhavnost predi dŭrzhavata; svrŭhfunktsii na bŭlgarskata vŭzrozhdenska zhurnalistika* (Sofia: Kliment Ohridski, 2000); as the title implies, the book argues that the press provided a form of state before the formation of the political state itself. The issue of literacy and reading, both in the vŭzrazhdane and after it, are discussed with much fascinating detail and considerable insight in Krasimira Daskalova, *Gramotnost, knizhnina, chitateli, chetene v Bŭlgariya na prehoda kŭm modernoto vreme* (Sofia: Lik, 1999). There is further useful material on this and adjacent themes in Raina Gavrilova, *Bulgarian Urban Culture in the Eighteenth and Nineteenth Centuries* (Cranbury, NJ: Susquehanna University Press, 1999) which also discusses the role of local councils and the formation of literary and other associations. The classic study of the Balkan town remains Nikolaĭ Todorov, *The Balkan City, 1400–1900* (Seattle: University of Washington Press, 1983). Most Bulgarian towns have had competent histories written of them, and these have useful data on the renaissance period. For a few examples, see St. N. Shishkov, *Plovdiv v svoeto minalo i nastoiashte; istoriko-etnografski i politiko-ikonomicheski pregled* (Plovdiv: Tŭrgovska pechatnitsa, 1926), and Ivan Undjiev, *Plovdiv 1878–1968; 90 godina ot osvobozhdenieto na grada i plovdivskiya krai* (Plovdiv: Hristo G. Danov, 1968); Ivan Undjiev, *Karlovo: istoriyata na grada do osvobozhdenieto* (Sofia: BAN, 1968); and for Svishtov, Konstantin Kosev, 'Ikonomicheskoto polozhenie na Svishtov predi osvobozhdenieto', in Ivan Undjiev et al. (eds.), *V Pamet na Akademik Mihaĭl Dimitrov; izsledvaniya vŭrhu bŭlgarskoto vŭzrazhdane* (Sofia: BAN, 1974), 617–23. This volume also contains a useful study of the village of Chupene, Strashimir Dimitrov, 'Selo Chupene prez xix v. (do osvobozhdenieto)', 23–37. Perceptive travel writers have much to offer on social conditions; see particularly, F. Kanitz, *Donau-Bulgarien und der Balkan: Historisch-geographisch-ethnographische Reisestudien aus den Jahren 1860–1879*, enlarged edition, 3 vols. (Leipzig: H. Fries, 1882), and Dr Constantin Jireček, *Das Fürstenthum Bulgarien. Seine Bodengestaltung, Natur, Bevölkerung, wirtschaftliche Zustände, geistige Cultur, Staatsverfassung, Staatsverwaltung und neueste Geschichte* (Vienna: F. Tempsky, 1891).

For a summary of social conditions, with an emphasis on rural areas and the land-tenure systems in the Bulgarian lands before 1878 see R. J. Crampton, 'Bulgarian Society in the Early Nineteenth Century', in Richard Clogg (ed.), *Balkan Society in the Age of Greek Independence* (London: Macmillan in association with the Centre of Contemporary Greek Studies, King's College, University of London, 1981), 157–204. See also: Dimitŭr Kosev, 'Kŭm izyasnyavane na nyakoĭ problemi ot istoriyata na Bŭlgariya prez xviĭi i nachaloto na xix v.', *Istoricheski Pregled*, 13/3 (1956), 26–62, and his 'Klasovite otnosheniya v Bŭlgariya prez vŭzrazhdaneto', *Istoricheski Pregled*, 7/4–5 (1950), 443–63; Hristo Hristov, *Agrarnite Otnosheniya v Makedoniya prez xix i nachaloto na xx v.* (Sofia: BAN, 1964); Bistra A. Tsvetkova, 'Turskiyat feodalizŭm i polozhenieto na bŭlgarskiya narod do nachaloto na xix v.', *Istoricheski Pregled*, 11/1 (1955), 59–86; Strashimir Dimitrov, 'Chiflishkoto stopanstvo prez 50–70te godini na xix v.', *Istoricheski Pregled*, 11/2 (1955), 3–34; Hristo Hristov, 'Kŭm vŭprosa za klasite i klasovite otnosheniya v bŭlgarskoto obshtestvo prez vŭzrazhdaneto (proizhod, sotsialna prinadlezhnostta i rolya na chorbadjiĭte', *Izvestiya na Instituta za Istoriya*, 21 (1970), 51–85; and N. G. Levintov, 'Agrarnye otnosheniya v Bolgariĭ nakanune osvobozhdeniya i agrarnyi perevorot 1877–1879 godov', in L. B. Valev, S. A. Nikhitin, and P. N. Tret'yakov (eds.), *Osvobozhdeniye Bolgariĭ ot turetskogo iga, Sbornik Statei* (Moscow: Academy of Sciences of the USSR, 1953), 139–221.

For the outbursts of unrest before the 1870s see: Lt. Gen. Sht. Atanasov, *Selskite vŭstaniya v Bŭlgariya kŭm kraya na xviĭi v. i nachaloto na xix v. i sŭsdavaneto na bŭlgarskata zemska voĭska* (Sofia: Dŭrzhavnoto voenno izdatelstvo pri MNO, 1958); Mark Pinson, 'Ottoman Bulgaria in the First Tanzimat Period—the Revolts in Nish (1841) and Vidin (1850)', *Middle Eastern Studies*, 11/2 (May 1975), 103–46; Strashimir Dimitrov, *Vŭstanieto ot 1850 godina v*

Bŭlgariya (Sofia: BAN, 1972), and also his 'Iz istoriyata na revolyutsionnoto dvizhenie v nishkiya vilayet prez 1850g', *Izvestiya na Instituta za Istoriya*, 16–17 (1966), 407–22. The April uprising has naturally attracted a huge amount of attention from Bulgarian scholars. Between 1884 and 1892 Zahari Stoyanov published his famous *Zapiski po bŭlgarskite vŭstaniya* which were republished a century later with an introduction by Nikolaĭ Genchev (Sofia: Nauka i izkustvo, 1981); they were translated into English by M. W. Potter and published as *Zachary Stoyanoff; Pages from the Autobiography of a Bulgarian Insurgent* (London: Edward Arnold, 1913); unfortunately the English version is a pale, anodyne, and much-curtailed version of the original. The most celebrated academic study of the rising is Dimitŭr Strashimirov, *Istoriya na aprilskoto vŭstanie*, 3 vols. (Plovdiv: 1907, republished Sofia: Marin Drinov, 1996). Another three-volume work is Ĭono Mitev, *Istoriya na aprilskoto vŭstanie 1876: v tri toma* (Sofia: BAN, 1986–99). See also Konstantin Kosev, Nikolaĭ Zhechev, and Doĭno Doĭnov, *Istoriya na aprilskoto vŭstanie 1876*, 2nd edition (Sofia: Partizdat, 1986), and Konstantin Kosev, *Aprilskoto vŭstanie—prelyudiya na Osvobozhdenieto* (Sofia: Hristo Botev, 1996).

FROM THE LIBERATION TO THE END OF THE FIRST WORLD WAR

The text of the Tŭrnovo constitution, along with that of other constitutions and constitutional drafts from 1879 to 1947 is included in Veselin Metodiev and Lŭchezar Stoyanov, *Bŭlgarski konstitutsii i konstitutsionni proekti* (Sofia: Petŭr Beron, 1990). For an invaluable guide to the composition of ministries from 1878 to the end of the twentieth century, together with short biographies of all ministers, see Tasho V. Tashev, *Ministrite na Bŭlgariya, 1879–1999; Entsiklopedichen spravochnik* (Sofia: Marin Drinov, 1999).

For the drawing up of the Bulgarian constitution C. E. Black, *The Establishment of Constitutional Government in Bulgaria*, Princeton Studies in History, vol. i (Princeton: Princeton University Press, 1943), remains of great value. See also Mariya Manolova, *Sŭsdavane na tŭrnovskata konstitutsiya* (Sofia: BAN, 1980). For more on the constituent assembly itself, see Elena Statelova and Zina Markova (eds.) *Spomeni za uchreditelnoto sŭbranie ot 1879g. Sbornik* (Sofia: Otechestven Front, 1979). There is useful information on the institution of monarchy in Bulgaria up to the end of the first world war in Dimitŭr Sazdov, *Mnogo-partiĭnata sistema i monarhicheskiyat institut v Bŭlgariya 1879–1918* (Sofia: Stopanstvo, 1993). Two further works by Mariya Manolova cover a significant proportion of the post-liberation period: *Istoriya na dŭrzhavata i pravoto: Treta bŭlgarska dŭrzhava, 1878–1944g.* (Sofia: Neofit Rilski, 1994), and *Parlamentarnoto upravlenie v Bŭlgariya, 1894–1912* (Sofia: Marin Drinov and Siela, 2000).

The reign of Alexander Battenberg was extensively covered in Simeon Radev's *Stroitelite na sйvremenna Bйlgariya* (Sofia: 1911). This magisterial work made extensive use of British parliamentary papers; the significance of its republication in 1973 (Sofia: Bйlgarski Pisatel) has been already been noted (see above, p. 367). The work of the Russian provisional administration in Rumelia is covered in Mariya Manolova, *Normotvorcheskata deǐnost na vremennoto rusko upravlenie v Bйlgariya, 1877–1879* (Sofia: Siela, 2003), which replaces her earlier *Rusiya i konstitutsionnoto ustroistvo na Iztochniya Rumeliya* (Sofia: BAN, 1976); Rumelia's relations with the principality are the subject of Elena Statelova, 'Razvoǐ i harakter na otnosheniyata mezhdu knyazhestvo Bйlgariya i Iztochna Rumeliya (1879–1885g)', *Istoricheski Pregled*, 35/5 (1978), 3–20. Also of use for Rumelia is Mihaǐl Iv. Madjarov, *Iztochna Rumeliya. (Istoricheski Pregled)* (Sofia, 1929). The reign of Alexander is treated intelligently in Ivan Stoyanov, *Liberalnata Partiya v knyazhestvo Bйlgariya 1879–1886* (Sofia: Nauka i izkustvo, 1989). There are English-language studies of Alexander in Egon Corti, *The Downfall of Three Dynasties*, trans. L. Marie Sieveking and Ian F. D. Morrow, (London: Methuen, 1934) and the same author's *Alexander of Battenberg*, trans. E. M. Hodgson (London: Cassell, 1954). Two other studies in English, which benefit greatly from close scrutiny of Russian source material and which provide a deeper analysis of the political problems of Bulgaria are Karel Durman, *Lost Illusions: Russian Policies towards Bulgaria in 1877–1887*, Upsala Studies on the Soviet Union and Eastern Europe, no. 1 (Stockholm: Acta Universitatis Upsaliensis, distributed by Almqvist & Wiksell International, 1988), and the same author's *The Time of the Thunderer: Mikhail Katkov, Russian Nationalist Extremism and the Failure of the Bismarckian System, 1871–1887* (Boulder, Colo.: East European Monographs no. 237, distributed by Columbia University Press, 1988). Other important sources for the decade after the liberation are Ilcho Dimitrov, *Knyaz, Konstitutsiyata i Narodйt. Iz istoriyata na politicheskite Borbi v Bйlgariya prez pйrvite godini sled osvobozhdenieto* (Sofia: Otechestven Front, 1972). For a survey of foreign policy see Elena Statelova, *Diplmoatisiyata na knyazhestvo Bйlgariya, 1879–1886*, Izsledvaniya po bйlgarska istoriya, no. 4 (Sofia: BAN, 1979). But this work is constrained by the political limitation of not being able fully to relate the extent of Russian pressure on Bulgaria in these years, though the book does not go to the absurd lengths of Dimitйr Kosev and Nikolaǐ Todorov (eds. in chief), *Vйshnata Politika na Bйlgariya. Dokumenti*, vol. i: *1879–1886* (Sofia: Nauka i izkustvo 1978), which manages to reproduce 463 documents in 779 pages without hinting that there were any tensions between Sofia and St Petersburg.

Recollections of the unification of Bulgarian and Eastern Rumelia were compiled in Elena Statelova and Radoslav Popov (eds.), *Sйedinenieto 1885: Sbornik ot dokumenti 1878/1886* (Sofia: Otechestven Front, 1980), an expanded version of which appeared five years later on the centenary of the unification under the Nauka i izkustvo imprint. The war of 1885 was described in Major A. von Huhn, *The Struggle of the Bulgarians for National Independence under Prince Alexander: A Military and Political History of the War between Bulgaria and Servia in 1885*, trans. from the German (London: John Murray, 1886). The centenary of the war produced another documentary collection: Hristo Hristov (ed. in chief), *Srŭbsko-bŭlgarskata voĭna 1885. Sbornik dokumenti* (Sofia: Voenno Izdatelstvo, 1985). See also Elena Statelova and Radoslav Popov (eds.), *Spomeni za Sŭedinenieto ot 1885g* (Sofia: Otechestven Front, 1980).

The first English biography of Stambolov was A. Hulme Beaman's *M. Stamboloff*, (London: Bliss, Sands, and Foster, 1895). There were few others of note until Duncan M. Perry, *Stefan Stambolov and the Emergence of Modern Bulgaria, 1870–1895* (Durham, NC: Duke University Press, 1993). Stambolov's stout defence of Bulgarian interests against Russian influences made him a dangerous subject for Bulgarian historians during communist rule but since 1989 curiosity has been reawakened and in the first half of the 1990s a number of important collations of source material were published, including Stambolov's letters, see: Milen Kumanov, *Lichniyat Arhiv na Stefan Stambolov*, 2 vols. (Sofia: Otechestvo, 1994 and 1995), fragments from his diaries in Milen Kumanov (ed. in chief), *Dnevnik. Stefan Stambolov* (Sofia: Kliment Ohridski, 1991), and a selection of his sŭbranie speeches, in Milen Kumanov and Dimitŭr Ivanov (eds.), *Parlementarni Rechi 1879–1894* (Sofia: Otechestvo, 1995). There is a great deal of thoughtful and perceptive analysis in Encho Mateev, *Dŭrzhavnikŭt Stefan Stambolov* (Sofia: Letopisi, 1992). On the events of 1886, see Radoslav Popov, 'Stefan Stambolov i Vasil Radoslavov v borba za politicheskata vlast v perioda na regentstvoto (1886–1887g)', *Istoricheski Pregled*, 37/1 (1991), 13–28. For a much earlier but still interesting assessment of Bulgarian-Russian relations see Ivan Panaĭotov, *Rusiya, velikite sili i bŭlgarskiyat vŭpros sled izbora na knyaz Ferdinanda, (1887–1896)* (Sofia: Universitetska Biblioteka No. 247, 1941). There is also relevant material in Andreĭ Pantev, *Angliya sreshtu Rusiya na Balkanite, 1879–1894* (Sofia: Nauka i izkustvo, 1972).

Stambolov inevitably features in the early sections of biographies of King Ferdinand. On internal evidence it is clear that John Macdonald, *Czar Ferdinand and his People* (London: T. C. & E. C. Black, London, no date) was written in the closing stages of the first Balkan war and treats the king as a liberator, whilst Hans Roger Madol, *Ferdinand of Bulgaria: The Dream of Byzantium*, trans. from the German by Kenneth Kirkness (London: Hurst & Blackett, 1933), attempts to redress much of the criticism levelled at Ferdinand after the first world war. Much greater objectivity is attained by Stephen Constant, *Foxy Ferdinand, 1861–1948, Tsar of Bulgaria* (London: Sidgwick & Jackson, 1979). The early years of the reign are excellently covered in Dr Ivan Panaĭotov's work cited above, and in Joachim von Königslöw, *Ferdinand von Bulgarien: Vom Beginn der Thronkandidatur bis zur Annerkennung durch die Grossmächte, (1886–1896)* (Munich: R. Oldenbourg, 1970). Fresh documentation on Ferdinand's last days as king have been published in Milen Kumanov (compiler and editor), *Abdikatsiyata na Tsar Ferdinand: dokumenti, spomeni, fakti* (Sofia: Otechestvo, 1993).

For many years the main sources for our knowledge of King Ferdinand's court and its political intrigues came from works such as Sultane Pétroff, *Trente ans à la cour de Bulgarie, 1887–1918* (Paris: Berger-Levrault, 1927), or, to a lesser degree, Nadezhda Muir, *Dimitri Stancioff, Patriot and Cosmopolitan, 1864–1940* (London: John Murray, 1957), but more colour and detail has recently been provided in the diaries of Robert de Bourboulon, see Zina Markova (ed.), *Bŭlgarski dnevnitsi* (Sofia: Kolibri, 1995); Bourboulon was private secretary and then court high chamberlain to Ferdinand.

Specific crises and incidents in Ferdinand's reign are covered in a multiplicity of monographs. For the question of the exiled officers and their return, see the relevant sections of A. K. Martynenko, *Russko-Bogarskie otnosheniya v 1894–1902gg* (Kiev: Kiev University Press, 1967), and Stiliyan Kovachev, *Zapiski na generala ot pehotata 1876–1918* (Sofia: Georgi Pobedonosets, 1992). The complexities of the parallel railway are explained in Theodor Beut, 'Baron Hirsch's Railway', *Fortnightly Review*, 44, new series (July–Dec. 1888), 229–39, and in Curt Gruenwald, *Türkenhirsch: A Study of Baron Maurice de Hirsch Entrepreneur and Philanthropist* (Jerusalem: Israel Program for Scientific Translation, 1996).

Ever since 1878 Bulgaria has produced masses of documents on Macedonia, and in subsequent years the Greeks and Serbs were no less industrious in the same endeavour. But objective studies are as rare as partisan ones are common. For the period before the Balkan wars objective treatments are to be found in H. N. Brailsford, *Macedonia, its Races and their Future* (London: Methuen, 1906), Fikret Adanir, *Die Makedonische Frage; Ihre Entstehung und Entwicklung bis 1908*, Frankfurter Historische Abhandlungen, no. 20 (Wiesbaden: Franz Steiner, 1979); Dorothy Buchholz Goodman, 'The Emergence of the Macedonian Problem and Relations between the Balkan States and the Great Powers, 1887–1903', Ph.D. thesis (London, 1955); and Duncan Perry, *The Politics of Terror: The Macedonian Revolutionary Movements, 1893–1903* (Durham, NC: Duke University Press, 1988).

The system of taxation, a fundamental cause of the social crisis of the 1890s, is succinctly analysed in N. Piperov, 'Danŭtsite v Bŭlgariya', *Misŭl* (Sofia), 11/3 (1901), 200–7. The growth of agrarian unrest at the end of the nineteenth century is covered in Petko Kunin, *Agrarno-selskiyat vŭpros v Bŭlgariya, ot osvobozhdenieto do kraya na pŭrvata svetovna voĭna* (Sofia: Partizdat, 1971); see also, D. Kosev, 'Selskoto Dvizhenie v Bŭlgariya v kraya na xix v.. Osnovavaneto na BZNS i otnoshenieto na BRSDP kŭm selskiya vŭpros', *Istoricheski Pregled*, 5/5 (1948/49), 549–86.

For the problem of the intelligentsia and its relationship to the people and the nation, see T. G. Vlaĭkov, 'Nashata inteligentsiya po otnoshenie kŭm narodnoto ni obrazovanie', *Misŭl* (Sofia), 3/1 (1893), 7–28; Vladislav Topalov, 'Otnoshenieto na sotsialistite kŭm dvizhenieto protiv naturalniya desyatŭk prez 1899–1900g', *Izvestiya na Instituta za Istoriya*, 18 (1967), 53–88; and two articles by Vivian Pinto: 'The Civic and Aesthetic Ideals of Bulgarian Narodnik Writers', *Slavonic and East European Review*, 32/79 (1953–4), 344–66, and 'The Literary Achievement of Todor Vlaykov, 1865–1943', *Slavonic and East European Review*, 37/89 (1958–9), 42–80. The evolution of the cooperative movement needs more attention but excellent introductions are to be found in Eric R. Weissman, 'The Cooperative Movement in the Bulgarian Village prior to World War One', Ph.D, thesis (University of Washington, 1977), K. Kozhuharov, *Selskoto kooperativno dvizhenie v Bŭlgariya pri kapitalizm* (Sofia: 1965), and D. Dobreff, *Die landwirtschaftliche Kreditgenossenschaften in Bulgarien* (Erlangen: Junge & Sohn, 1911).

The misdoings of the second Stambolovist ministry were laid bare to the public in *Doklad na izpitatelna komisiya po upravlenieto na stranata prez period ot 5 Maĭ 1903 do 16 Yanuarĭ 1908* (Sofia: Narodno Sŭbranie, 1910). For much fascinating detail on and intelligent analysis of the situation between Bulgarians and Greeks in Plovdiv before and during the crisis of 1906, see Spyridon Ploumidis, 'Symbiosis and Friction in Multiethnic Plovdiv/Philippoupolis: The Case of the Greek Orthodox and the Bulgarians (1878–1906)', Ph.D. thesis (London, 2004). The outburst of student radicalism in 1905 is described in Dr K. Krŭstev, 'Nashite universitet. Razmishlenie po povod na studentsko dvizhenie', *Misŭl* (Sofia), 15/6 (1905), 328–46. Documents on the declaration of independence were published in Mito Isusov, Tsvetana Todorova, et al. (eds.), *Obyavyavane na nezavisimostta na Bŭlgariya prez 1908g* (Sofia: BAN, 1989), and Tsvetana Todorova provided a monograph on the subject in *Obyvyavane nezavisimostta na Bŭlgariya prez 1908g i politikata na imperialisticheskite sili* (Sofia: BAN, 1960). Tsvetana Todorova also provided an exhaustive study of Bulgaria's foreign loans before the first world war in her *Diplomaticheska istoriya na vŭnshnite zaemi na Bŭlgariya, 1888–1912* (Sofia: Nauka i izkustvo, 1971).

For the beginning of political activity by the agrarians, see Vladislav Topalov, 'Politicheska deĭnost na bŭlgarskiya zemedelski sŭyuz prez 1900–1901g', *Izvestiya na Instituta za Istoriya*, 10 (1962), 61–119. For BANU in the subsequent decade, see Tsvetana Todorova, 'Kŭm istoriyata na Bŭlgarskiya Zemedelski Naroden Sŭyuz v navecherieto na voĭnite', *Istoricheski Pregled*, 11/5 (1955), 27–53.

The early history of socialism in Bulgaria has been thoroughly researched by Bulgarian historians, primarily those working between 1944 and 1990. The basic text is still Dimitŭr Blagoev, *Prinos kŭm istoriyata na sotsializma v Bŭlgariya* (Sofia, 1906); a more recent edition was published (Sofia: Partizdat, 1976). For the development of trade unionism, see Kiril Lambrev, *Nachenki na rabotnicheskoto i profsŭyuznoto dvizhenie v Bŭlgariya 1878–1891* (Sofia: BAN, 1960). An examination of strike activity in the early years of the labour movement can be found in Ivan M. Iliev, 'Stachno dvizhenie na bŭlgarskoto rabotnichestvo', *Arhiv za Stopanska i Sotsialna Politika* (Sofia), 2/4 (1926), 387–418.

There is a huge amount of published material on the Balkan wars. Bulgaria's role in the formation of the alliance of 1912 was described by Ivan Evstratiev Geshov, *The Balkan League*, trans. by C. C. Mincoff (London: John Murray, 1915). The campaigns were described by, amongst others, Noel Buxton, *With the Bulgarian Staff* (London: Smith, Elder & Co., 1913), and Lieutenant Hermenegild Wagner, *With the Victorious Bulgarians*, trans. from the German (London: Constable, 1913). Amongst the many Bulgarian memoirs see Aleksandŭr Girginov, *Izpitaniyata v voĭnata, 1915–1918g.* (Sofia: S. M. Staikov, 1936); a recent publication of value is Simeon Radev, *Tova, koeto vidyah ot balkanskata voĭna*, ed. Trayan Radev (Sofia: Narodna Kultura, 1993). There is political as well as military information and interpretation in Lt. Col. Reginald Rankin, *The Inner History of the Balkan War* (London: Constable, 1914). Few works contain as much detail as Andreĭ Toshev, *Balkanskite voĭni*, 2 vols. (Sofia: Fakel, 1929 and 1931). A more recent useful publication on the first Balkan war is Georgi Markov, *Bŭlgariya v balkanskiya sŭyuz sreshtu osmanskata imperiya, 1912–1913* (Sofia: Nauka i izkustvo, 1989). The previously unmentionable issue of the conversation of the Pomaks in the newly acquired territories is treated in Velichko Georgiev and Staĭko Trifonov, *Pokrŭstvaneto na Bŭlgarite Mohamedani v 1912–1913g* (Sofia: Marin Drinov, 1995).

The first world war remains the area of modern Bulgarian history most in need of further research and analysis. For nationalists, of left and right, it was frequently too painful a period to investigate but since 1990 there have been some moves to correct this omission, though even now most recent publications have been on the external or military aspects of the war rather than on domestic affairs. Bulgaria's entry into the first world war was documented in *Diplomaticheski dokumenti po uchastieto na Bŭlgariya v Evropeĭskata voĭna* (Sofia: Ministerstovo na vŭnshnite raboti i na izpovedaniyata, 1921). Reliable secondary works are available in Wolfgang-Uwe Friedrich, *Bulgarien und die Mächte 1913–1915* (Stuttgart: Steiner, 1985) and Richard C. Hall, *Bulgaria's Road to the First World War* (Boulder, Colo.: East European Monographs no. 560, distributed by Columbia University Press, 1996). Recent Bulgarian publications include: Tsvetana Todorova (ed.), *Bŭlgariya v pŭrvata svetovna voĭna: germanski diplomaticheski dokumenti: sbornik dokumenti v dva toma, 1913–1918*, 2 vols. (Sofia: GUAMS, 2002); Milen Kumanov (ed.), *Bulgaro-turski voenni otnosheniya prez pŭrvata svetovna voĭna (1914–1918): sbornik ot dokumenti* (Sofia: Gutenberg, 2004). There is very little available on domestic affairs during the war. Some information is to be found in Al. Ganchev, 'Bŭlgariya prez svetovnata voĭna', *Voenno Istoricheski Sbornik* (Sofia), 7/11 (1933–4), 1–30.

After the war Radoslavov attempted to justify his policies in Vasil Radoslawoff, *Bulgarien und die Weltkrise* (Berlin: Ullstein, 1923). There is much new material on Radoslavov in Ivan Ilchev (ed.), *D-r Vasil Radoslavov: Dnevni Belezhki, 1914–1916* (Sofia: Kliment Ohridski, 1993). The final year of the war and the social upheavals which it produced are treated in: Hristo Hristov, *Revolyutsionnata kriza v Bŭlgariya, 1918–1919* (Sofia: BAN, 1957); I. Draev, *Bŭlgarskata osemnadeseta godina* (Sofia: Narodna Prosveta, 1970); Lyubomir Ognyanov, *Voĭnishkoto Vŭstanie 1918* (Sofia: Nauka i izkustvo, 1988); and Ĭono Mitev, 'Voĭnishkoto vŭstanie v Bŭlgariya prez septemvri 1918 i uchastieto na germanskite voĭski v negovoto potushavane', in Hristo Hristov et al. (eds.), *Bŭlgarsko-Germanskite Otnosheniya i Vrŭzki; Izsledvaniya i Materiali*, vol. i (Sofia: BAN, 1972), 279–93. For a summary of the last days of the war in Bulgaria, see also, R. J. Crampton, 'Deprivation, Desperation and Degradation: Bulgaria in Defeat', in Hugh Cecil and Peter H. Liddle (eds.), *At the Eleventh Hour; Reflections, Hopes and Anxieties at the Closing of the Great War, 1918* (Barnsley: Pen and Sword Books, 1998), 255–65.

For the economic direction and effects of the first world war, see Georgi T. Danaĭlov, *Les Effets de la guerre en Bulgarie* (Paris: Les Presses universitaires de France, 1932); for social policy during the war, see Iliya Yanulov, 'Sotsialna politika na Bŭlgariya prez vreme na voĭnata ot 1915–1918g', *Spisanie na Bŭlgarskata Akademiya na Naukite i Izkustva* (Sofia), 42 (1941), 41–264.

The expansion of state institutions in the cultural sector is treated in Rumyana Koneva, 'Dŭrzhavnite kulturni institutsiĭ v Bŭlgariya (1912–1918g)', *Istoricheski Pregled*, 47/3 (1991), 52–66. There are earlier and more extensive treatments of this subject in Mariya Radeva, *Kulturna politika na bŭlgarskata burzhoazna dŭrzhava (1885–1908)* (Sofia: Nauka i izkustvo, 1982); and R. Manafova, *Kultura i politika. Bŭlgariya v navecherieto na Balkanskata voĭna* (Sofia: Nauka i izkustvo, 1987).

FROM THE END OF THE FIRST TO THE END OF THE SECOND WORLD WAR

The best treatment of the agrarian movement and government of the early 1920s is John Bell, *Peasants in Power; Alexander Stamboliski and the Bulgarian Agrarian National Union, 1899–1923* (Princeton: Princeton University Press, 1977). There is a great deal of interesting information in Konstantin Muraviev, *Sŭbitiya i hora: Spomeni*, ed. Ilcho Dimitrov, (Sofia: Bŭlgarski Pisatel, 1992). *Raĭko*

Daskalov—Politicheska i dŭrzhavna deĭnost. Privetstviya i dokladi, izneseni na natsionalnoto tŭrzhestveno sŭbranie i na nauchnata sesiya po sluchaĭ 100 godini ot rozhdeneto na Raĭko Daskalov, no editor named (Sofia: BANU, 1988), also has interesting material, including documents and is interesting in that, although published in the communist era—just—it does admit that relations between the BCP and BANU were not always rosy. The agrarian leader, Gemeto, is the subject of an English-language biography: Charles Moser, *Dimitrov of Bulgaria: A Political Biography of Dr Georgi M. Dimitrov* (Ottawa, Ill.: Caroline House, 1979). For a highly seasoned autobiography of another agrarian exile, see Kosta Todorov, *Balkan Firebrand: The Autobiography of a Rebel Soldier and Statesman* (Chicago: Ziff-Davis, 1943). For the agrarian government and for the years from the first world war to the advent of the communists there is a good deal of interesting, if sometimes tendentious material in Dimo Kazasov, *Burni Godini, 1918–1944* (Sofia: 1949, republished, Sofia: Otechestven Front, 1987).

For the period from the fall of the agrarian government to Bulgaria's entry into the second world war there are outlines of Bulgarian foreign policy in Panaĭot Panaĭotov, *Vŭnshnata politika na Bŭlgariya, 1919–1945* (Sofia: Agres, 1990, first published, Rio de Janeiro, Svoboden bŭlgarski tsentŭr, 1986); Georgi Markov, *Kambanite biyat sami. Nasilie i politika v Bŭlgariya, 1919–1947* (Sofia: Georgi Pobedonosets, 1994); and Krŭstyu Manchev and Valerian Bistritski, *Bŭlgariya i neĭnite Sŭsedi, 1931–1939. Politicheski i diplomaticheski otnosheniya* (Sofia: Nauka i izkustvo, 1978). For the wrangelist army, see Liudmil Spasov, *Wrangelovata Armiya v Bŭlgariya, 1919–23* (Sofia: Kliment Okhridski, 1999). The treaty of Neuilly is examined in G. P. Genov, *Nioiskiat dogovor i Bŭlgariya* (Sofia: Vanyo Nedkov, 2000); for the tsankovist period there is Veselin Stoev and Veselin Tepavicharov, *Politicheskata alternativa: yuni 1923–4 yanuari 1926* (Sofia: Kliment Okhridski, 1992). Freemasonry flourished in Bulgaria in the interwar years and there is a full description of it in Velichko Georgiev, *Masonstvoto v Bŭlgariya. Pronikvane, organizatsiya, razvitie i rolya do sredata na tridecette godini na xx vek* (Sofia: Nauka i izkustvo, 1986), the publication of which caused a sensation at the time. Most books on the Macedonian question are too biased to be of great value to the objective researcher. However, even if not confined to Bulgaria and the activities of the Macedonians therein, recourse should be made to Stefan Troebst, *Mussolini, Makedonien und die Mächte, 1922–1930*, Dissertationen zur neueren Geschichte, no. 19 (Cologne: Böhlau, 1987). J. Swire, *Bulgarian Conspiracy* (London: R. Hale, 1939), has a great deal of detail not only on Macedonian intrigues but also on Zveno and the coup of 1934. For that coup and the growth of royal power see Vladimir Migev, *Utvŭrzhdavane na monarho-fashistkata diktatura v Bŭlgariya 1934–1936* (Sofia: BAN, 1977). Bulgaria's rearmament in the late 1930s is described in Lyudmil Petrov, *Problemi na voennata politika na Bŭlgariya 1934–1939g* (Sofia: Voenno Izdatelstvo, 1990).

A useful introduction to the constitutional problems of the 1930s is provided in Nikolaĭ Poppetrov, 'Verfassungsrechtliche Probleme in Bulgarien während der Regierung von Zar Boris III (1918–1943)', *Südostforschungen*, 44/2 (1985), 205–21. There is also useful material on the early 1930s in Vasil At. Vasilev, 'Za politicheska obstanovka v Bŭlgariya neposredstveno sled parlamentarnite izbori ot 21 yuni 1931g', *Izvestiya na Instituta za Istoriya*, 19 (1967), 41–73. Both the 1930s and the war years up to August 1943 are naturally covered in studies and biographies of King Boris. The best of these, though greatly indulgent of its subject, is Stephane Groueff, *Crown of Thorns: The Reign of King Boris III of Bulgaria, 1918–1943* (Lanham, Md.: Madison Books, 1987). Shorter, even more indulgent, and less perceptive is Pashanko Dimitroff, *Boris III of Bulgaria, (1893–1943). Toiler, Citizen, King* (Lewes: The Book Guild Ltd., 1986). The fall of the communist regime produced a flurry of Bulgarian writing on Boris, see, *inter alia*, Hristo Dermendjiev, *Tsar Boris III; Zhivot i Delo v Dati i Dokumenti* (Sofia: Tsarstvo Bŭlgariya, 1990); Doncho Daskalov, *Tsar Boris III poznatiyat i nepoznatiyat* (Sofia: Agato, 2001); Nencho Iliev, *Boris III: Tsar obedinitel* (Sofia: Zharava, 2002); Albert Leverson, *Tsar Boris III: shtrihi kŭm portreta* (Sofia: Georgi Pobedonosets, 1995); and Nedyu T. Nedev, *Tsar Boris III: biografiya* (Sofia: Petŭr Beron, 2004). There has been considerable interest in the influence of Boris's various advisers particularly Lulchev, in, for example, Dinyu Sharlanov and Polya Meshkova (eds.), *Sŭvetnitsite na Tsar Boris III; Naroden Sŭd: Doznanie* (Sofia: Riana Press, 1993); Dinyu Sharlanov, *Taĭnite na dvoretsa: koĭ e bŭlgarskiyat Rasputin?* (Sofia: Ivan Vazov, 1999); Filip Panaĭotov, *Tsare i tsaredvortsi* (Sofia: Hristo Botev, 1993); Vano Vŭlkov, *Tsaryat i negoviyat sŭvetnik: kniga za tsar Boris III i negoviya sŭvetnik Lyubomir Lulchev* (Sofia: Georgi Pobedonosets, 1993); and for documents on Lulchev's trial see the anonymous, *Narodniyat sŭd sreshtu Lyubomir Hristov Lulchev, 59-godishen neosŭzhdan posledovatel na Byaloto Bratstvo taen sŭvetnik na tsar Boris III: dokumenti* (Sofia: Astrala, 1996). For the controversy surrounding Boris's last illness and the cause of his death, see Helmut Heiber, 'Der Tod des Zaren Boris', *Vierteljahreshefte für Zeitgeschichte* (Munich), 9 (1961), 384–416.

For Bulgaria's part in the second world war the best single-volume survey remains Marshall Lee Miller, *Bulgaria during the Second World War* (Stanford, Calif.: Stanford University Press, 1975). An excellent summary of Bulgaria's policy in the late 1930s and eventual signature of the tripartite pact is to be found in Nikolaĭ Genchev, 'Bŭlgarsko-germanski diplomaticheski otnosheniya (1938–1941g)', in H. Hristov et al. (eds.), *Bŭlgarsko-germanski otnosheniya i vrŭzki. Izsledvaniya i Materiali*, vol. i (Sofia: BAN, 1972), 391–433. There is a perceptive examination of Bulgarian-German relations in the 1930s in Georgi Markov, *Bŭlgaro-Germanski otnosheniya, 1931–1939* (Sofia: Kliment Ohridski, 1984). On the war itself, further essential reading is to be found in Filov's diaries, see Ilcho Dimitrov (ed. in chief), *Bogdan Filov. Dnevnik* (Sofia: Otechestven Front, 1990); sections of these diaries have been translated into English by Frederick B. Chary and published in *Southeastern Europe* (Pittsburgh), 1/1 (1974), 46–71; 2/1 (1975), 70–93; 2/2 (1975), 161–86; 3/1 (1976), 44–87; and 4/1 (1977), 48–107. The diaries of the German minister in Sofia are also valuable, see Vita Tohskova (compiler), *Iz Dnevnika na Bekerle—pŭlnomoshten ministŭr na tretiya raĭh v Bŭlgariya* (Sofia: Hristo Botev, 1992). Other valuable sources are: Vitka Toshkova, *Bŭlgariya i tretiyat Reih (1941–1944); politicheski otnosheniya* (Sofia: Nauka i izkustvo, 1975); Hans-Joachim Hoppe, *Bulgarien— Hitlers eigenwilliger Verbündeter: Eine Fallstudie zur nationalsozialistischen Südosteuropapolitik*, Studien zur Zeitgeschichte, Institut für Zeitgeschichte (Stuttgart: Deutsche Verlags-Anstalt, 1979); Vitka Toshkova, *Bŭlgariya v balkanskata politika na SASHT, 1939/1944* (Sofia: Nauka i izkustvo, 1985); and Nikolaĭ Georgiev Kotev, *Voĭna bez pravila: britansko razuznavane v Bŭlgariya (1939–1945)* (Sofia: Georgi Pobedonosets, 1994). Worth mentioning as an example of how stupid communist historiography could be is Stoyan Rachev, *Angliya i sŭprotivitelnoto dvizhenie na balkanite (1940–1945)* (Sofia: BAN, 1978). In absolute contrast, for the best material written on the allied bombing of Bulgaria, and on much else besides, see Irina Dimitrova Gigova, 'Writers Of The Nation: Intellectual Identity in Bulgaria, 1939–1953', Ph.D. thesis (University of Illinois at Urbana-Champaign, 2004).

The most recent, important works on the fate of Bulgaria's Jews during the second world war are: Tzvetan Todorov, *The Fragility of Goodness: why Bulgaria's Jews Survived the Holocaust*, trans. from the French by Arthur Denner (London: Weidenfeld & Nicolson, 2001), and Michael Bar-Zohar, *Beyond Hitler's Grasp: The Heroic Rescue of Bulgaria's Jews* (Holbrook, Mass.: Adams Media Corporation, 1998). Both use recently revealed documents but Todorov is as much interested in philosophical discussion as in history, whilst Bar-Zohar, whose English is dreadful, is not a trained historian. For a sound, historical treatment which places the question in its proper context, see Frederick B. Chary, *The Bulgarian Jews and the Final Solution, 1940–1944* (Pittsburgh: University of Pittsburgh Press, 1972). Books written in Bulgaria between 1944 and 1989 on this subject had to emphasize the communists' alleged role in saving the Bulgarian Jews and examples of such works are Albert Koen, *Spasyavaneto na evreite v Bŭlgariya, 1941–1944*, published simultaneously in English as *Saving of the Jews in Bulgaria, 1941–1944* (sic) (Sofia: Septemvri, 1977), and *Borbata na bŭlgarskiya narod za zashtita i spasyavane na evreite v Bŭlgariya prez vtorata svetovna voĭna: dokumenti i materiali*, compiled by David Koen and edited Voin Bozhilov (Sofia: BAN, 1978). More measured scholarship appeared in Bulgaria after 1989; see Hristo Boyadjiev, *Spasyavaneto na bŭlgarskite evrei prez vtorata svetovna voĭna* (Sofia: Kliment Ohridski, 1991), and the all-important memoirs, Dimitŭr Peshev, *Spomeni* (Sofia: Gutenberg, 2004).

For Bulgarian occupation policies see H-J. Hoppe, 'Bulgarian Nationalities Policy in Occupied Thrace and Aegean Macedonia', *Nationalities Papers*, 24/1–2 (Spring–Fall 1986), 89–100. For a detailed history of Thrace during the second world war see Dimitŭr Ionchev, *Bŭlgariya i Belomorieto (Oktomvri 1940–9 Septemvri 1944). Voennopoliticheski aspekti* (Sofia: Dirum, 1993). There is much useful information on Bulgarian policies in occupied Macedonia in Georgi Daskalov, 'Bŭlgarskite aktsionni komiteti v vadarska Makedoniya (april–avgust 1941)', *Istoricheski Pregled*, 47/8 (1991), 58–74; Vanya Stoyanova, 'Tsŭrkovno-administrativnata uredba na Makedoniya i Trakiya i izborŭt na patriarh na bŭlgarskata pravoslavna tsŭrkva (april–septemvri 1944)', *Minalo*, 1/2 (1994), 55–65; and above all in the thesis by Irina Gigova cited in the preceding paragraph. For the growth of resistance and the emergence of the Fatherland Front, see: Donko Dochev, *Monarho-fashizmŭt sreshtu narodnata sŭprotiva 1941–1944* (Sofia: Partizdat, 1983); and Kiril Vasilev et al. (eds.), *Otechestven Front: dokumenti i materiali*, vol. i: *1941–1944*, part i, *22 yuni 1941–april 1944*, part ii, *1 mai 1944–11 septemvri 1944* (Sofia: Otechestven Front, 1987). There is also much of value in Maj. Gen. Prof. Dr V. Zolotaryov et al. (eds.), *Bŭlgaro-sŭvetski politicheski i voenni otnosheniya (1941–1947). (Statii i dokumenti)* (Sofia: Voenno Izdatelstvo, 1999). The final, chaotic days of the war are treated in Georgi Mishkov (ed.), compiled by Georgi Mishkov and Todor Dobriyanov, *Dnevnik na Pŭrvan Draganov, bivsh ministŭr na vŭnshnite raboti ot 12 yuni do 1 septemvri 1944 godina* (Sofia: Georgi Pobedonosets, 1993).

SOCIAL AND ECONOMIC DEVELOPMENT FROM 1878 TO 1944

Social and economic development after the liberation is detailed in the multi-volume *Ikonomika na Bŭlgariya* referred to above. Other useful sources are: Georgi Georgiev, *Osvobozhdenieto i etnokulturnoto razvitie na bŭlgarskiya narod 1877–1900* (Sofia: BAN, 1979); Petko Kunin, *Agrarno-selskiyat vŭpros v Bŭlgariya, ot osvobozhdenieto do kraya na pŭrvata svetovna voĭna* (Sofia: Partizdat, 1971); Slavi Slavov, *Sotsialno-politicheski vŭzgledi v Bŭlgariya prez pŭrvoto desetiletie sled osvobozhdenieto* (Sofia, 1975); and Herbert Wilhelmy, *Hochbulgarien I; Die ländliche Siedlungen und die bäuerliche Wirtschaft*, Schriften des Geographischen Insituts der Universität Kiel, no. 4, series editors O. Schmieder and H. Wentzel (Kiel: Schmidt & Klaunig, 1935). On changes in the structure of village life after 1878, see Georgi Georgiev, 'Preustroistvoto na traditsionnata selska sistema v rezultat ot osvobozhdenieto', *Istoricheski Pregled*, 33/5–6 (1977), 111–26.

For the decline of traditional handicraft manufacturing, see D. Athanas Spassow, *Der Verfall des alten Handwerk und die Entstehung des modernen*

Gewerbes in Bulgarien während des 19 Jahrhunderts (Greifswald, 1900), and T. Obreshkov, 'Zanayatchiĭstvoto v Bŭlgariya', *Arhiv za Stopanska i Sotsialna Politika* (Sofia) 2/4 (1926), 374–86. There is a great deal of literature on the zadruga. Of particular value for Bulgaria are: Stefan D. Simeonov, *Die Zadruga und Ehegüterrectsverhälnisse Bulgariens* (Hamburg, 1931); Ivan Evstratiev Geshov, *Zadrugite v zapadna Bŭlgariya*, (Sofia, 1887); St. Savov Bobchev, 'Bŭlgarskata tselyadna zadruga v segashno i minalo vreme', in *Sbornik za narodni umotvorenie, nauka, i knizhina* (Sofia), 22 and 23/2 (1906 and 1907), part 2 *Dela za dŭrzhavni nauki*, 1–207. There is a classic study of Bulgarian village life in the inter-war years in Irwin Sanders, *Balkan Village* (Lexington, Ky.: University of Kentucky Press, 1949). A recent and very useful study of an intriguing but little known subject is, Svetla Baloutzova, 'State Legislation on Family and Social Policy in Bulgaria, 1918–1944', Ph.D. thesis (Cambridge, 2005). For the development of Sofia, see Petŭr Mirchev, *Kipezhŭt. Kniga za Sofiya 1878–1884* (Sofia: Otechestven Front, 1971). Four articles were published by D. Yurdanov under the title, 'Promishlenoto razvitie na grad Sofiya i Bŭlgariya', in *Arhiv na Stopanska i Sotsialna Politika*, 4/3 (1928); 4/4 (1928); 4/5 (1928); and 5/1 (1929). The creation of the Bulgarian state railways is well presented in Iwan Karasseroff, *Zur Entwicklung der bulgarischen Eisenbahnen*, Ph.D. thesis (Erlangen, 1907), and in G. Zgurev, 'Ravitie na eksploatatsiyata na Bŭlgarskite Dŭrzhavni Zheleznitsite za Vremeto 1888–1938g', *Spisanie na Bŭlgarsko Ikonomichesko Druzhestvo* (Sofia) 37/8 (1938), 489–95. The preceding two articles in the same journal deal with the question of BDZh's links to the networks of neighbouring states: see Bogdan Morfov, 'Politicheskite pregovori i spletni otnosno svŭrzvaneto na Bŭlgarskata Dŭrzhavna zhelezopŭtna mrezha c zhelopŭtnite mrezhi na drugite evropeĭski dŭrzhavi ot 1880g do 1938g', 462–78, and Ĭo. Danchov, 'Svŭrzvane na bŭlgarskite dŭrzhavni zheleznitsi s zhelezopŭtnitsite na sŭsednite dŭrzhavi', 479–88.

The history of the first fifty years of Sofia university is covered in Mihaĭl Arnaudov, *Istoriya na Sofiĭskya Universitet sv Kliment Ohridski prez pŭrvoto mu polustoletie, 1888–1938* (Sofia: Pridvorna Pechatnitsa 1939).

THE YEARS OF COMMUNIST DOMINATION, 1944–1989

Until 1989 scholarship concerning the assumption of power by the communists was bedevilled by ideological commitment. Anyone writing at this time, on either side of the divide, could not avoid bias, but if that can be discounted there is still useful information in such works as Mito Isusov (ed.), *Problems of the Transition from Capitalism to Socialism in Bulgaria* (Sofia: BAN, 1975), the same author's *Politicheskite partĭ v Bŭlgariya: 1944–1948* (Sofia: Nauka i izkustvo, 1978); Nikolaĭ Genchev, 'Okonchatelnoto ukrepvane na Narodnodemokratichnata

Vlast v Bŭlgariya (1947–1948)', *Izvestiya na Instituta za Istoriya*, 16–17 (1966), 25–64; and L. A. D. Dellin, *Bulgaria*, published for the Mid-European Studies Center of the Free Europe Committee, Inc. (New York: Frederick A. Praeger 1957). Since 1989 the immediate post-war period has attracted more attention from Bulgarian scholars than almost any other and much that is new, both in terms of evidence and interpretation, has come to light, rectifying and moderating the extreme views on both sides of the former ideological divide. Surprisingly, the diaries of communist leader Georgi Dimitrov add less than might have been expected; Dimitrov, unlike Winston Smith in *1984*, seems not to have had a secret alcove where he could pour out all his frustrations; or, more likely, he had no frustrations to pour out. The diaries appeared first in Bulgarian: Dimitŭr Sirkov (compiler and editor), *Georgi Dimitrov: Dnevnik (9 mart 1933–6 fevruari 1949)* (Sofia: Kliment Ohridski, 1997) and later in English: Ivo Banac, *The Diary of Georgi Dimitrov, 1933–1949*, trans. Jane T. Hedges, Timothy D. Sergay, and Irina Faion, (New Haven: Yale University Press, 2003). The best study of the communist takeover process is Vesselin Tzvetanov Dimitrov, 'The Failure of Democracy in Eastern Europe and the Emergence of the Cold War, 1944–1948: A Bulgarian Case Study', Ph.D. thesis (Cambridge, 1997); it is greatly to be hoped that this work is soon published. The trials of early 1945 have been treated in Petŭr Semerdjiev, *Narodniyat Sŭd v Bŭlgariya 1944–1945g. Komu i zashto e bil neobhodim* (Jerusalem: no publisher cited, 1997); this takes a very different line from Ivan Paunovski, *Vŭzmezdieto* (Varna: Georgi Bakalov, 1982); the latter contains much useful information. For the participation of Bulgaria in the latter stages of the war, see D. Dimitrov, 'Uchastieto na Bŭlgariya vŭv voĭnata sreshtu hitleristka Germaniya v razvŭrshvashtiya etap na vtorata svetovna voĭna (noemvri 1944–yuli 1945)', *Istoricheski Pregled*, 51/4 (1995), 27–38. For a really perceptive analysis of the changes in Bulgaria since the end of the second world war, see Evgeniya Kalinova and Iskra Baeva, *Bŭlgarskite Prehodi 1944–1999* (Sofia: Tilia, 2000), which was followed by the same authors' extended version of the same work, *Bŭlgarskite prehodi 1939–2002*, 2nd edition, (Sofia: Paradigma, 2002). Other works which concentrate on political events during the communist takeover include, P. Stoyanov and E. Iliev, *Politicheski opasni litsa: vŭdvoryavanya, trudova mobilizatsiya, izselvaniya sled 1944 godina* (Sofia: Kliment Ohridski, 1991); and Lyubomir Ognyanov, *Dŭrzhavno-politicheska sistema na Bŭlgariya, 1944–1948* (Sofia: BAN, 1993).

For foreign policy, and particularly the communists' contortions over Macedonia, see Magarditsch A. Hatschikjan, *Tradition und Neuorientierung in bulgarischen Aussenpolitik, 1944–1948; Die 'nationale Aussenpolitik' der bulgarischen Arbeiterpartei (Kommunisten)*, Südosteuropäische Arbeiten 86 (Munich: R. Oldenbourg, 1986). The interlaced problems of Macedonia, Bulgarian-Yugoslav relations, and a Balkan federation have been the subject of

a number of works since 1989: M. Lŭlkov, *Ot nadezhda kŭm razocharovanie.*
Ideyata za federatsiya v balkanskiya yugoiztok 1944–1948 (Sofia: Vek 22, 1993);
Leonid Gibianskiĭ, 'The Soviet Bloc and the Initial Stage of the Cold War:
Archival Documents on Stalin's Meetings with Communist Leaders of Yugoslavia
and Bulgaria, 1946–1948', in David Wolff (ed.), *Cold War International History
Project Bulletin*, No. 10 (March 1998) (Washington, DC: Woodrow Wilson
International Center for Scholars), 112–34; Dobrin Michev, *Makedonskiyat
vŭpros i bŭlgaro-yugoslovenskite otnosheniya, 9 septemvri 1944–1949* (Sofia: Kliment
Ohridski, 1994); and the same author's 'Yuzhnoslavyanskiyata federatsiya v
bŭlgaro-yugoslavskite otnosheniya, 9 septemvri 1944–1948 godina', *Voenno-
Istoricheski Sbornik*, 6 (1990), 24–57. Bulgaria's position in the foreign policy of
the great powers is assessed in Emanuïl Emanuïlov, *Bŭlgariya v politikata na
velikite sili 1939–1947* (Sofia: PAN–VT, 2000).

A summary of the process of the collectivization of agriculture is to be found
in B. Mateev, 'The Establishment of the Cooperative System in Agriculture in
Bulgaria', *Études historiques* (Sofia), 5 (1970), 619–46, and for a revisionist
interpretation, V. Migev, 'Kolektivizatsiyata na selsko stopanstvo v Bŭlgariya
(1948–1958). Tipologiya, etapi, problemi', *Istoricheski Pregled*, 50/4 (1994–5),
53–83; for details on the assault on the richer peasants, see the same author's,
'Borbata sreshtu kulachestvoto i negovoto likvidirane v Bŭlgariya (1944–1958)',
in Hristo Hristov (ed. in chief), *Iz istoriyata na stopanskiya i sotsialniya zhivot v
bŭlgarskite zemi* (Sofia: BAN, 1984), 40–84. The fate of the Bulgarian Orthodox
Church is described in detail in Daniela Kalkandjieva, *Bŭlgarskata pravoslavna
tsŭrkva i dŭrzhavata, 1944–1953* (Sofia: Albatros, 1997); this book contains
many documents; there is also Djoko Slijepčević, *Die bulgarische Orthodoxe
Kirche, 1944–1956* (Munich: R Oldenbourg, 1957). There is still no sober
assessment of the fate of Nikola Petkov. One need go no further than the title of
Michael Padev's, *Dimitrov Wastes No Bullets: The Inside Story of the Trial and
Murder of Nikola Petkov (leader of the Bulgarian Agrarian Party)* (London: Eyre &
Spottiswode, 1948) to realize that it has little to offer. Shorter but more delibera-
tive, is John E. Horner, 'The Ordeal of Nikola Petkov and the Consolidation of
Communist Rule in Bulgaria', *Survey*, 20/1 (90) (Winter 1974), 75–83. In
Bulgarian see Petŭr Semerdjiev, *Sŭdebni protses sreshtu Nikola D. Petkov prez
1947g*, (Paris: Fondatsiya Al Stamboliĭski-N. Petkov-G. M. Dimitrov, 1987) and
Georgi Gunev, *Kŭm brega na svobodata ili za Nilola Petkov i negovoto vreme* (Sofia:
Informatsionno obsluzhvane, 1992). Petkov's letter to the communist leaders
just before he was sent to the gallows has been published: *Predsmŭrtnite pisma na
Nikola D. Petkov do Georgi Dimitrov i Vasil Kolarov: 19 august–22 septemvri 1947*
(Sofia: Kliment Ohridski, 1992). For a relatively recent assessment of the Kostov
trial, see Mito Isusov, *Poslednata godina na Traicho Kostov* (Sofia: Hristo Botev,
1990). In English there is John E. Horner, 'Traicho Kostov: Stalinist Orthodoxy

in Bulgaria', *Survey*, 24/3 (108) (Summer 1979), 135–42. The situation in the universities is discussed in Bozhidar Doĭchinov, 'Promeni v strukturata na visheto obrazovanie v Bŭlgariya (9 Septemvri 1944–1948g), *Istoricheski Pregled*, 47/1 (1991), 43–55. For a chilling account of the methods used in the interrogation of communist victims of the purges see, www.yale.du/annals/Chase/Documents/doc71chapt7thm: Document 71 Letter from I. Terziev to Dimitrov and Kolarov. For recent examinations of the stalinist era in Bulgaria see, D. Draganov, *V syankata na stalinizma* (Sofia: Hristo Botev, 1990), and Mito Isusov, *Stalin i Bŭlgariya* (Sofia: Kliment Ohridski, 1991). Chervenkov, in his retirement, wrote notes justifying his conduct during the purges; they were published by his daughter after his death: *Vŭlko Chervenkov za sebe si i svoeto vreme* (Sofia: Hristo Chernev, 2000).

The western perspective of the takeover in Bulgaria is to be gleaned from the documents in Michael Boll (ed.), *The American Military Mission in the Allied Control Commission for Bulgaria, 1944–1947, History and Transcripts*, (Boulder, Colo.: East European Monographs, no. 176, distributed by Columbia University Press, 1985), and the same author's *Cold War in the Balkans: American Foreign Policy and the Emergence of Communist Bulgaria, 1943–1947*, (Lexington, Ky.: The University Press of Kentucky, 1984).

For an excellent guide to literature on Bulgaria during communist rule see Katya Yordanova (compiler) and Jordan Baev (ed.), *History of Bulgaria in the Cold War Era 1945–1990; A Bibliography (1989–2004)*, www.coldwar.hu/thml/en/bibliographies/bulgaria.thml. Essential reading for the entire history of communist rule and after is Kalinova and Baeva, *Bŭlgarskite prehodi* (see above). For the period of communist rule up to the mid-1960s there is a useful summary in English in J. F. Brown, *Bulgaria under Communist Rule* (London: Pall Mall, 1970), but more recent publications supplement this: D. Avramov, *Letopois na edno dramatichno desetiletie. Bŭlgarskoto izkustvo mezhdu 1955–1965g*, part 1 (Sofia: Nauka i izkustvo, 1994), and for a view of the 1956 plenum by a leading participant and then member of the politburo, Georgi Chankov, *Mezhdu istinata i lŭzhata. Aprilskiyat Plenum (1956)* (Sofia: 1996); the first part of the title means 'Between truth and falsehood'. For more on Chankov himself see Georgi Chankov (ed.), *Ravnosmetkata v dokumenti, spomeni, statiĭ, intervyuta, pisma* (Sofia: Hristo Botev, 2000). Also of use are J. F. Brown, 'Frost and Thaw in Bulgarian Culture', *Studies in Comparative Communism*, 2/3–4 (July/Oct. 1969), 95–120, and, on Bulgarian culture under the communists, two books by Atanas Slavov, *The 'Thaw' in Bulgarian Culture* (Boulder, Colo.:, East European Monographs no. 74, distributed by Columbia University Press, 1981), and *With the Precision of Bats* (Passaic, NJ: Occidental Press, 1986). There is also a great deal of information in Klaus-Detlev Grothusen (ed.), *Bulgarien*, Südosteuropa-Handbuch no. 6 (Göttingen: Vandenhoeck & Ruprecht, 1990). A somewhat eccentric treatment of Bulgaria under communist rule is Robert J. McIntyre, *Bulgaria: Politics, Economics and Society*, Marxist Regimes Series, series editor Bogdan Szajkowski (London: Pinter, 1988). In English the history of the communist party itself is admirably summarized in John D. Bell, *The Bulgarian Communist Party from Blagoev to Zhivkov*, Histories of Ruling Communist Parties, series editor Richard F. Starr (Stanford, Calif.: Hoover Institution Press, 1986); for its earlier years, Joseph Rothschild, *The Communist Party of Bulgaria: Origins and Development, 1883–1936* (New York: AMS Press, 1972), and for subsequent years Nissan Oren, *Bulgarian Communism: The Road to Power, 1934–1944*, East Central European Studies of Columbia University and Research Institute on Communist Affairs, Columbia University (New York: Columbia University Press, 1971), and *Revolution Administered: Agrarianism and Communism in Bulgaria* (Baltimore: The Johns Hopkins University Press, 1973).

Criticism of the Zhivkov regime is to be found in many works. After his death Georgi Markov became perhaps the most famous of the critics. For a collection of his writings see Georgi Markov, *Zadochni reportazhi za Bŭlgariya* (Zürich: Georgi Markov Foundation, 1980). See also Georgi Markov, *The Truth that Killed*, trans. Liliana Brisby with an introduction by Annabel Markov (London: Weidenfeld & Nicolson, 1983). For the Kostov affair, see Vladimir Kostov, *The Bulgarian Umbrella: The Soviet Direction and Operation of the Bulgarian Secret Service in Europe*, trans. Ben Reynolds, (Hemel Hempstead: Harvester: Wheatsheaf and St Martin's Press, 1988).

Amongst the welter of memoirs and exposés published in Bulgaria after 1989 those which stand out are Niko Yahiel, *Todor Zhivkov i lichnata vlast: spomeni, dokumenti, analizi* (Sofia: M 8 M, 1997); Todor Zhivkov, *Memoari* (Sofia: Abagar, 1997), a highly entertaining volume but hardly an objective one; Stanko Todorov, *Po vŭrhovete na vlastta* (Sofia: Hristo Botev, 1995); and Kostadin Chakŭrov, *Vtoriya Etazh* (Sofia: Plamŭk, 1990); this work was translated into English as *The Second Floor* (London: Macdonald, 1991). See also Angel Vekov, *Bŭlgariya v Taĭnite Arkhivi na Kremŭl. Sreshti i Razgovori s bŭlgarski premieri* (Sofia: Makros, 2002). For thoughtful reflections by an intelligent member of the pre-1989 establishment, see Ilcho Dimitrov, *Vsichko teche: spomeni* (Sofia: Tilia, 2000), though this also extends into the 1990s. There is useful information on opposition to Zhivkov in Dimitŭr Ivanov, *Zagovorite sreshtu Todor Zhivkov* (Sofia: ПеТекс-Petex, 1992). Some of the speeches and writings of Lyudmila Zhivkova are contained in (no author cited), *Lyudmila Zhivkova: Her Many Worlds. New Culture and Beauty. Concepts and Action* (Oxford: Pergamon Press, 1982).

An introduction to the study of the Agro-Industrial Complex is provided in Paul Wiedemann, 'The Origins and Development of Agro-Industrial Complexes in Bulgaria', in Ronald J. Francisco, Betty A. Boyd, and Roy D. Laird (eds.),

Agricultural Policies in the USSR and Eastern Europe (Boulder, Colo.: Westview Press, 1980), 97–135. For the economic mistakes of super-industrialization see M. Palairet, ' "Lenin" and "Brezhnev": Steel Making and the Bulgarian Economy, 1956–1990', *Europe Asia Studies*, 47 (1995), 493–505. The frenetic experiments of the 1980s are discussed in Richard J. Crampton, ' "Stumbling and Dusting off" or an Attempt to Pick a Path through the Thicket of Bulgaria's New Economic Mechanism', *East European Politics and Societies*, 2/2 (1988), 333–95.

The overthrow of Zhivkov is treated in Boyan Traĭkov, *10 noemvri prevratŭt 1989* (Sofia: Trud, 1999); Petko Simeonov, *Golyamata promyana. 10. XI. 1989–10. VI.1990 Opit za dokument* (Sofia: Otechestvo, 1996); and in Mladenov's memoirs, Petŭr Mladenov, *Zhivotŭt: plyusove i minusi* (Sofia: ПеТекс-Petex, 1992).

BULGARIA SINCE 1989

In the growing literature on Bulgaria since 1989 the starting point must be Vesselin Dimitrov, *Bulgaria: The Uneven Transition* (London: Routledge, 2001), and John D. Bell (ed.) *Bulgaria in Transition: Politics, Economics, Society and Culture after Communism* (Boulder, Colo.: Westview Press, 1998). Also relevant are Emil Giatzidis, *An Introduction to Post-Communist Bulgaria: Political, Economic and Social Transformation* (Manchester: Manchester University Press, 2002); and Albert P. Melone, *Creating Parliamentary Government: The Transition to Democracy in Bulgaria* (Columbus, Oh.: Ohio State University Press, 1998). The round table is examined in Wolfgang Höpken (ed.) *Revolution auf Raten: Bulgariens Weg zur Democratie* (Munich: Oldenbourg, 1996), and in Albert P. Melone, 'Bulgaria's Roundtable Talks and the Politics of Accommodation', *International Political Science Review*, 15 (1994), 257–83. For economic developments after 1989 see John A. Bristow, *The Bulgarian Economy in Transition* (Cheltenham: Edward Elgar, 1996); Derek Jones and Jeffery Miller, *The Bulgarian Economy: Lessons from Reform during Early Transition* (Aldershot: Ashgate, 1997); and A. Buckwell et al. (eds.), *The Transformation of Agriculture: A Case Study of Bulgaria* (Boulder, Colo.: Westview Press, 1994). Zhelyu Zhelev, *V Golyamata Politik* (Sofia: Trud Press, 1998) is essential reading for the period up to 1996.

Two electronic bulletins are invaluable for the post-communist period; they are RFE/RL's newsline-request@list.rferl.org and Transitions on Line, www.transitions-online.org.

MINORITIES AND ETHNIC QUESTIONS

The years since 1989 have produced major works of scholarship on the question of minorities and ethnicity. Some writing from before that date is still important, none more so than Bernard Lory, *Le Sort de l'héritage ottoman en Bulgarie: l'exemple des villes bulgares, 1878–1900* (Istanbul: Isis, 1985) which provides an entirely original approach to relations between Christians and Muslims. For the immediate post-second world war years, there is much, especially on educational provision, in Peter Bachmeier, 'Assimilation oder Kulturautonomie: Das Schulwesen der nationalen Minderheiten in Bulgarien nach dem 9 September 1944', *Österreichische Osthefte*, 26/2 (1984), 391–404. For the expulsions of the early 1950s see H. L. Kostanick, *Turkish Resettlement of Bulgarian Turks, 1950–1953*, University of California publications in geography, 8/2 (Berkeley: University of California Press, 1957), and in Joseph B. Schechtman, 'Compulsory Transfer of the Turkish Minority from Bulgaria', *Journal of Central European Affairs*, 12/2 (July 1952), 154–69. On the position of the Jewish minority, in addition to the sources cited above for the second world war, there is an excellent treatment in Stefan Troebst, 'Antisemitismus im "Land ohne Antisemitismus": Staat, Titularnation und jüdische Minderheit in Bulgarien 1878–1993', in Mariana Hausleitner and Monika Katz (eds.), *Juden und Antisemitismus im östlichen Europa*, Multidisziplinäre Veröffentlichungen des Osteuropa-Instituts der Freien Univeristät Berlins, no. 5 (Berlin: Harrassowitz, 1995), 109–25, and Nikolaĭ Todorov (ed. in chief), *Prouchvaniya za istoriyata na evreĭskoto neselenie v bŭlgarskite zemi, xv–xx vek* (Sofia: BAN, 1980). Official policies towards the Jewish minorities are also examined in W. I. Brustein and R. D. King, 'Balkan Anti-Semitism: The Cases of Bulgaria and Romania before the Holocaust', *East European Politics and Societies*, 18/3 (2004) 430–54. There is a rare study of the Germans of Bulgaria in Joachim Gerstenberg, *Bulgarien България: Ein Reisebuch* (Hamburg: Broschek & Co., 1940). For Bulgarian concerns at differential birth rates during the second half of communist rule see, Nikolai Mitchev, 'The Demographic Transition and Regional Variations in Birth and Death Rates in Bulgaria', in James H. Johnson (ed.), *Geography and Regional Planning*, Proceedings of the Second British-Bulgarian Geographical Seminar, Sofia 22–9 September 1981 (Norwich: Geo, 1983), 113–21. During the late 1980s the regenerative process focused more attention on the position of the Turks in Bulgaria. This prompted studies such as Kemal H. Karpat (ed.), *The Turks of Bulgaria; The History, Culture, and Political Fate of a Minority* (Istanbul: Isis Press, 1990), and Bilâl Şimşir, *The Turks of Bulgaria (1878–1985)* (London: K. Rustem & Brother, 1988).

Since 1989 the study of ethnic questions has moved to the forefront of the academic as well as the political stage. It has produced work of excellent quality which includes Valeriĭ Rusanov (compiler) and Lilyana Aleksandrieva (ed.), *Aspekti na etnokulturnata situatsiya v Bŭlgariya i na Balkanite*, 2 vols., vol. i, the proceedings of a seminar held in Sofia, 8–10 November 1991, vol. ii, 21–3 February 1992 (Sofia: Fumi Press for the Friedrich Naumann Foundation,

1992); Mary Neuburger, *The Orient Within: Muslim Minorities and the Negotiation of Nationhood in Modern Bulgaria* (Ithaca, NY: Cornell University Press, 2004); Ali Eminov, *Turkish and Other Muslim Minorities in Bulgaria* (London: Hurst, 1997). The assimilationist policies of the 1980s came under scrutiny in St. Mihaĭlov, *Vŭzrozhenskiyat protses v Bŭlgariya* (Sofia: M 8 M, 1992); Y. Konstantinov, and G. Alhaug, *Names, Ethnicity, and Politics: Islamic Names in Bulgaria 1912–1992* (Oslo: Novus Press, 1995).

The ethnic and minority policies of the post-1989 regimes are discussed in Stefan Troebst, 'Demokratie oder Ethnokratie? Nationalismus und Nationalitätenpolitik im Nach-"Wende"-Bulgarien', in Holm Sundhausen (ed.), *Südosteuropa zur Beginn der Neunziger Jahre: Reformen, Krisen und Konflikte in den vormals sozialistischen Ländern*, Multidisziplinäre Veröffentlichungen des Osteuropa-Instituts der Freien Univeristät Berlins, no. 4 (Berlin: Harrassowitz, 1993), 33–72, and in the same author's 'Ethnopolitics in Bulgaria: The Turkish, Pomak, Macedonian and Gypsy Minorities', in *Helsinki Monitor: Quarterly on Security and Cooperation in Europe*, The Hague, 5/1 (1994), 32–42. See also, A. Zhelyazkova, 'The Bulgarian Ethnic Model', *East European Constitutional Review*, 10/4, (Fall 2001), access at www.law.nyu.edu/eecr/vol10num4/focus/zhelyazkova.html, and U. Brunnbauer, 'Diverging (Hi-)Stories: The Contested Identity of the Bulgarian Pomaks', *Ethnologia Balkanica*, 3 (1999), 35–50. A first-rate and critical examination of the Bulgarian governments' minority policies is Bernd Rechel, 'Minority Rights in Post-Communist Bulgaria', Ph.D. thesis (Birmingham, 2006). Specific treatment of the Roma is to be found in the Helsinki Watch Report, *Destroying Ethnic Identity: The Gypsies of Bulgaria* (New York: Human Rights Watch, 1992); and J. P. Liegeois, *Romite-evropeĭsko maltsinstvo* (Sofia: Fondatsiya Mezhduetnicheska initsiativa za choveshki prava, 1998). The process of, and the difficulties caused by emigration and the movement of populations is treated in B. Vasileva, *Migratsionni protsesi v Bŭlgariya sled vtorata svetovna voĭna* (Sofia: Kliment Ohridski, 1991); D. Filipov and S. Tsvetarski, *Vŭnshnata migratsiya na naselenieto na Bŭlgariya* (Sofia, 1993); and D. Boveva, 'Emigration from and Immigration to Bulgaria', in H. Fassman and R. Munz (eds.), *European Migration in the Late Twentieth Century* (Cheltenham: Edward Elgar, 1994), 221–38.

For a pioneering study of a Bulgarian minority abroad see Rossitza Parvanova Guentcheva, 'State, Nation and Language: The Bulgarian Community in the Region Banat from the 1860s to the 1990s', Ph.D. thesis (Cambridge, 2001). And for the fate of Bulgarians from Ukraine who attempted to move to Bulgaria in the second world war, Boĭka Vasileva, 'Migratsiya na naselenie ot Ukraina v Bŭlgariya prez 1943–1944g', *Vekove*, 4 (1986), 36–40.

Index

Abdul Hamid II, Sultan 178
Abyssinia (Ethiopia) 252
Adrianople 28, 33, 34, 50, 69, 71, 137,
    152, 156, 167, 202, 204, 284
  Bulgarian traders in 28, 39, 284
  siege of (1912–13) 196–8, 200
Adriatic Sea 15, 198, 207, 251, 445
Aegean Sea 15, 33, 39, 93, 321, 445,
    446
Aegean coast, Bulgarian access to 202,
    222, 255, 258, 269, 308, 446
Afghan war, (2001) 416
Afghanistan 365, 416
Africa, north 267, 268
Africa, south 155, 367, 397
agrarian movement 159–62, 176, 180,
    290, 291, 453; see also
    Bulgarian Agrarian National
    Union, and cooperatives
Agricultural Academy 357
Agro-Industrial Complexes (AICs) 361
Akaev, Askar President of Kirghizia 6
Alamein, battle of 261
Albania 1, 6, 11, 94, 192, 195, 197–9,
    258, 338, 365, 410, 448
  Orthodox Church in 70
  Serbian aspirations towards 94, 193,
    199
Aleksandriyata 32
Aleksandrov, Chudomir 384
Alexander I, Tsar of Russia 36, 66
Alexander II, Tsar of Russia 93, 104,
    107, 173
Alexander III, Tsar of Russia 107, 108,
    113, 123, 125, 126, 128, 144
Alexander of Battenberg, prince of
    Bulgaria 101, 132, 134, 164,
    341
  abdication 128, 129 135, 139
  and the conservatives 101, 106, 109
  and the liberals 101–2, 104–8, 110,
    112, 114
  and the military 101–2, 106, 111,
    113, 118, 125, 127, 134

and the Russians 101–2, 104,
    110–11, 113, 116, 119, 122,
    123, 125–7, 341
  and Eastern Rumelia 118, 121–3,
    125, 126
Alexander the Great 32, 369
Alexandroupolis also 400, see also
    Dedeagach
Algeria 365
Alliance for National Salvation (ANS)
    407
Allied Control Commission (ACC)
    308, 313, 322, 435
allies, first world war 206, 207, 210,
    211, 216, 219, 221, 222; and
    Bulgaria after 1918 224–5,
    226, 233
allies, second world war 254, 271,
    272–4, 277–9, 310
alphabet, Cyrillic/Bulgarian 12–13,
    341
America, central 367
America, Latin 364
America, north 10, 220, 357
America, south 10
Anatolia 10, 24, 155, 197, 260, 426,
    430
Andonov, Ivan 451
Angista 199
Angola 365
Anhialo, see Pomorie
ANS, see Alliance for National Salvation
Antim I, Exarch 79
Antim VI, Oecumenical Patriarch 79
April uprising (1876) 1, 91–3
Aprilov, Vasil 50, 51, 65
Arabakonak 89
Archaeological Museum, Sofia 297
Argentina 266
Armenia 14, 144, 436
  Church 68; massacres of 144, 145
  minority in Bulgaria 8, 18, 20,
    260, 266, 429, 436, 437,
    438

army
  Austro-Hungarian 128
  British 268
  Bulgarian
    Alexander, Prince and 103, 106,
      111, 113, 118, 125, 134
    and Balkan wars 192–4, 196, 197,
      198–202, 203, 206, 305
    Boris, King and 245, 247–9, 252,
      253, 263
    communists and 250, 264, 275,
      276, 279–80, 308, 310, 312,
      341, 349
    communist purges of 314–15,
      321–4, 339, 351
    and coup and plots
      (1881) 113
      (1886) 127–8
      (Panitsa) 134–5
      (1923) 233–5
      (1934) 244–5
      (1965) 350–1, 359
      (1989) 388
    discontent in 113, 127, 131,
      134–5, 161, 200, 215, 218,
      231, 239–40, 247, 249, 261,
      279–80, 350–1
    in domestic affairs, use of 101–2,
      104, 111, 113, 138, 161, 172,
      178, 182, 223, 224, 254, 277
    Ferdinand, Prince and King and
      141, 149, 150, 162, 359
    in first world war 207, 208, 210,
      211, 213, 214, 218, 291, 307
    and Macedonian question 134–5,
      160–1, 164, 165, 167, 169,
      176–8, 196–7, 229, 239–40,
      247, 269, 280
    military units before the liberation
      81–2, 83–4, 86–92
    Muslims in 378, 429–30
    and NATO 410, 416
    and Neuilly, treaty of 222, 224,
      225, 231
    officer corps 101, 110, 113, 123,
      134, 150, 178, 211, 223, 231,
      247, 252, 297, 341, 382 *see
      also* Military League
    in post-communist era 390, 391
    and Rumelia 118, 121, 123

    Russian officers in 101, 103, 111,
      113, 341
    in second world war 261, 264,
      267–70, 272, 274, 275, 276,
      277, 310
    in Serbo-Bulgarian war
      (1885) 123–5
  German 206, 211, 268–9, 273, 277
  Greek 194, 197, 200, 238, 255
  Ottoman 41, 42, 44, 45, 46, 85, 92,
    175, 196, 197, 299
  Romanian 271, 305
  Russian 47, 83, 101, 131, 428, 446
    in Bulgaria 130–1, 428
    Bulgarians in 83–4, 88
  Serbian 15, 124, 200, 214
  Soviet (Red) 274, 278, 279, 280,
    314, 319, 321–2, 332
  Wrangel's (White Russian) 225, 231
  Yugoslav 397
Aromanians 438
Asen I, Tsar of Bulgaria 63
Asen II, Tsar of Bulgaria 15, 16, 17,
  194
Asenov, Hadji Dimitŭr 87, 120
Asenovgrad (Stanimaka) 202, 306
Asia 445, 446, 448
Asia, central 6, 14, 24; Russian interest
  in 118, 119, 122, 151, 153,
  271
Asia Minor *see* Anatolia
Asparukh, Khan 367
Ataka 420, 423, 443
Athens 86, 301
Athos, Mount 30, 31, 66, 68
Atolovo 2
Ausgleich, Austro-Hungarian (1867)
  76, 86
Austria 222, 304
Austria-Hungary 10, 154, 168, 176
  and Bulgarian declaration of
    independence (1908) 175–7,
    191–2, 204
  Bulgarians in 10, 29
  and Bulgaria 94, 119, 144, 153,
    175–7, 192, 204, 303–4, 446
  and Bulgaria in the first world war
    207, 208, 212–13, 214, 216
  and loans to Bulgaria 155
  and Macedonia 151–2, 167–8, 207

and railways in Bulgaria 106, 111, 112, 154
and Russia in the Balkans 152, 167, 168, 179, 204
and Serbia 124–5, 195, 206
and Serbo-Bulgarian war (1885) 125
shipping in Ottoman empire 42, 91
and vŭzrazhdane 42, 44, 54
Austro-Prussia war (1866) 76
Avars 7
Avksentiĭ, bishop of Veles 71
Axis powers 253–6, 258, 264, 266, 267–73, 274–5, 278–80

Baba Vanga 369
Bachkovo, monastery 78
Bagryanov, Ivan 277–9, 312
Bakalov, Tsanko *see* Tserkovski, Tsanko
Bakish, Sonya 386
Balabanov, Marko 97
Balchik 198
Balkan alliance, *see* Balkan league
Balkan federation 88, 132, 140, 152, 185, 229, 320, 321, 338, 453
Balkan league (1912–13) 178–9, 193–4, 198–201, 204
Balkan mountains 7, 11, 19, 35, 37, 52, 79, 94, 186, 288, 301, 433, 445
Balkan peacekeeping force 409
Baltic states 255
BAN *see* Bulgarian Academy of Sciences
Banat of Temesvar 9, 36, 426
banks
　Agricultural Credit Bank 186
　Agricultural Savings Bank 155, 158, 290, 304
　Alatini Bank 304
　Bank for Agricultural Credit 'Vitosha' 404
　Banque de Paris et de Pays Bas (Paribas) 157, 163, 165, 166, 301
　in Bulgaria 70.158, 226, 237, 246, 304, 329, 396, 402, 404–5
　Bulgarian Agricultural Bank 290
　Bulgarian Commercial Bank 452
　Bulgarian Credit Bank 246
　Bulgarian National Bank (BNB) 106–7, 115–16, 242, 304, 329, 403, 404

Central Cooperative Bank 290
　Cooperative Bank 262
　and corruption 404–5
　Deutsche Bank 155
　Discontogesellschaft 209
　Louis Dreyfus Bank 304
　State Savings Bank 418
　World Bank 409
Bansko 30, 60
BANU *see* Bulgarian Agrarian National Union
BANU-NP, *see* Bulgarian Agrarian National Union – Nikola Petkov
Banya 334
Basil 'the Bulgar-Slayer', Emperor 15
Batak 92
BBC *see* British Broadcasting Corporation
BCP *see* Bulgarian Communist Party
BDZh, *see* railways
Bebel, August 306
Beckerle, Adolf-Heinz 264, 266, 267
Belarus 401
Belasitsa 15
Belene
　labour camp 344, 346, 375
　proposed nuclear power complex 374
Belev, Aleksandŭr 265
Belgium 154, 303
Belgrade 26, 124, 206, 229, 232, 406
　Bulgarian revolutionaries in 63, 75, 77, 82, 83, 84, 86, 87, 89
Belogradchik 37
Benderev, Capt. Atanas 124, 127, 150
Benkovski 378
Berana 195
Berkovits 434
Berlin 149, 218, 256, 263
Berlin, treaty of (1878) 10, 94–5, 106, 107, 115, 119, 121, 176, 191, 202, 274
　and Macedonia 94, 121, 122, 202
　and minorities 422, 426, 438
　and railways 106, 115, 175–6, 175–5
　resentment at in Bulgaria 94, 97
　and tariffs 158, 303
Beron, Petŭr 10, 50, 51, 52, 55

Berov, Lyuben 399–400, 402
Bessarabia 9, 32, 35, 53, 174, 426
Biryuzov, Gen. Sergei 314, 321
Bismarck, Count Otto von 94
Bitola (Monastir) 39, 50, 137, 152,
    167, 193, 210
Black Sea 14, 15, 35, 93, 273, 342,
    379, 382, 433
Blagoev, Dimitŭr 9, 186–7, 215, 237
Blagoevgrad (Gorna Djumaya) 60,
    165–7, 320, 334, 337, 375,
    439
Bled 337
Blum, Léon 323
Blŭskov, Ilya 447
BNB, *see* banks
Boboshevski, Tsvyatko 309
Bobovdol 206
bogomilism 14–15, 17, 64, 234
Bogoridi, Aleko (Aleksandŭr) Pasha
    118
Bogoridi, Stefan 68
Bogorov, Ivan 56, 59, 61
Bolgrad 54, 57, 58
Bolsheviks 215, 221, 223
Boris I, King 11–12, 74, 367, 445
Boris III, King 140, 192, 197, 218,
    238, 270, 315, 336, 370
    conversion to Orthodoxy 144–5, 153
    and Germany 255, 258, 267–70, 271
    and Jewish minority 266
    marriage 251
    personal rule of (1935–41) 248–56,
        263–70, 449
    and second world war 258, 263, 266,
        267–8, 274
    and Stamboliiski 234–5
    see also army, Bulgarian
Borisov, Boiko 419
Bosnia and Hercegovina
    Austria and 26
    Austrian annexation of (1908)
        175–6, 179
    Austrian occupation of 94, 124
    refugees from 430
    revolt in (1875) 43, 90
    Serbia and 124, 179
Botev, Hristo 62, 63, 88, 90, 91, 120
    Hristo Botev radio station 276, 309
Boyana 16, 17, 383
Bozhilov, Dobri 271, 277, 312

Bozveli, Neofit 50, 66, 67, 68
Braila 10, 36, 62, 63, 86, 97
Brailsford, H. N. 2
Brannik (Defender) 262
Braşov 57, 61
Bratsigovo 92
BRCC, *see* Bulgarian Revolutionary
    Central Committee
Brezhnev, Leonid 353, 358, 363
British and Foreign Bible Society 58
British Broadcasting Corporation (BBC)
    380
BRSDP, *see* Bulgarian Workers' Social
    Democratic Party
BSP *see* Bulgarian Socialist Party
BTK *see* Bulgarian Telecommunications
    Company
Bucharest 86, 87–8, 89, 90–1, 93, 132,
    133
    Bulgarian communities in 10, 36,
        51, 56, 57, 69, 83
    treaty of (1812) 37
    treaty of (1886) 125
    treaty of (1913) 202
    treaty of (1917) 216
Budapest 10, 32, 310, 358
Bukhara 110
Bukovina 26
Bulgaria, relations with *see also* entries
    for states concerned
    Austria 304
    Austria-Hungary 153, 303, 304,
        446, 454
    Byzantium 13–14, 16, 445
    France 105, 209, 217, 252, 303,
        304, 309, 364, 384, 398, 446
    Germany 3, 12, 13, 103, 113, 319,
        446, 447
        economic 209, 212–13, 252, 253,
            275, 303–4, 318, 365, 373
        loans from 155, 205–6, 304
        over Macedonia 153, 207
        on railways 155
        and vŭzrazhdane 56
    Great Britain 1–4, 93–4, 252, 309,
        325, 337, 352, 448
        and anti-communist opposition
            313–14, 322, 334, 335
        and Balkan wars 199
        and declaration of Bulgarian
            independence (1908) 176

economic 1, 239, 299, 303
in first world war 207, 209, 217
over Macedonia 153
on railways 106, 115, 126–7
in second world war 254, 256,
   268, 270, 277, 280, 313
and treaty of Berlin 93–4
and union with Rumelia (1885)
   119, 126–7
and vŭzrazhdane 26, 42, 54, 58,
   73, 86
Greece 94, 171, 222, 238, 239, 243,
   251, 338, 343, 344, 365, 434,
   445, 448
in Balkan wars 193–4, 196–202
in first world war 207, 210
over Macedonia 15, 121, 126,
   136–7, 151, 153, 163, 168,
   169, 171, 179, 194,
   199–200, 202, 229, 238,
   247, 398, 434
in second world war 255–6, 258,
   259–62, 269, 272, 273, 275,
   278, 308, 311, 321
Italy
and Balkan wars 192, 195
economic 230, 303, 333, 409
in first world war 207
as diplomatic patron 251–2
in second world war 253–5, 258,
   260, 266, 267, 269, 271
in vŭzrazhdane 51, 73, 81, 88,
Japan 358, 365, 373
Macedonia (Former Yugoslav)
   Republic of 398, 410, 411,
   448
Montenegro 139, 153, 194, 202
Ottoman empire 97, 125, 131,
   445–6
and Bulgarian declaration of
   independence (1908) 174–7
cooperation with 137, 139, 150,
   151, 167, 168, 193
economic 284, 303, 304
in first world war 206–8, 210,
   211, 216
over Macedonia 121, 135, 141,
   145, 151, 153, 166, 167–9,
   174–5, 178, 179, 192–3, 207
over Muslims in Bulgaria 102,
   205, 426

over railways 111, 155, 175
tariffs 119–20, 303
and union with Rumelia (1885)
   120–1, 123, 126
Romania 36, 103, 132, 153, 164,
   198–9, 202, 203, 207, 210,
   215, 222, 251, 272, 301, 303,
   305, 368, 385, 410, 435
Russia
and Balkan league (1912–13)
   192–3, 204
and Balkan wars 201–2
and break in relations with 128–30
and Bulgarian declaration of
   independence (1908) 176–7,
   179
and BNB 106–7
and conservatives 109–12
and creation of Bulgarian state
   91–3
and Prince Ferdinand, question of
   recognition of 134–4, 137,
   138–9, 144–6, 150
in first world war 204, 206–7,
   209, 211, 214, 215, 454
ministers in Bulgaria (1880s) 9,
   101, 103, 106, 110, 112–13,
   129
unpopularity of 114, 116, 131,
   446
and Exarchate 100, 121, 150,
   194
liberals and 103, 106–7, 108,
   112–13, 114, 116, 126, 122,
   131–2, 450, 451, 453
and loans 163–4, 165, 205
and Macedonia 94, 118, 121, 122,
   132, 135, 136–7, 145,
   151–3, 157, 163–9, 178–9
post-communist Russia and
   Bulgaria 398, 400–1, 407,
   409, 410, 413, 417, 448, 449
provisional administration (in
   Bulgaria) 96–7, 110–11,
   296, 427, 429
and railways 106–7, 111
in Eastern Rumelia 119, 126
and Tŭrnovo constituent
   assembly 97
and Tŭrnovo constitution 101,
   104–5, 107, 108, 112

Bulgaria (*cont.*)
  and union with Eastern Rumelia
    (1885) 119, 123–4, 129
  and subversive activities in Bulgaria
    127, 134, 139, 142
  and vŭzrazhdane 1, 26, 30–1,
    35–7, 56, 57, 58, 77, 61,
    83–4, 87, 446
    Bulgarian support from 25, 30,
      73, 74, 85, 86, 87
    and Bulgarian Church 65, 68,
      70, 75–6
    and Bulgarian education during
      51, 53, 66, 87, 101, 102, 133,
      446
    see also Alexander of Battenberg,
      prince of Bulgaria, and the
      Russians; army, Bulgarian,
      Russian officers in
Serbia
  agreement with (1904) 168
  before Ottoman conquest 15
  and treaty of Berlin 94
  in first world war 206–8, 210,
    212, 214, 216
  and Macedonia 121, 124, 126,
    136–7, 151, 153, 163–6,
    168–9, 179, 192, 198–200,
    202, 207–8, 398
  in post-communist era 398, 410,
    412
  and railways 111, 154
  in second world war 11, 268–9,
    272, 273
  tariffs 303
  and union with Eastern Rumelia
    (1885) 123–4
  and vŭzrazhdane 30, 51, 61, 63,
    73, 75, 77, 82, 83–9, 90–1
  see also Balkan league; Serbo-
    Bulgarian war (1885)
Soviet Union
  and aid to Bulgaria 319–20, 330
  after 1989 397
  and Bulgaria (September 1944 to
    December 1948) 308,
    312–14, 321, 324–5
  economic exploitation of Bulgaria
    332–3, 336
  economic relations 332–3, 336,
    351, 357, 364, 372, 383

  and energy supplies to Bulgaria
    332, 357, 364, 383
  diplomatic relations with 225,
    246, 248
  under Gorbachev 370, 381,
    382–3, 385, 387, 388
  influence on BCP 237, 337,
    343–5, 349, 350, 363–4
  and Bulgarian police 310, 339, 366
  reparations after second world war
    318–19, 332–3
  in second world war 253, 255,
    256, 263–4, 267, 268, 269,
    272–4, 276–80, 310
  support for communists in
    Bulgaria 314
  Zhivkov and 350, 363–4
  see also army, Soviet
Turkey
  trade with 242
  relations in inter-war years 251
  relations in communist era 322,
    364, 365–6, 367, 376, 378,
    387
  relations in post-communist era
    397, 398, 448
  in second world war 255, 267,
    269, 271–2, 279
  population movements 365, 387,
    432, 433
Yugoslavia
  federation 88, 338
  and Macedonia 228, 229, 232,
    246–8, 258, 320–1, 337–8,
    366
  relations with in communist era
    320–1, 335, 337–8, 344, 366
  relations with in inter-war years
    244, 246–7, 249, 251–3
  relations in post-communist era
    397, 401, 403
  reparations 222, 337
  trade with 241
Bulgarian Academy of Sciences (BAN)
  36, 62, 297, 345, 357, 384
Bulgarian Agrarian National Union
  (BANU)
  agricultural reforms 228, 294–5 *see
    also* Bulgarian Agrarian
    National Union,
    redistribution of property

and army 161, 178, 182, 185, 218,
223, 224, 228–9, 230–1,
232, 233
and Church 185, 186, 230
in coalition governments 218,
241–4, 280, 316, 392,
400
and communists 221, 222–4, 226,
228, 230, 233–4, 236, 237,
280, 309, 324 350, 392
communist attacks upon agrarians
312–14, 316, 317
and cooperatives 184, 185–6, 226,
227, 228, 290, 292
and corruption 235, 243
and education 228, 230, 294
and foreign policy 204, 208–9,
216–17, 225, 228–9
foundation of 157–60, 180, 182–3
ideology 184–6
and Macedonia 176, 178, 185, 204,
225, 228–30, 231, 232,
234–5
and monarchy 178, 190, 209
Pladne faction 236, 250
becomes a political party 160–1,
182–3
redistribution of property 185–6,
226–7, 237
press 184
representation in sŭbranie 162, 174,
183, 190, 205, 221, 224, 313,
392
splits within 232, 236, 243, 317
strength of 161–2, 169, 183–4, 454
tax reform 228
anti-tithe agitation 160–2, 183
Vrabcha faction 236, 250
see also Gemeto; Petkov, Nikola; press,
Bulgarian, party political,
agrarian
Bulgarian Agrarian National Union—
Nikola Petkov (BANU-NP)
313, 314, 323, 331, 407 *see
also* Petkov, Nikola
Bulgarian Communist Party (BCP)
and agrarians 221, 222–4, 226, 228,
230, 233–4, 236, 237, 280,
309, 312–14, 316, 317, 324,
350, 392
April line 345–6, 354, 356, 358, 375

and army 250, 264, 275, 276, 279–80,
308, 310, 312, 314–15, 321–4,
339 341, 349, 351
and Bulgarian Orthodox Church
317, 318, 333–5
as Bulgarian Workers' Party (BWP)
239, 243, 250, 275, 276,
311–12, 322
cathedral outrage (1925) 237–8
congresses
fifth 326, 327–8, 331, 336, 341,
437
sixth 344
seventh 423
eighth 349–50
eleventh 380, 391
twelfth 358, 380
thirteenth 383
fourteenth 391
coup (attempted 1923) 236–7
(1944) 281–2
decline in power of 379–81, 384–7,
389–90, 403
July concept 375, 381, 383, 386
and Macedonia 238, 320–1, 337–8,
366, 367
membership of 224, 339, 380
and ethnic minorities 423, 435,
436–8 *see also* regenerative
process
origins
party programme
(1948) 327
(1971) 356–7
and police 264, 309, 310–11, 322,
325, 328, 339, 346, 350, 351,
359, 366, 386, 388, 390, 394,
403, 411
purges in 333, 336–40, 342, 345,
352, 359, 379, 384
representation in sŭbranie 221, 224,
232, 316–17, 325
in second world war 254, 263,
264–5, 266, 268, 276,
278–9
and social democrats 313, 315–16,
324
social policies of 371–2
and Soviet Union 314, 317, 321,
325, 328, 338, 340–4, 351,
363–4, 365, 366

Bulgarian Communist Party (*cont.*)
  and strikes 223–4, 242
  support for 223, 225, 230, 233, 236,
    239, 243, 244, 250, 309, 313,
    316–21, 454 *see also*
    collectivization of agriculture;
    Dimitrov, Georgi; Fatherland
    Front; regenerative process;
    Zhivkov, Todor
Bulgarian language 7, 11, 13, 16, 19,
    20, 25, 30, 31, 36, 37, 55–6,
    103, 156, 259, 425, 437
Bulgarian Legion, first 63, 82, 84,
    86, 89
Bulgarian Legion, second 89
Bulgarian Literary Society (Braila) 62,
    63, 297
Bulgarian National Council
    Constantinople 80
Bulgarian Olympic Committee 380
Bulgarian Orthodox Church
  in Constantinople 59, 63, 67–9, 71,
    74, 77, 78, 79, 118
  campaign for separate 13–14, 19–20,
    23–4, 27–8, 47, 55, 63–80,
    82, 84, 85, 96
  communists and 317, 318, 333–5
  Exarchate
    establishment of 77–9, 81
    location of 100, 194–5, 203
  and Greek Church in Bulgaria
    170–1, 202
  Holy Synod 100, 136–7, 194, 230,
    290, 317, 396
  and Macedonia and Thrace 71, 73,
    77–80, 93, 98, 100, 112, 121,
    136, 137, 140–1, 150, 153,
    194–5, 202, 229, 258–60,
    265
  mediaeval 12, 13, 15, 16, 17, 19
  modern Patriarchate 334, 396
  Ohrid Patriarchate 19, 28, 64
  and Rome 12, 16
  and schism in Orthodoxy 63, 73, 79,
    100, 334
    Russia and 100, 121, 150, 152–3,
      194
  split in (1992) 396
  Stambolov and 135–8, 139–40
  and state 100, 105, 137, 144–6, 190,
    193–5, 230, 247, 399

  synods 100, 136, 137, 194, 230,
    290, 317, 396
  see also bogomilism; Bulgarian
    Agrarian National Union and
    Church; monasteries;
    Stambolov, and Church
Bulgarian Revolutionary Central
    Committee (BRCC) 89–91
Bulgarian Revolutionary Secret
    Committee 88
Bulgarian Socialist Party (BSP) 392–5,
    400, 404, 405–6, 407, 414,
    415, 416, 417, 418, 420, 442
Bulgarian Telecommunications
    Company (BTK) 418
Bulgarian Workers' Party (BWP) *see*
    Bulgarian Communist Party
Bulgarian Workers' Social Democratic
    Party (BSDRP) 186–8
Bulgarian Workers' Union 245, 248
Bulgartabak 418
Bunar Hissar 196
Burgas 2, 34, 120, 127, 130, 154, 155,
    202, 213, 286, 301, 356, 400,
    428, 430, 433, 434
Burmov, Todor 72, 101, 102, 104
Burov, Atanas 236
Bush, President George (senior) 387
Buzludja 186
Byzantium, *see* Constantinople

Calcutta 44
Calendars, Gregorian and Julian viii, 211
Canada 349
Capitulations 95, 127, 130, 134, 174
Carol I, King of Romania 132
Catherine the Great, Tsarina of Russia 37
Caucasus 271, 448
Cavour, Count Camilio 195
Ceauşescu, Nicolae 353, 366, 368, 373
Chatalja 196, 198, 305
Chavdar partisan brigade 352, 388
Chelebi, Evliya 28
Chernobyl nuclear disaster, (1986) 382,
    385
Chernyshevki, Nikolaĭ 181
Chervenkov, Vŭlko 336–7, 340–1,
    344–7, 350, 352, 353,
    359, 433
Chesmedjiev, Grigor 275
Chile 397

China, People's Republic of 348, 350
Chintulov, Dobri 47, 62
Chiprovets 9, 36, 83
chitalishta 56–8, 96, 159
Chomakov, Stoyan 50, 51, 72
Churchill, Sir Winston 3, 207, 308
Circassians 8, 38, 73, 92, 285, 426
Citizens' Union Roma
CITUB *see* Confederation of
        Independent Trade Unions in
        Bulgaria
Clinton, President William 410
CLS *see* Compulsory Labour Service
Club for the Support of Perestroika and
        Glasnost' 386
Coalition for Bulgaria 415
collectivization of agriculture 318,
        328–31, 332, 333, 342,
        348–9, 355, 437, 440
Comecon (Council for Mutual
        Economic Assistance) 303,
        328, 342, 357, 383
Cominform 324, 325
Comintern 237, 250
commassation 160, 227, 292, 397
Commission on Security and
        Cooperation in Europe
        (CSCE) 387
Committee for the Defence of Religious
        Rights 385
Communist Party of the Soviet Union
        (CPSU) 345, 346, 349, 370,
        382
Compulsory Labour Service (CLS)
        226, 254
Confederation of Independent Trade
        Unions in Bulgaria (CITUB)
        390, 393
Congo, Republic of 365
conservatives 97, 98, 101, 102,
        104–6, 109, 110–16,
        118–19, 125, 134, 140,
        142–3, 148, 156, 173, 306,
        449, 452
Constantinople ix, 16, 18, 19, 27, 90,
        93, 153
    agreement (1886) 125
    Bulgarian aspirations to 13, 149,
        196–7, 445–6
    Bulgarian church in 59, 63, 67–9,
        71, 74, 77, 78, 79, 118

Bulgarians in 10, 36, 38, 39, 44,
        52, 54, 58–9, 61, 67–9,
        72–5, 82, 97, 131, 138, 203,
        284
    convention (1909) 176
    King Ferdinand and 149, 153, 178,
        445–6
    treaty of (1913) 202
    see also Istanbul
constitution
    Dimitrov 316, 322, 325, 327–8,
        331, 334, 337, 358
    of Exarchate 80
    of Oecumenical Patriarchate 69
    Rumelian 118–19
    Svishtov (1881–3) 109, 112
    Tŭrnovo 94, 98–101, 103, 104, 108,
        126, 162, 177, 203, 231–3,
        243, 271, 297, 422, 426–7,
        449, 452–3
        amendments to 139–40, 190–2,
            248, 250–1
        demand for restoration of 109,
            112–14, 116, 182, 452
        Russia and 104–5, 108, 112
    (1971) 356, 358, 390
    (1991) 392, 394–5, 406, 407, 418,
        419, 438, 439, 442
Constitutional Bloc 231, 455
cooperative movement 183–5, 186,
        226–7, 228, 237, 290–1,
        292, 304, 402
Copenhagen criteria 405, 418
corruption 160, 178, 183, 244, 274,
        379–80, 384, 396
    agrarian 230, 235
    electoral 100, 104 *see also*
        partizanstvo
    in Greek Church 63, 65
    in post-communist era 404–5, 408,
        411, 412–13, 415, 417–20,
        421
cotton cultivation 28, 242, 294
Council for Mutual Economic
        Assistance *see*
        Comecon
Council of Europe 378, 397
CPSU *see* Communist Party of the
        Soviet Union
Craiova, treaty of (1941) 255, 435
Crete 77, 81–2, 151

crime 1, 48, 87, 102, 105, 284, 293, 366
  by Macedonians in Bulgaria 142–3,
      164, 169, 173, 200, 208, 232,
      234, 229, 235, 238, 239–40,
      247, 451
  political murders 1, 138–9, 142–3,
      173, 234–5, 263, 275, 309,
      451
  in post-communist era 399, 400,
      404, 405, 408, 411–13, 415,
      417–21
Crimea 38, 73, 218
Crimean war 8, 25, 38, 47, 53, 62, 73,
      74, 86, 285
CSCE *see* Commission on Security and
      Cooperation in Europe
Cuba 365
Cubans in Bulgaria 9, 425
Cuban missile crisis 352, 365
Cyprus 378
Czechoslovakia 252, 358, 360

Dalmatia 26
Danev, Stoyan 162–6, 170, 197,
      201–2, 211, 232, 452
Danube Shipping Company 42
Danube, river 6, 7, 35, 37, 42, 83, 87,
      91, 92, 93, 94, 106, 111, 114,
      128, 210, 215, 280, 301, 385,
      410, 445
Darankulak 161, 182
Dardanelles 255
Daskalov, Gen. Teodosi 255–6
Daskalov, Raiko 218, 232, 238
Dedeagach (Alexandroupolis) 152,
      154, 202, 203, 207
Dedovo 21
Democratic Alliance 236–7, 239–40,
      241, 455
Democratic Labour Party 440
Democratic Party (DP) 115, 126, 137,
      144, 162, 173, 174, 177, 211,
      216, 221, 224, 233, 241, 316,
      406, 451, 452, 453–4
Democratic Romany Union 441
demography 29, 260, 282–4, 376–8,
      420, 443–4
Denmark 292
des Closières affair 209
Dibra 179, 192

Dimitriev, Major Radko 127, 130, 197
Dimitrov, Aleksandŭr 229
Dimitrov, Filip 395–9, 402, 406, 408
Dimitrov, G. M. (Gemeto) 313
Dimitrov, Georgi 2, 218, 237, 250,
      310, 314, 315, 316, 317,
      319–20, 321–3, 328, 334–8,
      340, 352, 353
Dimitrova, Blaga 385, 386
Djurov, Dobri 388
Dobrev, Nikolaĭ 406
Dobrovski, Ivan 50
Dobrudja 16, 39, 54, 79, 89, 97, 117,
      210, 213, 216, 279
  northern 94, 216
  organization 202
  southern 161, 198, 203, 210, 216,
      255, 288, 321, 330, 376, 432,
      433, 435
Dogan, Ahmed (Medi Doganov) 378
Doïran 76
Dondukov-Korsakov, Prince Aleksandr 97
DP *see* Democratic Party
Dragoicheva, Tsola 306, 366
Drama 210, 261
Drinov, Marin 32, 56
Drumev, Vasil Metropolitan Kliment of
      Tŭrnovo 63, 104, 136,
      139–40, 145
Dryanovo 300, 450
Dŭrzhaven Sigurnost (DS) *see* police, secret
Dumas, Alexandre 447
Dupnitsa 147, 434
Dyulgerov, Petŭr 384

Eagleburger, Lawrence 397
East Prussia 270
Eastern Rumelia
  and Bulgaria (1878–85) 97, 100,
      105, 109, 116–18, 284
  creation of 94, 95, 96
  ethnic composition of 118–19, 288,
      426–7, 429
  lobby in Bulgaria after union 126–7,
      143, 154–5, 451
  politics in 119–20
  organic statute (constitution) 101
  union with Bulgaria 120–3, 125–6
  as vassal of sultan 94, 95, 100, 175,
      176

EEC *see* European Economic Community
    see also European Union
Egypt 382
Ehrenroth, Gen. Kazimir 104–7
Ekoglasnost 386, 388, 400
Eksarh, Aleksandŭr 51, 59, 68
Elena 29, 35, 39, 48, 52, 57
Eliot, T. S. 349
encouragement of industry legislation
    154–6, 302–3
Enos-Midia line 207
esnafs, *see* guilds
Ethiopia, *see* Abyssinia
ethnographic museum
    Plovdiv 44
    Sofia 297
Eton College 396
Etropole 299
EU *see* European Union
Euro-Left 407
European Court of Justice 378
European Danube Commission 107
European Economic Community
    (EEC) 357, 378
European Peoples' Party 407
European Union (EU) 4, 397, 405,
    408–13, 415–21, 438, 448
Evangelical Union 73
Exarch, Ivan (John) the 13
Exarchate, Bulgarian *see* Bulgarian
    Orthodox Church
Expo70 358

fascism in Bulgaria 220, 244, 245, 246,
    250, 262, 309, 316, 342
  fighters against 347, 386
Fashizmŭt (Fascism) 385
Fatherland Front (FF)
  communist subversion and use of
    312–13, 317–18, 324–5,
    327, 328, 358, 438
  government 308–14, 334, 337, 371
  local committees of 281, 309, 319,
    325, 352
  in second world war 275–6, 279–81
Fatherland Union 399
Federation of Urban and Rural Labour
    316
Ferdinand of Saxe-Coburg-Gotha,
    Prince of Bulgaria, King of

    the Bulgarians 133, 149,
    153, 158, 173, 176, 179, 197
  abdication of 218
  and agrarians 161, 178, 190, 209
  and army 141, 149, 150, 162,
    359–60
  and central powers 206–7, 209, 211
  and Constantinople 149, 153, 178,
    445–6
  criticism of 170, 172, 177, 453, 454
    see also and agrarians
  and declaration of independence
    (1908) 174–6
  election of 132
  becomes King 176–7, 190
  and Macedonians 152, 162, 164,
    166
  marriage of 139–40
  personal regime of 149, 161, 179,
    190–1, 199–200, 203, 359
  question of recognition of 133–4,
    137, 138–9, 144–6, 150,
    346
  and religion 136, 137, 145, 190
  and Russia 152, 166, 191–2, 199,
    454 *see also* question of
    recognition
  and Stambolov 133–5, 138–43
FF, *see* Fatherland Front
Fichev, Gen. Ivan 203
Filov, Bogdan 253, 255, 256, 267,
    269, 271–2, 274, 277, 278,
    312
Finland 276
Firmilian, administrator of the diocese
    of Skopje 153, 157, 165,
    166, 168
Florence 73
Former Yugoslav Republic of
    Macedonia, *see* Macedonia
    (Former Yugoslav) Republic
    of
Fotinov, Konstantin 50, 56, 57, 59
France 74, 76, 153, 163, 254, 303–4,
    309, 335
  and Bulgarian education 53, 55, 57
  loans from 157, 163, 205, 304
  and vŭzrazhdane 53, 59, 86, 93
Franks 12
French Revolutionary wars 26

Gabrovo 44, 56, 57, 62, 75, 84, 108–9,
110, 215, 299–300, 450
schools in 51–2, 54, 55, 65
Gabrovski, Petŭr 254–5
Gagauze 8, 434, 438
Galaţi 74
Gallipoli 208
Ganchev, Georgi 395
Gandev, Hristo 58
Garibaldi, Giuseppe 82
Gashev, T. 451
Gaulle, Gen. and President Charles de 364
GDR, *see* German Democratic Republic
Gemeto, *see* Dimitrov, G. M.
Genadiev, Nikola 208, 238, 451, 454–5
General Workers' Trade Union 223
Georgiev brothers 36, 50, 91
Georgiev, Col. Kimon 245, 248, 254,
275, 280, 281, 315–16
German Democratic Republic (GDR)
364
German minority in Bulgaria 8, 435–6
Germany 215, 218, 222, 252–3
and Bulgaria
in first world war 204, 207–18
in second world war 253–6, 257,
259–61, 263–4, 266–9,
271–6, 278–80, 310, 319, 332
Federal Republic of 365, 373
policy in Balkans 153, 155, 255–6,
258–60, 261, 263
Gerov, Naĭden 52, 56, 62
Geshov family 1
Geshov, Ivan Evlogi 50, 91, 119
Geshov, Ivan Evstratiev 93, 177, 179,
190–3, 195–7, 199–200,
205, 232, 296, 452
Geshov, Ivan Stefanov 175
Gichev, Dimitŭr 236, 241, 250
Giovanna, Princess of Italy and Queen
of the Bulgarians 251, 266
Gladstone, William Ewart 1, 93
GNA *see* grand national assembly
Gogol, Nikolaĭ 447
Golem, Mount 193
Golovina, Atanasiya 52
Gorbachev, Mikhaĭl 370, 381, 382–4
Göring, Hermann 245, 263
Gorna Djumaya (Blagoevgrad) 60,
165–7, 320, 334, 337, 375,
439

Gorna Oryahovitsa 39
'Gorunya', *see* Todorov, Gen. Ivan
Gotse Delchev *see* Nevrokop
Graeco-Turkish war, (1897) 151, 153,
167
in Anatolia 260
grand national assembly (GNA) 99,
109, 126, 177, 178, 205, 271
(1881) 107
(1886) 129–31
(1887) 132, 146
(1893) 139
(1911) 183, 190–1
(1946) 316, 322, 323, 324, 325,
329, 341
(1990) 392, 394, 441
Great Britain *see* Bulgaria, relations with
Greece
ancient 7
autocephalous church in 65, 69
see also Bulgaria, relations with
Greek civil war 320, 325, 337, 434
Greek language and Bulgarians 10, 11,
13, 20, 28, 30, 71
Greek minority in Bulgaria 19, 97, 118,
124, 170–1, 266, 288, 423,
433–4, 436, 438
Greek war of independence 34, 41, 51, 84
Greeks and Bulgarians during
vŭzrazhdane 18–19, 25, 27,
31, 47, 49, 59, 74
in education 23, 47, 49–51, 55, 56,
63, 65, 85
see also Bulgarian Orthodox Church,
campaign for separate
Greeks, Phanariot 27
Green Party 395
Gregory VI, Patriarch 77, 79
Grekov, Aleksandŭr 235
Grekov, Dimitŭr 97, 112, 114, 156,
157
Grenada 365
Grey, Sir Edward 2, 199
Gudev, Petŭr 173
guilds 28–9, 44–9, 54, 68–9, 71–3, 79,
85, 97, 98, 120, 170, 172,
300
Guinea 365
Gulabchev, Spiro 306
Gŭlŭbov, Konstantin 423
Guzen, Georgi 83

Gypsies, *see* Roma
Gyumyurdjina 202
Gyumyushgerdan, Atanas 44

Habsburg monarchy *see* Austria-Hungary
Hadji, Mustafa 440
Hadjitoshev, Dimitraki 65
Hague Peace Conference (1907) 174
Haskovo 300, 387
 Third Company 124
health provision 148, 159, 185, 286,
  305, 355, 371, 386, 429
Heidelberg 50
Helsinki accords 364, 379
Helsinki, EU meeting in 409, 410
Hercegovina *see* Bosnia and
Herder, Johann Gottfried von 61
Herriot, Edouard 323
Hilendar, monastery 30, 31
Hilendarski, Paisiĭ 30–2, 34, 49,
  55, 56
Hirsch, Baron Maurice de 111, 115
Hitler, Adolf 244, 255, 267, 370
 and King Boris 255, 269–70
Hitov, Panaiot 87, 89
Holevich, Nikola 159
Holy Synod *see* Bulgarian Orthodox
  Church, synods
Hoxha, Enver 1, 353, 382
Hrabŭr, Monk 13
Hranoiznos 242, 295
Hristov, Kiril 422
Hugo, Victor 447
Hungary 9, 26, 222, 223, 274, 276,
  346, 347
Huns 7

Ignatiev, Count Nikolaĭ 87, 93
Ihtiman pass 118
Ikonomov, Todor 54, 75, 81
Ilinden rising 2, 167–9, 171, 229
IMF, *see* International Monetary Fund
IMRO *see* Internal Macedonian
  Revolutionary Organization
indebtedness, individual 32, 123, 140,
  158, 183, 241, 242, 274, 289,
  292, 441
indebtedness, state 122, 163, 304–5,
  362, 373, 389, 402
Independent Society for the Defence of
  Human Rights 385

India 44, 94
Indjova, Reneta 400, 438
inflation 103, 170–1, 212, 230, 274,
  289, 292, 318, 319, 394,
  396, 402–3, 404, 405, 408,
  413, 418
Institute for Molecular Biology 386
Institute for Nuclear Research 386
intelligentsia
 and agrarian movement
  159–60, 178–81, 220, 273,
  540
 attitude to foreign states 4, 111
 communists and 236, 311, 317–18,
  346–7, 353, 381
  intelligentsia opposition to
   communists 340, 368–9,
   387
 and Democratic Party 211
 formation of 51, 62, 426
 governmental use of 179–81, 187
 and NMSS 414
 as opposition force 140, 178–81,
  220, 273, 450
 Turkish 373
 in vŭzrazhdane 16, 43, 50–1, 61–2,
  63, 67, 89, 90
 and Zveno 244–5
Internal Macedonian Revolutionary
  Organization (IMRO)
  151–2, 164–5, 167,
  169, 229, 233, 249,
  265
International Monetary Fund (IMF)
  402, 405, 406, 409
Ioanina 196
Ionian Islands 196
Ĭosif, Exarch 98, 100, 112
Ipsilantis, Konstantinos 84
Iran 365, 376
Iraq 365, 401, 416
Islamic Conference Organization
  378
Israel 397, 435
Istanbul 334, 335
Ivan Alexander Gospels 16
Ivanchov, Todor 157, 162, 164

Jajce 320
Janissary Corps 20, 26, 34, 41, 48
Japan, *see* Bulgaria's relations with

Jews in Bulgaria 8, 18, 97, 380, 416,
　　422, 423, 424, 428, 434–5,
　　436–7, 438
　in Salonika 197, 199
　in second world war 254, 264–6,
　　278, 306, 311, 312
Jireček, Constantin 1, 108
John Paul II, Pope 366, 392

Kableshkov, Todor 93
Kádár, János 358
Kafka, Franz 349
Kalinova, Milka 363
Kalofer 35, 52, 300
Kaloyan, Tsar 16
Kampuchea 365
Kara Mustafa 34
Karadja, Stefan 87
Karadjić, Vuk 61
Karakachans 8, 437, 438
Karavelov, Lyuben 61, 87–9, 133, 447
Karavelov, Petko 97, 102, 105, 109,
　　174, 293, 450–1
　in exile 109, 114, 135
　as minister president 107–8,
　　115–17, 162–4
　and Macedonia 122, 164
　and railways 115–16, 126–7, 301
　as regent 128, 130
　and Russia 122–3, 130
　and Stambolov 128, 130, 131, 132,
　　139, 144, 453
　and union with Rumelia 122, 126
Karavelova, Ekaterina 132, 265, 306
Kardelj, Edvard 320
Karl, Emperor of Austria-Hungary 215
Karlovo 2, 34, 35, 50, 52, 57, 85, 89,
　　300
Karlsbad 171
Kaulbars, Aleksandr 110, 112
　Nikolaĭ 129–32
Kavalla 210
Kazanlŭk 35, 52, 57, 299
Kerbala 416
Kherson 66
Khrushchev, Nikita 344, 345, 347,
　　349–50, 360, 363–4
Kiev 53, 66, 74, 174
King Lewis, Miriam 2
Kinov, Col. Ivan 314
Kintex 367

Kirghizia 6
Kiril, Metropolitan of Plovdiv and
　　Patriarch 335
Kiril, Prince 197, 271, 311
Kiselev, Count Pavel 37
Kishinev 52, 66
Kisimov, Pandeli 81
Kliment, Metropolitan of Tŭrnovo *see*
　　Drumev, Vasil)
Kliment of Ohrid, Saint 13
Kliment Ohridski University, *see*
　　University in Sofia
Klokotnitsa, battle of 15, 16
Knyazhevo 280, 297
Kochane 195
Kolarov, Vasil 237, 336–7
Komi 10
komsomol *see* youth organizations
Konstantin of Preslav 13–14
Koprivshtitsa 35, 51, 52, 57, 61, 72,
　　87, 91, 92, 300
Kosovo 366, 376, 410, 416
Kosovo Polje, battle of 15
Kostov, Ivan 406, 407–10, 412–13,
　　416–18, 442
Kostov, Stefan 290
Kostov, Traicho 311, 321, 336–9,
　　345–6, 348, 352
Kostov, Vladimir 366–7
Kostova, Yelena 413
Kotel 31, 39, 44, 50, 52, 57, 85,
　　300
Kovačević, Stefan 68
Koyumdjioglu 44
Kozloduĭ 374, 411
Kraĭkov, Yakov 57
Kremikovtsi 356, 409
Krilov, Col. Vladimir 110
Kritski, Ilarion Metropolitan of
　　Tŭrnovo 65, 66
Krushevo 167
Krŭstev, Krŭstyu 181
Krŭstevich, Gavril 50, 51, 72, 77, 78,
　　80, 118–19
Kukush (Kilkis) 74, 76, 151
Kula 343
Kumanovo 106, 115, 153, 169, 178,
　　193, 301
Kun, Béla 223
Kunchev, Vasil *see* Levski, Vasil
Kŭrdjali 125–6, 202, 376, 394, 440

kŭrdjalŭstvo 24–5, 32–5, 42, 46, 57,
   64, 285
Kŭrdjiev, Georgi Antonov 186
Kutchuk Kainardji, treaty of 26, 70
Kyoseivanov, Georgi 249–51, 253–4
Kyulev, Emil 421
Kyustendil 43, 78, 122, 178, 218, 232,
   265–6, 301, 434

Laeken, EU meeting 417
Lamsdorff, Count Vladimir 166
Lankov, Nikola 349
Laos 365
Lausanne, convention on reparations
   222
League for Large Families 327
League of Nations 228, 238, 242, 243,
   251
Legionaries 262, 263, 385
Leipzig 28, 59, 446
Leipzig trial 2, 250, 323, 393
Lemberg (Lviv) 128
Lenin, Vladimir 223, 331, 340
Leningrad 368
Leo XIII, Pope 145
Levski, Vasil (Kunchev, Vasil) 62,
   87–90, 381, 422
Liberal Party/ liberals 98–9, 101–10,
   112–16, 118–19, 129,
   131–2, 136, 140–2, 147–8,
   153, 156, 167, 299, 449–50,
   453
Libya 365, 401
Lilov, Aleksandŭr 391, 400
Lobanov-Rostovski, Prince Alexeĭ 75
Lom 57, 91, 434, 442
London 86, 239, 366, 368
   agreement on terrorism (1933) 243,
     247
   conference (1912–13) 197–9, 201
London Club 402
Louis Napoleon 53
Louis Philippe, King of France 133
Lovchanski, Ilarion 80
Lovech 38, 52, 57, 67, 71, 72, 78,
   89–90, 353, 428, 439
Lublin 435
Luftwaffe 255, 267
Lukanov, Andreĭ 391–2, 393, 400, 402,
   404, 419
LUKoil company 409

Lukov, Gen. Hristo 263
Lulchev, Kosta 313–14, 324
Luleburgaz 196
Lutherans 8
Luxembourg 420
Lyapchev, Andreĭ 236, 239–40, 302
Lyaskovets 39, 55, 67

Macedonia
   in Balkan wars (1912–13) 192–4,
     197–200, 202, 293
   Bulgarian armed incursions into 118,
     120, 122, 151, 165, 239, 243
   Bulgarian aspirations towards 96,
     121, 126, 135, 168, 202, 216,
     253, 301, 321
   Bulgarian occupation of in first world
     war 210, 217
   Bulgarian occupation of in second
     world war 258–60, 261, 269,
     272, 280, 321, 435
   Bulgarian schools in 52–3, 136, 137,
     258–9
   Bulgarians in 9–10, 32, 80, 97, 106,
     117, 120, 192, 222
   economy 28, 45, 293
   Uniate church in 74, 76, 202–3
   see also army, Bulgarian; Berlin, treaty
     of; Bulgaria, relations with
     Austria-Hungary; Germany;
     Great Britain; Greece,
     Macedonia (Former Yugoslav)
     Republic of, Ottoman
     empire, Russia, Serbia,
     Yugoslavia; Bulgarian
     Agrarian National Union;
     Bulgarian Communist Party;
     Bulgarian Orthodox Church;
     crime; Ferdinand; Gorna
     Djumaya; Ilinden; Internal
     Macedonian Revolutionary
     Organization; Karavelov,
     Petko; Mürzsteg; Stambolov;
     Supreme Committee, Zveno
Macedonia, (Former Yugoslav) Republic
   of 9, 408–9, 410, 411, 448
   Bulgarian recognition of 398
Macedonia, People's Republic of (PRM)
   320–1
Macedonia, Stambolov and 132,
   137–8, 140–3

Macedonian
  folk lore 61
  language vii, 11, 320, 337, 411
  lobby in Bulgaria 121–2, 130, 134,
    137–8, 140, 151, 156, 164,
    167, 176–7, 183, 192–4,
    195, 200, 218, 225, 229,
    235–6, 244, 246–7, 453
  migrant labourers 37, 39
  minority in Bulgaria 320–1, 337–8,
    366, 436–7, 439, 440
Macedonians in Bulgaria
  restrictions on 122, 152, 164–6,
    221–2, 229, 246–7, 248
  refugees 27, 121, 168, 170–1,
    238–9, 303–4
Magyars 7, 15
Makariopolski, Ilarion 50, 67, 68,
    71, 74
Malinov, Aleksandŭr 174–9, 192, 202,
    208, 216, 218, 232. 240, 241,
    292, 453
Manchester 1
Mandradzhioglu, Konstantin 44
Marie Louise of Bourbon-Parma,
    Princess and Queen of
    Bulgaria 139–40
Marinopolski, Col. 239–40, 247
Marinov, Lt. Gen. Ivan 280, 312
Maritsa, river 39, 106, 207, 210, 296
Markov, Georgi 1, 349, 366–7, 392
Marmara, Sea of 39
Marne, battle of 206
Marseilles 86
Marshall Plan 324, 328
marxism and marxists 43, 48, 186–7,
    228, 309, 317, 346, 384
marxism-leninism 341, 370
Maxim, Patriarch 396
Mediterranean Sea 254
Melnik 50, 151, 202
Mesemvria, *see* Nesebŭr
Methodius, Saint 13
Metodi, bishop of Vratsa 65
Mexico 365
Midhat Pasha 292
Mihaĭlov, Ivan 265
Mihaĭlovski, Stoyan 447, 449
Mihov, Gen. Nikola 271
Miladinov brothers 61

Milan, King of Serbia 90, 123–4, 136
Mileti, Metropolitan of Sofia 111–12
Military Academy, Sofia 117
Military League 231, 233–4, 236–7,
    244, 248–9, 263
Mill, John Stuart 306
Milošević, Slobodan 406
Minev, Iliya 385
Mirkovich, Dr Georgi 75
Mirkovo 290
Mishev, Georgi 386
Mitterand, President François 384
Mladenov, Petŭr 387–93
Mlynář, Zdeněk 353
Model Agricultural School, Sadovo
    294–5, 297
Moesia 71, 93
Moldavia 9, 26, 35, 37, 52, 76, 81
Moldova 6
Molotov, Vyacheslav 321
Momchilgrad 378
monasteries 19, 20–1, 30, 31, 46,
    49–50, 66, 78, 96, 258, 368
  Bachkovo 78
  Hilendar 30, 31
  Petropavlovsk 55
  Preobrezhanski 60
  Rila 46, 60, 72, 230, 339
  Sokolski 75
  Zograf 30
Montenegro 77, 139, 153, 194, 196, 202
Morava, river and valley 79, 94, 97,
    117, 208, 210, 213, 216
Moravia 12–13
Moscow 10, 53, 61, 66, 87, 102, 237,
    268, 314, 333, 336, 338, 345,
    350, 363, 368, 395, 397
motor tractor stations (MTSs) 331
Movement for Rights and Freedoms
    (MRF) 392, 395, 399, 407,
    414, 415, 416, 420, 439
Mozambique 365
MRF, *see* Movement for Rights and
    Freedoms
MTS, *see* motor tractor stations
Multigroup conglomerate 419
Munich 50, 252, 253
Muraviev, Konstantin 279–80
Mürzsteg agreement 168–9
Museum of National History, Sofia 368

Mushanov, Nikola 241
Musina 159
Muslims 6, 7–8, 20, 29, 70, 102, 377
    Bulgarian 102, 125, 137, 178, 205,
        414, 426–9, 430–3, 439, 440
    emigration of 102, 288, 289, 291,
        299–300, 365, 401, 426–9,
        433
    regenerative process 375–8
    tensions Bulgarians and 102, 178,
        427–9
    and vŭzrazhdane 28, 92
    see also Circassians; Pomaks;
        regenerative process; Tatars;
        Turks in Bulgaria
Mussolini, Benito 231, 251, 255, 345
Mutafchiev, Petŭr 82, 181, 448
Mutev, Dimitŭr 58
Mutkurov, Sava 128

Nabokov, Capt. 127, 130, 134
Nachovich, Grigor 97, 111–12, 143, 452
Napoleon Bonaparte 368
Natanil, bishop of Ohrid 66
National Aid Society 2
National Liberal Party (stambolovist)
    129, 141, 156, 166, 167, 192,
    451, 454
National Liberation Revolutionary
    Army, *see* partisans
National Library, Sofia 297, 336, 447
National Movement Simeon II (NMSS)
    414–17, 419–20, 442
National Palace of Cultural (NDK) 90,
    368
National Party 143, 177, 178, 191,
    218, 221, 289, 452, 453, 454
National Social Movement (NSM)
    244–5, 249–50
National Statistical Institute 444
National Theatre (Sofia) 172, 242, 297
National Union Kubrat 262
Nationalist Party (Rumelian) 119
NATO, *see* North Atlantic Treaty
    Organization
Nazi-Soviet pact 253
NDK, *see* National Palace of Cultural
Nedelya, Sveti cathedral, Sofia 237
NEM, *see* New Economic Mechanism
Nenovich, Vasil 61

Nepal 369
Nesebŭr (Mesemvria) 78
Netherlands, The 303
Neuilly-sur-Seine, treaty of 222, 225,
    231, 252, 422, 438, 446
Nevrokop (Gotse Delchev) 141
New Economic Mechanism (NEM)
    361–3, 372–4
New Social Force 276
Nicholas II, Tsar of Russia 144, 145,
    165, 193, 199, 201
Nigeria 365
Nikich 83
Nikifor, Bishop of Plovdiv 66
Nish 38, 43, 78, 106, 229, 234, 301
NMSS, *see* National Movement
    Simeon II
Normandy landings 278
North Atlantic Treaty Organization
    (NATO) 364, 397–8, 401,
    407–11, 415–16, 420
Nova Zagora 155
Novi Sad 29, 87
NSM, *see* National Social Movement

O'Connell, Daniel 50
Obbov, Aleksandŭr 313, 317, 324
Oborishte 91
Obrenović, Michael 77, 87
Obrenović, Miloš 51
Obretenov, Nikolaĭ 91
Odessa 36, 51, 53, 62, 66, 74, 75, 76,
    83, 97, 133
Oecumenical Patriarchate,
    Constantinople 12, 24, 27, 55
    see also Bulgarian Orthodox Church,
        campaign for separate,
        Exarchate, and schism in
        Orthodoxy
Office of Young Writers 386
Ohrid 66, 67, 80, 82, 137, 198, 213
    see also Bulgarian Orthodox Church,
        Ohrid Patriarchate
Ohrid, Lake 139
Old Believers in Bulgaria 8
Omurtag 300
Omurtag, Khan 11
Operation Bogdan 277
Orange Guard 223, 224, 230–1, 232,
    233

ORC *see* Railways, Oriental Railway Company
Otets Paisiĭ 262
Ottoman empire 7, 8, 9, 19–20, 39, 43, 65, 68, 76–7, 83–4, 87, 90
  Bulgarians in 6, 10, 58
  conquest of and rule in Bulgaria 15, 17–21, 29, 37, 39, 49, 57, 64
  rebellions against 36, 48, 81, 89
  reforms in 23–4, 41–6, 68–70, 80
  and vŭzrazhdane 25–8, 41–6, 57, 63, 66, 68–73, 77–8, 82–3, 84–5, 88, 90
  see also April uprising; Bulgaria, relations with; *kŭrdjaliĭstvo*
Ottoman Public Debt 95

Paisiĭ, *see* Hilendarski, Paisiĭ
Paisiĭ bishop of Plovdiv 71, 72
Palauzov, Nikolaĭ 51
Pan Slavism 1
Panagyurishte 35, 45, 52, 57, 91, 93
Panaret, Metropolitan of Tŭrnovo 66
Panitsa, Capt. Kosta 120, 130, 132, 134–7
Pantev, Col. Atanas 263
Paprikov, Gen. Stefan 162
Parensov, Gen. Pyotr 103, 104
Paris 51, 52, 54, 73, 219, 221, 366, 368, 387
  Commune 106
  peace treaty of (1947) 315–16, 321, 337
partisans 264, 269, 272, 276–7, 280, 309, 310, 312, 320, 350, 352, 382, 388
partizanstvo 103, 112, 146–9, 161–2, 180–1, 183, 220, 230, 241, 246, 295, 305, 311
Pasi, Solomon 416
Pašić, Nikola 199–200
Patriotic Associations 129, 131, 170, 260, 451
Paul VI, Pope 365
Pavlov, Ilya 419
Pavlov, Todor 309
Pavlovich, Hristaki 50
Pavlovich, Parteniĭ 30
Pazvantoglu, Osman 33, 35
Pearl Harbor 256
Peć 27, 64

Pechenegs 7
Pekarev, Iordan 182
Pelin, Elin 181
Penev, Boyan 447
People's Bloc 240–4, 455
Pernik 206, 223, 228, 239, 285, 301, 309
Perushtitsa 92
Peterwardein 87
Petkov, Botyo 50
Petkov, Dimitŭr 166, 171–3, 183, 186, 451
Petkov, Nikola 275, 313–14, 316–17, 321–3, 334–5, 350
Petorka 250
Petrich 229, 232, 238–9, 243, 247, 251, 263, 369
Petrov, Dobri 454
Petrov, Gen. Racho 166, 168–71, 183, 186
Petrova, Sultane 306
Petrovich, Velko 83
Phanar, phanariots 27
Philological Society 61
Pikolo, Nikola 51
Piłsudski, Józef 245
Pimen, Metropolitan 396
Pinalov 83
Pirdop 290, 299
Pirin Macedonia 202, 235, 294, 320–1, 337–8, 439
Pirot 78, 244, 272
Pisa 73
Pladne (Noon) 236, 250
Pleven 160, 181, 182, 184, 233, 442
Pliska 11, 14
Plovdiv 21, 34, 52, 57, 58, 70, 73, 114, 126, 174, 177, 277, 295, 296, 306, 339, 409, 434, 450, 453
  and April uprising 92–4
  ecclesiastic affairs of 64, 66, 70–3, 78, 82, 100, 335
  economy 28, 44, 52, 299
  education 50, 52–3, 54, 61, 72, 87, 438
  garrison 128, 249
  Greeks in 47, 50, 65, 66, 70, 72, 170, 433
  guilds in 28, 47, 54, 120, 170
  International Exhibition 284
  Muslims in 427–9, 431
  and ORC 155–7

political protests and strikes in 213, 215, 237, 243, 246, 306, 343, 348, 378, 441
and union (1885) 117, 120, 122–3, 296–7
Podkrepa (Support) 385, 393
Poland 77, 208, 227, 245, 364, 379, 396, 434, 435
police 138, 147, 181, 186, 223, 229–31, 234, 241, 251, 276, 277, 280, 300, 306, 406
files 411, 412, 419
secret 350, 351, 359, 391, 394
see also Bulgarian Communist Party
Political Union 406
Pomaks 8, 19, 377, 423, 426, 432, 439–40
attempts at assimilation of 260–2, 375, 430, 432–3
Pomorie (Anhialo) 78, 170
Popov, Dimitŭr 393
Popov, Ivan 254, 255
Popov, Major 132
Popov, Raphael 76
Popovich, Raino 50, 56, 85
Porto Lagos 203, 205, 206
Potemkin 8
PR *see* proportional representation
Prague 238, 416
Pravets 352
Preslav 14, 15, 71, 451
press
Bulgarian
government control of 138, 172, 177, 210–11, 229, 245, 246, 250, 312, 399
for ethnic minorities 57, 320, 376, 431, 437
party political
agrarian 159–60, 182, 184, 313, 316
conservative 110, 140, 142–3, 450, 452
liberal 103, 108, 109, 115, 122, 167, 299, 450, 451
others 140–3, 169, 170, 173, 225, 231, 232, 270, 317, 419, 452–4
socialist 178, 315, 413
in Rumelia 117, 450

in vŭzrazhdane 23–5, 36, 41, 59, 60, 61, 68, 72, 86, 87, 93
foreign 86, 93, 132, 383
Prilep 39, 50, 54, 198
Prishtina 410
PRM, *see* Macedonia, People's Republic of
Progressive Liberal Party 162, 221, 309, 452, 453
proportional representation (PR) 118, 177, 186, 191, 205, 232, 240, 250, 392, 395, 442
Protestants 53–4, 68, 73, 139, 335, 337
Proto-Bulgars 6, 7, 11–12, 14, 82
Protogerov, Gen. Aleksandŭr 221–2, 231, 233
Provadiya 434
Prussia 73
Prussia, East 270
Przemyśl 211
Pŭrvanov, Georgi 417, 418

Radev, Simeon 367, 451
Radical Democratic Party (RDP) 453
Radical Party 215
Radomir 301
rebellion 218, 222, 238
Radoslavov, Vasil 127, 128–9, 132, 140, 142, 144–5, 192, 195, 202, 204–6, 209–11, 213, 215–16, 218, 222, 232, 430, 451, 453–4
Raĭkova, Teodora 307
Railways
Bulgarian State (BDZh) 115–16, 124, 154–6, 172–3, 175, 188, 203, 206, 215, 273, 279, 301–2, 356, 474
Oriental Railway Company (ORC) 153–6, 175–6
Rusé-Varna 106, 114–15, 126–7, 450
Vienna-Constantinople 95, 106, 111, 115, 154, 301
Rakovski, Georgi 41, 50, 57, 60, 62, 71, 75, 82, 84–9
Ralin, Radoĭ 349, 386
Razgrad 141, 387, 394, 434, 451
RDP, *see* Radical Democratic Party
Red Army *see* army, Soviet
regenerative process 375–8, 379, 381, 387, 389, 390, 391, 414, 423, 425, 438

Reichstag fire 2, 215, 250, 323
Reid, Mayne 447
Remlingen, Arnold 110–11
reparations 222, 239, 305, 318, 332,
   337, 344
   commission 225
Rhodope mountains 44, 296, 426
Riben Bukvar 55
Riggs, Elias 61
Rilski, Ivan 14, 334, 369
Rilski, Neofit 50–1, 56, 65, 68, 72
Robert College, Constantinople 53
Rodina 262, 432
Roma (Gypsies) 8, 414, 417, 423–5,
   433, 436–7, 439–42
   attempts to assimilate 375, 438
   discrimination against 414, 440–2
Roman Catholics in Bulgaria 8, 9, 64, 83
Roman Church and Bulgarians 16, 29,
   53, 59, 74–5, 136, 139, 153,
   335, 365, 379 *see also* Uniate
   Church
Romania 73, 76, 77, 82, 87, 89, 91–4,
   128, 243, 252, 255, 276, 279,
   314, 342, 351, 357, 390, 409,
   418, 420–1
   Bulgarians in 6, 9, 10, 36–8, 39, 51,
      56, 57, 60, 69, 83, 426, 435
   see also Braila; Bucharest;
      Bulgaria, relations with
Romanov, Manush 441
Romans in Bulgarian lands 8
Rome 12, 57, 75, 231, 365
Rozhen 60
Rumelia, Eastern *see* Eastern Rumelia
Rusé 2, 8, 29, 53, 90, 128, 137, 178,
   253, 295, 385–6, 434, 453
   bishopric of 67, 71, 78, 78 n
Rusev, Svetlin 386
Russia
   Bulgarians in 6, 9, 10, 35–6, 39, 53,
      54, 60, 69, 348, 426, 435
   see also army, Russian; Bulgaria,
      relations with; Bulgarian
      Orthodox Church, schism;
      Crimean war
Russian provisional administration
   (Rumelia) 96, 97, 102, 110,
   296, 427, 429
Russians in Bulgaria 130–1, 428
   Old Believers 8

White, in Bulgaria 8, 225, 231
Russo-Turkish wars
   (1769–74) 26
   (1787–92) 26
   (1806–12) 26, 34, 35–7
   (1828–9) 41
   (1877–8) 8, 93–4, 427

Sadovo *see* Model Agricultural School
Sainte Croix, Avril de 306
Saksekoburggotski, Simeon *see* National
   Movement Simeon II;
   Simeon II
Sakŭzov, Yanko 187
Salabashev, Ivan 118
Salonika 39, 58, 152, 156, 166, 195,
   197, 199, 203, 210, 218, 252,
   261, 269
Salzburg 265
Samokov 44, 55, 67, 71, 78, 108, 299,
   434
Samothrace 149, 258
Samuel, Patriarch 27
Samuil, King 15
San Stefano, preliminaries of peace 93–5,
   125, 145, 180, 219, 274, 422
Sarafovo 416
Sarajevo 10
Saranbeĭ 154, 155
Savov, Gen. Mihail 141, 201
Saxons 9
Saxony 28
SCBC, *see* Secret Central Bulgarian
   Committee
Schengen area 409
Schiller, Friedrich 447
School of Drawing, former School for
   Art and Industry, 297
School of Music 297
Scotland Yard 419
Scutari 193, 196
SDP, *see* Social Democratic Party
Secret Central Bulgarian Committee
   (SCBC) 86–7
Secret Revolutionary Committee
   (Rumelian) 120
Selim III, Sultan 34
Seliminski, Ivan 50, 51
Semerdjiev, Atanas 393
Serbia
   Bulgarians in 6, 10, 39, 426

Serbia and Montenegro 412
Serbian Orthodox Church 27, 64, 65,
 70, 73
Serbian war of independence 34, 83
Serbo-Bulgarian war (1885) 4, 7,
 123–5, 366
Seres *see* Syar
Sevlievo 29
Shakespeare, William 447
Shar mountains 193
Shipka Pass 93, 111, 166
 village 111, 428
Shtip 54, 192, 193
Shumen 29, 52, 54, 71, 78, 183, 232,
 235, 295, 299, 300, 394, 431,
 434, 451
Silistra 30, 57, 78, 84, 131, 198, 280,
 299, 434
Simeon II, King of the Bulgarians 271,
 395, 412, 414
Simeon the Great, Tsar 13–14, 445
Skobelev, Gen. Mikhail 105
Skopje 152, 193, 195
 in church affairs 65, 80, 137, 153,
 157, 165, 259
 National Theatre 337
 rail link to 106
 schools in 52
 university 259
Slaveĭkov, Pencho 38
Slaveĭkov, Petko 31, 52, 59, 62, 72, 75,
 80, 97, 98, 102–3, 109,
 114–15
Slavkov, Ivan 380
Slavs 7, 11–12, 14, 18, 31, 66, 73, 77,
 80, 82, 94, 105, 111, 117,
 121, 136, 164, 177, 201,
 447
Sliven 44–5, 47, 52, 62, 69–70, 71, 78,
 84, 91, 243, 300, 306, 437,
 438
Slivnitsa 124–5, 127, 200, 366
Smiles, Samuel 447
Smolyan 432, 439, 440
Smyrna (Izmir) 44, 50, 58–9
Sobolev, Gen. Leonid 110–12, 117
Social Democratic Party (SDP) 162,
 188, 221, 223–4, 233, 244,
 275, 280
socialism 9, 62, 140, 162, 178, 181,
 182, 186–8, 204, 205, 215,

 217–18, 220, 221, 223, 230,
 323, 422
 building in Bulgaria 24, 328, 331,
 341–2, 354–8, 360–2, 373,
 374, 376, 377, 382–3, 385, 437
Socialist International 188
Sofia 33, 48, 57, 90, 96, 110, 128, 173,
 194, 197, 202, 255, 280, 302,
 312, 428, 440
 bombing of 272–4, 276, 318, 319,
 435
 and Church 67, 71, 78, 100, 101,
 194, 203, 273, 428
 education in 52, 128, 434
 garrison 135, 202, 222, 351
 growth of 167, 295–7, 356
 industry in 29, 45
 minorities in 434–5, 436, 440
 municipal council 103, 243
 protests in 169–70, 128, 194, 195,
 215, 223, 231, 232, 266,
 306, 365, 388, 390, 392–3,
 405, 406
 social deprivation in 213, 227, 405
 violence in 173, 208–9, 237, 238,
 412, 428, 434, 440
Sofiyanski, Stefan 406, 409
Sokolski, Abbot Iosif 75
Soviet Union, Bulgarians in 10
Spanish civil war 252, 264, 339,
 345
Spiridon of Gabrovo 30
Sredna Gora 39, 277
Sremski Karlovtsi 30, 31
St Petersburg 66, 192
St Stefan's, Constantinople *see*
 Constantinople, Bulgarian
 church in
St. Antony's College, Oxford 368
Stalin 3, 279, 308, 319, 321,
 337–40, 343, 345, 349, 370,
 435
 split with Tito 338, 345
Stalingrad 261, 266, 269, 271
stalinism 329, 338–9, 341, 345, 353,
 356, 358
Stamboliĭski, Aleksandŭr 183–5, 209,
 214–16, 218, 221, 227, 228,
 230, 232–4, 279, 290, 455 *see
 also* Bulgarian Agrarian
 National Union

Stamboliĭski, Asen 323
Stambolov, Stefan 288, 341, 367, 433
  and Prince Alexander 122, 128
  and Church 135–6, 139
  early life 93, 102, 104, 133
  and Ferdinand 133–5, 138–43
  murder of 142–3
  and Macedonia 132, 135, 137, 138,
    140, 141, 143, 150, 164
  methods of rule 127, 129, 131–2,
    134–5, 138, 139, 140–1,
    142, 146–7, 181, 186, 451,
    453
  and union with Rumelia 117, 122
  and Russians 129–30, 132, 146,
    167, 341, 451
Stambolova, Poliksaniya 143
Stanchev, Gen. Kiril 323
Stanchov, Dimitŭr 142
Stanchov, T. H. 447
Stanimaka, *see* Asenovgrad
Stanishev, Sergei 420
Stanislavov, Filip 57
Stara Planina 39
Stara Zagora 34, 89–91, 102, 183, 184,
    237, 442
State Viticulture Institute, Pleven 181,
    184
Stefan, Metropolitan of Sofia 334
Stoilov, Konstantin 97, 101, 112, 114,
    142–5, 147, 156, 162, 451–2
  and Ferdinand 140, 143–5, 153, 156
  and Macedonians 150–2, 156
  modernization of Bulgaria 154, 211,
    302
  and ORC 154–5
  and Russians 143, 144–5
Stolipinovo 441
Stone, Ellen 164
Stoyanov, President Petŭr 405–6, 417
Stoyanov, Zahari 120, 451
Straits 26, 364
Strangford, Lady Emily Anne 2
Struma, river 196, 202
Strumitsa 151
Sŭbev, Father Hristofor 385
Suez Canal 94
Supreme Committee (Macedonian) in
    Bulgaria 151–2, 165–6 *see
    also* Internal Macedonian
    Revolutionary Organization

Suvorov, Count Aleksandr 83
Svishtov 42, 50, 52, 54, 55, 57, 58, 60,
    67, 74, 104, 107, 109, 428
Switzerland 303, 315, 323
Syar 67, 202, 210
Syria 14, 375

Tambuev, Georgi 384
Tanev, Vasil 2
tariffs 95, 120, 154–5, 158, 174, 302–3
Tatar Pazardjik 46, 60, 442
Tatars 7, 38, 285, 375, 426, 438
taxation 15, 18, 20, 21, 32, 35, 37, 38,
    43, 99, 105, 108, 126, 138,
    158–9, 169, 171, 177, 229,
    242, 247, 275, 298–9, 318,
    417, 444
  church 27, 33, 35, 63–5
  collection 27, 42–3, 45, 46–8, 51,
    85, 419
  devshirme 20, 26
  direct 33
  income 186, 227, 318, 330–1, 453
  indirect 103
  on land 155, 158, 289, 330, 427
  property 225
  sheep 45, 284
  tobacco 157, 163
  wealth 230
  see also tithe
television 355, 368, 373, 379, 383,
    387, 392, 394, 414, 439
Teodorov, Todor 452
Terpeshev, Dobri 353
Teteven 33, 54
Thassos 258
Thompson, Frank 277
Thrace 34, 35, 39, 53, 94, 97, 123,
    255, 269
  in Balkan wars 196–8, 200, 202, 204
  Bulgarian aspirations to 93, 117, 120,
    126, 132, 216, 321, 445, 453
  and Church 71, 77–9, 100, 258
  in first world war 207, 210
  Muslims in 205, 426, 430, 432–3, 435
  in second world war 255, 258, 269,
    279
    Bulgarian occupation of during
      258–62, 432–3, 435
    see also Aegean coast, Bulgarian
      access to

Timinski, Stanisław 396
tithe 42, 105, 120, 140, 142, 155, 158,
    160–3, 182–3, 427
Tito, Marshal Josip Broz 320, 321, 335,
    337–8, 345
    see also Stalin, split with Tito
TKZSs 318, 329–31, 342–3, 348, 349,
    360–1
    see also collectivization of agriculture
tobacco industry 157, 163, 229, 249,
    265, 293–4, 302, 303, 319,
    333, 343, 348, 399, 418
Todorov, Gen. Ivan 'Gorunya' 350–1
Todorov, Stanko 386–7
Todorov, Todor 218
Tolbukhin, Marshal Fyodor 310, 314
Tolstoi, Count Leo 447
Tonchev, Dimitŭr 142, 454
TopEnergy 400
Topencharov, Vladimir 346
Toshev, Andreĭ 248–9
Totyu, Filip 87
trade 1, 28, 34, 36, 41–2, 44, 329, 333,
    357, 362, 403, 408, 446
    agreements 120, 303, 318, 320, 373,
        400
    grain 226, 303–4
trade unions 172, 188, 223, 237, 239,
    245, 264, 323, 327, 352, 353,
    384, 385, 390, 393–4, 396,
    399
Traĭkov, Georgi 350
Transylvania 8, 26
Truman Doctrine 322, 324
Tryavna 29, 52, 57, 60, 67, 74, 300, 301
Tsachev, Mincho 452
Tsankov, Aleksandŭr 236–40, 244–6,
    250, 263, 265, 306
Tsankov, Dragan 97, 102, 109, 116,
    137, 450, 451–2
    and Church 105
    early life 56, 74
    in exile 131–2, 135
    as minister president 105–7,
        113–15, 288
    and Russians 106–7, 108, 112, 114,
        123, 126, 132
    and Uniatism 74–5
    in vŭzrazhdane 56, 58, 59, 61
    see also Democratic Party; Progressive
        Liberal Party

Tsanov, Naĭcho 215, 453
Tsaribrod 8, 106, 115, 200
Tserkovski, Tsanko (Tsanko Bakalov)
    182
Tulcha 54
Tŭmrŭsh 125, 126
Turan organization 432
Turgenev, Ivan 1, 447
Turkey 243, 259–60, 269, 271, 276,
    322, 364, 366, 397–8, 410,
    416, 432, 448
    Bulgarians in 10
    European 25, 58, 145, *see also*
        Ottoman empire
    Young Turks 174–6, 178, 192,
        194–5, 197
    see also Constantinople, Bulgarians in;
        kŭrdjaliistvo; Muslims,
        Bulgarian; Ottoman empire
Turks in Bulgaria 97–8, 118, 124, 205,
    260, 285, 380, 414, 418,
    422–7, 429, 442, 450
    (before 1878) 7–8, 18–20, 21, 39
    and education 375, 394, 409, 431,
        436, 439, 442
    discrimination against 104, 254,
        375–6, 399, 427, 429, 432,
        438
    emigration of 102, 288, 291, 375,
        399, 401, 426, 430, 431–3,
        450
    publications for 431, 436–7, 439
    see also Movement for Rights and
        Freedom; regenerative process
Turkish National Liberation Movement
    378
Tŭrnovo 29, 36, 39, 83, 108–9, 122,
    132, 136, 159–61, 177, 182,
    190, 231–2, 392, 442, 450
    Church in 19, 60, 64, 66–7, 72, 78,
        428
    constituent assembly 94, 96–101
    mediaeval 15–16, 17, 19, 30, 64
    in vŭzrazhdane 30, 50, 52, 57, 65,
        82, 91

UDF, *see* Union of Democratic Forces
Ukraine 6, 9, 278, 435
UN *see* United Nations
Uniate Church, Uniatism 73–6, 365
Union of Artists 385

Union of Democratic Forces (UDF)
    390, 392, 393, 395, 405–7,
    417, 420, 441
  extreme elements in 393, 394, 396
  in government 395–9, 403
Union of Journalists 346
Union of Teachers 386
Unionist Party 119
United Democratic Forces (UtDF) 407
  in government 407–15
  corruption and 413
United Nations (UN) 378, 401, 416
United States of America 58, 60, 215,
    216, 220, 256, 266, 268, 322,
    323, 338, 344, 367, 373, 397,
    410
Universal Israelite Alliance 434
University of Sofia 13, 36, 169–70,
    172, 173, 177, 228, 230, 294,
    297, 307, 384, 386, 431
UtDF, *see* United Democratic Forces
Uzundjovo 71, 284
Uzunov, Atanas 90, 92

Vardar river 33, 199, 445
Varna 52, 74, 78, 129, 159–60, 170,
    182, 192, 203, 255, 268, 273,
    278, 295, 299, 301, 378, 429,
    430, 433, 434, 451
Vasilev, Nikolaĭ 416
Vasilev, Slaveĭko 279
Vasilyov, Moma 54
Vatev, Atanas 245
Vatican 365
Vazov, Ivan 145, 194, 447
Velchev, Boris 359, 379
Velchev, Col. Damyan 245, 247,
    248–9, 281, 314–15, 323
Velchev, Milen 416
Veles 52, 71, 78–9, 141, 192, 193
Velichkov, Konstantin 447, 451, 452
Venelin, Yuri 56, 61
Venice 57
Verne, Jules 447
Videnov, Zhan 400–8, 413, 448
Vidin 8, 15, 16, 29, 33, 34, 37, 43, 65,
    66, 67, 71, 78, 102, 124, 214,
    299, 343, 410, 434
Vienna 26, 29, 44, 45, 54, 74, 97, 154,
    176, 200, 252, 256, 310, 368

Vietnam 364, 365
Vietnamese in Bulgaria 9, 425
Vinitsa 152
Vitosha, see for Agricultural Credit
    'Vitosha' *see* banks
Vitosha, Mount 382, 450
Vizantios, Neofit 66
Vlachs 8, 70, 438
Vladimirescu, Tudor 84
Vladislavov, Stoĭko, *see* Vrachanski,
    Sofronii
Vlaĭkov, Todor 159, 453
Voden 76
Volhynia 8
Vrabcha (Sparrow) agrarian faction
    236, 250
Vrachanski, Sofroniĭ 31, 49, 50, 57, 84
Vranya 216
Vratsa 31, 35, 38, 52, 65, 67, 72, 74,
    78, 91, 109, 112, 237, 361
Vŭlkanov, Velko 395
Vŭlkov, Gen. Ivan 236
Vŭlkovich, Georgi 138–9

Wallachia 9, 26, 35–6, 37, 39, 74, 76,
    81, 83
Warsaw pact 360, 364, 383, 397
Wilhelm II, Emperor of Germany 149
Wilson, President Woodrow 216
Witos, Wincenty 227
women 20–1, 45, 217, 285, 292, 371,
    429
  education of 52–5, 99, 306, 307,
    371
  in labour force 226, 299, 307, 317,
    371, 443
  in public life 45, 71, 132, 215, 265,
    305–7, 317, 324, 327, 380,
    400, 414–15
  reduction in restrictions on 285,
    305–6, 325, 429
  and votes for 186, 251
Wrangel, Gen. Pyotr 225, 231

Yambol 120, 154, 155, 243, 434
Yanev, Yanko 447
Yantra, river 7
Yeltsin, President Boris 398, 401
Yemen 365
youth, Bulgarian 4, 69, 159

organizations 239, 246, 262, 317,
323, 324, 327, 380, 390, 400
Yozal, Turgut 376
Yugoslavia 258, 275, 276, 277, 311,
320, 335, 338, 397, 398, 401,
403, 411
see also Bulgaria, relations with;
Macedonia, Bulgarians in;
Stalin, split with Tito; Tito,
Marshal Josip Broz
Yugov, Anton 347–50, 423

Zabunov, Yanko 181, 183, 184
zadrugas 46, 284–6
Zagreb 29, 61
Zaĭchar 89
Zaĭmov, Gen. Vladimir 264
Zambia 365
Zelić, Gerasim 64
Zhefarovich, Hristofor 30
Zhelev, Zhelyu 6, 385–6, 393, 395–6,
398–9, 404–6
Zheravna 44
Zhirov, Yuri 386
Zhivkov, Georgi 130

Zhivkov, Todor
decline in authority of 374, 379,
381, 383–8
early career 344, 352
economic policies 348–9, 356–7,
360, 374–5 *see also* New
Economic Mechanism
foreign policy 363–7
and police 350, 359
rise to power 345–50
as party leader 352–4, 358–60, 391
and Soviet Union 350, 360, 363–4,
367
trial of 391, 396
see also regenerative process
Zhivkova, Lyudmila 364, 367–70
Zita, Empress of Austria-Hungary 215
Zlatev, Petko 248, 252
Zocchi 173
Zograf, Zahari 60
Zürich 52
Zveno (Link) 244–8, 275, 280,
309, 316, 317, 324, 432,
449
and Macedonians 244, 246–7